1941

The Year That Keeps Returning

1941

The Year That Keeps Returning

Slavko Goldstein

TRANSLATED FROM THE CROATIAN BY
Michael Gable

NEW YORK REVIEW BOOKS

nyrb

New York

THIS IS A NEW YORK REVIEW BOOK

PUBLISHED BY THE NEW YORK REVIEW OF BOOKS

1941

THE YEAR THAT KEEPS RETURNING

An earlier version of the introduction by Charles Simic was first published as "He Understood Evil" in the July 2, 2009 issue of *The New York Review of Books* (Volume 56, Number 11).

Published by The New York Review of Books, 435 Hudson Street, Suite 300, New York NY 10014
www.nyrb.com

Goldstein, Slavko.
[1941. English]
1941 : the year that keeps returning / by Slavko Goldstein ; translated by Michael Gable ;
introduction by Charles Simic.
pages cm. — (New York Review Books classics)
Originally published as: 1941 : godina koja se vraca. Zagreb : Novi Liber, 2007.
Includes bibliographical references and index.
ISBN 978-1-59017-673-3 (alk. paper)
1. Goldstein, Slavko. 2. Jews—Croatia—Biography. 3. Croatia—History—1918-1945.
4. Vujicic, Milan, -1941—Assassination. 5. Usta°a, hrvatska revolucionarna organizacija.
6. World War, 1939-1945—Croatia—Karlovac (Karlovac) 7. Karlovac (Karlovac, Croatia)—
History—20th century. I. Title.
DS135.C75G65413 2013
949.72'022—dc23
2013011176

ISBN 978-1-59017-673-3
Available as an electronic book; 978-1-59017-700-6

Printed in the United States of America on acid-free paper
1 3 5 7 9 10 8 6 4 2

Contents

Introduction

I CAME ACROSS this remarkable book, which had not yet been translated into English, while writing about the wars in former Yugoslavia in the 1990s. It deserves attention, because it explains, perhaps better than any book I know of, how different ethnic groups, who lived side by side in peace, were made to turn against one another and become each other's executioners in that unhappy country. Written by the distinguished Croatian journalist and publisher Slavko Goldstein, whose father was killed by the Ustashas, the pro-fascist nationalists who were brought to power in Croatia by the Nazis when they occupied Yugoslavia in 1941, the book is a memoir of that fateful year, a meticulous historical recreation, and the cautionary account of the events that led to the deaths of some 32,000 Jews, 40,000 Gypsies, and 350,000 Serbs between 1941 and 1945.

"The great instrument of moral good is the imagination," Shelley wrote in *A Defense of Poetry*. Unlike many intellectuals who tend to rationalize and minimize the disagreeable chapters in their nation's history, Goldstein not only wishes to tell the truth, but to put himself in the shoes of various victims and even a few of their executioners. That makes 1941 a most unusual book, a story of one family's tragedy that is also a careful work of history that, because of its interest in a large number of individuals and their parallel stories, often reads like a novel.

The tale Goldstein tells starts in April 1941, after an uprising on March 27 in Belgrade led to a military coup. The army overthrew the Yugoslav coalition government that had been forced to join the Tripartite Pact with the Axis powers two days earlier; and the new government, consisting of Serbian officers, aware that the Nazis were making preparations to invade the country, tried to make itself more representative by also including some Croatian politicians. It was too late. Hitler declared that the uprising in Yugoslavia had drastically changed the entire political situation. Originally, he wanted to leave Yugoslavia alone, so that he could attack Russia. Now, he said, Yugoslavia must be regarded as an enemy and dismembered as quickly as possible.

The Germans encouraged Italy, Hungary, and Bulgaria, which had long-standing claims on Yugoslav territory, to participate in the invasion by extending to them the opportunity of annexing the Adriatic coast, Banat, and Macedonia respectively. Likewise, a promise of political independence was extended to the Croats. Days later, on April 6, Yugoslavia was attacked by Germany without a declaration of war, Belgrade was bombed, and the country was quickly occupied and partitioned. Croatia proclaimed its independence on April 10 and German troops were greeted as liberators when they entered Zagreb, the Croatian capital. For the Croats, after more than eight centuries of subordination to other powers, having their own state for the first time was a happy occasion.

Goldstein, born in 1928, was thirteen years old and living with his father, mother, and younger brother in Karlovac, a beautiful old city situated some fifty miles southwest of Zagreb, where his father owned a bookstore known as a meeting place of socialists, Communists, liberals, union workers, and other antifascists. There they bought, or borrowed from a lending library, books by such progressive writers as Gorky, Dos Passos, Upton Sinclair, Jack London, Thomas Mann, and Berthold Brecht. Goldstein recalls the day his childhood ended. On April 13, Catholic Easter, with the city already occupied by the Nazis, he recalls telling his father that he was going out to play with a friend. The father seemed surprised. There were German tanks and soldiers in the streets. After a bit of wavering, he gave his permission.

When the son came home for lunch, his father was gone, never to return again. He was rounded up with some twenty other well-known local Serbs, Communists, and Yugoslav sympathizers, the very day the future leader of the Independent State of Croatia, Ante Pavelić, returned from exile in Italy and passed through Karlovac on his way to Zagreb with two hundred Ustasha immigrants in Italian uniforms, many of whom had been interned for six years in various camps in Sicily, Sardinia, and the Lipari islands, and who were on their way to serve as the ruling elite of the new Nazi puppet state.

Most of the men arrested with Goldstein's father were soon released, but for reasons that are not clear to this day, he was kept in custody with a few other "unreliables," most likely because he was a known leftist. The new regime at the time didn't yet have a clear Jewish policy. The main enemies of the Ustasha movement were the Serbs and the Belgrade regime. Furthermore, some of the nationalist leaders of the earlier generation in Croatia, the so-called Frankists, were Jewish. It was only in the 1930s, under the influence of Hitler's ideas, that the Ustasha ideology, a blend of fascist and Nazi doctrines, became more and more anti-Semitic. Of course, anyone who was Jewish and had seen what had happened in Germany had to be worried.

What they did not know, and could not possibly imagine, is that it would be the local nationalists, rather than the Nazis, who would be their executioners. So they waited, expecting that the state would not harm peaceful citizens. This was true of local Serbs too. Not many of them were aware that Dr. Mladen Lorković, one of the future Ustasha ministers, had said that "the Croatian state cannot exist if 1,800,000 Serbs live in it, if at the same time we have a strong Serbian state behind our backs.... We, therefore, must strive to make the Serbs vanish from our midst." Supposedly, even Himmler was horrified when he heard from one of Pavelić's emissaries in 1941 that they intended to kill two million Serbs.

The most disheartening aspect of the early chapters of Goldstein's book is how long it takes for future victims under such a regime to realize that they are doomed, and how quickly others, who may have barely given them a thought a week before, become their eager persecutors. Since many of those in Karlovac who participated in the atrocities were either Goldstein's neighbors, school friends, or known to him as prominent citizens, he's able to tell us in considerable detail how they behaved during and after the war. It's a story made even more amazing by its close resemblance to the events in Croatia and Bosnia not long ago. A plan concocted by a small group of extreme nationalist intellectuals to undo the ethnic and religious mix of the population, which the wars with the Ottoman Empire and expulsions of peoples over the centuries had produced, was swiftly enacted. One day you were a citizen of Yugoslavia with full rights, and the next day you were told that unless you were a member of the Croatian nation by origin and blood, you did not exist legally. When it comes to this kind of evil, most human beings are innocents. Who can possibly believe that the prospect of having complete power over someone who has none would be such an enticement to people from all walks of life? Who can accept the idea that their school friends will turn into killers the first chance they get?

Goldstein describes the first political killings in Karlovac, of three prominent Serbian citizens who were taken from their homes on May 5, 1941, by five young men and shot in a nearby forest. The secret order came from Zagreb and was directed to officials in various towns whose job was to select the killers and their victims. This demonstration, of what Goldstein calls "synchronized violence," on St. George's Day, the Serbian religious holiday, was to show both Serbs and Croats that from now on blood would flow. The five who participated were known to Goldstein, one or two quite well. They were the usual small-town types from different social backgrounds, one a young lawyer, one a gifted high school student with a bright future, and the rest apprentices in various trades. As fanatical nationalists, all they needed was for some opportunist, who had rushed to embrace the new regime, to whisper in their ear whom to liquidate that day.

In the meantime, Goldstein's father had been transferred from Karlovac to a prison in Zagreb, despite his mother's frantic effort to have him released. In such situations, women can usually smell trouble better than men. Before he was arrested, both his wife and their house servant, a young woman from a nearby village, urged him to go and hide in the countryside. His son, who has made it his life's mission to hunt down everyone who knew his father in prison, has a fair amount of information on how he spent his time there. For a while, he and his mother were able to visit him and bring parcels of food to him in Zagreb and at the camp called Danica (Morning Star), to which he was next sent. Although it was not yet clear what the Ustashas intended to do with the Serbs and Jews they had rounded up, the signs were ominous.

One day while visiting the father in Zagreb, his wife noticed that he had bruises and that his face was swollen in places. In the Danica camp it was even worse. Torture is one of the perks of any regime that uses terror as a political instrument. Sadists get to have their fun and to pass themselves off as patriots. One of the camp officers even brought his sixteen-year-old son to participate in beatings. Goldstein has learned who some of these brutal characters were and what happened to them afterward. One of the worst among them, for instance, later switched sides, joined the resistance, and fought heroically against the Ustashas. After the war, a woman who had been an inmate recognized him and he was hanged in public on the site of the old camp.

The mass slaughter of Serbs began in late April 1941, less than three weeks after the proclamation of the new state, and continued throughout the war. The killing was done by special Ustasha units that would descend upon a village or town, round up all the Serb men they could find at home, and, after locking them up and mistreating them, take them out to a nearby forest and execute them. A few hundred people were killed on a typical night. The intention at first was to slay every man in the community; later, they didn't spare women, children, and old people either.

The local Croatian population did not directly participate in the killings. They dug mass graves and covered them and were told to keep their mouths shut. In the town of Glina, several hundred men were tricked into coming into the Orthodox church to be converted to Catholicism; they were slaughtered and the church set on fire. On another occasion, the Ustashas made the condemned roast suckling pigs and baby lambs for their executioners and dig their own graves while being forced to sing. As in Bosnia in the 1990s, the butchery was accompanied by pillage. The killers took everything that had any value, even clothes and shoes.

"We need to kill one third so that one third will run away and one third will convert," Ustashas used to say. That formula, Goldstein points out, was not invented by them. It originated in Russia in the years 1881 and 1882 and was attributed to Konstantin Petrovich Pobyedonostzev, close adviser of Tsar Alexander III, who commented on the latest wave of pogroms against the Jews: "Let a third immigrate, a third become Orthodox, and a third await their death." It made no difference to the leaders of the new regime that someone would have to pay for emulating the worst policies of Nazi Germany. As Goldstein observes, it was more important for Pavelić to kill Serbs than to stabilize Croatia.

Both Germans and Italians complained about the massacres of Serbs to Pavelić. They didn't care what he did with the Jews, but the commanders of the two armies could easily anticipate that they would have a rebellion on their hands. Ustashas, like the SS in Russia, believed that harsh policies would suppress any insurgency, but as one would expect, it only strengthened the resistance. For the desperate Serbs fleeing into the woods and mountains, there were two insurrections they could join: the Partisans, led by the Communists, or the Chetniks, who were led by pro-royalist officers. Communists called for an uprising against both the occupiers and the Ustasha with the aim of getting the Croatian population on their side, while the Chetniks wanted revenge against the Croats, and were willing to ally themselves with the Italians and Germans to ensure the survival of their people. This split between Partisans and Chetniks, into which the Serbian population was driven in 1941, has had tragic consequences and has not healed to this day.

Where was Goldstein's father while all this was going on? The family had no idea. To make matters worse, the mother, too, was imprisoned. Slavko's younger brother Danko was sent to his grandparents in Bosnia and he himself remained in Karlovac living with friends and waiting for his parents to come home. It was a period when, under the threat of arrest and severe punishment, all Jews and Orthodox Christians could move around town only between the hours of eight in the morning and six at night.

As is generally the case, the story of Goldstein's and his mother's survival is one of a few good people coming to their aid and one or two disreputable characters who decided to act decently for once.

That's how his mother got her "temporary" release from prison. The moment she was out, she took the only option a Jew who wanted to flee had in Croatia in 1941: she crossed over into the more moderately governed Italian occupation zone, and then, when things became dangerous for her there, she took both her sons and went over to the Partisans. Resourceful and tough, understanding better than others that one must act decisively, she reminds me of the women I grew up with during that same war, who found food where there was none and took care of their children and old people while their husbands and sons were either fighting with some army or insurgency, or were in prison or dead.

Goldstein's mother didn't say to her son that leaving Karlovac meant giving up hope that they would see his father again. Neither she nor anyone else knew that the Ustashas had already set up several extermination camps, one of them in the village of Jadovno near the town of Gospić among the deep woods and ravines of the Velebit Mountains. That particular camp existed for fifty-five days and had about four thousand prisoners, all of whom, except one who escaped, were killed. Most of the inmates were Serbs and the rest Jews. The method of killing was to take a group of about twenty people to the edge of a pit, tie the hands of all of them with wire, and then kill the first few with a sledgehammer, axe, or knife and let the dead pull the living down into their grave. This is where Goldstein's father ended his days.

Although the Ustashas tried to keep the existence of that death camp and the others in the region a secret, the local population began talking about seeing columns of badly mistreated people led toward the camp and hearing screams and shots in the night. The Italian occupying forces complained about "wild massacres" perpetrated in the proximity of their units, which forced the Ustashas to close the camps and relocate them farther up north and closer to

Zagreb. After the war, a number of camp guards were tried for crimes committed in Jadovno, but Goldstein admits that he couldn't bring himself to read their confessions. Besides, as he says, those who planned and gave orders were always of more interest to him than those who merely obeyed.

Goldstein's reason for his detailed documentation of terror in 1941 is the pain that he feels every time he finds the revisionist lie in one of his grandchildren's schoolbooks that the Ustashas' crimes were nothing more than a response to the Serbian uprising against the Croatian state. He is the kind of truth-teller even nations with far less on their conscience prefer not to hear from. In this book, in addition to the genocide of Serbs and Jews, he also writes about the slaughter of thousands of Ustashas, Chetniks, and other political opponents of the Communists, who were trapped in May 1945 as they were trying to escape into Austria, some of them with their families. This was a taboo subject in postwar Yugoslavia for forty years, and once it became possible to write about it, it was instantly used by the various nationalist factions to feed the passions of ethnic hatred. His wise book gives one hope. He is not an angry man, even though he has every right to be one when we consider how many members of his family were killed by Ustashas. He fought with the Partisans, became a Communist, but quickly turned against the Party and its repressive policies after being discharged from the victorious army after the war. He emigrated to Israel in 1948, but returned two years later, feeling that even with everything that happened to his family, Croatia was still his home.

While helping with the research for this book in the archives of the national and university library in Zagreb, the librarian in charge of old manuscripts and books found for Goldstein, among the papers of an Ustasha official (a minor poet and later the editor of a prestigious émigré magazine), two pages of a letter his father wrote while he was in prison, which the official, who had emigrated to Argentina and then returned to Croatia when it became independent in 1991, had kept all these years for some unknown reason. The letter is dated May 2, 1941. It says:

> Dear Slavko!
>
> I heard from mother that you cried last Saturday because I'm in prison. That news made me more sad than glad. I know that you didn't cry out of shame that your father is in jail! You should know that there are times when it's more honorable to be in prison than on the outside. Perhaps you cried because injustice is being done to your father. It's better to bear injustice than to inflict it. Or perhaps you cried because you feel sorry for me in my present situation. It's true that it's not nice and comfortable to be without freedom; still my situation is not such that you need to pity me. Even if it were much worse than it is, your tears would not be the right reaction. You are thirteen years old and I always wanted you to become—a champ. When you were a little kid, I showed you how one can be brave in a physical sense (better boxer than me, stronger than Prince Marko), but later I strove to show you another kind of courage. As much as your athletic and academic success make me happy, I would like you to become in that other sense, and primarily in that other sense—a hero. It's not a question here of just one but of many inner traits. I won't list them for you since I wouldn't remember them all, although I think I have indicated them to you all on different occasions.

Slavko Goldstein did not receive this fragment of his father's letter with its additional pages until sixty-five years after it was written, but the man he became in his long and rich life was the one his father wanted him to be. In the introduction to the Serbian edition of this book, he says of himself: I was a Jewish kid running to save his head from Croatian Ustashas, who survived thanks to good people in a Croatian village and who spent the remaining war years fighting the Germans while living in Serbian villages. On both sides, he made friends and found mutual understanding. Slavko Goldstein is an extraordinary man and this is an extraordinary book.

—Charles Simic

Part One

My Father

Ivo Goldstein (1900–1941)

I

The Two Ranks (1941–1945)

I WAS AN inquisitive young boy, not very tall, so I had to climb a fence to be able to see over the crowds of people. Good Friday, April 11, 1941, dawned bathed in spring sunshine, with tricolor flags fluttering in the breeze from the roofs, windows, and balconies. The sleet that had fallen on the streets of Karlovac the day before had melted overnight. From the Kupa Bridge toward Selce, rows and rows of residents stretched on either side of Banija Street to welcome the German army as it entered the city. Children were waving small paper flags, while from the ranks of people a jubilant refrain sounded: "No war and we have a state!"

The first tank of the German advance unit stopped at the corner of Banija and Kolodvorska streets in front of an improvised stage. Next to the stage, the brass band of the local fire brigade blared military marches and red-faced speakers recited welcoming speeches. I couldn't hear them—the loudspeakers were not very good—but from my elevated position on the fence, with my friends Tonček Strzalkowski and Bogdan Lasić, I had a good view and could see everything. Our curiosity was satisfied and we were happy not to be submerged in the multitude, whose joy we did not share that day.

Our schoolmate Lončarić, three or four years older than me and whom we called Lonac ("Pot") on the soccer field, was strutting along the rows of people with a rifle slung over his shoulder and a large insignia on his visored cap, obviously proud that he was one of those keeping order. Mr. Livadić, a Jew named Leitner who had recently converted to Catholicism and was the owner of a hardware store not far from our house on the promenade, was flaunting his swift accommodation to the new circumstances. Dressed in a guard's uniform with a newly sewn insignia on his cap, he carried a rifle and sported a conspicuous, man-in-charge attitude, like some kind of marshal (none of which saved him because as a Jew by birth he ended up at the concentration camp at Jadovno that same year). For a moment I thought that Smiljka Kozomarić, who was my age, was peeking out from behind the curtains of a first-floor window, the same Smiljka whom I had watched with that first shy yearning the previous summer at the swimming area on the Korana River exposing the roundness of her budding womanhood to water and sun. Her father was a wealthy Karlovac merchant and a prominent supporter of Serbian cultural associations and the Yugoslav Sokol,[1] so Smiljka certainly had little reason to be happy with the arrival of the Germans, the proclamation by the Ustasha of the Independent State of Croatia, and the celebration that was taking place in front of her house.

A young German soldier (or officer), visible from the waist up in the turret of a tank, was quietly, perhaps indifferently, listening to the welcoming speeches in a language that he didn't understand. From my distant vantage point he seemed to be furtively glancing at his watch. Sixty years later my friend Josip Vaništa, now a prominent Croatian portrait artist, told me how the youthful, handsome face of the soldier (or officer) surprised him—a beautiful, refined visage on top of an enormous, ugly tank.

Passing through the double ranks of people, the German advance unit paraded over the Banija Bridge, entered Karlovac, and spread throughout the city. "This is a power that no one can resist," Bogdan muttered dejectedly on his way home, the German tanks still fresh in his mind. Bogdan was a zealous sympathizer of the League of Young Communists of Yugoslavia; three years later he would be the commissar of a company in the Žumberak Brigade of the Partisan army. For the next two or three days we watched from our windows as German motorized units came and went, forming and re-forming their ranks in front of Zorin Dom, the local cultural center, as if they were being prepared for deployment. Armored cars were pulling artillery with barrels longer than the vehicles themselves. The Royal Yugoslav Army, which disintegrated in the face of the onslaught of the mechanized armor, also had artillery, but it was pulled by oxen. In the nearby town of Glina—as recorded by a local historian—an artillery division with harnessed oxen had camped one night in the courtyards and the town park. German tanks rumbled through the town in the morning, but the Royal Yugoslav Army's artillery crews had scattered in all directions overnight, leaving the oxen abandoned and lowing sadly on the streets of Glina, thirsty and hungry.

Four years later, on both sides of Banija Street long rows of happy citizens again crowded the street. It was late evening of May 8, 1945. The war was over. Through this clamorous cordon the Karlovac Shock Brigade was returning home. On the corner of Kolodvorska and Banija streets a brass band, perhaps the same band that had played four years earlier, was again blaring spirited marches. People in the crowd were waving small flags, loudly hailing and joyously welcoming soldiers in the ranks of the brigade. More than a thousand young people marching through the cordon could barely keep discipline in the ranks and would much rather have hurled themselves into the throng of citizens: They had returned from the war to their homes and families.

But this time there was no stage on the corner of Kolodvorska and Banija. The welcoming speeches were recited at the destroyed bridge, though I could neither see nor hear the speakers because I was far in the rear ranks of the brigade, in the Fourth Battalion. It seemed to me that among the many people in front of the Hotel Europa the man with the most luxuriant hair in town was again standing exactly where he had stood four years earlier. It was Kiš, the radio technician. The windows of Smiljka Kozomarić's house were not curtained this time and Smiljka was waving from one of them. From both sides of the cordon people would run into the ranks of the brigade to hug a son, a daughter, a brother, or a friend. The disciplined military ranks slowly loosened and were swallowed by the mass of people. Just before the bridge my mother suddenly ran up to me from the crowd and for a long time we cried—from happiness that we were together again and from sadness that those closest to us, and many others, were no longer with us. One war really was over. For many of us it was called the Liberation. Only later did we realize that this "liberation" did not bring happiness to all, that to some people it brought unjust suffering and pain. We were mature enough to resist evil, but we were not mature enough to crown our victory humanely. Like many military victories in history, ours did not remain untainted either.

Four years—between the first and second parades on Banija Street—was how long the war that had determined our fates lasted. It destroyed millions of families, tore apart countless others, and scattered people everywhere. It forced former friends and neighbors to look at each other down the barrel of a machine gun. The war left traces that endure to the present day. Although some years later the Germans, with some self-satisfaction, created the word *Vergangenheitsbewältigung* (overcoming the past), I fear that they still haven't fully confronted this past, even less so in the case of our eastern neighbors and here in Croatia. Hidden diseases still fester, the most stubborn roots of which lie in 1941, even if the years that came before and after it aren't guiltless either.

Writing this book about my family, I have tried not to separate what happened to us from the fates of many other people and of an entire country. The narrative follows friends and acquaintances, some of whom I might not have known at the time, trying to understand them even if we were not on the same side of history. I think that the fate of my family, which is my starting point, will fill in an overall picture of events, and that this picture, which I have outlined through a mass of researched documents and other sources, will help us all better understand what happened and why—to those closest to me, and to many others.

* * *

I think I can pinpoint exactly the hour and day when my childhood ended: Easter Sunday, April 13, 1941. On the promenade in front of Zorin Dom not far from our house, German tanks, armored vehicles, and military kitchens on large wheels with fat tires were neatly lined up. My friends Tone Oreškovič and "Cujo" Pasek came by so we could go out and play. My father stopped me at the door.

"Where are you going?"

"Out to play."

"To play?" My father looked at me with surprise. "Well, okay. Go, but don't be late for lunch."

When I came back, my father was no longer home. And he was never to return.

I don't remember if we actually played on the promenade that morning or if we gave in to our boyish curiosity and just walked around the neatly arrayed armored behemoths that we had only seen before in Fox Movietone newsreels. The German soldiers were chatting idly, sipping something from tin cups, joking around, and smoking. Stanko Lasić, a leading Croatian theoretician and literary historian, and my childhood friend, saw them at the same time and in the same place, and writes in his *Autobiografski zapisi* (Autobiographical Notes)[2]:

> Everything I thought about the Germans until that time I could put into a single phrase—an evil and ugly people. But the young ones who came to Karlovac were happy, smiling, polite, courteous, even kind, but above all, handsome. Nothing was too difficult for them. We watched them on the promenade in front of Zorin Dom, always doing something, cleaning weapons, polishing tanks, wiping mud from the wheels and treads, reading newspapers, listening to the radio, washing shirts, trimming fingernails—open toward us but closed within themselves. I immediately felt that they were being genuine, that they were not putting on a performance or playing a trick. They were what they were: an army, conquerors, disciplined killers.

"Why are they smiling? What are they saying," my friends kept asking, trying to persuade me to eavesdrop on their conversations. The German soldiers probably didn't realize that an inquisitive local boy understood German. They were laughing and chattering about girls, victories, letters home. I remember one conversation particularly well. Leaning back with one foot resting on the vehicle, a noncommissioned officer took a thoughtful puff of his cigarette and, wanting to test the knowledge of his younger charges, turned to two or three of his comrades.

"Well, what do you say? Where are we off to next?"

"To Turkey!"

"No way. To Russia!" the NCO declared with self-assurance, as if he knew something he could not tell the others.

"Why not Turkey? We can get to the Suez right away. The Spaniards at Gibraltar, and the Mediterranean is ours. And Iraqi oil and Persia, all the way to India."

"We're going to Russia, you'll see." The smug NCO pretended to know better.

The sullen face of Jaga, our housekeeper, greeted me when I got home. From 1932, when she first came to our home, Jaga was our ideal cook, housekeeper, nursemaid, teacher, confidante, peacemaker, and most reliable friend. She was also a full member of our family until the day in 1990 when my brother and I buried her in the family grave next to our mother at Mirogoj Cemetery. To this day, I find it difficult to comprehend where that young, inexperienced, semiliterate peasant girl from poverty-stricken Banski Kovačevac had gained such wisdom and where such an unerring instinct to distinguish good from evil came from.

An hour before I returned home that day, two young men had come for my father. Before the war they were well-known Frankists.[3] One was Ratko Demut, a law student; the other, Stjepan Augustinović, was a loafer. They were dressed in civilian clothes but had revolvers at their belts and newly sewn tricolor and Ustasha insignias on their sleeves. I was told that they were polite. "Excuse us, Mr. Goldstein, we just need you to make a statement. You'll be back in no time." My mother rushed after them, probably to the police station. Jaga could barely suppress her anguish. The evening before she had urged my father to go immediately to her village "until the first danger has passed, then you can decide what to do next." But my father and mother were trying to figure out how not to separate the family. They were hesitating, thought they had time. My younger brother, Danko, also remembers the look of anguish and fear on Jaga's otherwise stolid face when he came home that day just a bit after me.

This is how Lasić recalls my father's fate:

> Slavko's father had a bookstore and stationery shop right in the center of town, near the Church of the Holy Trinity. His business was doing very well. He was a capable man who in addition to the bookstore had a lending library in an extension of the main shop. Dark, but comfortable. Quiet. Books could be borrowed from but also read in that "library." Mr. Goldstein allowed me to read whatever I wanted, and from time to time he would talk to me about a book that I happened to be holding in my hands. Always gentle, always calm. Knowledgeable.... He was arrested early on and among the first to be liquidated, very likely thrown into one of the execution pits.... I would have been shocked if it had happened to any man, even the greatest criminal, because violent death has always horrified me. But how could I not be devastated when death had reached out and taken a man whom I considered to be full of goodness, from whom I had learned so much, who was a fine gentleman and like me in love with books, which he held in his hands as gently as if he were holding a child. I often witnessed in the bookstore his concern for other people. He knew how to talk with everyone; he was pleasant, unobtrusive, he was himself. It was said that he was a leftist; I heard that repeated many times, but also that he was never a member of any political party. He was spoken of as a humanist, which was how I learned that word, its meaning became equal with his character. Death came to him in the moment of our "resurrection." Why? Because he was a Jew. Because he was a humanist.

My father's arrest and those days of April 1941 are, in my memory, a distinct border in time. Until I was thirteen years old, memories were mostly brief flickering images, disconnected pictures pulled out of time and isolated from the contextual space. From that moment in

April I remember events in their entirety: moving pictures in a logical sequence, entire episodes immersed in space, steeped in time. I also remember some conversations, their context, here and there even sentences, word for word, though I'm not always certain which are actual memories and which are embellishments from subsequent conversations and insights. So, in writing this book, I have placed all of my memories under suspicion. I have filled in the gaps and sought to make sense of them by poring over newspapers, official documents, personal letters, and memoirs of the time. My recollections were also on trial in conversations with my brother and with friends from that time whom I still see today. For the description of these times I have relied on the many documents in which I discovered a variety of lesser-known or unknown details that shed better light on the important events of this period. I have tried to be faithful to myself, to future readers of this text, and to those about whom I am writing and who are no more.

"To the living we owe respect, but to the dead only the truth" is an often quoted aphorism of Voltaire. To me it seems that we owe the truth to everyone, living and dead, equally. And we owe respect to many, both the living and the dead, but not to everyone.

2

In the Jail of the District Court

ON THAT EASTER Sunday when my father was taken to the jail of the district court, about twenty or more Karlovac residents were arrested—the more prominent citizens of Serbian nationality, leaders of Serbian- and Yugoslav-oriented associations, several of the best-known communists (Ivo Vejvoda, Branko Priselac, Puba Drakulić), and just two Jews: my father and his close friend Filip Reiner, a lawyer and the leader of the Karlovac Zionists. No one ever told them or their families why they were in jail. Only later were we somehow able to piece events together.

On that same day—April 13, 1941—in the first failing light of evening at about eight o'clock, the Ustasha *Poglavnik* Ante Pavelić arrived in Karlovac from the direction of Duga Resa in the German army Mercedes of Lieutenant Colonel Saltzer, who was the deputy military attaché to the Kingdom of Yugoslavia. An hour or two later, a column of civilian Italian buses under the command of Lieutenant Colonel Sangiorgio arrived with about two hundred Ustasha émigrés, who were returning to the country after a long absence that included six and a half years of internment in Italy. They were "haggard-looking, with visible traces of their suffering and hardship in the camps on Lipari, Sardinia, and Sicily," as Eugen Dido Kvaternik described in *Sjećanja i zapažanja 1925–1945* (Memories and Reminiscences 1925–1945),[1] the most interesting of the Ustasha memoirs. They had traveled exactly twenty-four hours from Trieste to Karlovac and were undoubtedly happy at the prospect of a good night's sleep in the tidy barracks of the Karlovac Cadet School. But they were also undoubtedly disappointed that they had to spend all the next day and night there, impatient to start for Zagreb as quickly as possible to become the rulers of the country—powerful, rich, and honored—and also to reward and avenge themselves for their many years of patience, for every privation and suffering, for the painful uncertainties and the frequent crises of hopelessness, for all of the attendant maladies of political emigration, which now, in the explosion of this fortunate moment, had finally come to an end.

Pavelić was forced to wait in Karlovac for about thirty hours until Edmund Veesenmayer, an official from the German Ministry of Foreign Affairs, arrived from Zagreb and Filippo Anfuso, the Italian deputy minister of foreign affairs, arrived from Rome, so that they could dictate the Ustasha government's obligations to their respective countries. Only after Pavelić had promised Mussolini by telegram "to respect Italian rights in Dalmatia regarding the demarcation of the border," and had sent a telegram to Hitler to express his "gratitude to the German army" and his wish "that Croatia enter the new European order," and only after providing an additional guarantee—which Veesenmayer noted in detail—that "the Croatian army would march shoulder to shoulder with the German army in the struggle against the common enemy," was he allowed to continue on to Zagreb. He arrived on the still-dark morning of April 15, along with his fellow Ustasha returnees, and took his seat at St. Mark's Square, as Ratko Demut wrote in the Karlovac weekly *Hrvatska sloboda* (Croatian Freedom), "in order to take into his hands the helm of Croatia, which inadequate foreigners had guided through eight centuries." Demut went on to say that "Croats have waited eight hundred years for such a leader," whose personal qualities "raise him to the ranks of the greatest men in Europe," and that Karlovac "had welcomed with pride the opportunity given to it and had offered shelter to the greatest Croat of all time when on that first night he found himself in the homeland after a twelve-year absence, and that was the greatest day in the history of our city."[2]

The majority of people jailed because of the precautionary police measures during Pavelić's stay in Karlovac were quickly allowed to return to their homes after he departed, among them Filip Reiner and all of the communists. My father remained in jail with several of the "most politically undesirable." According to Milan Radeka, the only person from that group who survived to write his memoirs, Goldstein had too many black marks against him: He was a Jew, a leftist, a popular bookseller, a former Zionist pioneer in Palestine, and one of the leading Esperantists; the descendant of a native rabbinic-bookseller family who was thought to have some influence in the city. Residents of Karlovac who frequently dropped by his bookshop were said to be followers of Miroslav Krleža,[3] socialists, communists, extreme individualists, rebellious liberals, Zionists, Esperantists, antifascists, syndicalists, Popular Frontists—all of them politically undesirable. Father had already been questioned several times by the former Yugoslav police when packages were shipped from the bookshop to volunteers fighting in the Spanish Civil War and when he used each new publication by Krleža to decorate all three windows of his bookshop with Krleža's books and pictures and with quotes by and about Krleža. When he started the weekly *Karlovački novosti* (Karlovac News) in 1932, he was forced by the police to stop publication after a few issues.

In the bookstore my father heavily promoted antiwar writers (Erich Maria Remarque, Henri Barbusse), books with popular social content (Maksim Gorky, John Dos Passos, Upton Sinclair, Jack London), German anti-Nazis and émigrés (Thomas and Heinrich Mann, Erich Kästner, Bertolt Brecht, Alfred Döblin, Ernst Toller, Stefan Zweig), and first and foremost Krleža, including his complete works in the Minerva and Binoza editions and, with special personal affection and satisfaction, his famous *Ballads of Petrica Kerempuh* as soon as they appeared in 1936. My father tirelessly recited the *Ballads* to us at home in the Kajkavian[4] dialect as it was written. He urged Danko and me to try to follow the lamentations of poor serfs about the unbearable tributes and tolls, the verses about flowers without rights, and about Imbra Skunkač—chicken thief and petty crook—who succeeded in smuggling himself into paradise.

As an enterprising bookseller, my father made the circuit of village schools in the regions of Pokuplje and Kordun—first on a Dresch motorcycle and later in a rickety Fiat—supplying them with books and school supplies, becoming acquainted and establishing friendships with the more intellectually inquisitive and progressive teachers, especially with the teacher and writer Hasan Kikić, who often visited us while he was teaching in Gornji Sjeničak and Pisarovina (and whose handsome profile I remember to this today, as he was singing a nostalgic Bosnian song known as a *sevdalinka* and overpowering the rattling of our Fiat with his powerful but pleasant baritone on a bumpy road in Pokuplje or Kordun). When students in the senior classes of the teaching college and the high school organized protests and a strike in 1938 because of the transfers of two of their favorite teachers—a leftist by the name of Niko Pavić and a Croatian nationalist named Mirko Zelenika—several of the leaders of the protest came to our house to speak with my father and to hear his views. When Ivo Marinković, a leading Karlovac communist, returned home in 1937 after three years of imprisonment in Sremska Mitrovica and was not permitted to support his family in his profession as a high-school teacher of classical languages, my father found him a job as a bookkeeper with his friends the Veličković family, who owned the Podvinec leather factory. My father most frequently could be found in the company of his best friends: Mia Veličković, a Slovenian woman, and her husband, Aleksandar Veličković, a Serb; the Zionist Filip Reiner and his wife, Ružica Bonači Reiner, a literature teacher and poet from Split; and her best friend Marica Marinković, a high-school teacher and the sister of Ivo Marinković. Thus, as Milan Radeka said, Ivo Goldstein "had too many black marks against him."

My father was held in the jail of the district court in Karlovac from April 13 to 26. My mother brought him food every day and I accompanied her on several occasions. The superintendent of the jail, a man by the name of Berger, often arranged for us to speak with my father, alone, in a hallway. I don't know if this was permissible under the regulations or if the superintendent was simply being exceptionally kind. Berger spoke softly, with a pained and sorrowful expression, as if telling us something in confidence and expressing his regret that there was no more he could do. One of the guards, the mustachioed Đuro, out of respect for my father, called him "sir" and spoke consoling words to me. My mother was completely obsessed with all sorts of schemes to save my father, while he tried to stay calm, perhaps even confident that everything would end well. However, when I saw his face as he was waving goodbye through the barred window of the cell that faced the courtyard, I sensed a tension in his smile and a look of concern on his face. But today I don't know if this memory is genuine or some later embellishment.

April 16, three days after my father's arrest, was Danko's ninth birthday. Neither my mother nor Jaga had the will to arrange a birthday party, but Mia Veličković presented Danko with a wristwatch. In those days this was a rare and expensive gift—none of Danko's friends had a wristwatch. Jewish boys usually received such gifts on their thirteenth birthday as a bar mitzvah present. I was also promised a wristwatch for my thirteenth birthday, which was coming up soon. Mia had succeeded in easing Danko's sadness about a birthday without our father. Superintendent Berger allowed him a visit. Danko proudly showed his new wristwatch to my father, who smiled benevolently—but who knows what he was feeling in his soul.

I helped out in our bookshop for several weeks until it was sealed and confiscated as Jewish property. In the first days of the occupation our best customers were German soldiers, who paid with freshly printed notes stamped *Reichskreditkassenschein*, which we called "occupation marks." It seemed that the soldiers had an abundance of these marks and that they bought anything they could find to send home to Germany. "Wimpy eats everything," we would say, after the character in the Popeye cartoons. I saw soldiers with bundles of notes coming out of a large van parked on the promenade in front of the house of the Lukinić family. We boyishly surmised that they were printing the notes in the truck, but it was probably only serving as a cashier point for the troops—a portable warehouse for cheap money where the Wehrmacht rewarded its soldiers for yet another blitzkrieg victory. (According to the agreement of May 16, 1941, the Ustasha government had to cover all of the costs for maintaining the German army in the Independent State of Croatia (NDH)—the Croatian puppet state of Nazi Germany—and to provide the financial backing for the occupation money.) For the next several days, or as long as the Germans were in Karlovac, they emptied the shelves of many of the stores, leading to the first shortages of some articles in the town. Our head clerk, Mr. Rubčić, was elated by the rapid turnover in the shop. He wanted to go to Zagreb to purchase more items to restock the shelves, but my mother would not allow it. She did approve of having our most trusted assistant, Dragec Starešinić, a prewar member of the outlawed Communist Party, sneak out of the shop with two Olivetti typewriters, which Maca Majstorović and Josip Kraš, organizers of the local resistance movement, were said to have used to write antifascist propaganda two or three months later. I think that my mother also took "occupation marks" from the shop every day and exchanged them the next day for Yugoslav dinars, which she then used on the black market to purchase Italian lire, the only relatively reliable currency in Croatia at that time.

Although some people from the first group of the Karlovac detainees were released after several days, all three jails in Karlovac (county, district, and municipal) quickly began to fill up again. The corner of Haulik and Križanić streets in front of the district court became a gathering place for the relatives of those who had been arrested. They brought food and waited for news of their loved ones and for an explanation from the authorities. The ranks of the group swelled almost daily, becoming both larger and denser. Hungry for information about what was happening to their family members and wanting to help them, everyone exchanged news, advice, and other "confidential tidbits." New friendships were made in the kind of solidarity that is created among people struck by similar misfortune. Desperately wanting good news, the people produced it themselves: "Regardless of what they are, the Germans want order. I hear that they are asking Pavelić not to hold people in jail without a trial, and the courts, such as they are, will have to respect the law!" and other similar remarks. While many people were still happy because of the quick end to the war and the establishment of a Croatian state, the first acts of the Ustasha government had sparked fear in the population. People gripped by this fear had somehow understood that they were losing their status as equal citizens and perhaps also their jobs and property, but they still did not think that life itself was at stake. "As much as I read about Hitler's camps, which had been filled before the war with Germans and Jews, I held the firm conviction that this could not happen in Croatia. Croatian history and culture respected the sanctity of the law, which I learned as a student, and so any kind of illegal violence seemed impossible. 'Croatian-ness' for me is closely tied to the idea of justice," wrote Milan Radeka in *Sjećanjima* (Memories), one of the best memoirs about 1941.[5]

On Thursday, April 17, Radeka, who had been imprisoned in the Karlovac jail, was visited by Ivo Klarić, who was then a member of the municipal Ustasha leadership, a body of seven members that in those first weeks of the NDH was all-powerful in Karlovac. Klarić and Radeka were colleagues. They were both teachers at the Karlovac high school: Klarić taught language and literature and was known as a Croatian nationalist; Radeka taught religion and was also a lawyer and an excellent historian, and was well regarded in the city as a man of broad culture, democratic convictions, and religious and political tolerance. In the elections he had voted for Vladko Maček's United Opposition. Klarić had come to say that in the Ustasha leadership he had already removed Radeka's name from the blacklist twice, but the third time he was unsuccessful. However, he had arranged a "leave of absence" for Radeka from Friday to Monday so he could celebrate Orthodox Easter at home.

It is not completely clear if by granting Radeka this "Easter leave" Klarić wanted to give him the chance to disappear, or, which is more likely, that even as a member of the Ustasha leadership at that time he had no inkling that mass executions of prisoners were in the offing. In his memoirs Radeka does not say if he was seized by doubts and fears when on the evening of April 21, after spending Easter in the close circle of his family, he returned along the streets of Karlovac to the jail. Could he have known with great certainty that his head was on the chopping block? The majority of those whom Radeka joined in the jail that night would no longer be alive at the end of

1941. Radeka, however, was lucky. He was included in a decision by German generals and other officials from the area of the now-dismembered Yugoslavia in which, as part of a broader plan, Catholic priests from the Slovenian areas annexed to Germany were deported to Croatia, while an equal number of Orthodox priests were deported from Croatia to Serbia. Thus, on August 1, 1941, Radeka and his family were sent from a camp near the town of Sisak to Belgrade. Before leaving, they had to sign a document "renouncing all of their property in favor of the Independent State of Croatia."

Klarić was also lucky or, rather, had some common sense. He was a member of the municipal Ustasha leadership for a total of six weeks. He saw the evil that was being perpetrated and felt that there would soon be an even greater evil in which he did not want to participate. "From his exposed position [as a member of the Ustasha leadership] Ivo Klarić moved rather quickly into a sheltered position, having used his short-lived patriotic dedication to become the director of a high school in Zagreb where he was able to lie low," Radeka writes in his memoirs. Klarić later allegedly provided clandestine assistance for the Partisans, thanks to which he experienced no serious difficulties after the war for having been an Ustasha functionary in April and May 1941. He was transferred from the high school in Zagreb to a high school in the town of Glina. He soon returned to Zagreb, eventually retiring from teaching.

In the jail of the Karlovac district court Radeka became closer to my father and "got to know him as what is commonly called a 'baptized soul,' notwithstanding his Jewishness... Goldstein was always a man—selfless, human, but also practical and resourceful... gentle, kind, good-natured, and charitable." But I can also remember my father in less gentle moments, when his big blue eyes would flash in a quick explosion of anger, then he would just as quickly calm down, fall into a brief, dull silence, and regain his look of benevolence and self-confidence. Many people considered him to be a happy person because he knew how to create a cheery atmosphere, doing a prankish Cossack dance accompanied by boisterous shouting. But I have read stories and poems he wrote in his student days and in Palestine and published in Jewish journals, his letters to my mother, and his diary entries, in all of which I discovered—besides a lively spirit and a sense of irony—anxiety, melancholy, periodic doubts, and resignation bordering at times on depression from which he was rescued by the far less meditative, indestructible, and enterprising character of my mother. We love or mourn our parents not because they were perfect but because we are a part of them and they are the most important part of our lives. My granddaughter Tesa once wrote a homework assignment in the second grade entitled "My Father" that ended with the words: "I love my daddy because he is my daddy." In moments of his greatest trials my father tried to be calm and strong, but I also believe that the optimism he tried to convey was beset by inner doubts and torment.

A year before the war, my father gave Jaga's brother, Mata Đerek, several thousand dinars to build an extra room on his house in Banski Kovačevac because "bad times are coming and we will perhaps have to hide there." Mata was then a hardworking twenty-three-year-old farmer and carpenter, a strong and bright young man who would grow, without any schooling and only through life experience, into a man of astuteness and wisdom such as I have rarely encountered even among people of great intelligence and knowledge. He built the extra room onto his wooden house and "kept it for the Goldsteins, just in case bad times do come." For a long time my father knew very well that bad times were coming and that they most probably would not pass us by. He was even able to joke about it. Sometimes on Sundays he would take Danko, me, and several of our friends for a run around the moats of Karlovac, and on one such occasion a neighbor asked,

"Mr. Goldstein, why are you running so far?" "Eh, it's exercising," my father responded jestingly. "Bad times are coming and we're training. We might have to run farther."

For the two years before 1941, Jewish refugees from Vienna had been passing through our home—childhood friends of my mother, colleagues of my father from the university in Vienna, and other acquaintances and friends of acquaintances. My father was one of the organizers of assistance for more than two hundred of the refugees who were put up in the barracks next to the railway station in the nearby village of Draganić. He often visited them, sometimes taking me with him. My mother's friends from Vienna, Greta and Paul Hermann, stayed with us for several weeks while waiting for visas to Mexico. As emigrants with a one-way exit visa, they were unable to take anything of great value from their home, so my mother traveled twice to Vienna (which was still possible in 1940 for people with Yugoslav passports) and brought back Greta's more valuable jewelry and other items that were being held for safekeeping with friends. During the weeks that the Hermanns spent with us, my mother taught Greta the beautician's trade. With this training and the cash from the valuables they sold, the Hermanns were able to make a new start in Mexico. Several times after the war airline tickets would arrive with an invitation for my mother to come to Mexico as Greta's guest and stay for as long as she wished. In 1958, when Greta heard that my mother had become a grandmother and that the grandson's name was Ivo, a check arrived from Mexico with a note of congratulations and shared happiness that we again had an Ivo in the family and sadness that little Ivo would never see his grandfather, whom he would certainly love and admire, just as all of us did.

In the two years before the war, and especially in the summer of 1940, the Jews in Yugoslavia knew that if Hitler gained control of this area, they would be in trouble. The Karlovac Jewish Community organized training courses for its members in certain trades because "the time is perhaps approaching when we may need manual skills." My father studied glassmaking and brought home glasses he had "blown" in these courses. My mother had completed a sort of Jewish secondary school for social workers, with added courses in nursing, at home in Černovic from 1919 to 1922, and in 1936, she completed a course of several weeks in Paris as a beautician with Helena Rubinstein. She thought that with her practical disposition she would be able to cope well with any difficulties that might arise. In 1940 and at the beginning of 1941, the Jews here knew what was probably awaiting them—that they would face mistreatment, discrimination, and perhaps expulsion; that their shops and possibly their apartments would be confiscated; and that they might even be sent to concentration camps. But they were convinced that they would not be killed. Until April 1941, no Jews had been killed in the Third Reich (with the exception of the nearly one hundred Jews who had perished during Kristallnacht—the Night of Broken Glass—on November 9, 1938, and a few individual murders). The idea for the "final solution of the Jewish question" (*Endlösung*) by total liquidation matured among the top Nazi leadership only in March and April 1941. Prior to that, the prevailing idea had been for a mass exodus from Europe (*Gesamtlösung*, for example, "Plan Madagascar"). Reinhard Heydrich, the chief of the Nazi Security Service (*Sicherheitsdienst*) and Himmler's deputy, had not begun until May 1941 to prepare in great secrecy four "action groups" (*Einsatzgruppen*), each with five to nine hundred handpicked members of the Nazi SS, charged with the direct implementation of the radical *Endlösung*. The mass murder of Jews, which we today call the Holocaust, began in Kaunas (Kovno), Vilnius, Lvov, and Minsk in late June and early July 1941, following Germany's invasion of the USSR. On July 31, Heydrich received from Hermann Göring the authorization to coordinate the action that was then officially defined, for the first time in written form, as the "final solution of the Jewish question." The killing of Jews by the Ustasha in death camps on Mount Velebit and on the island of Pag also began in July 1941 (though the mass killing of Serbs had already begun in early May), but the knowledge that camps in the NDH were not just labor and penal camps but also death camps began to filter through to Jews only at the end of August and the beginning of September. For example, when the Jewish Department of the Zagreb Ustasha police sent 180 young Jews to the Danica[6] concentration camp at the end of May 1941, they had all answered the summons voluntarily, while a young man named Željko Šrenger, who had not been called, voluntarily appeared with a knapsack because he "wanted to go with his friends." An Ustasha policeman named Šuprina, a good friend of the Šrenger family, chased him home, shouting, "And don't let me see you here again!," saving him from execution at Šaran's cavern on Mount Velebit, where all of Željko's friends perished.

This is one of the possible answers to the tormenting question that has endured for more than sixty years: Why did they wait? Why didn't they flee while it was still possible to flee? It is also a partial explanation for why my parents hesitated on Saturday, April 12, thinking that they still had time, when Jaga urged my father to seek refuge in Banski Kovačevac, where "his" room was awaiting him at Mata's house. All evening, and late into the night, they had debated with Jaga whether the family should be split up during such times, whether my father should go to Kovačevac alone or all of us should go together. The next morning Demut and Augustinović came for my father and took him away, never to return.

I don't know when my father began to regret that he did not listen to Jaga that evening. I know my mother carried that torment with her for the remaining thirty-three years of her life. Sometimes, very rarely, she would drop a hint or the snatch of a sentence, but she never gave voice to a complete thought. I understood her abrupt silences and halting sighs, and I never asked because I knew that there were no answers.

3

Cell No. 15

LATE IN THE evening of April 26, six middle-aged men were put in a special second-class carriage at the Karlovac station under a police escort and sent to Zagreb. This was the first group of prisoners from the jail of the district court. They were to appear before a court in Zagreb. The group included Marko Sablić, the chief of the Karlovac Yugoslav Sokol and a lecturer at the teachers college; the lawyer Nikica Badovinac, a former representative in the national parliament from Karlovac and a leading politician; Milan Kozomarić, a wealthy merchant and supporter of Yugoslav-oriented societies; Josip Gjurić, a popular Karlovac journalist; and Milan Radeka and my father. Radeka writes in his *Memories* how "he slept well on the upholstered seats in the second-class carriage" on the trip to Zagreb. At that time, trains in Croatia had three classes: third class was the most crowded, "for common people," with wooden benches; second class was considerably more comfortable, with upholstered seats; while first class was different from second only in the width of the seats. The transfer of the six prisoners by a special second-class carriage was made in "comfort fit for a king," and was possible only in those first days of the NDH, when some consideration was still shown to prisoners.

Some twenty years after the war in Rijeka, I met several times with the youngest person from this group of six, Josip "Pepić" Gjurić, who was born in 1911. He was then a highly regarded and popular editor of the sports section of the daily *Riječki list* (later *Novi list*). Speaking quickly in his characteristically squeaky voice, accompanied by animated mannerisms and barely suppressing the emotions that such memories stir, he picturesquely described how in the dead of the night very early on April 27 they were "conveyed" through the deserted Zrinjevac Square in Zagreb to the police detention center on Petrinjska Street. It amazed him that Zagreb was totally blacked out, even though the war had been nowhere near the town for two weeks. All six of them were squeezed into the overcrowded Cell No. 15 on the first floor, where they stumbled in the darkness over the closely bunched sleeping forms of the other prisoners and were barely able to find a spot to sit on or curl up in and wait for morning. "Pepić, my God, is that you?" came the voice from the prison darkness of a Zagreb journalist named Turkalj, who had recognized the squeaky voice of his colleague.

"That chance encounter eased my mind a bit," Gjurić remembered twenty years later. "Also I think Turkalj helped me get out of jail."

Turkalj advised Gjurić that if he were interrogated he should refer to sports reporting as his primary professional interest, which was true anyway as sports were his passion while all other areas of journalism were only professional obligations that the talented journalist nonetheless carried out very well.

"You were a fan of Građanski, so you have to push that in their faces," Turkalj said, because the Građanski soccer club was a favorite of the more nationalistically oriented fans, in contrast to those of HAŠK and Concordia. Thus, according to Gjurić's story, at his first interrogation, the virtually omnipotent secretary in the presidency of the NDH—at that time Aleksandar Seitz—concluded, "Why Gjurić, you're a *purger*!,"[1] and Gjurić was released from prison.

Gjurić somehow got through the war working as a journalist for several marginal business newspapers. He lived, contrary to his temperament, by mostly keeping to himself, in all likelihood oppressed by a feeling of insecurity and more in fear for his wife, Mira (née Berger), who was a baptized Jew, than for himself. In the autumn of 1943, Josip Vaništa ran into him on the street in Zagreb and Gjurić bemoaned his situation, saying he was living like "some kind of animal." Only after the war was he again in his element in the Rijeka newspapers. I recently saw a picture of him from 1962 in *Novi list* in the column "Time Machine"—the distinctively "chubby" face of a man whose very posture exuded a lively energy and temperament and a kind of suppressed satisfaction. In the text below the picture he was described as "a legend of Rijeka sports journalism."

Working as a journalist in a daily newspaper is a profession deeply immersed in the present. The future is tomorrow's edition, while the past is over with yesterday's. Gjurić would occasionally bring up in conversation Karlovac in 1941, mumbling that he would have to write about it "once I retire." He did not make it to retirement. He died a sudden journalist's death at the age of fifty-eight, exhausted by the constant race to meet a deadline. But even if he had not met that unfortunate and untimely death, Gjurić would never have written anything about 1941 in Karlovac because he was unable to get over what was for him an unpleasant, if brief, episode.

In recent years, while doing research for this book, I gave closer attention to scanning the newspapers from that time. In *Hrvatski narod* (The Croatian Nation), dated April 27, 1941, I came across a short news item from Karlovac:

> Yesterday the first issue of the weekly newspaper of the Croatian Ustasha Movement, known as *Hrvatska sloboda*, was published. The editor is the writer Stjepan Mihalić. Since Josip

> Gjurić began to publish his weekly newspaper, *Hrvat* [Croat], several days ago, the Ustasha Council has decided to ban further publication of this weekly.

There was no explanation for the ban, but the coincidence of dates is telling. Gjurić's paper was banned on April 26; that same evening he was on his way to the prison in Zagreb in the same group as my father.

I was, of course, interested in what kind of crime Gjurić had committed. I searched in vain through the archives and libraries of Zagreb and Karlovac for his banned newspaper until Radovan Radovanović, a "know-it-all" from Karlovac, provided some photocopies—the only two editions of *Hrvat*, subtitled *A Weekly News Journal*, published on April 17 and 24, 1941. Each edition had four pages printed in the most economical format, A4. The name of the editor, Josip Gjurić, was signed at the bottom of the fourth page with the address of the editorial offices: Karlovac, Gundulićeva 3 (Gjurić's apartment). The first sentence of the opening text on page 1 of the April 17 issue announced, "On Easter, Karlovac experienced the greatest day in its history. After enduring more than a decade's exile the *Poglavnik*, the liberator and restorer of the great Independent State of Croatia, has returned to his homeland." On the last page of that same issue Gjurić, the ever-quick professional, was among the first in Croatia to publish "Song of the Croatian Victory," a march that had already been set to music by the maestro Lovro Matačić and whose lyrics by Jerko Skračić read: "Everywhere a single thought, everywhere a single voice; the Croat has a state, he is the master; the *Poglavnik* has brought salvation to his people," and then the chorus, "All Croats swear in unison to their leader, to place their lives in his hands, all will be for freedom, when he calls the troops to bloody battle."

The rest of the articles in *Hrvat* were proper journalistic pieces that would be of obvious interest to a local readership: “Rail Traffic Restored,” “A New Mayor of Karlovac,” “Black Marketeer Sentenced,” “Karlovac Residents Mobilized into the Defeated Yugoslav Army Returned Home,” etc. Both issues of *Hrvat* were filled with advertisements that Gjurić himself had probably gathered, thanks to his acquaintances and to the solid reputation he had acquired in the city. Thus, the newspaper carried advertisements by well-known Karlovac merchants with a Croatian Peasants’ Party orientation; a quilt manufacturer known to be a strong Nazi sympathizer; the producer of “renowned home furnishings,” Vejvoda (the father of the famous Karlovac communist and Spanish Civil War volunteer Ivo Vejvoda); and a large wood factory whose owner or co-owner was Josip Rendeli, the president of the Karlovac Jewish Community.

Encouraged by this wealth of financial support from such a great variety of sources, Gjurić announced in the second issue of *Hrvat* that the newspaper would be published every week instead of “occasionally.” This optimistic announcement obviously irritated Gjurić’s journalistic competition in the Karlovac Ustasha leadership, which just then was preparing to publish the first issue of its weekly, *Hrvatska sloboda*, with the subtitle *The Organ of the Croatian Ustasha Movement in Karlovac*. I am convinced this was the main reason for banning *Hrvat* and for Gjurić’s arrest—the quickest and simplest way of removing the competition was by banning and arresting, not an unusual practice in NDH. Thus, when the first issue of *Hrvatska sloboda* hit the streets on April 26, Josip Gjurić, that embarrassing competitor, was already on his way to the Zagreb jail on Petrinjska Street.

Within Karlovac journalistic circles Gjurić really was an inconvenient and, I would even say, formidable competitor. For more than ten years he had been a successful correspondent for the leading Zagreb daily *Novosti.* He was a skilled, diligent, aggressive, and talented journalist—inquisitive and ever-present in the life of the city, especially in sports—and generally regarded as an enterprising, hardworking young man. Every day the desk of his editor in Zagreb was inundated with brief, cleverly written, interesting tidbits about life in Karlovac, so the city was always well covered in *Novosti,* which sold very well in our city—far more than all the other dailies of that time combined. Once in a while Gjurić would throw in something like a children's column on the Karlovac pages of *Novosti,* articles and other items from the city's grade-schoolers. And so I also experienced the unique sensation of reading in a major newspaper for the first time a few sentences I had written. On Sunday afternoons hundreds of Karlovac residents would gather on Gundulićeva Street in front of Gjurić's apartment, which also served as the local office of *Novosti,* to follow a peculiar "broadcast" of the league soccer matches. With every change of the score Gjurić, one of the few people in Karlovac at that time who had a radio and a telephone, promptly informed the public of the score by writing in big letters on the windows of his office—to their joy and approval if the change was in favor of the Zagreb clubs and to sighs of disappointment if it was in favor of "those other guys." I remember his beaming face when he announced with a new posting another goal that his team, Građanski, had just scored.

But it has always been unclear to me what Gjurić wanted and what he was hoping for in those first days of the NDH when he rushed to start his weekly. Perhaps he believed that by doing this he would "wash away" his previous career as the longtime correspondent of *Novosti,* which under the leadership of Hrvoje Macanović and Ive Mihovilović, its editors in chief, had taken a pronounced pro-Yugoslav and antifascist stance in the years before the war. Gjurić had been the editor of *Karlovački novosti,* the weekly published by my father that neither the Yugoslav regime nor the "hard-line" Croatian nationalists approved of. Gjurić played tennis at and was in the leadership of the Karlovac Sports Association, where many Serbs also played, and where his regular playing partner and friend was Stanko Polak, a Jew. Gjurić's wife, Mira, was a Jewish woman who already had been baptized when she married. Under the criteria of 1941, Gjurić had a lot of "stains" that had to be washed away under the new government, and perhaps he thought he could best accomplish this by starting *Hrvat*. Or perhaps he was driven by the professional nerve of a passionate journalist in these uncertain times to try to have his own newspaper. But how could he have been so naïve as to believe that the jealous and ambitious arrivistes of the new government would tolerate him? Or was Gjurić so afraid, so spineless, that he believed opportunistic collaboration with the new government was the only possible chance for survival? Many people at the time believed that the NDH was bringing a bright future to Croatia, or at least saving it from a greater evil. But I do not believe that Gjurić—a politically savvy journalist, who must have known, or at least must have had a presentiment, about what the patronage of Hitler and Mussolini would bring to Croatia—was one of them. In crazy and uncertain times people may do many things that in normal times they would be reluctant or ashamed to do. For having temporarily curried favor with the Ustasha authorities, Gjurić was uneasy for the rest of his life. After the war, he did not return to Karlovac, which lost its best journalist ever, while Rijeka gained one.

Radeka is the only one who recorded his days in the jail on Petrinjska Street:

> The next day there were as many as fifty people in Cell No. 15; later as many as sixty. Only one typical prison window, small and high on the wall, was between us and the light of day. The cell had twelve hard cots, and twenty-four people were on

them. Another twenty-four were lying on the floor beneath them. The rest in any free space they could find. Fortunately, the floor was asphalt not concrete, easier to wash in the morning, dried quickly, not too cold to lie down on. I am lucky that I can sleep in any situation, even sitting on a train, and in my student days, on boards and a blanket, so here too I slept well lightly covered. During the day, when everyone was sitting, there was more room to move, you could get close to the window and breathe in a little fresh air, and even walk across the cell. In any case, there was too little air, which was suffocating and heavy with the smell of human sweat and fumes from the toilet. The toilet, an important part of the cell, was not a bucket but a Turkish-style toilet that flushed, separated from the rest of the cell by a small partition. Although the water flowed freely when the button was pushed, it was not enough so the flushing was never complete. That is why a chorus of "W-a-a-a-t-e-r!" could often be heard throughout the day. Later on, we wrenched a window slat, which let in more air and light. But there were also other ways to get fresh air. For an hour in the morning the cell door was opened: for airing out, washing the floor; washing ourselves, our socks, our underwear; chats in the hallway, etc.—a regular prison routine. But at night the cell created something that was outside of that routine. We organized performances that included singing, news, reports, recitations, anecdotes, jokes, and reports on life in the cell, all in the dark and all by heart. The chief editor was Turkalj, who was assisted by Gjurić and Ivo Goldstein. The composition of the cell was so diverse and rich that there was no shortage of performers. We had an expert singer of light melodies, a little dark Jew from Niš. And at the beginning of the performance, which was right after the lights were officially turned out for the night at nine

> o'clock, the guards in the hallway would usually open the doors to hear the program. Then the cool breeze of the May evening would flow through the cell and all of us would clear our lungs of the humid, stale air.[2]

The administration and the guards of the jail on Petrinjska Street were still from the old regime, although Ustasha officials were coming to interrogate the prisoners and decide their fate. The old rules were maintained in the jail, as much as that was possible in such overcrowded conditions. It was a so-called "primary jail of the general type," a huge reception center that was open day and night for the temporary holding of all kinds of misfits, suspects, and accused, a great waiting area for transfer to somewhere else—no one knew where.

During the six weeks that my father was in Petrinjska, my mother visited him regularly. At that time, it was possible to travel between Karlovac and Zagreb with only the mandatory police permit, which, it seems, my mother obtained with no difficulty. Once or twice she took Danko with her, and once or twice she took me. The overcrowded jail did not allow a separate area for conversation between the prisoners and visitors. We stood with my father next to a window in the wide hallway of the jail under the supervision of a polite guard who moved away so we could speak more freely. I don't know what my father asked me or what I answered, what my mother said to my father or what he said to her. I remember the view from the window—the empty, gloomy courtyard of the jail and my father's large blue eyes that did not pretend to be cheerful. Then the doors of Cell No. 15 closed on my father and the guard turned the key twice in the large lock.

In the same cell was "a young Dalmatian man," recounted Radeka, "a doctor of law, refined, a youthful-looking gentleman, elegant, a man of the world in that motley crowd. An only child, and still a bachelor, he received every day a tastefully prepared lunch under a clean napkin in a basket. It was the best lunch in the cell and, naturally, there was always something for the others." In later years I saw this "Dalmatian man" often. We became friends and sometimes took walks together in the hills of Kalnik and Medvednica near Zagreb. His name was Ante Mladineo. For several years after the war he had a modest job in the film business and later became a prominent and respected Zagreb lawyer and the president of the bar association. He was the defense attorney for Danko, who was jailed in 1966 for his activities in Mihajlo Mihajlov's dissident group that called for the democratization of the Titoist regime.[3] In contrast to Gjurić, Mladineo did not promise to "write down everything some day" about the jail on Petrinjska, but to my occasional questions, he would respond willingly, if somewhat tersely, in a precise and stark legal manner. Mladineo was jailed in 1941 because before the war he had been a supporter of Yugoslavism and a member of the Yugoslav Academic Club. He was released from jail because he had been born in Zadar and raised in Split, and therefore was considered a citizen of Italy under the Rome agreements of May 18, 1941, by which Pavelić had ceded Dalmatia to Mussolini's Italy.

Mladineo remembered my father as "the guardian of Cell No. 15." According to the prison rules, lunch could be delivered from outside to the prisoners between noon and 1:00 p.m. Because of the overcrowding, the distribution of packages to different cells went slowly, sometimes lasting until 4:00 p.m., by which time lunches were often delivered to their intended recipients cold—until, as Mladineo recounted, my father took over. He ordered tags of various colors from our bookstore, assigned a different color for each floor, and there was a clearly written number for each cell. After inspecting the package, which usually went quickly, the guard simply had to put the appropriate tag on each basket and the deliveries went considerably faster. By 2:00 p.m. everyone had his lunch.

As Radeka recounts in his memoir:

> Goldstein deserved most of the credit for everything that the cell had at that time. It had its own cash fund made up of contributions by individuals who had been released. One day Goldstein called my attention to an old priest who was collecting garbage in the courtyard and putting it in the sleeves of his cassock. Goldstein was quickly able to find out that it was an Orthodox priest named Popović from Bosnia. He succeeded, who knows how, in collecting eight hundred dinars and delivering them to the old man through one of the guards. Another time, in our hallway the usual fingerprinting was being conducted. A single cleric was standing in the midst of this throng of prisoners. By the red trimmings on his soiled and torn cassock, we could tell that he was an Orthodox bishop. Indeed, it was the Zagreb Metropolitan Dositej, whom I knew personally, but who was now so battered, bruised, and swollen that I could not recognize him. Goldstein then remembered to do something that would never have occurred to me—he put a lemon and an orange in Dositej's pocket. Goldstein later learned from some guards that Dositej had been tortured the night before in the middle of Zagreb.[4]

In May 1941, the older guards at the jail on Petrinjska Street did not mistreat the prisoners. They tried to be correct, as much as that was possible. However, beatings and torture had already become a systematic part of the investigations by the newly appointed Ustasha investigators and police officers. Therefore, among the prisoners there was a "rule to eat less because of the rumor that being beaten with a full stomach could cause a rupture of the intestines. Another trick was to wrap a towel around your body before an interrogation. It was said that each blow would be better heard, so the Ustasha were satisfied, and your kidneys better protected and hurt less."[5]

My father was subjected to a cursory interrogation at Petrinjska but not tortured. His greatest torments during the imprisonment were, I believe, the gloomy news in the daily newspapers, which, thanks to the relatively lenient prison regime, arrived every day to Cell No. 15. If my father could discern his fate in the newspapers he was reading, he must have been filled with dark forebodings.

In those weeks of May 1941, Hitler was at the height of his power. In yet another blitzkrieg, German armored divisions had occupied Greece, pushed a British expeditionary force into the sea, and, by the end of the month, captured Crete with a powerful parachute assault. The Afrika Korps of General Rommel had forced the British army back from Cyrenaica in a twelve-day armored assault and had reached the border of Egypt. Rashid Ali, the new prime minister of Iraq and a Nazi sympathizer, requested that the British abandon the airfields and military bases that they maintained in Iraq under the Anglo-Iraqi Treaty of 1930. Then on May 2, 1941, Ali personally approached Hitler with a request for military assistance. The puppet government of Vichy France had placed the airfields and ports in the French colonies of Syria and Lebanon at the disposal of the German army. The ring formed by Crete, Cyrenaica, Iraq, Syria, and Lebanon was tightening around Egypt and Palestine, the last British bastions in the eastern Mediterranean. The focus of military action quickly moved away from Croatia and with it the forlorn hope of everyone imprisoned and threatened in the NDH that some good news might before long come from the major battlefields of the Second World War.[6]

In May 1941, a weakened Britain stood almost completely alone against the might of the Third Reich, Italy, and a subjugated Europe.

The submarine war in the Atlantic and the air attacks on Britain during the Blitz were threatening the British populace with starvation while Stalin's Soviet Union calmly watched and, as a loyal signatory of the German-Soviet Nonaggression Pact, continued to feed Hitler's war machine with regular deliveries of wheat and raw materials.

My father used to say that one should read newspapers "between the lines." But in reading the newspapers of May 1941 today, it is sufficient to check the headlines and be able to guess the feelings of those being threatened. When I visited my father in the Karlovac jail, he did not seem to me to be overly worried, but when I saw him in the hallway of the jail on Petrinjska, his speech was less animated, his eyes flickered with uneasiness. Or is that how I see it today, as I leaf through the ominous newspaper headlines my father must have been reading back then?

The only thing that the prisoners could possibly think would save them was Article Six in the "Decree of *Poglavnik* Ante Pavelić" published in *Hrvatski narod* of April 29: "All persons arrested must be immediately interrogated according to the regulations of the law and a decision about them must be rendered according to the law within forty-eight hours." The other articles limited the power of local Ustasha Councils by transferring it to the ministries, police, courts, and other institutions. Someone was obviously trying to curb the growing chaos and introduce some kind of order. But that "legal order" was also threatening, beginning with the first Legal Decree for the Defense of the People and the State passed on April 17, 1941, the second day under the Pavelić government in Zagreb. It called for the death sentence for anyone "who in any way commits or has committed an offense against the honor and interests of the Croatian people, even if that act was only in the planning stages." This decree was the quasi-legal underpinning for all kinds of violence committed in the NDH, including the mass killings in Orthodox villages and in the death camps. From this decree also evolved the courts-martial that handed down death sentences with no possibility of appeal.

Although *Hrvatska sloboda* was not delivered to Petrinjska, the prisoners in Cell No. 15 could, of course, read the news in Zagreb's *Novi list* on May 11, which quoted *Hrvatska sloboda*: "Ivo Lipovščak, former police chief; Milan Radeka, teacher; Marko Sablić, former schoolteacher; Ivo Goldstein, engineer and bookseller; Josip Gjurić, journalist; [and twelve other Karlovac residents] were brought before the court in Zagreb on suspicion of working against the interests of the Croatian people." With such an indictment before a court-martial or an extraordinary peoples' court, and in accordance with the laws of April and May 1941, only one sentence awaited the defendants: death. None of the people on this list ever appeared before a court and had only rarely been interrogated. With the exception of Radeka and Gjurić, they all lost their lives without an interrogation and without a court trial, by that other channel of the Ustasha regime that ran parallel with the legal one, or the ostensibly legal one, for as long as the NDH endured. Partially concealed, this extralegal channel of authority was even more brutally devised than the legal one and caused far greater suffering and death.

4

The Camp with the Beautiful Name

ON JUNE 6, 1941, my father was transferred from the jail on Petrinjska Street to the Danica concentration camp on the outskirts of the town of Koprivnica with several townspeople from Karlovac and another group of prisoners. Radeka remembers that day on the train from Zagreb to Koprivnica as being particularly beautiful; the prisoners thoroughly enjoyed the fresh air and the light of day, the gentle fields, the forests, the open view. On arrival in the camp, they saw the Ustasha face-to-face for the first time. Until then, in the jails of Karlovac and Zagreb, they had been guarded by regular police, who were rarely harsh. The camp inmates immediately warned them to be prepared—after lunch would come the beatings and robbing of new inmates. And indeed, after lunch the guards came with full stomachs and half drunk and immediately began with the searches and petty extortions. Soon after that, as Radeka recounts in his *Memories*,

> A stocky, ruddy-faced young man in a uniform and boots hit Kozomarić only once and that powerful man fell, without a groan. Then he hardly touched the little bowlegged Jew Adler, who fell unconscious into my lap as I sat on my suitcase against the wall. He had to hit Goldstein several times before he fell.

> "Are you a Jew," he asked. "Yes, I'm a Jew, so what; I've never committed an evil deed against anyone!" Later, Goldstein was upset for not having realized that this man was testing how many blows it would take to bring the men to their knees and that if he had thought of this sooner he would have been able to shorten the blows right away. However, they were not able to knock down Vojo Besarović from Sarajevo. They were punching him, in vain. He did not fall. Stevan Ćurčić, a well-known member of a cooperative and a rector of Serbian Orthodox parishes, first in Bović and then in Ogulin, had come with us from Zagreb. Tall, handsome, with a full dark beard, a younger man, now in a torn white shirt, with bruises on his body. They beat him savagely, even when he was on the ground. In the end, someone, screaming, pulled a large horse-collar hook from the wall and hit him several times on the shins. They asked another one what he was. Policeman. "Oh, you're a policeman, son of a bitch," "Don't hit me, I'm a Croat!" "On top of that you're a Croat," and they went wild. The whole time I sat on my suitcase with Adler in my lap, scared to death.[1]

"After all of this," Radeka continues, "we spent half an hour in dead silence." He does not say what thoughts tormented him in that half hour of "dead silence." He did not find the words then that would break that silence, nor did he later find the words that could describe it. In a single day they had been hurled from an intoxicating, seductive spring landscape into the depths of humiliation in which a half-drunk, heavyset young bully had stripped them of their humanity. "I then felt for the first time that there are no words in our language that would express this violation, this destruction of a human being," wrote the Italian writer Primo Levi, who experienced that "first-day shock" in the Monowitz camp next to Auschwitz. In the words of Immanuel Kant, they had all been touched by "radical evil."

Levi's feeling that there were no words and Radeka's "dead silence" endured in my late wife, Vera, for almost ten years. Because she had spread, and perhaps made up, some political jokes as a twenty-one-year old student, she had been jailed for six months, then sent for a year to a prison camp on the island of Sveti Grgur (St. Gregory) between 1951 and 1953. A senior officer of the State Security Administration, who sentenced her to eighteen months of "administrative punishment" for "subversive propaganda in support of the Cominform" (Communist Information Bureau), added a verbal justification to his written decision: "The jokes that you and your group at the School of Journalism and Diplomacy thought up and spread were directed against the organs of the people's government and its leadership, and they were harmful. Since in our country's current political situation the main front of the people's government is turned to defense against the Cominform, your subversive jokes were objectively working to the advantage of the Cominform." When Vera was released after serving her eighteen-month sentence, she resumed her studies and, thanks to her father's prewar friendship with Ivan Šibl, got a job at Radio Zagreb.[2] This is where we met and fell in love. She rarely mentioned anything about her days in jail and at the prison camp, only sharing occasional hints in which she could not hide the pain of those memories and experiences. She finally bared her soul to me one beautiful summer day in the fifth year of our marriage during a carefree walk on the island of Krk.

From the beach in Baška, Vera stared at the sea and the surrounding hills. She wanted to climb the hill overlooking Stara Baška from where we would be able see the island of Grgur. It was a bright day; the visibility was excellent. The setting sun brilliantly illuminated Velebit, Senj, the island of Prvić and the Senj channel below us, and the peaks of the island of Rab in the distance. In front of Rab was Grgur and, behind it, Goli Otok (Bare Island). Here on this hill above Baška, a scene that elevates the soul, Vera opened up to me. Eight years earlier, in the late spring of 1952, she had been taken through this same Senj channel from Bakar to Grgur. She had already spent six months behind bars in the dark cells of the Glavnjača jail in Belgrade. Although she was a prisoner belowdecks, she could enjoy the expanse of the open sea and the blessed rays of the sun on the peaks and slopes of the island and coastal hills through a porthole. As they were approaching the pier on Grgur, she heard singing, a chorus of women's voices. It was high noon. The rocks glimmered in the sunlight and Vera breathed in the fragrance of the sea. She knew that she was going to be in the camp for a year, but that camp—under the sun, by the sea, accompanied by song—held out the promise of a respite, of a way station from the darkness of the jail to the light of freedom. She knew the song well, it sounded enchanting, but the words were unfamiliar. Although she couldn't make them out exactly, they sounded threatening. Once she was on shore the words became clear: "We'll kill every bastard who's against the KPJ" (Communist Party of Yugoslavia). And then loud chanting: "For whom? For Tito. For the party. All, all, all!"

The guards forced them to pass one by one through a cordon of the camp inmates, who spat on them, hit them, and shouted in their ears, "Pig, whore, traitor!" Vera staggered through the cordon, bracing herself against the blows, wiping the spit from her face and the tears from her eyes. She was helpless under the heavy blows that were meant to show zeal and inflict pain, and she was grateful for the lighter blows that simulated heavy ones. After passing through the cordon, she fell to the ground. The guards let her come to her senses. In an instant her illusions about humane behavior on that island of brilliant sunshine and fresh sea air had vanished.

In the concentration camps of the Nazis, communists, and other dictatorial regimes the methods of "greeting" new arrivals were diverse but always had the same purpose—to show new inmates right away who was in charge and who was a nobody, new prisioners had to be humiliated and subjugated, and their humanity had to be annihilated. According to the detailed procedures at Mauthausen and Buchenwald, any personal belongings of new arrivals were taken away—shoes, clothes, wallets with photos of children—in exchange for a tattooed camp number to which they had to respond because they no longer had a first or last name. For those going to Auschwitz and Treblinka the "greeting" had started with a trip that lasted several days in sealed cattle cars without a scrap of food or a drop of water, on the way to the gas chamber. At Norilsk, one of the northernmost sites of the Gulag, Karl Steiner was greeted, in weather of minus forty degrees, at the door of his camp hut by the frozen corpse of an inmate with the sign: "This is the fate that awaits anyone who tries to escape from Norilsk."

The organization of the Ustasha Danica concentration camp, including the "greeting" on arrival, was rudimentary, primitive, and subject to whim. Although the inmates at Danica were accommodated separately—Orthodox believers in their huts, Jews in theirs, and Catholics and a small number of Muslims in a former factory—Radeka and my father managed to stay together, jammed with several other people from Karlovac into a former coachman's cramped quarters called "the little cage." Their close friendship, which had begun in jail in Zagreb, eased somewhat during the thirty-five days they spent in Danica. But their "first-day shock" extended into their first night in the camp: "Nighttime brought restless sleep," writes Radeka.

> We could hear the muffled sounds of the beatings and howls of pain from the other side of the wall, from the coach house

> where some Serbs from Ogulin were housed. They had been brought in by local Ogulin Ustasha, were beaten and tortured the entire night by the camp Ustasha. The next day a railway worker named Jovetić, the father of six children, was loaded unconscious into a car and taken to the hospital. There the doctors certified in writing that he had died of a weak heart.[3]

Radeka's description of the first day in the Danica camp also has its epilogue, which occurred ten years later:

> I've already mentioned that the main camp thug was that young man, that heavyset Ustasha bull. He was always looking for a chance to hit someone. With a piece of rubber hose in his hands, it was impossible for him to pass without lashing out. He was said to have forced men to take out their penises so he could hit them with the hose. After the war he was tried. Accused by a woman who had lost her father at Danica. Somehow they found me to testify at the trial. During the lineup at the Karlovac Secretariat of Internal Affairs, I immediately recognized him. I was told that in 1941 he had joined the NOB [National Liberation Struggle][4] and had been a good fighter! He later married and at the time of the trial had two young sons. When I testified at the trial in Varaždin, he barked, "You hate me! Don't you?" I was upset because just seeing his face reminded me of the camp, so I turned and said to him, "While I am testifying here, I am not thinking of you, but of your two sons!" Afterward in the hallway, his wife and father-in-law came up to me and the old man said, "Thank you, sir, you treated him well!" I asked them if his father ever struck him, and they replied, "Not struck but regularly beat him like an ox." This would explain why the son of such a father would take inhuman enjoyment in torturing

helpless people. For him it was like a "parental" practice. He was sentenced to several years in prison. He is now free and has his work and family. Only God knows if he also beats his own children![5]

* * *

Radeka called Danica "the camp with the beautiful name." It was the first concentration camp in the NDH, situated in the abandoned Danica Chemical Products Factory. The factory had several advantages: room to accommodate prisoners in the main factory building and its warehouse buildings; proximity to the Koprivnica railway station (about three kilometers away) and a railway siding that entered the factory compound; and a large fenced-off area that was not difficult to monitor. In the documentary records it is referred to by several different names: "work camp," "transit camp," and, most frequently, "Danica concentration camp." In some documents, especially from the early period, it was also called "camp Drnje," after the Drnje suburb of Koprivnica where the post office for the camp was located.

The NDH Ministry of Internal Affairs established the Danica camp on April 15, 1941. At dawn that day about two hundred Ustasha émigrés led by Pavelić arrived in Zagreb from Italy via Karlovac and assumed power. That same day the Ustasha main headquarters issued "assignments" for the arriving Ustasha. Thus, Stjepan Pižeta, a captain in the *Poglavnik*'s bodyguard battalion, was assigned as a "political camp officer at the Danica collection camp," and along with him seven other Ustasha émigré returnees were "assigned duties" in the camp. Since all had spent several years as émigrés, they received three days of leave to visit their homes and families. They assumed their duties on April 18, 1941, and took over the administration of the camp.[6]

The initial prisoners at Danica were the more prominent people of

Serbian nationality from Koprivnica and the surrounding area. The first large transport of prisoners arrived from Grubišno Polje, where about 530 Serbian men had been rounded up in a massive operation on April 26 and 27. Then on April 30, the first transports of prisoners—still mostly Serbs but also now some Jews and "undesirable" Croats—arrived from Bjelovar and Zagreb. Throughout May 1941, the camp filled with more new arrivals every day. According to regular reports, there were 763 prisoners in the camp on May 4; 1,007 on May 18; and between 2,000 and 3,000 during June. In the spring and summer of 1941, a total of about 5,600 prisoners passed through Danica. Zdravko Dizdar has collected the names and personal data of 3,358 inmates of Danica: 2,259 Serbs, 600 Jews, 434 Croats, and 65 of other nationalities. He established that 2,862 camp inmates were killed (the majority of them on Mount Velebit or on the island of Pag), while 496 were released or saved in some other way.

Camp security and the supervision of the inmates were carried out from May to August 1941 by about 100 to 120 Ustasha guards and officials. The aforementioned seven Ustasha émigré returnees who had founded the camp were also among its guards and the camp administration during the first weeks. All the others were younger people from Koprivnica and the surrounding area—mostly half-trained tradesmen and poor peasants who in April and at the beginning of May volunteered for service in the Ustasha army hoping for regular pay, free food, clothing, and other benefits. According to the testimonies of camp survivors, the Ustasha returnees frequently acted more brutally in their dealings with the inmates than the local Ustasha, among whom there were major differences: Except for a few utterly brutal individuals, like the previously mentioned perverse "boxer," the majority of the local guards were satisfied with "revenues" from bribery and petty theft. There were also those who tried to establish some kind of human relationship with the inmates, complaining how misled they had been when, enticed by various promises, they had "voluntarily changed from civilian clothing to military uniforms."

The inmates remembered Martin Nemec as the most brutal. He was a merchant in Koprivnica until 1933, an Ustasha émigré, and then for a short period in May 1941, the commandant of the camp. In 1946, the District Court in Bjelovar sentenced him to death by hanging. The public execution was carried out on March 17, 1947, in front of former Danica inmates. Nemec's successor, a barber from Koprivnica named Nikola Herman, was executed by firing squad in the summer of 1945. Pavel Gaži-Jandrin, the commander of the camp guards, shared a similar fate. Although he could be considerate and occasionally prevented a prisoner from being beaten, a military court sentenced him to death after his capture in November 1943. Of the senior officers in the camp, only Stjepan Pižeta succeeded in fleeing to Austria in 1945, and then via Italy to Spain, where he was active in Ustasha émigré activities and also contributed to the Croatian programs of Radio Madrid.

* * *

At the beginning, Danica was envisioned as a work camp. In the course of the first few weeks of operation, able-bodied prisoners filled in the antitank trenches that had been dug in the fields around Koprivnica and repaired roads. This did not last long because some of the prisoners took advantage of the outside work details to escape, while some local peasants complained that the prisoners working on their fields were being treated cruelly and they wanted nothing to do with it. When at the beginning of June my father was sent to Danica, there was hardly any outside work detail and, as far as I know, he never worked outside the camp. Thus, Danica remained only a receiving and transit camp for the great majority of prisoners, who would be sent to other camps after only a month or two. At Danica they helplessly awaited their fate, not knowing who was making the life-or-death decisions or where those decisions were being made. They were subject to occasional mistreatment and humiliation, but for the most part they were free to move about the camp because the area was too large to be strictly controlled. In such circumstances, an inmate, crippled in his humanity, clings to its bits and pieces as his only source of resistance to the inhuman circumstances in which he finds himself.

Primo Levi has spoken most eloquently about this tragic but frequently admirable effort to preserve one's humanity in his book *If This Is a Man*. This effort is succinctly expressed in the monologues of the camp inmate Steinlauf, a sergeant in the former Austrian army who of all the prisoners in the hut most eagerly washes up, scrubs his clogs, washes his shirt, for "he didn't give up": "Precisely because the *Lager* was a great machine to reduce us to beasts, we must not become beasts....We are slaves, deprived of every right, exposed to every insult, condemned to certain death, but we still possess one power, and we must defend it with all our strength for it is the last—the power to refuse our consent."[7]

That is why Sergeant Steinlauf walks in Monowitz with a military bearing, even though he is starving and at the end of his strength. And despite wearing worn-out clogs that make every step difficult, he walks rhythmically and briskly. Hungry and dying, the Parisian professor of philosophy Maurice Halbwachs speaks in a weak voice, in Block 56 of Buchenwald, not far from Weimar, with his colleague Henri Maspero, unraveling the thoughts of Goethe, while through the nearby beech trees on the hills of Ettersberg, where Goethe once walked with Eckermann, gray smoke now rises, carrying the stench of burning bodies from the camp crematorium, where the bodies of Halbwachs and Maspero will soon end up. In Stara Gradiška, the prisoner Ilija Jakovljević, through the bars of his cell, recognizes by

Portrait of Milan Radeka by Zlatko Prica, 1941

moonlight the faces of his friends whom the Ustasha guards are taking to their death and listens to the footfalls in the hallway that perhaps are coming for him, while at the same time, he secretly writes the notes that will provide testimony of the greatest literary value about the Ustasha concentration camps. In the "esplanade" of the Danica camp, Zlatko Prica draws portraits of the haggard faces of the camp inmates on smuggled paper. Radeka keeps his portrait, a miniature masterpiece that testifies to his time in the camp—it is reproduced almost sixty years later on the cover of *Ljetopis* (Chronicle), in which his *Memories* are published.

In the Jewish huts of Danica, Radeka relates, "it was always lively, constant discussion, no quarrels, no confrontations." All of the fifty communists in Danica held their meetings in groups, each had its own leadership, and they regularly distributed "red assistance" in money and food that arrived through secret channels. From the better-supplied Jewish inmates my father collected food for the starving Serbian prisoners from Bosnia, and he helped them himself, as some of the survivors recalled in statements they made after the war. The Hieromonach Nektarije Dazgić, the abbot of the Gomirje Monastery in 1941, also mentioned him. Dazgić was brought to Danica with about a hundred prominent Orthodox from Gomirje and its vicinity after five nights of brutal treatment in the tower of Ogulin. The camp guards at Danica greeted them in the usual fashion, mercilessly beating them on the first day. Dazgić offered the following testimony in 1962:

> People were, quite simply, screaming like beasts. Most of us were bruised and bloodied. There were more than thirty priests here....The rest were teachers, merchants, and local government officials, peasants, workers, rich villagers with their sons. After this ordeal, each of us was allowed to lie down on the concrete floor without straw or anything else. We spent several nights on this bare floor until along came a rich Jew, the bookseller and engineer Ivo Goldstein, a merchant from Karlovac, and gave us some money to buy several bales of hay.[8] We received food at eleven o'clock in the morning and at six o'clock in the evening the next day. Just enough to have something warm in the gut. Other food we got from Jewish prisoners, who received packages from home, and who shared it with those who did not have any....[9]

Some camp inmates have remembered my father for his supreme optimism and alleged gullibility, which Radeka also mentions. On the eve of June 13, a rumor spread that Danica would be disbanded in honor of Pavelić's name day and my father, probably too optimistically, passed along the rumor. Did he really believe it or was it a kind of forced optimism—less than wishful thinking but more than playacting—in which he wanted to give himself and his fellow sufferers several days filled with a glimmer of hope? Of course, nothing came of the amnesty and the disappointment must have been that much greater. Was it worth awakening a hope that would only be killed by disappointment? Or was hope, however illusory it may have been, necessary to persevere in the face of the inhuman conditions?

In June 1941, the Jewish Department of the Ustasha police began to require that the Jewish communities bear the costs of feeding the Jewish prisoners in the concentration camps. The Zagreb Jewish Community still had enough money to deliver plentiful provisions to Jews in Danica on a regular basis. They went through the Jewish Community in Koprivnica, which for some time was able to maintain an agreement with Nikola Herman, the Ustasha camp commander in Koprivnica, by which a good portion of the food that was sent in fact reached the Jewish inmates. Since many prisoners received packages from home, although they were "censored," the Jewish prisoners in Danica could help some of the other inmates who were literally starving on the weak soup they received once a day. This lasted until June 22, 1941, when all of the Jews in Koprivnica (with the exception of ten, who thanks to a variety of circumstances avoided capture) were arrested in a major roundup and sent to Danica. There were 337 of them. By July 24, they had all been shipped to other camps, the majority of them to Gospić. They disappeared somewhere on Mount Velebit or on the island of Pag, along with the great majority of about 600 remaining Jewish prisoners from Danica, only twelve of whom were said to have survived.

* * *

Every Sunday in June and the first week of July, and frequently during the week, my mother went to Koprivnica to visit my father. Once or twice Jaga went with her. At a designated time at the camp's main entrance packages with food and other necessities could be handed over, with no certainty how much of it would reach the prisoner for whom it was intended and how much of it the Ustasha guards and the camp administrators would "censor." My resourceful mother quickly got to know two or three guards who gladly accepted "a reward for their effort" and so her packages regularly reached my father, sometimes even "uncensored." In a similar way, and perhaps also through regular channels, my mother was frequently able to speak with my father. I don't remember what and how much she told us about these conversations, but I do know that she came back from the visits deeply concerned and no longer feigning any optimism.

On Sunday, June 29, 1941, my mother took me to see my father. There are few events in my memory I recall so clearly as that visit to Danica. A long column of women with baskets, bags, and backpacks stretching along the road from the Koprivnica railway station. At the camp's main entrance Ustasha guards brusquely taking the food and packages for the camp inmates. Rumors circulating that conversations with prisoners would not be permitted. Off to the side my mother whispering to a young Ustasha to whom she gives the food for my father and something is furtively agreed upon. My mother and I waiting in front of a small, isolated rear gate of the camp. The young Ustasha, a carbine slung over his shoulder, finally shows up, pushing my father in front of him as if escorting him somewhere. They stop behind a bush, which is where we are permitted to speak with my father. Afraid that someone will come along and discover his offense, for which my mother has paid a substantial sum, the Ustasha is constantly glancing around and rushing us. Trying at least to appear to be carrying out his guard duties, he does not allow us to speak alone for a moment, stands right next to us the entire time. My father and mother speak in code.

"I saw Mr. Iton yesterday," my father says. "He tells me things are not good at Uncle Šaju's place."

"Iton" is Hebrew for "newspapers," and "Šaju" is the name of my mother's brother in Černovic, which was annexed in 1940 by Russia. Obviously, my father has heard news about the German victories in Russia and is worried.

"Mr. Iton is exaggerating and he lies a lot. Uncle Šaju is perhaps a bit surprised, but he will recover quickly," my mother replies, trying to be convincing.

"I thought so, too." My father sounds consoled.

On the train back to Karlovac, my mother said, "Father was a bit swollen and he looked a little strange, did you notice?"

"I didn't."

"I think they are beating him," she said. "He didn't want to admit it, but I am certain, they have beaten him," she concluded dejectedly.

I probably said nothing, but I didn't believe her. From my boyish perspective I simply could not believe that someone would beat my father, a person whom I had set on the highest pedestal as the epitome of authority. Although we often saw each other in Karlovac between 1945 and 1947, the considerate Radeka never mentioned this to me, not wanting to touch upon the boyhood traumas that were healing—but which never did fully heal. When I read the third installment of Radeka's memoir in the weekly *Oko* (The Eye) in 1981 and learned of the humiliating mistreatment my father had suffered, I was unable to calm down for some time. The scenes Radeka described were painfully amplified in my head—and torment me to this day.

On that Sunday in June 1941, on the train from Koprivnica to Zagreb and Karlovac, my mother had guessed correctly that my father had been beaten on that very day. She saw it in his eyes and on his face and hands. Who knows, he may have been beaten by that same Ustasha who had accepted a substantial sum of money to bring my father for a brief meeting—which was the last time we saw him.

* * *

In the Croatian National Archives in Zagreb, in the file labeled "Ustasha Commission for the City and County of Koprivnica, NDH Box 1," under number 887/41 there is a document about one of the last attempts my mother made to save my father. It is a request my mother had addressed to the Ministry of Internal Affairs with the heading "Subject: Ivo Goldstein from Karlovac in the Drnje Camp—Release." I don't know who recorded this request, probably some not very literate lawyer, but it is correctly worded in legal terms and clearly summarized in content, without trying to curry favor, as was usual in such documents at the time. I reproduce the letter here in its entirety in all of its stylistic awkwardness.

> My husband Ivo Goldstein, the owner of a bookshop in Karlovac, was imprisoned in the jail of the district court in Karlovac from April 13–26, 1941, during which time he was not interrogated, and on April 26, 1941, he was transferred to the jail in Zagreb, where he stayed until June 6, 1941. While he sat in the jail of the Zagreb police he was interrogated one time, on the occasion of which interrogation he was asked why he was publicly known in Karlovac as a communist, since there was nothing to suggest that. The interrogation produced nothing that he could be charged with.
>
> On the day of June 6, 1941, my husband was transferred to the Drnje [Danica] camp near Koprivnica, where he still is today.
>
> During the entire time that he lived in Karlovac for the last twelve years, he never had any problems with the authorities.
>
> From the above it follows that my husband has been imprisoned for more than two months even though there have been no complaints against him, therefore I humbly ask this illustrious ministry to please determine what is necessary for Ivo Goldstein from Karlovac to be released after enduring more than two months of prison because of the difficult material circumstance in which we find ourselves, and we have two boys,

one of whom has completed second grade in primary school, while the older has finished the second grade of high school, and we need father's help.

Karlovac, June 18, 1941
—Lotte Goldstein, wife of Ivo Goldstein

This time the legal channels of the Ustasha regime functioned efficiently. It is apparent from the document that my mother's request was received in the NDH Ministry of Internal Affairs on June 19, and that on the same day it was forwarded to the Directorate for Public Order and Security (RAVSIGUR) under document number 10038 with the comment "Forward for Action." The request was received in RAVSIGUR on June 20 and sent to the Ustasha commission in Koprivnica on June 23 with the comment "Sent for Action" and the signature of "Chief of Department, Aleksandar Benak." The document was received in the Ustasha Commission for the City and County of Koprivnica on June 24 under the number 887 with the signature of Nikola Herman and immediately forwarded to the "Command of the Danica Camp—for the interrogation of the interned, document to be returned with summary."

However, the document was not returned from Danica. It is not in the neatly arranged folder 887/41 or in the box of the archive file "Ustasha Commission for the City and County of Koprivnica." The legal channels of the Ustasha regime functioned efficiently only to a certain critical point, while all further action flowed through that other channel, the extralegal one. My father wasn't interrogated at Danica, even though an interrogation was officially ordered. He wasn't informed, either verbally or in writing, of what was to happen to him. His fate was decided by a single verbal command, issued in the Ustasha main headquarters in Zagreb on June 30, 1941. On that day, Herman, the Ustasha commissioner for the city and county of

Koprivnica and the temporary commander of the Danica concentration camp, was ordered to send all Serbs and Jews from Danica to the Directorate of the Provincial Police in Gospić within a month. For the great majority of those sent under this order, Gospić was only a stopping point on the road to Jadovno on Mount Velebit or to Slano on the island of Pag, the first two death camps of the Ustasha NDH.

5

The Letter

AFTER THE FIRST part of this book had already been written, I received unexpected news from the National and University Library that left me deeply shaken. Ivan Kosić, the director of the Collection of Manuscripts and Antiquarian Books, told me that the archivist Drago Pažin, while arranging the bequest to the library of Vinko Nikolić's papers, had discovered two pages of a letter that my father had written to me from the Zagreb jail in 1941. They sent me a barely legible photocopy. Yes, this was indeed a letter from my father; it was in his handwriting. The date and place—Zagreb jail, May 2, 1941—could be clearly seen in the upper-right corner. The letter was headed, "Dear Slavko!" It had traveled for sixty-four years to reach me; I felt as if my father were writing to me from his grave in the Mount Velebit caves.

The next day, in the depository of the National and University Library, I held in my hands a sheet of yellowed paper. Both sides were written in pencil in the neat, fluid handwriting of my father. The paper was carefully folded eight times into a very small square, the customary way that prisoners secretly sent letters to their families. The thin prison pencil writing had faded with time. In some places the words were difficult to read, but with the help of a magnifying glass and a scanner the entire text could be deciphered. It was clear that the letter had been written calmly and without haste because from the first to the last line the handwriting was steady and uniform. The spacing between the words was also uniform: on the first page there were thirty lines, on the second thirty-one. At the end of the second page a thought was interrupted in the middle of the sentence. What happened to the rest of the letter? That has raised several unanswerable questions. How did a letter meant for me come into the possession of Nikolić, a nationalistic poet and official in the Ustasha propaganda service and the armed forces of the NDH until 1945, and then editor of the émigré newspaper *Hrvatska revija* (Croatian Review) from 1950 to 1990? Why did Nikolić need this letter? Why did he hold it for half a century in his files and drag it with him while he wandered as a refugee to Buenos Aires and Barcelona and back again to Zagreb? And why did he never mention to me that he had it, even though we met several times and talked about many things?

Here is the letter:

Zagreb jail, May 2, 1941

Dear Slavko!

I heard from mother that you were crying last Saturday because I am in prison. That news saddened me more than it pleased me. I know that you were not crying from shame that your father is behind bars! You should know that there are times when it is a greater honor to be in prison than outside it. Perhaps you were crying because your father is suffering an injustice. It is better to bear an injustice than to commit one. Or perhaps you were crying because you are saddened by my present circumstances. True, it is neither pleasant nor comfortable not to have freedom. But my position is not so bad that you have to grieve

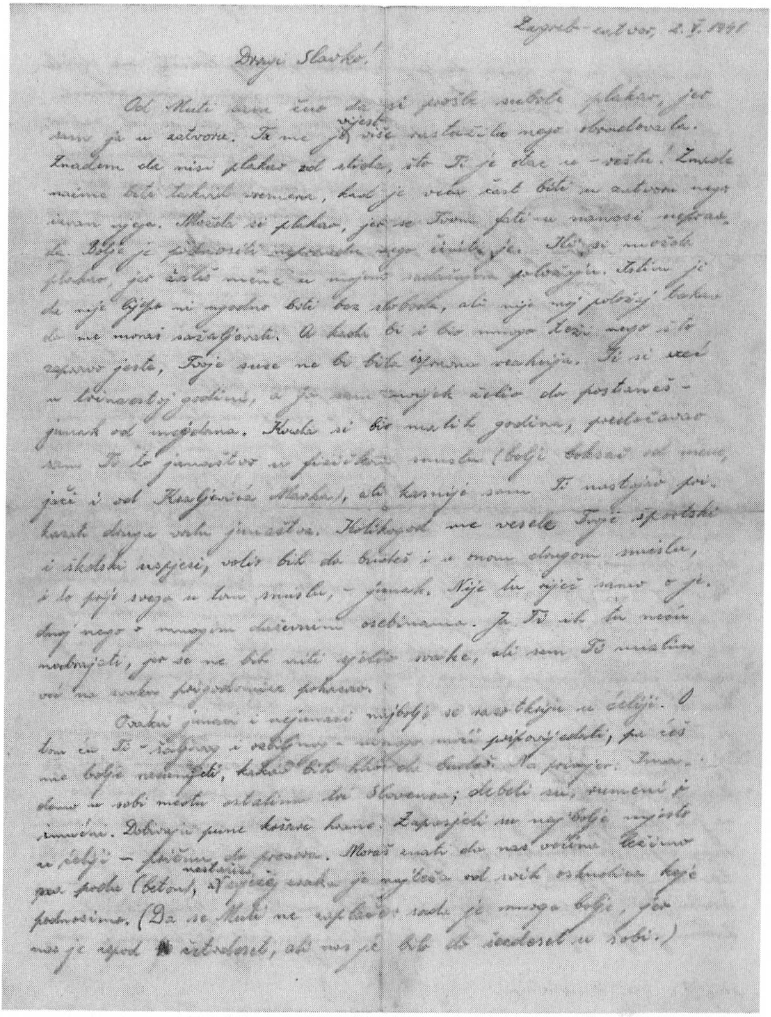

Zagreb–četvrtak, 2. V. 1941

Dragi Slavko!

Od Muti sam čuo da si [illegible] plakao, jer sam ja u zatvoru. To me je vijest više rastužila nego obradovala. Znadem da nisi plakao od straha, što Ti je otac u zatvoru! Znade naime biti takovih vremena, kad je veća čast biti u zatvoru nego izvan njega. [illegible] si plakao, jer se Tvom oci nanosi nepravda. Bolje je podnositi nepravdu nego činiti je. [illegible] si mogao plakati, jer [illegible] u mojem sadašnjem položaju. Istina je da mi nije [illegible] ni ugodno biti bez slobode, ali nije moj položaj takav da me moraš sažaljevati. A kada bi i bio mnogo teži nego što zapravo jeste, Tvoje suze ne bi bile ispravna reakcija. Ti si sada u trinaestoj godini, a ja sam uvijek želio da postaneš junak od [illegible]. Kada si bio malih godina, predočavao sam Ti to junaštvo u fizičkom smislu (bolji boksač od mene, jači i od Kraljevića Marka), ali kasnije sam Ti nastojao prikazati drugu stranu junaštva. Kolikogod me vesele Tvoji športski i školski uspjesi, volio bih da budeš i u onom drugom smislu, i to prije svega u tom smislu, – junak. Nije tu riječ samo o [illegible] nego o mnogim duševnim osobinama. Ja Ti ih ne mogu nabrajati, jer se ne bih [illegible] svake, ali sam Ti [illegible] na svakom pojedinom pokazao.

Ovakvi junaci i nejunaci najbolje se razotkriju u ćeliji. O tome ću Ti – [illegible] – mnogo moći pripovijedati, pa ćeš me bolje razumjeti, kakav bih htio da budeš. Na primjer: Imamo u sobi među ostalima tri Slovenca; debeli su, [illegible] i imućni. Dobivaju pune košare hrane. Zaposjeli su najbolje mjesto u ćeliji – [illegible] do prozora. Moraš znati da nas većinu ležimo na podu (beton), a nestašica [illegible] svaka je najteža od svih oskudica koje podnosimo. (Da se Muti ne [illegible] sada je mnogo bolje, jer nas je ispod četrdeset, ali nas je bilo do šezdeset u sobi.)

for me. Even if it were or would become much more difficult than it really is, your tears would not be the correct reaction. You are now thirteen years old, and I've always wanted you to become a hero. When you were younger, I showed you how one can be brave in a physical sense (a better boxer than me, stronger even than Kraljević Marko), but later I tried to show you another kind of heroism. As happy as your athletic and academic successes make me, I would like you to be both in that other sense, and primarily in that other sense, a hero. It is not a question here of a single quality but of many inner traits. I will not number all of them here because I would not remember them all, but I think that I have indicated all of them to you on different occasions.

Such heroes and nonheroes are best revealed in the cell. I will be able to tell you much about that—funny and serious—so that you will better understand what I would like you to be. For example, we have in the cell, among others, three Slovenes. They are fat, red-faced, and rich. They receive baskets full of food. They've taken possession of the best spot in the cell—the bunk next to the window. You should know that most of us are lying on the concrete floor, and that the shortage of fresh air is the hardest privation of all we must bear. (So that your mother doesn't break down in tears, it is now much better because there are fewer than forty of us in the cell, and there had been as many as sixty.) These three don't move from their spot day or night. They don't share their food or cigarettes with anyone, not even with their less fortunate countrymen, to whom no one sends food.

You should know that it isn't possible to survive on prison rations. They are handed out only once a day and consist of a quarter loaf of bread, with which we get, every other day, a

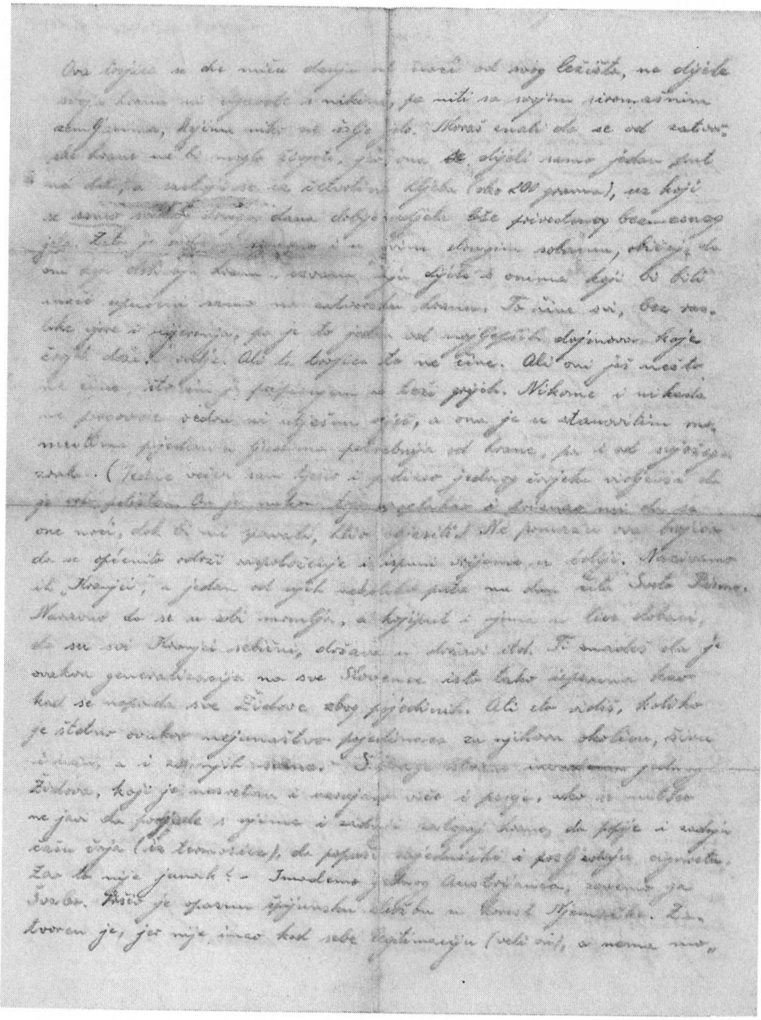
Ova trojica se [illegible] miču danju [illegible] noću od svog ležišta, ne dijele
svoje hrane [illegible] s nikim, pa niti sa svojim siromašnim
zemljacima, kojima niko ne šalje ništa. Moraš znati da se od zatvor-
ske hrane ne bi moglo živjeti, jer ona se dijeli samo jedan put
na dan, a sastoji se od [illegible] kruha (oko 200 grama), uz koji
se [illegible] dobije [illegible] bezmasnog
[illegible] sa svim ostalim sobama, [illegible] da
su [illegible] hrane, [illegible] dijele s onima koji bi bili
inače upućeni samo na zatvorsku hranu. To čine svi, bez raz-
like vjere i [illegible], pa je to jedan od najljepših dojmova koje
čovjek dobije ovdje. Ali ta trojica to ne čine. Ali oni još nešto
ne čine, [illegible] Nikome i nikada
ne ponude [illegible], a ona je u stanovitim mo-
mentima [illegible] potrebnija od hrane, pa i od [illegible]
vode. (Jedne večeri sam [illegible] da
je [illegible]
one noći, dok ti [illegible] Ne pomaže ova trojica
da se općenito održi [illegible] u sobi. Nazivamo
ih „Kranjci", a jedan od njih [illegible]
Naravno da se u šali [illegible], a [illegible],
da su svi Kranjci [illegible] Ti znadeš da je
ovakva generalizacija na sve Slovence isto tako [illegible] kao
kad se napadaju sve Židove zbog pojedinih. Ali ti vidiš, koliko
je štetno ovakvo [illegible] pojedinaca za njihovu okolinu, širu
[illegible], a i [illegible] S druge strane [illegible] jednog
Židova, koji je [illegible], ako se [illegible]
ne javi da podijeli s njima i [illegible] hrane, da popije i [illegible]
čašu čaja (iz termosice), da popuši [illegible] cigaretu.
Zar to nije junak? – Imademo jednog Austrijanca, zovemo ga
Švaba. [illegible] Za-
tvoren je, jer nije imao kod sebe legitimaciju (veli on), a nema [illegible]

lean, poorly prepared dish. That's why here, and in all the other cells too, the practice is that those who receive food "from outside" share it with those who otherwise would have only prison food. Everyone does this, regardless of faith or conviction, and it is one of the nicest things that a man can experience here. But those three don't do this. And there is something else they don't do, which I consider an even graver sin. They never speak a word of comfort to anyone, and at certain moments that is more necessary to some people than food, or even fresh air. (One evening I consoled and tried to cheer up a man, seeing how dispirited he was. He broke down and cried and confessed to me that he wanted to hang himself that night.) These three do nothing at all to keep our spirits up or to help pass the time in the cell. One of them reads the Bible several times a day. Of course, the other people in the cell grumble and sometimes bluntly call them "Kranjci" as everyone from Kranj is selfish, a state within a state, etc. You know that such generalizations about all Slovenes are just as true as when all Jews are attacked because of certain individual Jews. Still, you can see how such a nonheroic attitude of some people damages their surroundings, near and far, and themselves. On the other hand, we have a Jew who becomes unhappy and upset and shouts and swears if no one shares with him his last morsel of food, and drinks the last cup of his tea (from a small thermos bottle), and smokes his last cigarette. Is he not a hero? We also have an Austrian, we call him the Kraut. He carried out dangerous spying work for Germany. He was locked up because he did not have the proper identification (so he says) and he co—

The last word at the bottom of the second page breaks off. There is no third page. What more did my father want to tell me? Where is the rest of the letter? Or was my father perhaps prevented from finishing the letter in jail?

I read the faded print letter by letter; I read the words again, and then again, pausing after every sentence. I can see my father in the semidarkness of an overcrowded cell, under the feeble light from a miserly prison window, leaning over the wooden frame of a prison bed on which he is writing this letter because there probably wasn't a desk in the cell. In each line, in every sentence, I read my father's desire to act calmly and serenely, which today makes the letter seem even sadder. But was my father really as calm then as he wanted this letter to imply, so much stronger than the situation in which he found himself? Had he still not been seriously concerned? I remember he once explained to me, with a smile, how a person sometimes has to read between the lines, but even reading this letter between the lines, I find neither strained consolation nor self-comfort. Am I imagining his anxiety? A man writes a letter to his son from jail in which he wants to say so many things, but the conversation is denied him. He senses that more difficult times lie ahead for him and his son, so he insists that "tears are not the correct response" and that the son must be a "real hero." What more did he tell me, or did he want to tell me, in the missing part of the letter? At that time, arrests had become widespread, but killings were still rare—they had only just begun. Perhaps something was already known about them in Cell No. 15. Is it possible that my father feared it was his last letter to his son, his final message?

As much as I blame Nikolić for not giving me my father's letter, I am grateful that he kept it through his whole émigré odyssey. He made it possible for me to listen again to my father's voice, recalling so many images of long ago, as well as pain and sad awareness of the father I had lost too early. "*Ihr naht euch wieder, schwankende Gestalten*" (Once more ye come, wavering forms)—the first line in

Faust, which my father loved to quote when he wanted to express his own feelings or thoughts more beautifully. Here is the "Dedication" I've adapted from Tito Strozzi's translation that captures the feelings I have about my father's letter:

Once more ye come, ye wavering forms that passed
In earlier days before my troubled sight...
A vision of happier days ye now unveil,
And wraiths of friends once dear to me arise;
As in an ancient, half-forgotten tale,
First love and childhood pass before my eyes.
Through plaintive echoes sorrow is revived,
Life's labyrinthine path again I see;
They are recalled who were by fate deprived
Of happy years, and so were lost to me.[1]

Although my father spent much of his free time with me and my brother, I cannot claim that I knew him really well: a thirteen-year-old boy has barely begun to sense the anxieties and dilemmas of adulthood. I think that I only began to understand my father better once I was nearing his age and read his published works and travelogues, and his unpublished notes and letters that, by some miracle, were preserved.

Some of my father's letters to my mother were material for fine literature—thoughtful and sometimes self-mocking and funny or intimate and tender. As a student in Vienna, my father had published some interesting prose pieces in Jewish journals in Zagreb and Sarajevo. His travelogues and journalistic pieces from Palestine, frequently filled with contrived, and not always convincing, optimism, made much less of an impression. The weekly journal *Židov* (Jew) published six of his poems under the heading "*Palestinski prvijenci*"

(First Poems from Palestine) in February 1927. Contrary to the editor's praise in his introductory remarks, I think my father's poetic gifts were far behind his unrealized gift as a prose writer. But poetry, even when not especially good, speaks rather intimately about its author, usually more so than good prose.

The poems published in *Židov* are dated 1925, from the period when my father had just arrived in Palestine, full of enthusiasm to build a new Jewish homeland, though he encountered many disappointments. The titles of the poems indicate the range of his moods: "Dreaming," "Wounds," "Zeal," "Fall," "Rise," and "Fantasy." In the poem "Wounds," he is nostalgic for his former home, lonely in his new surroundings:

The jackal cries in the distance,
His voice in the air suspended.
I am alone in the silence,
By the night befriended.

In "Dreaming" he is already thinking about a girl, my future mother ("she conquered me with her soul"), but in the other poems he weaves his activist resourcefulness with a painful resignation:

Do not lose heart, plant and sow,
Raise a house, build a road,
Fortify thyself with firm faith
And to God new roads do take!

But almost at the same time:

Lies and hatred, every ill
Where my foot touches the soil...

Whips and tears and lies and dark
Of the light ne'er a spark.

From its opening stanzas, the long final poem returns to idealistic delight though its title, "Fantasy," betrays his skeptiscm:

Come, let us build a temple,
To God and to people a home
Come, that I am not alone,
Arise, do not be slow!...
Foundations firm
As of precious stone
Come, a temple let us erect,
For justice and truth to protect!

But this was preceded by the utter gravity of the poem "Fall":

To you heart and soul and all I gave,
But no peace to me did you save...
Would that you grant in peace I die
In unfettered dreams sleep shall I.

Thinking about my father's verses from Palestine and their mixture of enthusiasm and desperation, I am convinced that in the Zagreb jail on May 2, 1941, my father sensed that he was possibly writing his last letter to his son. But at the same time he still believed, or at least hoped, that he would return once again to his family. And so, when he promised that he would be able to tell me about life in jail, "funny and serious," it was neither self-deception nor a false consolation but an activist's optimism, which didn't abandon him.

I can feel the effort and pain it took for this letter to be written, for my father to express concern for his son while not betraying any fears or misgivings. And though it is enormously difficult to write such a letter and distressing to think of my father writing it, I am so grateful that he did.

* * *

Besides my father's unfinished letter, there were five more pages in Niklolić's archive written in his widely spaced handwriting: a word-for-word copy of my father's letter, accompanied by some brief data about my father, mother, brother, and me. From these notes something can be concluded about the circumstances under which Nikolić, the Ustasha propaganda officer, came to possess the letter and the reasons he kept it for so long in his files.

At the top of my father's letter Nikolić had written: "Letter of a Jew to his son Slavko, fourteen years old, from jail in Zagreb, son with mother in Karlovac." At the end of the letter he had noted in his own hand:

> Ivo Goldstein, engineer of agronomy, had a bookstore in Karlovac "Reich" (named after father-in-law). Zionist. Arrested in 1941 and sent to Zagreb, around June 1941 from Zagreb to Danica, a temporary transit camp in Koprivnica. Disappeared.
>
> Wife had a beauty salon in Karlovac, Romanian Jewess, son Slavko and one other small son in Tuzla. Beginning of August wife Lea also arrested. *Bogoš. občina* [religious community] took son, placing him with a Jew. Wife released in October, returned to Karlovac, stored possessions at a friend's, a non-Jew, and with son Slavko joined Partisans. There she was a nurse. Son Slavko a courier in 1943 near Ogulin, in the spring arrested by the Italians with important documents. The Italians brought him before the military court in Rijeka.
>
> Before 1930 Goldstein was in the Yugoslav Jewish Commu-

> nity in Palestine, worked to improve the soil and life, organized life for Yug. Jews. In diary wrote that he was disappointed. Zionism is a lie. They don't want to work. He does not believe in the possibility of a Jewish state. Nobody wants to work, it is all phony. They only want to be involved in commerce. That is why he—returns.

I am no Maigret or Poirot and I will never solve all the puzzles surrounding my father's letter from jail, but the information in Nikolić's notes and the manner in which they are placed have allowed me to piece some things together. The information about my family dates back to the spring of 1943. In the summer of that year the details would already have differed: Italy had capitulated, the military tribunal in Rijeka (Fiume) had recently ceased to function, and I did not appear before it. It is true that I was captured as a Partisan "courier" that spring not far from Ogulin and that I was carrying some propaganda circulars from the County Committee of Ogulin of the Communist Party of Croatia (KPH) and the League of Young Communists of Yugoslavia. But I wouldn't call them "important documents." After several days of questioning in the Ogulin jail, the Italian carabinieri told me that I would be sent to the military tribunal in Rijeka. My interrogator, Lieutenant Giustini, consoled me by saying that although I was imprisoned "like an armed bandit" and could therefore expect the death penalty, I would not be sentenced to death because according to their law the death penalty for anyone under fifteen years of age was automatically reduced to a sentence of twenty years imprisonment. To convince me of his goodwill, Giustini gave me a small Italian-Croatian dictionary and a book by Benito Mussolini, *The Doctrine of Fascism*, which was written in the "beautiful Italian language" and which would help me improve my scant knowledge of that language while I was in jail waiting to be brought before the tribunal. While he was questioning me, Giustini didn't allow his men to torture or beat me, although there were two or three times when it looked as if they wanted to. He let me drink as much water as I wanted, but he gave me nothing to eat. I thought that they wanted to starve me, to squeeze information out of me, though I had very little and what little I did have I denied or avoided disclosing. For several days, or as long as the interrogation lasted, Giustini held me in isolation in the Ogulin jail, with a short period each day in the courtyard, just enough to take "the pot" out and clean it, wash my face, and breathe a little fresh air, but without the usual meager prison meals of rice and macaroni. It never occurred to him that pressure through starvation wasn't going to work because I was almost never hungry.

On one of my first nights in jail an unforeseen guardian angel, my unexpected savior, appeared out of the darkness. Through the four-cornered "spy hole" in the isolation cell, an Italian soldier, the guard on the night shift, woke me and furtively passed me some bread, cheese, and salami, and the narrow neck of a bottle from which I drank as much as I could. This was repeated the next night, accompanied by greetings from the prisoners in the neighboring cells. They encouraged me to "keep your spirits up; at least you won't go hungry." Then one night a letter from my mother in Partisan-held Drežnica arrived in the same way, and several days later, when I was already in the common cell, my guardian angel passed me a message from Maca Gržetić, the secretary of the District Committee of the KPH for Gorski Kotar: They had captured an Italian officer and four soldiers and had offered them in exchange for several Partisan prisoners, including me.

But the exchange never happened. Perhaps there were some disagreements between the Italian military and civilian authorities, sufficient to postpone my transfer to the tribunal in Rijeka. The guardian angel who had brought me food during my days in isolation continued to help me in many other ways. His name was Vinci. He was a short, thin, dark-skinned Sicilian. He had a close friend, also a Sicilian, in the guard unit. Together they maintained secret contacts with the Partisans through agents in Ogulin. One hot summer day, during the exercise period, Vinci's friend (whose name, unfortunately, I've forgotten) approached and quietly confided to me, "Vinci was suspected by the carabinieri—they were following him. He's had to escape to the Partisans. The link will continue through me." With the first news of the capitulation of Italy on the morning of September 8, 1943, that friend of Vinci's unlocked the doors of our cells in the Ogulin prison, helped us get through the rear exit and on to the suburb of Žegar, then past a large bunker and the perplexed guards, on to Krpelj Hill and the Partisans.

Nikolić could not have known all of this when in the spring of 1943 he prematurely noted that I was sent before the military tribunal in Rijeka. At that time, Nikolić taught Croatian literature in the First High School in Zagreb and was also a prominent official in the Ustasha movement, assigned to the Propaganda Department of the headquarters of the Ustasha Youth Movement. In April 1943, Rome allegedly tried to have him relieved of his duties and punished appropriately because he had broadcast poems on Radio Zagreb in which he used metaphors to express dissatisfaction over his native Šibenik and Dalmatia having been taken from Croatia. Nevertheless, he retained his position. Nikolić outlined these in greater detail in a polemic with the Chetnik newspaper *Protest* in Buenos Aires in 1949, emphasizing that "even then he was proud to have been an official in the service of his people."

As a propaganda officer, Nikolić must have been acquainted with a memorandum sent out from the chief of RAVSIGUR in the spring of 1943. Signed by the head of the Newspaper Section, a person named Ivančević, the memorandum contained a directive that "it is necessary once again to start writing about the Jews.... Therefore materials with the exact information will be delivered to the editorial offices of newspapers at the beginning of next week," etc. The renewed anti-Jewish propaganda campaign had been ordered by the police as part of the preparations for a major deportation of the remaining Jews from the NDH to Auschwitz. The deportation was agreed upon at a meeting of the directorate on January 16, 1943, at which Franz Abromeit, the Nazi SS representative, confirmed the details with the leaders of the NDH police regarding the cooperation of the two police services in organizing and carrying out the deportation. With the detailed preparations, which also included coordinated anti-Jewish propaganda, the last great deportation was carried out on May 3, 1943. About 1,600 Jews, mostly from Zagreb—including the prominent chief rabbi Miroslav Shalom Freiberger; the popular young artist Lea Deutsch; and the president of the Jewish Community of Zagreb, Hugo Kon—were sent to Auschwitz. As far as is known, only four people from this group returned after the war.

Everything that I was able to establish through my amateur investigation allows me to make the well-founded assumption that my father's letter was delivered to Nikolić in the spring of 1943 as part of the directive for a coordinated campaign in which "it is necessary once again to begin to write about the Jews." Until then, the letter had languished for two years in some police file, probably the one on the Goldstein family in the municipal police station in Karlovac. The police managed to get it when my father tried to send the letter through one of the usual channels by which prisoners communicated with their families: with the assistance of a well-intentioned or bribed guard, with one of the released prisoners, or concealed at the bottom of food containers that were being returned. It seems that the connection had broken down somewhere. It might also be that the letter was neither finished nor sent because my father had been prevented from doing so by a search of the cell. In any event, instead of reaching my mother and me, the letter was delivered to the Ustasha police and then to Nikolić in the Propaganda Department of the headquarters of the Ustasha Youth Movement.

In accordance with the directive from the directorate, the letter was forwarded with "exact information materials," which Nikolić summarized in his accompanying notes. As I have already indicated, the "information" was partially correct, partially incomplete, or inaccurate, while the last part of his comments contain a deliberate falsehood. It was not difficult for me conclude that the information originated from Franjo Družak, the chief of the municipal police in Karlovac. Only he could have been familiar with the details, and what he didn't reveal was in his interest not to do so.

One morning at the beginning of August 1941, I was alone in our apartment. My father was in the camp in Jadovno, my mother and Jaga were in the Karlovac jail, and my brother was being cared for by family friends, the Trontls. A man of medium build, rather slender, and dressed in a handsome summer suit, rang our doorbell. He introduced himself as Franjo Družak. Before he crossed our threshold, he showed me a paper that said our apartment had been assigned to him. I cannot say that he was brusque or rude. To the contrary, when I recall the scene at the door of our apartment, Družak seemed to feel uncomfortable about taking over someone's apartment in this manner and throwing out a young child from his home. To ease the situation, he immediately told me that the Jewish Community would take care of me and that this had already been arranged with its president. He added that I didn't have to vacate the apartment right away; I had three or four days because he would not need the apartment until his wife came from Samobor with their child. When he began to look around, however, he immediately told me to leave the furniture in the apartment since I had nowhere to store it. I could take my family's personal belongings and also all of the bedding, but I was to leave the carpets behind. He hesitated about the books and photographs. He later said that I could take them, but that I could also leave them if I didn't have a place to store them. "If you need any of the books, you can always come for them," Družak concluded. So the photographs and books remained with Družak, but we got them back, along with the furniture, when Družak fled via Austria to Argentina in the spring of 1945, and my mother, brother, and I, a broken family without a father, returned from the war as Partisans to our Karlovac apartment.

In 1941 and 1942, Družak was in charge of propaganda for the Ustasha Council in the province of Pokuplje in Karlovac. The son of wealthy village merchants from Šišljavić, he had contacts with an Ustasha organization while a student at the Faculty of Law in Zagreb. In the early days of the NDH, he was credited with carrying out an Ustasha mission—he led about three hundred armed members of the Peasants' Defense of the Croatian Peasants' Party on a raid through villages in the Pokuplje region in the direction of Karlovac, disarming the disintegrating elements of the Yugoslav army and establishing a new government. Although he forced me out of our apartment in the summer of 1941, I didn't feel that Družak was an evil man, though he was portrayed as such in some documents I subsequently read. For example, in a report to the appropriate ministries on March 3, 1944, Provincial Governor Ivan Betlehem accused Družak of abusing his position as the director of the municipal police in 1943 to his material advantage, of sexually blackmailing female prisoners and co-workers, and of assisting another provincial governor in arranging several sexual escapades. Perhaps this is just more proof that the absolute power of an uncontrolled government can morally corrupt many seemingly gentle people.

Among the information forwarded to Nikolić in the spring of 1943, only Družak could have known that in August 1941 the Jewish Community had taken over my care and had settled me with a Jew; that my grandfather had come for my brother and taken him to Tuzla; and that when my mother was released from jail in October, Družak's wife permitted her to take some of her things from our apartment (documents, my father's papers, some porcelain, crystal, and other small items), which my mother then stored at "a friend's, a non-Jew," Pavica Vine. As the director of the municipal police, he might have found some of the other information in our police dossier or he could have learned it from other policemen.

My father's disappointing stay in Palestine was no secret in Karlovac. When along with my father's confiscated letter Družak had to provide information about us, it seemed most appropriate to him to forward the "materials" about Palestine: enthusiastic Zionist, pioneer in the establishment of the Jewish state who was disappointed and who writes that Zionism was "a lie" and "phony," and that among the Jews "nobody wants to work . . . they only want to be involved in commerce." Of course, my father never expressed himself in writing or otherwise about Zionism or Jews and his Palestinian disappointments in such a crude manner. After his return from Palestine he was active in the Karlovac Jewish Community, and he remained a slightly passive Zionist sympathizer who sent his sons to Zionist youth athletic competitions and summer camps. He also periodically contributed money for construction in Palestine, mostly through a blue-and-white "cash box" from the fund Keren Kajemet le Israel, which I still keep today on a bookshelf among my father's mementos. But before he became the director of the municipal police, Družak had worked in Ustasha propaganda for almost two years. He had accepted the idea that propaganda is not a slave to the truth, that truthful information is only a useful starting point for a superstructure that can thus better support the fog of massive fabrications. I found Družak's major text in the journal *Pokuplje* of the spring of 1942, under the title "Croatian Blood Has Spoken," an incredible misrepresentation of the facts surrounding events in Kordun, the incitement to genocide against Kordun Serbs, filled with shallow pathos about the "first Croatian Sovereign, the Great *Poglavnik*." In the article "Facing the Second Revolution," Družak was very pleased that the Jews "had ceased to be the ruling caste" and that they "had been removed from public, political, cultural, and economic life." With such an approach—a grain of truth accompanied by a wealth of exaggeration and lies—it was not difficult for an experienced propagandist like Družak to paint my father as anti-Zionist and anti-Jewish.

Nikolić received the "material" and conscientiously made additional editorial notes for further use. However, he didn't publish any of it. As a skillful editor, he may have felt that my father's letter didn't provide proper "material" for anti-Jewish propaganda, and the text about my father's Palestinian disappointments, without citing the prison letter, simply didn't contain enough information. Or maybe my father's letter moved Nikolić, the Ustasha official, when he read it a little more closely. In the concluding portion of the notes, and after copying the letter, when Nikolić must have pondered a bit more deeply the individual sentences he had copied from the original, Danko is suddenly no longer an "other son" or a "younger son" but the "little son."[2] Perhaps there was a twinge of sadness in his heart as he tersely wrote in his accompanying notes that this man had "disappeared" in the Ustasha camps, knowing full well what that word meant for Jews in the NDH.

Nikolić would describe himself as mild-mannered, a "peace-loving man" with "a sensitive poet's heart." Yet he wrote hundreds of inflammatory texts filled with hatred against the Serbs. But I never found any similar writings by Nikolić against the Jews. After all, it was well known that his main financial supporter for *Hrvatska revija*, the prominent Ustasha émigré Ivo Rojnica, tried hard to establish business and other connections with Jews in both Argentina and Israel. It is probable that during the time of the NDH, Nikolić was among those Ustasha intellectuals, not especially numerous, who reluctantly accepted Ustasha persecution of the Jews as the unavoidable price to be paid to Hitler for his benevolent patronage in the establishment and continued maintenance of the "independent" Croatian state. This assumption, if it is indeed correct, might explain why Nikolić so carefully guarded my father's letter.

In 1992, Nikolić's archive, which he had compiled while in exile, was sent from Barcelona in a special truck to the National and University Library in Zagreb. It contained about twenty thousand letters, about eight thousand published and unpublished articles from the forty-year span of *Hrvatska revija* (1951–1990), and Nikolić's private papers. This mass of documents was wrapped in sheets of old, unidentifiable newspapers. The archivist Drago Pažin, who had completed the processing of Nikolić's bequest in 2005 and had found my father's letter within the stack, convinced me that each of the twenty thousand letters delivered from Barcelona originated from Nikolić's émigré days and were dated after 1945. My father's letter was the exception. It was the only original document among the twenty-eight thousand documents processed that was dated May 1941. Neither Pažin nor his superior, Ivan Kosić, nor I knew how this letter from wartime Zagreb ended up with Nikolić in exile, but there were only two possibilities: either Nikolić took it with him when he fled from Zagreb in early May 1945, or the letter was part of a larger consignment of Ustasha documents sent abroad before the breakup of the NDH and Nikolić had found it. He would then have preserved it in his archive as a rarity because, I am convinced, he had plans for my father's letter, along with his own notations and comments.

Nikolić had some reservations about Ustasha actions against the Jews in the NDH that, of course, deepened during his years as an émigré in the West. In some of his writings and statements he used the word "remorse" and said "cleansing" was a necessary act. He was inclined to statements and gestures of great pathos. Was he touched by the photograph of Willy Brandt, who in the name of Germany had knelt at the monument to the Warsaw Ghetto Uprising in 1970? I have reason to believe that Nikolić was thinking that *Hrvatska revija* should publish a statement of repentance for the Ustasha crimes against the Jews and also for the Ustasha's crimes in general. My father's letter might have served as both the reason and the argument. Nikolić never did this; and in the spirit of his lifelong hesitation to confront the truth about the Ustasha NDH, he hesitated for too long.

I met Vinko Nikolić at the Frankfurt Book Fair in 1980.

A heavy, mustachioed elderly man approached our Liber University Publishing booth in the company of two younger men and, with strained politeness and self-satisfaction, extended his hand to me.

"What's the matter, Slavko, you act like you don't recognize me."

It was Franjo Pavičić, the prewar table-tennis champion in our high school, whom I had not seen since 1941. I heard that he had become an Ustasha lieutenant in the *Poglavnik*'s bodyguard battalion; that he had been in prison several times after the war; that he had nevertheless obtained a degree in forestry and then fled to Germany, where he was politically active in the more moderate Croatian nationalist émigré circles, a contributor to *Nova Hrvatska* (New Croatia), and a member of the Croatian National Council. In this, our first meeting after so many years, he was trying to be casual and hearty, while I was surprised and rather reserved. He gave a cursory look at the Liber publications on display, bought two books by Petar Šegedin, and invited me to the *Hrvatska revija* booth to take a look at their books and magazines. "Your colleagues, the Croatian publishers, are afraid to come to our booth, but you're probably not afraid are you, you old partisan?" Pavičić added.

I must admit that this invitation was not very welcome, but I still went. I was not about to let Pavičić tell his friends that I was a coward. At the booth they barely gave me two or three minutes to leaf through the latest issue of *Hrvatska revija* when a man close to seventy came up to me and in a kind tone of voice said, "Mr. Goldstein, I am honored and very happy that I can welcome you to our booth. I am Vinko Nikolić."

He extended his hand, and while we were shaking hands, almost at the same moment, two cameras flashed, one on each side of us. One photographer probably worked for some émigré organization; the other for the Yugoslav intelligence services.

Nikolić knew something about Liber's publications and praised them, while I casually inquired about their books and magazines. We spoke briefly, not even ten minutes, repeatedly photographed with flashes from the "watcher in the wings." I remember his strikingly luxuriant gray hair, courteous manners, and the pleasant tone of a soft Croatian dialect. I saw him eleven or twelve years later, in the Zagreb café Dubrovnik, after he had returned permanently to Croatia. I think he had already been named an honorary representative to the Croatian parliament. He was sitting in the café with his wife and kindly waved to me. We exchanged a few formal words and he invited me to join them. I hesitated. He wasn't insistent, and his sullen wife was even less so.

Starting in the 1950s in Buenos Aires, under difficult circumstances and with great editorial passion and effort, Nikolić succeeded in publishing and maintaining *Hrvatska revija* for forty years as the richest and most important source for the political and cultural history of the nationalist Croatian émigré community after the Second

World War. His instincts as an editor led him to define the most valuable possible mission for his magazine: the examination of the NDH phenomenon, and confronting Croatian Ustasha émigrés and pro-Ustasha émigrés with the whole truth, urging them to suppress the self-consoling stories, falsifications, myths, and arbitrary accusations in which everyone else is guilty, but not we who avoid looking at ourselves in the mirror. Stimulated by Nikolić's editorial inspiration, thousands of pages of memoirs and historiographical literature about the NDH appeared in the forty years of *Hrvatska revija*. In addition to uncritical panegyrics and jeremiads, it published historiographical information and texts that aspired to truthfulness and even critical reflection: analyses of the ideological trends within the Ustasha movement, an examination of the role of Ante Pavelić, and the government's internal policy. In a major interview in the newspaper *Šibenski list* in 1997, Nikolić nevertheless greatly exaggerated his contribution when he stated that the "magazine guided our people to a democratic orientation to respect human beings and human dignity." After the independence of Croatia in 1990, an unexpectedly small number of contributors to and readers of *Hrvatska revija* returned to the country, and only rarely were they someone "with a democratic orientation," such as Mate Meštrović, Boris Maruna, and Jakša Kušan. The majority arrived with the baggage of their old prejudices, as champions of an autocratic regime and political and national intolerance, to prove Aleksandr Herzen's adage that political émigrés do not forget anything, but they also do not learn anything.

Despite all of Nikolić's efforts with *Hrvatska revija*, a critical examination of the NDH phenomena in its pages went only so far, to a clearly marked border. On the other side of that border some important topics remained untouched: the fetishism of nation and state; the totalitarian essence of Ustasha ideology; its genocidal character and the scale of the crimes committed; the criminal character of the regime. The critical sense of the editor also suffered from the same limitations and shortcomings, which were reflected in the choice of contributors, their texts, and the entire magazine. Indeed, the editor was able to touch superficially on some of these topics, but not on that sacred idol, the state, or more exactly, on the NDH as the embodiment of the state of the Croatian people. Before that idol he knelt and prostrated himself for his entire life in shallow, inhibited thoughts.

In the polemical exchange with the Chetnik journal *Protest* in 1949, Nikolić wrote that he "was always against all forms of violence, whoever committed it." In the next half century or so his thinking evolved. In the interview with *Šibenski list* he was a little more specific: "We have a right to defend ourselves, but some borders should never be crossed. However, crimes were also committed by our side. A crime should be condemned, whoever committed it. We must have the strength to admit our mistakes. Anyone who does not have that strength cannot be redeemed and elevated." Upon receiving the news of the assassination of Vjekoslav Maks Luburić[3] in August 1969, Nikolić wrote, "Jasenovac remains the great Croatian wound, and an even greater disgrace, and because of it, to this day our souls are pained and our cheeks burn with shame." In his statements and writings he would mention the words "remorse" and "cleansing," but he never achieved a true "remorse" or "cleansing." He never got beyond generalizations and never tried to step beyond them. Remorse requires exceptional courage, something that Nikolić did not possess. He was also traumatized by a personal wound. One of his brothers was tortured and killed by the Chetniks; another brother was condemned to death and executed by the Partisans ("And for us that means Serbian communists," Nikolić added). He wrote hundreds of pages about the crimes against Croatians that were perpetrated by Serbs, Chetniks, communists, Italians, English, Russians, and even Germans, but nothing about what the Jasenovac camp really was and how widespread and frightful the "crimes committed by our side" really were. His "sensitive poet's heart" many times spoke of its empathy for the innocent victims of his side but not for the equally innocent victims on that "other side." For him Jasenovac was "the great Croatian wound," but he forgot to say that Jasenovac is just as great a wound to the Serbs, Jews, and Roma. He lived with a permanent division between ethical sensitivity and a fetish for the state that relentlessly crushed ethics.

Of the contributors to *Hrvatska revija*, one of Nikolić's favorites was Eugen Dido Kvaternik. This is understandable only from the narrowest professional-editorial viewpoint: Kvaternik was one of the most literate and by far the best educated of the contributors to *Hrvatska revija*. He held some of the greatest secrets of the NDH, and in *Hrvatska revija* he even revealed a few of them. But of all the contributors to *Hrvatska revija*, Kvaternik was also by far the greatest war criminal. He issued the direct orders for the first massive and genocidal killings in April and May 1941; he was the originator of the death camps that spread from the island of Pag and Jadovno to Jasenovac; and he was the commander of the unified Ustasha and regular police during the harshest period of political and genocidal terror. An old maxim says that the greatest criminals are sometimes capable of the greatest remorse, and beginning in 1952, Kvaternik several times expressed in *Hrvatska revija* words of remorse more radical than all the other contributors to Nikolić's journal put together, and more radical than Nikolić himself:

> Our national fall so shortly after its rise in 1941 was caused by the constant and repeated violation of fundamental ethical and moral principles....The notorious fact that we cannot deny is that during the last war the Croatian side also committed serious transgressions, which can be called sins from a moral view-

> point, crimes from a legal viewpoint, and insanity from a political one.... That is why no one will be able to erase our responsibility before history.

Kvaternik never wrote one word about what made up this "sin," "crime," and "insanity." He blamed only one man for everything: "that psychologically unbalanced Balkan man" Ante Pavelić who, according to Kvaternik, was the primary, and practically the only, cause of everything bad that happened in the NDH. About his own role in this evil Kvaternik wrote only three very general and unfinished sentences in his fascinatingly contradictory writings: "There is no doubt that the writer of these lines was for seventeen months a weapon in the hands of a despot, carrying out his orders. This was a mistake caused by my youthful and boundless faith in the patriotism and ability of Pavelić. But it was only because I no longer wanted to be or could be that weapon that our breakup occurred...."

For Nikolić this was enough to call Kvaternik, at his memorial service in a Buenos Aires cemetery in 1962, "a veteran who pledged all and gave all for the good of his people" and that someday "in a liberated Croatia... he will receive the honor he deserves. He judged himself the most harshly for the mistakes and delusions in his life, and suffering and remorse have purified his soul, which lived only for patriotic ideals. If he made mistakes in that love, like each of us, it was because he loved it so much, and much has been forgiven him...."

Sublimated in this aphoristic pseudo-philosophy are all of Nikolić's cognitive and political and moral limitations. If you loved Croatia very much, you must be forgiven completely even if in its name, in the name of its state, you persecuted people, drove them into prisons and camps, killed them, or had them killed on a massive scale. If you have expressed remorse with a few general phrases, you have been "purified" and you will receive the honor that you deserve. This perverted logic arises from a fetishism of the state and a fetishism of the nation, caused by a disease from which neither Nikolić nor the contributors to *Hrvatska revija* were able to recover. Modern Croatia has not been freed from this disease, and it is only in the last few years that the country has begun to treat it. Albert Einstein was right in his claim that it is more difficult to break human prejudices than to break the atom.

Part Two

The “Vujičić Affair” and the Roots of Evil

Hrvatski Blagaj: until April 1941 an elementary school; in May 1941, a jail and torture area; in the summer of 1942, a Home Guard[1] stronghold; in September 1942, gutted in a battle and left in ruins

6

The "Vujičić Affair" and the Roots of Evil

THERE ARE TIMES in our lives when it seems that we decide our own fates. We freely choose our company, friends, and profession; we start our families; our success depends on our own knowledge and effort; we calmly prepare ourselves for old age. But there are moments, and even entire periods, when our fate is in someone else's hands. Then, that someone or something outside ourselves, some inexorable power that we are unable to resist, makes decisions for us. We can try to escape it or resign ourselves to it. For my family, and for many other families, 1941 was such a period. Remembering what happened, I began to wonder about the roots of the evil that had befallen us. It is difficult to explain our fates without some explanation of the general circumstances that determined them, which is not easy to do. No final answers can be found. As for the evil, I got to know its mechanisms a bit better, which I offer to readers in this chapter.

* * *

In the early evening of May 5, 1941, five well-known members of the Karlovac Ustasha Youth Movement forcibly entered the apartment and office of the lawyer Milan Vujičić on Lopašićeva Street. Quickly, nervously they searched the desks, cabinets, and shelves, and set fire to many legal documents in his office. They took Vujičić away with them and told his wife, Anastasia, that they were taking him to the court in Zagreb. That same evening they arrested two other Karlovac residents of Serbian nationality: Captain First Class Gojko Janjanin of the defeated Royal Yugoslav Army and Dušan Dokmanović, a railroad worker.

Vujičić was known in Karlovac as a respectable and brave man. He was one of the few lawyers who, after the January 6 dictatorship was established,[2] spoke out against the regime and stood up to the police and other organs of power for persecuted members of the United Opposition and other political opponents of the regime. A Serb from Banija, he had grown up and been educated in Karlovac and had married a Croatian woman. He had completely assimilated into the city in which he had become a well-known and respected citizen. As the leading figure in the Independent Democratic Party in the city, Vujičić was a major advocate in the 1930s of cooperation between Karlovac and Krajina Serbs[3] and the United Opposition of Vladko Maček, for whom he had voted in 1938. After the Cvetković-Maček Agreement of 1939,[4] Ivan Šubašić,[5] the newly appointed Croatian governor, proposed Vujičić as his deputy; the appointment was rejected by the central government in Belgrade, allegedly because Vujičić was considered to be a republican. Because of Vujičić's anti-regime views, his wife lost her teaching position at the Karlovac High School in 1935 during the Jevtić government.[6]

Even as the Ustasha Youth were taking her husband away, Anastasia Vujičić set off the alarm on all sides. Through her mother she was descended from the old Karlovac family Blašković, whose several members were prominent in public life. Anastasia's first call was to her uncle Petar Blašković, a former Austro-Hungarian and Yugoslav officer, and before the war, the president of the Croatian Club in Belgrade. He was also among the first officers to be promoted to the rank of general in the Independent State of Croatia. That same night, the leading members of the Karlovac Ustasha Council discussed Vujičić's arrest. Vladimir Židovec, the secretary of the Council, during his interrogation in the State Security Administration (UDBA) prison in Zagreb in 1947, stated:

> If I am not mistaken, it was the evening of May 5, 1941, when Mane Bilović, a member of the Ustasha Council, called me. In an agitated voice he told me that several armed men had entered the apartment of Milan Vujičić, arrested him, put him into a car, and driven him away. He had already called Nikšić, who could only express his shock and amazement, but who professed to be powerless and had no advice.... I immediately sensed danger and gave an order, in my capacity as a member of the Ustasha Council, to block all exits from the city and not to allow a single car to leave. I telephoned the police with the same order. Unfortunately, it was too late. The car with Vujičić had left the city a short time earlier via a secondary road heading toward Rečica....That same evening we, the members of the Ustasha Council, met to discuss this affair. Though we knew nothing for certain, we were filled with foreboding.[7]

What happened next is in "Memorandum of May 22, 1945, written in the office of the District Commission for Establishing War Crimes of the Occupiers and Their Collaborators," which I found in the Karlovac Archive. It was used as material evidence in the criminal proceedings against Aleksandar Šantić in Karlovac in 1948. Luka Šprajc, "fifty years old, born in Brinje, now residing in Karlovac at Matko Laginja 6, Roman Catholic, nationality Croatian, profession gendarme sergeant,[8] married without children," gave the following statement before the commission:

In 1941, after the breakup of the former Yugoslavia, I was commander of a gendarme station in Karlovac. At the beginning of May, a peasant, whose name I cannot remember, reported that he had seen three bodies covered with leaves in a ditch in the forest of Pomrčica near Karlovac. I reported this event to Captain Marković, then-commander of the gendarmes, and requested permission to investigate. Captain Marković advised me not to get involved because this was an Ustasha matter, and if I involved myself I might suffer. For that reason I did not conduct an investigation because I knew that Captain Marković knew more than I about the activities of the Ustasha in the city.... That same day, before evening, Hinko Karl, the chief of police in Karlovac, came with a truck to my gendarme station with two or three other men and asked for a patrol to accompany them on some official business. I gave him the patrol and they departed in the same truck. When I came back the next day, I saw in front of the station the same vehicle, all bloody inside and out, and I remember seeing on the floor of the vehicle human brains. I asked the man on duty at the station what had happened, why the vehicle was bloody. He answered that they had taken the bodies from the forest of Pomrčica and buried them in the cemetery in Šišljavić. Subsequently, I learned from the patrol that they had traveled with Karl in the direction of Rečica and along the way Karl had told them they were going to bury those bodies, but not to say a word about it to anyone under penalty of death. Reaching the spot in the forest where the bodies were, they loaded them into the vehicle, took them to Šišljavić, and buried them in the cemetery, having called a parish priest whom they also threatened with death if he told anyone.... Later I found out in Karlovac that these were the bodies of Gojko Janjanin, former captain first class of the Yugoslav army; Milan Vujičić, a Karlovac lawyer; and a third person [whose identity] I don't know to this day.

Hinko Karl, who so vigorously tried to cover up the evidence of the crime, was until the outbreak of the war a senior supervisor in the Karlovac police. After April 10, 1941, he was a member of the Ustasha Council and was the Ustasha commissioner of police for the city of Karlovac. However, the crime could not be covered up as it wasn't just one peasant who had seen the bodies under the leaves in the Rečica forest; a large group of hunters had also seen them. Deep shock spread through the city and fear crept into many homes. "They've killed Vujičić... they've killed Vujičić," our Jaga was repeating in disbelief when she returned home from the market. I can imagine my mother's anxiety: Until then there had only been arrests and the hope that it would end there. But now there had been killings and not even a month had gone by since the Ustasha had come to power.

Only a few days before this news came, Pavica Vine, my mother's best friend, had mentioned Vujičić. She and my mother had been constantly thinking about how to save my father, who had been languishing in an Ustasha jail since Easter Sunday, April 13. I would sometimes listen to their plotting and scheming, which they didn't seem to mind. When Pavica once said that it might be worth hiring Vujičić to intervene on behalf of my father, my mother was surprised. "But he's a Serb! He has to think about himself, how can he take care of someone else?" But Pavica was of a different opinion. Her husband, Ivo, was one of the leaders of the Croatian Peasants' Party (HSS) in Karlovac and a former representative in the national assembly from the Rečica district. Pavica knew that many Croatian politicians considered Vujičić to be a valuable partner of the United Opposition and that he had once been close to Ante Nikšić. In any event, Vujičić was the last Serb in Karlovac who should feel threatened, said Pavica—a woman of gentle disposition and great virtue, often inclined to see at least a little light even in the most impenetrable darkness.

But if the "last Serb in Karlovac who should feel threatened" was killed, who is not in danger?

Five Young Killers

According to the detailed description given by Vladimir Židovec during the discussion of the eight-member Ustasha Council, at least three members—Feliks Židovec, the mayor of Karlovac; Vladimir Židovec, his son; and Mane Bilović, the commander of the municipal Ustasha organization—firmly demanded an investigation into the murders in the Rečica forest and the punishment of the perpetrators. They were supported by Ivo Klarić, a high-school teacher, and Zdravko Berković, a Karlovac merchant and until April 10 the commander of the local HSS Civic Guards. Giving a variety of excuses, Ante Nikšić, the Ustasha commissioner for the city and county of Karlovac and the former president of the Karlovac district court, blocked the investigation with the support of Hinko Karl, the Ustasha commissioner for the municipal police, and Ivan Gromes, his close associate who would soon replace Karl as the head of the police.

The discussion at the Ustasha Council became increasingly heated, especially after the perpetrators were revealed. After all, they had not concealed their identities when they had carried out the search of Vujičić's apartment and burned his papers; his wife had recognized almost all of them. The families of the other two people they had taken away also recognized them, and it was known whose truck had been used to transport the victims. In *Moje sudjelovanje u političkomživotu* (My Participation in Political Life), Vladimir

Židovec writes that the entire affair was made worse by the fact that those young men, whom everyone in the city knew to be the killers, were behaving so brazenly and provocatively, feeling safe under the powerful protection of Nikšić.

The young men who had so suddenly become killers belonged to a group of about twenty people—university and high-school students, commercial and shop assistants—who in the immediate prewar years had been known as Frankists. I once saw several of them on a rainy day, a tightly packed group, fidgeting and sheltering under umbrellas next to the rear wall of the Edison cinema. When they moved away, the word "ŽAP" materialized on the wall in large black letters. My father later explained to me that this meant "*Živio Ante Pavelić*" (Long live Ante Pavelić). At the time Pavelić was the leader of a small group of militant émigrés living under the protection of Benito Mussolini in Italy and advocating the separation of Croatia from Yugoslavia with Italian assistance.

In the first days of the NDH the young Karlovac Frankists were the most active and reliable supporters of the new Ustasha government. The power and authority that they so unexpectedly acquired turned some of these ideological fanatics into arrogant thugs and bullies and some into murderers. But some backed away from such behavior and took refuge in their studies or their professions. Nikola Marić, a wise Karlovac builder, sent his son to Switzerland to study in order to rescue him from the clutches of a group that had already begun to impress upon him the meaning of being a commander in the Ustasha Youth Movement and a camp officer in the Labor Service of Karlovac Youth.

I personally knew two of the five young men whom everyone recognized as the killers of Vujičić. It was generally assumed in Karlovac that the leader of the group and the main perpetrator was Aleksandar "Saša" Šantić, but the documents that I reviewed in the last several years state that he was only a participant. Šantić was a handsome, well-built young man with excellent posture and a self-confident walk. At that time he was a twenty-one-year-old law student. His former high-school teacher, Milan Radeka, describes him in his *Memories* as an "outstanding student, a bright, intelligent boy, darkly handsome, but a spoiled brat through and through, and also an ardent Ustasha." I remember his self-assured, derisive smile, which he flashed at me more than once. In the winter of 1940–41, I often hung out with some older boys and played hockey with them on the skating rink in front of the Hrvatski Dom. Once when I was skating after Šantić, he hit me hard with the rear point of his skate in the lower leg. At first I thought it was unintentional, but while he was helping me up, his roguish smile told me that he was not at all sorry to have dealt me such a painful, vicious blow. In the spring of 1941—I don't know if it was before or after Vujičić's murder—while playing cops and robbers with my friends, I had forgotten that Jews weren't permitted access to the cinemas, parks, and walking areas, and I dashed off to the promenade in front of the Edison cinema. There I ran into a strolling Šantić. He was in a uniform with the embroidered gold band of a commander's rank around the upper part of his Ustasha cap. He was surrounded by two or three young girls, one of whom was also wearing an Ustasha cap. When he caught sight of me, he laughed out loud in a happy, almost friendly way, flashing that malicious smile: "Hey, you little Jew! What are you doing on the promenade?" And, as if he had made a good joke, pleased with himself, he turned to the girls while I rushed away. When I heard that "handsome Saša" had become a killer, I was surprised but not too surprised.

I was, however, very surprised when I heard about Jožica Gombač. I knew him as a pleasant, chubby fellow who didn't say much and who was an especially gifted mechanic. I visited him several times in the beautiful garden his family had on the banks of the Korana River above Fogin's swimming area. Here Gombač made and tested small model airplanes, which he did far better than any of us. He had turned eighteen right before the war and his wealthy parents had bought him a small two-seat Fiat Topolino. It was one of the first luxury cars in Karlovac and we were all envious of him. Gombač wasn't previously known to associate with Šantić and his Ustasha group, and I don't know how they coaxed him into driving them in his father's truck from the meatpacking plant on their terrible mission. I doubt they told him beforehand what the plan was and can only imagine that scene in the darkness of the Rečica forest: The truck stops along the country road, the lights are extinguished; Gombač sits stunned in the driver's seat, trembling with fear while four armed young men force three bound and frightened prisoners to march into the forest; desperate cries for help from the edge of the forest pierce the dark silence and are immediately extinguished by a fusillade of revolver shots; Gombač can barely contain his anguish and, trembling as he starts the engine, rushes with the four killers from the scene of the crime back to the city. Did anyone have the strength to speak on that drive through the darkened city, or did each of them, for himself and within himself, stifle the hollow shuddering of their first murder? Or perhaps not all of them felt that shudder; perhaps some tried to overcome the uneasy silence with cynical comments, or with a suppressed spasm of their numbed conscience felt a sense of satisfaction about crossing the Rubicon in the first real "settling of accounts with dangerous enemies of Croatia."

It was rumored that the first to shoot the victims was Stipe Augustinović. Before the war he was said to be by temperament the most ardent, the bravest of the young Frankists. Židovec remembers that one night Augustinović had to be dissuaded from tossing a bomb at the Sokolski Dom and that on April 5, the eve of the war, he had "cut the telephone line between Karlovac and Ogulin ... thus fulfilling for the first time his burning desire for 'action.'" After April 10, he quickly became known for participating in many arrests (including my father's), and also allegedly in beatings, as well being the most inclined to "revolutionary methods," that is, violence. But Augustinović was never a leader, only the most ardent follower.

The leader among the five was probably a young lawyer named Josip Željko Kurelac. Two weeks before the murders in Rečica forest, he was appointed the commander of the Ustasha Combat Unit for the City and County of Karlovac. In an interview in the May 2, 1941, issue of the Karlovac newspaper *Hrvatska sloboda*, Nikšić says that of the young men in the prewar Ustasha movement, he most valued Kurelac, "who had won over many students to 'the Croatian cause.'" Thanks to him the Ustasha movement had spread into the ranks of Karlovac students—until that day they had been recruited as "democratic sloganeers, lost in empty discussions and idle talk." A selfless, intelligent, and tubercular fanatic, Kurelac had been closely connected to Nikšić before the war and he remained so after April 10. He received advice, instructions, and assignments directly from Nikšić. As the commander of the Ustasha Combat Unit he led a group of the most passionate followers. Among the Karlovac Ustasha they were known as "Nikšić's boys." Židovec maintained that "these extremist Ustasha youth ... did not need anything other than a quiet word in their ear that Vujičić was a danger to the new Croatian state ... and that was motive enough to move them into action."

"All for Our Cause"

For a long time in Karlovac there was speculation as to the motives for the Vujičić murder, though it was rather clear that the motives were concealed in the legal and private documents that the Ustasha

Youth Movement so zealously incinerated in his office. Radeka, who was personally close to Vujičić, says in his *Memories*:

> As a lawyer, Vujičić knew some unpleasant things about Nikšić, now the Ustasha provincial governor.... After World War I, Nikšić as a Yugoslav had gone with a delegation of the Adriatic Guards, a monarchistic organization, to the tomb of the late King Alexander in Oplenac in 1935.[9] And on April 13, 1941, the *Poglavnik* himself was staying at his house. However, that intellectual, doctor of law, and senior judge was involved in one piece of dirty family business: the falsified signature of his brother on a bill of exchange.

In short, Nikšić had conducted some compromising financial transactions and in the past he had played a double game between the Royal Yugoslav government and the illegal Ustasha movement, and Vujičić was an inconvenient witness to it all. However, it is not likely that Nikšić, a cautious man and an experienced opportunist, would have had enough nerve to issue an order for the first three murders without having someone covering his back or protecting him "from above."

That same night of May 5, when Vujičić, Janjanin, and Dokmanović were murdered not far from Karlovac, other similar murders took place in Croatia, Bosnia, and Herzegovina. They were also the first of their kind in those regions. On the evening of May 5, Asim Đelić, a bodyguard for Viktor Gutić, the Ustasha commissioner for western Bosnia, took the Orthodox bishop Platon Jovanović and the priest Dušan Subotić from their cells in the Banja Luka prison and brought them to the banks of the Vrbas River, where he brutally murdered them and threw their bodies into the river. That same night in Glina, Adam Resanović and Stojan Slijepčević were arrested, brutally beaten, then taken away with a group of several village teachers, Orthodox priests, and former noncommissioned officers from the surrounding villages, never to be seen again—victims of the first mass murder in that area. In Lika the infamous Macolina cavern swallowed its first twenty-six victims: Serbs who had been arrested in Gračac and the surrounding area. Also during this time two Ustasha columns from Petrinja raided Serbian villages in the Banija region and carried out the first public executions of several prominent villagers. On Tuesday, May 6, self-organized Ustasha groups, or "wild Ustasha," as they were subsequently called, raided the villages around Sanski Most, where they encountered the first spontaneous Serbian resistance in the village of Srpsko Kijevo. This resistance was crushed on May 8 with the help of a Wehrmacht unit that also carried out reprisals: One hundred hostages were selected from among villagers who had been arrested, then twenty-seven of them were summarily executed, their bodies hung from the trees in the park in Sanski Most, and their houses burned.[10] The slaughter of Kordun Serbs in Blagaj, not far from Slunj, also began on that same day. It was the largest crime committed in the first month of the NDH, about which more will be said in later chapters.

The coordinated violence, clearly directed from a single central point, can be explained by the date of the atrocities. According to the Orthodox calendar, May 6 is Đurđevdan (Saint George's Day), and according to the old Serbian saying, "*Đurđev danak, hajdučki sastanak*" (Saint George's Day, the outlaws' get-together).[11] It is not clear if Pavelić and Kvaternik actually feared that some Serbs might arise as outlaws on Đurđevdan, or if the date for the first killings was chosen for its symbolic meaning, as a demonstration of power to sow fear and contrition among the local Serbian communities by killing their leaders.

In the torrent of the initial exemplary killings, Nikšić, as the Ustasha commissioner for the city and county of Karlovac, likely received from "on high" in Zagreb an order or recommendation that something similar should be staged in Karlovac on Đurđevdan. According to the testimony of Židovec, Nikšić went to Zagreb several times for discussions in April and May. He came home from one of these meetings and said in passing that "there will still be blood up to the knees in our revolution." All Nikšić had to do was select the first victims. But how did he convince his young "praetorians," his "boys," the five young men from Karlovac, suddenly to become killers as Pyotr Verkhovensky did in Dostoyevsky's *The Possessed*?

According to available information, it appears that Nikšić didn't have to work hard to convince his five boys that it was both useful and necessary to kill Vujičić, Janjanin, and Dokmanović "for our cause" on the eve of Serbian Đurđevdan. Nikšić's five had just become part of an all-powerful government, intoxicated with a feeling of daring and doing anything, and no one could stop them.

The Dilemmas of the Ustasha Leadership

Regarding the twists and turns of the story that followed, Stjepan Vukovac, the assistant minister of Internal Affairs of the NDH, described the key moments of the case in his statement made in 1952, when he was serving as a lawyer in the Municipal Archive of the City of Zagreb:

> At the end of April or the beginning of May, young Židovec came to my office. He told me about an official report regarding a terrible crime in Karlovac that his father, Židovec the elder, was sending personally to Artuković, the minister of internal affairs. It involved a group of Ustasha Youth criminals who

forcefully broke into the apartment of a Karlovac lawyer, Vujičić, set fire to official documents in his office, tied him up, packed him into a car, then killed and buried him in a forest.... Vujičić was a man of rare worth and honesty, he said, and regardless of the fact that he was a Serb, he was held in high regard by everyone in the city and in the surrounding villages... that he was a republican, which is why he could not be nominated as the deputy of Ivan Šubašić. He also told me that the deceased left a widow, a Croatian woman, who had close, friendly, or even family ties with many senior Ustasha officials...the report concluded that the criminals were protecting the interests of the president of the district court in Karlovac, Nikšić.... Motives for the murder of Vujičić and the burning of some of his papers could be found in the accusation of unpaid bills of exchange, and in some notes on the management of Sokol society in Karlovac, which implied the double role of Judge Nikšić—on the one hand he prospered under the Belgrade regimes, while on the other hand he suddenly stood prominent as a longtime, ardent Ustasha. I immediately went with Židovec to Artuković. He quickly read it and then listened to statements by me and Židovec, pretending to be appalled and surprised that these young men had not yet been arrested. It was apparent that he had already been informed about the affair. He said that the investigation was the official responsibility of the Directorate for Public Order and Security, but that he would act immediately to have the perpetrators arrested and charged according to the law....

Well acquainted with Andrija Artuković's manner of speaking and working, Vukovac immediately understood that nothing would come of the promise to act "according to the law" and he said so openly to Židovec and fellow Ustasha Council member Bilović. Since the Directorate for Public Order and Security (RAVSIGUR) was heading the investigation, Vukovac was convinced that Nikšić would enjoy the full support of Kvaternik and people like him, and given the attitude of Artuković, "there is no longer any use in speaking to him about the matter." In these initial discussions Vukovac quickly sensed that he could trust Židovec and Bilović. He complained to them that unfortunately the "incident" in Karlovac was not the only one. For fifteen days there had been reports of similar "arbitrary acts," and he had already been to the minister several times in an attempt to initiate investigations, to stop the spreading evil, but had been unsuccessful.

Kvaternik, the head of RAVSIGUR as well as the deputy minister for internal affairs and a state secretary, held all the cards. He had an unlimited authority that rendered Vukovac simply powerless. "One day," Židovec writes, "they were both called to Artuković, who listened to Dido Kvaternik speak about the revolutionary needs of our times. He then listened to Vukovac's views on the need for legal, rational, and thoughtful procedures. After hearing each of them, Artuković rubbed his hands in satisfaction and wisely pronounced the judgment, 'You see, I really need both of you. You, Dido, represent one extreme, which is radical and revolutionary; and you, Vukovac, represent the other extreme, which stands for strict legality and moderation. In that way the two of you complement each other, however much you may disagree. You are just what I need so that I can always choose the middle way!'"

But Artuković made no attempt to choose "the middle way." His actions demonstrated his sympathy for the "radical" Kvaternik, who was Pavelić's favorite and his confidant from their years as émigrés. Vukovac finally involved Minister Milovan Žanić in the affair, convinced that he, if anyone, would be able to do something.

At that time Žanić was a prominent minister in the NDH government and the president of its Legislative Commission, which oversaw various aspects of the Ministry of Justice, the Ministry of Internal Affairs, and other ministries. Known as a successful lawyer in the town of Nova Gradiška and in Zagreb, he was respected in Ustasha circles for his long years of support for and activity in the Croatian Party of Rights, which is why he frequently had difficulties with the former royal regime and was imprisoned several times. Žanić maintained that Vukovac "was without a doubt our best legal mind and was at the highest European level," so consequently he had full confidence in Vukovac's recommendation to receive Židovec and Bilović. Židovec writes:

> When I visited Minister Žanić and briefly told him about the case, he immediately put one of his offices at my disposal, gave me a trustworthy typist, and asked me to prepare a detailed report. I actually dictated a report of some twelve pages, signed it, and immediately delivered it to Žanić. Mane Bilović was present while I was preparing the report. We then met with Žanić, who promised to take decisive action to resolve this matter in the way that I proposed in the report, that is, that the guilty be brought before the law in the interests of the "Croatian cause" and the country's reputation.... I warned him of the careless conduct of the killers and of Nikšić, as a result of which Nikšić had been seriously compromised before public opinion in Karlovac. I therefore concluded that Nikšić should be removed from Karlovac.... Minister Žanić promised to do all that he could.

Since Žanić had mentioned another minister, Lovro Sušić, who was also considered a member of the "moderate wing," Bilović and

Židovec went to see if they could win him to their side. "When I explained the matter to Sušić and showed him what Nikšić had done, he held his head in his hands, 'terrible, terrible,' 'incredible, terrible,' he moaned and promised to do everything he could."

All of this happened in the week of May 12–16. Židovec claims that he and Bilović did not expect much from the lamentations of Sušić, but the calm and energetic Žanić made a convincing impression on them. "We were in a state of expectation about the results of our efforts. My father, I, and some other members of the Ustasha Council had made a firm decision to resign if our action was not successful.... I didn't remember how long we waited for a decision from Zagreb. I think it was about two to three weeks, not more."

These twenty or so days in the second half of May and at the beginning of June 1941, during which the Karlovac Ustasha Council awaited the resolution of its internal divisions, was also a period during which the initial wave of mass killings of Serbs in Croatia was temporarily halted. The "Vujičić affair" in Karlovac had been only one of the incidents that had inundated the senior Ustasha leadership with complaints that they could not easily dismiss. When Židovec saw the seriously ill Žanić for the last time just before his death in Fermo, Italy, in the summer of 1946, Žanić told him how in May 1941 "he had fought and strained to achieve something in the 'Vujičić affair,'" with the hope of stopping the wave of illegal Ustasha violence and thus saving the NDH from sinking into evil, but unfortunately he was "unable to accomplish anything." Žanić's predicament is even more explicitly described in a very interesting and intelligent report on the Ustasha movement written by an anonymous UDBA collaborator using the pseudonym "Dizdar" in the spring of 1952. With respect to Žanić, the report claims that "he wanted to use the Vujičić case as an opportunity to alter the course that Pavelić and Kvaternik had set, but it became clear that it was not a question of random events or of the guilt of individuals but of a deliberate plan, so that it was impossible to do anything," and that later as an émigré Žanić "was deeply bitter and said that Pavelić had not only personally destroyed us and an entire generation but the idea of a Croatian state as such."

In his 1947 *Memoirs* written while in prison, Slavko Kvaternik, Deputy Prime Minister and head of the military in the NDH from 1941 to 1942, also wrote about the unwillingness of some Ustasha ministers to be identified with Pavelić's genocide policy: "Except for Puk and Mile Budak, not a single member of the government approved of the persecutions, but they came to their senses only when they were already powerless." Although such claims are only a feeble defense by a prisoner accused of serious crimes and of a weak character, I think that they can be accepted as yet another sign that there really was a dilemma within the Ustasha government regarding the justifiability of such massive crimes. According to various testimonies, Žanić spoke most openly about this in internal discussions, but his resistance to Pavelić's policy in mid-May 1941 was not as decisive as Židovec, "Dizdar," and Žanić himself subsequently suggested.

At a large Ustasha gathering in Nova Gradiška on June 2, 1941, Žanić was the main speaker. According to the June 3 issue of *Novi list*, he said:

> Ustasha! Know this! I speak openly. This state, this homeland of ours, must be Croatian and no one else's. And that is why those who have come here must leave. Events through the centuries, but especially in the last twenty years, have shown that any compromise is out of the question. This must be a country of Croats and no one else, and there are no methods that we, as Ustasha, will not use to make this country truly Croatian so

> that we can cleanse it of the Serbs, who have been threatening us for hundreds of years and would threaten us again at the first opportunity. We do not hide this, it is the policy of this state, and when we carry it out, we will only be carrying out what is enshrined in our Ustasha principles.

Does this mean that after the discussions within the Ustasha leadership in May 1941 Žanić had promptly stopped opposing Pavelić's policy and accepted it? Or had Žanić maintained that Serbs in Croatia "must leave" without being killed and that, as a lawyer, he was looking for some semblance of legality, while Pavelić and Kvaternik considered killing to be the primary tool and didn't concern themselves with legalities? Žanić's words in the speech above—"there are no methods that we, as Ustasha, will not use"—are indication enough that the opposition within the leadership of the NDH to the mass killings of Serbs during this time was not exactly strong. Or was Žanić only resorting to a "cunning," opportunistic tactic to show public solidarity with Pavelić's unscrupulous policy while at the same time trying to soften it in internal discussions? Žanić continued to be a member of the Ustasha government and the president of the Legislative Council until February 1942. He signed the laws that opened the way for the genocide policy and political violence. He also signed the race laws, but he was able to insert exception clauses, by which he was able to protect his wife, Alma (née Stöger), who was Jewish, from persecution. Žanić began to distance himself publicly from Pavelić's policies only at the beginning of 1942, when he ceased to hold influential political posts, remaining only as the president of the Croatian Red Cross. In November 1943, he sought and was granted retirement, and at the beginning of 1945 he publicly refused to accept a medal from Pavelić.

Pavelić's Genocide Plan

The Ustasha *Poglavnik*, Ante Pavelić, took power in Zagreb in April 1941 with the firm intention of creating an "ethnically pure Croatia," but he seemed to lack a precisely prepared plan to implement it. He relied on improvisations dictated by the circumstances. Mladen Lorković, one of the leading interpreters of Ustasha ideology, expressed its basic precept most concisely: "The Croatian state cannot exist if 1.8 million Serbs are living in it and if we have a powerful Serbian state at our backs... therefore, we are trying to make the Serbs disappear from our regions."[12] In this spirit Ustasha organs inspired a cult of revenge and hatred during their ten or so years in exile. "KNIFE, REVOLVER, BOMB, AND TIME BOMB, these are the idols, the clarions that will announce the dawn of a new day and the RESURRECTION OF THE INDEPENDENT CROATIAN STATE!" read the banner in the newspaper *Ustasha—The Journal of Croatian Revolutionaries* above an editorial titled "Fed Up with Slavery" signed by the *Poglavnik* in its first issue in February 1932. Subsequent issues of the newspaper made statements such as "we need bloodshed to wash away the stain," "when the blood flows, it will be in rivers," "drops of blood will be transformed into whole streams and rivers of our enemy's blood and bombs will scatter their bones like chaff in the wind," "every Ustasha is waiting to be called... to throw his body and soul at the enemy, to slaughter and crush him," and "the dedication, revolvers, bombs, and razor-sharp daggers of the Croatian Ustasha will cut out all the rotten flesh from the body of the Croatian nation and will have the final word." In September 1932, it printed a slogan in capital letters, "*PREKO DRINE OTJERATI PSINE*" (Drive the dogs across the Drina), and a month later it hailed the leader who "*Gdjegod stiže i Srbe pristiže, tragživota svakuda im briše*" (Wherever he finds Serbs, he wipes away all traces of their lives).

The spring of 1941 showed that these were not just idle threats and metaphors for Pavelić and his hard-core émigrés. Having returned to the country, according to Slavko Kvaternik's *Memoirs*, Pavelić, senior government officials, and other Ustasha émigré returnees were seething with hatred toward the Serbs. Living abroad as émigrés for twelve years, during which time they lived only in the yearning for revenge, had turned them into psychopaths, mentally deranged people with a desire for revenge. Slavko Kvaternik witnessed this firsthand, and those who were not with them were branded as traitors to the Croatian people. General Edmund Glaise von Horstenau, the Wehrmacht representative to the NDH from April 1941 to the summer of 1944, also testified to this derangement. In his diary he noted, "In April 1941, Pavelić set foot on the soil of the homeland with no less an intention than to exterminate by fire and sword the 1.8 million Serbs, who were living in the country mingled with 4 million Croats and 700,000 Muslims."[13] Even Heinrich Himmler was said to be horrified when Dido Kvaternik told him during their first meeting in late May 1941 about the plan to kill two million Serbs in the NDH.[14]

Pavelić entrusted the organization and implementation of this program to Dido Kvaternik: "When we triumphantly returned home from abroad and when Pavelić decided that I should take over the implementation of the measures against the Jews and Serbs, I obeyed immediately and without hesitation... because I knew that this question had to be resolved for the future of the Croatian people and state and that someone had to make the sacrifice so that these odious but necessary measures would be carried out." Kvaternik confided this to his close friends in 1944, when he had already been relieved of his duties and banished from Croatia. Regarding the details of Pavelić's orders against the Jews and Serbs, the younger Kvaternik is silent. They were in all likelihood never issued to him in writing, only orally and in private. How these orders were implemented is probably the best indication of what they contained.[15]

Dido Kvaternik selected a broad area around the town of Bjelovar, with a mixed population of Croats and Serbs, for the beginning of his "historically necessary mission." This was the area in which the 108th Regiment of the Slavonia Division of the Royal Yugoslav Army rebelled on April 8, 1941, after refusing to take part in any resistance to the approaching units of the German Wehrmacht. With the support of Julije Makanac, the nationalist mayor of Bjelovar, several officers and noncommissioned officers sympathetic to Ustasha ideals took power with their units in Bjelovar and in some other nearby towns the next day. This was the only instance of a pro-Ustasha uprising of any significance in Croatia and Bosnia before the entry of the German army into Zagreb and the declaration of the NDH. Ustasha propaganda celebrated it as an uprising of the Croatian people against the April war and for the destruction of Yugoslavia.

Kvaternik was obviously counting on the fact that his first drastic action against the Serbs would find approval and even active support in this militantly Croatian region. For several days after the rebellion of the 108th Regiment, from April 9 to 14, groups of armed soldiers from the disbanded Slavonia Division roamed the area looking for a way home, but there were also armed Serbian officers who had refused to surrender and were carrying out raids to obtain food, money, and civilian clothing that would make it easier to pass through any checkpoints. In some villages local units of the Peasant Guards disarmed the defeated army and plundered its warehouses. Some of these units, especially in the Gudovac district, became a local unit of the Ustasha army, known as the "readiness battalion."

There were numerous incidents in this region during the disarming and arresting of members of the former Yugoslav army in which some twenty military deserters and civilians were killed. These incidents were another reason why Kvaternik, when he heard the rumors from Grubišno Polje on April 26 that the Serbs there "were preparing something for a Đurđevdan rising," immediately rushed "to the field" to begin his first major operation. With Ivica Šarić, his closest and most reliable assistant (and future best man), and about thirty other Ustasha returnees, he carried out massive arrests of Serbs from Grubišno Polje and the surrounding areas on the night of April 26. Đoko Starčević, a well-educated villager from nearby Pavlovac, noted in his diary how "Pavelić's Ustasha" (that is, the Ustasha who had returned from exile) brutally mistreated the detainees, but in his village "Pavelić's Ustasha made no arrests; these were made by the Peasant Guards from Dražica, by people we knew. Although deadly serious and formal, we cannot complain about their conduct because they were rather courteous for these troubled times."[16] "Pavelić's Ustasha" transferred about 530 prisoners from the Grubišno Polje area first to the Danica camp and then on to their calvary through the Ustasha camps in Gospić, on Mount Velebit, or on the island of Pag, all the way to Jasenovac or Stara Gradiška, which very few of them survived.

On April 28, Kvaternik had already moved on to the other side of Bjelovar to the village of Gudovac. The day before, as two peasants were being led from their homes to jail, Đuro Miketić, a Croatian guard, and Milan Radovanović, a Serb villager, were killed in a skirmish. That same afternoon, a stray bullet or an unknown assailant killed Đuro Raptavi, a member of the Home Guard on leave, in his yard. In "retaliation" Kvaternik ordered and supervised the arrest of about two hundred Serbs from Gudovac and the neighboring villages. They were arrested by members of the local Peasant Guards, which had been transformed into a quasi-military unit under the command of Martin Cikoš, a "sworn" prewar Ustasha. Most of the people arrested were well-to-do or more prominent villagers, teachers, and priests. According to one testimony, late that afternoon Cikoš was in a restaurant "upset and uneasy, his mind somewhere else . . . in no mood to talk." At the last minute he separated from the group a neighbor of his and a good friend, a Serb, telling him, "Now get lost and quickly!"—then gave the order that all two hundred detainees be lined up. Kvaternik stood before them and asked, "Are there any Croats among you?" Four came forward, three of whom were allowed to go home after their identification was checked, while the fourth was sent back into the ranks of Serbs.

The detainees had been told that they would be taken to Bjelovar for interrogation. When they were ordered to move off in the opposite direction, toward the field where the weekly village market was held, they realized that great evil was in store for them. The column was escorted by about seventy armed guards who had been transformed into Ustasha under the supervision of Cikoš, by Kvaternik and his retinue, and by several other newly appointed Ustasha officials from Bjelovar. The prisoners were led through the village in the twilight and brought to the field in the falling darkness. Here they were ordered to line up in ranks and to make "a left face": they collapsed, cut down in a fusillade from two light machine guns and many rifles. The scene was observed from the road, at a distance of about fifty meters, by Kvaternik; Mijo Hans, the Ustasha commissioner for the city and county of Bjelovar; Josip Verhas, the acting head of the county; and Mirko Pavešić, the head of the Gudovac district, a man who had long been closely linked to the Ustasha leadership and who had driven Kvaternik to Gudovac in his own car that day.

Gruesome cries rose from the scene. At the last moment some of the executioners had second thoughts about murdering their neighbors, and so many of the victims were struck in the legs. Some of the wounded were screaming for help, some were begging, some were cursing the killers, while Pavešić ordered Cikoš to "finish the job!" But before Cikoš and several of his paramilitaries were able to "finish the job," five of the more lightly wounded managed to escape in the darkness. Their detailed testimonies, then and later (the testimony of Ilija Jarić is especially detailed), present a graphic and deeply shocking picture of the horror that took place in Gudovac on April 28, 1941.

In any case, Kvaternik never tried to hide his first major crime. On the contrary, it seems that everything was intentionally carried out in front of the entire village and with the knowledge of everyone in the area, who heard the deadly fusillade at the first fall of darkness. The Gudovac villagers were later forced to come to the field with lanterns to dig a pit measuring forty-two by two meters. They covered the bodies of almost 200 of their friends with lime and then buried them. The sources generally agree on the number of victims: at least 187 and at most 196 innocent people were killed without any interrogation or trial. Their sole crime was that they were of the Orthodox faith and perhaps a little more prosperous than their neighbors.

The next day Bjelovar was buzzing about the incident. The wife and daughter of Nikola Gvozdenčević heard that their husband and father was among those executed. Not believing it, and deeply upset, they rushed to the command post of a German military unit that was still in the city. Mrs. Gvozdenčević spoke German and reported what she had heard. The mother and daughter led two German officers to the scene in Gudovac. With their usual efficiency, the German officers immediately informed their headquarters and complained that the "disorder" in their area of responsibility was beyond their control. Exhumations in a part of the burial site were ordered and the corpses photographed. An investigation, arrests, and punishment for the perpetrators were requested. At the order of the local German commander, about forty of those involved in the shootings were arrested. Their weapons were confiscated and they spent the next night as prisoners in the Bjelovar high school.

The commander of the temporary German garrison in Bjelovar,

whose name and rank I have not been able to establish, obviously belonged to that segment of the German officer corps that abhorred the brutal violence of the Nazi government and the SS. Starčević has written how his group of Serb detainees from Pavlovac was mistreated in the Bjelovar jail on April 27 and 28, until "a German officer appeared in the corridor with an interpreter. When I passed by them, I heard the officer say, '*Ist so was möglich?*' [Is something like this possible?]. And from that moment life got better for us; the harshness was gone." From the very first weeks of the NDH some German officers could sense the danger caused by the brutal behavior of the Ustasha authorities and they warned their superiors that it threatened to "transform the entire country into an inferno that will not be easy to extinguish"—but at the highest levels of the German government at that time opinions favoring Pavelić and the Ustasha violence had the upper hand.

On the evening of April 29, the day some of the killers from Gudovac were arrested, Mladen Lorković, the state secretary in the NDH Ministry of Foreign Affairs, requested an urgent meeting with Siegfried Kasche, the German ambassador to the NDH. According to Kasche's report, Lorković informed him that Serbs in the area of Bjelovar had killed eleven Croats and that retaliatory attacks in the village of Gudovac followed on April 28 in which 192 Serbian men had been killed. Lorković maintained that this was an internal political issue under the jurisdiction of the Croatian government. He therefore requested that the men detained by the Germans be handed over to Croatian authorities, who would carry out a further investigation. Kasche, probably with the agreement of his superiors, accepted Lorković's proposal. After twenty-four hours in custody at the Bjelovar high school, the perpetrators of the Gudovac massacre were released and their weapons returned to them. The promised investigation, of course, was never carried out.[17]

In an attempt to convince Kasche, Lorković had made up the number of eleven Croats killed as the reason for the so-called retaliation. Kvaternik had been more systematic in an attempt to be more convincing. He had requested from the Bjelovar police chief a list of names of all Croats killed in that area between April 8 and 27, 1941. On April 30, the police provided a list of twenty-seven names of those killed, with the date and place of each death. It was apparent that the first twenty-five victims on the list were killed between April 8 and 14 during the rebellion of the 108th Regiment, in military operations, or in skirmishes with remnants of the fleeing Royal Yugoslav Army. After April 14, there were no casualties—peace reigned. Only on April 27 were the previously mentioned two Croats and the Serb detainee killed—hardly a convincing reason for the massacre of 192 innocent people.

The National Archive in Bjelovar contains rather exhaustive material about the crime in Gudovac. There are also documents identifying the victims that district officials of Gudovac compiled in May 1941, a neatly filled out form from the medical examiner for each of the 187 identified victims with detailed information in all of the numbered sections, including in some places "Shot as a Chetnik," accompanied by a starkly bureaucratic notation that "State of death routinely confirmed—Gudovac, May 9, 1941," with the signature of the district notary, a man named Pokopac. A statement speaks of the "fright" of the Serbian residents because of such Ustasha acts and of the "distress" of the Croatian population. The majority of local HSS activists and the party's leadership distanced themselves from the crime committed by former members of their party in the Peasant Guards, which had been incorporated into the Ustasha, and condemned their actions. A substantial number of the prominent HSS members who cooperated with the national liberation struggle from the very beginning and then joined the Partisans were from the

Bjelovar region, and I believe the primrary motive was the need to disassociate themselves from the Gudovac crime. According to some sources, even Julije Makanec, the former mayor of Bjelovar, had tried to distance himself from it, allegedly protesting to the "appropriate authorities" in Zagreb. His protests could not have been particularly urgent as Makanec quickly rose through the Ustasha hierarchy: From the fall of 1943 until May 1945 he was the minister of national education in the NDH government and in that capacity, officially and in the name of the government, criticized Archbishop Alojzije Stepinac in an article in *Hrvatski narod* for too openly disapproving of some of the Ustasha government's measures in his sermons.

An ossuary and mausoleum were erected in 1955 at the edge of the village of Gudovac on the field where the massacre took place. A monument called *Gudovac—Before the Firing Squad*, by Vojin Bakić, one of Croatia's greatest sculptors and a native of Bjelovar, was also erected there. In 1991, the ossuary was destroyed, the mausoleum demolished, and the field laid to waste. At the same time, one of Bakić's most famous monuments, *Bjelovarac*, was demolished and removed from the center of Bjelovar because Bakić was a Serb and the monument had been dedicated to his brothers, who had been killed by the Ustasha. In 2002, the remains of the ossuary in Gudovac were removed. Bushes and weeds covered the remains of the mausoleum. That same year, a large number of cultural and public officials signed a petition to erect *Bjelovarac* again on the same site where it had been destroyed in 1991. The city of Bjelovar promised half of the amount required for the restoration of the monument and the Ministry of Culture informed the petitioners that they should apply for the other half of the amount through a tender in 2005. The petitioners applied for the tender but the monument has not been returned to the center of town. As far as I know, there has been no further petition for the return of the Gudovac monument.

Veljun and Blagaj

The intervention of the local German command in the Gudovac crime did not deter Kvaternik. The Ustasha police continued their increasingly frequent arrests in the cities. In early May, they even carried out the first coordinated killings of prominent Serbs in several cities. However, when the first occasion for a mass killing appeared, Kvaternik was somewhat more cautious: He tried to find a new "pretext" for his quasi-legal action.

On the night of May 5, 1941, in the canyon of the Korana River below the ruins of the castle of Hrvatski Blagaj,[18] two unidentified persons robbed a miller by the name of Josa Mravunac and killed him, his wife, his mother, and two of his children with knives. Mravunac's twelve-year-old daughter, Milka, saved herself by jumping into the river. Nikola Lasić, the investigating judge from Slunj, and Eduard Lenčerić, the county commissioner, filed a report from the scene of the crime the next morning, citing "murder-robbery by unknown perpetrators," but two Ustasha officials from Slunj, Nikola Zdunić and Gerdhard-Đeranda Jelečanin, expressed their suspicion that it was a "political crime, which was probably carried out by Chetniks from Veljun and the surrounding area." Kvaternik, who was in Zagreb, had already decided that it was a "Đurđevdan uprising" of Kordun Serbs[19] against the new Croatian state. He immediately sent Ivica Šarić, his most trusted aide, and Vjekoslav Maks Luburić with about ten Ustasha émigré returnees, from Zagreb to Blagaj. Under their supervision, and with the assistance of other Ustasha units, they rounded up nearly four hundred Serbs from surrounding villages. In the meantime, Kvaternik was pulling the strings from Zagreb. He was in a rush to create some "legality."[20]

In a telephone conversation late in the evening of May 6, Mirko Puk, the NDH minister of justice, ordered Vladimir Židovec, the secretary of the Karlovac Ustasha Council, to select from among Karlovac lawyers those who were "certified good Croats," people suitable for a Special People's Court that would try Serbs suspected of a serious political crime in Blagaj on the basis of the Legal Decree for the Defense of the People and the State. Half an hour before midnight, Židovec dispatched messengers from the Ustasha Council to the people he had selected telling them that they should be ready to set out at five the next morning for Blagaj as members of the Special People's Court. The people chosen included Mirko Mikac, the president of the county court in Karlovac, as president of the Special People's Court; Ivan Betlehem, the assessor of the county court, and Zdravko Berković, an Ustasha Council member, as members of the Special People's Court; Milan Stilinović, the clerk of the district court, as the deputy judge; Ivan Gromes, the secretary of the district court, as the state prosecutor; and Berislav Lukinić, a Karlovac lawyer, as the public defender for the accused.

All of those appointed, with the exception of Lukinić and Stilinović, were proven partners or sympathizers of the new Ustasha government. Early in the morning of May 7, Minister Puk confirmed the appointments by a decree of the Ministry of Justice while they were still at "the scene of the crime" in Blagaj. According to the subsequent corroborating statements of Betlehem, Stilinović, and Lukinić, they encountered in the Blagaj school a large group of detainees and alleged suspects who were already "in a sad state, beaten and obviously tortured," and the gendarmes and the Ustasha were bringing still more new "suspects" from Veljun. According to testimony by Momčilo Kozlina, Milić Duduković-Strojić, and other detainees, they had been abused mostly by Ustasha émigrés commanded by Luburić, but several Ustasha from the local readiness units, which now numbered about fifty armed peasants, also participated. Angered by the massacre of the Mravunac family, Ustasha from Blagaj and Pavlovac,

who had recently taken up arms, willingly participated in bringing their Serbian neighbors in for questioning, but the majority became more restrained when the mistreatment and the beatings began.

Judge Lasić repeated before the court his opinion that there was no evidence that identified the assailants or a political motive for the crime. He stood behind his report about a "murder-robbery by unknown assailants." Šarić, the representative of RAVSIGUR, demanded that the court immediately establish that the murders were part of a politically motivated uprising of Serbs, and that his service would later prepare a report with the material proof. Milka was unable to identify the killers in a police lineup. Deputy Judge Stilinović conducted another investigation of the scene of the crime. The court then met in session in the Blagaj school, stated that there was no evidence to justify a trial, and reached a unanimous decision that the trial would continue once evidence had been gathered. By that evening, the judges were on their way home to Karlovac.

But Kvaternik was not about to suffer any delays. That same evening, Vlado Singer, Kvaternik's friend from émigré days and the head of the personnel section of the Ustasha main headquarters, formed a new senate of the Special People's Court that would not put off the deliberations but would "try cases in the Ustasha way." On the morning of May 8, Minister Puk immediately signed off on the composition of a new court, which included Joso Rukavina as president of the court; Josip Majić and Jakov Jurag as members; Josip Raspudić and Grga Ereš as deputy judges; and Vladimir Vranković as state prosecutor. Rukavina was an Ustasha émigré returnee and later a commander of the Ustasha military police. Majić was an adviser to ministers Artuković and Puk. Ereš was a sworn prewar member of the Ustasha who was convicted of the murder of the left-wing student activist Krsto Ljubičić in 1937. The other members of the court were reliable members or supporters of the Ustasha movement. This time no public defender was appointed.

In the haste dictated by Kvaternik the court convened in the Blagaj school on May 8. During his interrogation by the UDBA on July 24, 1947, Ereš described how they conducted an investigation for two full days. Šarić roasted a lamb especially for them. Milka again had to identify suspects and this time, allegedly, she recognized one of the assailants. The Ustasha investigators interviewed several dozen prominent people: a priest, the former president of the district, activists of pro-regime parties, alleged members of Chetnik societies, and avowed communists. The next afternoon, thirty-two suspects were sentenced to death by firing squad "for an attempted Chetnik uprising against the Independent State of Croatia and the murder of the Croatian family Mravunac." Dušan Nikšić, the only survivor from this group, claimed in a postwar statement that thirty-six people were convicted; that they were immediately taken to the execution site, a pit behind the Blagaj church; and that he was the only one who managed to escape. The court concluded that there was insufficient proof to convict the other people who had been arrested. "I later found out that Luburić killed all of the remaining detainees," Ereš remarked in his 1947 statement, adding that Šarić and Luburić were dissatisfied with the court's relatively lenient decision, which wasn't rendered "according to Ustasha regulations."

A Slunj parish priest named Ivan Nikšić, who was also the Ustasha commissioner for the county of Slunj in the first months of the NDH, wrote in his *Spomenici ožupi slunjskoj* (Testimonies About the County of Slunj) that 440 Serbs were killed in Blagaj on the night of May 9. Other sources cite both lower and higher numbers of victims: the lowest being 150, the highest 600. Zvonimir Martinčević, a captain at army headquarters in Zagreb, noted that at 11:00 p.m. on May 9, he called the gendarme station in Veljun and that the "duty sergeant, Andrija Smiljanić, answered and said that in the last three days 377 suspected Chetniks from the area had been arrested," that they "had been taken to Blagaj six kilometers away, and that a court there was carrying out further investigations." There is no information on whether any of those taken to Blagaj returned alive, with the exception of Dušan Nikšić. Captain Martinčević's notes fail to mention that in addition to the 377 people "taken to Blagaj" about 80 other people were arrested in the surrounding villages. They were not taken to Blagaj but were released from the jail in Veljun on May 10 at the intervention of the commander of an Italian military unit that had arrived in Slunj. I think Captain Martinčević's notes are the most appropriate starting point for establishing the number of people killed in Blagaj. I also found indirect confirmation in an unpublished manuscript by Tomo Žalac, an excellent, knowledgeable researcher about the Slunj region who reviewed the list of victims from almost all of the villages from which people were taken to Blagaj and who subsequently disappeared. He counted 118 men killed from Veljun, 49 from Lapovac, 34 from Šljivnjak, 21 from Točak, and another 112 from the smaller villages in the area, for a total of 334 people listed as having been killed in Blagaj. Žalac had no information on the victims from the towns of Gornji and Donji Poloj, so his estimate should probably be increased by several dozen.

A completely accurate number of victims will never be established, but I believe it can be concluded on the basis of the data above that in one night Luburić and his squad of Ustasha returnees killed more than three hundred and probably closer to four hundred people in the pits behind the Blagaj school. Prematurely aged women from Blagaj and the old school janitor, Mr. Muić, with whom I spoke in the 1960s when I was writing a ten-part newspaper series about this region, told me how they heard periodic shooting from the valleys below the school that night. One woman told me that the morning "after that night" she saw the men commanded by an Ustasha "who was called Maks" pouring water from a well by the bucket so he could wash the blood from his hands and sleeves. Luburić and his squad departed from the village that same morning, leaving behind murdered Serbs and an eternal stigma over Croatian Blagaj.

The women of Blagaj claimed that "not one of our men" was at the pit that night. In fact, some of them were around the school and the pit as armed guards and some had to pour lime on the dead and cover up the pit with stones and earth, but not a single Blagaj villager, according to the people from Blagaj, killed his neighbor from Veljun. But, after the war, two Blagaj Ustasha prisoners confessed to investigators from the Department for the Protection of the People to their participation in the killings. The entire village knew what had happened that night behind their school and they participated in a conspiracy of silence that lasted three full months. When women from Veljun arrived on the morning of May 10 at the Blagaj school with baskets of food for their fathers, brothers, and husbands, Šarić told them that the men had been sent to work in Germany. They believed him because none of the women from Blagaj would tell them the truth. The one to escape, Dušan Nikšić, knew the fate of only thirty-two or thirty-six of those who had been convicted. However, the worst was suspected because after three months none of the people who had been taken away had been heard from. The full truth became known when the first Partisans of Veljun captured a teacher by the name of Ivan Šajfar, the Ustasha commissioner for the district of Veljun, at the beginning of August. Under interrogation he told the Partisans exactly what had happened that night behind the Blagaj school. In his defense he claimed, probably truthfully, that neither he nor the villagers of Blagaj had participated in the killings, that at the last minute he had tried to save some of his good friends, "honest men," to which Šarić had allegedly responded, "I know there are honest men among them and you can do them a favor—don't torment them, shoot them in the back of the head!" None of this helped Šajfar. After the interrogation, the Veljun Partisans executed him as punishment, or revenge, for the Blagaj massacre.

The consequences of the crime in Blagaj in 1941 resonate to this day. The crime that Pavelić initiated, that Kvaternik ordered, that Šarić organized, and that Luburić carried out has left a stigma on a small village in Kordun and its impoverished population. For Kordun Serbs, Blagaj has become a symbol of the most evil Ustasha atrocity. In Veljun's scattered hamlets horror stories spread of the Blagaj curate Blaž Tomljenović, who was to blame for all of this: knife in hands he had butchered the Mravunac family so the neighboring Serbs could be accused of the crime and their mass arrests and killings organized, those who were left expelled to Serbia and their abandoned property shared among the Blagaj Ustasha. Some of these horror stories entered into postwar historiography, in which we can read that the "godly saint," the priest Tomljenović, "with his knife took part in a slaughter" that "only human beasts in a wolf's skin can commit," and that "in Blagaj and Pavlovac . . . the priest from his altar and the teacher from his blackboard taught young and old how to become executioners and butchers."

When two battalions of the First Primorsko-Goranski Partisan unit and the First Proletarian Battalion of Croatia attacked Blagaj in September 1942, the Home Guard garrison (about 120 men) scattered in all directions and surrendered after desultory resistance. But about 30 of the local Ustasha defended their homes almost to the last bullet. Some of them were able to escape, several others killed themselves rather than fall into the hands of the Partisans, while the rest were captured by the Partisans and summarily executed. Serbian widows from the surrounding villages ransacked and then set fire to twenty-six houses in Blagaj, about one-third of the village, as an act of revenge. They would have torched all of the houses if the Partisans had not stopped them. The women claimed that they set fire to the houses in which they had found their property, the property the Blagaj Ustasha had plundered from Serbian villages during one of their "cleansing actions." In the fall of 1943, when as a Partisan I was going on foot from Veljun to Slunj, an old woman looking out the window of one of the last houses by the road asked me, "Where are you taking this road, my son?"

"To Slunj," I replied.

"Don't go through Blagaj, my son, they might kill you the way they killed my son! Why don't you take the upper road through Cvijanović Brdo?"

After the war, a memorial tomb was built in the small valley behind the Blagaj school. The remains of those killed were later transferred to Veljun, where a mausoleum had been erected. Until 1990, every year in early May commemorations were held at each of these sites, with the mandatory attendance of schoolchildren. Children from Veljun would hear how, in this place, their grandfathers had been killed and that the Blagaj Ustasha were the ones who killed them. Children from Blagaj would hear how their grandfathers had been killers, how with no reason they had murdered the grandfathers of the children from Veljun, with whom they went to the same school. But at home, behind closed doors and windows, the children from Blagaj also heard a completely different story: Chetniks from Veljun, Poloj, and other Serbian villages were guilty of all this. They had raised a rebellion on Đurđevdan in 1941 and massacred the Mravunac family. They had been tried and executed according to the law by a court from Karlovac and Zagreb and not by local people, nor were four hundred or five hundred Serbs killed, but far fewer, only those who had been convicted—a hundred or a hundred and fifty at most.

For decades after the war animosity smoldered between Veljun and Blagaj. It would die down then flare up, but the political authorities did not know how to calm it, and some of their actions only inflamed the situation. When Frane Barbieri, the editor of the leading Belgrade daily *Politika*, published my ten-part series on the sorrowful history of Veljun and Blagaj in June 1969, I received about fifty letters and postcards at my office and home. Most of them were reproaches, signed and unsigned, claiming that I was feeling too sorry for the current residents of Blagaj—"So what if they don't have electricity or a school, they deserve this and worse." There were also complaints that I was again bringing up that unfortunate crime in Blagaj, but I was not saying loudly and clearly that it all began with a Chetnik uprising and crimes and that I was again tarnishing the name of a poor Croatian village—"Hasn't it suffered enough, and how long will the children have to atone for the sins of their fathers?" However, half of the letters commended the attempt to arrive at the whole truth without political prejudice and empty talk, and in some of the letters there were also well-intentioned comments about details that I was unaware of or that I had not considered.

In 1991, only 200 residents remained in Blagaj and Pavlovac out of a prewar population of 708. In Veljun and the neighboring villages of Lapovac and Točak there were still 700 residents from a prewar population of 1,297. The younger people had gone to the cities, the older ones were eking out an existence by cultivating the increasingly less fertile fields—the usual depopulation of villages in the majority of Croatia's regions. After exactly fifty years, revenge again rained down on Blagaj and Pavlovac: In 1991, all of the remaining residents of these two villages were forced from their homes, the villages were completely deserted, and the majority of the houses were robbed and leveled to the ground. Then in 1995, Veljun and all the surrounding Serbian villages were also deserted after the major exodus of Kordun Serbs. In the post–Operation Storm frenzy, all of the abandoned houses in Veljun were robbed, many were set on fire, and several old men who had remained in their homes were killed.[21]

The expelled residents of the Croatian Blagaj and Pavlovac began to return to their destroyed homes in 1996 and, with government assistance, gradually began to rebuild them. Some weekend houses also sprang up, built primarily by younger people who lived in the cities and returned to their ancestral villages from time to time. Then people started to return from exile to Veljun, mostly the elderly. A bit of life returned to the entire region, but it was an imperfect life that flickered weakly in the widespread desolation. However, even in that imperfect renewal of life, on May 6, 1999, some residents of Veljun wanted to remember their ancestors who had been killed fifty-eight years ago in Blagaj and wanted to honor them at the Veljun mausoleum. They were prevented from doing so by about one hundred people who came from Slunj, led by Dragan Hazler, a well-known Ustasha nostalgist living in Switzerland, and by Tomislav Turek, a prominent activist in the Slunj Croatian Democratic Union, a conservative political party. More numerous and stronger, they forced the elderly Serbs from the mass gravesite in full view of the police, who were standing nearby with their arms crossed. Then a woman named Biserka Legradić dropped her underpants in front of the entire mass of people and police, squatted down, urinated on the ossuary, and, to loud laughter and approval, rejoined the group and returned to Slunj.

And so Veljun and Blagaj concluded the twentieth century with a desecrated memorial tomb behind the Blagaj school and a mass grave that had been urinated on at the Veljun cross. But had they concluded the century, or were they just entering the twenty-first century with a defiled mass grave?[22]

Glina

Glina was the scene of the third mass murder of Serbs organized by Kvaternik. In contrast to the first two atrocities, there was no pretext for the Glina massacre in May; it was not preceded by any local incidents. The mass killing could not be rationalized by "retaliation" as in Gudovac and there was neither a brutal murder of a Croatian family nor a staged trial as in Blagaj. "Out of the clear blue sky," as the saying goes, eloquent proof that the intent was genocide and not repression in response to a provocation.

On the eve of the war in 1941, Glina was a small town of less than three thousand inhabitants, but it was the seat of a relatively large county of more than fifty thousand residents. All of the county administrative offices, the county court, the tax office, the regional police and gendarmerie headquarters, a high school that drew students from a wide area, and a new and fairly large hospital were located there. Glina was also an active commercial center with regular weekly markets. It had two local banks, prospering shops, and a variety of restaurants and cafés. According to census data going back a hundred or more years, the population of the county was about two-thirds Serb (Orthodox), while within the town itself a little more than half of the population was Croat (Catholic). Almost all of the villages in the rural areas of the county were divided into those whose residents were exclusively Serbian or exclusively Croatian, while in the town there was no such division. Glina's Croats and Serbs lived next door to each other, house by house or apartment by apartment, and not a single street could be called primarily Croatian or Serbian. Local patriotism was widespread. The interests of the town were represented jointly and everyone rooted for the Glina Sports Club, in which neither the players nor the club management were divided along ethnic lines. There were also more than a few intermarriages, friendships, and marriage and baptismal sponsorships that crossed religious and ethnic lines. However, this micro-idyll in private life did not cross over into a macro-idyll in public life among the political parties. Although at the beginning of the twentieth century a Croatian-Serbian coalition dominated for a brief time—with Svetozar Pribičević,[23] a Serb, and Frano Supilo, a Croatian politician and journalist, representing Glina in the national assembly—a hard-core nationalist orientation soon emerged on both sides. In 1932, at the very beginning of the formation of the Ustasha movement, the lawyer Mirko Puk had already gathered about twenty to thirty supporters, whom Glina's residents called "Frankists" or "*pravaši*" ("rightists" after the Croatian Party of the Right), and who, in fact, were already a well-organized body that would be at the core of the future tragic events. It worked to their advantage that at the same time a small group of rabid extremists, supporters of a radical nationalistic rightist named Svetislav Hođera, emerged among Serbs in Glina and that the pro-regime Yugoslav Radical Community was relatively strong in number.[24]

In the 1930s, Puk was known in Glina as a man of the most deeply rooted intolerance. On the street he refused to greet either his Serbian neighbors or Croats who were known to be friends or doing business with Serbs. Until April 1941, his pro-Ustasha group did not grow significantly. It never had more than about fifty active supporters, but thanks to the tenacity and energy of Puk's ardent leadership, the group was active and even influential in some situations, "one of the most important centers of the Ustasha movement" according to one commentary. In the years prior to the war, Mirko Jerec, a Glina lawyer and Puk's closest political collaborator, was the "roving emissary" of Slavko Kvaternik, whose "instructions for the impending, inevitable political events he transmitted... on a special mission to all regions of Croatia."

In the critical days at the beginning of April 1941, Puk's small apartment in Zagreb was the key center from which the Ustasha leadership in the country coordinated preparations for the takeover of the government and held meetings with German agents. In these early days Puk was a vice president in the provisional Croatian government formed by Ustasha activists. On April 16, 1941, he became the minister of justice in the first NDH government. As the author of the drastic laws on the emergency courts, he quickly acquired a reputation as the top hard-line supporter of political terror. On June 10, 1942, the canon Augustin Juretić, an important Yugoslav intelligence agent, sent a detailed report on the situation in Croatia from Switzerland to Juraj Krnjević, the vice president of the Yugoslav government in exile. In item 27 of the report he states: "The greatest instigator of violence is Puk, followed by Budak, while the executor is Eugen Kvaternik."

All relevant sources unanimously claim that the idea for the May massacre of Serbs in Glina came from Puk. The most precise description was provided by Juraj Rebok, briefly the Ustasha commander for the county of Glina in the summer of 1941. In his *Memoirs*, written in exile in Argentina, under the heading, "Who is guilty for the massacre in Glina," Rebok says:

> I went to Minister Puk to protest the actions of some so-called Ustasha who had raided neighboring Orthodox villages to steal and rob. The majority were supporters and friends of the minister. This was not part of being an Ustasha but of being the most common Chekhist. To which Puk replied: "I know what I will do. I will send some Ustasha returnees to impose order." "Anyone is fine as long as they bring order," I answered, not suspecting what kind of demonic plan he had in mind.[25]

That same day or the next, either May 8 or 9, Puk was allegedly already in Glina to make some secret arrangements, about which there is no reliable information. All that is certain is that on Saturday, May 10, probably while traveling from Blagaj to Zagreb, Ivica Šarić, now Dido Kvaternik's specialist for such operations, arrived in Glina. Šarić held a meeting in the office of Vilim Klobučar, the director of the hospital, with a small circle of the local Ustasha leadership from which some information "leaked out." With little prior discussion the group proceeded to draw up a list of names of all the Serbs in Glina between the ages of sixteen and sixty, who were to be arrested. The discussion dragged on only when Šarić requested that the list also identify those to be executed immediately after arrest because in the Kingdom of Yugoslavia they had been prominent enemies of the Croatian ideal. Allegedly Rebok, with the support of several others, voiced the opinion that this could not be decided without a trial.

Nikica Vidaković, a member of the municipal Ustasha organization, and Josip Misson, a local merchant and the president of the Glina Sports Club, were the most vociferous at the meeting. After much back and forth about the composition of the execution list, they allegedly suggested that there was no sense in having a list because "they should all be killed," meaning everyone who was to be arrested. Šarić, in his capacity as the "representative" from Zagreb, wholeheartedly supported this opinion. The next morning, a Sunday, Šarić held one more meeting, this time only with the hard-liners in the local leadership, at the inn of Jurek Muretić, an Ustasha sympathizer. They obviously reached their final conclusions at this meeting. The future course of events is known in detail because they unfolded before the entire town.

On Sunday, May 11, at five o'clock in the afternoon, two gray buses arrived in Glina from Zagreb. They were carrying around fifty well-armed Ustasha, the majority of whom were émigré returnees, members of the *Poglavnik*'s bodyguard unit in their yellow uniforms brought from exile. They stopped in front of the house of Mato Vidaković, a carpenter and the first Ustasha mayor of Glina, whose house before the war and at the beginning of the NDH was the main meeting place of Glina's Ustasha. Some of the newly arrived "yellows" went to the local Ustasha headquarters next to the Hotel Kasina, while the others joined the local Ustasha in Muretić's inn. Some of the Ustasha returnees in the restaurant were said to be speaking Italian with each other.

On that Sunday, a slightly larger group of local Ustasha, about twenty men, assisted in the planned action by performing some auxiliary tasks or by providing information. Secrecy could no longer be maintained; rumors had begun to circulate through the town. On the afternoon of May 11, Zlatko Pinotić, the son of the principal of the Glina elementary school, who just the month before was triumphantly parading through the streets of Glina carrying an unfurled Croatian flag, rushed to warn his Serbian friend Boro Meandžija that a mass arrest of Serbs was being readied. That night Meandžija hid himself, avoided arrest, and survived. At around noon on Sunday, Joso Zibar approached a merchant named Marko Vujasinović on the Glina promenade and told him in confidence how several Ustasha were drinking *rakija* that morning in Zibar's father's café in Jukinac (near Glina) and "talking about how something was in the works for the Serbs." He advised Vujasinović to hide somewhere temporarily. Vujasinović replied that he was not guilty of anything, that he was not afraid of anything, and that he would remain with his family; that same evening he was taken to his death. Many of Glina's Serbs heard the rumors that something bad was in store for them on that Sunday, but only about ten of them heeded the warning and took refuge. The great majority remained in their homes. They could not believe the impossible that awaited them. Few understood that "some insane wind had struck the heads and souls of people" (Ivo Andrić) and that the "insanity of history" (André Malraux) was about to strike.

As soon as night had fallen on Sunday, the arrests began. One local Ustasha led two Ustasha returnees from one Serbian house to another. The returnees brutally entered homes and took away all males older than sixteen. Those arrested were told not to bring many belongings because they would be released immediately after interrogation. The majority of the men went without protest or resistance, convinced that nothing would happen to them. Yet weeping, begging, and cries for help were heard from some homes.

The streetlights had been extinguished; Glina lay in darkness. The Ustasha were rushing the detainees along, trying to complete the roundup before morning. Ilija Letić, a baker, was not given the time to dress; he had to put his clothes on over his pajamas. He protested and in the quarrel that followed refused to leave his house. He was killed on his doorstep. His son, sixteen-year-old Dušan, and his apprentices, Rade and Slavko (the list of victims does not give their surnames), who were trying to help Ilija, were also killed on the spot—all in front of Ilija's wife, Marija, their two daughters, and their seven-year-old son, Đorđe.

Judge Stjepan Detoni, a Croat, protested to the Ustasha while they were taking away his landlord, Gajić, a Serb, so they took him to jail too. By morning all of those arrested had been squeezed into a small holding area in the building of the former gendarmerie. In the cramped cells, along the narrow hallways, and in the small courtyard, the closely packed mass of Glina Serbs sat under heavy Ustasha guard. They were office workers, tradesmen, merchants with their assistants and apprentices, innkeepers, butchers, and students—according to one report, "373 Orthodox men." Among them were Jovan Mirković, the former president of the county court; Živko Radojčević, the president of the local Serbian Bank; the lawyers Milan Metikoš and Stevan Branković; high-school instructors and religion teachers. There were also several Croats—in addition to Detoni there was Ante Šešerin (an electrician and the future Partisan committeeman for the Glina district), Miroslav Štimac, and others—who had spent the night trying to protect their Orthodox neighbors or fellow tenants and complained about their arrests. After the morning roll call, the Croats were released, but all of the Serbs were kept in jail. Around noon they were allowed to receive food sent from their homes, but they were not able to see their families. No visits or conversations were permitted. They spent the day in the torment of uncertainty, gradually fearing the worst. Around midnight the Ustasha began to tie them up in pairs and put them onto two trucks, about twenty tightly bound men with several Ustasha guards to each truck. After approximately thirty minutes the trucks would return for a new group of detainees.

All of this has been described in great detail by Nikica Samardžija, a strong, athletic young man, the only one of the three hundred or more detained Serbs who lived to greet the next day. Bound and jammed together on the tarpaulin-covered beds of the trucks, the detainees did not know where they were being taken. When the Ustasha unloaded them in a field, Samardžija recognized the banks of the Glina River behind the village of Prekopa, about six kilometers from town. The Ustasha were leading them to a large, long pit that peasants from the surrounding Croatian villages had to dig and then remain silent under the penalty of death. However, some of them did not stay silent, neither then nor later; nor did some of the mobilized Croatian peasants who had to guard the area during the night of May 12. The conspiracy of silence could not be kept.

The killings at the pit were carried out by Ustasha returnees, mostly with guns. On the morning of May 13, Petar Erent, a peasant from Prekopa, and Joso Šešerin, a miller from Jukinac (and the brother of the aforementioned Ante Šešerin), along with some of their neighbors were forced to cover the bodies in the pit with lime and to fill it with fresh earth. They witnessed how Nikica Vidaković, the Ustasha commander and son of Mato Vidaković, the Ustasha mayor, shot in the head anyone in the pit or next to it who still showed signs of life.

Earlier in the evening of May 12, the rebellious and physically strong Samardžija, while still in the Glina prison, had tried unsuccessfully to convince some friends to rush the Ustasha guards in the courtyard, seize their weapons, and escape. That night, while they were being driven in the truck, Samardžija found that he was not securely bound and, as soon as they unloaded him from the truck, freed his hands. While on his way to the pit under an armed escort, he passed closely by a local Ustasha named Mato Kihalić-Brko. The powerful Samardžija grabbed him in a skillful hold, flung him across his back, stepped into the pitch-black night, and threw himself into the Glina River. The alarmed Ustasha immediately began to shoot wildly into the darkness. The quick-thinking Samardžija stripped off his coat, threw it into the middle of the river, then dove underwater and swam to the opposite bank. The Ustasha fired at the coat, but Nikica was already under the bushes on the other side of the river, slightly wounded in the thigh. Under cover of darkness, he dragged himself along a small creek and stayed hidden the entire day in the reeds. Later that evening, he slipped into the nearby village Majske Poljane and found the house of some acquaintances. They courageously took him in, warmed him up, fed him, and gave him shelter for several days until he recovered his strength. Samardžija then fled to relatives in Belgrade and survived the war.

In his memoirs, Juraj Rebok claims that Samardžija also turned to him for help:

> One of the victims (who had been taken to the banks of the Glina River to be shot) succeeded in jumping into the river and was struck by a bullet in the leg. He saved himself and later sent for me to give him medical assistance. I sent word to him that I too would be in danger if it were discovered that I was helping him, but I gave him instructions on how to treat his wound temporarily and how to reach a doctor in Karlovac, where he would not be suspected and would be out of danger.

Then, at the end of this description of the May 1941 Glina massacre, Rebok laconically concludes, "Deep shock and indignation among Croats. Is this the Croatia that we longed for?"[26]

About Victims and Numbers

According to the 1931 census, Glina had 2,315 residents. In 1941, when the regular ten-year census was not published because of the war, it might have had 2,800 residents. More than half were Catholic and Croat. Based on this data, in April 1941 there could have been around 450 to 500 men in Glina between the ages of sixteen and sixty of Serbian nationality registered in the city records. On the night of May 12, most of these men were killed, save Samardžija and about 30 Glina Serbs who survived because they had been warned and escaped, were well hidden when the Ustasha patrols pounded on their doors, or by accident weren't at home that night (for example, Milan Brakus who had fallen asleep drunk in a nearby barn and thus avoided arrest). There were also about 50 more Serbs listed as residents of Glina who were not in town on May 11: officers and soldiers captured in the April war; people away on business; several who were hospitalized in Zagreb and elsewhere; several students who had not returned from Belgrade or Zagreb; about 10 people who had been arrested earlier and were already in the Danica camp or in jails outside of Glina and at least another 10 who were by pure chance traveling, visiting relatives, or far away from home for some other reason.

Various publications and sources have cited different figures for the number of victims in Prekopa on the night of May 12: 260, 307, 322, 370, 373, 391, 437, 520, and 582. I am not taking into account here the claim by Rebok in his memoirs (written in Argentina in the 1980s) that states: "According to my information, about one hundred Orthodox believers were killed and not two hundred and sixty." Later in the text Rebok refutes himself when he describes how they prepared "to round up all of the Orthodox in Glina," how the arrests were carried out the next night, and "the next day we learned that they had been taken to the banks of the Glina River and killed," and that "only one of the victims had succeeded in jumping into the river." But in fact the number of all the Orthodox Serbs in Glina between the ages of sixteen and sixty was not "about one hundred"; it was closer to five hundred.

In my opinion the most useful source for establishing the number of victims is the list published in *Ljetopis* (number 6, 2001) under the heading "A List of Serbs from Glina and Environs Killed in the Spring of 1941." It contains 388 names and surnames, along with basic information about almost all of the victims. After publication, the editor received numerous letters with confirmations of and comments about the published information. A year later, *Ljetopis* (number 7) included corrections and additions to the information. The list now included 391 victims and is probably complete. However, there are 40 names and surnames of people on the list from the area around Glina, and it is not clear if they were killed on the night of the massacre in Prekopa with the Serbs from Glina or before or after that night at some other location. There are also other names on the list—including Milena Gajić, Đuro Sužnjević, Adam Resanović, Stojan Slijepčević, Stanko Rebrača-Šlik, Stevo Jelovac, Miloš Živković, and others—who are known to have been killed before or after the mass murder in Prekopa. Nevertheless, I consider the list to be credible because the authors correctly state in the heading that it pertains to victims in "Glina and Environs" in the spring of 1941. Therefore, we can reliably conclude that the number of victims in Glina's equally tragic version of the Saint Bartholomew's Day massacre was less than four hundred, but certainly higher than three hundred.

This unprovoked and monstrous crime traumatized Glina for a long time, more so because less than three months later it was repeated in an even crueler manner: some one hundred Serbian Orthodox men from the area of Vrginmost and Topusko were lured to the Orthodox church in Glina, misled into believing that they would be converted to Catholicism, and on August 2, 1941, all of them except one were killed with knives, bayonets, and clubs. At the end of August, just after receiving her degree, Benedikta Zelić, a family friend of Rebok, arrived in Glina to take up a position as a history and

Italian-language teacher in the Glina high school. In her memoirs, published by the journal *Marulić* in 1991, she describes in detail the painful atmosphere in Glina at that time:

> Even if I had searched through all of Croatia, it would have been difficult to find a more dismal place than Glina.... A very somber mood prevailed in the small town, a consequence of two bloody mass crimes against the Serbian Orthodox population that had been committed a short time before.... Today, when I think about this, it is a little difficult for me to understand how I could have so eagerly accepted a position in an Ustasha camp as the leader of the organization of Ustasha Women Youth. Probably the ecstasy of having my own country and my youth contributed to this, so that I was aware of those crimes only superficially. Nevertheless, in spite of my ecstasy and youth I felt that it was inappropriate in that environment to make effusive speeches glorifying Croatia to children who had just recently lost their parents.[27]

The scale of the Glina tragedy was such that it must have resonated far beyond the town itself. As the seat of a large county with many institutions, Glina had active communications with Petrinja, Sisak, Karlovac, and Zagreb. Šime Balen, an active Croatian nationalist during his student days in the 1930s who later joined the Communist Party of Yugoslavia, once told me that he had already heard in May 1941 about the killings of the Glina Serbs. He was horrified, but what made the deepest impression upon him was that some close acquaintances and friends from his student days were among those who had been killed. Around that time he bumped into Vlado Singer, an Ustasha returnee whom he also knew well from their student days, in Zrinjevac Park in Zagreb. At the beginning of the 1930s, Singer had been the chief organizer of the first pro-Ustasha student groups at the University of Zagreb and the founding editor of the first pro-Ustasha magazine in the homeland, *Croatian Land*, first published in 1933 and banned after two issues. Balen sympathized and collaborated with active Croatian nationalists, but he was not as radical as Singer. He also had friends among leftists and even among communists. That is why in 1932 Singer asked him to act as intermediary between the communists and the Croatian nationalists in an effort to coordinate their activities against the common enemy, the royal dictatorship in Belgrade. When Singer and Balen accidently met in Zrinjevac Park eight years later, Singer was in the uniform of a senior Ustasha officer, as he was the head of the personnel department of the Ustasha main headquarters and a chief in the intelligence service. Although a Jew by birth, Singer had early on renounced his heritage, both religious and ethnic, convinced that the only real option for Jews in Croatia was complete assimilation and total identification with Croatian nationalism. Enterprising and capable, wisely distancing himself from the intrigues and compromising disputes within the émigré community, Singer had returned with Pavelić to a senior and highly responsible position in the Ustasha hierarchy, giving him the power to become the protector of his old colleague Balen. But at first Balen was taken aback by that meeting in Zrinjevac Park: He had in the meantime spent four years in jail for organizing anti-regime activities as a Croatian nationalist, and during his incarceration he had drawn closer to the communists, especially to Andrija Hebrang,[28] under whose influence he had become a communist. He had reason to fear that the Ustasha government would treat him as an enemy, but Singer reassured him: "Šime, you were imprisoned for Croatia, we all know that. You have nothing to fear while I am here!"

They continued their conversation somewhat more openly, during which Balen cautiously touched on "the unpleasant excesses against the Jews and Serbs," while Singer spoke without any great passion about the national revolution and the inevitability of revolutionary measures. Then Balen plucked up his courage and mentioned Glina. At that moment Singer grimaced and suddenly grew very serious. It was obvious that he knew what had happened there, saying "All right, Šime, since you've asked, I will explain it all to you, completely openly. The world is at war, and it will be at war for some time. Our revolution is taking place in the middle of that great war. In such circumstances things happen that otherwise would not happen. One can do things that are not possible in a time of peace. We have to take advantage of the opportunity. For three hundred years the Serbs have been our biggest problem. Because of the way they are and because they multiply as they do, there will never be happiness in our Croatian state. Now is the chance! We have to kill one-third of them, one-third of them will run away, and one-third will be converted to Catholicism and become Croatian!"[29]

It seems that this frequently mentioned formula—one-third, one-third, one-third—was very popular within Ustasha circles in 1941. It has the overtone of a cynical joke, but it is also a laconic summary of clearly menacing intentions and unformulated plans. A later senior representative of the Third Reich for southeastern Europe expressed his shock at this horrifying phrase as "the prescription of the Ustasha leader Ante Pavelić for action against Orthodox Serbs that recalls the religious wars of the bloodiest times."[30] However, the phrase didn't originate with the Ustasha. It was formulated in Russia in 1881, when Konstantin Petrovich Pobedonostsev, the chief adviser to Tsar Aleksandar III and a fanatical Orthodox believer known as the "Grand Inquisitor," used almost the same words about the great wave of pogroms against Russian Jews: "Let one-third emigrate, let one-third become Orthodox, and let the other third be killed."

A Temporary Halt to the Genocide

On Wednesday, May 14, Franjo Žužek, the parish priest of Glina, sent an urgent report to Archbishop Alojzije Stepinac about the mass killings that had taken place two nights ago in his parish. I believe that during the previous month Stepinac had heard several times about Ustasha crimes in various parts of his diocese, but the Glina incident was the first about which he complained in writing to *Poglavnik* Pavelić. That same day, Pavelić had the archbishop's letter on his desk:

> I have just received news that Ustasha in Glina have executed 260 Serbs without a trial and without an investigation. I know that the Serbs have committed serious crimes in our homeland during the twenty years of their rule. But I nevertheless think that it is my duty as a bishop to raise my voice and say that this is not permitted by Catholic morality, so I ask that you undertake the most urgent measures throughout the Independent State of Croatia to prevent one Serb from being killed if he has not been proven guilty of something that deserves the death penalty. Otherwise, we cannot count on the blessing of heaven we need to succeed. I hope that you will not take exception to my speaking so openly. With utmost respect.[31]

Here we must pay close attention to the chronology. On May 14, or a day earlier, Pavelić had on his desk the memorandum from Karlovac that Židovec and Bilović had written on May 12 in the office of Minister Žanić. He knew that because of the genocidal action in Karlovac he was threatened with the collapse of the local Ustasha Council. He also knew about the obstructionism of the Special People's

Court in Karlovac and the partial obstruction by the Zagreb court in providing some legality to the genocidal actions in Blagaj. He must have heard from Dido Kvaternik and Minister Puk that many prominent Croats in Glina did not approve of the crime committed there and that some of them had opposed it. From his old collaborator, the Frankist veteran Professor Marko Veršić (the state secretary in the Ministry of Religious Affairs and Education), he had recently heard in private that "the course of events in the NDH, that is, the mass killing of Serbs . . . can lead to a national and popular catastrophe." Pavelić, of course, knew about the first Serbian resistance around Sanski Most and he was present at the meeting when Vukovac had cautiously warned of the "arbitrary behavior by local Ustasha in some areas" that had to be brought under control, and to which Budak had mockingly responded, "And I thought you were an intelligent man, Vukovac!"

But more than anything, Pavelić was concerned by the increasingly frequent complaints from General Glaise von Horstenau, the chief representative of the German army in the NDH. At a later date, Glaise von Horstenau summarized his objections in an ironic question to Pavelić in the presence of several of their associates: "Tell me frankly, *Poglavnik*, do you really intend to kill all of the Orthodox Serbs?" In his reports to the Supreme Command of the Wehrmacht and in his other official dispatches, beginning on April 23, 1941, Glaise von Horstenau frequently warned that Pavelić's genocidal policy against the Serbs would lead to a chaotic situation (Glaise von Horstenau never objected to the Ustasha genocide against the Jews). The German army would have to keep some of its troops in the NDH, instead of the NDH assisting the German army in its military efforts on all fronts outside of the NDH. At that time Pavelić knew that the Ustasha policy enjoyed the full support of Siegfried Kasche, the German ambassador to the NDH, but in May 1941, it still was not clear which of the concepts would prevail among the German representatives. Pavelić had to be cautious.

After his April political triumph, in the first days of May Pavelić was faced with energetic Italian demands for prompt payment of the price he had promised in advance of granting him power. Using all the newly established diplomatic channels, he frantically appealed for German support in reducing, at least a little, the concessions promised to the Italians. The Germans offered no assistance. At a meeting with Mussolini in Monfalcone on May 7, Pavelić initialed an agreement that met almost all the Italian demands: Croatia without Dalmatia, an occupied Croatian northern coastal region, and the Italian Crown on the throne in Zagreb.[32] Until the last moment Pavelić kept secret, even from his closest collaborators, what he would have to sign on May 18 in Rome. He was in a precarious position and knew that signing the Rome agreements would be a serious disappointment for those who had so firmly believed in him. He feared that it might weaken what had been until then his undisputed leadership of the Ustasha movement. He must also have surmised that the tensions with the "milquetoasts" in the Ustasha hierarchy, with German military representatives, with the leadership of the Croatian Catholic Church, and with the broader Croatian public were problems he did not want. On May 14, 1941, he halted the massacres of Serbs—until further notice.

After the massacre of Serbs in Glina, arrests of those few Serbs from the surrounding villages still filtering into the town for whatever reason continued for the next two days. By the afternoon of May 14, about thirty Serbs were in jail. They were certainly candidates for death in a second round of killings at Prekopa. Then suddenly and unexpectedly Nikica Vidaković, the Ustasha commander, appeared. He quickly interrogated the detainees, all of whom were immediately released and sent home.

From that day until July 1, a period of about six weeks, there were no mass killings of Serbs in Croatia like those in Gudovac, Blagaj, and Glina, though in Herzegovina such killings started in early June. The Ustasha authorities, however, did intensify other types of persecution. In May, measures against the Jews expanded almost daily and in some places they were being taken away to camps in large numbers. The arrests of prominent "undesirables" continued in the cities, and the jails were filled to overflowing. By the end of May, there were already several thousand detainees, mostly Serbs, in the Danica camp. The emergency courts were announcing their first convictions. A series of new laws threatened even harsher punishment. In many villages, especially in Lika, Bosnian Krajina, and Herzegovina, Ustasha and gendarme patrols were terrorizing the population, in some cases robbing them, in others taking away prominent Serbs, leaving no trace of them.

According to the already quoted statement of Židovec, the Karlovac Ustasha Council was in a state of expectation. The more moderate members were encouraged by the arrest of the four Ustasha youth who had murdered Vujičić, Janjanin, and Dokmanović on the night of May 5. Milan Radeka briefly saw them in the Zagreb jail on Petrinjska Street in the second half of May and describes it in his *Memories*:

> They were all in uniform, with open collars on their coats and shirts, faces completely different, thickset, tanned, swollen, distorted as if from feasting and drinking. Completely different faces from those boys of just barely a month ago. The duty officer said to me, "It's forbidden to talk to the prisoners." "What do you mean forbidden," I shouted, "these are students from my school!" When I went by again, the little pudgy Jožica

> Gombač said, "This is a mistake. They'll let us go right away. . . ." Nevertheless, they spent that night in jail, not in the cells but in an office, and the next day they were indeed released. . . .[33]

The arrest of the four young men was not a "mistake," as Gombač was trying to convince himself. It was an attempt to try to deceive the unsettled residents of Karlovac and to calm the disgruntled members of the Karlovac Ustasha Council, at least for the time being. When these four were released the next day, Kvaternik's RAVSIGUR arranged some other duties for them outside of Karlovac, and they returned home to Karlovac after several weeks as if nothing had happened.

On May 23, Feliks Židovec, the father of Vladimir Židovec, gave the following statement to the Karlovac newspaper *Hrvatska sloboda*: "Many citizens have recently turned to me as the mayor requesting that I intervene in the matter of the arrests. I wish to state that I have no competence over any arrests, and therefore I cannot intervene. I ask that no one come to me anymore regarding these matters." Residents of Karlovac, of course, understood this laconic "statement" as Feliks Židovec disassociating himself from the wave of arrests that had not stopped spreading through the city. But perhaps the elder Židovec also wanted to announce what he did just fifteen days later—he resigned. Key directives from central government institutions were already bypassing the moderate faction of the Ustasha Council and going directly to Nikšić, the commissioner for the city and county of Karlovac. Commenting on those few days, Vladimir Židovec wrote: "One day I heard that Dido Kvaternik was visiting Karlovac and that he was seen in the Grand Café with our chief of police, Hinko Karl, but they did not call on me or ask for me, so we understood from this visit that Nikšić had become the absolute master of the situation." Besides, Nikšić made frequent trips to Zagreb and it was also known that he had met with Pavelić. It was becoming increasingly clear which way the wind was blowing.

It is not known how the discussions went in the narrowest circles of the Ustasha leadership at that time, or whether there was any discussion at all. Some of the veterans, such as Žanić and Veršić, perhaps dared to say something privately to Pavelić, to ask a question, or even to express doubts, but there was very likely nothing more than that. Pavelić continued to decide everything himself. And he was not sitting idle: He was seeking support from the supreme arbitrator—he was doing all he could to be received as soon as possible by Adolf Hitler.

Kvaternik was not resting either. From the first days of the NDH he had become friends with Lieutenant Colonel Willy Beissner, the German SS police representative to the NDH, with whom he worked closely. Through Beissner, and bypassing other official channels, he received an invitation to visit SS headquarters in Berlin at the end of May. In these meetings, it helped that Kvaternik spoke excellent German (and, almost equally well, French, English, and Italian).

Accompanied by Beissner and several of his closest associates in RAVSIGUR, Kvaternik spent several days in Berlin, returning to Zagreb on June 2. He had also been received by Reichsführer Heinrich Himmler, the leader of the SS, but he spent most of his time in discussions with General Gottlob Berger. They announced an agreement for the training of one hundred Ustasha security personnel by various services of the SS, but the most important talks centered on the establishment of a system of concentration camps in the NDH. Kvaternik began to work on this issue immediately upon his return to Zagreb. On June 4, he appointed Mijo Babić commander of all the transit, labor, and concentration camps in the NDH. Babić, an émigré, was known as Pavelić's most merciless liquidator of "undesirables" in the Ustasha ranks, the Italian police considering him a "most dangerous person, capable of any crime." Kvaternik immediately sent Babić to the island of Pag to select the locations for camps in the inaccessible rocky terrain. Kvaternik himself began to organize a system of camps in Gospić, Velebit, and Pag, with a death camp at Jadovno, and to search for suitable people to manage them. It is obvious that Kvaternik had been advised in Berlin to carry out his radical plans for an ethnically pure Croatia more rationally—in inaccessible camps, far from the eyes of the populace, and not in full public view, as in Glina.

The day Kvaternik returned from Berlin, Pavelić received a message from Joachim von Ribbentrop that Hitler would receive him on June 6 at the Berghof, not far from Salzburg. No coincidence here. Kvaternik perhaps did not know it, but in fact he had served as Pavelić's precursor for discussions with Hitler. The most delicate topics, including above all the policy toward the Serbs, had been discreetly discussed in the office of General Berger in the main headquarters of the SS on Albertstrasse in Berlin. The agreements were confirmed in private during Kvaternik's audience with Himmler. I assume that Kvaternik made an excellent impression on the SS men (he was the prototype for what they aspired to: tall, fair-haired, intelligent, well-educated, fanatic, unscrupulous), and that Hitler was informed of this in detail.

That is how the doors of Hitler's Berghof opened wide for Ante Pavelić.

Hitler's Green Light

Hitler received Pavelić on June 6, 1941, at three o'clock in the afternoon. The audience lasted exactly two hours. Paul Otto Schmidt, the chief translator of the German Ministry of Foreign Affairs, recorded detailed minutes of the meeting.

German diplomats had made their usual thorough preparations. On June 4, Ambassador Kasche transmitted to Foreign Minister Ribbentrop an elaborate report about the members of Pavelic's entourage along with a reminder about the eleven topics for discussion. At eleven in the morning on June 6, Ribbentrop greeted Pavelić at the railway station in Salzburg and before lunch discussed the proposed topics with him: the deportation of Slovenes from Styria and Carinthia to the NDH and Serbs from the NDH to Serbia; the open question about the NDH's borders with the Third Reich, Hungary, and Serbia; the NDH's relations with Italy; the status of the German ethnic minority in the NDH; economic cooperation; anti-Jewish measures; the special status of Muslims; and the relationship with Maček and the HSS. Pavelić presented the most flattering picture possible and humbly agreed to all of Ribbentrop's suggestions. He behaved like an obedient schoolboy, an "eager beaver" in a colloquium with a much respected professor. Ribbentrop carefully skirted the "hot topic" of interethnic relations, that is, the "Serbian question" in the NDH. It seems that he had intentionally reserved that topic for the discussion with Hitler.

Pavelić began the meeting with Hitler by expressing gratitude to the leader of the Third Reich for making it possible for the Croatian people to establish their own independent state. With false modesty Hitler replied that "recent history had made him the unintentional instrument for the liberation of Croatia" because, in fact, he had not intended to move against Yugoslavia and destroy it, but circumstances had forced him to do so. The conversation then continued in a more conventional vein, touching on the traditional friendship between the two peoples and the outstanding prospects for future cooperation. However, Hitler warned Pavelić that "Germany and Italy were the closest of allies in the war and thus Germany was obligated by bonds of great loyalty to Italy. Il Duce must be allowed succeed." In other words, the Italian demands about the borders and other issues with the NDH must be met, yet Hitler was personally sympathetic to the Croatian people, and as a "sincere friend" of Croatia, he was prepared to act as an intermediary and offer advice on any difficulties that may arise. Pavelić responded that a "brave and powerful Croatia with tremendous gratitude accepted the Führer's offer of mediation and advice"—and in this context he broached the "Serbian question" in the NDH. Hitler initially praised the plans for the relocation of Slovenes to Croatia and of Serbs from Croatia to Serbia proper. The discussion about the "Serbian question" then concluded with Hitler's famous and frequently quoted sentence that was probably prepared in advance because it is quoted exactly in the minutes of the meeting: "After all, if the Croatian state aspires to be truly stable, it will have to carry out a policy of ethnic intolerance for fifty years because excessive tolerance on such issues will only cause damage."

On June 7, Pavelić returned to Zagreb from the Berghof full of newly acquired self-confidence that radiated from his first public statements. Hitler's pronouncement about fifty years of ethnic intolerance was a sign of firm support for the rigorous anti-Serb policies in the NDH. The policy was immediately put into effect by hurried and more frequent political and legal measures that reinforced the system of terror: the establishment of mobile emergency courts; the Extraordinary Law Decree and Command, which for the first time legalized mass arrests and deportation to camps without investigation and trial; the Decree on the Composition of the Ustasha Movement and Its Activities, which among other things established the Ustasha Surveillance Service (UNS), with practically unlimited authority to carry out terror.

Kvaternik continued to be the chief organizer of the genocidal actions, but his tactics were new and more discreet: No more public mass killings on the outskirts of cities and towns, such as those in Gudovac and Prekopa. Ad hoc actions and other improvised operations were to be avoided. Genocidal persecutions were to be planned more systematically and in a more orderly fashion. Kvaternik applied the models with which he returned from his discussions in Berlin on June 2, 1941: concentration camps and death camps.

In the Croatian National Archive in Zagreb, Document USIKS 337/41, Collection MUP RH, Document II-91, Box 150 contains the actual statements of Eugen Dido Kvaternik, Vjekoslav Maks Luburić, Stjepan Rubinić, Juco Rukavina, Jurica Frković, and others relating to the closing of the Jadovno camp in August 1941. For the attentive reader, who also knows the circumstances surrounding this topic, these documents are a good basis for establishing a clear picture of this phase of Pavelić's genocidal activities, which were no longer focusing solely on the Serbs but also on the Jews. In the middle of June, Kvaternik sent Rubinić—the Ustasha commissioner for the districts of Kostajnica, Dvor na Uni, and Bosanski Novi—to Gospić to head the Directorate of the Provincial Police. His orders were to "establish a camp in Jadovno and temporarily to supervise the camp on the island of Pag." The site was chosen by Ustasha veterans Rukavina and Frković, who as participants in the Velebit uprising in 1932 were well acquainted with the remote areas around the mountain, including its deep caverns. The first transports for Jadovno arrived in Gospić on June 18. The arrests of Serbs in villages throughout Lika followed soon after. They were taken to the police prison in Gospić and then transported to other facilities, most frequently to Jadovno. On June 23, the first Jews from Zagreb arrived. They were immediately sent on, some to Jadovno and some to Pag, where a camp had been set up in the most deserted part of the island, known as Slana. Then came the women detainees, who were to be the first prisoners in the women's camp at Metajna on Pag. The end of the month saw the arrival of detainees from the Danica camp to Gospić and immediately on to Jadovno and Pag.

On June 18, when the death camps in the Gospić-Jadovno-Pag system were being set up, the Ustasha headquarters of the province of Bribir and Sidraga in Knin sent order No. 10/41, entitled "To the Fraternal Ustasha Camp Knin, the Camp Drniš, the Camp Promina":

> I. Acts of violence, that is, confiscation of property, killings, and beating, are not to be carried out in the presence or proximity of the Italian army or Italian soldiers.
>
> II. All arrests of Serbs are to be carried out without noise and commotion, as quietly and peacefully as possible, removed from the scene as quickly as possible.
>
> III. No mass arrests are to be made, but rather individual ones so as not to attract attention.
>
> IV. No beatings in public view.
>
> V. The theft of Serbian property must be prevented, and all requisitions made legally, a list of confiscated items recorded, which items become the property of the state and for which you must be responsible.
>
> VI. An investigation of robberies committed by individuals in Drniš and the surrounding area must be carried out.
>
> VII. Italians should be treated in a friendly manner, nor should Ustasha be permited to speak against them or to provoke them by saying the annexed territory will be ours.[34]

This order, signed by the Ustasha commander Marko Roša, remains somewhat unclear about where any Serbs "removed from the scene as quickly as possible" were to be sent—to the local jail, to some nearby execution site, or to Gospić and Jadovno. Since RAVSIGUR had sent instructions in June and at the beginning of July that "politically suspect persons" and other undesirables should be sent to Gospić, the assumption is that those arrested in the area of Dalmatinska Zagora had been marked for execution at Jadovno at the order of Roša.

One episode from Rebok's memoir provides a good picture of how some of the Ustasha leadership was still in a dilemma during that time about the methods for resolving the "Serbian question" in the NDH but not about its goals. On June 29, 1941, the Feast of Saint Peter, Puk gathered a select company at his father-in-law's inn in Glina: Mile Budak, Mirko Jerec (the governor of the province of Gora in Petrinja), Filip Crvenković (soon to be the successor of Kvaternik as the chief of the UNS and RAVSIGUR), Josip Rožanković (the commissioner of the Ustasha government in Sisak and the commandant of the province of Gora), Ivica Cvitković (Kvaternik's personal secretary and brother-in-law), Rebok, and several other leading Ustasha from Glina. The conversations around the table were relaxed and open, a result of the success of the German army in the first week after the invasion of the Soviet Union, and Rebok turned to Budak, saying, "I do not think that minority questions have ever been resolved by slaughter anywhere in the world. If we kill, let's say, one hundred thousand Serbs in this region, all of our pits and trenches will be filled with corpses and we'll still have 1,300,000 even angrier Serbs."

"And how would you solve this problem?" Budak inquired.

Rebok replied, "The other day a newly married Serbian woman came to my office and asked the following question: 'What do you plan to do with us, what do you want from us, Doctor, that we convert to Catholicism? We will. To tell you the truth, I won't be much of a Croat, but my son might make a good one!'"

Budak was not pleased with the implied suggestion by Rebok,

who had been reproached before for wanting to solve everything with a rosary: "I don't know that we will have time for that, my good Doctor. I will feel safest when they are all under ground."

This last comment ended the conversation, but according to Rebok, Puk and Cvitković were in obvious agreement with Budak.

The Uprising in Lika

In the second half of June, the Serbian villages in the southeastern parts of Lika and the northwestern section of Dalmatinska Zagora were deeply alarmed. The greatest tensions were in the district of Donji Lapac. Ustasha from the garrison in Boričevac were raiding Serbian villages, encircling individual homes and hamlets, conducting searches for weapons, looting along the way, and in some places killing. One hundred and forty Serbian men were arrested between June 14 and 29 in the district, many more were arrested in some other districts of Lika (especially in Gospić). The majority of those arrested were taken to Jadovno and Pag, while some were killed along the way and thrown into pits. In some places in neighboring Bosanska Krajina the persecutions, organized by Viktor Gutić, the Ustasha commissioner and head of the county, who was a resolute advocate and strident executor of genocidal terror, were even more drastic.

Nothing was ever heard from the men taken through Gospić to Jadovno. Any access to them was forbidden. However, the truth "leaked out" from the ranks of the Ustasha in Gospić, and it became clear to the Lika peasants that none of them would be coming back from Jadovno alive. When Ustasha and gendarme patrols from Gračac, Gospić, and other garrisons moved on the Serbian villages, many of the men in the villages no longer waited in their homes, and no one responded to the persistent calls of the Ustasha authorities to turn in the weapons that many Lika residents had brought home after the dissolution of the Royal Yugoslav Army.

Early on the morning of June 29, Ustasha units from Bihać suddenly appeared in front of Serbian homes in the villages of the district of Plitvice Lakes: "Be ready to depart within half an hour! You are going to Serbia. Each family member can take fifty kilograms of possessions." Driven by shouting, swearing, and rifle butts, about 1,200 people had to abandon their fields before the harvest, their cows in their barns, their sheep in their pens, and their homes that had been built through centuries of toil.

A column made up of mostly women and children stretched for miles. The men had been more cautious; the Ustasha raid did not catch them at home—they had fled into the nearby forests and shepherds' huts. Peasants from the Korenica district were forced to transport the exiles in their wagons because the deportees had to leave behind their own wagons, horses, and oxen. Thus, the region around the Plitvice Lakes became the first area of the NDH to be cleansed of Serbs. Allegedly the intention was to construct a residential and tourist paradise for *Poglavnik* Pavelić and important dignitaries from Germany, Italy, and other allied countries, and thus no Serbs could be in the area. According to another interpretation, the cleansing around the Plitvice Lakes established a breach and broke up the concentrations of ethnic Serbian communities between Lika and Kordun. In any event, it was the first great deportation under the German-Ustasha agreement of June 4, 1941, for the forced emigration of Serbs from the NDH to Serbia.

After several days of suffering without food and with no roof over their heads, and under an Ustasha escort, the deportees arrived in Drvar. They were lodged in the surrounding Orthodox villages with the understanding that this was "temporary accommodation on the journey to Serbia." Most of the refugees were warmly received in the homes of the Krajina Serbs, who were naturally concerned about their own fates.[35] The Ustasha authorities did not foresee that the expulsion of the Lika Serbs into Bosnian Krajina would strengthen the solidarity of the Serbian population and that it would become the nucleus of the joint Krajina-Lika uprising a month later.

The homes of the Serbs exiled from Lika were given to Ustasha supporters in the neighboring Plitvice and Kordun districts. Some even moved in, but for only a brief time. By the beginning of August, they had to flee when the expelled Serbs, supported by the first Partisan units, returned to their looted and demolished homes in Končarev Kraj and other villages around the Plitvice Lakes.

The news of the brutal cleansing of the Plitvice region reached Serbian villages throughout Lika on the day it occurred. Not only the men fled into the forests but also their families and, indeed, entire villages. On June 30, 1941, the headquarters of the Vrhbosna Divisional Area reported:

> We still do not have clear information about the motives and extent of the disorder in the district of Donji Lapac. It is probable that the people are alarmed and frightened by the Ustasha actions against the Serbian inhabitants carried out in the province of Psat and Krbava. On June 24, about 1,200 Jews and Serbs were evacuated from Bihać to Kulen Vakuf and the surrounding villages, that is, the total Serbian population of Bihać. Since entire families were roused at four o'clock in the morning and evacuated with only hand luggage and five hundred dinars per person, it is understandable that there was concern and fear about their future. These desperate families were relocated to a purely Serbian area around Kulen Vakuf, which borders on the district of Donji Lapac, also purely Serbian. . . . [The report continued and concluded:] a) a military patrol from Donji Lapac

> came under fire in the village of Srb and there are allegedly about 2,000 Chetniks and refugees in the area; b) it was necessary to send the army immediately to the district of Donji Lapac to establish peace and order; c) nothing can be sent from Bihać because of a certain operational situation in the area of the Plitvice Lakes....

The gunfire mentioned here occurred not far from Srb, near the village of Suvaja, when refugees fired from the edge of the forest to stop the pursuing Ustasha. There is no information that any Ustasha troops or gendarmes were killed anywhere in this area before July 27. The uprising was still a month away. Moreover, the number of "about 2,000 Chetniks and refugees" cited in the report must refer only to the fleeing population because there were not many armed units in the area, barely a few dozen people with carbines and hunting rifles, and they had not yet been organized, as either Chetniks or Partisans.

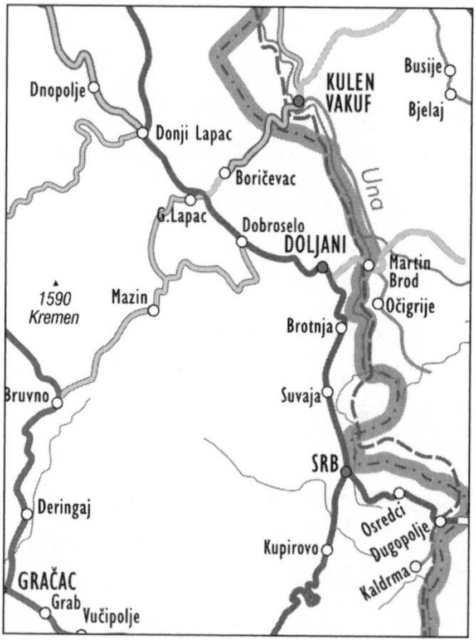

In a statement on November 5, 1941, Luburić comments that because of the events in the region at the end of June he was sent "on a special assignment to the province of Psat and Krbava to carry out a cleansing operation." He goes on to say: "I was given only one general order: that in the territory of Krbava and Psat all the authorities in the region, including military, were to report directly to me until the designated cleansing operation was completed." Such powers are only given to people who enjoy the greatest possible trust of their superiors and who have already shown themselves to be reliable in carrying out "special assignments." The fact that Luburić received such powers and that they were frequently entrusted to him later clearly demonstrates that Kvaternik and Pavelić were behind this "special assignment" and that they had approved of and initiated such cleansing methods. I could not establish the exact date Luburić arrived in Bihać with this mandate, so I cannot be sure if the deportation of Plitvice Serbs on June 29 was carried out under his command. What is certain is that Luburić suddenly appeared in the villages of Gornja and Donja Suvaja in southeastern Lika on July 1, where he carried out the cleansing operation. He had about 150 men at his disposal from the Ustasha Auxiliary Force, a unit notorious for "special assignments" made up of handpicked Ustasha from towns in Lika and from Bihać. For additional security during the operation Luburić directed about 250 members of the Home Guard from the Twenty-second Infantry Battalion in Gospić. Luburić and his Ustasha entered Suvaja on the morning of July 1 in several trucks from the direction of Srb. He immediately ordered looting, burning, and mass killing. Many men of the village had fled into the nearby forests, leaving primarily women, children, and the elderly. Some women and children in houses at the edge of the village were themselves able to escape into the forest, but all of those in the central part of the village were killed. The burning and massacre lasted about two hours. Survivors claimed that they could hear automatic rifle fire only here and there. The killing was done primarily with weapons other than firearms—knives, clubs. According to the list of names of the victims, 173 people were killed that day in Suvaja, and according to some sources, more than 200. Luburić's operation was the first Ustasha massacre in which mainly women and children were killed.

For the next two days Luburić's expedition carried out similar cleansing actions in the villages of Bubanj and Osredak. According to one gendarmerie report, "during this operation, 152 people were killed in Bubanj." A subsequent list of victims has 83 names, of which only 6 are men, while the rest are women and children (among them ten who were younger than five years old). In three days in these three Lika villages at least 279 people were killed, maybe as many as 330.

On July 3, one of Luburić's smaller units carried out a different kind of "resettlement" in the village of Nebljusi. They arrived with a list of fifty-three people who were to be "moved out," all members of several of the more prominent and wealthy families in the area, including ten children under the age of twelve. To this group they added twelve adult men who had been arrested earlier, then took the entire group by horse-drawn wagons to Boričevac. There the detainees were crammed into a barracks to await the night. As soon as darkness fell, Luburić's men tied them together in groups of eight and led them away from the village on foot. Above the cavern known as Bezdanka they killed them group by group and threw their bodies into it. One detainee, Đuro Balać, was able to untie himself in the darkness and escape before reaching the cavern. Another, Dara Škorić, was only wounded and lay low among the dead. After a while, she managed to drag herself out of the cavern and, completely distraught, ran into Luka Miškulin, a resident of Boričevac and the father of two of the Ustasha who had participated in the killing. He revived her with some water and food and guided her on the road to her people, evading the Ustasha guards and patrols along the way.

Thus, in Suvaja, Bubanj, Osredak, and Boričevac, Luburić marked out the road of no return that led to rebellion. Lika could no longer be pacified. Armed men now guarded some villages, while the inhabitants of others fled en masse into the hills and forests. Luburić and his superiors had wrongly calculated that the brutal killing of an innocent population would quash any embryonic resistance to their plan for the creation of an "ethnically pure area." Their actions had provoked the completely opposite effect. The attempts of some of the more reasonable Ustasha (for example, Jure Pavičić in Donji Lapac) to calm the Serbian population through well-intentioned gestures (material assistance to the villages that had been destroyed, the release of some of the arrested) were in vain.

After the German invasion of the Soviet Union on June 22, a new factor had a major impact on the events in the region: The Comintern had mobilized communists everywhere with the directive that it was "essential to take all measures to support and facilitate the just struggle of the Soviet people" because "the defense of the USSR is the defense of the nations occupied by Germany." According to data given by Jakov Blažević in *Prva godina narodnooslobodilačkog rata* (The First Year of the National Liberation War), there were about 245 members of the Communist Party of Croatia and an equal number of League of Young Communists of Yugoslavia members and active collaborators in Lika at the time.[36] Many of them, especially in the districts of Korenica and Donji Lapac, had already taken to the forests by the beginning of July, offering organized resistance to protect the fleeing Serbian population. Individuals who supported the Chetnik program of resistance and retaliation were also on the rise.

In the villages and forests of Lika and Krajina "revolutionary committees," "guerrilla units," and "Chetnik headquarters" were being set up. In this initial phase the Chetniks advocated defensive tactics with retaliatory raids on Croatian villages and collaboration with the Italian occupation forces as protection against the Ustasha. The communists called for offensive tactics and an uprising against the Ustasha regime and the occupying forces, while also attempting to win over the Croatian population wherever possible. From the outset of the rebellion, the communists were more dominant in the leadership of the rebellion in Lika, Bosanska Krajina, Kordun, and Banija, while Chetnik leadership was predominant in Dalmatian Zagora and eastern Bosnia and Herzegovina.

A coordinated uprising broke out on July 27 from both sides of the upper reaches of the Una River in the territory of southeastern Lika and southwestern Bosanska Krajina. Within a matter of days a rather large portion of the heart of the NDH (Drvar, Glamoč, Bosansko Grahovo, Donji Lapac, and Srb) was in the hands of the rebels. The communists led the rebellion in these early days, although some groups under Chetnik leadership also participated. The latter were responsible for the mass killings of Croats as "an eye for an eye" revenge in Brotnja, Boričevac, Vrtoča, and Krnjeuša. According to Ustasha sources (the so-called *Gray Book*), about 170 Croatian men and women, including many children, were killed in these villages on July 29 and August 2, 1941. (There were considerably more victims in later Chetnik crimes in some parts of eastern Bosnia and Herzegovina.)

The Ustasha government reacted to the July 27 uprising and to the Chetnik crimes of July 29 and August 2 with Luburić-style reprisals against unprotected Serbian villages. Major massacres occurred in Banija, Kordun, Cazinska Krajina, and those parts of Lika that the rebellion had not yet affected. Thus, the last days of July and the first days of August 1941 proved the bloodiest period of the Ustasha's four-year rule in the NDH. According to Ivan Nikšić, the Ustasha commissioner for the county of Slunj, "for that entire time [that is, from July 30 to August 8] from three to four thousand Serbs in the district of Slunj were killed, among them only one hundred to two hundred men able to bear arms, the rest were the infirm, women, children, and the elderly."[37] According to Partisan sources, another 1,755 Serbian civilians were killed in the Ustasha reprisals in Gospić in August.

The immediate consequence of these Ustasha reprisals was the rapid spread of the rebellion from Lika Kordun and Banija to Dalmatia and the regions of Gorski Kotar, Hrvatsko Primorje, and gradually throughout all of Croatia. Lika had been the initial flashpoint and it remained so for the first year of the war. According to a report from the supreme command of the National Liberation Partisan Units of Croatia, on December 31, 1941, all of the Partisan units in Croatia numbered about seven thousand armed troops, exactly half of whom were from Lika. And it is important to keep in mind that the Lika-Krajina uprising of July 27 did not lead to the horrors at Jadovno and Suvaja. It was just the opposite: Jadovno and Suvaja led to the Lika-Krajina uprising.

I felt I had to address some of the details of this history, at least in summary, even though it lies outside the intended framework of these memoirs of the year 1941. I did so because I believe that everything that happened to my family and to me in 1941 might not be sufficiently clear without some of the background that this chapter provides. To this day it pains me to read in the school textbooks of my grandchildren the pallid justification that the Ustasha crimes were a response to the rebellion of the Serbs against the Croatian state. As one of the witnesses, I think it is my duty to state how I personally experienced these crimes that in truth began in my hometown on the night of May 5 with the murder of three innocent men in the Rečica forest near Karlovac—two of the perpetrators were acquaintances of mine—when there was not even a trace or rumor of a rebellion. The culmination of these crimes was the camp at Jadovno, where my father disappeared, among the many thousands who were taken there, before a single bullet was fired at their murderers.

The Outcome of the "Karlovac Case"

Hitler's green light for the half century of Pavelić's ethnic intolerance indirectly brought a resolution to the "Vujičić affair." The sharp divide within the local Ustasha leadership in Karlovac was, indeed, only a marginal issue in regards to the central question of May 1941: *Quo vadis*, NDH? However, the manner in which the "Karlovac case" played out and how it was finally resolved was indicative of the general conditions in the country. Indeed, it did not leave much doubt about the political direction in which the Ustasha state was moving and would continue to follow more decisively.

Even before the audience with Hitler, it was clear which of the opposing groups in the Karlovac Ustasha Council Pavelić and Kvaternik supported. But after Pavelić had met with Hitler, there was no longer any question. Feliks Židovec, the mayor of Karlovac, had received no response to his request for a legitimate investigation into the "Vujičić affair" and measures against such murders. Mane Bilović and Vladimir Židovec, two other members of the council, never received an answer to the memorandum they had drafted on the same issue on May 12 in the office of Minister Žanić and which was forwarded to the *Poglavnik* Pavelić. Although the *Poglavnik* responded neither in writing nor verbally, his answer was nonetheless eloquent.

When the provinces were established as the main regional administrative units of the NDH on June 10,[38] Pavelić's favorite, Ante Nikšić, became the provincial governor of Pokuplje, whose seat was in Karlovac. At the same time, Hinko Karl, Nikšić's most devoted associate, was appointed head of the Directorate of the Provincial Police, and Ivan Gromes, another confidant, became chief of the Karlovac police. Hard-liners now occupied the most influential positions, tacitly blessing the crimes that had been committed and encouraging continued terror. Members of the "moderate wing" of the

Independent State of Croatia, June 1941

Ustasha Council were simply isolated from any duties and appointments. Vladimir Židovec wrote about this state of affairs in *My Participation in Political Life*:

> It now became clear that all our efforts to remove Nikšić from Karlovac were a complete failure. It was equally clear that our demands to punish the guilty parties in the "Vujičić affair" had also failed.... In consequence all of the members of the Ustasha Council in Karlovac, except Hinko Karl and Gromes,

> immediately submitted written resignations. My father and I prepared the document, which was delivered to Blaž Lorković, the *Poglavnik*'s assistant, who was at that time overseeing the organizational activities of the Ustasha main headquarters. In the resignation letter we expressly stated that the work of Nikšić was damaging the interests of the Ustasha cause and the Croatian state, and since we did not want to share responsibility for such activities, we were submitting our resignation....[39]

Writing his political autobiography in an UDBA prison in 1947, Židovec inevitably tries to paint a sanitized picture of his actions in the NDH. His claim of a joint resignation is not altogether accurate. There is no trace of this resignation letter anywhere on record—not in the archives or in the statements of other witnesses to events in Karlovac at the time. The Ustasha as an organization would never have tolerated such autonomy of thought and action as a demonstrative collective resignation of five members as the younger Židovec claims. The signatories of such a document would have suffered unpleasant consequences to say the least. They would have fallen into political disgrace and certainly would not have been appointed to new, relatively senior positions within the NDH, which is what happened to at least two of the members Židovec claims had signed the joint resignation. I think that their membership in the Ustasha Council and the council itself simply withered away, ceased to operate with the establishment of the provinces and with the Decree on the Composition and Activities of the Ustasha Movement, and no resignations were called for.

The only person on the Usasha Council who in fact submitted a resignation, and did so publicly, was Vladimir Židovec's father, Feliks. In an inconspicuous corner of *Hrvatska sloboda* (issue 7) a small note was published under the title "Resignation of the Mayor": "The mayor of Karlovac, Feliks Židovec, today submitted his resignation. He has remitted his salary as mayor of 6,000 dinars to the municipal welfare department." And that is all. No word of explanation, but to anyone slightly better informed it was enough. Feliks Židovec signed the resignation on June 7, or as soon as he officially learned that Nikšić would be named provinicial governor. A part of the Karlovac public ascribed this act to a rivalry between the Frankist veteran Židovec and the fledgling Ustasha activist Nikšić. If such a rivalry did exist, their conflict had not manifested itself until the "Vujičić affair" and it concluded with Feliks Židovec withdrawing to his legal profession and not accepting any public position for the duration of the NDH. However, he remained until the end a staunch supporter of the ideal of an independent Croatian state. When Vladimir suggested to his mother and father on May 6, 1945, that they go with him into exile, Feliks refused. He scornfully condemned Pavelić's decision to flee instead of placing himself at the head of the army at Zagreb and dying there, which in Feliks's opinion would at least to some degree salvage the *Poglavnik*'s reputation and the idea of Croatian statehood.

And so on May 7 Vladimir Židovec joined the great exodus, while his mother and father remained in their apartment in Zagreb. At the end of his political autobiography Židovec writes, "On Easter 1946, already deep in exile, I learned the terrible and shattering news that my parents—around May or June 1945 when the current regime in Yugoslavia was newly established—had been arrested in Zagreb, taken to Karlovac, and there executed . . . I am convinced that this could only have happened in 1945 and that it certainly would not have happened later."

After the dissolution of the Ustasha Council, Vladimir Židovec was without a position in the Ustasha hierarchy for about a month. He worked in the law offices of his father. In July 1941, Mladen

Lorković, the new NDH minister of foreign affairs, invited him to become the NDH ambassador to Bulgaria. He spent two full years in that position and a similar amount of time in various senior positions in the Ministry of Foreign Affairs. In March 1947, the British authorities arrested him in Genoa, Italy, and extradited him to Yugoslavia in April. He spent almost a year in prison, where he wrote nearly a thousand pages about political life in the NDH. Read with the required skepticism—the author was in prison and the possibility of the death penalty always loomed—portions of these writings, I think, are among the most interesting source of information about the socio-psychology and political character of the Ustasha hierarchy and some of its most important actors. Židovec's descriptions are relatively nuanced, with a sense for detail that gives credibility to the overall picture. To the very end he writes from the perspective of a Croatian nationalist and a Catholic, embittered by Pavelić's style of governing and by the crimes committed, but always dedicated to the political orientation he called his "youthful ideals." He discreetly offered his services to the communist authorities in the form of further writings about all aspects of the Ustasha cause and the NDH if they would spare his life. On January 22, 1948, the district court in Zagreb sentenced him to death by firing squad. The Supreme Court confirmed the sentence; the presidency of the National Assembly of the Federal People's Republic of Yugoslavia refused his request for a pardon and, according to the official register, the sentence was carried out less than two months later at three o'clock in the morning on March 3. Some researchers have claimed that the register was a forgery since Židovec allegedly lived for at least six more years, writing reports on various topics for the UDBA under the alias Dizdar. I cannot say that there is no truth to this claim, but I strongly doubt it. I once compared the style and sentence structure of Židovec's prison writings with the documents signed by Dizdar and can say with complete confidence that the same man didn't write them.

Nikšić was the commissioner in Karlovac until the spring of 1942. He then became the minister of internal affairs, followed by a posting as the NDH ambassador to Italy. The end of the war found him abroad. His eldest daughter, Dunja, married the son of the Italian general Vittorio Ambrosio. Through various connections Nikšić managed to reach Argentina, where he lived peacefully until his death in 1962. He and Vladimir Židovec met each other in exile only once, in Genoa on March 3, 1947, as they were boarding a ship to Argentina. Stephen Clissold, a British army major and the intelligence officer responsible for Croatia, was standing guard at the gangway. His assignment was to identify wanted war criminals and prevent them from boarding. He prevented Židovec but allowed Nikšić to travel to Argentina. By what strange criteria? In his prison writings Židovec provides a bizarre explanation: In the early days of the NDH, a British diplomat, late in escaping from the newly occupied country, was rushing from Ljubljana through Karlovac to the coast. Recently installed as the Ustasha commissioner for Karlovac, Nikšić provided some papers and an escort for the diplomat, making it possible for him to reach the coast. But the diplomat first had to provide Nikšić with a written confirmation of this service and express his gratitude, in a diplomatic memorandum in English, which Židovec claims permitted Nikšić to become a persona grata for Clissold. Židovec wasn't as cautious or farsighted; he never requested a similar diplomatic memorandum, even though in Sofia there might have been an opportunity to do so. And this is how he ended up in a jail in Zagreb instead of free in Argentina.

Aleksandar Šantić, the most notorious Ustasha among the young killers, spoke German well. Kvaternik included him in a group of one hundred of the more promising Ustasha policemen who were sent for training in Germany. Šantić ended up working for German military intelligence, the Abwehr, and in that capacity was assigned to Ogulin and Karlovac. He spent most of the war years in Croatia as a German intelligence officer. In May 1945, he managed to escape to Austria. After spending two years in camps and prisons, the British authorities extradited him to Yugoslavia as a wanted war criminal. The UDBA investigators promised to spare his life if he cooperated, an offer Šantić accepted. However, at a spectacular public trial in Karlovac in the fall of 1948, he was condemned to death—among other reasons because of his participation in the murders of Milan Vujičić, Captain Gojko Janjanin, and Dušan Dokmanović. After the sentencing, the investigators continued to press Šantić for information, promising that the death sentence would be overturned, but he no longer believed them. Without waiting for a possible reduction of his sentence by the Supreme Court, at an opportune moment he overpowered his guard and was wounded while trying to escape. Returned to his cell, he unsuccessfully tried to commit suicide and then was immediately executed.

Stjepan Augustinović, one of the young men who had taken my father away, became an agent for the UNS, serving the entire time in the NDH. He disappeared in the last days of the war. He was allegedly killed in battle during the liberation of Karlovac by the Partisans on May 5 or 6, 1945.

Jožica Gombač's wealthy parents sent him to finish school in Germany in the fall of 1941. From that time on he never again set foot in Karlovac. I was told he became a mechanical engineer in Germany, lived a quiet life, and broke off all contact with Croatia.

Of all of the members of the Ustasha Council, I knew only Mane Bilović personally. He was a rather corpulent, friendly man, given to jokes and having a good time. He worked as the chief accountant in the local electric company. A Croatian nationalist before the war, he liked to sing proscribed songs in jolly company and several times spent a few hours or even an entire night in jail on account of it. Bilović took none of it seroiusly and it made him more popular among the city's residents. On the basis of these "merits" he was co-opted into the leadership of the Ustasha Council in April 1941.

After the dissolution of the council, Bilović did not seek a new position. When the reorganization based on the Decree on the Composition and Activities of the Ustasha Movement came into effect, he was offered the position of the commander of the municipal Ustasha organization. Bilović hesitated for several days before accepting the position. Danica Banda, a friend of the Bilović family, a Serbian, and a teacher, told me how she and a friend had urged Bilović to accept this position because he might be useful to many people and be able to forestall disaster here and there. I don't know if this was one of the reasons that Bilović agreed to become the commander of the Karlovac Ustasha organization in July 1941 or why he remained in that position for the duration of the NDH. However, I do know that he used his position to help many people, including my mother.

My brother, Danko, was best friends with Bilović's son, and I sometimes played with them and also socialized with his daughters. After my father was sent to Jadovno, my mother was arrested and taken to jail in Zagreb, and my brother and I were thrown out of our apartment, I mustered the courage to knock on Mrs. Bilović's door and ask for help. She brought me into the apartment and cried with me. She kept me there until her husband came home from work. We didn't wait long before he appeared at the door in the uniform of an Ustasha commander, with a large officer's cap that he removed from his sweaty head. Mrs. Bilović did not give him time to breathe: "Mane, look what's going on!" and brought me before the Ustasha commander. "This is terrible, it's a scandal!"

Bilović listened calmly, asked a question or two, and said he would see what he could do. He wasted no words in comforting me, but he did what he had promised to do. It was a lucky coincidence that at that time Ivan Gromes, the hard-line chief of police, was transferred (to Bihać, I think), and that Milan Stilinović, a longtime friend of Bilović, replaced him. After some time, my mother was transferred from jail in Zagreb to the Karlovac jail "for further investigation and interrogation." She was held three or four days and after an interview rather than an interrogation, Stilinović gave her a travel permit to Kraljevica in the Italian zone of occupation. He pointed out that the permit was valid for only four days and that it would not be easy to get an extension. He also conveyed greetings from the Ustasha commander, Mane Bilović.

My mother understood the message and immediately traveled from Karlovac to the Italian zone of occupation, which at the time was a temporary safe haven for persecuted Jews. As enterprising as ever, my mother quickly succeeded in bringing my brother and me to Kraljevica, and in the spring of 1942 the three of us joined the Partisans.

After the war was over, my mother, brother, and I happily returned to Karlovac, each from a different direction as it were. Bilović was in jail. His daughter Neda was collecting statements from the people he had helped. She had gathered fifty-four signed statements. Among them, of course, were those signed by my mother and me. I believe that these statements helped to save Bilović's life. Nevertheless, on June 26, 1945, the military court sentenced him to seven years of forced labor and the loss of civil rights for "membership in the Ustasha movement and spreading hostile propaganda."

After many requests and interventions, the district court in Karlovac submitted a "proposal for a special reduction of the sentence" to the Supreme Court of the People's Republic of Croatia on September 14, 1950. Thus, after five and a half years of forced labor (some of which he spent as the accountant for the construction of the Vinodol hydroelectric dam), Bilović was released and allowed to return home. He found employment as an accountant with the local department store.

All of us who were deeply indebted to him looked forward to seeing him smiling again at work or on the streets of Karlovac. We always felt that we had not repayed him as much as we should have.

Part Three

One Spring in Karlovac

The Karlovac promenade. We lived in the ground-floor apartment in the left foreground from 1929 to 1935. There was also an exit onto Zrinski Square from the opposite side of the building

7

The Yellow Symbol That I Did Not Wear

THE GERMANS LEFT Karlovac after about two weeks and the city's many army barracks were not large enough to accommodate all the Italian troops that descended on the city. According to the demarcation line established on April 23 between the German and Italian military commands, Karlovac fell into the Italian sphere of military influence. The Second Italian Army took possession of the girls' school as its headquarters, and about four thousand officers and soldiers spread through the city's barracks, schools, government buildings, and apartments, along with about a thousand former Yugoslav soldiers who had been regrouped into the Home Guard of the Independent State of Croatia. The old garrison town of Karlovac had never had to accommodate so many soldiers.

The Italians resembled something from an operetta. With their helmets decorated by feathers, arranged in straight rows of six, the *bersaglieri*[1] paraded around town at their distinctive jogging pace, accompanied by lively military bands. It all sounded cheerful and benign, in contrast to the more menacing and harsh Erika Division of the local Kulturbund, in their shiny black boots and snow-white shirts with a huge swastika on one sleeve, stepping in unison to a rhythmic beat that sounded like a powerful drum. The Italians dug trenches around the old town of Dubovac, and before the cameras of an Italian film crew, they staged a mock assault on the town. The film was said to have been shown later in a newsreel depicting "the heroic capture of an enemy fortress" in the recently ended war. Residents of Karlovac scornfully laughed at it, saying, "They are making fools of us."

The military loudspeakers blared popular songs like "Rosamunda," "Vento," and "Siciliana Bruna," while the soldiers hummed or whistled the tunes during off-duty hours. Later it became a regular Sunday-morning feature for the Second Army's orchestra to perform popular arias from operas by Verdi, Rossini, Donizetti, and Mascagni on the promenade at the monument to Radoslav Lopa.[2] The Italians could be voluble and sociable in their dealings with the local residents. They would flirt with the young girls and court them, sometimes successfully, which would lead to angry comments from the young men of Karlovac.

Stanko Lasić remembers the Italians in Karlovac as "insolent, arrogant, and dangerous because of their capriciousness . . . the impression was that they could kill for fun, whenever the mood struck them." Perhaps my recollection has been colored by the attitude of the Italians toward the Karlovac Jews. I know several Jewish families with whom Italian officers were quartered. They were mostly kind, sympathetic men who helped their hosts in various ways with the dangers they were facing, even making it possible for some to escape to Italy to save themselves. That was also one of my mother's more optimistic schemes. She was buying lira on the black market: "When we get your father out of jail, we are all off to Italy."

But a year and a half later, in September 1942, from the slopes of Mala Kapela I watched with Drežnica refugees while Italian soldiers and officers of the Sassari Division, guided by Chetniks from Gomirje, mercilessly robbed and set fire to the houses around Drežnica and

Jasenak—to the last house, the last barn, the last hayloft. Everything that could be burned, except the church, was destroyed: in total, several hundred houses and nearly a thousand farm buildings, leaving about eight thousand residents of Drežnica, Jasenak, and Gornji Kraj without roofs over their heads or provisions for the winter. Watching all of this, I wondered, "Were the men committing this evil—looting, robbing, burning, leaving only desolation in their wake, and taking 1,100 innocent villagers away to internment—the same good-natured, cheerful soldiers who softly sang "Mama son' tanto felice" on the Karlovac promenade and played the melody of the "Chorus of the Hebrew Slaves" from *Nabucco* in front of Lopašić's monument, and the same polite officers who brought sweets to the children of their landlords and saved those in danger?"

I searched for an explanation much later in Elias Canetti's *Crowds and Power*, which abounds with interesting examples and observations, while also avoiding firm answers: "The destructiveness of the crowd is often mentioned as its most conspicuous quality, and there is no denying that it can be observed everywhere, in the most diverse countries and civilizations. It is discussed and disapproved of, but never really explained." Every explanation, however lucid, inevitably poses new questions. Goethe also examined this question, as if he were looking one hundred years or more into the future: "I have often felt a bitter grief at the thought of the German people, which is so noble individually and so wretched as a whole." Of course, a man is not the same when he is alone or isolated as when he is in a group. But what is it in a human being that a crowd can arouse, sometimes to unimagined evil and more rarely to a surprising good? I think that Tolstoy came closest to an answer in *War and Peace*—in the descriptions of the peasant revolt on the estate of Bogucharovo, in the contradictory actions of the French soldiers during the occupation of and their retreat from Moscow. He articulated the "dialectic of the soul of a soldier in war," as Viktor Shklovsky so brilliantly wrote about Tolstoy in analyzing *The Sevastopol Sketches* and *War and Peace.* But when Tolstoy distanced himself from the characters in his literature, when he went in search of a comprehensive explanation of the "differential of history," even he fell into generalizations that leave much to be desired.

Under the burden of having to feed so many soldiers, in May 1941 Karlovac was already gripped by serious shortages of grain, meat, dairy products, and eggs. Even potatoes and bread had to be purchased on the black market, and everything was subject to rapidly increasing prices, especially meat. *Hrvatska sloboda* complained that even the children of well-to-do families went to the military barracks with containers to beg for food. Black marketeers were threatened with "having their fingers burned" because "the mayor, Židovec, has taken matters in hand, and will soon be imposing order." On May 10, the newspapers published a notice that for the next eight days the buying and reselling of "the necessities of life" would be temporarily banned throughout the NDH and rationing introduced for these items. The majority of residents still believed that such difficulties were only temporary because life had begun to return to normal in many other ways. "Karlovac streets are again lit," *Hrvatska sloboda* joyously proclaimed, and freedom of movement around the city was extended until midnight. Rail and bus service became much more regular. The cinemas, coffee shops, and bowling alleys reopened and sporting events resumed. The promenade was full of strollers in the early evening. There were no classes in schools because the army had taken over all of the school buildings, so that secondary-school students, freed from their obligations, filled the promenade, the streets of the city, and the parks along the Korana with their youthful good cheer. I believe that only a minority of the residents were happy when on April 26 the Ustasha Council renamed the Korana gardens the

Park of the Poglavnik and the main promenade Ante Pavelić Promenade.

The initial enthusiasm associated with the slogan "We have a state" had apparently died out rather quickly. With his usual dose of irony, General Edmund Glaise von Horstenau wrote in his diary on May 30, 1941:

> Regarding the orders that in Croatia only what is urgently needed is to be confiscated, our troops have evidently considered everything that comes to mind as urgently needed, so that anything and everything they want rather than what they need is confiscated. The residents of Zagreb watch as our military trucks, fully loaded with all kinds of goods, leave their city and their country, while our good Croats in the second month of their freedom eat bread of poorer quality than the bread they ate during the famine in the last world war.

In his first report on April 23, 1941, General Glaise von Horstenau's best intelligence officer, Captain Arthur Haeffner, warned about the first improper actions of the Ustasha government and the announced plans that could provoke serious trouble in the country. Haeffner also reported that "the Ustasha movement has attracted many new adherents and since moral character was not an issue, the worst rabble can be found in its ranks." In his summary report to the German high command on July 10, 1941, Glaise von Horstenau concluded that "the entire country is gripped by a feeling of complete legal uncertainty," and on the same day Troll-Obergfell, the chargé d'affaires of the German embassy, informed the Ministry of Foreign Affairs that "the ruthlessness with which the mass expulsions are being carried out, as well as the many accompanying violent acts . . . are a cause of serious concern even to more sober Croatian circles." Haeffner, in a report to Glaise von Horstenau on July 18, 1941, said: "It is regrettable for us Germans to state that as a result of the Reich's policy toward this country virtually nothing was left of the enthusiasm of the Croatian people that greeted the arrival of our army at the beginning of April, and that today a deep distrust of Germany reigns in this country because it is supporting a regime that has no right to exist in either a moral or political sense." Haeffner concluded that the Ustasha crimes against the Serbs threatened "to transform the entire country into a red-hot volcanic eruption that will not be easily extinguished."[3]

Some German representatives, especially those in the army and in military intelligence, accurately assessed that such Ustasha policies were damaging German interests, that instead of the NDH assisting them in their military and military-economic efforts, it had become a dead weight that the army of the Third Reich would have to help maintain. However, German SS and SA police representatives in the NDH, and also Ambassador Siegfried Kasche and even Hitler himself several times ("*Die guten Kroaten mögen sich austoben*": The good Croats should be allowed to unleash their rage), tolerated, approved of, and to some extent encouraged the Ustasha government and its methods. This dual track in German relations with the NDH also resulted in some dilemmas, and even divisions, within the senior Ustasha leadership. As a result, it vacillated in resolving the so-called "Serbian question": from the initial drastic persecutions to its temporary halt, and then the renewed persecutions, followed by occasional conciliatory gestures, which were most frequently hypocritical and deceitful.

At the same time, German representatives never objected to the Ustasha measures against either the Jews or the Roma. On the contrary, in 1942 and 1943 they were encouraging those measures and participating in them. There was no hesitation or disagreement in the

Ustasha leadership with regard to the "Jewish question," although compared to the "Serbian question" it was of secondary importance, almost marginal. Moreover, the Ustasha's hatred of the Jews was never as passionate as their hatred of the Serbs—it might even be said that there was no deep-rooted anti-Semitism among some part of the Ustasha leadership. Nevertheless, the Nazi prescription for a "final solution to the Jewish question" was systematically transferred to the NDH, with the unanimous participation, or at least submissive approval, of all the Ustasha leadership. Before investigators of the postwar military court in March 1947, Mile Budak and Slavko Kvaternik described how during the adoption of anti-Jewish laws in the sessions of the NDH government there was never a single opposing vote because, according to Kvaternik, "we all considered them to be necessary, we felt that we were being forced to adopt them." It began with

The house in the right foreground: Zrinski Square No. 9, the apartment of the Goldstein family, 1935–1941

the shameless looting of property, continued with all means of legal and social discrimination, and culminated after several months in massive deportations to the camps and mass killings.

* * *

On May 9, the Karlovac Directorate of the Provincial Police issued the following order: “All persons of the Jewish and Orthodox faiths are permitted to move about the city only between the hours of eight o’clock in the morning and six o’clock in the evening.” Anyone violating this order was threatened with being arrested on the spot and punished severely. Several days later a regulation was issued that required Jews to wear a yellow symbol. I never wore it because in Karlovac it was required only for persons above the age of fourteen. My mother had to wear it, and she certainly did so when she was on the street, as did my older Jewish friends and acquaintances, because the punishment for noncompliance was harsh. Nevertheless, I don’t remember that symbol on my mother’s chest. She said that she was not ashamed to wear it; those who ordered her to wear it should be ashamed. I can vaguely remember once holding that symbol in my hands, both the early cloth one and the later metal one, but I don’t remember seeing it on my mother, or on Filip Reiner, Mrs. Eisler, Saša Glück, or any others in our family’s narrow circle of friends and acquaintances. Nevertheless, it is possible that they did wear it. Obviously, in each of us there is a blackout mechanism for some of the images from our pasts, so one must be careful when calling upon one’s memory. And so, as I have already said, I am trying to confront my memories with notes and documents of the time, and in other people’s reminiscences that verify my own.

Despite the drastic anti-Jewish measures and the immediate sufferings of my family, I cannot say that in the spring of 1941 in Karlovac I felt persecuted. Perhaps that feeling was there from time to time, but I have pushed it into the recesses of my memory, like the yellow symbol on my mother's chest. Perhaps a boy of thirteen is not yet emotionally mature enough to feel the torment that is taking place around him and inside him. Leo and Eko Beljan, the sons of the owner of an ice-cream parlor near our apartment, still asked Danko and me to go with them to the islands in the Korana to play a strange game of hide-and-seek that Leo called "*tabona.*" I still ran through the trenches around Zorin Dom with Bogdan and Stanko Lasić and dropped in to see Edo Lukinić, who drew cartoons for Mišo Dozet and me of his imaginary characters Sojnici and Hrozotnici, and of the giant Zdravljak, who for morning exercise from a running start at a spot across Lake Bohinj, jumps over Zagrebačka Gora, and all that was accompanied by Edo's funny improvisation on the piano. The mothers of my friends Tonček Strzalkowski, Vlado Samardžija, and the Lasić brothers warmly received me in their homes in a gesture of sympathy.

I don't remember any of my friends or classmates in 1941 not socializing with me because I was a Jew and because my father was in jail. Unfortunately, my older friends, both Serbs and Jews, frequently experienced such unpleasantness. Something similar had happened to me only once, as far as I can recall, two or three years before the war.

In the building next door to ours on the Karlovac promenade lived Beno Jaroš, a long-legged boy who was in the same grade as me but in a different class. We were the main competitors in running races—he won in the shorter distances, while I won in the longer ones. Since Beno had problems with mathematics in school, his mother often invited me to their cramped, neat attic apartment so I could tutor him. This is how I met Beno's father, a housepainter and an amateur painter of still lifes on canvas. Who knows what led him to Hitler, but sometime at the beginning of the war I was no longer invited to this house. Beno confided to my brother and me that his father had forbidden him to play with us because we were Jews. However, Beno couldn't resist the temptation and would sometimes secretly join us in our races and other games, and was beaten several times by his father for doing so. Later, Mr. Jaroš moved to Germany with his family and I don't know what happened to them. Beno never again appeared in Karlovac.

* * *

In the last years before the war ping-pong was the main sport among high-school students of Karlovac. It was played in the courtyards, basements, gardens, and apartment building hallways, on professional tables and on improvised ones. Competitions between youth clubs sprang up like mushrooms after a rain, disbanded, and formed again. This obsession with ping-pong continued for at least several months during the NDH.

With about fifteen of my friends and some older students I played at the Pubi Club, which was based in Dražen Blazina's courtyard and basement on Domobranska Street. Even today, in wistful conversations with Vlado Samardžija that I dare not call an old man's idle talk, I remember the boyish faces of our ping-pong friends, whom life and events scattered all over. Jole Dasović was killed as a Partisan "courier" in 1944 while trying to escape from pursuing Ustasha over a picturesque waterfall not far from Stativo, at the gentlest bend of the Dobra River. Miro Šrenger disappeared at Jasenovac with his entire family. Bogdan Lasić even then might have been a member of the League of Young Communists of Yugoslavia (SKOJ), and a year later he was a company commissar in the Zumberak Brigade. After the war, he became a political functionary in Karlovac and the director of the Museum of the Revolution in Zagreb. The driving force behind the Pubi Club and the organizer of all of our matches, Blazina, distraught by the unrequited love of the most beautiful girl in our school, turned into a notorious drunkard and bohemian in Karlovac in the years just after the war, only to be transformed by a happy marriage into a fine architect and the director of a large construction company in the city of Varaždin. To this day I remain very close to Stanko Lasić, thanks to the bonds of friendship and trust from childhood that, with a few bumps, we have essentially kept.

The competitions between the clubs continued for a time after the establishment of the NDH, perhaps with a bit less intensity. Preoccupied with other worries and obligations, I was no longer able to attend the training sessions regularly, but when I did no one disputed my place on the team. We once played against our closest neighbors, the Bobi Club. Their base was in the courtyard of the apartment building for employees of the local electric company on the corner of Zajčeva and Lisinski streets. Besides "Brcko" Rastovski and "Gaga" Bivala, both of whom were future members of SKOJ and future participants in the resistance movement, the other Bobi Club members were Marijan Koob, their best player, who was briefly a member of the Nazi-inspired Kulturbund, and Miro Sedlaček, a longtime and unrelenting sympathizer of Hitler and the NDH. Miro was a brilliant mathematician and the best student of his generation, but he was also one of the weakest players. When the match with Bobi was arranged, I was reluctant to take part—I don't know if it was because of my uneasiness at having to play against a member of the Kulturbund and a self-declared Nazi, or if it was out of fear that the two of them would demonstratively refuse to play with me. But nothing like that happened. Marijan, who was by nature an introvert and uncommunicative, was a little more restrained toward me than usual, but without a single insulting word or gesture. When he easily defeated me in the match, he didn't make a big show nor did he gloat. On the other hand, Miro was constantly talking to me, jovially but in a pushy, alternately pitying and patronizing way (he was four years older than me), with no nasty allusions but with an undisguised tone of affected superiority. It was all the sweeter for me when I defeated him in a match.

The best player by far in our club was Dori Kurelac, an exceptional ping-pong talent. He easily won all of the intra-club tournaments. Although I usually finished third or fourth in these competitions, Dori gladly accepted me as his partner in the doubles competition and, thanks to his skill, we usually won. I cannot say that we were close friends because we rarely socialized outside of the club, but we spent a lot of time together at the ping-pong table. For a time I went to his mother for French instruction. Mr. Kurelac was a widow who supported her two sons, Hanzi the eldest and Dori the youngest, by giving private German and French lessons. When the NDH was established, Hanzi quickly became active in the Ustasha Youth, but Dori never got involved. Ping-pong remained his favorite preoccupation.

I don't remember at whose invitation Dori and I, on borrowed bicycles, carrying our paddles and balls, went one May morning in 1941 to play an unusual match near Draganić. I have already mentioned that about two hundred Austrian Jewish refugees, mostly from Vienna, were living there in abandoned, dilapidated dwellings next to the railway station. Between 1934 and 1941 about fifty-five thousand refugees from the Third Reich passed through Zagreb. A reception office at the Zagreb Jewish Community helped the great majority of these refugees, about fifty-one thousand of them, obtain travel documents for Palestine or another country where they could settle. About four thousand of them didn't obtain visas in time; they were swept up in the war of April 1941 and the powerful fist of the Third Reich again hung over them. The two hundred refugees in Draganić were among the unfortunate ones. They included several musicians, some fine singers and scriptwriters, and a comedian who acted as a master of ceremonies. When my father and I visited them before the war, they put on a small show that I remember as being funny and cheerful, although the cheerfulness was certainly only a façade behind which I was too young to detect their concerns. That façade was no longer there when Dori and I came to play the scheduled ping-pong match on that spring day in 1941. In the early days of the NDH this place was still not a real camp. It appeared to be free and open, with no armed guards around it. But these people were caught in a trap—with no passports or any other kind of travel documents, there was nowhere to go, and they were condemned to wait helplessly for whatever might come. Some asked Dori and me who we were and where we were from; some recognized me from my earlier visits; some were amazed that we had come at all. I don't remember how the match went. But I think that Dori and I were subdued on the ride home through the forest around Draganić, still filled with the sadness that characterized that strange match in the refugee camp "*na bijelome hljebu.*"[4]

I don't know if any of the Viennese Jews at the Draganić refugee camp survived the war. Several were said to have left for Italy in the summer of 1941—with travel documents they had purchased, or perhaps without them—but who knows if they ever got there. In the fall of 1941, the Ustasha rounded up everyone who was left in Draganić. The entire group is said to have experienced real suffering in several transit camps, and if some remained alive in the NDH until August 1942, they were shipped in one of the four major transports of Jews from the NDH to Auschwitz. In Draganić only the memory remained of these two hundred unfortunate Viennese about whom even today, among the older people, many anecdotes are told, only one of which seemed like it would have a happier ending but still ended sadly, like the most sorrowful of ballads.

The tragic protagonist of that ballad is Oto Eisler, a violinist in a Vienna orchestra, who in 1939 found himself in the Draganić refugee camp along with two hundred of his Jewish compatriots. According to the original, romantic version, Oto was a sociable and charming man, so it came as no surprise when the most beautiful "white widow" in Draganić, whose husband was working abroad, fell in love with him. Oto fell in love with her, too. When the Ustasha police came to round up all the Jews, Oto happened to be at his lover's home. She artfully concealed him and kept him in hiding for the next three and a half years of the war. No one, not even her closest friends, knew her secret. In early May 1945, Oto was listening closely from his hiding place to the machine-gun and mortar fire approaching Draganić and, finally, to the skirmishes in the village itself. Everyone knew that the end of the war was near and that the German and Ustasha armies were withdrawing through Draganić to Zagreb. Once the firing had died down, Oto happily thought that it was all over at last. He came out of his hiding place to greet the Partisan liberators, but instead ran into the last Ustasha rear guard that was withdrawing from the village. He fell, cut down in a hail of gunfire, the last shooting in Draganić of the Second World War.

Mišo Klarić, my slightly older colleague from the Karlovac gymnasium and one of the first from Draganić to join the Partisans, told me this story forty years ago. But he didn't tell me what happened to Oto's unhappy, beautiful companion. She didn't stay in Draganić; perhaps she joined her husband, who never returned from overseas.

Recalling Mišo's story now, it sounds a little too much like a fairy tale. Mišo died a long time ago, so I had to turn to his friend Martin Vajdić and Martin's older brother, Francek. From them I learned a second, slightly less romantic but equally tragic and considerably more realistic story of the Viennese refugee, the violinist Oto Eisler. The father of the Vajdić brothers had been a successful businessman in Draganić as a pig breeder and producer of meat products. He exported goods to Austria, frequently traveled to Graz, and could speak German. He met and became close with some of the Jewish refugees housed in Draganić on the eve of the war. The refugees were not permitted to leave Draganić without special permits, but they were free to move about the village. Some of the refugee families had been given permission to move in with village residents, so the Vajdićes took in a married couple named Streicher. Some established close friendships with their hosts and the Vajdić brothers do not remember any frictions or difficulties in their relations with them. Speaking from my own knowledge and experience, I believe that incidents of anti-Semitism in Croatian villages were rare, certainly rarer than in some cities and towns.

The Vajdić brothers knew Oto, who, though he was said to have been a violinist in Vienna with a famous orchestra, was happy to play in restaurants and at various events in the village. His fiancée, a Croatian woman named Štefica, came several times from Vienna to visit him. She had been born in Sarajevo, but she had attended school in Vienna, and after graduating from higher music school had found work there as a singer in the Volksoper. This is where she had met Oto.

After the April war and the proclamation of the race laws in the NDH, Oto stopped playing in public in the village. The prevailing concern among the Jewish refugees was what the next day would bring. Francek remembers that their tenants, the Streichers, suddenly decided to cross Žumberak into a part of Slovenia that had then been annexed to Italy, but they returned after two or three days, disheartened. No one knows what prevented them from reaching Italy and escaping the fate of Jewish refugees that hung over them in the NDH.

Immediately after the establishment of the NDH, Štefica moved permanently to Draganić to be with Oto. They were quickly married and moved in with a widow at the lower end of the village, not far from the refugee camp and the railway station. The Catholic Church in the NDH had managed to arrange that Jews in mixed marriages be exempt from deportation to the camps, so Štefica hoped to save her Oto by marrying him. When in the late fall of 1941 a rather large Ustasha unit from Zagreb came to Draganić to round up the Jewish refugees, Oto was the only exception, thanks to his marriage to Štefica.

All the others were loaded into cattle cars and dispatched somewhere, no one knows where. The Streichers sent a letter to the Vajdićes from a transit camp, and the Vajdićes sent them a package of food. There was no response from the Streichers. The Vajdićes wrote two or three more times, sent another package or two of food, but there was still no answer. Nor were some of the other families from Draganić who inquired about the Jewish refugees able to learn anything.

Oto and Štefica remained in Draganić for the duration of the war. As a Jew, he was not able to obtain a permit to travel, but in the village, where they had made friends, they felt relatively safe. Because of the NDH's anti-Jewish laws, Oto was not allowed to perform publicly, so he worked at various jobs in several homes in the village in order to provide for Štefica and himself. Just before the end of the war, in April 1945, he was working in a hamlet not far from the railway station. A group of exhausted, draftee German soldiers were guarding the railway and had built a bunker next to the station. A man named Miha, an outsider from some distant region who was always trying to curry favor with his German bosses, was working on the construction. He denounced Oto as a Jew to a German noncommissioned officer. The German was a zealous soldier of Hitler's to the last breath. He arrested the denounced Jew and, since the battle was drawing near and a German retreat was imminent, had him executed on the spot—the last victim of the Holocaust on the territory of the NDH.

The aggrieved Štefica, with the help of several residents, laid out Oto's grave at the spot where he was killed, at the edge of the forest not far from the railway station and the bunker. After the war, some of the villagers would leave flowers on the grave from time to time. His widow went away, perhaps to Vienna or to Sarajevo. She returned after several months to Draganić. She had the remains of her husband exhumed and transferred, most likely to Sarajevo, where she continued to live after the war. Štefica remarried a well-known engineer, never returning to Draganić.

In the immediate postwar days in Karlovac, I also learned of the fate of my friend Dori Kurelac, who was my ping-pong partner on that last visit to the Viennese Jews in Draganić. I don't know under what influence or at whose urging, but in 1943 Dori was registered in the officer's school of the NDH Home Guard. He was killed in 1944 in his first skirmish with the Partisans; he was only eighteen years old. It saddened me to hear this right after I had returned to Karlovac, but at least, I thought, we didn't end up shooting at each other, for Dori had been killed in Slavonia, while at that time I was a commissar in the First Company, Second Battalion of the Karlovac Partisan detachment somewhere between the Kupa and Dobra Rivers.

Dori's brother, Hanzi, became a junior official in the Karlovac Ustasha Youth and a member of its elite unit known as the "storm troops." In the fall of 1944, he found a contact through whom he began to send intelligence information to the forest and quickly thereafter joined the Partisans. Allegedly, at the beginning of 1945, he was unmasked as an Ustasha double agent and executed.

Not long after the war, on a Karlovac street, I recognized a woman dressed in mourning. It was Mrs. Kurelac, visibly older, but still with her luxurious hair carefully groomed. Undecided about whether to go up to her or not, I greeted her awkwardly. Today, when I recall that scene, I am sorry that I did not approach Mrs. Kurelac. But what could or should I have said to a woman whose two sons had been killed only several months before by the hand of the army to which I belonged? That I am very sorry, but you know, it was wartime? Mrs. Kurelac wouldn't have known how to reply and would only have greeted me coldly. I don't remember if I ever saw her again.

8

The Strange Suicide of Filip Reiner

IN MY MOTHER'S terminology our living room was called the *Wohnzimmer*, but to Danko and me it was the "blue room" because everything in it—the upholstery of the armchairs, the wooden frames of the glass bookcases, the table and chairs—was blue. Early in May 1941, our friends Filip Reiner and his wife, Ružica Bonači Reiner, sat with us in that room.

Filip had been arrested on April 13, the same day as my father, and had spent about two weeks with him in the district court jail. When my father was sent to Zagreb with the first group of prisoners on April 26, Filip had been released from jail. During his interrogation by the State Security Administration in 1947, Vladimir Židovec claimed that it was through his intervention that Filip, his colleague from the bar association, had been freed from jail (which Židovec was in a position to do at that time as an influential member of the Karlovac Ustasha Council). Another version has it that Filip had been released because of the great services the Reiner family had rendered to the city of Karlovac and the unanimous respect they enjoyed in the city.

Filip's grandfather, who was also named Filip, had been the president of the Karlovac Jewish Community for thirty-five years (from

1863 to 1898); he was also the first well-to-do Jewish businessman to have a visible role and influence in the social life of the city. In his youth he had supported the Illyrian Movement,[1] which was popular in Karlovac. His wife, Tereza, had been the driving force behind the establishment of the City Beautification Association in 1886, while Filip senior was known as a patron of cultural and humanitarian activities. His younger brother Vilim, the longtime president of the choral society Zora, also promoted and organized the construction of Zorin Dom City Theater, the centerpiece of Karlovac cultural life from its opening in 1892 to this day. Filip's son Vatroslav, the father of our Filip, was the president of the Karlovac Jewish Community for thirty-two years (from 1908 to 1940) and a longtime member of the city council. He had served as the president of the Jury Commission of the Karlovac city council in the 1920s, which formulated an urban renewal plan that focused on the construction of pedestrian areas, gardens, parks, and the cultivation of green zones. Vatroslav was also the first Jew to become the deputy mayor of Karlovac. In the years before the war he made for quite a sight on the streets—the striking figure of an upright elderly gentleman with a neatly trimmed white beard, returning greetings from the many passersby by waving his cane, which he did with an elegance so typical of him. When he died in the fall of 1940, his was the largest funeral the Karlovac Jewish Cemetery had ever seen.

I don't remember what Filip said in our blue room about his time in jail with my father. I only remember that he was depressed and commented on the bad news in the newspapers, which he avidly read. Today, reading the newspapers of the NDH from April and May 1941 in the National and University Library, it is not difficult to imagine why Filip was depressed. The entire first page of the May 1 edition of *Hrvatski narod* is taken up with a headline in two rows of large red letters, THE BLOOD AND HONOR OF THE CROATIAN PEOPLE

PROTECTED BY SPECIAL DECREES, and two full pages of text stipulating three racial laws that stripped the Jews of their citizenship and deprived them of all legal protection. Just two days later, decrees for seizing the property of Jews and Serbs were published; eight days later came the decrees on the forced expulsion of Serbs and Jews and the confiscation of their apartments in the more attractive areas of the city; then the decree that made wearing the yellow symbol mandatory, followed by a whole series of increasingly harsh legal decrees on emergency and summary courts; and finally, in June, the first decree on sending people to the "transit and work camps." In its second edition of May 2, the Karlovac weekly *Hrvatska sloboda* had a commentary on these developments under the seemingly benign heading "Events in Croatia" and ominously threatened:

> Law after law is being enacted, one better than the next.... A thousand unnecessary existences will vanish, all of those who have lived here in propserity but have not benefited the people, only harmed them. Croatia will not remove that large, poisonous boil either with injections or pills. It will remove it, as it should, by a surgical procedure... [because] if you want to live as you should, the first rule is to get rid of the enemy in your house. This is surely clear to everyone,... Croatia is moving forward... it will crush whatever gets in its way.

It is also clear that after reading this proclamation Filip must have concluded that he could not survive long in Karlovac. Ružica had been born in Split, where the rest of her family still lived. Under the agreement between Italy and the NDH, she had a right to obtain a permit to travel to the place of her birth with her husband. I now think that when the Reiners were at our home in May 1941 they had come to say goodbye to us.

The closeness between my father and Filip had probably originated in the traditional friendship of the two families: my father's grandfather, my great-grandfather Aron Reich, the rabbi of Karlovac from 1853 to 1876, and Filip's grandfather, Filip Reiner, had jointly started the construction of the Karlovac synagogue, which was dedicated and opened in 1871, four years after the Zagreb synagogue. They were both Reform Jews, and as a result of their harmonious cooperation, Orthodox Jews never dominated the Karlovac Jewish Community. Their sons became friends, as did their grandsons, Filip junior and my father, during their student days in Vienna, when both were fervent Zionists. Their friendship continued after my father returned to Karlovac in 1929, after having lived for three years in Palestine. What brought them together was their shared intellectual skepticism of former Zionistic idealists who questioned, but never really abandoned, their youthful ideas. Filip was completely given to such skepticism, while characteristically my father's skepticism was tempered by his curiosity, activism, and powerful belief that in spite of everything one has to try to improve things.

When she came to Karlovac in 1934, Ružica—a language and literature teacher at the Karlovac high school, a poet, and a great lover of books—immediately became one of the most frequent visitors to our bookshop and a user of our lending library, as well as a frequent guest in our home. This is where Ružica and Filip were introduced and got to know each other before they eventually married. They lived in the Reiner family home (built in 1892), the most beautiful house in my memories of Karlovac, which also housed the law offices of Filip and his father. Today it is a music school.

Filip was a corpulent man, slow of movement, prone to reflection and, I think, to resignation. He spoke in a quiet, almost timorous voice but was always thoughtful, to the point, sometimes even bitterly humorous. Ružica was the opposite: short, thin, always lively, enterprising, and determined. They were the first married couple to escape in the direction that many others would follow—to areas under Italian authority, where the chances of survival for Jews were better.

The Reiners were warmly received by the Bonači family in Split. Between 1941 and 1943 the plucky Ružica was one of the organizers and instructors in the illegal Split high school. According to one of her poems, the school was "a cauldron of revolt, a beacon of defiance." With the increasingly sad news from Karlovac, Filip fell into a deep depression. Ružica told us after the war that he was full of dark foreboding and so never wanted to have children.

The capitulation of Italy in September 1943 and the arrival of the Partisans in Split gave the Reiners some short-lived encouragement. They both joined the auxiliary services of the National Liberation Army. When the Partisans had to abandon Split because of the advance of a German motorized column, Ružica and Filip went with them to join other Partisan units in Bosnia. They walked toward Omiš, south of Split along the coast, from where transport to Bugojno in Bosnia was to be organized. During the trip, Ružica became completely exhausted. A Partisan truck came along, picking up the sick and infirm. Filip put Ružica on the truck and told her to wait for him in Bugojno, but he never arrived. For days she anxiously waited for him, then for more than a year she looked for him, made inquiries in the Partisan commands in Bosnia and Dalmatia, but no one could tell her anything. It was only after the war that she learned what had happened to Filip. But what she learned was neither clear nor logical.

Filip never reached Omiš. He took the road back to Split. By the time he arrived, the Germans had entered the city. He didn't go to the Bonači family, so as not to expose them to danger. Instead, he went to the German headquarters and told them who and what he was. They put him in jail and several days later shipped him somewhere else.

This Ružica learned from a man who was in jail with Filip in the first days of the German occupation of Split. Another man reported that Filip had been sent from the jail in Split to a camp in Zemun, a suburb of Belgrade, and from there to his execution at Banjica.[2] But why didn't Filip continue on to Omiš after parting from Ružica? Why did he return to Split and calmly turn himself in? Ružica traced the explanation to the depression that had gripped Filip on several occasions in the past. In those moments he was convinced he would not survive the war. With his bleak sense of humor, he would imitate the ominous announcement in Hitler's speech to the Reichstag on January 30, 1939, that "if it comes to a world war, the consequence will be the complete destruction of the Jewish race in Europe." Filip had become obsessively convinced that Hitler would achieve his goal at any price, even if he lost the war. In such moments he surrendered to feelings of helplessness. He insisted that he was only a burden to Ružica and her family, he was beyond help. He perked up a bit during the brief Partisan occupation of Split. When he was forced to escape again into uncertainty, it seems it was too much for him. He said nothing to the exhausted Ružica, her well-being was his only concern, and when he put her into the truck on the road to Omiš, Ružica guessed that Filip surrendered to his obsession with the futility of the situation. If he had headed back to Split suffering such anguish, he did so believing this would free Ružica from her burden, her concern for him, a concern that was, in his eyes anyway, hopeless. He knew that surrendering to the Germans was tantamount to a suicide that he didn't have the strength to commit, so he consigned himself to the hand of fate.

For the rest of her life Ružica carried the trauma of her parting from Filip on the road to Omiš. After the war, she became a senior editor of *Kultura* in Zagreb and later of the Split newspaper *Slobodna Dalmacija* (Free Dalmatia) and a contributor to the Zagreb weekly *Naprijed* (Forward). She married Špiro Janović from Split, who like her had lost his spouse during the war. He was a highly regarded specialist in pulmonary diseases. They spent fifteen years in Sarajevo, where Janović organized a campaign to combat tuberculosis in Bosnia and Herzegovina. During and after the war, Ružica wrote poetry but was so harshly critical of her own work that she rarely published it. Only when she returned with Janović as a pensioner to Split (where they both died in 1986) did she edit and publish two collections of her poems, both dedicated to Filip.

9

The Sealed and the Unsealed Bookshop

AMONG THE LAWS that *Hrvatska sloboda* announced on May 2, 1941, was the Legal Decree on Normal Business and the Prevention of Economic Sabotage by which our bookstore would later be confiscated. Then on May 9, the Karlovac Directorate of the Provincial Police ordered that "all Jewish merchants must have a sign with 'Jewish Merchant' written in large letters on their shops within forty-eight hours." Trustees with great powers were appointed for those properties whose owners had fled, been expelled, or been arrested. We were fortunate because Mr. Rubes, a considerate and compassionate man, was made the trustee of our bookstore. As the director of the Municipal Savings Bank, which owned the building in which our bookstore was located, Mr. Rubes probably could not escape this responsibility.

Under his supervision the bookstore continued to operate for several more weeks, perhaps until the end of June, while my father was in jail in Zagreb. Then one morning, at the order of the Office for Economic Renewal, my mother and the bookstore manager, Mr. Rubčić, handed over the keys to Mr. Rubes and he locked up the shop. Yellowish-gray packing paper covered the display window and door was secured with an enormous black padlock and impressed with a large red wax seal. But before that, and since becoming "our" trustee, Mr. Rubes had allowed my mother to take all of the money from the daily receipts after business hours. Indeed, from the moment the sign "Jewish Merchant" had gone up business was considerably slower, but there was enough so my mother could exchange some of the earnings for Italian lira, which would later prove to be a lifesaver. A month or two later, when my mother was in jail, Mr. Rubes called me to the bookshop two or three times. We entered through the rear door in the courtyard each time and he allowed me to take some possessions, such as the gold Pelikan fountain pens. Thus, when the Directorate of Economic Renewal took over our bookshop officially in October, there was nothing of any real value in its inventory.

I don't think my mother was too saddened by the loss of the bookstore. As a child she had learned that, when life was at stake, it was not worth worrying about property. She had grown up on a large farm near Czernovitz in Bukovina (today part of the Ukraine), managed by her father, Salamon (Shlomo) Bril, who owned eight hundred sheep, forty cows, and many horses. My mother had just turned ten when the Cossacks swarmed out of the Carpathian Mountains and plundered all of Bukovina, including the area around Czernovitz, during the Russian offensive of 1914. My grandfather Shlomo (who died in 1922 and whom I know only from stories) loaded his four daughters and two young sons, his wife, Sabina, and her brother and his family into four horse-drawn wagons and headed west in a small convoy. They wandered as refugees for four years across half the Austro-Hungarian Empire, stopping for the longest stretch at a private camp near Vienna and at Budejovice, where my grandfather sold the horses and with the money joined in the production and sale of canned pickles.

According to my mother's sisters, it was at this time that my mother revealed her toughness in difficult circumstances and her talent for business, from purchasing cucumbers to decorating labels and selling canned pickles. When she returned to Czernovitz after the war, not quite sixteen years old, she was already making decisions for herself and knew what she wanted. She had become enthralled by Zionism, by the idea of a new homeland that she would build with her hands, and when she was barely eighteen she joined the first group of young people from Bukovina that went to Palestine. Before leaving, she had completed courses at an improvised secondary school in Czernovitz as a nurse and social worker. Like all Jews in Czernovitz, her education had been in German, but her schooling remained incomplete because of wartime circumstances. She spoke only German at home and never did learn to speak any other foreign language well, including Hebrew and Croatian. But she had other gifts: She was enterprising and diligent. She had a lively personality, resilience, and the ability to handle difficult situations, but she could also be rash. She was always ready to help, but also to seek help. Although she was short, she was very beautiful. In many ways my mother was the opposite of her future husband, who was a relatively tall man, prematurely bald, introspective, more inclined to books, dreaming, and intellectual pursuits.

My mother spent most of her five years in Palestine at the Bet Alfa kibbutz on the slopes of Mount Gilboa at the edge of the Jezreel Valley, where everything was communally owned. This probably deepened her sense that value lay in "being" and not in "having." And so in Karlovac in the 1930s when the bookstore had become successful enough for my parents to acquire things, it wasn't difficult for them to resist the temptation. We didn't become owners of either the house or the apartment we lived in, or of any property. As a passionate bookseller, my father used the earnings from his prospering business to expand the range of titles and other goods (typewriters, radios), while my mother preferred to spend the generous household allowance on outings into the surrounding countryside; on visits to relatives in Tuzla and Sarajevo, Bucharest and Czernovitz; on long summer vacations with her children at the seaside and in the mountains—basically on everything we would today call "quality of life," rather than on acquiring four walls and a bit of land.

I don't know how much my father was affected in jail by the news of the confiscated bookstore. The Karlovac cultural historian Marija Vrbetić has lauded my father as a "torchbearer of culture," the man for whom his "bookshop was the meaning and content of his life. He gave his bookshop the widest range of titles and the most noble meaning. He was the most humane connection between the written word and man."[1] True, my father spent a great deal of time in the bookshop, but it wasn't the only thing that gave "meaning and content" to his life. He also had other interests, pleasures, and concerns, such as family, friends, and public life. He took over the bookshop from his uncle Lisander Reich after returning from a three-year stay in Palestine at the beginning of 1928. He had moved to Palestine from Zagreb in January 1925 with a group of nine young men who had decided to build "a new homeland for the Jewish people," being among the first to do so from the Kingdom of the Serbs, Croats, and Slovenes.[2] My father had made his decision to go to Palestine while still in high school in Vinkovci. For this reason, after graduating in 1919 he studied agronomy in Vienna to build the most vital foundation of his new homeland, agriculture, instead of pursuing his deeper inclinations in literature and history.

In Palestine my father wasn't able to apply his knowledge of agronomy because the group encountered insurmountable difficulties. After two years of negotiations, they were unable to purchase the land for a collective farm in the immediate vicinity of Haifa because the British mandate authorities had decided to build a railway maintenance shop on the site. Palestine was in a serious economic crisis and unemployment was high. While waiting to acquire the land, my father and the other members of the group were barely able to survive by working from time to time as unskilled laborers in road construction and on the agricultural estates of Arab landowners.

Finally, by practically exhausting their budget, they managed to buy a parcel of land, smaller and less fertile than they had hoped, next to the Arab village of Jedda, about twenty kilometers southeast of Haifa. They then suffered through the drought and poor harvest of 1927, living a spare existence in four 3.5-square-meter huts—one was the common kitchen and dining area, another was used to store food and tools, and the other two served as sleeping quarters. Under such difficult living conditions the group began to break up: By the end of 1927 only three people remained of the original group along with three new arrivals. By then my father had married, my mother was pregnant, and they shared a small hut with two others from the group. Although my father tried to put a good face on this sad picture of his dream of a collective farm in his reports to the Zagreb weekly *Židov*, and probably in his letters to his parents, his shrewd and resolute mother, my grandmother Adolfa, saw the truth. At the same time, she knew that her elder brother Lisander wanted to stop working but had no one to whom he could entrust his well-established bookshop. So she arranged for Uncle Lisander to invite his nephew Ivo to come back from Palestine and, with a reasonable sale price and a satisfactory schedule of payment, to become the owner of the L. Reich Bookshop in the center of Karlovac. A passionate book lover living in extremely difficult conditions in Palestine simply couldn't resist such an attractive offer.

With a great deal of entrepreneurial zeal and well-conceived innovative ideas, my father threw himself into the business. The shop quickly expanded, and of the seven bookshops in Karlovac ours became by far the most successful. Some book lovers counted it among the cultural institutions of the small city in the 1930s.

My mother later told me that at first they had problems making payments to Uncle Lisander. They overcame them thanks to a substantial loan from their wealthy friends the Veličkovićes, whom they repaid within ten years. My father truly loved that bookshop. It allowed him to provide his family with a high living and cultural standard, and it kept him involved with books and with men of letters. Through books he acquired many acquaintances, several close friendships, and a fine reputation in the city. But I recall that at home he often showed fatigue from the demands and responsibilities of the work. One time my mother forced him to take a ten-day vacation on Lake Bohinj in Slovenia, but he brought me along and I am not really sure if my youthful curiosity and pestering afforded him a true vacation. However, another time he hastily packed his suitcase, took his three-volume edition of John Ruskin's *The Stones of Venice*, and went for eight days to Venice, a city that he loved passionately.

Again, I don't know how my father took the news in the Zagreb jail in June 1941 that the bookshop was no longer ours. I don't remember if he mentioned it at all when my mother and I visited him at Petrinjska Street and later at the Danica camp. He probably felt that the bookshop was no longer important because lives were at stake. His life and those of his wife and children.

* * *

The winds of war also scattered the staff of our bookshop. Zvonko Jaklić was originally a trainee with us for three years, then in 1938 he became an assistant. He loved motorcycles and speed. He learned to ride on the bookshop's old Dresch motorcycle, then two or three years before the war he bought his own bike with my father's assistance. He was a reliable delivery driver for books and other goods and a good assistant at the counter, even though he was often rash

Our bookshop and our old Fiat, Radić Street, a postcard from 1935

and sloppy. He enjoyed rushing around the city and making lots of noise, just like today's immature drivers with their powerful BMWs and Yamahas. He also took part in some local races. He could often be seen in the company of Josip Zgurić, a young boy with a violent temper, short and muscular, with a barely noticeable malicious grin. Zgurić and Zvonko were members of the United Workers' Union and some other leftist organizations.

I don't know when Zgurić joined the Karlovac Frankists, but on the evening of April 10, 1941, he was patrolling the city with a badge on his cap, a rifle on his shoulder, and a pistol in his belt. He immediately recruited his friend Zvonko, who obviously could not resist this new adventure. Jaga once saw them from our window, rushing through the square on Zvonko's motorcycle, both armed.

On Sunday, April 13, Zgurić participated in the first arrests. With a rifle held at the ready while crossing the railway bridge, he led Professor Sablić from his house in Banija to the city jail. The sense of power transformed the violent Zgurić into a dangerous brute. He quickly became the cruelest policeman in the city, a merciless torturer of prisoners and a killer, quick with knife and gun. In *Autobiografski zapisi* (Autobiographical Notes), Stanko Lasić cites documentary evidence that Zgurić killed twenty-two people with his own hands in 1944 in Stativo not far from Karlovac. He remained a troublemaker to the very end, always spoiling for a fight, as he was when he was killed on May 6, 1945, in Karlovac, on the left bank of the Kupa River during the last resistance to the Third Montenegrin Division of the National Liberation Army as it entered the city.

But Zvonko didn't follow Zgurić. I don't exactly know when he realized what evil Zgurić was drawing him into, but it must have been early on. After April 10, Zvonko didn't show up at our bookshop. Jaga had heard that Mr. Jaklić, Zvonko's prudent father, had forced his wayward son to leave Karlovac, quickly enrolling him in a recently established aviation school. Zvonko soon became an expert on aircraft and engine maintenance, and I don't know when or how, but definitely sometime during the war, he joined the Partisans.

For a long time after the war Zvonko did not show his face in Karlovac. Jaga attributed this not only to his shame for having associated with the notorious Zgurić but also to his fear that he might be prosecuted. Several years after the war, he suddenly appeared at our door in Zagreb in an air force uniform with the rank of captain. He had aged and was visibly heavier but was essentially the same person with his directness, harmless boasting, and tasteless humor. He told us that he was working at air force headquarters in Zemum outside of Belgrade, where he was a favorite of General Nenad Drakulić, "and we have known each other since before the war, when he was a regular in our bookshop." Mentioning my father, "the boss," Zvonko said that he was a "great authority figure," whom he nevertheless did not fear because my father was never unfair or rude. Of course, Zvonko no longer treated me as he had before the war, as a boy who was eight years younger, still a child, but as a man from whom he had come to ask a favor. The time had now come for his promotion to major. He had prepared for the examinations and was sure he would pass them, but his past would again be scrutinized, this time more closely because he was being promoted to the rank of a senior officer. Would I write a statement that while he had been employed in our bookshop he had been engaged in disseminating progressive literature and had been a member of leftist organizations? Together we drew up a statement that I signed for him. Zgurić wasn't mentioned either in the signed statement or in the course of our long, and generally pleasant, conversation that day.

A month or two later, an air force officer whose name and function I have forgotten called on me. I remember clearly that he immediately said he wished to discuss "your statement, Comrade Goldstein, about Zvonimir Jaklić" and that he was bringing greetings from General Drakulić, my good acquaintance from Karlovac and from my Partisan days. Without mincing words, the officer asked why I had not mentioned Jaklić's association with the "criminal Zgurić" in my statement, about which they had some knowledge but wished to be fully informed since it pertained to Jaklić's promotion. I told the truth: Zvonko did associate with Zgurić, but it was more a matter of a misguided youthfulness that should not influence any current judgment about him. In my opinion, Zvonko had gradually distanced himself from Zgurić and had not been involved in Zgurić's crimes or, more generally, with the Ustasha regime.

I don't know what happened to Zvonko, but I heard that he retired relatively young with the rank of major from the Yugoslav air force. This might have meant that his commanding general, Nenad Drakulić, the youngest member of a prominent Karlovac family and the commander of the Yugoslav air force until his unexpected death from a stroke, had given his townsman the gift of a promotion to the rank of major in spite of the misgivings, but didn't allow him further promotions and quickly retired him.

* * *

My father was considerably closer to our slightly older assistant, Dragec Starešinić, than to Zvonko, and I remained close to him for my entire life, until the day in 1993 when we said our last goodbyes to him at his grave in the Miroševac Cemetery, and where at the request of his family I was the last speaker. Dragec had come to our bookshop to serve his apprenticeship in 1929 as a fourteen-year-old boy whose poor family with seven children couldn't afford to support him after his completion of the second year of gymnasium. They lived in Logorište, an outlying village that today is a suburb of Karlovac. Working hours in the bookshop were from 7:00 a.m. to noon and from 4:00 p.m. to 7:00 p.m., and the distance from Dragec's home to the bookshop was about six kilometers. Dragec had to cover this distance on foot at least twice a day, and frequently four times a day if he wanted to go home for lunch during the afternoon break because he didn't have the money to buy lunch in the city. My parents quickly noticed that he had a weak physical constitution and was always tired. One day my mother invited him to come to our house for lunch instead of going to Logorište. Dragec became animated and immediately offered to repay my mother by doing odd jobs around the house for the remainder of the break. He regularly came to our house for lunch during the entire time he was a trainee and an apprentice in the bookshop. He would do favors for my mother, but more often he would go around town and offer people books from our bookshop. Marija Vrbetić recalled this in her already quoted *Karlovac Anthology 1579–1979*: "Dragutin Starešinić, better known to the people of Karlovac as Dragec or 'the little Reich,' the apprentice and later the assistant in the Goldstein bookshop, distributed newly published books and magazines to the homes of those residents he thought would be interested, 'Please, look at it, if you don't like it, return it,' he would say, but very few people ever returned the book." Dragec's nickname "little Reich" made him feel honored; after taking over the bookshop, my father had kept its old name, "L. Reich," which had been introduced in 1885 after the shop's cofounder Lisander Reich.

Dragec loved books, but he didn't read many. He had the rare bookseller's ability to understand the contents and attributes of a book by listening to other people talk about it, thereafter convincingly passing this information on to an interested customer. That pleasant intimacy—warm, unobtrusive, and honest—was the nicest of Dragec's qualities. He was not excessively intelligent or an interesting conversationalist, but his directness, honesty, and readiness to help, with no expectation of payback, won him many friends.

Before the war Dragec was friendly with Branko Priselac, our bookkeeper, who became the director of the Zagreb edition of the daily *Borba* after the war, and with Veco Holjevac, the future mayor of Zagreb, who at one time was an assistant in the textile shop of Šandor Weiss, which was next door to our bookshop. The three of them were also members of the United Workers' Union and the SBOTIČ (Alliance of Bank, General, Commercial, and Industrial Clerks), and a leftist scouting group (as a young boy, I went with them on some of their outings). At the beginning of 1938, they came to the attention of Ivo Marinković, a teacher of classical philology, the leader of the Karlovac communists, and an energetic party organizer, who also frequented our bookshop. After the war, Dragec told me how one night after the close of business Marinković invited him for a short walk and suggested he become a member of the clandestine Communist Party. Dragec was confused; he told Marinković he would ask "what the boss thinks of this," meaning my father, but the boss told Dragec that he would have to decide for himself. Thus, Drago, the popular "little Reich," along with Priselac and Holjevac, became a member of the first communist cell within the Karlovac branch of the leftist SBOTIČ.

When the Independent State of Croatia (NDH) was established, Dragec continued to come to our house and to help out in the bookshop. After the war, we retrieved some of our more valuable items that my mother stored in his house, save two typewriters that Dragec gave to the Karlovac resistance movement and my father's winter coat. Dragec wore the coat when he joined the Partisans. My mother burst into tears when she met Dragec in newly liberated Slunj in November 1942. I don't know whether it was from the joy of seeing Dragec or from seeing my father's coat. Danko, who witnessed that emotionally charged meeting in Slunj, remembers how funny Dragec was, tongue-tied and befuddled about how to address my mother, the wife of his former employer: with the prewar "madam" or with the Partisan address "comrade," or as "Mrs. Goldstein," or simply as "Lea." At my mother's insistence he used "Lea," but for a long time, he would still get confused and slip into using "madam."

The physically frail Dragec was assigned to the rear services in the Partisans, first as a commissar in a hospital in Lika and then for a time as the chief of some supply section. After the war, he briefly headed a department in Jugoslavenska Knjiga, a publishing house in Belgrade. Since he was not cut out for a supervisory position, they sent him first to Tirana and then to Prague to set up small bookshops in Yugoslav cultural offices. It soon became obvious that he wasn't capable of independent organizational work, so at his own request he was transferred to Zagreb. I think that the personnel section of the Central Committee of the KPH faced a quandary: a party veteran with prewar membership and a clean record—in the terminology of the day a "deserving comrade"—whom they could not possibly assign to a low-level position but who demonstrated neither the capability for nor the willingness to accept a more senior position. So, as a "verified cadre," Dragec was assigned to internal affairs, but even there they did not know what to do with him. With his easy-going character, good-natured, sociable and talkative, he obviously was not suited to the "hard" jobs in a ministry of internal affairs, but he was a "deserving comrade" and they had to give him a job. Finally he was appointed the chief of control in the department for the importation of books, magazines, and newspapers as a censor of sorts. In practical terms, he had to decide what could and what could not be delivered to the addressee. I don't believe that he ever became a good chief of censorship, but I do know that he always was, and he remained, a loyal friend. During this time, in the 1950s and 1960s, he would knock on our door, unannounced, and in a muffled, conspiratorial voice warn me, "Be careful, you've been blabbering again.

They're reading your mail. And I think they're listening to your telephone conversations, be careful what you say." When we moved from apartment to apartment, he was of assistance to my mother, brother, and me, especially with books, among which he happily, if wistfully, recognized those from our bookshop, and which "your dad, the boss, liked very much." Later he quickly became close with my wife and then with my sons.

I think he was one of those rare people who didn't know how to be unhappy. And his death too was gracious: It had let him live in peace for seventy-eight years and then quickly took him away, when a heart attack made his memory weaker and made it difficult for him to walk. Dying did not torment him long.

* * *

Our chief assistant and head clerk in the bookshop, Miroslav Rubčić, was of all of us the most deeply attached to the book trade. I don't think he had any other interests or pastimes, with the exception of occasional solitary jaunts into the nearby woods to hunt. He was a man of great restraint and little humor, exceptionally tall, a little stooped, and of a timid character. He spoke slowly, calmly, and never raised his voice. He often stayed in the bookshop after hours to settle the accounts, straighten the items on the shelves, and, just in case, remove the gold Pelikan fountain pens from the display window and lock them in the cash box overnight.

Two or three years before the war, Rubčić married Marija Šomek, a saleswoman in the local shoe store. Her brother, a bank clerk named Franjo Šomek, became an active member of the Ustasha movement immediately after the proclamation of the NDH, and perhaps secretly before then. On July 16, 1941, he was appointed to a prominent position in the Ustasha organization for the Karlovac district. At the very beginning of the NDH, when the bookshop was still under our ownership and open for business, Rubčić managed it conscientousły and promptly carried out my mother's directions. However, in the fall of 1941, when none of the Goldstein family was in Karlovac any longer (and my father was no longer alive), Rubčić started a procedure with the assistance of his Ustasha brother-in-law to acquire the bookshop. In the spring of 1942, according to the regulations on the disposal of nationalized Jewish property then in effect, he took over the bookshop and registered the ownership in his name. This was nominally a purchase, but one reserved for privileged buyers such as Rubčić, thanks to his relationship with Šomek. The purchase price was minimal, practically a gift. In May 1942, the "L. Reich" sign disappeared and was replaced by "Miroslav Rubčić, Bookseller and Stationer." Who knows, perhaps this was Rubčić's long-nurtured secret dream and he could not resist the temptation to realize it, even though it was on terms that were unpleasant to him, I believe.

For the three remaining years of the war Rubčić managed the bookshop diligently and successfully. When he took it over the stock was lean because the trustee, Mr. Rubes, had allowed my mother and me to take quite a few items, and the rest was snapped up by various Ustasha institutions scrambling over the abandoned property of Karlovac Jews.[3] Branko Mikašinović told me after the war that in front of the Ustasha Council in the fall of 1941 he saw a large pile of books from our lending library, probably books considered "objectionable," readied for burning. He had apparently succeeded in pulling from the pile Maxim Gorky's *Childhood*. Rubčić, of course, didn't try to replenish the lending library—the expense would have been too great—but he was a capable businessman and regularly restocked the shelves with the most sought-after items, especially school necessities and paper products. And so, when we returned to Karlovac immediately after the liberation in 1945, the stock was not what it had been at the beginning of 1941, but it was more than what Rubčić had received in 1942.

Two or three days after we had returned, and my mother, brother, and I were still settling in, an officer from the Department for the Protection of the People, by the name of Ivo Trgovčić, a tailor in prewar Karlovac, came looking for us. "We have arrested Rubčić because he appropriated your bookstore. We have him in jail, but he claims that he did it in agreement with you in order to save the bookshop, and he is asking to see Slavko, whom he had last seen in the fall of 1941," Trgovčić reported. With mother's approval I went with Trgovčić to the district court jail, and he arranged for me to speak to Rubčić in private.

At this time I was still wearing my olive-drab uniform (compliments of the British) with Partisan insignias for my rank of lieutenant and a revolver at my waist. Rubčić was visibly frightened. In a trembling voice he gave me a muddled account of how in "those days," when the Germans had invaded Yugoslavia before the NDH had been proclaimed, "our boss, your father" knew that the Germans would be victorious and that "Hitler would also become the master here." He then alleged that my father had told him it was possible that the property of the Jews would be confiscated, just as in Germany and Austria. If it came to that, "the boss said he would turn the bookstore over to me, sign it over to me, in order to save it, and after the war I would return it to the boss, your father." He said he was sorry about what had happened to my father, but he would continue faithfully to manage the bookshop for my mother, brother, and me, as, of course, it was still ours, and he, of course, didn't deny that. He also mentioned something else, rather unconvincingly, about how he had mentioned to me, and just to me, all of this when we had last seen each other in front of the closed bookshop in the fall of 1941, but "you don't remember this, it's understandable, you had bigger concerns, you didn't know at the time if your father was still alive and how to save your own head."

My mother thought that there was no truth in any of Rubčić's story. If there had been any such conversation with Rubčić, my mother claimed "Fati would have at least mentioned it."[4] But she added that if Rubčić had not taken over the bookshop, someone else would have, and perhaps it would have been worse and nothing would have remained of it. At least this way there was something left of the bookshop. "To hell with him. Go and sign, no sense in him losing his life because of us, but I won't sign anything for him," my mother concluded.

I didn't really believe Rubčić's story about his agreement with my father, either, and I was certain that Rubčić hadn't mentioned anything to me during our last conversation in the fall of 1941. However, knowing that my father had given money to Mata Đerek to build an extension on his house for us "just in case," I allowed myself a few more doubts than my more resolute mother: Perhaps my father had hinted at something to Rubčić, perhaps Rubčić had not made all of it up. And so, with my mother's blessing—"to hell with him"—I signed a statement for Trgovčić that got Rubčić out of jail, where he had spent four days. I don't have that statement, but in Rubčić's folder there are two statements that I signed for him to confirm his employment record and his right to vote: "I confirm that Miroslav Rubčić, my late father's business manager, per previous agreement with my father, in May 1942 purchased our confiscated bookshop from the Hrvatski Radiša cooperative in order to protect the property from plundering by the occupier and his allies. It was expected under the agreement that after the war the property would be returned to the owner, i.e., my father, but since my father was killed, Miroslav Rubčić has transferred it to me, as a completely proper transaction, as an inheritance... SFSN[5]—signed: Slavko Goldstein." By a decision of the People's District Court of Karlovac of June 15,1945, the bookshop was restored to our family, but now we faced a decision: What do we do with it? Both my mother and I knew that in the new Yugoslavia private ownership had no future. Although the government leadership had not yet announced anything official, it was clear to anyone who had tried to penetrate the foggy phraseology of the long articles by Edvard Kardelj[6] being published in the Serbian newspaper *Borba* that the country would be moving toward a Soviet model: industry and commerce under state ownership, collectivized agriculture, centralized power, and a one-party political system. I have to admit that at that time I saw nothing wrong with this. I was seventeen years old. I had not attended school for four years. I had been in the war for three years, a member of the League of Young Communists of Yugoslavia for three years, and a member of the Communist Party for almost a year. An inclination for critical thinking had been planted in me by my father, but he had been absent too long to cultivate and develop the seed. It had been stunted by the war years and only in the months after the war had it begun to awaken, in a disappointing encounter with the "brutal reality of the new era." During the war, I only rarely saw my mother, just here and there on a given day, too little to absorb her common sense and logic of life. My war experience had rendered me totally indifferent to ownership, to the small-minded obsession with property. Influenced by communist ideology, the only one I was exposed to in my three war years, I found commerce repulsive, and since in the early postwar period a new bureaucracy demanded the filling out of endless forms, I felt uneasy every time I had to fill in the box "profession" with "merchant." I said to my mother, "Let's donate the bookshop to the state before the state takes it from us!" I thought that would be a nice gesture of solidarity with the new state, in which I still strongly believed. The state had grown out of a movement that was on the right side in the war, opposing what was then the most murderous horror, and in those first weeks I still had no inkling that our new state would betray that movement.

My mother, of course, was more sensible than I and did not share my boyish enthusiasm. She agreed that I had to make up for the school years that had been taken from me, to finish gymmnasium and enroll at university in a course of study that suited my inclinations (which at the time were philosophy, literature, and history). There was no sense in devoting myself to a commercial enterprise, my mother agreed, even if it meant the selling of books. Under socialism commerce would be neither attractive nor profitable. My mother had already taken a job as the director of a large foster home for children who had lost their parents in the war, a job in her professional calling as a social worker that she took to enthusiastically. She agreed to donate the bookshop to the government, but not right away. We had to build a home for ourselves from scratch, we needed everything—clothes, shoes, healthy food for my brother and me to make up for years of poor nutrition—and only the bookshop could provide that for us. We had to keep it going, at least until the new year.

We hired Rubčić as the business manager. He wholeheartedly threw himself into the work and, before long, convinced us to give him greater responsibilities. My mother authorized me in her name and in the name of my underage brother to represent all three of us in the management of the bookshop. And so during the day I was studying for my high-school examinations and enjoying the return to a normal life, the rekindling of old friendships, my first great love, and lovers' walks along the Korana, but every evening at seven I was in the bookshop, where Rubčić reported on the day's activity and I dealt with any problems that might have come up. He left all decisions to me. I, of course, consulted with my mother, and I think that in those six or seven months—observing capable Rubčić at work and with commonsense advice from my mother—I did learn something about the bookselling business.

Rubčić brilliantly organized the fall school season. The bookshop was swarming with old and new students and residents and had more customers than all of the other Karlovac bookshops combined. Sensing that we were pleased with his management, Rubčić requested a salary increase, or two percent of the total amount of sales. My mother and I approved both because it was obvious that the bookshop would give us what we had expected from it: resettling into our home and a return to the standards of a normal urban life—far from our prewar standards, indeed, but adequate given the circumstances in a country devastated by war.

Early in 1946, I went to the publishing-bookselling company Kultura in Zagreb, where our friend Ružica Bonači Reiner was working. I proposed that the Goldstein family donate the bookshop to them under certain conditions: Until the transfer was finalized we would not restock the inventory and the proceeds of the sale of the remaining stock would belong to us. I recommended that they retain Rubčić as the manager. My mother didn't want to participate in the negotiations or in any other part of the transfer because she was overcome with grief. She said her "heart ached" that we were letting go of my father's bookshop, even though she herself maintained that it was the most logical course of action, and it was she who formulated the conditions of the transfer that I was negotiating.

On January 31, 1946, Kalman Vajs, a representative of Kultura, came from Zagreb to inspect the inventory and records, and we signed a contract on the donation and transfer. I don't remember why the procedure lasted until June 28, 1946; I only know that during that period I went to the bookshop less frequently. It was a transition period, in accordance with the contract. Rubčić continued to manage the business and reported to both me and Vajs on anything of importance. On August 1, 1946, the small temporary sign "Owner, Slavko Goldstein" disappeared from the façade and was replaced by "KUL-

TURA: Bookseller and Stationer." My mother was pleased when the transfer was completed and we received the remaining cash due us under the contract, but for a long time she would not walk past the bookshop.[7] For my part, I was relieved that I no longer had to write "merchant" in the box under "profession" on official records. I had been appointed director of the local movie theaters Edison and Banija, and on my official records I could now write "cultural worker" as my profession.

Rubčić continued to manage the Karlovac bookshop Kultura, as a branch of the Zagreb company that was later renamed Naprijed (Forward). Marija Vrbetić wrote that this bookshop, thanks to "the oldest living bookseller in Karlovac, Miroslav Rubčić, before the war an assistant and manager in the Reich-Goldstein bookshop," was the best in Karlovac, "approaching the range of books and book-related items and various cultural activities of today's large bookselling establishments." In his quiet, persistent way Rubčić rather quickly entered the political life of the city. In one document from his folder, dated December 16, 1950, he writes: "From the liberation of our country until today I have actively worked in the building of socialism and actively participated in all mass organizations and worked on all issues in the city of Karlovac. I am a member of the Executive Committee of the National Front for the City of Karlovac and this year in the elections for the organs of the people's government, I was elected a commissioner for the National Committee for the City of Karlovac." It is apparent from the document that during this time Rubčić was a member of the Communist Party, of which I had not been a member for some time.

After 1947, I didn't go often to Karlovac and was only in the Naprijed bookshop that Rubčić managed a few times. He would greet me with a strange combination of friendly talk and cold restraint. Timid by nature, perhaps he was afraid I would bring up unpleasant topics from 1941 and 1942. I never mentioned them. He spoke rather optimistically about the good sales but complained about the limited interest in publications of literary value, more limited than before the war. Rubčić retired in 1970 and I did not see him again.

Five or six years ago I had a call from someone who had moved into Rubčić's apartment after his death. He told me that in some out-of-the-way corner he had found a fat folder with Rubčić's papers, among which was a document with my signature about Rubčić's acquisition of our bookshop. Was I interested? Of course I was interested. That was how I came by documents that have assisted me in faithfully reconstructing the story of our bookshop.

10

Cherchez les Juifs

ON SATURDAY AND Sunday, June 21 and 22, 1941, my mother was in Koprivnica with Jaga, visiting my father. Three days earlier she had sent a request to the Ministry of Internal Affairs that my father be interrogated in the camp, then permitted to go home. Knowing her, I assume she had found a connection or had obtained a referal to someone in Koprivnica through whom she hoped to sway the local authorities to act on her request.

So as not be left alone for two nights and a day, Danko and I had gone with Dragec Starešinić to his house in Logorište. The village extended along the Korana River and a road that meandered toward a cluster of military barracks at the end of the village. The Starešinić family lived in a single-story brick house that was rather cramped for Dragec, his parents, and his two younger brothers, so Dragec's mother made beds for Danko and me in the barn behind the house, where we enjoyed the fragrance of the hay, a rare experience for city kids.

There was a meadow behind the house that extended to the banks of the river, visible in the distance. The days were sunny and warm. We walked along the overgrown riverbanks, watched men fishing, and briefly swam in the cold waters of the Korana. Dragec forced us to learn how to say quickly "*Kotlokrpa kotle krpa iza kotlokrpine kuće*"[1] and another tongue twister that began "*Jakci, Jakci drakci, Jakci droni.*" Dragec's mother was forever urging us to eat and to drink "the healthiest milk in the world, still warm, right from the cow." She was especially affectionate with Danko, more affectionate than the usual hospitality dictates. A woman exhausted by many births and a difficult peasant life, stooped a bit and appearing older than her years, she hovered over Danko with care and attention.

When today I read the anti-Jewish Ustasha laws, I again feel grateful to the Starešinić family. They had taken some of our posessions for safekeeping, knowing that they were exposing themselves to danger. But they showed no signs of concern. The Laws on the Registration of Jewish Property of June 5, 1941, called for strict penalties in "criminal acts" like those that the Starešinićes had committed, taking in unregistered "persons of the Jewish race" and accepting their property for storage and safekeeping. After the war, I would mention this to Dragec, but he did not respond. Only once, when we were reminiscing about his mother and I asked him about her special affection for Danko, did he talk. It was in the summer of 1987. My eldest son, Ivo, was about to get married and we had moved from a larger apartment into two smaller ones. Dragec, of course, had come to help us move. A master at packing books, he was preparing our library for the move and I was helping him. That was when he told me the strange story about his mother.

In 1929, when my parents invited the new apprentice, the young Dragec, to have lunch with us every day, his mother was very happy. Her reed-thin fourteen-year-old would no longer have to walk home to Logorište and back during the afternoon break. She boasted in the village that her son was employed by "kind people" and would soon be an assistant in a good bookshop.

All went well until the beginning of 1932, when Dragec announced at home that my mother was expecting a baby. Dragec's mother was flabbergasted. "My son, don't go to their house anymore," she cried out, "I pray to God and implore you!" For the baby to be born healthy, she explained to Dragec, Jews had to drink virgin Christian blood. Dragec's mother knew this for certain because when she was a child, some Jews in Hungary had slashed the throat of a young Catholic girl so they could drink her virgin blood, and this had become known around the world. "Maybe they don't slash throats anymore, maybe they just make a small wound in a Christian child to get a little blood, but my son, just wait until your kind mistress gives birth. They have to drink at least a little virgin Christian blood to wash away their original sin, which they carry in themselves for nailing our Lord Jesus Christ to the cross."

The then seventeen-year-old Dragec, a boy who had for three years grown up among books and book lovers, didn't believe a word of this, but he was unable to dissuade his mother. She had decided to seek the counsel of their parish priest, which is how she found out that long ago there had been cases here and there of Jews being convicted of taking the blood of Christian children, and even though nothing had been heard about it in more recent times, one had to be cautious—the Devil never sleeps. Maybe the Jews are now taking only a little blood from the wound of a child; maybe they believe this is the only way to wash away their original sin.

To calm his mother, Dragec had to promise that he would be careful when in our house. However, every morning that spring his mother would see him off with great anxiety and would greet him with relief when he returned home in the evening. He continued to have lunch with us without any worry and was ashamed to mention his mother's fears to us. The poor woman finally breathed more easily and was again happy when my mother gave birth to a healthy boy on April 16, 1932, and Dragec was still alive and healthy. Later, Dragec's mother invited Danko and me several times to come on weekends, like the weekend in June 1941, for "fresh cheese and cream" and "fresh milk right from the cow." It was her modest, religious way of atoning for the "sin" she had committed because of an ugly suspicion.

After hearing the story of Dragec's mother I immediately wrote it down. As I started writing this book, I searched for the sources of her story and may have found them.

In the spring of 1882, Eszter Solymosi, a fourteen-year-old Catholic girl, disappeared in the northern Hungarian town of Tiszaeszlar on the eve of Passover. Rumors quickly spread, followed by a public accusation that Jews from Tiszaeszlar had lured the girl into the synagogue, cut her throat, and mixed her blood into the ceremonial unleavened bread for Passover. This is one of several variations of the classic accusations of ritual murder that led to the mass persecutions of and innumerable deaths among many members of Europe's Jewish communities from the twelfth century on.[2]

At that time, Tiszaeszlar was a town of about 2,700 residents, including twenty-five Jewish families, and Dragec's mother was an infant. The district chief, a local priest, and a local representative to the Hungarian parliament publicly supported the rumors that local Jews had carried out the ritual murder of Eszter Solymosi. On that basis the district court in the neighboring town of Nyiregyháza initiated criminal proceedings against fifteen Jews from Tiszaeszlar who had been arrested as suspects. The trial lasted more than a year. It gave rise to sharp polemics in the parliament in Budapest and divided the public in the countries of the Austro-Hungarian Empire between liberals and anti-Semites. Its echoes reverberated throughout Europe: In France the voice of the great poet and national tribune, the elderly Victor Hugo, once again sounded the alarm against the wave of anti-Semitism, as a kind of prelude to the Dreyfus affair against which Émile Zola would thunder some fifteen years later. In several regions of Hungary there were pogroms that destroyed a great deal of Jewish property and led to the mistreatment of many Jews and several deaths. Göyzö Istóczy, the leader of the anti-Semitic movement in Hungary at that time, founded a political party that advocated the forced emigration of Jews to Palestine. Even after all fifteen of the Tiszaeszlar suspects were acquitted by the district court in Nyiregyháza, and after that decision was upheld by the Supreme Court in Budapest in May 1884, Istóczy's anti-Semitic party won seventeen seats in the Hungarian parliament in elections that same year, despite condemnations of the anti-Semitic hysteria by the Hungarian prime minister Kalman Tisza, the state prosecutor Sandor Korma, and even Emperor Franz Josef himself. Nor did the campaign cease later, when circumstances and subsequent information clearly proved that Eszter Solymosi, alleged to have been murdered by local Jews, had committed suicide by throwing herself into the Tisza River.

Independently from the trial in Nyiregyháza, disturbances had broken out in many parts of Croatia in 1883 to protest the placement of bilingual (Hungarian and Croatian) coats of arms in institutions in Croatia. However, influenced by the wave of anti-Semitism in Hungary and rumors of the trial in Nyiregyháza, the anti-Hungarian demonstrations in some places in Croatia were accompanied by loud demands of "Jews out!"—because they were Christ-killers, child-killers, blood-drinkers, loan sharks, and pro-Hungarian unionists. In Zagreb and Samobor and in some villages in the provinces of Varaždin and Koprivnica the initial anti-Hungarian slogans were accompanied by calls of "Let's get the Jews!", the breaking of Jewish shop windows, and the destruction and looting of wine cellars and commercial establishments.

For the most part, the Croatian intelligentsia, political leaders, and newspapers opposed the wave of anti-Semitism. On August 9, 1883, *Pozor* (Attention), the most influential newspaper of the time, wrote: "If these Jews were murderers, and they are not, that guilt should not be placed on all Jews." And in the issues of September 7 and 14, *Pozor* reported: "There are people who would gladly provoke anti-Semitism at any price," therefore "everyone should be on guard against scoundrels who come here from Hungary to incite people against the Jews, to turn our poor people into criminals, the same as those in Hungary." On June 25, 1883, *Narodne novine* (National News) called the accusations of ritual murder "a medieval assassination of the Jews" and "an act of savagery." During the Nyiregyháza trial, only *Slododa* (Freedom), the newspaper of the Croatian Party of Rights, expressed anti-Semitic sentiments in its editorials, such as these from August 5 to 15, 1883: "The Jews are guilty of a crime that, if it were proven, would have to prompt the Christians to expel all the Jews from their countries. Thus...Jews would be bribing anybody and everybody.... As long as the Jews ruthlessly exploit the Christians, as long as the Christians have no legal protection, there will be no peace between them." Once the Nyiregyháza trial ended in late August with the acquittal of the accused and a clear understanding that the entire affair had been fabricated as a political attack against liberals, such editorials no longer appeared. However, several politicians in the Croatian Party of Rights continued to cultivate aggressive anti-Semitism. Among the most vehement was Grga Tuškan, who became the chief advocate of anti-Semitism in Croatia at the end of the nineteenth and the beginning of the twentieth century.

In 1883, Dragec's village was part of the district of Švarča, where Tuškan was sowing his anti-Semitic hatred. As a child, Dragec's mother may have frequently heard the gruesome stories about the fourteen-year-old girl whose throat the Jews had cut in some Hungarian village and about the fourteen-year-old Jewish boy watching his father drain the blood from the open wound into a pitcher.[3] The fears of Dragec's mother for her son in 1932 show that while the ghost stories from childhood may have faded, they were not completely forgotten. Her insistent hospitality in 1941, when conditions were extremely dangerous, was her way of apologizing to the Jewish boy whose birth had aroused the grotesque suspicion that her son would be killed. I wonder to what degree such stories of evil from long ago were still in the subconscious of people in 1941. To what degree did those old stories account for the suffering that year and in the succeeding years? And to what degree did some other stories of evil account for the sufferings in 1945, 1991, 1995, and many other years?

* * *

After sleeping in the hayloft that June, Danko, Dragec, and I drank fresh milk "right from the cow" on the small back porch of the Strarešinićes' house. As on the previous day, Dragec's mother continued offering us cheese, cream, and homemade bread. The sun had already risen high in the southeast above the Slunj hills. In the meadow leading to the Korana River the dew was disappearing into a mist. Veco Holjevac emerged from that mist, beaming with a broad smile and happy news: "Russia is in the war! Everything is all right now. Russia is at war with Germany. Hitler is in for it now. The Red Army will show him!"

I don't know if the famous Partisan commissar and mayor of Zagreb was ever again as glowingly optimistic as the morning he heard on the radio that the German army had invaded the USSR. He and Dragec were talking, laughing, and clapping each other on the back. Veco pushed a small bundle, perhaps some leaflets, into Dragec's hand and rushed off. Perhaps he had already seen himself running to meet the Red Army and submitting a report as an underground communist activist to the first Red Army officer he encountered. Even Danko understood that something good and great was happening—"The Russians will come!" We told him that it was indeed so, that it was wonderful, but that he had to keep quiet about it, say nothing to anyone, because it was dangerous. Danko understood because the times were such that even a nine-year-old boy knew whom and what to fear.

Perhaps I still could not understand, but I must have had some inkling that my family and I were no longer deciding our fate. It was being decided someplace far from us, in cities and towns that we did not know and had never heard of, cities and towns named Mozhaysk, Vyazma, and Bryansk, or Sidi Barrani, Marsa Matruh, and Tobruk. That is why I anxiously stopped every day at the side wall of Mataković's coffeehouse, where there was a large map of the Ukraine, Byelorussia, and Russia labeled "The Eastern Front." In the last days of June pins with small German flags were rapidly spreading to the east, leaving ever farther behind large dots marking places called Lvov, Vilnius, Kovno, Bialystok, Riga, and Minsk. Every time the small flags with the swastikas moved closer to Moscow on this map of the eastern front, I would feel a sharp pain deep in my chest. I can vividly recall this pain, even today.

Someone, I don't recall who, once whispered to me in front of this map, "Propaganda!" I tried hard to convince myself that all the little flags that were rushing eastward were indeed only propaganda, but it didn't work.

My somewhat older friends Tonček Strzalkowski, Bogdan Lasić, and Tone Orešković did not hide their disappointment and concern. Only Jaga showed no concern. Someone, probably from the United Workers' Union, perhaps her quiet suitor Mića Katarinčić, had told her that once long ago the powerful French emperor Napoleon had made a move toward Moscow and had even captured it. He then was forced to beat a hasty retreat in the dead of winter and didn't stop until he was back in Paris. "You'll see, that's what will happen now," Jaga claimed, with so much confidence that one could believe her for a moment.

Part Four

Jadovno

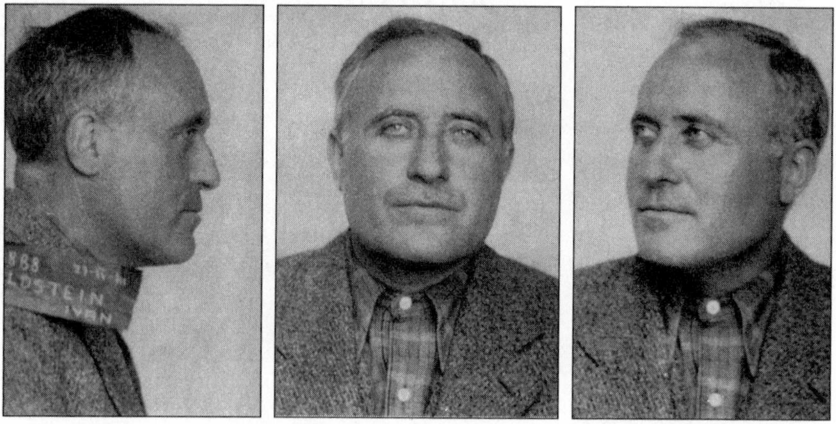

Ivo Goldstein, photos from the files of the Zagreb jail on Petrinjska Street, April 1941

11

"We Are All Hostages Now"

THE MISFORTUNE THAT had befallen my family in the spring of 1941 came in quick blows, one after the other, early in the summer. On Thursday, July 10, all the daily newspapers as well as prominently placed posters carried the announcment of the Ministry of the Interior of the Independent State of Croatia (NDH) informing the Croatian public that a mobile summary court had sentenced ten "spiritual initiators" to death for the murder of a policeman. Today we know this was not the first execution of hostages in the NDH (this distinction belongs to Jura Francetić, who ordered the execution of twenty hostages not far from Gacko in Herzegovina on June 10, 1941). However, July 10 was the first time that such a horrifying act had been so widely publicized. Among those executed were several well-known names in Croatian and Yugoslav intellectual circles. Although this announcement has been recounted in many memoirs of and historiographical works on the NDH, it is worth recalling the announcement in its entirety:

> On July 2, 1941, the disfigured body of policeman Ljudevit Tiljak, 37 years old, Roman Catholic, born in Gračac, was pulled from a pond in Petruševać forest next to Radnička Street in

Zagreb. Subsequent investigations have established that the crime was the work of communist agitators.

The following have been detained as the spiritual initiators of this crime:

Božidar Adžija, 50 years old, Roman Catholic, born in Drniš, District of Knin

Ognjen Prica, teacher, 41 years old, Orthodox, born in Ilidža, District of Sarajevo

Ivo Kuhn, lawyer, 38 years old, Jew, born in Slavonski Brod

Zvonimir Richtmann, engineer and teacher, 39 years old, Jew, born in Zagreb

Ivan Korski, engineer, 32 years old, Jew, born in Hrastovac, District of Garešnica

Viktor Rosenzweig, graduate student in agronomy, 27 years old, Jew, born in Ruma

Alfred Bergman, private office worker, 39 years old, Jew, born in Visoko

Sigismund Kraus, bank clerk, 31 years old, Jew, born in Sarajevo

Otokar Keršovani, journalist, 39 years old, Catholic, born in Trieste

Simo Crnogorac, 40 years old, housepainter, Orthodox, born in Polača, District of Knin

The senate of the mobile summary court condemned all ten to death. The sentence was carried out on the ninth of this month by firing squad.

My father had been a close friend of Alfred Bergman, a close acquaintance of Zvonimir Richtmann and Ivo Kuhn, and he knew Božidar Adžija and perhaps a few of the others. When my mother read the announcement, she must have known that what she had quietly feared for weeks was now knocking at our door. After the German invasion of the USSR on June 22, Ustasha political terror took on ever more drastic forms and spread in new directions. The main targets were now communists, and leftists in general, especially intellectuals and people of influence within those ranks. The list of the ten chosen for execution revealed a racist component of the political terror, now more vigorously directed against Jews.

These were my father's final days in Danica. The first transport of prisoners from Danica to Gospić took place on June 20, with additional movements of prisoners in early July. The transports included Serbs and Jews, and my father probably knew that his turn would be coming soon. If he saw the newspapers from July 10, and he probably did, he would have realized that being sent to places unknown was less ominous for him than the more likely prospect of being "promoted" to a "spiritual initiator" like his friends Bergman and Richtmann, who had no idea who Ljudevit Tiljak was but lost their lives because of him.[1]

My father had become close friends with Fredi Bergman in the early 1920s, when both were studying in Vienna. Their political ideas, which at the time they called "ideals," caused a rift between them in 1925 and each went his own way: my father, the ardent Zionist, to Palestine to build a "new old homeland," and the communist Fredi to the perilous life of a party professional, a "soldier of the Revolution," with assignments that took him around Europe, from one danger to another. In Vienna, at the headquarters in exile of the Central Committee of the illegal Communist Party of Yugoslavia (KPJ), Fredi organized the printing of party materials and their smuggling into Yugoslavia. He set up clandestine communist cells in Sarajevo and Mostar and served three years in the prison at Sremska Mitrovica. In Vienna he used the pseudonym "Lenz" in the minutes of a session of the Central Committee in the fall of 1934, where it was decided to organize provincial party conferences in Yugoslavia in preparation for the Fifth Congress of the Comintern in Moscow. During a brief respite between two party assignments he married Braina Fos, a communist émigré from Latvia who had graduated with a degree in medicine in Berlin, had been accepted as a member of the Communist Party, and had escaped in 1933 from Berlin to Vienna, where she became a party professional and, like Fredi, a "soldier of the Revolution." They were "kindred spirits," devoted each other, but unhappily torn apart by party assignments that sent them in different directions.

Between 1935 and 1936, Fredi was at the International Lenin School in Moscow, and then in Prague and Paris as a delegate to the General International Secretariat of the Comintern for Assistance to the Spanish Republicans. At the same time, Braina was carrying out party assignments between Vienna and Yugoslavia with a forged Austrian passport, until March 1937 when she was arrested on one such assignment. She was cruelly mistreated in jail in Belgrade but, because of the lack of solid evidence, was sentenced to only six months in prison for traveling on a forged passport. A 1937 article signed by "T.T." (Josip Broz Tito) in issue number 13 of *Proleter*, the newspaper of the Central Committee of the KPJ, lauded Braina for her "heroic conduct before the class enemy."

When Tito took over the leadership of the Central Committee of the KPJ in August 1937, Fredi was removed from leadership responsibilities and "transferred" as a volunteer to the International Brigades in Spain. Braina came with him since she had completed her prison sentence in Yugoslavia. She served as a doctor in the medical corps of the Republican army, while Fredi served at the front in the Fifteenth International Brigade. With the fall of the republic in 1939, they were separated again, this time for good: Braina was recalled to Moscow as an indispensable "Latvian cadre," and Fredi was sent to a camp in southern France for refugee members of the International

Brigades. At the party's orders, he returned to Yugoslavia in 1940 "to become legal." The police of the Banovina of Croatia arrested him, sent him to jail, then handed him over to the Ustasha authorities, who first dispatched him to Kerestinec, then to Gospić, then back to Zagreb, and finally directly to his execution at Dotrščina. Braina died in Riga in what was then the Soviet Union in 1973. In 1970, she traveled to Belgrade at the invitation of the Institute of Contemporary History of Yugoslavia and gave a detailed presentation about cooperation with the Yugoslav communists in the 1930s and about her memories of her husband.

Youthful friendships can last forever, and this was true of the friendship between my father and Fredi, regardless of their different ways of life and political reasoning. I don't recall exactly when Fredi stayed at our house in Karlovac, but I believe it was in 1934, after serving time in prison and after he was under police surveillance but not yet a wanted person. For me he was Uncle Fredi, a friend of my mother and father. I remember him playing with little Danko, bouncing him on his knee; his melancholic eyes behind thick glasses. Fredi had worked in Karlovac as a shop manager. I think my father helped him get this job, which he soon quit, responding to the call of his party. My mother told me that she had later seen Fredi in Paris, when she had brought supplies for the International Brigades in Spain and Fredi was one of the main organizers for the assistance in the Paris headquarters. Fredi visited us at home rarely in those days, either because our house was not a safe refuge for an illegal or because he did not want to risk putting us in danger. For a long time after the war my mother and I would reminisce about Fredi, his sadly disjointed life and its end. When she read Fredi's name among those executed on July 10, 1941, what until then had been only a vague sense of foreboding suddenly burst forth with penetrating clarity. She told me, "*Jetzt sind wir alle Geiseln*!" ("We are all hostages now!").

I remember Ivo Kuhn from the streets of Karlovac—his striking profile, his thick curly reddish-brown hair—riding on a loud red motorcycle, dressed in the pump pants that were then in fashion, sometimes with a female companion on the rear seat. Our Jaga described Kuhn as a "womanizer," thus dismissing him in every respect. In the mid-1930s, he was a law clerk in the firm of my father's friends Vatroslav and Filip Reiner. In some communist historiographical literature I read that as a student Kuhn had been a communist, but in view of his legal career he had ceased any active involvement in the party. Nevertheless, he continued to move in leftist circles. In the years immediately preceding the war, he opened his own law office in Zagreb, defended political prisoners in court, and acquired a reputation as a brave and capable attorney. He was arrested on April 30, 1941, and sent to Kerestinec in a group of seventy-nine Jewish lawyers from Zagreb. When virtually everyone in this group was released on June 7—thanks to the intervention of the Bar Association and a contribution of gold and stocks from the Zagreb Jewish Community—Kuhn remained at Kerestinec and was one of the first ten to be executed.[2]

In the last few years before the war Zvonimir Richtmann frequently came to Karlovac, where his closest friend, Vera Šarić, a doctor in the clinic of the high school, lived. Richtmann was a handsome man, eloquent and funny, with a tireless curiosity and a broad education. During his studies in Vienna, he was carried away by the ideas of Einstein's theory of relativity and the elaboration of Max Planck's quantum theory. He was the first in Zagreb to popularize Einstein. Later he embraced psychoanalysis and, in 1937, he was the first in Yugoslavia to write and publish an original monograph on Sigmund Freud.[3] Primarily as a scholar, and then also as a leftist, Richtmann tried to adapt Marxist materialistic philosophy with the achievements of modern science. To orthodox Marxists and the party faithful, who were firmly committed to Lenin-Stalin dialectical materialism as the sacrosanct view of the world, this was blasphemy.[4]

The leader of the aggressive campaign against Richtmann was Ognjen Prica, a member of KPJ and one of the founders of the League of Young Communists of Yugoslavia. His polemic marked an earlier phase of the conflict among leftists (1933–1938) in which the central question was the relationship between science and philosophy. According to Prica, Richtmann was an "idealist," a "fideist," a "revisionist," a "knight of revisionism," a "would-be theoretician," an "unhealthy and suspicious element," and a "moral and political dead man," who defended himself more than he attacked. Richtmann called Prica a "doctrinaire," a "typical example of a dogmatic spirt and an empty phrase-monger," who "does not know how to think logically" and "automatically fabricates falsehoods, and doesn't even know it." And after all of the squabbling the two men found themselves together in jail and then shoulder to shoulder before a firing squad. I've often wondered if they uttered a word of reconciliation to each other, or if they shook hands at the last moment.

On March 25, 1941, Prince Paul of Yugoslavia, acting as regent for the seventeen-year-old Peter II, declared that the Kingdom of Yugoslavia would join the Tripartite Pact. On March 27, Serbian military officers staged a coup d'etat. Prince Paul was overthrown as regent, while Peter II was proclaimed of age and installed on the throne. In the critical days after the March 27 putsch in Belgrade, the police of the Banovina of Croatia arrested twenty-five prominent communists as a preventive measure. Richtmann was among them, although he had never been a party member. The group also included Prica, Otokar Keršovani, Božidar Adžija, and other lesser-known opponents of Richtmann from the prewar leftist conflicts. They were all held in the Zagreb jail on Savska Street. Under the orders and strict supervision of Andrija Žaja, a member of the Central Committee, no party member in the jail was permitted to speak to Richtmann. For six weeks, or as long as they were together in the common cells, Richtmann didn't exist for members of the Communist Party.

On Saturday, June 5, a small police van drove into the courtyard. The commander of the unit and two prison guards rushed into the main hallway of the building and called out the names of Adžija, Bergman, Simo Crnogorac, Keršovani, Ivo Kuhn, Ivan Krndelj, and Prica: "Get ready! With all of your belongings!"

The seven men were taken to an unknown location. On Sunday morning, a "green police van" took Krndelj back to Kerestinec and picked up Viktor Rosenzweig and Sigismund Kraus, as well as Richtmann and Ivan Korski. No one knew where they were taken, although there was anxious guessing: To one of the Zagreb jails? To Gospić? To the Danica camp?

Only after the war did investigators establish that the first group taken from Kerestinec was sent to Gospić by a night train on the evening of June 5, and the next night from Gospić back to Zagreb. The other four—Korski, Kraus, Richtmann, and Rosenzweig—were held in the jail on Petrinjska Street. This confusing routing of Zagreb–Gospić–Zagreb and the urgent substitution of Rosenzweig for Krndelj suggests that Dido Kvaternik needed several more days to discuss with Pavelić and the senior Ustasha leadership which hostages were to be killed, and the names then released *urbi et orbi* with terrifying effect.

Grgo Gamulin was likely the last person to speak with Richtmann and Korski in the jail on Petrinjska Street. Through the bars of his cell he saw the two walking along the hallway escorted by a guard.

"Where are you going," Gamulin asked them.

"Well, to our execution," Korski said, then added, "Say hello to my children for me."

And Richtmann said, smiling, "Give my greetings to all our friends."

A few minutes later Gamulin saw them getting into a police van. It was their last contact with a world that stayed behind.

* * *

For many years after the war the first ten executed hostages in the NDH were announced as "Božidar Adžija, Otokar Keršovani, Ognjen Prica, and others." At the first postwar congress of the KPJ in 1948, only these three were mentioned in a positive light, while Richtmann continued to be described as a "revisionist." In Jewish circles I heard the comment that this was a disguised form of anti-Semitism: six Jews, two Croats, and two Serbs had been executed, but only two Croats and one Serb were ever mentioned. I saw it in a completely different light. It wasn't anti-Semitism—anti-Semitism didn't exist either among the higher levels of the KPJ or with Tito himself, not even during the break in diplomatic relations with Israel. The criterion for granting the aura of heroism was loyalty to the party line and the party leadership. Richtmann was a priori a longtime, stubborn opponent of party policy at that time; Bergman was "Gorkić's man"; Rosenzweig was a silent supporter of Krleža; Kuhn and Kraus were activists who had become inactive; Korski was a "factionalist"; and Crnogorac must have had some stain on his record that I was unable to discover. That left only Adžija, Prica, and Keršovani with clean party records, unquestionably "fit" for the hero's pedestal. The injustice of the unfairly granted honor was not remedied until the 1970s and 1980s in a number of books and in some Jewish publications.

My father was never a member of the KPJ, although he had several friends who were communists and whose activities he occasionally supported (for example, assistance to the International Brigades in Spain). He could not easily be counted among the "communist agitators," such as the ten who were executed, but the epithet "spiritual initiators of the crime" was sufficiently absurd to have included anyone. My parents knew that. Ivo Goldstein fell under that category: He was a leftist and a Jew; he associated with known communists, even with some of the ten who were executed. His bookshop had been a gathering place of the local leftist intelligentsia; he promoted leftist and antifascist literature; and he had influence within the community in which he lived. My mother also was not far removed. She knew what she knew when on July 10, 1941, she said, "We are all hostages now!"

12

On the Road to Jadovno

ON SATURDAY, JULY 12, a brief article appeared in *Hrvatska sloboda*:

> Who doesn't know the teacher Ružica Reiner née Bonači? We believe everyone in our city knows her. She is "nationally conscious," "endowed with the Yugoslav spirit," and, we hear, also "tainted red."
>
> If this description does not sound familiar we should point out that she was most often found in the company of the following individuals: Prof. Marica Marinković, Vera Šarić, Prof. Lazo Avramović, and Milan Radeka, as well as the wife of the bookseller Goldstein.
>
> Together they raised high the flag of "equality," "brotherhood," and "freedom" in our city. However, that has now come to an end.
>
> Let them forever "rest in peace."

Being singled out in *Hrvatska sloboda* usually meant that prison or a camp would soon follow. Today I can vividly imagine my mother's torment: She was not a person who closed her eyes to danger. Always active and of an enterprising temperament, she tried to anticipate events, to influence them, to avoid them. This time she found herself in an impossible situation. What could she do to deflect a threat announced in several thousand copies? To run away, to hide and leave her children behind—that was out of the question. To escape with the children, but to where? Any idea of escape, with her children or without them, meant breaking contact with my father, who was languishing in Danica: To leave him without that bit of hope he was still nurturing, to endanger him further, although he was already in danger—to betray him? And to run away with the children, does that not mean dragging them into some unforeseen peril? Perhaps she thought that there was still a little more time because until then, until July 12, 1941, only "undesirable" men, and not a single woman, had been arrested in Karlovac and sent to the camps. Who knows what my mother was thinking and planning in those days. I am certain that she had discussed in detail with her friends Mia Veličković and Pavica Vine what they could do for my father and what to do with the children if she were arrested. She gave her instructions to Jaga and me: The money is here, the jewelry there, if anything happens, call Mia and Pavica right away. Her only consolation was that the children would find refuge with our reliable Jaga. She would take them to Kovačevac and having the children with her might not be a bad thing at all.

On that weekend in July, while my mother was waiting to be arrested, all of Karlovac, either voluntarily or under coercion, was decked with flags with the new Ustasha symbol. On the first page of Saturday's *Hrvatska sloboda* under the headline WELCOME TO KARLOVAC was the following announcement:

> On Sunday, the 13th of this month, the free and royal city of Karlovac will have its great day. On this day, a major gathering will take place of Ustasha intellectuals connected to the 362nd

> anniversary of the founding of our city. On this day, the city of Karlovac is especially honored that two of the leading men of Croatia, Mile Budak and Lovro Sušić, will be in attendance.... So, Croats, residents of Karlovac, gather before the emissaries of our glorious leader to hear his message....

At nine o'clock on Saturday evening a procession of Ustasha members accompanied by music passed through the city. At six o'clock on Sunday morning we were awoken by a patriotic song wafting through the city. At eleven o'clock we watched from our window as on the opposite side of Zrinski Square the mansion that belonged to a Jewish family, the Fröhlichs, was "consecrated" as the new headquarters of the Great Parish of Pokuplje. At twelve o'clock in Jelačić Square, the old heart of the city, a "major political meeting" was held, which, according to the newspapers, "gathered old and young who feel and think Croatian, to hear the manly words of the government ministers who spoke to them in the Ustasha language of a free homeland." Half of Budak's speech, printed in its entirety in *Hrvatski narod* on July 14, glorified Pavelić: "And when you celebrate it is the great *Poglavnik* you celebrate. The *Poglavnik* is the sole standard-bearer of our statehood, pride, and honor. It is his work and if it were not for him all of us together would mean nothing." The second half of the speech included praise for order, work, faith, the Croatian people, a little for the city of Karlovac, and a lot of ridicule for Vladko Maček, the Croatian Peasants' Party (HSS), Bolsheviks, and "Orthodox of all types" to whom Budak addressed his favorite message: "*Ili se pokloni, ili se ukloni!*" (Bow before us, or get out of our way!) According to the newspaper reports, Sušić's speech was considerably shorter but more direct: "The cleansing in the Croatian state has begun... as it's written in the Ustasha principles."

And what this cleansing meant to hard-core Ustasha was made

clear by Budak at a reception for a small circle of invited guests at the Franciscan monastery in Karlovac. According to Vladimir Židovec, who was present, Budak was in a rather jovial mood and explained that in this closed circle he was able "to speak openly about one thing that is becoming increasingly urgent... the question of what will become of the Jews and Serbs in our state," and then he continued:

> You are intelligent people who do not need much explaining, so I will illustrate the matter best with a simple anecdote from our Ustasha émigré days. On a visit to an Ustasha camp, the question came up about the Jews and Serbs, about what they were doing in our homeland, and how we would resolve the issue when we returned home. An Ustasha, a good man, came up to me and said, "When we get home, then you, sir, will certainly be a minister and a representative of the Croatian government. And I will continue to be a soldier and a representative of the fighting spirit of the Croatian state. What will we Croatian soldiers ask for and expect from you ministers and representatives of the Croatian government? Nothing more nor less than the following: When we soldiers take care of the Serbs and Jews, then you as representatives of the government will have to come and investigate what has happened. All we expect from you is that you always come half an hour too late!"

According to Židovec, in his book *My Participation in Political Life*, Budak was "unusually happy... obviously feeling himself to be in the middle of a mission assigned him by Providence." So that the Italian and German representatives who were present could understand, Budak personally translated his remarks, first into Italian and then into German.

At about seven o'clock in the morning on Monday, July 14, Danko and I were still sleeping when two well-known Karlovac detectives, Mihelčić and Saletto, came for my mother. She was horrified when the detectives showed her an arrest warrant listing not only her name but also Jaga's (Agata Đerek). In a life that had had more than its share of difficult situations, I don't believe my mother had ever been in such despair. Jaga was her last guarantee that someone would be there to take care of her children. I don't know how my mother was able to be so collected when she gently woke me: "Get up, brush your teeth, get dressed, don't cry, get in touch with Pavica and Mia right away, they will know what to do."

The detectives took Jaga and my mother away; Danko and I remained in the apartment alone. That same morning, Mia engaged the services of a lawyer to make inquiries about my mother and Jaga. Pavica arranged with Mrs. Klobučar to deliver food to us from her restaurant, and by about noon I was in the courtyard of the local police station with containers of food for my mother and Jaga. Every day I visited the jail and the guards would permit my mother to come into the courtyard, receive the food, and speak a few words to me. Several times Danko came with me. He remembers that the guards once allowed him to go with my mother into her cell "to see where she was sleeping now." In the cell with my mother and Jaga were several prominent women leftists. Apparently the time had passed to spare "politically undesirable" women. Equality of the sexes had been established for arrest and persecution, the only area in which the government of the Independent State of Croatia (NDH) recognized such equality.[1]

A day or two after the arrest of my mother and Jaga, again at about seven o'clock in the morning, I was awoken by the doorbell. I rushed to open the door. A middle-aged man in a railway worker's uniform stood at the entrance.

"Does Mrs. Lea Goldstein live here?"

In a quandary, I avoided a direct answer.

"She is not at home, but she will be coming soon. I am her son."

"When your mother comes home, give this to her right away. Tell her it was found at the railway station late last night, next to a freight train on the third track."

He pushed a rolled-up paper into my hands, turned, and hurriedly left. I never saw him again and never found out who he was.

My father's handwriting was on the rolled-up paper: "I would be grateful if any honest passerby would deliver this note to my wife, Mrs. Lea Goldstein, Karlovac, Zrinski Square 9, first floor." There was a short note inside that, unfortunately, in our wartime wanderings, we were unable to save, several lines addressed to my mother, written hastily and in German, perhaps while the train was stopped at the Karlovac station. They were being taken to Lika, probably to Gospić, my father said, and he would be in touch from there soon. He said that he is with us in his thoughts, he loves us all, and he hopes to see us soon.

By the strange coincidence misfortune tends to create, my father's transport to Lika began on the same day, perhaps at the same hour, that my mother and Jaga were arrested and taken to the local jail. I found confirmation of the date in Dizdar's research on Danica, that the fourth transport of camp inmates from Danica to Gospić embarked on the morning of July 14. That night my father passed through Karlovac. At the railway station he tossed the rolled up paper through a small window of the freight car, hoping that the short letter would find its way to my mother.

"The honest passerby," a night worker for the railway, found the letter and bravely brought it to the given address immediately after his shift was over. I have not written the word "bravely" by accident. At that time, compassion and honesty were not enough for a person to take a prisoner's randomly thrown letter so promptly to an unknown addressee, the prisoner's wife. Indeed, the man must have possessed courage.

I am not prone to tearful scenes. In this book I have often skipped over them, thinking of how my mother bravely controlled her tears during four years of war. But this time she did not even try: When I handed her Father's note in the prison courtyard that afternoon, she quietly wept, letting her tears flow freely.

At the end of that week, probably on Thursday or Friday, Mr. Trontl, a calm, heavyset man of few words, appeared on our doorstep.

"Is Danko at home?"

Mr. Trontl was the father of Tomica, Danko's schoolmate and good friend. Danko would frequently play at Tomica's house on the banks of the Kupa River.

"Come on, Danko, Tomica is asking for you, you can play together at our house. Bring some clothes, maybe you can stay a few days."

Mr. Trontl said to me as the elder brother that Danko could stay with them while our mother was in jail or for "as long as necessary."

When I told this to my mother the next day in the prison courtyard, she was deeply moved, speechless. She quickly collected herself and said she was sure Danko would be well taken care of by the Trontls.

With his calm, measured manner, Mr. Trontl generally inspired trust. He had a small grocery store on Riječka Street and was said to be an honest man. Although he had never been active in politics, the local branch of the HSS had elected him to a variety of committees because he enjoyed a good reputation in the city. As far as I know, my parents barely knew the Trontls and the friendship between their children was the only connection.

Danko spent several untroubled weeks with the Trontls. He and

Tomica were only nine years old. They got along well and spent the hot summer days in the garden around the house or on the Kupa and Korana Rivers, playing with neighborhood children. In the house Danko was treated as a family member. When I would sometimes go around to see Danko, Mr. Trontl would ask how our mother was and if I had heard anything from our father, always adding that Danko was a good boy, that he was welcome there, and could stay "as long as necessary."

And so I was a thirteen-year-old alone in our apartment, but not for long. Barely ten days after the arrest of my mother and Jaga, Franjo Družak appeared at our door with the written order that our apartment be turned over to him. I have already described that he was neither brusque nor rude. He immediately told me that he was not throwing me out onto the street, that they had taken care of housing, and that the Jewish Community would "take charge" of me. I later read and heard of evictions that were considerably more brutal—leaving an apartment within twenty-four hours and, in the most extreme cases, within one hour. Družak gave me three to four days, and a day longer if I needed it. He specified what I could take from the apartment and all that I had to leave behind.[2] In the chapter "Evictions from Houses and Apartments" in his book *Holokaust u Zagrebu* (The Holocaust in Zagreb),[3] my son, Ivo, describes at great length the legal basis, the procedures used, and the many arbitrary actions taken during the confiscation of Jewish homes and apartments in the NDH. As a relatively senior Ustasha and government official, Družak had received our apartment on the basis of the Legal Decree on Vacating and Settling Residential Dwellings for Reasons of Public Security of May 31, 1941. Of course, I didn't know anything about this when Družak showed me the confiscation order at the door of our apartment. I had already learned that Ustasha decrees against the Jews were final. And if I had asked Družak or, possibly, our lawyer Longhin, I would have received the response that according to the law the eviction was to take place "with no delay or compensation" and that "no appeal had power to postpone it."

Therefore, I had three or four days to pack the clothes, shoes, undergarments, all of the bedding, porcelain dishes, and vases, at least some of the books, and hundreds of other things belonging to my father, mother, Jaga, Danko, and me—with the exception of the furniture, carpets, and most of the paintings, which I had to leave for Družak. I was, of course, confused and helpless. Again, my savior was Pavica Vine. She and her husband, Ivo, managed the most successful retail and wholesale grocery in Karlovac, which she had inherited from her father, Mr. Bakšić. Ivo's nephew Fabo, a capable and intelligent man, able to do "one hundred things at once," worked in the retail store. He came to our apartment with wooden crates and in one day everything was done: All of our things were properly packed in separate crates and containers. On each crate Fabo noted the contents; everyone would be able to find what they needed, there could be no mistake. A worker from the Vines' warehouse arrived with a horse-drawn wagon; the crates were loaded and taken to Pavica's attic. We took a few things from the crates when we left Karlovac in the fall; all the rest of it was there waiting for us when we returned after the war. One must recall that during this time anyone who hid Jewish property, according to the Legal Decree on Preventing the Concealment of Jewish Property, was subject to a prison sentence of at least one year, to which Pavica, Ivo, and Fabo paid little heed.

When Mrs. Družak arrived from Samobor three or four days later to take over our apartment, everything that we were allowed to take and could be taken had been carted off. It was then that I saw Družak for the second time, this time in uniform and with a large Ustasha cap on his head. It seemed to me that the uniform didn't fit him nearly as well as his meticulously tailored civilian suit had. He was not unpleasant this time, either. He spoke to me not in a commanding tone but calmly, almost softly, as if we were discussing some mutual agreement that I leave my own apartment. His wife was more nervous and hurried, disgusing her uneasiness. She was a young woman from a middle-class Samobor family, and I don't believe she had a clear conscience about moving into someone else's apartment and evicting a boy who was barely thirteen years old.

I turned the keys over to Družak. He accompanied me down our long hallway to the front door and extended his hand.

"If you've forgotten anything, or if you need some of your books, just come, don't hesitate."

Loaded down with two full suitcases—the last possessions that I took from our apartment—I went to Mr. Šandor Weiss, who, at the suggestion of Mr. Rendeli, the president of the Jewish Community, agreed to take me into his apartment and feed me for as long as necessary.

* * *

If my memory isn't deceiving me, I first heard about Jadovno from Mr. Weiss. He and his wife, Tina, put me into the room of their son, Vlatko, who had been arrested with a group of young Jews on July 8 and sent to Gospić. Everything in Vlatko's room was still neatly in its place, as if he would be coming home at any moment, but Mrs. Weiss had also found a way to make me feel at home in this room. The Weisses were warm and considerate to me and I felt that they were trying to ease my difficult days. On the first evening, Mr. Weiss told me in some detail everything he had done to learn the news from Gospić "about our people, where they are, and how they are doing." About thirty Jews and at least twice as many Serbs from Karlovac had been sent from Danica or directly from Karlovac to Gospić. News from Gospić was constantly circulating among the families in Karlovac through a variety of contacts and acquaintances, but not a single detainee had been in touch directly, either in person or by letter in his own hand. Mr. Weiss told me that the most reliable news was from the Zagreb Jewish Community because it maintained official contacts with the Red Cross and the appropriate police authorities. Moreover, the community had been able to send its representative, a doctor, to Gospić to inquire about the situation of "our people" and to deliver food and medicine to them. I believe I heard from Mr. Weiss that "our people" from Koprivnica, meaning also my father, first spent a day or two in the jail in Gospić and then all had been sent to the Jadovno camp on Velebit. Allegedly, they were building a road through the forest. Almost nothing was known about the camp because access was strictly forbidden. He added that the Zagreb Jewish Community was seeking permission to send packages through the Red Cross, and that as soon as it obtained that permission, we would be informed.

Mr. Weiss was in his fifties, a gentle man with a mild character and a pleasant voice who spoke in measured words. Until the war he had a large textile shop in the center of the city, right next to our bookstore. He had fifteen employees and paid them a relatively good salary. Today, Dane Maješki, one of Weiss's employees at that time and in 1944 my immediate "boss" as the commissar of a battalion in the Karlovac Partisan detachment, can confirm this. As I write this, Dane has just turned eighty-six and walks with great difficulty, but he reads all of the newspapers and follows politics and other "scandals." He still calls me, especially when he is angry that in some article or interview, in his opinion, I have not spoken harshly enough about fascism, the Ustasha movement, or today's "Ustashoid recidivism." I usually say that he is to blame for it because he didn't train me well enough in politics when he was my commissar in the Partisans. According to Dane, Mr. Weiss was a fine gentleman and a good boss. He behaved correctly to his employees and they appreciated him as a considerate and just man. Although early on Dane was a communist sympathizer and since 1940 a member of the Communist Party of Yugoslavia, he never portrayed his employer as a stereotypical exploiter of the working class.

The Weisses lived in a large apartment on the second floor of Gundulićeva Street 3. They were forced to give the rear, smaller, and partially detached portion of the apartment to an Italian officer, a colonel—an arrangement that later proved to be fortuitous. Mrs. Weiss treated me like a nephew, worrying if I had clean underclothes, if I had gone to see my younger brother at the Trontls or had taken food to my mother and Jaga at the jail. In the evening I stood at the window of Vlatko's room and observed the promenade, on which, as Jews, we were no longer permitted to stroll, and at the lighted windows of my former apartment. Tea, the Weisses' sixteen-year-old daughter, whom I knew from meetings of the Jewish organization Kadima, would come by my room before going to sleep to say good night and kiss me on my forehead, awakening in me pubescent thoughts. Every morning Mr. Weiss conscientiously went "to work," to the shop that was no longer his. A tall, strong man in an Ustasha uniform now sat at the cash register. He was from Imotski and his name was Mate Brekalo. Until the war he had very successfully peddled goods among Croats in western Europe and had provided material assistance to the Ustasha movement and to individual Ustasha émigrés. He was given a high Ustasha military rank and Mr. Weiss's shop, first as the trustee and then as its owner. Dane told me that Brekalo quickly realized he was more interested in business than in politics. He got rid of his uniform, resigned his political positions, and, shrewd and intuitive as he was, immediately grasped that managing a large shop with fifteen employees was not the same as being a competent peddler. He had established good relations with the employees and did not fire or replace any of them with a politically "more desirable" person. He asked Mr. Weiss, in return for a bonus, to teach him about the business. Mr. Weiss agreed, though his primary motive was probably the hope that through Brekalo he would be able to get his son out of Jadovno.

When he came home in the early evening, Mr. Weiss liked to talk to me. He of course was worried by the disappointing news from the Russian front and even more by the shortage of news about our people in Jadovno. He didn't try to hide his concern and spoke to me like an adult. Mr. Weiss perked up one day when he learned that the Jewish Community would be permitted to send packages to Jadovno via the Red Cross. At least fifty Karlovac families put together packages with hearty food, sugar, lemons, and the most essential medicines. Mrs. Weiss immediately prepared three packages: one for Vlatko and two for other relatives. Pavica made a package for my father and carefully measured out the maximum allowable quantity and weight. My mother too was thrilled by the news that we were sending the packages.

Much later we learned that not a single package ever reached the prisoners at the Jadovno camp.

* * *

That summer Serbs and Jews were forbidden to move through the city from nine o'clock in the evening until five o'clock in the morning. One evening, when the hour of the curfew was drawing near, the doorbell of the Weisses' apartment rang loudly. On the dim street at the main entrance of the building stood my grandfather Aron Goldstein. He had come from Tuzla to see what he could do for us in this dire situation. In fact, he wanted to take Danko and me to Tuzla "until your mother and father come back home," he said using the customary expression for those times.

That evening my grandfather conferred for a long time with Mr. Weiss and very briefly with me. The unavoidable questions all Jews faced at that time were: What else is awaiting us? Should we sit at home or should we flee? And if we leave, where to? My grandfather still believed nothing would happen to him and his family in Tuzla. He was handsome, a prominent and esteemed citizen. I enjoyed strolling with him through the market and wandering around the city on our prewar visits to Tuzla. I felt a childish pride seeing how everyone greeted my grandfather with respect, spoke to him in a warm and friendly manner. He said that the nuns who lived in a convent nearby were paying back a favor from before the war and helping in every way possible to protect them from the Ustasha. Admittedly, his glass factory and shop had been confiscated, as had all Jewish businesses, but "some senior people" would assist him. The new mayor, a Muslim, was an old acquaintance, one might say a friend, who always purchased glassware for his house through the shop, as did the local mullah. Even now they were sending him some encouraging messages.

Mr. Weiss was more suspicious. He mentioned David Meisel, the senior cantor of the Karlovac synagogue, the soul of Karlovac musical life for thirty years, the conductor of Zora, the First Croatian choral society, which performed to international renown. Meisel composed and arranged choral music for all of the Karlovac choirs and organized many musical performances at Zorin Dom. His friends in the music world convinced him that nothing would happen to him, that he was a Croatian conductor, a credit to Karlovac and to Croatian culture, and, moreover, he was married to a Croatian woman. When he was detained in the first wave of arrests, some people from Karlovac cultural life interceded on his behalf and rescued him. However, he had barely got home when he was picked up again, sent to Danica, and from Danica to Jadovno, where no interventions could help him. Meisel's son Zlatko, a student, was also in Jadovno, along with about thirty other Jewish men from Karlovac and certainly even more Serbs. Mr. Weiss was afraid that few would be freed as long as the war continued. He held out much greater hope for the more imminent return of my mother, and cautiously mentioned to my grandfather that, who knows, perhaps the people in Tuzla are not safe either. Well, what will happen to Danko, a nine-year-old boy, if, God forbid, something bad happens to them in Tuzla? Here Danko is among good people who are taking care of him, and if worse comes to worse the Jewish Community could place him somewhere "with our people."

My grandfather wasn't going to change his mind. He said that though these were terrible times, nothing bad would happen to them in Tuzla. The Ursuline nuns had convinced him that they would alert everyone if any danger threatened. My grandfather explained to Mr. Weiss and me that Danko would be well taken care of and safe with them in Tuzla, that in times such as these a child should be with his own family and not with outsiders, however well-intentioned they might be. There was another matter for me staying with the Weisses. I had my friends, and would be among my own people, but someone had to wait for news of my father and take food to my mother in jail, and it was our good fortune that I was old enough to do this. My grandfather patted me on the shoulder with a forced smile as he tried to encourage me and perhaps hide his grief.

In 1941, my grandfather was sixty-nine years old and still walked with long, measured strides. He dressed carefully, shaved regularly, and trimmed his long gray mustache. He liked hot paprika, Yiddish songs, Hungarian czardas, and good-natured jokes. He opened his glass workshop and store in 1908. Over time he had acquired a great reputation in the city as a fine craftsman, an honest merchant, and a pleasant and sociable man. He had provided half of Tuzla with glass, including the new city hall. He had taught his eldest son, Oto, the trade for the last ten years, and before the war he only signed contracts while Oto managed the business. He lived with my grandmother Adolfa, their youngest daughter, Berta (the only one of four daughters not married), and Oto, his wife, Greta, and their ten-year old son, Darko, in a spacious house with a courtyard, some outlying buildings, and a garden. My grandmother was in many ways the complete opposite of my grandfather: She was short, serious, the well-educated daughter of a rabbi who wrote beautiful letters and enjoyed reading fine literature, unlike my grandfather who only read the newspaper and Jewish publications. A few years before the war my grandmother lost the use of her legs. She was confined to a wheelchair and my grandfather treated her with touching attentiveness. He may have been the boss in the factory and the shop, but my grandmother was the boss at home right until the very end.

The next morning my grandfather picked up Danko from the Trontls. I wasn't there, but Danko clearly remembers that the discussion went on forever. Mr. Trontl repeatedly said that Danko would be safest with them and that he could stay "for as long as it might be necessary." My grandfather reiterated that Danko would be just as safe with them in Tuzla and that he would be with his family. Faced with the demands of Danko's family, now represented by my grandfather, Mr. Trontl was forced to relent. And so Danko went to Tuzla with my grandfather.

I don't remember if my grandfather also talked with my mother in jail or how he obtained her agreement to take Danko away. I only remember her favorite expression from that time: "*Schöne Zeiten! Die Wahl tuht einen Weh!*"—which more or less means "What wonderful times! Every choice is painful!" or whatever choice you make is the wrong choice because you have to choose between two evils and you are never certain which one is the lesser.

* * *

Mr. Weiss, a man who rarely showed his emotions, couldn't hide his agitation one day when he came home early from the shop: The previous day Nikola Adler had returned home from Jadovno. He lived close by, in the building of the First Croatian Savings Bank. That morning some of "our people" with family members in Jadovno had already gone to see him, but Adler had been curt. "He barely wants to speak," complained Mr. Weiss, and he asked me to go see Adler immediately. "Maybe he will tell you something more; perhaps he has a message from your father. Ask him about Vlatko, too."

Adler, a timid, frail man, was a thirty-four-year-old Jew who had worked until the war as a clerk in the Karlovac company Impregnacija, d.d. He was in Danica with my father and Milan Radeka and on July 14 was sent in the group of Karlovac men to Gospić and on to Jadovno. His wife, a German and a person of "pure Aryan descent," had somehow managed through her German or Volksdeutsche connections to get Adler released from the camp at Jadovno. But it was neither easy nor quick, even for her, for her husband had spent two full months in the camps and I don't know how long in jail prior to that.

Adler said no more to me than he did to the others. He was probably forbidden to talk about the conditions there, and he was certainly afraid: Of course, he had seen my father every day; they had worked together once on the construction site of the forest road. Yes, everyone is there, Mr. Weiss's son; the Glücks, father and son; and the Meisels, Professor Sablić, and others. Well, you know, they are all well; it's not as bad for them as it could be.... Listening to Adler, the fearful look on his face and the sound of his voice more than what he was actually saying, made me feel overcome with the most terrible forebodings: Was he hiding something with his silence, some terrible thing happening there that he wasn't able to share? I don't know what the Ustasha authorities had against Adler because despite his frightened caution, despite his marriage to a "pure-blooded" German, he was arrested again in November 1941 and before the end of that year killed at Jasenovac.

In the evening Mr. Weiss frequently spoke with his "tenant," the Italian colonel, a jovial and talkative man. He had promised Mr. Weiss that he would inquire about "our people" in Jadovno, but even he had been unable to learn anything. However, a day or two after the conversation with Adler, the first (and only) official announcement came out, which could be taken as a ray of hope. Mr. Weiss brought home a copy of a letter from the Jewish Community of Zagreb:

> The Jewish Community, Karlovac, number 760/1941 of August 10, 1941.
>
> We are pleased to inform you that we have received information that the following members of our community in Jadovno on Velebit are healthy and well:
>
> Blau, Zvonko, private clerk, 22 yrs.
> Braun, Herman, traveling salesman, 40 yrs.
> Brauner, Gjuro, photographer, 30 yrs.
> Danon, Elias, private clerk, 30 yrs.
> Deutsch, Aleksander, merchant, 43 yrs.
> Eisler, Ernst, merchant, 55 yrs.
> Eisler, Pavao, merchant, 29 yrs.
> Fischer, Leo, director
> Glück, Rudolf, merchant, 51 yrs.
> Glück, Boris, student, 20 yrs.
> Goldstein, Ivo, eng., merchant, 41 yrs.
> Gomboš, Ljudevit, private clerk, 54 yrs.
> Heksch, Tibor, med., 25 yrs.
> Lederer, Salamon, private clerk, 31 yrs.
> Leitner, Dragutin, merchant, 41 yrs.
> Meisl, David, private clerk, 56 yrs.
> Meisl, Zlatko, student, 21 yrs.
> Mattersdorfer, Slavko

Moses, Zlatko, clerk, 32 yrs.
Polak, Stanko, 44 yrs.
Reisner, Gjuro, merchant, 35 yrs.
Rosenfeld, Samuel, merchant, 37 yrs.
Stern, Izidor, merchant, 52 yrs.
Stern, Hinko, private clerk, 50 yrs.
Spitzer, Hugo, private clerk, 30 yrs.
Schlossberger, Geza, merchant, 49 yrs.
Vadaš, Andrija, student, 21 yrs.
Weiss, Vlado, clerk, 20 yrs.

If you would like us to continue sending them additional food, we kindly ask that you instantly pay the amount per our circular no. 760-0/VI.

If we receive further information about the members of our community, we will notify you immediately.

President	Secretary
Hugo Kon	J. Abraham

My mother was delighted by this news, but Mr. Weiss was still skeptical. He was concerned by the paucity of the information and the clichéd expression that they are "healthy and well." Why then did they not give the men the chance to write a postcard home? Mr. Weiss had also learned at this time that Milivoj Schwartz, an emissary from the Zagreb Jewish Community, had not been able to go farther than Gospić because he was not granted access to the camp at Jadovno. So what else were they hiding up there on Velebit?

* * *

After an endless series of shocks, the middle of August was to bring one more blow, one that struck me the hardest. I wasn't able to find the exact date in the police records, but I know that it was before August 22, my birthday. When I went, as I had gone every day, to the jail with lunch for my mother and Jaga, the guard coldly refused to admit me.

"They are not here anymore."

At my incessant questioning, and after some hesitation, the guard relaxed a bit: Early that morning about thirty people, including four women, therefore meaning my mother, had been taken to Zagreb, perhaps to the main police station on Petrinjska Street or else to the jail on Savska Street—that was all he could tell me—but they certainly went to Zagreb. And yes, they took Jaga out of the group and returned her (under escort) to her native village on the Kupa River.

That same day, some residents rushed to Zagreb and returned with the news that "all of our people" were there, in the jail on Savska Street. Netica Šuman passed me a message from her sister, Metka Šuman-Drakulić, that my mother was with them. Netica offered to take me with her when she went to Zagreb the next day. I could bring my mother a food parcel, and perhaps I might find a considerate person who'd let me to speak to her.

I immediately went to the local police station to request a travel permit for Zagreb. When I explained to the clerk the purpose of my trip, the man's shoulders sagged. Such a permit could only be approved by "the boss," that is, the chief of police.

I don't know how I managed it or who let me into the office of the Karlovac police chief, at that time the all-powerful Ivan Gromes. Heavyset, with a large head, he sat leaning over his immense desk. Next to him stood the even more powerful chief of the provincial police, Hinko Karl, who kindly smiled at me.

"Well, young Goldstein, tell us, what brings you here?"

I don't remember what I said to them, but I can imagine it: My mother is in jail in Zagreb; my father is in the camp on Velebit; please let my mother out of jail or give me a travel permit so I can see her and bring her food. Gromes remained quiet the entire time, while

Karl continued to be chatty and kind. He said that my mother was under investigation but that I did not have to worry, she would be coming home. There was no sense in traveling to Zagreb because while the investigation is on, visitors are not permitted. I can send my mother packages and I can write to her, and he will make certain that she receives them and that she can write back to me. My father will be in the camp for a long time, but he will be all right, nothing will happen to him. He is healthy and strong, he will easily put up with the camp and its routine. And I should not be sad; my mother would be coming home soon. Karl escorted me to the door. I went into the street with the sickening feeling that his words were empty promises and that I could expect nothing, not even a travel permit, from him and Gromes.

A few days after that encounter was my thirteenth birthday, my bar mitzvah. I could now be counted among the minyan, the quorum of ten adult males required for regular prayer services. In Jewish families in prewar Croatia the bar mitzvah was a major ceremony. In addition to the traditional rituals, a boy would receive many gifts. One custom was that one of the gifts should be a wristwatch, an expensive gift for that time. My father also once promised me that for my bar mitzvah, either he or my mother would take me to Paris.

For my bar mitzvah I sat in the big parlor of the Veličkovićes' home in Banija. Mia and I were alone; Aleksander was out, perhaps at work in the factory. I had not even thought of a birthday celebration, nor could there have been a birthday celebration. Not a word from my mother and father. A congratulatory telegram might have arrived from Tuzla, but I don't remember. Mia knew of my father's promise of a "real" watch. From a drawer she pulled out a Swiss watch, an Eterna, and put it around my wrist. That was my bar mitzvah, a small assurance that I was not completely alone, that someone was here to ease my pain, inasmuch as that was possible.

Years later my mother often remembered the August 22 that she spent in the jail on Savska Street. She was quietly hoping I would visit her that day, but there was no word from me. She asked to send her son a letter that she had written for his birthday, but the commander of the Ustasha guards did not allow it. One of the guards promised to put the letter in the mail without permission; all my mother could do was hope that he would keep his promise. She spent the entire day trying to envision us together, whenever and wherever, but all four of us together. However, by that day the Jadovno camp no longer existed and my father was no longer alive.

On the morning of August 23, several transports filled with prisoners from Gospić and the island of Pag passed through Karlovac. Mr. Weiss found out that they had been housed temporarily in Jastrebarsko, where representatives of the Zagreb Jewish Community were permitted to visit and deliver food and medicine. Some of them had already been sent on to Jasenovac and to some point in Zagorje (Lobor). The camps in Lika were said to have been disbanded, but there was no one from Jadovno in the transports. None of "our people" were seen in Jastrebarsko nor did any of them get in touch.

Mr. Weiss had probably learned from his Italian colonel that on August 23, because of the unrest in Lika and other regions, the Italian army had reoccupied the island of Pag, all of the region of Primorje, and almost all of Lika. The Ustasha in these areas had to hand over power to the Italian command, while they withdrew some of their military units and the camp prisoners. The colonel could not have known anything about Jadovno.

And if you, my readers, were to ask me today what I felt then besides sadness and torment, I would be forced to admit: I don't remember, I don't know. Was I dispirited, despondent, and prone to desperation or depression? Although at thirteen years of age we don't have the benefit of experience, we certainly have a world of emotions.

Was I mourning for Danko, for my room, for our bookshop, for our confiscated apartment? Perhaps these emotions were overwhelmed by the instinct for survival, which after every new shock had to be and was more pronounced. Or perhaps there was not much room for emotion because each new situation demanded greater toughness and activity, not wallowing in self-pity. At that time I also feared for the lives of my mother and father, and that fear could have suppressed all other fears and emotions. I remember images and events from those times in more detail than from any other period of my life, but I can barely remember the emotions. Perhaps they have died away; perhaps they have been transformed because six and a half decades have passed, almost an entire lifetime. The images I recall are certainly authentic because they are so detailed that they cannot be a trick of my imagination. I have checked them in documents and books and against the memories of others. But we cannot verify our emotions from times past; they are always only personal, subjective. I am describing them with restraint and caution, perhaps even starkly, trying not to deceive myself or the reader.

13

The Velebit Death Camp

FANTASTIC STORIES IN which imagination defended itself against a vanishing hope circulated among the families anxiously awaiting news from Jadovno. According to one story, the Italians had taken control of "our people" on Velebit, but this was kept secret, so "our people" were not yet allowed to get in touch; or "our people" had managed to escape from the camp and were hiding in the Velebit forests; or Lika guerrillas had liberated the camp and "our people" had "gone underground" with them...etc. In still another version, the BBC had reported that Italian occupation authorities had been horrified at the conditions in the Ustasha concentration camps and would disband them. By their number and many contradictions the stories refuted one another, and instead of offering encouragement, they deepened the sheer depression. After the August 10 letter from the Zagreb Jewish Community, there was no reliable news about our people in Jadovno. A complete silence descended and hope was fading. Even so, after my mother escaped from Karlovac to the relative security of the Italian zone of occupation (Kraljevica) on October 20, she still thought it a good idea that I wait in Karlovac for news from my father, for God willing, "if Fati turns up, it will be in Karlovac." Even as a refugee in the Kraljevica camp at the beginning of 1942,

Hinko Gottlieb nurtured the slim hope that he would get some word—somehow, somewhere—from his son, Danko, who had disappeared in Jadovno in August. The elegant Gottlieb was a poet who to this day is the best translator of Heinrich Heine into Croatian, but he was also a successful lawyer. With the severe logic of a good lawyer, he realized that Danko was gone, but with the imagination and soul of a poet, he still hoped for a miracle.

* * *

Jadovno was the first death camp in the literal sense of the term in the Ustasha's Independent State of Croatia (NDH). As a part of the Gospić-Velebit-Pag camp system, which had several purposes, Jadovno was designated for the outright killing of its prisoners. The July 8 order of Dido Kvaternik outlines the genocidal component: "When the interests of public security require the deportation of undesirable persons from their places of residence, all Greco-easterners[1] and Jews will be sent to Gospić, whereas Catholics and Muslims will not." The implication here is that "undesirable" Croats and Bosnians would avoid death, but that the criteria of a selective political terror was applied to them, while a nonselective genocide was applied to Serbs and Jews.

Kvaternik was the creator of the Gospić-Velebit-Pag camp system. He began to work on it in June 1941, immediately upon his return from Berlin, where he'd had several days of discussions at the SS headquarters. During that time, the SS leadership had completed the preparations for the start of the action that came to be called the "final solution of the Jewish question," so Kvaternik probably received some advice for a similar action in the NDH. The timing is not a complete coincidence: four *Einsatzgruppen* (special task forces), each with five to nine hundred SS members, had begun a series of mass killings of Jews and other "undesirables" on occupied territory immediately after the invasion of the USSR, and the first group of camp inmates arrived at Jadovno two days later, on June 24.

The Gospić-Velebit-Pag camp system was under the immediate operational authority of the Directorate of the Provincial Police of Gospić County. Kvaternik appointed Stjepan Rubinić chief of police and sent him to Gospić on June 18 with orders to "establish a camp in Jadovno and to carry out temporary supervision of the camp on Pag." In his memoir, *Konclogor na Savi* (Concentration Camp on the River Sava),[2] Ilija Jakovljević describes Rubinić in vivid detail. The boastful "confidences" that Rubinić shared with Jakovljević in Stara Gradiška in 1942 reveal the criteria Kvaternik used to select Rubinić for this assignment, which he euphemistically called "the establishment of a camp in Jadovno." We learn the rest from Rubinić's statement of October 29, 1941, and other testimonies before the Ustasha Disciplinary and Criminal Court in Zagreb.[3]

Born in Jastrebarsko in 1909, Rubinić completed a two-year commercial school and became a traveling salesman and, briefly, a manager in the nationalistically oriented prewar societies Ante Starčević and August Šenoa. By distributing propaganda materials, he qualified for membership in the Ustasha, took the Ustasha oath, and was immediately activated on April 10, carrying out a variety of assignments at Ustasha headquarters in Zagreb. Two weeks later Kvaternik appointed him the Ustasha commander and state commissioner for the district of Kostajnica, Dvor na Uni, and Bosanski Novi with special powers and assignments. He boasted to Jakovljević in Stara Gradiška how one of those assignments was so "special" that he could describe it in general terms only. It involved a group of undesirable "volunteers" that "the Hungarians during the collapse had expelled to their Bosnian homeland," and that Rubinić had to get rid of. Jakovljević writes in his memoir what he was told by Rubinić:

> I invited them to meet and they accepted. They were told that they would be temporarily sent to a village where their security

> was absolute. After making a list of their names, I made sure they were fed well. Then I sent them away in sealed wagons to a station. You won't believe it, but it took only a few young men to do the job.... Gypsies carried out the liquidation. They also dug a common grave. Afterward we took care of that scum too. I'm sorry that along with the Gypsies I had to liquidate some of our people who participated in that business.... Too bad, but the homeland demands victims from among its best sons.

I believe it was the way in which Rubinić had carried out this particular assignment—perfidiously, cynically, and brutally, and all in the name of the homeland—that encouraged Kvaternik to entrust him with Jadovno.

In his statement on October 29, Rubinić complained that the "public in Gospić and Lika were not well-disposed toward me because I, an outsider, had been appointed chief of police in the heart of Lika." The local Ustasha veterans probably felt Zagreb was wrong to send them a "greenhorn" with an inferior pedigree in the Ustasha movement and with no police experience for such an important position—moreover the "outsider" was bringing with him four assistants with the approval of the young Kvaternik, as if there were not enough trustworthy Ustasha in Lika capable of doing the job.

Despite the initial animosity, Rubinić managed to get along with local Ustasha. The site of the Jadovno camp was selected by two men well-acquainted with the terrain—Jurica Frković, the first Ustasha commissioner for Lika and the governor of Gacko and Lika, and Juco Rukavina, the first commander of the combined Ustasha armed forces. In 1932, both men had participated in the Velebit uprising, and so had become familiar with the terrain around Jadovno.

The village of Jadovno is situated deep in the forests of the Velebit massif in a one-and-a-half-kilometer-long clearing 805 meters above sea level and about sixteen kilometers northwest of Gospić. According to the 1931 census, the village had 106 residents. In 1948 it had 92, and by 1971 it had 51. In the summer of 1994, I counted only seven inhabited homes, with barely twenty residents. From the northern edge of the town a dirt road leads into thick forest and winds up into the trackless waste. After eight kilometers a single narrow path breaks off from the road and descends into a valley, nearly two hundred meters long and one hundred meters wide. It is called variously Čačić-draga or Čačić-dolac. This is where the camp was situated. Today there are no longer any traces of it and one has to scratch hard under the bushes or turf to find the remains of barbed wire or shell casings. All around is thick forest and gray stone rising from the ground, a remote, forsaken place.

The entire Velebit area is known for its bottomless karst caverns. The best known is Šaran's cavern about one and a half kilometers from the village of Jadovno next to the forest road that led to the camp. The cavern is forty-two meters deep and its floor is layered with the skeletons of the camp inmates. It is impossible to establish the number. A large monument was erected in their honor and the road to the cavern was paved and bordered with a stone wall marked with verses from the poem "Cave" by Ivan Goran Kovačić. When I was there in the summer of 1994 with a Dutch film crew, the large monument above the forest road had been completely demolished and the road to the cavern vandalized. But between 2010 and 2012 the road was repaired and the monument reconstructed.

* * *

Rubinić set up his Directorate of the Provincial Police in the building of the provincial headquarters in Gospić on the same floor as the office of Frković, the provincial governor. In a statement four months later, he complained that because of the large number of prisoners "the job that fell to me was too great to be carried out as it should be." The prisoners arrived from all over Croatia and Bosnia and Herzegovina in overcrowded cattle cars and in daily shipments to the railway station in Gospić. They were being delivered from the surrounding districts of Lika in trucks, in horse-drawn wagons, and even on foot. Many were starving and exhausted by cruel treatment along the way. They were received at the railway station and were supposed to be registered by Janko Mihalović, Rubinić's deputy, and sometimes by Rubinić himself. It wasn't unusual for prisoners to enter the transit center or one of the camps unregistered.

The main holding and transit center was the old jail attached to the Gospić courthouse. The local nickname for it was the "Gericht" or the " Štokhauz." It was a large, two-story building, a hundred and thirty meters square. About two thousand and sometimes as many as four thousand prisoners were routinely crowded into the building. At the time of the greatest number of transports, in the second half of July and the first days of August, not even the huge old jail was large enough to hold everyone and arriving prisoners were housed in other public buildings in Gospić, most frequently in the local cinema and its courtyard. Some groups of Jewish and Serbian women with children and older men were taken from the railway station directly to an agricultural property called the Ovčara, which had been transformed into an auxiliary holding and work camp.

During these hot summer weeks, Gospić lived with the painful scenes of columns of prisoners trudging through the town, "not only at night but also in the middle of the day. Those columns made me feel terrible," Mićo Jelača, a witness, told researcher Đuro Zatezalo in 1987.[4]

> The sad column of people, haggard and wearied from the journey and by hunger and thirst, joined together with a chain that ran the length of the column and also by a two-by-two with a

> wire, passed down the middle of the street. On both sides of the column the Ustasha escorts beat them with rifle butts, swore at them, and made them sing.... Our people were horrified at seeing all of this. I remember one of my relatives wept while watching those exhausted people, but her daughter, who was an Ustasha sympathizer, shouted with joy. Both knew these people were on their way to the scaffold.[5]

Interrogations were being conducted in the Gericht, accompanied by a variety of tortures, and the fates of the prisoners were determined: directly to execution or to the camps on Pag and Velebit or to the Ovčara and rarely—and only as an exception—home, to freedom. "We frequently heard cries for help from the cells, where the Ustasha were beating and torturing people. Some in those cells had been condemned to death by starvation and beating. When the lights went out at night, we knew what that meant: The dead were being removed from the cells, we saw it from the windows," testified Terka Gojmerac, a woman from Zagreb who had gone through several Ustasha prisons and camps as a suspected communist only to be exchanged in 1942, later joining the Partisans and surviving the war.

Prisoners assigned to the island of Pag were most frequently transported in trucks from the Gericht to Baške Oštarije or Karlobag, where they were taken over by members of the Thirteenth Ustasha Battalion. Under the command of Ivan Devčić Pivac, an Ustasha émigré, the battalion was responsible for the camps of Metajna and Slana. There were also groups of prisoners who had to make that journey from Gospić to Baške Oštarije or Karlobag on foot, in columns joined lengthwise by a chain and a two-by-two with wire. Very few of these unfortunates survived the trek to Pag. They were either killed at a cavern not far from the village of Stupačinovo near Baške Oštarije, or ended up in the caverns on the coastal side of Velebit around Karlobag, or were thrown into the sea while being transferred by boat from Karlobag to Pag.

The prisoners transported to the camp at Jadovno from the Gericht or directly from the railway station were usually taken by truck for 11 kilometers to the village of Trnovac. They had to cover the remaining 12.5 kilometers walking uphill on the bumpy forest road with the customary shoving and beating with rifle butts by their Ustasha guards. Rarely would a truck bring a group to the village of Jadovno and almost never to the area of the camp itself. More frequently columns of prisoners had to cover the entire distance of 23.5 kilometers on foot, chained and tied together. Nikola Kosović of Lički Novi saw such columns of prisoners on a daily basis, and in 1981 gave the following account:

> In the summer of 1941, at the end of July and the beginning of August, as a twelve-year-old boy, I was guarding a herd with other shepherds in the area we call Novoselo, which is right where the road for the village of Trnovac turns off from the main Gospić–Karlobag road. At that time I saw almost every day the Ustasha leading long lines of prisoners in the direction of the village of Trnovac, three or four groups in the morning and two or three in the afternoon. The lines were long, about forty or fifty meters, with a gap of about fifty meters between one group and the other. The Ustasha escorted them. The prisoners were tied together two by two as well as lengthwise, end to end. Some were dressed very well, like real gentlemen, and even carried suitcases. Many were barefoot and naked, wearing only shirts and underwear. I didn't know who these people were. It was said in the village they were Serbs and Jews and they were being taken into the caverns at Jadovno. There were no women and children among them. I remember clearly how

> some people from these columns asked us shepherds while we were watching from the side of the road, "Is it far to Jadovno?" We would point to the direction with our hands but we didn't tell them how far it was because we didn't know how far Jadovno was, we were children.[6]

* * *

The first prisoners to arrive in Jadovno on June 24, 1941, were Zagreb Jews—from a group of about two hundred people who had been transported on the night of June 22 from the Zagreb transit center to Gospić. In Gospić at the Gericht about thirty able-bodied men were separated out and, under a heavy Ustasha escort, loaded onto a truck with bales of barbed wire and sent to Jadovno (according to the statement in 1946 of Bela Hochstädter, one of the group who survived the war). The prisoners cleared an area at Čačić-dolac and enclosed it with the barbed wire. After several days, ever-larger contingents be-

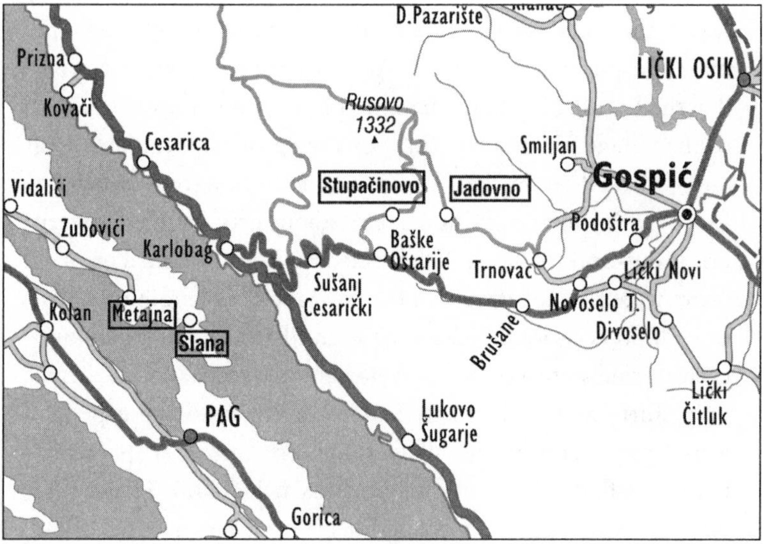

gan to arrive with increasing frequency. Two barracks were constructed for the Ustasha guards, while the inmates slept under the open sky. Only later were prisoners permitted to build shelters for themselves roofed with pine and beech branches and ferns. They called them "dwellings." They were up to two meters in height and about thirty people could be crammed into each. They were laid out in the shape of a horseshoe: one for Jews, one for the far more numerous Serbs, and one for about thirty politically suspect Croats.

The first encounter of the newly arrived prisoners with the camp was grim: a small valley, oval in shape with a double fence of thick barbed wire about four meters high. Machine-gun nests and guard posts were strategically placed around the fence and there were four observation posts for guards within the camp. Upon entering all personal items and money, if anyone still had any, were confiscated. The "dwellings" were crowded and provided no protection against the rain and the cold nights. All around were the craggy mountains, with no access roads or paths, and the impenetrable forests, with deafening silence perhaps more ominous than the barbed wire and the watchtowers. There was such a sense of impending death that there was no need for a prisoner to use his imagination.

The isolation of the camp was complete. In contrast to all of the other camps in the NDH, no one in Jadovno received a single letter or package, nor were they permitted to get in touch by letter or messanger. There were no visits by relatives or friends; access to the camp was not permitted to anyone except the Ustasha. No investigator ever came to the camp. In the period from July 7 to August 22 the Zagreb Jewish Community several times requested, proposed, and demanded that it be allowed to deliver packages to Pag and Jadovno via the Croatian Red Cross. The Red Cross of the NDH accepted the proposal, the Jewish Department of the Zagreb Ustasha Police issued an approval on July 23, and on August 11 the Directorate for Public

Order and Security in Gospić County confirmed in writing the receipt of a large number of packages. Some of these packages reached the camps at Metajna and Slana on the island of Pag. Not a single one arrived in Jadovno. The camp had disappeared into silence.

The researcher Franjo Zdunić Lav has traced fifty-six camp inmates who were transferred to other camps or were released before the Jadovno camp was dismantled: thirty-one prisoners of Croatian nationality (of whom ten from Gospić were released and twenty-one were sent to other camps); ten young Jewish men from Zagreb, who were pulled out by their schoolmate, the Ustasha lieutenant Janko Mihalović, allegedly to clean streets in Gospić but really to save them from execution (seven of them later ended up in Jasenovac, but three survived the war); five Serbian prisoners from the surrounding villages near Velebit, who saved themselves by escaping (two were subsequently killed fighting with the Partisans, but three survived the war as Partisans); and around ten other prisoners released at the intervention of higher authorities as members of mixed marriages (among whom were Nikola Adler of Karlovac and Bela Hochstädter of Zagreb).[7] On the basis of survivor statements, several researchers and historians—Đuro Zatezalo, Franjo Zdunić Lav, Mirko Peršen, Ivo Goldstein, Đuro Vezmar, and others—have reconstructed and described the conditions in the Jadovno camp before its final dismantlement.

The Jadovno camp at Čačić-draga was in existence for slightly less than two months, barely fifty-five days. Lav writes in his book on Jadovno:

> For the entire existence of the camp the prisoners were engaged in leveling the ground and other jobs related to the maintenance of the camp. They cut down trees within the barbed-wire fence and they cleared rock and dug up the upper part of the clearing. The work was hard and exhausting, it went on from

> morning until evening. . . . The food in the camp was miserable, some beans and hot kasha once a day dispensed at the entrance gate to each prisoner, one by one, separately to the Jews, then to the Serbs and to the Croats. The prisoners brought water for cooking and drinking from a spring, located about five to six hundred meters from the camp, in five cauldrons under an Ustasha guard. . . . The nights were particularly unbearable because of the low temperatures and humidity. One sat or lay on the bare earth. Some of the prisoners would sleep on a piece of tree bark or branches or ferns gathered from the area around the camp under the supervision of the Ustasha.

Mane Čanak, one of the four men who managed to escape from the camp, remembers being among eleven prisoners under an Ustasha escort who went one afternoon with the cauldrons for water: "When we arrived at the spring, they beat us, and before returning to the camp they forced us to sing Chetnik and communist songs. They made Savo Zaroja from Vrepac sing 'Pavelić, long live the hand that killed the Serbian bandit.'"

At the beginning, the Ustasha would lead small groups of eight to ten prisoners out to cut down trees and gather branches and ferns. After two successful escapes and one failed attempt, such work outside the fence was halted. Thus the prisoners languished, squeezed into the small area within the fence, forced to work endlessly on meaningless tasks, with the sole purpose of making them more exhausted and powerless, incapable of any kind of resistance.

* * *

The capacity of the camp, given the area and the circumstances described, could have been about 1,500 to 2,000 prisoners. For a brief time, probably in the middle or the latter half of July, the camp was overcrowded with roughly 3,000 prisoners. Among the survivors, the highest estimate was made by Božo Švarc, who in 1945 claimed that upon his arrival at the camp, in the middle of July, 4,000 prisoners were there, but in a statement in 1972 he corrected this and said roughly 2,000 to 3,000 Serbs and several hundred Jews. Dizdar identified by name 2,167 prisoners transported from Danica via Gospić and on to Jadovno, where they disappeared. Prisoner transports through Gospić for Jadovno also arrived from Zagreb, Osijek, Varaždin, Sarajevo, Vinkovci, Koprivnica, Slavonski Brod, Banja Luka, Karlovac, and other towns of northern Croatia, Bosnia, Herzegovina, and Srijem. There is no doubt that many more prisoners started out for the camp at Jadovno than reached it. They were killed along the way. Columns of prisoners that numbered one hundred or more arrived daily from Gospić until the middle of July as the camp filled to its maximum capacity. In the second half of July and the beginning of August, when the greatest number of prisoners was sent from Gospić to Jadovno, entire columns no longer arrived there, only one or two small groups each day with ten to twenty new prisoners. According to the postwar testimony of some residents of the village of Jadovno, complete columns arrived in their village, eight and a half kilometers away, but not at the camp. The execution site for many was Šaran's cavern, at the top of the road leading to the camp, only one and a half kilometers from the village. Once the columns passed through the village, gunfire could be heard from the forest fifteen to thirty minutes later, allegedly to the sound of gruesome cries and the pleading of the victims.[8]

At the peak of the transports the "surplus" prisoners were killed in the camp itself. This was the duty of two Ustasha camp commanders, First Lieutenant Rudi Ritz (a teacher before the war) and Ante Bešlić (a student in Split before the war), who took turns with the assignment. Summarizing the memories of the surviving camp prisoners, Lav vividly describes how this worked:

> Before nightfall Ritz would separate groups of eight to ten people from the camp based on a list of names jotted on a small sheet of paper. He did this two or three times for a total of about thirty to forty prisoners. They were taken, unbound, along the path that led to the camp. Whether they were tied together once they were away from the camp was not known, but an hour or an hour and a half after their departure, gunshots could be heard. The prevailing opinion among the camp inmates at the time was that those taken away were going to their death.... It is understood that the executions were carried out at a cave below Grgin Brijeg [Grga's Hill], as indicated by the statements of the camp survivors. The cave has not been investigated by speleologists to this day.

I imagine my father in the Jadovno camp, in the evening shade, as he listens to the shooting from Grgin Brijeg. He had arrived in Jadovno from Danica via Gospić on July 17 or 18, when the camp was already overcrowded and the executions of the "surplus" prisoners had already begun. One evening, did Ritz call out my father's name and send him off to Grgin Brijeg, or did my father lose his life in the final extermination of the camp? I know I will never find out, but I cannot help but think of my father's last days, last moments.

During these first evenings, the dreamer in my father may have believed that the salvoes from Grgin Brijeg were an exercise in firing or shooting during a search for escaping prisoners. To break away, to disappear into the thick forest, protected by the Velebit wilderness and the impenetrable darkness? But then, how to go on, to where? My father certainly considered such possibilities until the last moment and thought of ways not to surrender helplessly like a lamb. Only a single, inevitable question stopped him: What would happen to his two sons and their mother? He would expose them to the danger of becoming hostages of his actions.

Since the evening shootings from Grgin Brijeg monotonously followed one after the other, with no machine-gun fire or excitement among the Ustasha guards, the inmates were painfully aware that the liquidation of the "surplus" was proceeding, that there were no escapees, and that there was virtually no possibility of escape. The guards bound the prisoners they were leading to Grgin Brijeg with a chain and a wire outside the camp to forestall a prisoner revolt. "That feeling of helplessness was strange," wrote Branko Cetina, one of the five prisoners who succeeded in escaping. Cetina fought the helplessness from the moment they took him out of the Gospić jail toward Jadovno, looking for any opportunity to escape, until one proved to be lifesaving.

What did my father feel and think in those moments? What passed through his mind, his consciousness? How did he look death in the face?

In his youthful writings my father indicated that he had ceased being a practicing Jew early on, but that he remained a great admirer of Jewish traditions. Did he turn back to God when facing death? Did he address Him with reproachful questions? The father of Søren Kierkegaard, feeling the injustice of having to live wretchedly as a village servant though he was an intelligent and enterprising young man, in an act of anger left his sheep, climbed a hill, and unleashed that anger in the face of unjust God. My father couldn't climb a hill—he ended up in a bottomless pit.

* * *

On August 16, Mussolini sent a telegram to Pavelić ordering the reoccupation of Zone A by Italy "due to the urgent needs of military security." According to the Rome agreements of May 18, 1941, Zone A (parts of the regions of the Croatian coastline and Gorski Kotar, northern and central Dalmatia, and almost all of the Adriatic islands) was annexed to the Kingdom of Italy. But if security reasons required, Italy also had the right to place a far greater portion of Croatian territory, known as Zone B, under its control. Zone B was made up of all of the remaining islands, the entire Adriatic coast, and major portions of the littoral area, including Gorski Kotar and almost all of Lika, the Dalmatian hinterland, and Herzegovina. This meant in effect that the Ustasha camp system of Gospić-Velebit-Pag would have to be withdrawn from the area under Italian authority.

Vlado Singer, at that time the chief of the Ustasha intelligence service, had warned Kvaternik and Pavelić at the beginning of August that the headquarters of the Italian Second Army (responsible for Slovenia and Croatia) had plans for the military occupation of the above-mentioned regions. From the Italian perspective, the need for the occupation was justified by the uprising that had broken out at the end of July and the beginning of August in these regions, disrupting communication and threatening the security of the coast. In addition, General Vittorio Ambrosio, the commander of the Second Army, in a report to the army chief of staff on August 24, claimed that his troops were "unwilling witnesses to the savage massacres the Ustasha were carrying out, while honest Croats were ashamed." These "savage massacres," in the view of Ambrosio and his subordinate commanders in Croatia and Bosnia and Herzegovina, caused unrest among the Orthodox populace and could only be quelled by assuming full responsibility—that is, occupation. In the background, not publicly stated of course, were the enduring imperial aspirations of fascist Italy to rule the entire Adriatic coast and greater parts of the interior.

Through the month of August, Pavelić and other senior NDH officials frantically but unsuccessfully tried by diplomatic means to convince Ribbentrop and Hitler to intervene with the Italian leadership to forego the occupation or at least to reduce its scope. Choosing between two allies, the leadership of the Third Reich felt it more important to support fascist Italy than the Ustasha NDH. Besides, the Italian arguments that the Ustasha's repressive measures were inciting unrest and rebellion were considered plausible by the German leadership, who had already received similar warnings from Glaise von Horstenau and other German representatives in the NDH. Thus the Ustasha authorities had to withdraw their military units from the designated areas by the end of August and turn over police authority to the Italian carabinieri.

At a hearing before the Ustasha Criminal and Disciplinary Court on October 29, 1941, Rubinić described how "a panic arose among his police and Ustasha in Gospić and its surroundings" after the news of the Italian reoccupation in August. The real victims of that panic were the remaining prisoners at Jadovno and the majority of those remaining on the island of Pag.

The truth about those killed at Jadovno, Pag, and ten other execution sites in the Velebit region was uncovered during a sanitation inspection by the Italian occupation forces in the first days of September 1941. Spurred by reports from various Lika localities about "temporary graveyards" from which "the disgusting stench of decaying corpses is spreading," the health service of the Fifth Army Corps based in Crikvenica sent two sanitation inspection teams on a tour of the area—to "prevent the possible polluting of the water supply." The chief of the first inspection team, Vittorio Finderle, described his four-day tour of one location on the island of Pag and some villages in the Velebit region in a detailed report. He established the existence of caverns in which "the bodies of the victims of the most recent political events in Croatia were discarded"—in particular, two caverns not far from Baške Oštarije near the village of Stupačinovo:

> Here we found fragments of shirts and men's clothing. Next to the cavern there was human hair, photographs, and empty and torn coin purses, as well as wallets, shell casings, and other objects. It is said that about two thousand Serbian men were brought here and thrown into the cavern and that the most recent massacre was about three weeks ago. No sanitary procedures were carried out by the Croatian authorities. I mixed a large amount of chemical cleaning solution with water from a nearby spring and poured it into the cavern.

And then in another report:

> I returned to the starting point and began a search with the army. I was able to discover another chasm, called the Duliba cavern. It was covered with tree branches and leaves and was well-concealed. On a path near the cavern we found fragments of clothing, handkerchiefs, personal documents, shell casings from military rifles, small toothbrushes, and even a man's broken wristwatch. I ordered the peasants to remove the branches. The sharp, penetrating odor of decayed flesh drifted out. The entry of the cavern measured eight by eight meters. The stones in the immediate vicinity of the opening were covered with bloodstains and human remains. About two hundred people had been thrown into this cavern and the murder had been carried out a month or so ago. No disinfecting agent had been thrown into this cavern. Here too I put in a chemical solution.

From a tour of the area, the statements of neighboring residents, and the information from an army patrol that searched parts of Velebit, Finderle identified execution sites at six main locations. These included Jadovno, which he noted held "the most victims." However, the Italian inspection teams in the Velebit forests had been ordered to perform sanitation tasks exclusively. They were not engaged in collecting the data of the crimes committed or establishing the number of victims. Only one disinfection team, while cleaning up a grave site in September near the former Ustasha camp of Slana on the island of Pag, exhumed bodies from a shallow grave and burned them. In a detailed report dated September 22, 1941, Lieutenant Santo Stazzi, the head of the group, stated:

> Thus, 791 bodies found at various sites were burned, 716 of these at the main cemetery in Malin.... Of these bodies, 407 were men, 293 were women, and 91 were children between the ages of five and fourteen.... I learned from the person who served as my guide to the clean-up that the greatest number of those deported to Slana had been thrown into the sea, weighted down with large stones, and that many others took their own lives by drowning.[9]

* * *

The Italian military and political authorities did not publish the reports of their sanitation inspections of Ustasha genocidal crimes during the war, but they did use the information and the documentation as arguments in their political negotiations and quarrels with NDH leaders. This is how they justified their patronage of the Chetniks, their occupation of Zone B, and the military control of areas all the way to Karlovac and Sarajevo. It was eventually reported that the Italians had requested that the Ustasha authorities extradite Rubinić so he could be publicly tried for the crimes at Jadovno.

On orders from Kvaternik, Rubinić was arrested on September 13, or after the Italian discoveries of the Velebit caves and the Pag burial sites had been presented to the Ustasha leadership. Kvaternik obviously didn't want the Italians to conduct a public trial about Ustasha crimes or to give the Chetniks satisfaction. He felt the need, nevertheless, to show that the senior Ustasha leadership did not stand behind these misdeeds, which is how the trial of Rubinić before the Ustasha Criminal and Disciplinary Court was staged.

The trial was a transparent tragicomic farce. The procedure was conducted in secrecy and the final report for the public was window dressing. In his testimony Kvaternik outlined what the trial was about only in turgid phrasing and in code interspersed with obvious lies. In his testimony before the court Rubinić claimed that he had done nothing without the knowledge of Kvaternik and had relocated the Jadovna camp to Maksimović, the Ovčara station in Gospić.

Rubinić was telling the truth when he said that he didn't do anything without instructions and orders from Kvaternik, but he was lying when he said that everyone and everything except for the kitchenware was relocated to Ovčara when the camp had already been liquidated. Kvaternik was also lying when he said that he wasn't aware of what Rubinić was doing at Jadovno, but Kvaternik was perhaps speaking the truth when he expressed surprise that what had been done was handled so quickly. In every way, Rubinić was the ideal sacrificial lamb to the Italians, and possibly to other causes.

The rest of the participants in the trial, witnesses and suspects, spoke about everything but the subject at hand. They knew the trial was about Jadovno, but that it couldn't be stated openly. They knew that Rubinić had been chosen as the sacrificial lamb, so they attributed to him transgressions that by Ustasha criteria were minor or even meaningless: unclear accounting of the money taken from camp prisoners, unlawful use of automobiles, sexual relations with a female prisoner. At the end Rubinić was accused and convicted as Kvaternik wished, that "as director of the county police in Gospić," he willfully misused the prisoners in the Jadovno camp, and he had willfully relocated the camp from Jadovno to Gospić and from there to Jastrebarsko.

On January 29, 1942, Rubinić was sentenced to expulsion from the Ustasha movement and a year of forced labor in a camp. The sentence was published in the newspapers, but with a general formulation about the abuse of power and with no mention of Jadovno. Kvaternik had what he needed: public acknowledgment that the worst crimes committed had been "willful" and not the result of a decision by the Ustasha authorities. This sentence could now be used as an instrument in internal disputes with the Italians, with some German representatives, and with weaklings in their own ranks, as well as for a general softening of the harrowing stories about Jadovno and Pag circulating in Croatia and Bosnia. And Rubinić himself told Ilija Jakovljević how for some acts, just in case, they always had to have in reserve some "cover," and it had turned out that he had been sacrificed as "cover" for his boss, Kvaternik, to whom he was always the loyal underling.

Nevertheless, Rubinić did not exactly pay a heavy price for being sacrificed. Kvaternik had to be careful not to instill doubt among the hard-core Ustasha, who did not see guilt but merit in Rubinić's actions at Jadovno. Rubinić spent a year at Stara Gradiška, where he enjoyed "special" treatment, that of an honored guest of the camp. He was housed in the headquarters building, received the same quality food as the senior officers, and spent evenings in their company. He slept on clean bedding, freely walked around the camp, worked a little in the office sorting prisoner files, and sometimes assisted in investigations of individual prisoners.

After serving his one-year sentence, Rubinić was released. He was not reactivated in the Ustasha organization, but as a consolation he was granted two confiscated Jewish companies, which he managed until the end of the war. Nothing was known about him in the fall of

1945, so in the files of the National Commission for the Investigation of War Crimes it was noted mistakenly that he had "allegedly been killed by the Ustasha." It wasn't until three years later that a report dated October 17, 1948, by a State Security Administration agent indicated that Rubinić was frequently seen in the company of Ustasha émigrés in Salzburg, Austria, especially with Vjekoslav Blaškov. The report said that the last time he was seen was between September 12 and 25 in the Grossglockner Café. However, when it was later learned that Blaškov had been arrested while trying to enter Croatia illegally, "Rubinić had disappeared without a trace.... He is well off financially, and Hotko and Kovačević think that he is living in Austria or Germany, withdrawn from public life...."

* * *

No one knows, and it seems impossible to establish, the day the Jadovno camp was liquidated. The lawyer Edo Neufeld claims that it occurred in the first days of August 1941, "since there was no sign of life of those people at that time and the Ustasha had brought us [the prisoners at the Ovčara] several cooking pots and pans, saying they were from Jadovno as the camp had been abandoned." This probably isn't accurate because on August 10 the Jewish Community had official information that Karlovac Jews at Jadovno were "healthy and well." But perhaps their information wasn't accurate either. I think Lav's guess is probably the closest:

> The liquidation of the Jadovno camp was carried out between August 15 and 20. On August 15, 1941, Fascist Italy issued an order to the Second Army for the reoccupation...the Ustasha and Pavelić were faced with a fait accompli. Therefore, they quickly carried out the liquidation of the camps at Slana and Jadovno and removed the traces of their crime. At that time, about 1,200 prisoners—900 Serbs and 250 to 300 Jews—were

> in the Jadovno camp. Most of these prisoners were killed in the immediate vicinity of the camp and their bodies thrown into the karst caves. The largest cave entrance has a diameter of about two hundred meters and is located about forty to fifty meters south of the camp. The Ustasha threw stones, tree trunks, and branches over the murdered victims.

I don't know in which cave my father is lying. The researcher and historian Đuro Zatezalo has established that eighteen caves contain the remains of the victims of Jadovno. I don't know, and there is no way to find out, when and how my father was killed, by what weapons or means. There were no surviving reliable witnesses. Only one man, Serđo Poljak, from the village of Šibuljine near Velebit, managed to escape from the Jadovno caverns. Before he was killed as a Partisan, in a battle against the Ustasha in 1942, he spoke in detail to his family and friends about his Jadovno calvary. Pavle M. Babac described Serđo's escape in his book *Velebitsko podgorje* (The Velebit Foothills).[10]

On the way to the cavern Poljak had managed to free his hands from the wire that bound them. When the Ustasha started shooting with machine guns and rifles from above the cavern, Poljak hid himself among the dead and wounded. During the night, he crawled out of the cavern and somehow reached his village. Stevo Pjevač from Lički Čitluk escaped from the immediate vicinity of the cavern and his testimony corroborates Poljak's. The other three fugitives from Jadovno escaped while working in the forest and they did not witness the liquidation.

A considerable number of the Lika Ustasha, the actual or alleged perpetrators of the crime at Jadovno, were convicted by courts after the war. I have read three or four of their testimonies, and I did not want to torture myself by reading the rest. They are terrifying. I never know if these are truthful or forced confessions. And those who planned and issued the orders for the killings have always interested me more than those who actually carried them out.

The perpetrators of these crimes state in their testimonies that they killed with hammers, axes, knives, and only sometimes with a rifle or revolver. They say that many were beaten and wounded and tossed, still alive, into the cavern. I didn't want to see my father that way. I tried to force such images from my mind when in 1994 I was at Čačić-draga and at Šaran's cavern. The historian Antun Barac was a prisoner in Jasenovac in 1941, and in his posthumously published *Bijeg od knjige* (Escape from a Book) he says that after his first trembling brush with death in the camp, repeated experiences with death did not bring feelings of fear but "only hardness and an even greater contempt for our oppressors." I tried to picture my father at the last moment—when he realizes that it is the end, that there is no escape, hope, or rescue—not kneeling, not pleading, but feeling contempt for his killers and for those who gave the orders for the killing.

Part Five

My Mother, the Ustasha, and the Partisans

Lea Goldstein (1904–1974)

14

Cell No. 20

THE TITLE OF an article in the Zagreb newspaper *Novi list* on August 4, 1941, read "On the Romantic Mrežnica Enjoy Fishing, Rowing and Swimming." The reporter was charmed by the luxurious vegetation of the islands and the shady backwaters of the Mrežnica, its low-lying and hilly banks, its gurgling waterfalls, and its picturesque old mills. He delighted in the many picnickers, patient anglers, powerful rowers, and the idyllic scenery with four gently winding rivers—the Korana, the Mrežnica, the Dobra, and the Kupa—that surround Karlovac.

By that time the Jews had been banned from public bathing areas, so from time to time I went swimming with friends across the old wooden bridge and downstream to several small islands in the Korana. When Josip Vaništa, Lasić, and I recently went on an old men's nostalgic walk along the Korana, we quietly enjoyed the beauty of "our" islands and the river backwaters that surround them. I don't remember if I enjoyed the Korana's beauty with such intensity at any time in 1941, or in the subsequent war years, when I had many occasions to cross all four of the Karlovac rivers. Marching as a Partisan across the Mrežnica waterfalls that the Zagreb reporter so admired, I saw them as an obstacle and a danger, sometimes a hiding place and protection, and least for their beauty. May I then conclude that beauty in nature does not exist in and of itself but arises through interaction with our predisposition and experience?

In August 1941 much of Karlovac still tried to live a normal existence. Judging from the newspaper reports, the summer was pleasantly warm, mostly clear, and sunny, with only occasional clouds and gentle rains. Most residents still had not been touched directly by the evil of the times. Schoolchildren enjoyed a longer vacation—no school from April 10 until the early fall. The soccer matches were well attended. On August 5, *Novi list* noted a "successful concert by the main headquarters of the Ustasha army band at Croatia House." The factories of Karlovac granted a one-month salary to the families of workers serving in the army. Groups of twenty-five children from the city's poorer families were sent on holiday in fifteen-day shifts to Kraljevica at the expense of city hall. At the fairgrounds horses were on display for export to Germany. On August 10, the cornerstone was laid for the workers' housing project for forty-eight families on the left bank of the Kupa River. *Poglavnik* Pavelić issued a decree on extensive public works, which included the modernization of the Zagreb–Karlovac road.

At the same time, bread was rationed. People knew that Croatia had to feed the Italian occupation forces and that wheat was shipped to Germany by the wagonload, but the newspapers blamed only smugglers and speculators, which usually meant Jews and Serbs. But by August most of them had lost their businesses, so guilty parties had to be found among Croatian merchants.

Before long another harbinger of evil hit Karlovac: the mobile summary court from Zagreb. My mother was among the first to be aware of it. One day when I brought her lunch, as I did every day, a thin slightly bent old woman was feverishly caressing and hugging a pretty young girl in the jail courtyard. I found the scene disturbing.

"They are mother and daughter," my mother explained, "both seamstresses. The daughter is in the cell with us. A lovely girl. Her prospects are grim. She is going before the summary court. When we clean the hallway, just the two of us, she talks to me about herself, taps the middle of her forehead with her finger: 'They will shoot me here... right here.'"

The girl was Herta Turza, for whom the elementary school in Banija was named after the war.

Herta was arrested on July 21, along with about twenty other members of the Communist Party and the League of Young Communists of Yugoslavia (SKOJ). The next day the mobile summary court arrived in Karlovac from Zagreb. On July 23, it held its first trial. In eight sessions, as many as the court had held in Karlovac in total in the previous months of 1941, and after brief deliberations, it handed down forty-five death sentences and one prison term.

At the municipal police station, in a cell with my mother and ten other women, Herta awaited her turn to stand before the summary court. It is human nature that in such situations there is hope until the last moment, but in talks with my mother Herta did not deceive herself. Although they were in the cell together for only twelve days, and had not known each other before, they became close. She needed someone with whom she could speak openly and frankly, and my mother, friendly and understanding, was that person. My mother later recalled that Herta did not shed tears or lament her fate. She accepted it as a hard, inexorable fact, as some natural disaster that one knows about in advance but cannot escape.

In *Zapisi iz rodnog grada* (Notes from My Birthplace),[1] Veco Holjevac writes that Herta was "a quiet and modest twenty-two-year-old girl... kind and sensitive, seemingly fragile, so it was hard to understand from where she drew her tremendous strength for clandestine party work. She became a member of the Party District

Committee"—of which Holjevac was also a member. At the first meeting of the committee after the German invasion of the Soviet Union, in the last days of June, Josip Kraš read a telegram sent to the Central Committee of the Communist Party of Yugoslavia (KPJ) through a secret Comintern radio station:

> The perfidious German attack on the USSR is a blow aimed not only at the socialist countries but at the freedom and independence of all people. All measures must be undertaken to support and facilitate the just struggle of the Soviet people. The defense of the USSR is the defense of the countries Germany has occupied.... A movement must evolve under a united front... and protect the subjugated countries from fascism—an act that is inseparably linked to the victory of the USSR. At this stage it is a question of liberation from fascist subjugation and not of socialist revolution.

For fanatical communists, disciplined "soldiers of the revolution," this was a clear call to battle. Based on a decision of the District Committee, Holjevac became the main organizer of shock groups in the city, while Herta became the main link between the groups. In a matter of days they had ten such groups under their control, each with three to four mostly young members of the KPJ and SKOJ. On Thursday night, July 3, 1941, at nine thirty, Karlovac was suddenly without power: lights went out in homes and on the streets, in cinemas and in cafés. In their first action the shock groups had knocked out the power lines. For about an hour, under the cover of darkness, Herta and several activists wrote in huge letters on walls in Karlovac "Long live the Soviet Union!" and "Long live the Communist Party!"

A number of other attacks followed over the next few days in which the telephone lines between Karlovac and other cities were cut, as well as an unsuccessful attempt to sabotage the rail line between Karlovac and Zagreb. Then, on the evening of July 19, twelve young men, again under the command of Holjevac, demolished the main railway line between Karlovac and the coast at Mrzlo Polje. The detonation was powerful and was heard as far as Kordun.

Although insignificant in military terms, these first acts of sabotage were a courageous and far-reaching announcement of Croatia's stance in the Second World War. At that point, a clear division had been formed between fascism and antifascism in Europe and in the rest of the world, between the forces that threatened human civilization and those that opposed them. The newly installed government of the Independent State of Croatia unequivocally stood on one side of that divide, on the fascist side. With the German invasion on June 22, 1941, the Soviet Union, against Stalin's will, found itself on the antifascist side of the divide, becoming a great power through force of circumstance. At Moscow's behest, Croatian and Yugoslav communists followed the lead of the Soviet Union. With their first acts of sabotage, Holjevac and his shock group made it known that Croatia was not completely on the fascist side, that the global divide of the Second World War also ran through Croatia. The authors of the ancient Qumran texts would have said that Croatia was caught up in a great war between the Sons of Light and the Sons of Darkness, in which the victory of the Sons of Light wasn't certain because in the end it was shown that many of the victors carried within them a new darkness. But the earliest protagonists of this apocalyptic war in Croatia paid a heavy price, and this included the Karlovac shock groups.

Nikola Šavor, a twenty-year-old baker's apprentice and the secretary of the Municipal Committee of SKOJ, took part in the majority of the acts of sabotage in and around Karlovac. Holjevac describes him as a young man who "spoke with emotion...that betrayed a lively and energetic nature and made an excellent impression." Ivo Marinković described him as "first-rate, the best of the SKOJ members." With enterprise and ingenuity Šavor had managed to obtain or purchase a variety of weapons from Italian and Home Guard soldiers. All of his SKOJ comrades in the shock groups had revolvers; some even had hand grenades. Even as they were returning from the nighttime sabotage of the rail line at Mrzlo Polje, Šavor was frantically looking for partners among his SKOJ comrades for a new, more spectacular operation.

At around midday on July 20, Šavor and his partner, Milan Vidović, stood before an Italian guard at the gate of the large barracks in the main square of the old center of Karlovac. Šavor was acting on his own initiative. While Vidović distracted the guard's attention with questions, Šavor threw two hand grenades through the open gate and into the courtyard of the barracks. Neither grenade exploded. Nevertheless, all hell broke loose. Šavor and Vidović tried to escape, but soldiers from a neighboring barracks blocked their way. Šavor shot at them with his revolver, but he and Vidović were quickly caught and overpowered. Božo Piškulić, the leader of one of the SKOJ shock groups, started to fire in an effort to help Šavor and Vidović escape. He couldn't save them and himself fell into the hands of their pursuers. All three were taken to the nearby police station and subjected to a brutal interrogation. Vidović and Piškulić did not break under the heavy beatings, but Šavor, perhaps under harsher torture, gave in late that night and talked. Grga Milašinčić, who had been arrested that same night, later recalled: "Šavor was beaten savagely, all bloody, his teeth broken, his face covered with bruises, his hands swollen. He lay flat on the floor because he couldn't stand." Before morning Šavor divulged the names of some twenty members and leaders of the shock groups. Almost all were arrested early in the morning, among them Herta Turza.

Holjevac managed to hide for two days and later escape to the nearest village in Kordun. A week later at Petrova Gora, he stood along with several local communists before a crowd of one thousand or more people of Kordun who had escaped into the forest in the face of a new wave of Ustasha massacres. Only about fifty had weapons, mostly hunting rifles and a few carbines, but they were prepared to fight rather than wait like sheep for an Ustasha knife. They accepted the leadership of the communists because no one else offered them better organization and more decisive solidarity in combat.

The remaining members of the shock groups who had evaded arrest, along with other communists, quickly joined Holjevac in Kordun. Thus, the uprising in Kordun evolved from the symbiosis of threatened Serbian peasants and well-organized communists.

* * *

Herta faced the summary court with six of her shock-group comrades on August 7, 1941. The hearings were conducted under an "expedited procedure" and were completed for all seven defendants in three hours. The court considered the statements made by Šavor under torture as sufficient proof against them. At exactly one o'clock in the afternoon, the chief judge read out the seven death sentences then left for lunch at the nearby Hotel Central. At the same time, Mirko Gantar, the clerk of the district court who recorded the proceedings of the summary court, was seen leaving the hearing wiping his glasses and hiding his tears. A good friend of our family, Gantar told us after the war that writing that transcript was the most difficult day in his forty-five years of service in the court.

The Law on Summary Courts required the execution to be carried out within three hours of sentencing. There was virtually no possibility for an appeal. The condemned spent their last three hours of life together in a special cell of the court jail. Several minutes before four o'clock a flatbed truck pulled up to the rear exit of the jail. A large group of people, some gloating but also friends who had the courage to come and bid farewell, were crowding around the truck on Križanićeva Street. At exactly four o'clock, policemen with bayoneted rifles escorted the seven condemned prisoners out. The gathered crowd made their farewells in silence. On the bed of the truck Herta sang the "Internationale" and "Down with Force and Injustice."

The flatbed truck drove through the city with the bound prisoners on display. Herta, as many of the observers later reported, was singing martial songs, while some of her comrades were shouting slogans to the glory of the Communist Party and to Comrade Stalin. They were transported to an execution site on the outskirts of the city. An hour later the echoes of gunshots resonated through the city. The residents of Karlovac knew that at that moment seven of their fellow citizens had been executed.

In the morning posters appeared on the news kiosks and other prominent places in the city:

Independent State of Croatia
Ministry of Internal Affairs

ANNOUNCEMENT

Following the frequent communist actions in Karlovac and the surrounding area, a police investigation has identified the perpetrators.

After conducting hearings, the mobile summary court, having established the guilt of the accused, today sentenced them to death by firing squad:

Milan Vidović, Orthodox, 21 years old
Herta Turza, Protestant, 22 years old

Božo Piškulić, Roman Catholic, 22 years old
Josip Milašinčić, Roman Catholic, 20 years old
Josip Bukvić, Roman Catholic, 28 years old
Risto Konstantinović, Orthodox, 35 years old
Mate Jakšić, Orthodox, 41 years old

The death sentence was carried out in the legally prescribed period after the announcement.

Ministry of Internal Affairs
Karlovac, August 7, 1941

Few residents of Karlovac, I believe, remained indifferent when they read the names on this poster on the morning of August 8. People stood in small groups before the posters, all dumbfounded, each thinking their own thoughts in silence. Such an announcement of the executions of seven fellow citizens sowed varying degrees of uneasiness in the small city, and among many residents, a hollow fear—which is precisely what the posters were meant to do.

Šavor was not taken before the summary court. The Ustasha authorities spared his life and released him when he had no one else to betray. Of course, it was not easy for him to live in a city where many people knew that he had betrayed twenty of his comrades. He went into hiding with his relatives in a village not far from Karlovac. In the spring of 1942, he was discovered by a Partisan unit. An improvised a military court was formed and he was sentenced to death. Šavor accepted the sentence. His final words standing before the firing squad were, "Long live the Communist Party!"

* * *

My mother spent nearly two months in the jail on Savska Street in Zagreb, in Cell No. 20 on the ground floor. She was sent to Zagreb from Karlovac in the middle of August with Vera Šarić, Metka

Šuman-Drakulić, and Mika Godler. On October 16, all four were sent back to Karlovac. By prison standards Cell No. 20 was medium-sized, about five meters long by four meters wide, with two small barred windows that looked onto a courtyard, part of Savska Street, and the railway line.

Between fourteen and twenty women prisoners were routinely crowded into the cell. They slept on straw mattresses in two rows with a narrow aisle down the middle. In the corner next to the window was a wooden partition, behind which was the washbasin and a bucket used as toilet. There was a faucet but no water.

The jail, administered by the Ustasha police of Zagreb, was considerably harsher than the civilian jail on Petrinjska Street where my father had spent six weeks in the spring, or the jail of the Ustasha police in Karlovac, where my mother had spent a month. The prisoners were locked in all day. In the morning they were permitted to go to the bathroom, to wash, and to empty and clean the bucket. They were not permitted to write letters home or to receive letters from home. Their only connection with the outside world was the food they were allowed to receive. Every day between noon and one o'clock, two or three Ustasha guards would accept pots with food and packages and inspect them, slicing open the cakes and loaves of bread. If a package was refused at the gate or returned undelivered, that meant the prisoner was no longer there. A search would follow through all the police stations for the missing person, often in vain because the missing person was no longer among the living. Many brought at least something to the gate every day at noon because that was the most reliable way of finding out whether their son, brother, daughter, or sister was still there.

The Savska Street jail was a transit center from which prisoners left in one of three directions: usually to the Jasenovac camp, sometimes to the execution site at Rakov Potok, and, rarely, to freedom.

The jail on Savska Stret in Zagreb was demolished in 1958.

Since they had not been interrogated, the women in Cell No. 20 feared that they were simply being held in reserve for a time when it became necessary to fill the quota for Rakov Potok.

I owe many of the details from Savska Street to Vera Gerovac-Blažević, who was only eleven when she was in Cell No. 20 with her mother and older sister. Vera told me the story of nineteen-year-old Laura—a slight woman with a very light complexion and delicate fingers and hands. Laura was quiet and withdrawn until she felt provoked by a conversation in the cell that didn't please her, whereupon she'd vigorously defend her views. She never hid her Jewish identity. When two Jewish women from Zagreb flaunted their wealth a little, Laura attacked them and defended the poor, though it seems she herself was not poor. When they called Laura to ready herself for departure, she put on her blue shoes, neatly gathered her things, and calmly said goodbye to everyone in the cell.

A few days later, a barefoot Vera was guarding the vegetable garden from the chickens when the manager of the jail's warehouse, an Ustasha émigré and peasant from the village of Lika, noticed that the little barefoot Vera was shivering.

"Hey, little girl from Lika, where are your shoes?"

"I don't have any, sir."

"Then come with me."

The manager took her to the large warehouse where there were several stacks of clothing and accessories by the door.

"There, find a pair of shoes for yourself."

Vera began to search through a pile of shoes, and finally found a pair that fit her. She put them on, took a few steps, and suddenly froze. She stared down at the familiar blue leather and laces and in a moment it flashed through her mind: These are Laura's shoes! She started to cry and ran out of the warehouse, to the astonishment of the manager. The eleven-year-old child had suddenly realized the terrible truth: Laura was dead.

* * *

One Friday Jaga's sister Jana brought me a message from Jaga that I could stay with her in Banski Kovačevac if I needed to. Expelled from Karlovac by the police, Jaga wasn't permitted to leave her village, but Jana came every Friday to the market in Karlovac. Jana claimed that all was calm and safe in their village, and that perhaps it would be better for me to get out of the city.

Mr. Weiss and Pavica Vine said this was good to know, but there was no danger for me in the city for the time being. No Jewish children under the age of sixteen had been arrested. The uncompromisingly optimistic Pavica convinced me that if my mother was lucky she would soon be returning home from the Zagreb jail. She thought it was impossible that at least one of the ways she was trying to get my mother out of jail would not succeed.

Mia Veličković (1899–1960)

I spent two months hoping that we would get my mother out of jail, often having to shoulder the responsibilities of an adult while still a child. But I had not been left on my own; quite a few people were trying to help. None of my close friends had stopped seeing me and some in fact invited me to their homes more than they had before that summer of 1941. However, in September they went back to school. By a government degree, Jewish children were no longer permitted to attend public schools, but I don't think this had too much of an effect on me because I was increasingly preoccupied with far more serious concerns and obligations. Our lawyer had approached the authorities regarding my mother's release and information about my father. He needed documents that I was allowed to remove from our apartment. The bookshop was "under lock and key," but we were still its nominal owners, so the trustee allowed me to take some things from the shop. Vlado Samardžija recalls that once I sold old, valuable postage stamps to my friends on the promenade. I don't know why I did this, perhaps to have something to do, because I could always get spending money, as much as I needed, from Mia Veličković.

I often went to the Veličkoviće's in Banija. They were my parents' closest friends during the ten years before the war. They owned two-thirds of the "Podvinec" factory, the second largest leatherworks in Croatia. The Veličkoviće's didn't have any children, so they often took Danko and me with them on excursions and treated us as their own. He was a Serb and she was a Slovene, and in the NDH they had suddenly become *personae non gratae*. However, by bribing almost everyone, the shrewd Ane provided them with a kind of security and a partial continuation of the operations of the factory. In the summer and early fall of 1941 they were put under police surveillance and a form of house arrest—only allowed to walk from the apartment to the factory and from the factory back home, and nowhere else. When I visited them, a police detective, usually Saletto, the one who took my mother and Jaga to jail with Mihelčić on July 14, would be standing in front of their house. He always spoke to me kindly, almost like an old friend or protector, and without any trouble he allowed me to pass and visit the Veličkoviće's on the first floor. I cannot say that I liked Saletto's attention.

Ane was usually in the factory all day, while Mia stayed at home alone. I would usually find her reading a book or playing patience at the large table in their living room. Here, with the Veličkoviće's, I felt perhaps the most comfortable in 1941—if I can say that I felt comfortable anywhere. Even in this catastrophic situation, Ane radiated a persistently enterprising spirit, while Mia exuded a calmness and genuine tenderness. As paradoxical as it may sound, I felt that they were my protectors. I knew that they both had contacts with people from whom Mia received warnings—information which they then shared with trusted friends. I think that the most important of these contacts was Ivo Rukavina, a senior financial advisor in the City Hall, later also chief of the tax administration. He knew who and how much had to be paid to get someone out of jail or a camp. And fortunately, it was not difficult for the Veličkoviće's to pay.

Despite repeated requests, I was unable to obtain a permit to travel to Zagreb. Yet even with a permit I would not have been able to visit my mother, not even briefly, as I did when she was in jail in Karlovac. I regularly sent packages to her though—Pavica or Mrs. Weiss would put them together and I would take them to Netica Šuman on Masaryk Street not far from the train station. Netica traveled once or twice a week to Zagreb with a package for her sister Metka and carried the package for my mother too.

One time I waited for Netica on the platform of the Karlovac railway station with a package for her to take to Zagreb. The train from Kordun pulled in and stopped at the siding. From the first car Franjo Pavičić, the table-tennis champion at our high school, descended, dressed like some kind of paramilitary, with a rifle slung over his shoulder. In one hand he was carrying a rooster by the legs. He spotted someone he knew on the platform, triumphantly raised the dead rooster aloft, and in his powerful, shrill voice shouted, "Hey, look, an Ustasha kill! Come see, an Ustasha kill!"

For Pavičić this was obviously a good joke, but I was frightened. I rushed from the platform and remained hidden until I was certain he was out of sight.

I saw Pavičić again forty years later, at the Frankfurt Book Fair in 1980 (which I described in Chapter 5). "Of course, I would not have arrested you, we were friends from ping-pong," Pavičić said with a laugh when I mentioned how I had hidden from him at the Karlovac railway station in 1941. He was then an eighteen-year-old student, a functionary in the Ustasha Youth, sent on a temporary assignment to Vojnić in charge of supervising the wheat harvest, the first step in his brief Ustasha career. Two years later he had finished high school in Gospić and an accelerated officer's school in Varaždin, and had become a lieutenant in a unit of the *Poglavnik*'s bodyguard in Gospić. The Partisans captured him a month before the end of the war.

Pavičić managed to remove all of his Ustasha insignias in time and present himself as an officer in the Home Guard, saving his own life. After a relatively brief imprisonment, he was released in the fall of 1945. In 1952 he graduated from the Faculty of Forestry in Zagreb. During his studies, and even later when he was employed in the forestry office of Klana near Rijeka, he was arrested, questioned, and held in jail for several days, until he escaped across the border. He ended up in Germany, employed as a forestry engineer in the Saar region, and became active in Croatian émigré circles. He was the main distributor of Jakša Kušan's *Nova Hrvatska* in Germany and reproduced a mini-issue of this newspaper at his own expense, surreptitiously sending copies, disguised as letters, by post to newsstands in Croatia. Because of these activities, the State Security Administration (UDBA) allegedly broke into his apartment in February 1988 and tried to assassinate him. Having acquired a wide reputation in the more moderate factions of the Croatian political émigré community, Pavičić was elected to two terms in Mate Meštrović's Croatian National Council.

After our meeting in Frankfurt, Pavičić called me several times, and less often he also began to call Josip Vaništa, with whom he had attended the Karlovac gymnasium for six years. In long telephone conversations he asked about Karlovac, books, our health, the general situation, but little about politics. Pavičić was clearly lonely in exile, nostalgic for Zagreb, Karlovac, the homeland. He is said to have attended the first congress of the Croatian Democratic Union (HDZ) in Zagreb in February 1990, but he didn't get in touch with us. As far as I know, he was no longer coming to Croatia. He called Vaništa and me less frequently and was more sentimental each time. He complained of painful arthritis, but he wasn't giving up and walked using crutches. I didn't have the courage to ask the indiscreet question of why he wasn't returning to Croatia. I did ask his collaborators in exile, Jakša Kušan and Mate Meštrović, who, independently and after a bit of hesitation, gave me similar explanations: Pavičić had been a useful and valued collaborator for them, but when the HDZ came to power in Croatia in 1990, his "Obligation" from 1945, signed at the Department for the Protection of the People in Karlovac, had been found in the records of the Republic Secretariat for Internal Affairs.[2] Thus, Pavičić was marked as a traitor within the circles of former political émigrés and was reluctant to appear in the homeland.

Neither Kušan nor Meštrović think that Pavičić was working for the UDBA in exile. When Kušan was writing his book *Bitka za Novu Hrvatsku* (The Battle for New Croatia)[3] at the end of the 1990s, he was permitted to review some UDBA files on Croatian political émigrés. That is how he came across Pavičić's "Obligation," a photocopy of which I received from Kušan and reproduce here in its entirety:

> I, Franjo Pavičić, pledge on this day that after my release from jail I will never again go against the interest of my people. I admit that I am guilty because I belonged to fascist organizations and throughout the occupation of our country served in satellite units. I am aware that I could and should have been punished, but when you release me I will try with my work and my professional knowledge to compensate my people for the crimes I have committed against them. If in the future I show the least evidence or trace of hostility to the National Front, I signify in this obligation that I assent to being punished for all that I have done until now and for that which I might do to be taken into account as an especially aggravating circumstance.
>
> In Karlovac, this day of September 5, 1945
>
> Signed,
> Franjo Pavičić

Kušan believes that Pavičić signed this "Obligation" to save his life and to gain his freedom, not to work for the UDBA. However, the new government in Croatia in 1990–1991 was embracing some parts of the extreme neo-Ustasha émigré community and marginalizing the more moderate nationalists gathered around *Nova Hrvatska*. In his book, Kušan maintains that

> as a rule extreme elements from the émigré community were brought in and given senior political, military, and police positions. In many places former UDBA collaborators could be found standing shoulder to shoulder with the "biggest Croats." This policy of the most shameless Balkan opportunism was given the cynical name of "reconciliation of the Partisans and Ustasha." In fact, it was simply confirmation of our frequently noted observation that there never was much difference between communist conformists and nationalist extremists.

Furthermore, Kušan believes that Pavičić became a victim of the political conflicts between the extreme and moderate wings of the Croatian political émigré community. Having assumed important positions in the Croatian government in 1990–1991, the extremists also got their hands on the UDBA files on Croatian political émigrés. They selectively chose documents that could compromise "moderate" émigrés, while withholding files that could compromise "extremists." According to widespread rumors, Vice Vukojević, the deputy minister of internal affairs, played the lead role in this manipulation.

And that is why Pavičić remained in the village not far from Saarbrücken, walking on his crutches.

15

Fanatics, Yes-men, Killers, and Saviors

AT THE END of September or in early October, Mr. Weiss asked to speak with me in private. Hesitant, visibly uneasy, he told me that he, Mrs. Weiss, and their daughter, Tea, would be leaving Karlovac in a day or two. He quickly added that I should not worry because they had already arranged for me to stay with Mrs. Eisler.

I know Mr. Weiss sensed how sad I was about them leaving. I had lived in their home, where all three of them had treated me as a member of their family. I had shared their worries about their son and brother, and they had shared my concerns about my mother and father. They had very much eased those last two months for me, the months which I think today, looking back many years later, were the most difficult in what has now been a fairly long life.

But the departure of the Weiss family also awakened in me dark forebodings that until then had been dormant. Many of the evening talks with Mr. Weiss had been filled with speculations about his son and my father, who were in Jadovno. What was going on? Why had they not been in touch for so long? Mr. Weiss had a calm manner, but as time went on he admitted that he was increasingly concerned and feared the worst. However, he had not lost all hope. Every rumor about our people in Jadovno, however fantastical, awakened hope in

Mr. Weiss, and he would go out to verify and investigate the source of such rumors. But why did the Weisses decide to leave their apartment and Karlovac, the only place their son knew where to reach them? Did it mean that they thought they'd never receive news of him again?

Much later, I learned why and how the Weisses left Karlovac at the end of September 1941. The Italian colonel who was staying in their apartment had access to the September 6 report of the Italian sanitation team on the fate of the Jadovno camp. He alerted Mr. Weiss to the news, and a subsequent report on September 22 was only definitive confirmation of the worst. Mr. Weiss accepted the painful conclusion that there was no longer any reason to wait. Out of compassion, or else for a large sum of money, the colonel had provided travel documents for the Weisses and helped them get first to Ljubljana and then to Milan, where Mr. Weiss's wealthy brother lived. Much later, after the war, they contaced me from the United States. As far as I know, they never came back to Karlovac, not even as tourists.

For the next two months I stayed with Mrs. Eisler, to whom I am grateful to this day. A vital, energetic widow in her late fifties, Zora Eisler managed her hardware store, kept house, and took care of her children and grandchildren. Unlike Mr. Weiss, she did not establish a close relationship with me, but could always find an appropriate way to remind me of my responsibilities and the rules of the house.

In their tireless scheming to free my mother from jail, Mia Veličković and Pavica Vine sent me to see people who they thought might intercede to have my mother released. They spoke less and less about my father, as if there was nothing left to do except wait. And so I once went to see Peter Prebeg, a Croatian party veteran and an honorable man who was a friend of my father. A prominent judge, he received me kindly in his office in the district court and promised he would try to intercede on behalf of my mother through a relative of his. Although I clearly sensed his good intentions and his sincere desire to help, I left his office with little hope. It wasn't easy for me to travel around the various offices with such requests, so perhaps I have repressed the memories of some of these visits, as I had the yellow symbol. But full of hope I went to see Mrs. Peschke because I knew that her powerful husband could easily get my mother out of jail.

From 1930 to 1934 the Peschke family lived in our apartment building. They were from Germany and spoke German at home. Mrs. Peschke spoke little Croatian, like my mother, and the two had become friendly. Mr. Fritz Peschke was the owner of a small sock factory. I played with their daughter, Pipi, a year older than me, and son, Peter, a year younger. I still have photographs of us children at play from 1931 and 1932. However, a coldness set in at a certain point, undoubtedly the decision of the perpetually scowling Mr. Peschke, and perhaps against the will of the good-hearted Mrs. Peschke. Then the Peschkes moved to a house that had been built next to their factory. Mr. Peschke wore a swastika on the lapel of his suit coat and became the leader of the Nazis in Karlovac. On the promenade Pipi coldly avoided me, but in chance meetings Mrs. Peschke still greeted my mother and exchanged pleasantries. In the summer of 1941, Mr. Peschke was considered the most powerful man in Karlovac. He was chief of the Abwehr, the military intelligence service for central Croatia. It was Pavica who urged me to see Mrs. Peschke to ask her for help: "She could do it, she was always good with your mother and he is not an evil man." So I went to the Peschkes' house. A uniformed guard stood at the foot of the stairs. I told him who I was and what I wanted. He went up the stairs and rather quickly returned: "Madame Peschke would like you to know that she is sorry that she cannot receive you and that there is nothing she can do for you or your mother." Mrs. Peschke later told Pavica that she was truly sorry she did not receive me, that she had wept over our situation, but really there was nothing she could do for me or my mother.

* * *

From July 10, when the names of three acquaintances appeared on a poster of those executed, I approached each new poster with dread. Obviously I feared I would see a name I recognized—of my mother or father. "Death prowled the city," wrote the Karlovac poet Oto Šolc.

My fears were not unjustified because my mother was accidentally placed in a group that was to be executed. She happened to be in the hallway of the prison on Savska Street as the Ustasha were taking prisoners from their cells. In the tumult an Ustasha guard pushed my mother into the group. Only when an officer counted off the fifty prisoners from the list was it established that my mother was an "extra." She later found out that the fifty people on the list were hostages executed in retaliation for the murder of the police officer Ivan Majerhold by a shock group.

By August, the posters no longer listed the names of those executed, just numbers. Because of a grenade attack on the Ustasha University Battalion at the Zagreb Botanical Garden on August 4, the mobile summary court had condemned to death and executed "the intellectual instigators of that attack, ninety-eight Jews and communists"; and a day later, on August 5, by a decision of the same summary court, eighty-seven "Jews and communists" were executed who had been "discovered as additional participants and intellectual instigators" of that same attack. On September 11, the execution of "fifty Jews and communists" was carried out for the murder of Majerhold, and on September 14, fifty "Jews and communists" were executed for a bomb attack on the telephone switchboard of the main Zagreb post office—and so on and on throughout the Independent State of Croatia (NDH), without end. "If a man wanted to live peacefully, he was wrong to have been born in the twentieth century," scoffed Leon Trotsky, one of the great instigators of the stormy unrest that characterized the century. With the decline of religion as the only absolute spiritual authority, fanaticism in the service of ideology had become the inheritor of fanaticism in the service of religion. It grew out of a human need to believe in absolutes, to be faithful and loyal to them, to fight and sacrifice for them, to the point of intolerance toward the Other and anything that is different. In its effects and consequences that fanaticism has branched off into a variety of currents, more destructive than constructive, and frequently contradictory. The most pernicious is the fanaticism of hatred, a fanaticism tied to hatred, but there is also revolutionary fanaticism that begins with a justification for the destruction of evil but often carries within it the seeds of a new evil. It is not right to evaluate them unambiguously, to celebrate them without reserve or ignore them without due consideration.

Albert Camus writes in *The Rebel* that the true revolutionary ends up as either a tyrant or a heretic. Twenty and thirty years after the war, my work as a publisher gave me the satisfaction of being able to associate with people who in their youth were among the most ardent fanatics of revolution but who in their later years had become downright heretics. They paid for their heresy with the loss of their powerful positions and privileges or they were subjected to harassment—here I can mention Milovan Đilas, Veco Holjevac, Jovan Barović, Marijan Stilinović, and Gojko Nikoliš, but I would also add Veljko Mićunović, Vojo Kovačević, and Koča Popović among others. They questioned the idea of revolution and became critical of their own revolutionary fanaticism, with the exception of the year 1941. They unanimously maintained that their actions that year were beyond reproach, their moment of glory.

The official postwar historiography and political propaganda put communist *prvoborci*[1] onto an inviolable pedestal of heroism and self-sacrifice for a brighter future. Any doubts about the validity of the suicidal forms of the struggle and its many victims were simply not permitted. Commemorative plaques sprang up on every street corner and every member of the League of Young Communists of Yugoslavia who fired more than three bullets in the summer of 1941 had a street named after him. The commemorations of heroes became routine, boring, and tiresome, like any routine, while schoolchildren were forced to write class assignments that retold one-sided stories of heroism full of pathos. In 1990, the reaction had set in. After the disintegration of Yugoslavia and the fall of communism, the nationalistic Tuđman government removed from their pedestals most of the heroes of communism, the rebellion, and anti-fascism. It did away with their monuments and busts, changed the names of streets, and dropped them from school textbooks, trying to cast them into oblivion. A book published by the Alliance of Antifascist Fighters of Croatia described the vandalism that included the destruction or removal of 2,964 antifascist monuments and memorial plaques, while many of the remaining 3,000 were damaged or had fallen into disrepair. There were rare exceptions, mainly based on a contrived division between those who were antifascist but allegedly fought for Croatia and those who were antifascist but allegedly fought for Yugoslavia. The criteria were warped, but then so were the artificial divisions applied to the communist *prvoborci* of 1941. A false picture of the key years of the recent past was created and new animosities arose.

With Stjepan Mesić, Franjo Tuđman's successor as president, the relationship of national government to its past became healthier. In 1959, the modernized elementary school in the Banija section of Karlovac was named in honor of Herta Turza and a bust of her was placed at the entrance to the school. In 1971, a bust of Veco Holjevac was installed in the charming little park behind the Edison cinema. In 1991, the name of Herta Turza was removed from the elementary school in Banija and the bust carted away, leaving the empty pedestal. The bust of Holjevac was also removed from the little park along with the busts of seventeen communist and antifascist *prvoborci* from Karlovac and the surrounding area, among them one of Nada Dimić. In 2001, the bust of Holjevac was restored to its old place, but Herta's pedestal in front of the Banija school remained empty. Nor had any of the other seventeen busts been returned. Would Herta or any one of the other seventeen join Holjevac in their former places? By what criteria? In the fall of 2001, at the request of Holjevac's daughters, I spoke about their father at a large commemoration for the sixtieth anniversary of his actions in Karlovac during the war. I concluded my remarks by saying, "Veco's former comrades and friends are grateful to the current Karlovac authorities for returning his bust to the place where it belongs. Unfortunately, I must add that if Veco could witness all this today, he would not be happy that he has returned alone, without Herta, Nada Dimić, and some others who were once here with him."

* * *

The Ustasha regime was the failed illusion of a legal state, a poorly organized combination of draconian legality and chaos. The legal credibility of the regime was annulled by the ever-present extralegal terror, which was in part directed by the government leadership and was in part tolerated and controlled. From time to time it was suppressed, but only when the terror got out of control. The summary courts were intended to provide a degree of legality to the terror, but because of their rigidity and extralegal procedures they did not give even a semblance of such legality.

In the NDH a total of eleven summary courts and seven mobile summary courts were established. They operated on the basis of legal decrees published in the spring of 1941, and then were diligently supplemented with increasingly stricter provisions by Mirko Puk, the chief promoter of the draconian legislation. Thus, on July 5, they were supplemented with the provision that "those in possession of a leaflet, book, or newspaper whose contents lead to the promotion of communism or which contain any other type of criminal act against the survival of the state and its order, or against government authority or against the public peace and order, or against the *Poglavnik*, or against those who constitutionally succeed him, or against the Ustasha movement, or against Ustasha units" would be brought before the summary courts and the mobile summary courts. By July 10, a new supplement was promulgated: "anyone who without government approval 1) listens to news broadcasts from the enemy countries of the Independent State of Croatia or of the Axis powers or 2) listens to news broadcasts that are unfriendly to the existing order in the Independent State of Croatia, will be brought before the summary courts and the mobile summary courts." Despite these drastic threats, at night behind well-sealed windows and doors massive numbers of people listened to the BBC, Radio Moscow, and Free Yugoslavia. One night an anonymous resident of Karlovac hung a sign on a monument to the local historian Lopašić that read: "I am the only resident of Karlovac who did not listen to Radio London last night."

The quasi-legality of the summary courts was irreparably compromised in the summer of 1941, when these courts sentenced hostages to execution, for which until October 2 there was no basis even under the most rigorous NDH laws. While the mobile summary court from Zagreb under Ivan Vidnjević was in session in Karlovac from July 23 until August 7, that same judge, in the name of the same mobile summary court in Zagreb on August 4, had sentenced to death four people named as the alleged perpetrators of an attack on the Ustasha University Battalion and ninety-eight unnamed "Jews and communists... co-participants and the intellectual instigators" of that attack, and on August 5 sentenced another eighty-seven Jews and communists who had been subsequently "discovered" as "additional co-participants and intellectual instigators." Of course, in two days

Vidnjević and his mobile summary court, even with the expedited procedures, could not have questioned, let alone sentenced, a total of 189 suspects, so it is obvious that the procedure involved randomly selected hostages whom the court never saw. At a hearing before the Military Tribunal of the Command of Zagreb in 1945, Vidnjević still justified the legality of the proceedings. He signed two memoranda, a total of two and a half closely typed pages from which I have selected the most representative passages:

> The creation of the NDH found me in Zlatar as a judge...on June 24, 1941, I was appointed president of a summary court. On that same day, the law outlining how we should judge cases was issued. Minister Puk had determined where we should go and what cases would be put before us. I voted for acquittal when there was no proof, but never when there was proof. I always voted for the death penalty if the law required it. We administered justice according to the law, our consciences, and the facts. We were sentencing to death those who had made paltry financial contributions to the National Liberation Front. The police carried out the sentences, and I would issue them a written order....I think in Zagreb I sentenced about one thousand people, in Karlovac sixteen, in Petrinja about forty. In these four years, while I was the president of the summary court, I went to confession four times. I told the priests everything that I had done and not one of them told me that what I was doing was wrong....I have made this statement under no pressure and everything has been entered accurately in the record.

At the end of both memoranda are two signatures: "Accused: Ivan Vidnjević" and "Investigator, V. Berčić."

Vidnjević is a perfect example of the syntagma of "the banality of evil," the frequently cited phrase by Hannah Arendt from her book *Eichmann in Jerusalem*. However, let's avoid generalizations: Evil is not always so banal and the criminal is not always as bland and colorless as Eichmann and Vidnjević. In totalitarian regimes evil is diverse and has many faces. In his book *Das Gesicht des Dritten Reiches—Profile einer totalitären Herrschaft* (The Face of the Third Reich: Portraits of the Nazi Leadership),[2] Joachim Fest provides brilliant psychological biographies of Hitler and fourteen of his more prominent associates. Some, perhaps the majority, were banal, one-dimensional personalities, but they also had distinctive characteristics: The propaganda genius Joseph Goebbels, who "transformed propaganda into an ideology" and an ideology into the fanaticism of the monstrous killer, marked the failure of the Third Reich by poisoning all five of his children, his wife, and finally himself; or Hermann Göring, the insatiable power seeker, and hedonist; or the perfect technologist of the regime and its moral blind man, Albert Speer; the diabolical "man with the heart of iron," Reinhard Heydrich; the split personality of Heinrich Himmler, who simultaneously embodied the petit bourgeois and grand inquisitor; or the butcher Rudolf Höss, for many years the commandant of Auschwitz, who wrote in his memoirs that he saw himself as a great sufferer but also as a hero because he had to sacrifice himself to carry out a command that was odious to him: the murder of more than a million human beings. But before and above all, their link and source of power, Adolf Hitler—the great fanatic of hatred and the visionary of evil.

Evil also had a variety of faces within the Ustasha hierarchy. Shortsighted patriots, who in good faith and in great numbers joined the Ustasha movement in 1941, did not give that movement its character. The majority of these people rather quickly came to their senses; they were disappointed, became passive, and only rarely held positions of influence. Ustasha institutions abounded in yes-men like

Vidnjević, a diverse group of fellow travelers characterized by ambition or material interests, and in local thugs with violent mentalities, but even they were not the motivating force of the regime or its real power. Actual power in the NDH, especially in 1941, rested with the Ustasha émigré returnees, supported by the few hard-core members of the national organization. They were united by a fanaticism of hatred that relied on a mythomanic view of themselves as part of a holy mission to create "a nationally pure area": Croatia to the Drina River without 1.8 million Serbs. Four protagonists, each in his own way, gave expression to the characteristics of this obsession: the most vociferous propagator of hatred, Mile Budak; the consistent instigator and legalist of hatred, Mirko Puk; the architect of the crimes, Dido Kvaternik; and their most brutal executor, Vjekoslav Luburić. And above them all, Ante Pavelić, who united all these obsessions and fanatical hatreds in his person and was their prime mover and sponsor, the lawgiver and the commander, the undisputed autocrat and the owner of hundreds of thousands of lives and deaths.

In 1941, I doubt there was a single person in the upper echelon of the Ustasha hierarchy capable of seeing that Pavelić's "fire and sword" policy would destroy the country. If any of these people quietly harbored such fears, they were not recorded, with the exception of the comments of Milovan Žanić that Vladimir Židovec and the anonymous "Dizdar" described. Žanić's muted desires to curb the extralegal terror were a sterile call for justice amid injustice because Pavelić's dictatorial power was supreme. Only in the lower structures of authority, at the local level, could one find people who were ready to temper the evil. I met two such men: Mane Bilović, the longtime Ustasha commander of Karlovac, and Milan Stilinović, the director of the municipal police in Karlovac and one of the deputy directors of the provincial police in Karlovac.

* * *

In the summer of 1952, a tall, heavyset, well-dressed middle-aged man, with the shadows of strain on his face, visited me in the apartment I was then renting. He introduced himself, saying, "Milan Stilinović, perhaps you remember me from Karlovac in 1941." I immediately remembered him. He thought that as a member of the editorial board of the newly established *Vjesnik u srijedu* (Vjesnik on Wednesday), perhaps I could help. He had been in prison for four years and eight months. "Still, I got through it all right," he added, with a forced smile.

Several people whom he had released from jail in 1941 to 1942, or had helped save, had provided certified statements about his conduct immediately after the war. Joža Mađar, a member of the Communist Party before the war and a Partisan *prvoborac* in 1941, who after the war held influential positions in the state administration of the People's Republic of Croatia, was one of them:

> I have known Milan Stilinović since before the war, when he was a court assessor in Karlovac. In August 1941, he became deputy chief of the district police [then quickly the chief of the Karlovac municipal police].... He made every effort to bring back to Karlovac a group of twenty-four prisoners who had been sent to Zagreb because he knew that they would be killed in Zagreb. He finally succeeded in this at the beginning of October and so saved from certain death twenty-four men and women comrades, setting them free upon their arrival in Karlovac and issuing them permits to leave Karlovac....They all later joined the Partisans.

The group of people saved included the author of the statement, Joža Mađar, and my mother.

Mađar's statement, supported by other depositions, saved Stilinović's life, but it did not save him from prison. The district court in Karlovac sentenced him to three years of hard labor on August 5, 1946, but the Supreme Court of the Republic of Croatia increased the sentence to six years on November 6, 1946. The same court subsequently approved a reduction in his sentence, and he was released sixteen months early. This was a relatively mild sentence for a former chief of the NDH police. In the immediate postwar years the courts would sentence such people to at least fifteen years in prison.

The court proceedings considered the fact that on his own authority Stilinović had freed from jail more than one hundred people who had been threatened with death and had warned many to flee when their arrest was imminent. At the same time, the court had before it a poster with Stilinović's signature on it, limiting the movements of Serbs and Jews and calling on Serbs and Jews to report to the municipal police within forty-eight hours, among other incriminating documents. The court also knew that during his mandate more than one hundred people had been sent to Jasenovac, few of whom returned home. Stilinović did not make the decision regarding these mass arrests, that decision was made by the Ustasha Intelligence Service. However, the decisions were carried out and the arrests made by detectives and policemen of the Karlovac police whose director was Stilinović. Why then did he not resign? Or at least feign illness and seek a transfer? Why did he remain in this position for a full nine months? These were some of the logical questions that the investigating judge asked Stilinović. I did not ask him about it, and he volunteered nothing about his personal conflicts.

In the summer of 1941, Ante Nikšić, who was until the beginning of the war the president of the district court and Stilinović's immediate superior, was an Ustasha commissioner, the provincial governor, and the most powerful man in Karlovac. He issued the order for the young Judge Stilinović to be transferred from the court service to a relatively senior position in the police. Could Stilinović have refused that order? It would have been difficult. He wasn't a member of the Ustasha movement and, according to the statements of witnesses, didn't show sympathy for the Ustasha ideal. To refuse a transfer to the police, which certainly required a lawyer, could have been interpreted as obstruction of the young state, an anti-Croatian act. Moreover, Stilinović's wife had been an Orthodox Serb, though she converted to Catholicism after they married. And these were not times when one could easily refuse the order of those who wielded such power and who ruled the country and the people with an iron fist.

Stilinović may have accepted the position of deputy director of the provincial police on the assumption that he would be dealing only with legal matters. But once in that position he probably realized that he had made a Faustian pact with the devil. He thought that tricking the devil and wresting some of his victims from death now and then would soothe his conscience, but his conscience would not grant him pardon. Only in later years did it become evident that the price of the pact with the devil was a high one, considerably higher than the rewards for his charitable deeds. The prison calvary through which Stilinović passed was tortuous and painful. Stilinović's daughter, Branka Stilinović-Petrović, a judge in the Higher Commercial Court in Zagreb, later told me that her mother, when she first obtained permission to visit him in the prison in Stara Gradiška, was shocked because she could barely recognize her husband.

We can reduce the entire story to a hypothetical question: What would have happened if Stilinović had refused to become chief of the Karlovac police in the summer of 1941, if he had wriggled out of it or, let's say, found refuge in the legal department of the Karlovac sock factory or at the Red Cross? He would have saved himself, but he would have saved no one else. After the war he would not have been sent to Stara Gradiška, but my mother, Joža Mađar, and perhaps hundreds of other people would have ended up in Jasenovac. Does this mean that he should have been given an award for agreeing to become chief of police, even though in that position he also committed acts that, objectively speaking, were punishable? Based on the hard laws of the administration of justice, I think that he should have been punished (but the punishment should have been milder), but based on the moral sense of justice I think he should have been given an award. Or more in the style of King Solomon: in the implacable Court of Justice he would be punished, but in the higher Moral Court he would have been freed and awarded a special certificate of Gratitude. Unfortunately, I gather there are no such courts, not even in Utopia.

After leaving prison, Stilinović wasn't able to work in his profession for nearly two years, even though lawyers were in demand. He had a difficult time trying to feed his family by playing the violin in a bar and working as a bookkeeper. When he came to see me in the summer of 1952, he had the prospect of a job as a lawyer in a construction company, but they wanted additional testimonies about his conduct during the war. I provided a statement, as did several others, and he was hired. A professional, conscientious employee, Stilinović quickly advanced to the position of legal adviser. His subsequent request for judicial reinstatement was granted.

Stilinović ended his working career in the construction company and retired when he reached the normal retirement age. He died in 1978 at the age of sixty-seven. In 2005, his daughter, Branka Stilinović-Petrović, a judge in the higher commercial court in Zagreb, initiated the procedure with Yad Vashem in Jerusalem that her father posthumously be proclaimed Righteous Among the Nations. Mađar and I supported the proposal with detailed statements. The nomination is still pending.

On two separate occasions, in 1952 and in 1961, Stilinović gave me some details of the release of my mother. When he assumed his duties as the chief of the municipal police, he learned about the group of thirty Karlovac residents, four women and twenty-six men, that had been sent to the Zagreb jail on Savska Street. None had been interrogated. Most had family and friends in Karlovac who through lawyers or personal contacts had interceded for their release. He remembered my mother well because she was the only Jew in the group. There had been several interventions on her behalf; he particularly remembered the efforts of the Ustasha commander of the city of Karlovac, Mane Bilović, who cited humanitarian reasons for his actions.

Stilinović based his request for the return of the entire group to Karlovac on the fact that the investigation of the group of thirty had not yet been initiated, that he needed to question the prisoners personally to establish their guilt or innocence and, if possible, to uncover their contacts.

The news that the prisoners from Savska Street had returned to Karlovac quickly spread through the city. I think Mrs. Klobučar was the first to tell me. She and I brought food from her restaurant to the city jail—she to her son-in-law and I to my mother. Again the guards were kind: They let my mother and me hug and kiss in the jail courtyard. After so many months, it was a rare moment of happiness.

Stilinović began the questioning that same day. Among the first was his good friend Mađar, in whom he confided that he intended to release everyone. Stilinović interrogated the prisoners himself, five to six each day, and immediately released them. Mađar testified that Stilinović was hurrying because he was taking advantage of Nikšić's absence from Karlovac.

My mother's interrogation was on the third or fourth day. It lasted about twenty minutes. Stilinović told my mother to go back to her cell and pack her things. She would be released, but she would be called to sign the minutes that he still had to review and complete. When she returned, the court reporter was no longer in the room. Stilinović handed her a completed travel permit for Kraljevica, valid for four days. My mother was surprised and, as she told me later, asked, "Why Kraljevica?" After two months in prison, Stilinović said, she needed fresh sea air and an extended stay at the seaside. My mother understood the message. On parting, he shook her hand and gave her greetings from friends; he mentioned only Mane Bilović by name.

During that week, about the middle of October, Stilinović freed the entire group from jail. He provided them with permits to leave Karlovac, and my mother later met many of them in the Partisans.

The freeing of such a large group of prisoners, mostly people well-known in the small city, was a brave act, exceptional given the circumstances. Stilinović suffered consequences, fortunately not too severe. He was transferred to a provincial police district in a position that was less sensitive and responsible; then in May 1942, he was moved to an even lower-ranking position with the provincial police in Knin. In 1943, Stilinović reached Zagreb, where he was employed as a lawyer in the Ministry of Social Welfare. He remained there until the end of the war. He was arrested in the spring of 1946 at the request of the district prosecutor of Karlovac.

I vividly recall the number "20" on my mother's travel permit for Kraljevica. I don't know if this meant that the permit was issued on October 20, or that it expired on October 20, so I say that my mother was released from jail in the middle of October and that she traveled to Kraljevica in the second half of that month. During the four days she spent in Karlovac, she stayed with Mrs. Eisler. I know that she went to our apartment and that Mrs. Družak allowed her to take some of her necessities. My mother found most of her possessions in the boxes at Pavica's house and she carefully packed into two heavy suitcases what she needed for the long journey into uncertainty. She wasn't afraid to go to Kraljevica. She knew that Jews were not being arrested in the Italian zone; they were allowed to live peacefully, at least for now. She took the most counsel with the Veličkovićes and consulted about everything with me, as never before. She didn't spare me from even the most difficult questions; she wanted to hear my opinion, as if we were equals, but she continued to make the important decisions herself and I gladly accepted them.

Decisions in those difficult times were a serious business, as each one might be fatal for us, but my mother did not hesitate much. As soon as she reached Kraljevica, she would send someone for Danko in Tuzla. Then I would also come to Kraljevica. The times were such that we had to be together. It would be easier to decide where to go from there if something more suitable turned up, or if we had to escape. My mother mentioned as possibilities Italy, or the refuge at Jaga's, or some other out-of-the-way village where the Ustasha authorities had not yet set foot. We had enough money for now, but if necessary my mother would sell her gold or some of her jewelry. We could also borrow from Mia Veličković at any time.

My mother spoke little about my father, only a word here and there with a muted sigh. One could sense this was her greatest distress, the one before which she was powerless. In those four short days she asked around and, I think, realized that nothing more could be done except wait. Hopes were fading, although they still flickered. "If Fati sends news," she once said, "it will be to Karlovac. Our friends will know how to get in touch with us, wherever we are."

Of course, my mother departed for Kraljevica with a heavy heart—she was leaving me alone. I didn't have a permit to go with her and, as a Jew, I couldn't obtain one in the regular way. Three or four days was not time enough to acquire one in an irregular way, but my mother assured me that I would get the travel documents for Kraljevica in due time. Until then, I had to be careful. Jewish children under sixteen had not yet been individually arrested anywhere, but we knew that in some places—Varaždin, Koprivnica, and elsewhere—entire Jewish communities, with small children and sick elderly people, had been sent to the camps. If that was to happen in Karlovac, the Veličkovićes would know in time and get in touch, my mother was certain. She gave me exact instructions about what to do in such a situation.

It was then that my mother mentioned the Partisans for the first time as a possibility for us and perhaps as some vague hope in general. She mentioned in passing how she had heard that the Partisans were quickly becoming stronger and held a number of villages in Kordun. She said nothing directly, but I think she had begun to think about the possibility of all three of us—my mother, Danko, and me—finding refuge with the Partisans. Perhaps she had discussed this with Marica Marinković, the sister of Ivo Marinković, with whom she had met before her departure for Kraljevica, and perhaps they had reached some agreement.

This was my mother's first contact with the Partisan movement, and to its beginnings I devote the following chapter.

16

The Uprising in Banija and Kordun

ON AUGUST 8, 1941, the city of Karlovac received two messages: The morning posters declaring the execution of Herta Turza and six of her comrades were a message from the Ustasha authorities that the terror had become increasingly merciless, and the afternoon burial of the first two Karlovac Ustasha to be slain was a message from Kordun that resistance to the terror had erupted. Under the headline SOLEMN BURIAL OF THE USTASHA RUDI STARIČ AND DRAGO MIHELČIĆ IN KARLOVAC, *Hrvatski narod* of August 9 described the two slain men as "Ustasha who were prepared to sacrifice all for Croatia, even their young lives."

Karlovac was a small city and I personally knew both Mihelčić and Starič. Mihelčić was one of the two detectives who took my mother and Jaga from our home to the city jail in the early morning of July 14. Before the war, he had been friends with our apprentice, Zvonko Jaklić—they both shared a love of motorcycles and fast driving. Rudolf Starič (who was, in fact, a Croatized Slovene) was an auto mechanic in the garage of Mr. Prahić in the courtyard behind our bookshop. When we bought the used Fiat, Starič taught my father how to drive it and, when necessary, he repaired it. He tried several times to explain to me the "soul" of an automobile engine, which I don't understand to this day.

Twenty years later, while preparing materials for the book *Okrug Karlovac 1941* (The District of Karlovac in 1941), Ćanica Opačić told me how Starič and Mihelčić were killed. It was on the Vojnić–Krstinja road on August 6, 1941. The major Ustasha cleansing operations in Kordun, Lika, and Banija had abated somewhat, although they were still under way. As the commander of the Debela Kosa Partisan unit, Opačić led his soldiers for the first time in an ambush on one of the roads around Petrova Gora. Until then, the unit had carried out only several small acts of sabotage at night: the destruction of telegraph and telephone poles, cutting the lines, and the destruction of the post office in Tušilović. This was the first time that armed Partisans, about thirty of them, moved in broad daylight to openly engage the enemy.

Starič and Mihelčić were scouts for an Ustasha company that had departed Karlovac on July 30 and was now in its eighth day in Kordun. At about eleven o'clock in the morning the two of them, on a motorcycle, had driven far ahead of the company and rode into the ambush Opačić had set up at a bend in the road near Vilin Točak. Starič and Mihelčić, along with their motorcycle, were knocked into a ditch by the road in the first volley. The Partisans took their rifles, revolvers, hand grenades, and other equipment and returned to their nearby base in a small forest. They left the motorcycle in the ditch by the road, and surprisingly it remained there for the rest of the war as a kind of monument to the first Partisan raid at Petrova Gora and to the first two Karlovac Ustasha killed in Kordun.

Two days later the bodies of Starič and Mihelčić lay in state in the Croatia House in Karlovac. A stream of Karlovac citizens, students, and soldiers filed by their caskets in the morning. The burial was in the afternoon. I stood in a small group of mute onlookers at the corner of Radićeva Street while their bodies, covered with wreaths, slowly passed by. Black flags hung from roofs and balconies and all of the stores were closed. One part of Karlovac, publicly and ostentatiously, mourned Starič and Mihelčić; the other part, quietly and in secret, mourned for Herta and her comrades. There were certainly those wiser ones who knew that they should mourn the dead on both sides, but there were also many who were indifferent, who thought that none of this affected them, not knowing that the time had come when no one, literally no one, would be spared.

From that day until the end of the war the echoes from nearby Kordun reverberated through Karlovac. I knew that my fate and that of my family would be decided on faraway battlefields in Russia, Libya, and the Atlantic, and perhaps I had an inkling that events in Kordun would also have a direct effect on us. Later I often thought about these events, their causes and their outcomes, how and why all of this happened in Kordun and turned our lives upside down. While preparing this book, I have researched and added to my knowledge of the initial uprising, which I now offer to the reader in this chapter.

* * *

After the May massacres at Hrvatski Blagaj and Glina, a relative calm descended on Kordun, even as disturbing news was reaching the region's Orthodox residents from many sides. In the neighboring region of Banija, Ustasha from Petrinja and other garrisons continued to attack Serbian villages in small groups, to mistreat and rob villagers and prominent individuals, and to arrest and take them away or kill them on the spot. In Lika the violence was much greater, culminating in massacres at Suvaja, Bubanj, and Osredak in early July. The people of Kordun also knew about Jadovno because the arrests of Serbs and Jews from Karlovac, Ogulin, Plaško, and other towns in the Kordun region had become more frequent. They had most likely heard rumors from some parts of Bosnia, Herzegovina, and northern Dalmatia, where mass crimes against Serbs were already intense in June. However, an apparent peace still prevailed in Kordun, so Mirko Marušić, the commander of a gendarme platoon in Slunj, claimed in a later report that "until July 27 the situation was largely satisfactory with regard to the blow the Serbian population received with the establishment of the Independent State of Croatia. A good portion of the population has accepted its fate. Many have sought conversion to the Catholic faith."

The gendarme commander in Slunj perhaps didn't know, or perhaps he didn't want his superiors to know, that the Kordun Serbs, even prior to July 27, were upset and unsettled, primarily because of clear indications that preparations were under way for their forced expulsion to Serbia and the confiscation of their property. Under instructions from the National Directorate for Reconstruction, all of the district heads had to form special departments for the expulsion of Serbs and the admission of transplanted Slovenes. On June 7, an order was announced for the registration and listing of certain categories of the Serbian population and some registrations had begun. The brutal expulsion on June 29 of the Serbian population from the neighboring area, the district of Plitvice Lakes, caused the greatest alarm. When the first six hundred Slovenes were settled in villages in the counties of Vojnić, Vrginmost, and Kostajnica at almost the same time, it became clear to the Kordun and Banija Serbs that their turn was next.

In the villages people held meetings, wondering what to do, but no one was able to come up with a sensible plan. At meetings in late June and early July local communists came up with fuzzy slogans and arguments against the expulsions, such as the one at the meeting of about thirty members of the Communist Party, the League of Young Communists of Yugoslavia, and their sympathizers in Tušilović when it was decided that "broad agitation should be initiated against the expulsion of Serbs from their homes."

In the large village of Luščani in the region of Banija, with no connection to the communists, the brothers Tanasije, Đuro, and Dušan Bakrač organized a village guard as a standing precautionary measure. On the morning of July 12, the guards raised the alarm that an Ustasha unit had arrested a merchant named Vilus in the lower part of the village and had occupied his house. Word quickly spread that the Ustasha had come to register people, to put them on a list for expulsion. The villagers grew uneasy; many began to leave their homes and flee into the forest. The Bakrač brothers, along with several other determined young men, stopped them and guided them to the lower part of the village. Armed with hunting rifles, pitchforks, and clubs, they surrounded Vilus's house, where the Ustasha were drinking wine and *rakija*. There were six of them, mostly young men from the neighboring Croatian village of Pecki. They apparently came to Luščani with an order to arrest several prominent people, but they paused in Vilus's shop for a bit of thievery and a lot of drinking. They became frightened when outside the window they caught sight of the mass of people that had surrounded them. "Give yourselves up!" Đuro Bakrač ordered. The Ustasha hesitated, called on the people to disperse, and allegedly threatened to shoot, but they didn't. Someone from the group outside promised that nothing would happen to them if they released Vilus, surrendered their weapons, and peacefully left the village. The Ustasha were losing their nerve. Finally, Đuro Bakrač jumped in among the totally befuddled men with a pistol and easily disarmed them. The villagers allowed all six of the drunken Ustasha to leave the village peacefully, but their carbines remained with the village guards of Luščani.

Having raised their hand against a dangerous authority, the Bakrač brothers, out of necessity, began to seek contact with people who were also at war with that authority. That is how Đuro Bakrač learned of Ranko Mitić, the Secretary of the Glina District Committee of the

KPH, who lived in hiding in villages around Glina. Đuro's older brother, Tanasije, got in touch with Vasilj Gaćeša, who was the leader of a newly formed combat unit in the neighboring village of Vlahovići.

* * *

Toward evening on Saturday, July 19, 1941, Rade Končar, the secretary of the Central Committee of the Communist Party of Croatia (KPH), and Josip Kraš, another member of the committee, arrived in the Abez forest, an hour's walk north of Vrginmost (today called Gvozd) and transmitted a directive to eight of the leading local communists for the beginning of the uprising. The meeting lasted seven hours, until one o'clock in the morning. They concluded that the uprisings had to begin on July 23 in the counties of Glina and Vrginmost and four days later in the district of Vojnić. They identified nine facilities to be attacked on the evening of July 23: Communist activists would carry out all of the operations, signaling the general uprising in Banija and Kordun that many threatened Serbian villagers would join.

Of the nine attacks planned for the night of July 23, only one was carried out: Eight of the nine combat groups of communist activists failed to carry out the orders. Some groups discovered they had no weapons or the guides who knew the terrain didn't show up, and some others had heard that the garrisons they were supposed to attack had received strong reinforcements. Many communists openly expressed doubt about the planned attacks and maintained that their villages and innocent people would suffer as a result and that communists would be blamed for the suffering. Obviously it was not easy, even for communists inspired by revolution, to stand barehanded against a heavily armed power. Stanko Bjelajac, whose party assignment was to organize the groups for the attacks on Maja and Jukinac, in his lively memoir claims that the "plan devised for carrying out the operations was overambitious."[1]

On the evening of July 23, a group of about thirty handpicked members of the village guard from Vlahović, Lusčani, Šušnjar, and Gornji Drenovac gathered in Lavčanske Livade, less than a kilometer from the railway station in Banski Grabovac. They waited until midnight for another group from Donji Drenovac, which never arrived. "We're going!" decided Vasilj Gaćeša, the unquestioned leader of the group of brave young men.

About an hour after midnight the fighters from Gaćeša's group carried out a skillfully planned attack on the railway station, the district building, and the brickworks in Banski Grabovac. According to Đuro Bakrač, twenty-two fighters armed with five carbines, about ten hunting rifles, and several old pistols took part in the attack.[2] Two gendarmes and the owner of the brickworks, who had put up some resistance, were killed in the attack. The rebel units confiscated nine military carbines and a great deal of equipment and ammunition. They suffered no losses of their own. They executed a captured district clerk and the chief of the railway station, allegedly because they were active Ustasha collaborators, but they released the district police and other captives. They set fire to the district building, the railway station, and the brickworks; destroyed the equipment in the station; and before dawn withdrew to villages close to the Šamarica forest.

The harsh retribution of the Ustasha authorities started immediately. Trucks with Ustasha and Home Guard units from Petrinja and Glina arrived in Banski Grabovac and the surrounding villages in the early morning of July 24. Božidar Cerovski, the commander of the Ustasha police, accompanied them, followed by the arrival of Dido Kvaternik from Zagreb.

That same morning Cerovski marched into the nearby Orthodox villages of the districts of Banski Grabovac and Kraljevčani with a platoon of Ustasha and students from the police academy. They arrested all men between the ages of sixteen and sixty found in or around their homes. At about three o'clock in the afternoon they returned to Banski Grabovac with, according to some sources, about four hundred villagers. The number is likely exaggerated, but there is no doubt that the arrests on that first day were indiscriminate and massive. Of the many eyewitness accounts, I consider the statements of Dragutin Laboš, the chief of the railway station in Petrinja, to be the most accurate:

> On July 24, 1941, in the morning, I came across a group of Ustasha in Banski Grabovac, among them Ivan Turki [the Ustasha commander for the district of Petrinja]. About fifty people who had been arrested were there. The Ustasha had removed Orthodox men from trains; they brought them on foot from the surrounding villages. All Orthodox, Turki said, are the same and they should all be killed. At five o'clock in the afternoon I went to Petrinja, where three hundred detained villagers were still at the station. On the morning of July 25, when I returned, about two hundred of the three hundred had been killed during

> the night. That evening there were again about three hundred detainees. When I returned to Grabovac on July 26, only eighty to one hundred of those three hundred detainees were left. "Tonight your railway workers were also killed," Turki said. On July 27, the dispatcher Šikić came to the station. He said he had never seen the horror of the kind the Ustasha had committed here in Grabovac.

In his testimony before the district court of Zagreb on January 10, 1947, Cerovski said in his defense that he had gone to Banski Grabovac only to provide security for the mobile summary court from Zagreb. According to him, "The trial lasted three to four hours and seventy to eighty people were convicted." He did not try to explain a trial that was able to examine and hand down death sentences in three to four hours for seventy to eighty people, none of whom were participants in the incriminating attack. Gaćeša's people didn't wait for the Ustasha at their homes; they were already in Šamarica forest.

The execution of the condemned men was carried out under Cerovski's supervision immediately after the sentencing, and the court returned to Zagreb. Then the major portion of the cleansing began. The orgy of killing next to the train station in Banski Grabovac lasted for four days. The killers were drunk. The prisoners had to roast lamb and pig for them; they had to dig graves for themselves and sing under the threat of being shot. The dead were buried by their neighbors, who stood in line for the next round of executions. Peasant women from Vlahović and Luščani brought food for their husbands and sons, but were forced to sing and dance with the drunken Ustasha. The testimonies of the seven prisoners who escaped from the execution site are shocking.

At Cerovski's trial before the district court in January 1947, the number of victims of the Grabovac cleansing in 1941 was cited at about 540, which was based on information then available to the Commission for Establishing War Crimes. In later years more detailed research was carried out that listed 977 people identified by name in the district of Glina and 288 for the district of Petrinja as victims of the reprisals in Banski Grabovac. I am aware that such lists are not always reliable, yet at Banski Grabovac, and I dare to say this with complete confidence, in four days more than 500 Orthodox men were killed, not one of whom participated in the uprising.

On July 27, 1941, the Zagreb daily *Hrvatski narod* carried a brief item: "Today the commander of the Ustasha police for the NDH, Božidar Cerovski, is returning to Zagreb from Glina, where with the police academy cadets he had captured a large number of Chetniks and so cleansed that entire area of Chetnik bands."

In addition to covering up the truth about the events in Banija, this news item served to suggest that Cerovski's operation had quelled the disturbances in the region. The truth was that they had just begun.

* * *

While the four days and four nights of gunfire from the execution site next to the railway station at Banski Grabovac periodically announced the murder of new groups of prisoners, people from the surrounding villages began their mass exodus. "Those who managed to escape arrest in the villages of Luščani, Grabovac, Vlahovići, Bačuga, Veliki, and Mali Šušnjar, as well as those from the districts of Mali Gradac and Klasnić, withdrew toward the Šamarica forest, carrying on their backs rolled-up bedding and food, taking their children and the elderly with them, many also taking their farm animals. Šamarica quickly became a refuge for thousands of people from the areas of Glina and Petrinja," Stanko Bjelajac wrote in *The Glina Anthology*.[3]

Gaćeša was furious. He was sitting at the edge of the Šamarica forest above the village of Miočinovići with his fifteen carbines, powerless to stop the evil that was destroying his region. When the communists, neighbors from his village, persuaded him to carry out an attack on Banski Grabovac, he was told that the same night attacks would be launched in the surrounding area and that a general uprising in Croatia and Bosnia would follow. The Ustasha would have no time for reprisals; they would have to defend themselves. When they met in Šamarica, Gaćeša attacked Bjelajac, who Gaćeša knew was a party functionary (a member of the Provincial Committee for Glina): "Who gave the order for an uprising and claimed that in a single night the whole country would rise and the enemy be expelled and the cities and countryside liberated ? It's a lie, don't you see, nothing like that happened, and the Ustasha killed many innocent people in Grabovac. What do we do with the many who escaped to save themselves?"

Gaćeša suspected that either the communist activists were deceiving him or else they were cowards and traitors afraid of raising their hand against the government and who would in the end betray him. He ordered his men to find Ranko Mitić, arrest him, and bring him to Šamarica to be questioned so that they could find out what was going on.

The confrontation between Gaćeša and the communists was preempted by events that followed one after the other with frightening speed. The actions of the Ustasha were forcing Gaćeša and the Serbs into an ever-closer alliance with the communists, and Gaćeša grew convinced that among the communists there were capable people courageously moving the uprising forward. The "reprisal action" in Banski Grabovac had not yet completely ended when on July 27 the first mass uprising in Bosanska Krajina and southeastern Lika erupted. By the end of the first day, the rebels controlled several county and district centers (Drvar, Srb, and Bosansko Grahovo) within an area of about two thousand square kilometers in the very epicenter of a shaken Independent State of Croatia (NDH). At the same time, news arrived of increasingly frequent minor acts of sabotage throughout the region: the Zagreb–Sušak rail line was destroyed at Moravice; south of Karlovac the telephone and telegraph lines were destroyed on two consecutive nights; and on July 23, in the village of Stipan (near Vrginmost) in a clash between two communists and two Ustasha the first shots were fired in Kordun, killing one Ustasha.

Poglavnik Pavelić had to make a decision. He might have considered the experience in Herzegovina, where the uprising had broken out a month earlier. General Vladimir Laxa, his special representative, reported to him: "The Serbian population has been incited to rebellion by the actions of the Ustasha who are carrying out random cleansings and mass killings, not only of men but of women and children, taking them from their homes whether they are guilty or not, throwing the corpses into caverns and rivers," and in doing so the "so-called 'Ustasha' have trampled underfoot the exalted ideals of the Ustasha movement, have buried its reputation and incurred the hatred of the populace." Instead of halting the massacres in peaceful villages that encouraged the rebellion, and trying to suppress it by attacking the rebels themselves, Pavelić decided to do the opposite: He launched cleansing operations against peaceful Orthodox villages in central Croatia with handpicked Ustasha units, and against the core of the uprising he sent weak forces that lost battle after battle. For example, in a two-day battle in August on the Boričevac–Kulen Vakuf road, the Gračac unit, according to its own report, lost 212 Home Guard troops, including 23 officers and noncommissioned officers. Partisan sources claim that rebel losses were 3 dead and 2 wounded and that in the two days they killed 110 members of the Home Guard; seized 195 rifles, 13 submachine guns, and 7 heavy machine guns; and captured 90 Home Guard troops, whose weapons and equipment were taken before they were released.

The major Ustasha cleansing operation began on the morning of July 29 and lasted until the evening of August 8. Based on the number of people killed, this was the largest Ustasha operation of its kind in the history of the NDH, with the exception of the even more brutal and extensive Kozara cleansing in the spring of 1942. Of the 16,535 documented Orthodox Serbian civilian victims in Lika during the Second World War, 96 percent were victims of Ustasha violence and slightly more than one-quarter of the total number were killed in these ten terrible days at the end of July and the beginning of August 1941. This time the hardest-hit counties in Banija were Hrvatska Kostajnica and Dvor, then the district of Glina again, culminating in the horror at the Glina Orthodox Church, in which more than one hundred people were deceived into believing that they would be converted to Catholicism and all but one were killed inside the church. In many places cleansing instantly sparked a rebellion, especially in Kordun.

After the experience of the rebellion of Serbs in Herzegovina, which broke out on June 25 in response to the Ustasha massacre in Orthodox villages, it is not easy to explain why a month later Pavelić would repeat the same suicidal crime in Croatia and parts of Bosnia. Was he so obsessed with hatred that killing Serbs was more important than stabilizing the state and creating peace in the country? Mladen Lorković, the minister of foreign affairs of the NDH, tried to explain this blind logic when Vladimir Židovec asked about the situation of Croatia in June 1942:

> You are our ambassador in Bulgaria so it is useful for you to be informed about the true state of things in Croatia. I have recently returned from the scene of a battle in Kozara. It is a large area, many square kilometers, but today there is not a living soul there! This whole area was settled by Serbs. Here is the thing: it is not true that the NDH authorities could not confront and destroy the Partisans. The truth is we are not rushing into these operations and we wish to use them for another pur-

> pose. Croatia cannot continue to live undisturbed if it does not get rid of the Serbian parasites who came to this area at the end of Turkish times. The battles with the Partisans give us the opportunity to finally resolve this general problem.[4]

I don't know how widely these perverted justifications were circulated among the Ustasha leadership. They can be glimpsed in the statements by Kvaternik, Mile Budak, Mirko Puk, and others, recorded by those who spoke directly with them. Of course, there were never any public statements that the uprising and the Partisans were welcomed as an excuse to kill more Serbs, but it is obvious that such interpretations were circulating within the inner circles of those who were deciding the fate of the country. Above all, these justifications served as a hypocritical self-justification for the failure in the fight against the increasingly successful Partisans. They could also be understood as an indirect justification for the commission of crimes that nothing else could justify. In fact, it involved the grotesque logic that springs from the fanaticism of hatred. The perverted conclusion that the difficulties posed by the uprising were useful could arise only from blind fanaticism. It enabled actions (the growing number of genocidal massacres) because of which the existing difficulties (the uprising) spread and sharpened ever more. For those who started this vicious circle (the Ustasha government), failure was inevitable.

There is no doubt that the genocide against the Serbs in the NDH was planned and carried out before the uprising. The only question is whether the plan was curbed by the uprising or whether the uprising provided the impetus that expanded it to catastrophic proportions.

* * *

The center of the major cleansing operation was Kordun, where the first three or four days of the campaign were under the direct command of Cerovski. On the morning of July 29, Cerovski set off from Glina toward Vojnić in a private automobile with a convoy of about ten trucks and approximately one hundred and fifty Ustasha gathered from various sources. In addition to émigré returnees (members of the *Poglavnik*'s bodyguard), the group included Ustasha selected from Petrinja, Glina, Sisak, Bosanska Krajina, and Cazinska Krajina. On the way to Vrginmost, they arrested about fifty Serbian men on the road and took them along. In Vojnić they arrested an even larger group of Serbs, but several Croats working in Vojnić spoke out on their behalf, and some of the Serbs were released. The Ustasha expedition then broke up into smaller groups that moved from Vojnić in various directions. After speaking by telephone directly from the district headquarters with Kvaternik, his immediate boss, Cerovski issued orders to the commanders of the individual groups and returned to Karlovac. The next day, July 30, he was again "in the field" in Rakovica, and on July 31, Colonel Tomašević, the commander of the Karlovac garrison, reported to his headquarters: "Ustasha commissioner Božidar Cerovski has passed Petrova Gora and arrived in Krstinja, where he has made contact with the Ustasha company from Karlovac that was moving from Tušilović to Krstinja. . . . The northern front of Petrova Gora is full of Chetniks. Lukas and Kvaternik are fighting them, while Cerovski is advancing from Cetingrad toward Topusko. No major resistance."[5]

Of course there was no resistance as Cerovski passed along the Cetingrad–Topusko road through villages that had not yet been engulfed by the uprising. Strong patrols under the command of Lieutenant Venturo Baljak, an Ustasha returnee, were picking up anyone they could find in the Orthodox villages along this same road. They were primarily noncombatants because the adult men had been alerted and had fled into the forests. The Ustasha took all the prisoners to Mehino Stanje, a hill by the road on the border between the counties of Slunj and Velika Kladuša, where the Royal Yugoslav Army had dug deep antitank trenches on the eve of the April war. On July 31, Baljak's Ustasha slaughtered the prisoners above these trenches, for the first time mostly women, children, and the elderly, and filled the trenches with their bodies. Mehino Stanje became the deadliest execution site in Kordun during the Second World War. And the commander of the Ustasha police, during his inspection trip on that very first day, drove right by that execution site and reported that "there is no major resistance."

The group of Ustasha that Cerovski sent in three trucks at about noon on July 29 through Tušilović to Krnjak was under the command of Ivan Turki, the Ustasha commander from Petrinja. The trucks stopped at the intersection at Brezova Glava before Tušilović. Some of the Ustasha stayed with the trucks, the others dispersed through the village, calling to the residents to come out of their homes. Almost no one responded. Only a few people were arrested because the men had hidden and women weren't arrested that day.

Veco Holjevac, with about ten armed men from Tušilovic and the surrounding villages, observed this from a distance of some three hundred meters from the hill of Babina Gora at the edge of the nearby forest. That day they were the first and only Partisan unit in Kordun. Watching the Ustasha arrest people, the first Kordun Partisans hesitated and argued about whether they should fire at the Ustasha or let them leave with the prisoners.

Seven days prior to that, on July 22, Holjevac had arrived in Tušilović from Karlovac, assigned by the Communist Party to form Partisan units with the leading local communist, Ćanica Opačić, for the planned rebellion. During his meetings with local communists, he immediately saw the main obstacle: a shortage of weapons. The local people in Kordun had some hunting rifles but only a few carbines. In May, Holjevac and some friends had acquired ten carbines from the military depot in Jamadol and hidden them in the military cemetery at the edge of the town. Thus, while the first operations in Kordun had to start virtually without weapons, the weapons were lying in the grave of an Austrian officer from the beginning of the twentieth century.

Opačić's wife, Dragica, a woman of great composure and courage, agreed to go with Holjevac on the dangerous assignment to recover the weapons. On Friday, July 25, Opačić hitched up his two horses and furnished the wagons for the journey. Dragica found some blacksmith's clothing, smeared paint on Holjevac's face and hands, and disguised him as a village blacksmith. In this guise, Holjevac believed there would be little danger of his being recognized in Karlovac. Two peasant boys, Nikola Basara and Mićo Đipalo, members of a local combat group, went with Dragica and Holjevac.

Friday was market day in Karlovac. Dragica drove the wagon and Holjevac sat next to her, with Basara and Đipalo in the back. Like everyone else, they paid at the tollgate below Turanj and just as they had hit the road to the cemetery an unexpected complication arose: One of their horses threw a shoe and they had to go to the blacksmith. Here they ran into an Ustasha official named Augustinović, who eyed them suspiciously. Sensing the danger, Basara and Đipalo wondered whether it might be better to turn back to Kordun, but Dragica prevailed and with great determination urged the horses on to the cemetery.

The military cemetery at Kozjača is almost always empty; visitors are rare. The three young men easily raised the covering of the crypt that concealed the weapons, carefully wrapped in rags. Just then they noticed two old women sitting on a bench some way off who, frightened by the sight of three strangers pulling something from an open grave, screamed and ran from the cemetery as fast as they could.

Dragica waited outside the cemetery next to a hedge with the horses and wagon. So as not to raise the suspicions of the few passersby, or of the city policeman who happened by, she had taken off a rear wheel, as if to repair it. The three men came through the hedge, loaded the guns under some hay, helped put the wheel back on, and they set off through the same tollgate below Turanj they had passed when entering the city.

A single policeman was monitoring the carts; people returning from the market formed a long line at the tollbooth. The policeman would take a look into some wagons, but he let most pass through, including Dragica's. Finally, she and her three companions breathed a sigh of relief. It seemed to Veco as if the horses felt the same relief as they happily rushed through Turanj and over the hills of Slunj. On the downhill stretch on the Kordun side Mićo and Nikola burst out into thunderous song in rhythm to the trotting horses. Dragica and Veco joined in, relieving themselves of the tension that had been oppressing them all day. Ćanica had been waiting for them since noon, near the most visible stretch of the road to Tušilović. Twenty years later I heard him say how he had never in his life waited so anxiously for his horses as when he caught sight of them returning home on that road.

The first Partisan unit in Kordun was formed the evening of July 25, on Glavica above Tušilović, with the guns, ammunition, and hand grenades brought from Karlovac. The people of Kordun were grateful to Holjevac and gained a new confidence in him: In Kordun guns and courage were always highly regarded. The unit chose Opačić as the commander of the Babina Gora unit and Holjevac as its political commissar. The next evening, they destroyed telephone and telegraph lines on the Karlovac–Slunj road and repeated the operation the following night.

The guns delivered from the military cemetery in Karlovac didn't fire a shot in the first encounter with the enemy. "Perhaps it all would have been different if Ćanica, the commander of the unit and a man

Veco Holjevac, the political commissar of the headquarters of the National Liberation Movement of Kordun and Banija (1941–1942)

whom the men had trusted, had been with us," Holjevac later commented. He had to reconcile himself to the fact that many of his *prvoborci*, Kordun communists, were not yet prepared to attack and expose their village to danger.

But everything in Kordun changed in a single day on July 29, 1941.

* * *

An Ustasha group under the command of Turki arrived in Krnjak from Tušilović with three trucks at about four o'clock in the afternoon. A little later, a second Ustasha group, which had traveled from Vojnić on the southern road through Kolarić, also arrived in Krnjak. They brought with them more than fifty prisoners, all of whom had been arrested along the way from Vrginmost to Krnjak. They were late in arriving because they had briefly stopped in Vojnićki Grabovac for a little drinking and plundering. At a convenient moment Ante Salomon, an Ustasha from Barilović, whispered to Marko Todorić, his friend who had been arrested, to flee into the corn while no one was looking. Todorić survived.

In Krnjak that morning Dragutin Muić, the Ustasha *povjerenik*, had ordered some Serbs from Krnjak and the surrounding villages to bring food and other supplies to the district building for Slovenes who had been resettled in the area. The Ustasha arrested these Serbs, roped them together, and held them prisoner in the building. "There, you see, it is your own fault," Muić explained to them. "It's not worth defying the government because the government is the government. When it was your government, Serbian, you didn't tear down telephone lines, and now you do to defy us. We are not joking around, this is Croatia, not Serbia." Whereupon Muić left and several Ustasha émigrés entered the room and beat the prisoners savagely. A second group of Ustasha went to Krnjački Grabovac to carry out more arrests. Their trucks stopped in front of the home of Zorka Maćešić, who made the following statement to the researcher Đuro Zatezalo in 1975:

> Trucks with Ustasha stopped that day in front of my house and they ordered the Serbs they had picked up along the way to get off and sit next to my house near the ditch by the road. Several Ustasha stayed behind to guard these people; the others went to the village of Krnjački Grabovac, where they seized more Serbs. Among those arrested I recognized the priest Mile Peruča; he had been badly beaten....They tied up my husband, Mihajlo Maćešić, and Nikola Pribić, who was visiting us from the village of Zagorje at that time, and hit them both several times with rifle butts and ordered them to lie down by the house. Five of them then entered my house and hit me with rifle butts. When my daughter Radojka, who was then seventeen, saw this, she started to cry and jumped to defend me, begging them not to beat me. But those criminals hit my Radojka in the chest with their rifle barrels and she fell to the ground. After this abuse, they pounced on me and my aunt Mila Mihajlović. They threw us to the ground and raped us. We were crying, pleading for help, begging them not to torment us, but we could not get them to stop. The men tied up outside, my poor Mihajlo too,

> could hear our screams. You can imagine what it was like for them to hear all of this.... After the rape, the Ustasha kicked us and went on searching the house and what they liked they took, whether it was clothing or food; I had some money from the sale of horses, they took that too. When the Ustasha and the gendarmes brought the duped and arrested Serbs from the gendarme station in Gornji Krnjak to my house, they then locked me, my aunt Mila, and my daughter Radojka in a room, and ordered us to stay put. I couldn't bear not knowing what they were going to do to the bound prisoners and I managed to sneak into the courtyard through a different door and through the gate. I saw them beating the men. Those who put up resistance they beat until they were unconscious with blows all over their bodies. They threw the beaten men onto the trucks as if they were not living beings....[6]

At nightfall the Ustasha brought the beaten men in trucks to the house of Marko Ivanović. From there they forced them to walk, bound in small groups, along a short road across a bridge over the Rijeka creek to the edge of the Loskunja forest, where they brutally murdered them with knives, clubs, and axes. Three of the men were able to save themselves: Mirko Trkulja, by jumping from the truck while it was headed to the execution site; Nikola Bižić, by escaping from the execution site; and Ljubomir Vukmirović, whom an Ustasha officer (Turki?) strangely released. I think their eyewitness accounts are reliable because they were recorded independently from one another and the details are precise and generally consistent. The executions were so horrendous that I will skip the details and describe them only in generalities.

Again, the number of victims is in dispute. The monument at Ivanović Jarak, which was heavily damaged in 1995, states that 350 people were killed. Some publications and statements speak of 400 victims. Captain Haeffner, a German intelligence officer, also claimed in a report to General Glaise von Horstenau, his chief, that 400 people from Krnjak, Vojnić, Tušilović, and Krstinja were killed there. In his book, *Notes from My Hometown*, Holjevac claims that "about one hundred and fifty peasants" were killed. The list of victims in the book *Kotar Vojnić u narodnooslobodilačkom ratu i socijalističkoj revoluciji* (The District of Vojnić in the National Liberation War and the Socialist Revolution) contains 203 names, which is probably the closest to the true number.[7]

In any event, the number of victims at the Ivanović Jarak was nowhere near the largest execution in Kordun, but it had a far greater resonance and more immediate consequences. It was, literally, the trigger that set off the general uprising.

The victims were from a wide area—from the Glina River to the Korana River. They were killed within sight of other people, right next to the main road, and the killers didn't try to hide anything, nor could they have done so. Half of Kordun knew that the Ustasha punitive expedition was arresting whomever it came across throughout the area, that people were taken away and never heard from again. The shots echoed some distance from the execution sites and people in nearby houses could hear the screams. On the night of the killings the three escapees told their fellow villagers what had taken place at the Ivanović Jarak. Through the night the alarming news swept from village to village. By the morning of July 30, the forests were full of fugitives. In some places entire families had fled. Word also spread that the main gathering point was at Petrova Gora, that a large store of weapons was there, and that the communists were forming a front for protection from the Ustasha. In the course of that day, about one thousand people had gathered at Crna Lokva in Petrova Gora. By the next day the number is said to have increased to three thousand.

Panic and fear among the people quickly subsided in the security of the deep forest, but rebelliousness, a desire for revenge, a fighting spirit, and fury were rapidly growing. Many were looking for weapons, but there were none: The myth of weapons magazines in Petrova Gora was quickly dispelled. Only several dozen hunting rifles and barely five or six military carbines were on hand. Žarko Čuić, the secretary of the District Committee of the KPH in Vojnić and a sympathetic and popular teacher who had been chosen as the commander of Petrova Gora, stood before the people. Some asked him to lead them to Vojnić to attack its garrison with pitchforks and axes so as to capture its weapons. They sought a true popular uprising. Čuić was confused. He believed the garrison in Vojnić was well-armed. It would defend itself, he said, and there was nothing they could do—a lot of people would be killed, more evil would come. He advised that those who were able should cautiously go home during the night, take their farm animals and as many of their possessions as they could, and return in the morning to Petrova Gora. Some dispersed in disappointment, others remained at Crna Lokva, their fighting spirit waning. The communists were criticized for calling people to fight bare-handed when they themselves were bare-handed. Ivan Furlan, an enterprising teacher and a member of the District Committee of the KPH of Vojnić, nevertheless managed to collect several small groups of fighters from the villages on the south side of Petrova Gora and to establish a kind of "front" facing Velika Kladuša and Krstinja. Rade Bulat and Bogdan Oreščanin organized a front on the eastern side of Petrova Gora in the direction of Vrginmost and Topusko.[8]

The news of the massacres at Miholjsko, at Mehino Stanje, and around Topusko deepened the bitterness and fear of the people in the central refuge at Crna Lokva. But the appearance in Petrova Gora of about thirty fighters of the Babina Gora and Debela Kosa units, armed with twelve carbines and twenty hunting rifles, restored the will for armed resistance and battle.

* * *

Babina Gora, the first Partisan unit in Kordun, quickly paid the price for its inexperience. On the morning of July 30, the unit was resting on Glavica above the villages of Brezova Glava and Tušilović when they were surprised by the attack of a Home Guard company. With

rifle and machine-gun fire the approximately 120 Home Guard soldiers put to flight about 15 Partisans. The Home Guard unit did not pursue them or prevent their escape. The scattered Partisans regrouped in the Loskunja forest, realizing they'd had a lucky escape. Opačić, the commander, and Holjevac, the political commissar, quickly agreed that the location of Babina Gora was untenable as a permanent base for the unit—it was too exposed to Karlovac and the nearby gendarme and military garrisons. They led the unit closer to Petrova Gora, to the small forest of Debela Kosa, where a recently formed rebel unit of about twenty people from the nearby villages was encamped. The two groups joined forces and the Debela Kosa unit was created with about thirty-five fighters. In the first months of the uprising it was the best-armed, best-organized, and most successful Partisan unit in Kordun. The men of the new unit reelected Opačić as the commander and Holjevac as the political commissar.

The next day, on July 31, the Debela Kosa unit circled part of Petrova Gora and made its presence known to the fleeing people. At Crna Lokva, Opačić made a fiery speech to the refugees. A temperamental thirty-five-year-old, he was a persuasive speaker with a powerful voice, prone to earthy expressions. He enjoyed a good reputation and the trust of many people in Kordun. His speech resonated throughout the region and without a doubt encouraged the formation of new Partisan units in refugee camps and villages at the edges of the forests on all sides of Petrova Gora. The former peasant guards, combat groups, and fronts were growing into small military units trained in guerrilla warfare. They each numbered between ten and thirty volunteer fighters. At the beginning they were mostly local communists and their sympathizers, but in time they were joined by Kordun villagers with no political persuasion, encouraged by the initial successes in resisting the Ustasha terror.

In the early phase the units usually formed their bases at the edge of forests above villages or in an out-of-the-way hamlet below the forest itself. At their backs were the deep forests of Petrova Gora, which provided sanctuary and security; and in front of them were their villages and families, on whom they relied and without whose support they would not have been able to survive. From home and village they received food, vital equipment, and contact with the outside world. The units also wrangled the last hidden carbines of some former soldiers and the last hidden hunting rifles of former hunters that the populace of Kordun, raised in warfare, jealously protected in some hidden bunker—and now they had to turn these over to the first Partisans or go into battle and use the weapons themselves. In these early days, therefore, each unit had at least two or three, and as many as ten, military rifles, and for every fighter a hunting rifle, or at least an old pistol. The continued strengthening of the units depended almost exclusively on the weapons they were able to take from the enemy. Their first significant success in this regard was on August 31, 1941, when the Debela Kosa unit attacked the gendarme station in Perjasica and acquired sixty-six guns, and a day later, when the Vojišnica and Radonja units attacked a garrison at the Vojišnica mine and seized their first machine gun. According to reports from the first conference of Kordun and Banija, on September 19 and 20 Partisans in Crna Lokva (the first district consisting of Petrova Gora and its surrounding villages) already had 190 armed fighters, fifty-six of whom were members of the Communist Party, while all of Kordun, which was divided into four districts, had a total of 688 fighters, 131 of whom were Communist Party members.

The major Ustasha cleansing operation in Kordun lasted until August 8. It began at Ivanović Jarak and continued with increasing force throughout the region. It subsided most quickly around Petrova Gora, although even there the Ustasha continued to hunt for people. Nevertheless, the weak rebel fronts and their units provided some protection to the endangered population. They warned them of Ustasha movements, and people were able to flee into the forests of Petrova Gora. Through several small raids and nighttime sabotage operations, some rebel groups made it appear that their strength was greater than it was. The myth spread that Petrova Gora was "buzzing with rebels," and the reports at the time from the gendarme stations and the Ustasha authorities list many hundred "armed Chetniks and communists." For example, on August 12, the gendarme section in Petrinja reported that "about three hundred armed Serbs had attacked the village of Bović in the district of Vrginmost" when, in fact, eleven armed Partisans assisted by a group of unarmed peasants attacked the district building and disarmed one gendarme and one policeman while two other gendarmes fled.

After Ivanović Jarak, the forest refuges became permanent havens for many of Kordun's Orthodox Serbs. People abandoned their property, but their lives were saved. The Ustasha avoided battle with the rebels. In skirmishes around Petrova Gora during these ten days, only two rebels and seven or eight Ustasha, gendarmes, and members of the Home Guard were killed. The uprising in Petrova Gora saved many Serbs of the surrounding villages from the much greater evil planned for them. The main strike of the Ustasha cleansing operation was now directed at the district of Slunj, which until then had been a relatively peaceful part of Kordun.

* * *

Ivan Nikšić, the parish priest of Slunj, was born in 1910. He was more than just a humble man of the church. In fact, he showed himself to be a fiery exponent of Croatian nationalism, maintaining that even Vladko Maček was "a servant of Belgrade" and that he "had betrayed Croats in the most shameful way" because he had led a policy of cooperation with the Belgrade government. In his book *Spomenici ožupi Slunjskoj* (Testimonies About the County of Slunj),

Father Nikšić described with undisguised delight and in great detail for fourteen full pages how he had led the small group of Ustasha supporters that disarmed 1,100 soldiers and officers of the Royal Yugoslav Army between April 10 and 12 in Slunj and had set up an Ustasha government. Father Nikšić was appointed the Ustasha commissioner for the district of Slunj. In that capacity he personally, skillfully, and courageously disarmed two Yugoslav generals and their entourage. He distributed large quantities of seized weapons to local volunteers, with whom he organized a successful defense against the remaining Royal Yugoslav Army units that had not surrendered and were intent on occupying Slunj. Then on the evening of April 12, Father Nikšić, as the representative of the new government, formally and warmly welcomed German troops to Slunj.

In his memoir, Father Nikšić recalls with considerable reserve the massacre of the Veljun Serbs in Hrvatski Blagaj between May 6 and 10, which was preceded by the brutal murder of the Mravunac family of Blagaj. He describes how on May 7 a mobile summary court arrived from Zagreb with a company of Ustasha émigrés to conduct an investigation, which produced evidence that the Orthodox inhabitants had been organized as so-called Chetniks in an uprising, and therefore the summary court in Blagaj condemned to death 440 men found in possession of "subversive material." Further on Father Nikšić puts an ever-greater distance between himself and the events in Blagaj: "The summary court conducted the subsequent trials independently and did not inform the Ustasha Council, the district, or the court in Slunj."

By consciously distorting important facts, Father Nikšić, like Pontius Pilate, "washed his hands" of the mass murder in Hrvatski Blagaj, but he did not expressly condemn it. Only with the major cleansing operation carried out in the district of Slunj was Father Nikšić's level of tolerance for the Ustasha crimes challenged. In his memoirs he gives a two-page, detailed description of the event, which I cite here because of its historiographical value and interest:

The Massacre of Orthodox in Slunj
(the so-called cleansing)

At the end of July came the surprise arrival of Ustasha émigré lieutenant Vital Baljak[9] in a truck loaded with several hun- dred rifles (allegedly four hundred). He did not report to the district authorities, the Ustasha Council, or the gendarme station, but on his own called on the people of Slunj to take up arms and ordered all of the Orthodox residents of Slunj imprisoned.

The Ustasha commisoner, Father Nikšić, and the head of the district, Lenčerić, protested, but Baljak said that he had a special mission, that he was responsible only to Zagreb, that his operation did not concern us, and that we should let him get on with his assignment. It was still not known what would become of the Orthodox Serbs, but the Kovačević brothers said that they would all be shot. Further, Nikšić immediately sent a telegram to the *Poglavnik* himself, a telegram of more than one hundred words. As he received no reply, he telephoned the *Poglavnik*'s office. He was told that the telegram had arrived and that a response was forthcoming. Father Nikšić went directly to Karlovac to the *veliki župan* (grand chieftan) Ante Nikšić, who had also intervened with Zagreb, but with no results. Father Nikšić then went personally to Zagreb, but while he was on the way, all of the Slunj Orthodox were murdered, thrown into a pit, and buried.

In Zagreb, Father Nikšić resigned his duties as the Ustasha commissioner and Žarko Kovačević was appointed the commissioner and later the commander.

When Slunj was thoroughly cleansed, they began to hunt Orthodox in the villages, and those caught were immediately killed. Every able Orthodox man fled to the forests, and those killed were mostly women, children, and the elderly who could not flee. This rampage lasted for about ten days. During this entire time, Father Nikšić was in Zagreb protesting with all authorities, but in Zagreb they did not believe that this was going on. It did not stop until the émigrés, at the order of the *Poglavnik*, were called to Zagreb and all of the Ustasha in top positions were relieved of their duties.

The three Kovačević brothers from Slunj participated in the operation along with Mile Katić, a bootmaker from Podmelnica; Ivan Skukan, an unemployed worker from Rastoke; Marko Obajdin, a peasant from Podmelnica; and less actively, Predrag Neralić, a noncommissioned naval officer dismissed for supporting the communists, and Milan Kovačević, a shoemaker's apprentice. The other peasants called to arms did not want to participate in the killing; they only carried out the arrests. The most bloodthirsty of all was Zvonko Kovačević, the humpbacked organist. A conscientious organist who came exactly on time for every devotion in the church, but from the start of the killing was never to be found near a church. He walked the streets, head down, timidly, did not dare to look anyone in the face. But he has a conscience! The saying from the Holy Scripture was fulfilled: "Beware the mark of the beast!"

According to the statements of the bandits themselves, during that time they had killed about three to four thousand Orthodox throughout the district of Slunj, among whom only one to two hundred were capable of bearing arms; the rest were the infirm, women, children, and the elderly. This was a sad page in the history of Slunj and of the Croatian state because the guilty were

> not called to account by the government authorities, but for Slunj there was some comfort because such a small number of individuals participated, and then only those who even before were the rabble and dregs of society. In addition, the other good thing is that these people finally showed who they really were and that everyone avoided them and held them in contempt. When the operation was over, the Orthodox returned to their homes, but they had lost their trust in the Croatian government.[10]

The statements of many other witnesses confirm the credibility of Father Nikšić's text, except for his estimate of the number of victims. It seems that "victim-mania," with an uncritical inflation in numbers, is a widespread disease among chroniclers of the events of that time, and unfortunately we also have the "victimology hypocrites" who either crudely reduce the number of victims or cover up the events completely. It is curious that Father Nikšić belongs to the former group: His claim that three to four thousand Orthodox were killed in those ten summer days in the district of Slunj is grossly exaggerated. The anthology *Kotar Slunj i kotar Veljun u NOR-u i socijalističkoj izgradnji* (The Counties of Slunj and Veljun in the National Liberation War and the Socialist Revolution), edited by Đuro Zatezalo, listed the names of the victims of the cleansing operation, giving what I think is closer to an exact number. It cites a figure of 2,139 civilian victims of the Ustasha terror in the district of Slunj in 1941, not including the wartime district of Veljun. Of that number, about three-quarters were killed in the major cleansing, that is, about 1,500 to 1,600 people killed in about ten days.[11]

By the beginning of August 1941, Father Nikšić was no longer an Ustasha functionary, but he didn't distance himself from the Ustasha movement. In the later pages of his memoir, he continues to glorify the Ustasha movement and the NDH, even if he mentions Ustasha crimes here and there and condemns them. Regarding Ljubomir Kvaternik, he writes that Kvaternik's "rule in Bihać was one of the regrettable episodes in Croatian history. His entire effort, instead of building the young state, consisted of butchering and killing the Orthodox and stealing their property. He himself stated that in Slunj he killed more than ten thousand of them."

When the Partisan National Liberation Army seized Slunj in November 1942, Father Nikšić fled to Karlovac. There he became the chaplain of the Eighth Ustasha Slunj Battalion. In 1943 and 1944, he was engaged in battle several times in Slunj and Bihać counties. He had the rank of an Ustasha captain; and in the several months in 1943 when Ustasha authority was reimposed on Slunj, he also carried out the duties of the head of the district. He demonstrated some military skill; it was said that he commanded parts of the Slunj battalion, but I could not verify this. At the beginning of 1945, he was imprisoned by the Partisans, then all trace of him was lost; he was probably killed shortly after his imprisonment.

In addition to Father Nikšić's text about the summer cleansing operation in the district of Slunj in 1941, I think it is worth citing the main portion of the report of the Command of the First Croatian Regiment:

> The Command of the Gendarme Platoon in Slunj by letter, Office No. 89, of August 13, 1941, reports the following:
>
> On July 29 the cleansing by the Ustasha began. This caused panic among the Serbian population and they have all fled into the forests.
>
> The work of the Ustasha, among other things, was tactless because those cleansed were less dangerous and less guilty, such

as the elderly, women, and young children, while others fled to the forests. It can be summed up in one sentence: noncombatants were cleansed, while fighters remained in the forest. Those who were more naïve, and with a clear conscience, did not flee in the first wave because they thought nothing would happen to them.

The cleansing was successfully carried out in the city of Slunj and around Slunj, while in the more distant places less so.

The current situation cannot be supported with accurate data because the people have stayed in the forests, but it is certain that a great many families have lost members.

The Ustasha cleansing activities were carried out in public, which is one of the reasons people fled. The cleansing occurred in the home, the courtyard, on the road, with parents in the presence of children or vice versa. They robbed homes and property, scrambling to get into richer households and cleanse the more wealthy. In the recent cleansing, they stole clothing and there were arguments among the Ustasha over this. There were drinking binges; there were barbarous scenes of cleansing children in the cradle, the elderly, entire families together, sadistic enjoyment of terrible tortures before the final cleansing. Such acts provoked disapproval among honest and solid Croats, and whispers could be heard: this is a disgrace for the people of Croatia, our culture, and the Catholic faith. Most of the pits were dug beforehand. There were cases in which those being cleansed carried shovels, etc. Some were buried while still alive, the rest not buried or poorly buried so their relatives, as well as those who fled to the forests, came to see.

All this has instilled fear in the people and also bitterness so that there can be no hope of reconciliation. If some laws existed, there might be a possibility, but here there are no such laws and there are none to this day.

> I, as well as the gendarmes in general, have been powerless. It was all done without our knowledge and with great distrust toward us. If I were to complain, no matter how trivial the complaint, my life would be endangered with threats, directly or indirectly. You could hear pronouncements like: "Now it's the gendarmes' turn."
>
> Perhaps the main reason for the distrust of the gendarmes was that they were not prominent in the cleansing, although they had a hand in it. I explained to them that we are an organ of the government and therefore obliged to protect the reputation of the government.
>
> Among the Croatian population (among many) we have noticed disapproval of this method of cleansing because they know some of those who have been cleansed, they know that they did nothing against Croats, on the contrary they were shunned by the earlier regime because they favored Croats. These people would be useful now because they could influence those who have fled.
>
> The order to halt the cleansing and invite people to return to their homes has met with little success. They have lost their trust, as each one of them is aware of the horrible reason that made them flee to the forests. I state again that a complete return of the population from the forests will be difficult to achieve.[12]

This report was written by Mirko Marušić, the commander of the gendarme unit in Slunj, on August 13, or five to six days after the end of the cleansing. However, even during the killings, if not before, some gendarme commanders warned in their reports that Ustasha actions against the Orthodox were leading to resistance, a variety of disturbances, and perhaps rebellion. In fact, the gendarme reports can be considered among the most reliable regarding the situation in 1941. For example, in its routine report of August 6, the Command of the First Croatian Gendarme Regiment warned that the majority of Serbs participating in the uprising were doing so "in reaction to their cleansing by our Ustasha units. By cleansing we mean destruction: the killing and butchering of Serbs, regardless of gender and age, as well as the destruction of their personal property."

The first discussions between the peasants and the local communists on armed resistance and rebellion in the district of Slunj were held in Gornji Primišalj on the second and third days of the genocide. The first skirmish between the rebels and the Ustasha was on August 3 in Zečev Varoš, in the immediate vicinity of Slunj. The Ustasha fled in the face of an assault by a poorly armed mass of peasants. From that moment the uprising in the district of Slunj spread relatively quickly, which I consider proof that the cleansings were the main impetus for the spread of the rebellion and not the other way around. According to reports at the conference of September 19 and 20, of 688 armed Partisan fighters throughout Kordun, there were 190 in the first district (around Petrova Gora), 138 in the second district (the central portion of Kordun, the wartime district of Veljun), 46 in the fourth district (the southernmost part of Kordun), while the third district (Slunj) had 314, by far the most. The numbers speak for themselves: in the fourth district, where there had been relatively few cleansings, there were also far fewer Partisans, among whom 27 (about 59 percent) were communists; in the third district, which was the hardest hit by the Ustasha cleansing operations, there were far more Partisans with a far lower share of communists (a total of 30, or about 9.5 percent).

* * *

On the front page of *Hrvatski narod* on August 10, 1941, a decree of the *Poglavnik* was published, which I provide verbatim:

Zagreb, August 9. This decree is issued today from the Ustasha main headquarters:

In reference to Articles 4 and 13 of the Ustasha Constitution by this decree I RELIEVE FROM ALL DUTIES ALL HIGH-RANKING USTASHA AND THEIR ADJUTANTS on the territory of the Independent State of Croatia.

In line with the above they must cease each and every activity.

Ustasha organizations must remain within their units in an inactive status until officials are appointed, which will follow immediately.

All units formed as armed auxiliaries, that is, the so-called "wild Ustasha," must cease all activity at once.

This decree does not apply to regular Ustasha units in the Ustasha army under regular Ustasha command, to those units that are serving with the National Directorate for Renewal, to those units on the national borders and in national transportation facilities and government buildings, and to those assigned to the Ustasha intelligence service.

FOR THE HOMELAND!

Issued in the Ustasha Main Headquarters on August 9, 1941.

Administrative Commander	*Poglavnik*
Organizational Office of G.U.S.	Dr. ANTE PAVELIĆ (signed)
Poglavnik Adjutant	BLAŽ LORKOVIĆ (signed)

Although it was not explicitly stated, in effect this decree meant the end of the cleansing operation, or the mass killing of Serbs, in many parts of the NDH. The same front page of *Hrvatski narod* also carried the order that "all Ustasha members of the *Poglavnik*'s bodyguard on leave or on temporary duties must return immediately to Zagreb," which meant that the leaders of the cleansing, such as

Venturo "Vitala" Baljak in the district of Slunj, were being withdrawn from all locations.

The dismissal of all local Ustasha functionaries, although stated in the decree, was only superficially significant. Within the next few days Pavelić appointed mostly the same people to duties in the Ustasha hierarchy, with only slight reassignments, based on the needs of the organization. However, the halt to the cleansing was indeed real, at least until further notice. Ustasha patrols stopped their raids of Serbian villages and the majority of the Ustasha units sent to Kordun from Zagreb, Karlovac, and Ogulin returned to their home garrisons. Minister Andrija Artuković and some local government authorities sent public invitations to the fleeing residents to return to their homes. Gendarme stations in the field were ordered to calm the population and to guarantee their peaceful homecoming. The response to these calls was restrained. After the killing of so many men, women, and children, the Serbian peasants could no longer trust the Ustasha government. Those who did return to their homes continued to rotate as village guards and maintain their refuges in the forests—just in case they were needed again. The young men more inclined to fight didn't return from their safe havens. They joined Partisan units, which in August were springing up throughout Kordun, especially in those regions that had been hit the hardest by the killings. The displaced people quickly sensed that the Partisans were providing relatively greater security than the promises of the Ustasha government.

In his decree, Pavelić had implied that the so-called "wild Ustasha," whom he defined as "armed auxiliaries," were the ones guilty of committing the crimes. Accordingly, the residents of Slunj, who had received arms from Baljak at the beginning of the cleansing operation, were "wild Ustasha," a sort of outlaw or irregular unit. Some were indeed wild in their actions, but as a "unit for armed assistance" they were not some "wild" unit outside the control of higher authorities. They received weapons and operated under the direct command of Baljak, an officer in the *Poglavnik*'s bodyguard; the operation in which they participated was under the supervision of Cerovski, the director of the Ustasha police of the NDH, who carried out the orders of Dido Kvaternik, the chief of all of the security and police services of the NDH, and a man to whom Pavelić personally entrusted the "resolution of the Serbian question." In this strict hierarchy there were individual cases of a lack of discipline (robbery, corruption, revenge for personal motives, rape), which were frequently tolerated, and sometimes, at the insistence of Kvaternik, punished. There could be no self-initiative when it was a question of major decisions that embraced many districts and several counties. The responsibility of the Ustasha leadership for the genocidal killing of Serbs was not only implicit, what today we would call "command responsibility," but the most direct executive responsibility.

Those who carried out the will of the supreme authorities in Banija and Kordun were Cerovski and Baljak and in other areas Juco Rukavina, Ljubomir Kvaternik, Viktor Gutić, and Jure Francetić, among others. After the summer of ethnic cleansing operations, they all remained in their senior positions, and the majority were promoted. The same was true in the lower ranks: Father Nikšić was replaced as the Ustasha commissioner by Kovačević, the notorious leader of the Slunj Ustasha, who was quickly appointed by Pavelić as the Ustasha commander for the district of Slunj upon completion of the operation. Pavelić acknowledged the mass killings in the Serbian villages and never disowned that crime. He halted the cleansing on August 9 for tactical reasons, because of pressure from all sides, which I summarize here:

1. It had become obvious that the cleansing operation was not suppressing but was inflaming the rebellion; the scale of the

incidents quickly outgrew what Pavelić might have considered a desirable motive for launching genocidal "reprisals"; the rapid spread of the uprising threatened the country's economy, the infrastructure of the state, and the stability of an already unstable regime.

2. Because of the rapid spread of the uprising, Italian military commanders announced a significant expansion of their zones of occupation. In some places they protected endangered Serbs, made pacts with the Chetniks, and called into question the competence of the Ustasha authorities.

3. German military and other representatives, some of whom were skeptical of the Ustasha ideal, openly expressed fears that the spread of the uprising would threaten some of their vital land routes, make it impossible to exploit the mineral wealth they were counting on, and tie down their troops in the region; they were contemplating, it was rumored, the possibility of offering the government of the NDH to Vladko Maček instead of to Pavelić and his Ustasha.

4. The complaints of Generals Prpić, Blašković, Laxa, and other senior officers of the Home Guard about the cleansing operation in the field were becoming more frequent; dire warnings also came from senior gendarme commanders and lower-ranking Ustasha officials like Father Nikšić in Slunj.

5. In the orgy of cleansing, a lack of discipline flourished in the Ustasha units with excesses that were not to the liking of those who issued the orders. It became necessary to place the unruly units under firm military discipline.

6. There were protests by groups and individuals among the Croatian population, accompanied by a chill in attitudes toward the Ustasha authorities, which grew with the awareness of the scale of the crimes committed.

Although Pavelić halted the major cleansing operation against the Serbian villages on August 9, neither he nor his most trusted subordinates renounced the genocidal character of their plan for resolving the "Serbian question" in the NDH. They had cultivated the fanaticism of hatred for too long, which made them incapable of perceiving reality and understanding that by killing everyone around them, they were, in fact, killing their own idea, their state, and their government. Indeed, the mass murder of Serbs and Jews in the Ustasha death camps on Mount Velebit and the island of Pag reached its culmination in August 1941. In the second half of August the Jasenovac camp system, at the time the largest site of genocidal and political terror, began operations. Maček, who was a prisoner at Jasenovac in the winter of 1941, asked Ljubo Miloš, the camp commander, whether he feared God's punishment for the godless acts he was committing, to which the Ustasha fanatic Miloš responded: "Say nothing to me. I know I will burn in hell for what I have done and for what I will do. But I will burn for Croatia." It is difficult to imagine a more descriptive characterization of the fanaticism of hatred.

In carrying out the cleansing of villages, Pavelić and Kvaternik merely changed their tactics after the summer of 1941. There was no longer a synchronized, simultaneous cleansing throughout the country but numerous local operations of a similar character. Prepared in more precise military detail, these attacks were usually launched against the centers of the uprising, such as Petrova Gora and Kozara. In those areas the killing was directed not only toward the Partisan units, who avoided major losses through the use of guerrilla tactics, but more so toward the local population: the burning of entire villages, robbery and the destruction of property, killing regardless of age and gender, the desolation of a region, and mass deportations of the population to Jasenovac and other camps. In public and to their allies the Ustasha defined such actions as "operations of reprisal," even though the actual effect was ethnic cleansing no less brutal than the other genocides in the summer of 1941. In some places Partisan units were able to provide at least some protection to the civilian population, but in other places they could not. The "operations of reprisal" aimed at the civilian population devastated the northern portions of Kordun and Banija at the end of 1941 and the beginning of 1942, followed by the villages around Petrova Gora in May 1942, then Kozara, part of Srijem, and many other localities in sad succession.

A state erected on such a foundation could not survive. It had also quickly antagonized the greater portion of the Croatian people whose name it had invoked without basis. I will make use here of the aphoristic conclusion of Ante Ciliga, an early forerunner of communist dissidents turned Croatian nationalists: "Pavelić divided the Croats, united the Serbs, strengthened the communist Partisans, and blindly tied himself to powers that were condemned to lose the war. It is difficult to imagine a more disastrous, suicidal policy." The conclusion is witty though oversimplified. Pavelić's policy did not unite the Serbs everywhere—it divided them into Partisans and Chetniks. And it did not fragment Croats everywhere—they remained united on one side or the other. However, in regard to Kordun, Ciliga was right: Pavelić's major cleansing operation in the summer of 1941 divided the Kordun Croats and united the Kordun Serbs, who became the most organized Partisan entity in the very heart of Croatia.

Nothing changed when the Ustasha government established the Croatian Orthodox Church in 1942 and tried to "pacify" the Serbs with several similar actions. This indeed alleviated the position and fate of the remaining Serbs in some cities, but it made no impression on Serbs in Kordun, Banija, and Lika. And nowhere did it overcome the general distrust of the Ustasha government. While a relatively milder policy toward the Orthodox population was proclaimed in Zagreb in 1942, at almost the same time the Ustasha army was carrying out its most brutal cleansing operations (Petrova Gora and Kozara). Such operations were repeated right to the end of the war, reaffirming the trademark that the year 1941 had left.

* * *

The Kordun Croats had many reasons to be dissatisfied with their situation and the general conditions in royalist Yugoslavia. They lived off land that was rocky, hilly, difficult to cultivate, and largely unproductive. In the county of Vojnić in 1931, families had an average of 6.3 members, about 1.8 hectares of tillable fields, and about 1.6 hectares of pasture. With a yield per hectare several times lower than in Slavonia and Vojvodina and with poor stock, there was not much surplus to sell—barely enough for a meager self-sufficiency. In the county of Slunj circumstances were more difficult. In the county of Vojnić there was one doctor for every 35,000 residents, while in the county of Slunj in 1940, 65.5 percent of the population was illiterate. Croats and Serbs in Kordun suffered all of this together, although with some differences: from the former Military Frontier some Orthodox villages inherited better land than their Catholic neighbors; the fields of Veljun were more fertile than those in Blagaj; life in Primišalj was slightly better than in neighboring Nikšić. When one considers that all of the county officials, all of the commanders of the gendarme stations, and almost all of the district heads were Serbs, the unproductive Kordun soil suddenly became fertile ground for the rise of interfaith and interethnic animosity. This occurred most frequently in Slunj, the poorest county. The centralizing policies of all of the Belgrade governments up to 1939 contributed to the deepening of these local animosities.

In the counties of Vojnić and Vrginmost relations between the Croatian and Serbian populations frequently oscillated between cooperation and polarization; in the county of Slunj polarization was virtually constant. In the last years before the war, Pribičević's Serbian

Women from the region of Slunj, photographed in 1964

Democratic Party and Maček's Croatian Peasants' Party also established political cooperation between the Croats and Serbs in Kordun, and coalition electoral lists enjoyed increasingly frequent success in local elections. Lovro Sušić, a national representative from the county of Slunj, emerged as the most forceful voice against such a policy of agreement. At a session of the Croatian National Assembly on August 29, 1939, he was the only member to oppose the Cvetković-Maček Agreement and resigned his electoral mandate. Before 1941, the national Ustasha organization, despite its small numbers, was the most popular in Slunj, Glina, and Gospić. At the same time, an equally small and equally militant Chetnik organization appeared in the 1930s around Slunj.

The majority of the Croatian people happily accepted the establishment of the NDH, but that happiness was most evident in Slunj. Baljak had no difficulty on July 29 in distributing four hundred rifles to people from the Slunj area who were ready to fight for Croatia.

However, in the succeeding days, when people witnessed the brutal scenes of the cleansing operations and realized what kind of "action for Croatia" they had been invited to join, many backed away. I think we have to believe Father Nikšić when he reports that with the exception of a small group of homegrown extremists, "the other villagers called to arms did not want to participate in the killing but only in the arrests." Even the following day some avoided joining the operation, citing a variety of excuses. The villagers were told that killing their Serbian neighbors was "retribution for all of the evils they committed against us during the late monarchy," but people remembered that while the royal government had inflicted injustice, it had not killed. There were frequent clashes with the gendarmes and arrests, there were also occasional beatings of Croatian peasants, but during the twenty years of royal government there were only three or four individual murders that could be considered politically motivated, and in all of Yugoslavia from 1919 to 1941, a total of 230 Croats were killed because of their ethnic identity (according to the data of the well-informed canon Augustin Juretić, who from 1924 to 1928 had served as a young priest in Lađevac in the county of Slunj). Women and children were never killed, so no sane person could accept the Ustasha justification that the murders of thousands of Serbian women, children, and elderly were an appropriate response for everything that had happened to the Croatian people in the Kingdom of Yugoslavia.

The ten-day cleansing operation led to a clear differentiation among the Slunj Croats. In his memoirs, Father Nikšić rightfully claims that "only a small number of local individuals participated" in this massive crime, but that small number compared to the total number of Croats in Slunj was proportionally among the highest in Croatia. However, nowhere else in Croatia during that time was there recorded as brave a public protest of Croatian citizens against the cleansing of their Orthodox neighbors as occurred in Slunj: two residents of the town, Ivan Gračan and Ivan Modrušanin, collected 120 signatures of prominent Croats of the town and its surrounding area demanding that the mass killings of Serbs stop immediately. In the atmosphere of unbridled violence and terror, many citizens of Croatia needed courage to lend their names to such a protest. The initiators of the protest were immediately arrested, but their action echoed throughout the region. Franjo Rajković, the district notary in Rakovica, had telephoned six of his colleagues, district notaries in the county of Slunj, on July 30 and encouraged them to write reports on how the Croatian population deplored the killing of Serbian residents in their towns. All of them except one sent reports to the appropriate higher authorities. Janko Jurčević from Gornja Glina was forcibly mobilized into an auxiliary Ustasha unit, but when he saw what was being done in the Serbian villages, he refused to participate and publicly protested. His behavior won over several other people in the unit. They were quickly arrested and Baljak himself publicly executed Jurčević and two of his comrades in Velika Kladuša. In their own way Eduard Lenčerić, the district head, and Mirko Marušić, the local gendarme chief, as well as Father Nikšić, also condemned the cleansing. Since the spring, Father Dragutin Štimac in Drežnik had been calling on his parishioners in his sermons not to join the Ustasha units. During the cleansing operations, Rajković recorded Štimac's words from the pulpit: "God sees everything, let us not stand before his judgment with blood on our hands and let us help our brothers who are in distress!"[13]

For understandable reasons the protests of the Croats of the Slunj region were not recorded and perhaps were not intended to oppose the Ustasha government as such, but only as repudiation of the mass crimes. Nevertheless, those protests were not in vain. They may have influenced the Ustasha government in reining in the cleansing, and I know that they helped the initiators of the uprising in fighting the vengeful Chetnik mood reflected in the slogans "All Croats are Ustasha" and "Revenge is sweet and bloody." The rebellion in the Slunj region and in the rest of Kordun didn't escalate into a war between Serbs and Croats but became a struggle against the Ustasha government and the occupiers. During the four years of the war, Chetnik sympathies were a rare phenomenon in Kordun, always isolated or limited to small groups without a broader influence.

In its first months the uprising rapidly strengthened and spread through Kordun and the surrounding areas, culminating on January 12, 1942, when Vojnić was liberated after a siege lasting several days and a three-hour battle. Three hundred eighty Home Guard members were captured and 410 rifles, thirty-two submachine guns, six heavy machine guns, and a great variety of equipment were seized, all without the loss of a single Partisan. However, this explosive development of the uprising in Kordun was not without its ups and downs, internal difficulties, and friction. The minutes of the first conference of delegates from Kordun and Banija record the discussion of the Partisan commander Robert Domani who "points to the appearance of robbery" to which individuals in some units are subject and proposes energetic measures to suppress it (in the first and second year of the war it was successfully suppressed with drastic measures, but became an increasingly frequent occurrence after the summer of 1943). Circular No. 3 of the Central Committee of the KPH of September 30, 1941, criticized "some comrades in Primorje who have adopted a passive attitude toward the Italian occupier" and warned that there were "also similar errors in Lika and Kordun," where "Italian officers, agents of Italian fascism, are trying to take advantage of uprising for purposes of imperialistic conquest." They are ostensibly shocked by the atrocities that Ustasha bands under their protection are carrying out against the population in those areas, portraying themselves as "protectors of the people.... Some comrades have not seen through this double game of the Italian fascists and their Frankist mercenaries."

In Lika and Kordun the communists had many problems until they convinced the local rebels that the National Liberation War was being waged not only against the Ustasha but also against the occupiers. In the first days of August the command of the Italian occupation forces in the NDH was already trying in various ways to establish cooperation with the threatened Serbian population. It promised them protection against Ustasha crimes, while demanding that they halt rebellious activities and distance themselves from the communist leadership. This tactic had only minor success in individual locations in Lika and Bosanska Krajina and slightly greater success in the Knin region and Herzegovina (but was most successful in Montenegro, where in the spring of 1942 the rebellion was de facto extinguished). In this way a division emerged in some parts of Croatia and Bosnia and Herzegovina among the Serbian population between supporters of the Partisans and the Chetniks.

The communists prevented such division in Kordun. In some places this was achieved by political persuasion and in others through force. In early December 1941, Dušan Korać, a district official, organized the signing of "minutes" in the villages of Radonja and Jurga below Petrova Gora with the following "unanimous conclusions":

> 1. The delegates reached a conclusion that the command of the National Liberation Army will not carry out attacks anywhere in the field during winter.
> 2. The delegates unanimously conclude that the same number of Croatian homes be burned as Serbian homes.

The remaining eight points include similar topics, while emphasizing that the Italians should not be attacked. The minutes were read to the more than one hundred delegates, at the conclusion of which the following was added: "After reading the minutes to those assembled, it was unanimously agreed to drop point 2 cited in these minutes."

The Partisans executed Korać, the initiator of this action, and two or three of his closest collaborators who gathered the signatures, as traitors, while the remaining signatories of the minutes were dissuaded from their program at meetings in their villages. The search for plunder by Italian soldiers through the villages of Kordun (people called them "roosters" after their feathered helmets) and the burning of entire villages in some centers of the uprising (for example, Perjasica was torched along with several surrounding hamlets) were additional reasons the Orthodox in Kordun did not trust the occupation army. Although they remained dedicated to the Partisans for the entire war, dissatisfaction did erupt from time to time because of the troubles that the Serbs in Kordun were experiencing. For the four years of the war they had to feed their Partisans, while they themselves lived in want. They were subject to occasional enemy offensives and the majority had to protect themselves at least two or three times by fleeing into the forests and returning to the charred remains of their homes. They constantly looked with resentment at the neighboring Croatian villages that were attacked far less. While few Orthodox houses in Kordun survived the war, the majority of the houses in the Croatian villages remained untouched. A Croatian village had to provide food for the Partisans only in the second half of the war and until that time was spared from making contributions to the Partisans and from looting. Until the fall of 1943, there was no forced mobilization of Croatian peasants into the Partisan army and the majority survived the war in the less dangerous Home Guard or as military deserters in hiding places near their homes. Many lives were tragically lost on both sides, but the losses were greater on the Orthodox side. The grumbling of the Kordun Serbs because of their disproportionate share of the wartime burdens occasionally broke out into loud accusations and, rarely, opposition to the communist leadership.[14] From the narrow view of the Kordun Serbs, the Serbian village bore the main burden of victory and deserved the right to be rewarded for that burden and victory. Part of that price was paid by some of the Catholic villages of Kordun, to which many young men and providers did not return after Bleiburg and the Way of the Cross.[15] Thus, instead of seeing the wartime animosities subside with the end of the war, we have seen them deepen and take on new forms. And when with the passing of years and the new generations these animosities, begun in Kordun in 1941, were slowly starting to fade away, or were only smoldering, they suddenly burst into flame in 1971 and then erupted even more catastrophically exactly half a century later, in 1991.

* * *

The initiators of the uprising in Kordun were the communists, among whom were about thirty Croats: communists from Karlovac, Zagreb, Duga Resa, and some other nearby Croatian villages. Holjevac, who was also the first Partisan to be wounded in Kordun in an attack on the post office in Tušilović on August 2, 1941, brought the first weapons from Karlovac. The first medical personnel were Dr. Savo Zlatić and Jakov Kranjčević Brada, a qualified medical attendant who founded the first Partisan clinic at Petrova Gora and who attended not only the Partisans but also the people from the surrounding area. Former volunteers from the Spanish Civil War deserve the most credit for the successful and stable development of the uprising in Kordun and the relatively light losses during the first year of the war. In the first week of August there were seven such veterans in Kordun—five Croats and two Jews. They brought combat experience to the Partisan units and acquired a fine reputation among the Partisans and in the villages that supported the Partisans. The Sisak Partisan unit joined Gaćeša's Kordun Partisans in neighboring Banija, and on September 28, 1941, a total of 220 fighters—150 Serbs and 70 Croats—took the first Partisan oath at Šamarica before Ivo Rukavina, the commander of Kordun and Banija.

During this time, there were not more than ten Partisans from the Croatian villages of Kordun and about twenty active collaborators prepared to work secretly for the Partisans. They were primarily prewar members of the Communist Party or close sympathizers. To a great extent Croatian villages tried to maintain their neutrality, as much as that was possible in this time of insanity. In the late fall of 1941, I spent a month in one such village (Banski Kovačevac) and became somewhat familiar with that defensive neutrality. The major summer cleansing operations in the nearby Serbian villages made a powerful impression on that Croatian village. I believe that before the cleansings the peasants, in their cautious way, approved of the new Croatian government and were prepared to support it, but the reverberations from the killings disenchanted them. My hosts wondered how so-and-so from the neighboring Croatian village could have participated. They did not recount the horrible details in front of me but only mentioned in general "the extermination of many who were complete innocents." With scorn, they once mentioned someone from their village who "had gone to Petrova Gora to steal, but the fool doesn't know he is taking on a debt he will have to repay some day." Peasant wisdom told them that the number of crimes being committed would not leave the perpetrators untouched. They were afraid the blame might fall on all of them, the Croats of Kordun and on those who were not blameless—which, in fact, is what happened.

The Kordun Croats greeted the arrival of the Partisans with distrust, and many with fear. That fear eased when they realized that there would be no Chetnik-style reprisals: The Kordun Partisans didn't burn homes or kill civilians in the Croatian villages, and in the first year of the war robbery, which the Partisans strictly forbade in their ranks, was the exception rather than the rule. The Partisans neither killed nor mistreated captured members of the Home Guard. They would disarm them, force them to listen to political speeches, take their equipment and uniforms, and send them home in rags. All of this lessened the fear of the Partisans, but the distrust of Croatian peasants lingered. While Croats in some neighboring areas had begun to favor the Partisans heavily in 1942 (parts of Pokuplje, the region between the Kupa and Dobra Rivers, and Gorski Kotar), some Kordun villages had been irretrievably drawn into the "witches' dance" on the Ustasha side, but they were in the minority. The majority of the Croatian villages of Kordun and Banija tried to remain neutral, but in a war that was rapidly becoming a total war, neutrality was difficult to maintain. A commitment to one side or the other was becoming unavoidable and led to divisions, all too often with tragic outcomes.

Having taken over the organization and leadership of the uprising in rural Kordun, the Croatian communists had to change the rhetoric they had used in the cities. On July 25, 1941, the Central Committee of the Communist Party of Yugoslavia concluded its call to rebellion, "To the Peoples of Yugoslavia" (written by Tito), with eight slogans, the first two of which were "Long live the Soviet Union and the heroic Red Army!" and "Long live Comrade Stalin!" It was difficult to win over fleeing peasants in Petrova Gora with such slogans, so on August 10 another slogan materialized: "Death to fascism, freedom for the people!" The next acclamations were for "our heroic Partisans," "to the brotherhood and harmony of Croats and Serbs in Croatia," and "to the brotherhood and harmony of the peoples of Yugoslavia in the battle for freedom and national independence." And while the "Long live"s for Stalin, the Soviet Union, and the Red

Army receded, "Long live the World Antifascist Front!" surfaced. The frequently trumpeted slogan "There is no going back to the old ways!" was interpreted by different people in different ways: to Croats it promised national equality in a postwar federal state, to poor peasants a just division of the land, to workers better pay and more social rights, and to everyone "power to the people," that is, democracy.

The change in rhetoric reflected an adaptation to real-life practice that also required some changes in political conduct, at least temporarily. The communists in Croatia and Yugoslavia had to take into account the general course of the Second World War. At that time, on August 12, 1941, Churchill and Roosevelt had signed the Atlantic Charter on the British battleship *Prince of Wales*, in which they formulated the principles of the democratic component of antifascism. On the same day, they sent a joint telegram to Stalin. Churchill was corresponding with Stalin about a bilateral agreement and a public declaration in which the "two governments are mutually obligated to provide each other assistance of any kind in the present war against Germany." Responding to a parliamentary question of whether this close understanding with yesterday's enemy was excessive and whether his traveling to Moscow was necessary, Churchill replied, "If I find that the devil is prepared to wage effective war against Hitler, I am ready to journey to hell and sign a pact with Satan himself."

Thus, the antifascist coalition of the three great powers was created. The historian Eric Hobsbawm has defined antifascism as a temporary and short-term alliance (of former enemies) of liberal capitalism and communism against the deadly danger that threatened each of them equally. For the sake of that alliance both sides had to renounce temporarily some of the immanent methods and goals in their mutual rivalry and struggle. By the same token, the communists in Yugoslavia, Croatia, and even in Kordun had to adapt to this change.

If they wanted to succeed before the deadly danger called the

Ustasha ideal, Nazism, and fascism, the Croatian communists had to seek an alliance with the Serbs facing death in Kordun and throughout the NDH, with nationally endangered Croats in Dalmatia, and with freedom-loving Croats wherever they were. That meant waging a national liberation war instead of a socialist revolution—temporarily. That was how Croatian antifascism evolved.

The communists should be recognized for waging this antifascist war bravely and with great sacrifice, sparing neither themselves nor others. To a great extent, they prevented the forced expulsion of Serbs from Croatia to Serbia, they made the planned genocide against Serbs from Croatia more difficult, they saved the Croatian people from being shamefully stamped as Nazi-fascist allies, and they aligned their movement with the victorious side in the Second World War. Significantly, they prevented the return of Serbian monarchy to power in Yugoslavia, which would have meant—if it had happened—the fulfillment of Chetnik plans for brutal reprisals against the Croatian people.

However, in waging the antifascist struggle, the Croatian and Yugoslav communists did not for a moment lose sight of their ultimate goal: the establishment of a communist government and the revolutionary transformation of society into a socialist and communist one. After all, the aspiration to achieve power is inherent to every political party. From the very beginning of the uprising, the communists occupied all of the leading military and political positions and consistently reinforced them with military successes. They had no competition in this effort because no other antifascist political party was their equal in military decisiveness and organizational skills. In areas under Partisan domination, the national liberation committees were the nominal authority, but in fact the party committees made the decisions. A federation of autonomous republics was proclaimed, but the central power of the party leadership and Josip Broz Tito personally was systematically being consolidated. From time to time this power became oppressive. Instead of a democratic antifascism that had won over the population, brutal revolutionary principles prevailed. "We treated every complaint about our authority as enemy activity...for the revolution and the totalitarian idea do not recognize anyone except themselves," wrote Milovan Đilas, one of the leading actors at that time, in his memoir.[16] The communists carried out "purges" of the politically undesirable on liberated territory and within their own ranks. They called it "leftist deviation," and they realized, usually with considerable delay, that such actions resulted in the loss of support among the local people and of the allegiance of many in the Partisan ranks. The "leftist deviation" in Montenegro, Herzegovina, Serbia, and to some extent in Bosnia was more frequent and more drastic than in Croatia, which is why the Partisan struggle in Croatia evolved with greater stability than in the other parts of Yugoslavia.

However, over the long term the deeply embedded communist ideology was stronger than the logical conclusions that the negative experiences of "leftist deviation" had imposed on them. The communists leading the antifascist struggle increasingly injected elements of socialist revolution into that struggle. Toward the end of the war this fact was no longer even disguised. Instead of the former term "national liberation war," the term "national liberation war and socialist revolution" was used more frequently. With the end of the war, this was shortened to only "socialist revolution." Indeed, this was never publicly acknowledged, but it had become the actual state of affairs.

Citing the example of his village Kupinec, which the Partisans had captured in the fall of 1943, Maček described in detail the transformation of communist antifascism into a communist revolution:

> Their conduct in Kupinec was reasonable until the beginning of March 1944. They appointed Ivan Tor as their commissar.

> While in that position, Tor protected the population from being robbed as best he could.... In addition, he permitted the manager of my property to send as much food as was needed to me and my family in Zagreb.... At first the Partisans did not reveal their communist identity. When they took a village, they asked the priest to hold a service in the church. Not until the beginning of 1944 did they begin to attack the HSS and me personally in their leaflets. In contrast to the Chetniks and the Ustasha, the Partisans committed no mass killings anywhere. Wherever they could get their hands on some village leader, they would force him, at least formally, to join the Partisans. If he resisted, one way or other they would liquidate him.... The Ustasha and Chetniks killed people in massive numbers in blind hatred. The communists killed with cold logic those they considered an obstacle to the consolidation of communism.[17]

Revolutions contain a violence that rarely ends with victory and the elevation of revolutionaries to power. To the contrary, only then do the obstacles to violence disappear, and violence transforms into a system. Antifascism, as an alliance of ideologies and social systems, carried within itself both the potential for democracy and the potential for violent government. Victorious in the antifascist war, Stalin immediately restored the prewar practice of violent personal power, while Churchill respected the results of a democratic election and peacefully relinquished power. The postwar fates of individual countries were dependent on the political forces and personalities that led the antifascist struggle. In France, this was the resistance movement led by Charles de Gaulle; in Yugoslavia, it was the Communist Party led by Tito.

The Yugoslav communist leadership had a major opportunity to bring the promised freedom and to carry out a renewal of the country by democratic rather than revolutionary methods. They would have kept the support of the majority of the population, which they had gained by being on the winning side in the war. Enslaved to their revolutionary ideology, the leading communists could not imagine, let alone carry out, such a program. They fell into the trap of "leftist deviation," which was considerably deeper and more pernicious than during the war. When they became more sober after four or five years, the Yugoslav communists redefined the "leftist deviation" into "Stalinism." And as in wartime, they realized too late the damaging effect of "leftist deviation," so after the war they realized too slowly the degree to which the several years of "Stalinism" had damaged the country. When they tried to mend it, the ideology again proved to be too strong a barrier to overcome. Forty years of attempts to overhaul the system were not enough to repair the damage inflicted in the first four years. And thus the communists lost power, and in the 1991 war of insanity their state disintegrated, their ideal was compromised, and even their historic contributions in 1941 are now no longer recognized.

17

The Refuge at Banski Kovačevac

WHILE MY MOTHER was in Kraljevica, Danko in Tuzla, and I in Karlovac, my grandmother regularly wrote letters to me in her calligraphic handwriting and always about the same two things: Danko was fine, all was going well for him; and was there any news from my father in Jadovno. I don't remember how I responded to this repeated question from my grandmother. It was the beginning of November, a full three months since the last news about Jadovno. I probably didn't want to admit to myself that I should no longer expect news from my father.

The mail continued to function smoothly. Postcards from Tuzla arrived in two to three days and from Kraljevica within two. My mother wrote from Kraljevica in German, in her wide-spaced handwriting and clear thoughts. Because of the possible censorship, she used many allusions that Mia Veličković and I understood easily (for example, "Aunt Rut" was Palestine and "Uncle Romano" was Italy).

One day at lunch my landlady, Mrs. Eisler, noticed that I was constantly scratching swollen bumps on the fingers of both hands. She immediately took me to her doctor, a man by the name of Hruby, who diagnosed the problem at first glance: scabies. Where did I pick up this silly disease? wondered Mrs. Eisler, since she made sure that

I washed my hands and changed my clothes regularly. We concluded that I had gotten this unpleasant infection in the courtyard behind Mrs. Eisler's house where I often played with the apprentice Milan, a strong and cheerful sixteen-year-old who entertained me with jokes filled with sexual innuendos and who taught me to handle the horses that were usually kept next to the large warehouse.

Dr. Hruby suggested that I stay in the municipal hospital for several days; I would recover there safely, and the possibility that I might pass on this easily transmitted disease to someone else would be eliminated. Mrs. Eisler hesitated. She felt responsible for me, and wondered if it was too dangerous in these times to leave a Jewish boy alone in a large hospital. Who knows what might happen to him. Hasn't enough happened to him already?

I listened silently, a bit dispirited, to the conversation between Mrs. Eisler and Dr. Hruby. I remember the overwhelming odors of Hruby's office, his pleasant deep voice, and the polite tone that inspired confidence. When he mentioned to Mrs. Eisler that he had been a frequent visitor to our bookshop, that he knew my parents well and respected them, she was convinced that I was safe under his care.

In some partially preserved hospital records I found my name on a list of patients in the infectious-disease ward from the first half of November 1941. I had stayed in a small one-bed room on the first floor of the ward in the front part of the building. I remember the strong smell of the sulfuric ointment a nurse would apply every day and the bleak view from the window of the late-fall desolation of the Katzler and Kopriva parks. I don't think anyone visited me other than the nurses, a young doctor, and a medical attendant, a nun, who regularly brought me meals. I remember the utter despair of loneliness I felt. To this day, I don't know if the strict isolation was meant as a quarantine or a wise precautionary measure on the part of the hospital administration offering treatment to a young Jew. I was happy when I returned to Mrs. Eisler's care, cured of an unpleasant disease and of my loneliness.

In the late afternoon of Monday, November 17, Veco Holjevac, leading twenty-four Partisans dressed in the uniforms of the Home Guard, walked into Karlovac over the old footbridge. The disguised Partisans, singing popular Home Guard marches, walked through the city toward the old hospital. However, they didn't find the man who was the cause of their reckless adventure: Marijan Čavić, whose pseudonym was "Grga," and who was the secretary of the Karlovac municipal committee of the Communist Party of Croatia. In fact, he had been under guard in the hospital for several days after slitting his wrists, but he had been returned that morning to investigative detention at the request of the Ustasha police. There was nothing for Holjevac and his Partisans-Home Guards to do except return the way they had come and leave their job unfinished. On the circuitous route out of town they killed two Ustasha, and upon exiting the city, at a bunker on the Korana River, they attacked and disarmed the Italian guards and disappeared into the thick blackness of the night to Kordun.

Just two days after this action, on Wednesday, November 19, Ivo Rukavina sought me out with a message: "Slavko, a major roundup is in the offing. It might also affect you. Mrs. Veličković thinks that you should go to Jaga in Kovačevac. When the roundup is over, we will obtain a travel permit for you to join your mother in Kraljevica."

Before her departure for Kraljevica, my mother had made arrangements for just such a contingency: I immediately packed all of my belongings and went to Pavica Vine. I told Mrs. Eisler in confidence what was going on and she too left (many years later I visited her in Israel). I spent the night at Pavica's and did not leave her apartment the entire next day. Late that evening, in the deep November darkness, Pavica accompanied me to the dock on the Kupa River at Gaza, to the ferry for Banski Kovačevac. On the ferry we found Jaga's sister Jana. The owner of the ferry was Jaga's distant relative Mika Mihalić, who before the war had supplied us with firewood.

Every Thursday, early in the afternoon, the ferry left Banski Kovačevac, and at all of the villages along the banks of the Kupa people boarded for Karlovac for market day. The ferry docked in Gaza in the evening. Those who had no place to stay in Karlovac would sleep on the ferry and early Friday morning they would go to the fair, the market, and the shops. In the afternoon the boat returned the twenty-two kilometers down the Kupa to Kovačevac.

Mihalić let me sleep in the ferry's cabin and in the morning slipped a peasant's coat over my city clothes for protection. He generally behaved toward me in a caring way.

The announced roundup, the reason for my flight from Karlovac, was carried out three days later, on the evening of November 23. Rukavina told me after the war that his friend Milan Stilinović had warned him of the impending roundup. Stilinović had already been relieved of his duties as the chief of the Karlovac police and returned to the position of the deputy chief of the county police, but in that capacity he was still privy to orders from the Ustasha Intelligence Service.

According to some reports, 220 people were arrested on the night of the roundup, while according to other sources, 260 people were arrested as a reprisal for the attack by Veco Holjevac and his Partisans on Karlovac. Most of the arrested were men of Serbian nationality, with a smaller number of Jews and "suspect" Croats. Because I was still underage, the roundup probably wouldn't have included me, but after everything I had gone through, I was better off in Kovačevac. Among the arrested was my slightly older friend Brano Majder, who after the war became a well-known sports official in Karlovac and

Zagreb. He told me that he had been arrested with his father, Aleksandar, because of their family's very distant Jewish heritage. Brano's father was a prominent citizen in Karlovac, for many years the chief of the district office for health and social services. A police agent named Foschio noticed him in the mass of detainees and persuaded his superiors to release Mr. Majder, who refused to go home without his son, so Brano was released too. Foschio also gave them the password for that night, which Brano remembers to this day: "Opasač-Otočac." While returning to their nearby home in the early hours after midnight, they encountered three patrols making arrests in the surrounding houses. If they had not known the password, they would have been arrested again, and who knows what might have happened. The next morning more than two hundred detainees were sent in cattle cars to Jasenovac and, as far as I know, not one came back.

Also among those arrested that night were the father and brother of my high-school classmate Danica Kos. After half a century, she wrote down her recollections so that her grandchildren would know what had happened. She provided me with photocopies of six handwritten pages. She describes how in the first hours after midnight on November 24, 1941, she was sleeping with her mother and father in their bed when they were awoken by knocking on the kitchen door: "Two agents in civilian clothes entered the apartment and asked for my father. He stood up. They ordered him to get dressed, they were taking him for interrogation. Nikola was sleeping in the other bedroom. 'Who is that?' they asked my mother. When she replied that it was her son, they said that he too should get dressed and come with them." And so based on their list they took away the railway worker, a Serb, Simo Mamula, and as an "extra," who was not on the list, they took away his twenty-three-year-old son, Nikola. Nothing was heard from them again. Danica didn't even know for certain when and where they were killed. In the book *Jasenovac: žrtve rata prema podacima Statističkog zavoda Jugoslavije* (Jasenovac: Victims of the War Based on Information of the Statistical Bureau of Yugoslavia)[1] I found both their names with the terse notation: "Killed by the Ustasha in 1941 at the Jasenovac camp."

* * *

I spent exactly four weeks in Banski Kovačevac, where I stayed in the wooden house of Mata Đerek with Jaga in a room built with the money my father had given to Mata a year or two before the war—"just in case." Jaga's unmarried sisters, Jana and Draga, slept in the large front room, which was also the kitchen. Mata was serving in the Home Guard in Karlovac and every other Saturday he came to Kovačevac on a weekend pass. He was a handsome twenty-three-year-old, intelligent, with a level-headed peasant's wisdom, an unobtrusive self-reliance that inspired confidence—a bachelor whom the most attractive single women in the village wanted for a husband. The Đereks were a happy family in which Jaga was the authority and Mata, the only male in the house—the brother of six sisters—the favorite. Three of the sisters were married—the beautiful Berta lived nearby and Mara and Kata lived in Selnica and Lasinja. Jaga was then thirty-five, while her younger sisters, Jana and Draga, were old enough to be considered "old maids." They owned five acres of cultivated fields, along with some pasture, forest land, and two cows and two oxen in a stall. However, they didn't live in want because Mata was known as an excellent carpenter, hardworking and reliable, sought throughout the area for work and well compensated. During the war years, when Mata was away from home, the "old maids" Jana and Draga, sometimes with Jaga's assistance, diligently "kept the house."

In Banski Kovačevac I felt safe and sheltered, after those tumultuous weeks in Karlovac when barely a day passed without bad news and new dangers. I was pampered in the Đereks' home and moved freely through the village. Everyone knew who I was and why I was staying with the Đereks, yet Jaga had no fear that anyone would "squeal" on me. She claimed with confidence that if any danger arose, we would hear about it in time and find a solution.

Although the disturbing echoes of that insane time reached Banski Kovačevac, I think the village was united in its desire to remain neutral. "We will not get involved" was the phrase that I heard several times in chats with neighbors in the evening by the large stove in Jaga's kitchen. The local Ustasha and gendarmes from Lasinja, seven kilometers away, had not come to Kovačevac for some time, not since groups of armed men had appeared in the Serbian villages and disarmed several patrols. Not one of those groups from the Serbian villages had yet appeared in Kovačevac, and Jaga told me that she knew some of the people who were "in the forest" and that I should not fear them. Banski Kovačevac existed as if it were an extraterritorial entity, some temporary area that neither the fist of the Ustasha authorities nor the din of the Partisan war had yet reached.

With a tinge of self-satisfied local pride, Jaga took me to their large wooden church, the work of an excellent carpenter's artistry, built more than two hundred years earlier. Milovan Gavazzi[2] cited this church in his works as having an ethnographic value in the Kupa River region. Jaga also took me to meet the teacher Jurica Oklopčić, whom I saw frequently afterward. He loaned me some books that I hungrily read by the light of an oil lamp in those late-fall evenings (my favorite author was Jack London). Oklopčić gladly talked with me about our bookshop, where he had made many purchases for the Kovačevac school, and he remembered my father, who, as a trained agronomist, was always interested in village life.

According to the 1931 census, Banski Kovačevac was a Catholic (Croatian) village with 555 residents. Ten years later, on the eve of the war, it numbered about 600. The village was picturesquely nestled into the hillsides of the Bukova Glava forest, above a large field on the right bank of the Kupa River. On a third small hill, right next to Banski Kovačevac, lay the Orthodox (Serbian) village of Prkos. According to the 1931 census, it numbered 570 residents, and on the eve of the war it probably had more than 600 residents, like Banski Kovačevac.

Agata (Jaga) Đerek (1906–1990), who was granted recognition as Righteous Among the Nations from Yad Vashem

From Karlovac downriver, close to fifty kilometers, all of the villages on the right bank of the Kupa were Catholic (Croatian) with the exception of Prkos, which was surrounded by Banski Kovačevac, Novo Selo, and Lasinja. But on the small hills, behind the thin belt of Croatian villages on the right bank of the Kupa, there was a dense network of Serbian villages that dominated the northern portion of Kordun. And while Pokuplje on the left bank of the Kupa was Croatian, the right bank was an ethnically mixed area that drew its character from Turkish times and the Military Frontier. Just a half-hour walk from Prkos or Banski Kovačevac on the other side of the Bukova Glava forest lay Sjeničak. A village scattered over about fifty square kilometers with more than 3,500 residents, before the war Sjeničak was one of the largest and oldest Serbian villages in central Croatia, a center of cultural, intellectual, and political life of the northern Kordun Serbs, a village known as the birthplace of Sava

Mrkalj,[3] for the peasant rebellion of 1907, and for the young men from the village who went to Spain as members of the International Brigade in 1936–1937. Sjeničak had been established as a parish of the Serbian Orthodox Church, to which Prkos also belonged, in 1715. In religious and political life, in cultural and intellectual endeavors, Prkos was always influenced by Sjeničak.

Between Banski Kovačevac and Prkos winds the Vezovnik, a small turbulent creek that ultimately flows more calmly into the Kupa. From the last house in Kovačevac to the first house in Prkos is about two hundred meters. The Croatian word *vez* means binding, connection, tie, and is often used as the root or stem for many other words. And so the Vezovnik creek from time to time indeed joined the two villages, but from time to time it also rigidly divided them. The twentieth century began in alliance: In the parliamentary elections of 1901 Orthodox Prkos and Catholic Kovačevac both voted for Josip Pasarić, the opposition candidate and the editor of the Zagreb daily *Obzor*. The alliance was amicably negotiated by Antun Radić and the Sjeničak Orthodox priest Mihajlo Nikoliš, both of whom had considerable political influence throughout the entire region. Subsequently relations between Prkos and Kovačevac through the rest of the twentieth century oscillated between cool and warm and back again, until in 1991 and 1995 when the final chill set in. Today there is virtually no communication between Banski Kovačevac and Prkos. Old acquaintances, who at one time helped each other repair burned houses and build the road that connects the two villages, today pass by each other without a greeting, "like passing a Turkish cemetery." Other people would greet each other coldly, but it was rare that anyone would stop and ask an old friend, "How are you? How are the wife and children?" Just as the broad-minded politicians of one hundred years ago had forged an alliance between the two villages, ninety years later narrow-minded ones incited a bloody separation. I had good friends in both villages—in Kovačevac Mata Đerek; in Prkos, Vaso Roknić. Both died in 2005. When I visited them from time to time after 1995, I sat with each separately in his own home. Even though both were reasonable men and close collaborators on joint projects that brought advantages to both villages, after 1995 they barely greeted each other and I was no longer able to get them to sit at the same table. Perhaps their souls had frozen; perhaps they shrank from entering each other's homes because their villages would have held it against them. The next chapter is devoted to their unhappy story.

* * *

In retrospect it is clear that the hyperborean shelter of Banski Kovačevac in the late fall of 1941 could not last. In the early morning of December 2, a loud clamor of voices from Jaga's kitchen woke me. Several men from the neighborhood were telling Jaga about what had happened in the village the night before. A group of armed men, half dressed in civilian clothes, half in military uniforms, with red stars on their caps, saying they were not Chetniks but Partisans, made the rounds of the village at about midnight and took five hunting rifles, a military carbine, and an old pistol. They knew exactly who in the village had arms because they went only to seven specific houses. The residents of Kovačevac recognized people from the neighboring Serbian villages among the Partisans, including Mile Kličković from Stipan, whose comrades called him "commissar" and who was a baker in Karlovac before the war. Someone claimed that this was all the doing of Čedo Bućan from Prkos, who led the group but kept to the cover of darkness and didn't approach the houses. They didn't take anything except guns, ammunition, and military equipment, and they explained that they were not against Croats but only against the Ustasha and the occupiers. Upon leaving, one of them a bit disdainfully thanked a peasant: "Thanks for the gun, it will be returned after the war." Especially angry about all of this was the bargeman Mika Mihalić, whose expensive hunting rifle was taken, even though before the war he "had carried all of Prkos on his barge though they didn't have the two dinars to pay him."

After that, communication between Banski Kovačevac and Prkos was kept to an absolute minimum. For the residents of Kovačevac, Prkos became a territory they didn't enter without a great need. Perhaps only Jaga and two others who felt as she did still secretly maintained contact with Prkos, because in his book Dušan Korać mentions three Kovačevac residents as "activists who worked as illegals for the National Liberation Movement."[4] Jaga wisely kept quiet about this, although two or three times she told me that she was going "to the forest," where she would meet people from Prkos or Sjeničak who had frequented our bookstore before the war.

The excitement in Kovačevac after the first Partisan raid had not yet died down when the news arrived that on the night of December 7,[5] the gendarme station in Pisarovina had been attacked. Although the operation was only partially successful, its reverberations quickly spread throughout the Pokuplje region. It was the first armed Partisan operation on the left bank of the Kupa River, not far from Zagreb. The Partisans had crossed the Kupa from neighboring Prkos and had returned the same way before morning. The war drawing closer to Kovačevac caused concern among the villagers. In Jaga's kitchen there were loud comments: "The government is the government, it will not look on quietly. It will strike back at Prkos and it might even find fault with us in Kovačevac." Jaga led me to the woods on the nearby hill and showed me where I would be hidden "if something happens."

I think it was Tuesday, December 16, when Mihalić came rushing to Jaga. "Slavko, be ready on Thursday, I will be taking you back to Karlovac," he told me firmly. "Home Guard troops and gendarmes will be here any day. You are no longer safe. Jaga says that everything has been arranged, your friends in Karlovac will put you up somewhere safe—you have to go on the first ferry!"

On the way to the ferry on Thursday afternoon, Jaga went down a list of instructions—everything I had to know, what to do, in what order, how careful I had to be. She tried to be calm and encouraging, but she didn't quite succeed, probably wondering whether we would see each other again.

On the barge Mika again disguised me as a peasant boy and again looked after me the entire trip. We arrived at the Gaza docks in Karlovac in pitch-darkness. Mika kept me in his cabin overnight, since he was concerned about me walking through the city after curfew. In the morning he helped me get ready and, big and strong, he picked me up and kissed me on both cheeks. He was still waving to me from the barge as I walked away, across Gaza to the house of Pavica Vine.

Two years and two months passed before I saw Mika again. I was climbing the hill Gornji Budački heading toward the command post of the Kordun Partisan region when I heard his agitated voice calling out to me: "Slavko, hey, Slavko!"

He was in a group of five or six men escorted by two armed guards. He tried to talk to me, but one of the guards pushed him back into the group. Mika was visibly frightened.

"Slavko, please help me! I've been arrested, I don't know why, you know me, please speak up for me."

The guard rushed him along. I promised Mika I would intervene on his behalf with the commandant of the region.

I was on my way to the command post for a pass to the Karlovac detachment, to which I had been reassigned at my own request. Joco Eremić, the commandant, whom I knew from several large agitprop District Committee meetings, received me. He babbled on about his days in Karlovac and about our bookshop, which, he said, he frequently visited. I mentioned Mika, wondering why he had been arrested, saying that I knew he wasn't an enemy and that he had helped rescue me. Eremić promised he would see what the problem was and said everything would be all right. The Regional Intelligence Center was responsible for prisoners, but as commandant of the region, he would have some say in the matter, Eremić confidently added. Reassured, I went across the Korana, Mrežnica, and Dobra rivers to the Karlovac detachment.

Three months later, in May 1944, we in the Karlovac detachment learned that Eremić had gone over to the Germans. He had been discovered taking bribes from mobilized individuals, children of well-to-do peasants, whom he approved for release from service in the National Liberation Army. He hid in Kordun for about two weeks, then surrendered to units of the 392nd Croat Infantry Division[6] in Oštarija near Ogulin. In the official version of the Partisan authorities it was established that Eremić had for some time been secretly linked to a Chetnik group and that he was, in fact, a Chetnik agent. (After the war, he managed to reach Canada, where he was openly active in Chetnik émigré circles; he died in 2005.)

In Banski Kovačevac several months later, I found out that my intervention on behalf of Mika had been in vain: He was executed based on a decision of the military tribunal in the spring of 1944 at Gornji Budački. I cursed Eremić: I cursed him as a traitor, as a Chetnik, and as someone who had lied to me.

I only learned the truth twenty years later from some documents in the archives, while collaborating on the book *Okrug Karlovac 1941* (The District of Karlovac in 1941):[7] Mika had been part of a delegation of twelve peasants from the Pokuplje region that had had an audience with Ante Pavelić on December 15, 1941, to request that an army unit be dispatched to their region for protection from the Partisans.

Poglavnik Pavelić satisfied their request, but in his own way. Instead of Home Guard or gendarme units, he sent Ustasha under the command of Maks Luburić, Juco Rukavina, and Ante Moškov, who carried out the typical Ustasha cleansing operation: In Prkos on December 21 they rounded up more than four hundred people, mostly women, children, and the elderly, and for the next several days executed them in the nearby Brezje forest. Today it is impossible to establish if Pavelić ordered the cleansing operation independent of the request of the twelve-member delegation that included Mika, or if the delegation's request encouraged Pavelić to implement the cleansing operation.

However, returning home on Monday, December 15, 1941, after the visit to Pavelić, it occurred to Mika that the arrival of the units might threaten the refugee in the Đereks' home, the young Goldstein. It was my good fortune that he foresaw the danger because Luburić's cleansing operation was thorough. In Banski Kovačevac on December 21, the Ustasha rounded up refugees from Prkos, the majority of whom were captured and killed. And had it not been for Mika, I might not have escaped the Ustasha's cleansing.

And to this day, it makes me uneasy to think that I was not able to save Mika.

* * *

I spent three days in Karlovac and slept four nights in the home of Pavica Vine. I did not leave the house, even though I don't think I was in any immediate danger. After the major roundup of November 23 and 24, there was no new wave of arrests, and it turned out I had not been on the list.

But one never knows, as the old saying about the wisdom of caution goes. Zgurić or some other Ustasha policeman might have spotted me on the street and purely on a whim taken me to jail or put me onto a transport to Jasenovac. Nor did I go to the Veličkovićes because their house was under constant surveillance. From Mia Veličković I received an encouraging message along with a long letter and package for my mother. In Pavica's home I was "safe," but she wisely hurried to obtain a travel permit for me to join my mother in Kraljevica. This was no time to be hesitant.

On Saturday, December 20, there was a small "party" at the Vines' on the occasion of their eldest daughter, Dorica's, thirteenth birthday. About ten or so friends of Dorica and me—high-school classmates, the carefree children of Karlovac doctors, lawyers, and other members of the city's "upper crust"—gathered. I remember the beautiful Milena Krefl, Tomica Huzjak, Božidar Oršanić, and especially Dražen Blazina in an elegant suit with a tie, barely a year older than me and even then fatally and hopelessly in love with haughtily beautiful Dorica. He kept insisting that we play *fote*, a kissing game, in the hope that he would be able to kiss Dorica. Pavica encouraged me to join the raucous company; my classmates pulled me into their games, which I never managed to surrender to completely. Perhaps that evening I felt most acutely that I no longer belonged to the company of the carefree.

On Saturday or Sunday, December 20 or 21, Slavo Srića delivered a "legitimate" travel permit in my name for the journey to Kraljevica. At that time Srića worked in the city administration in various official capacities, among which was the issuing of travel permits. It wasn't difficult for him to fill in my name on an already stamped form and to move it along to the authorized supervisor for signature in a heap of similar papers—or perhaps he signed the name of the supervisor himself. I heard that over time he had helped a number of people in trouble in the same way. After the war, Slavo was for many years the director of the "Predrag Heruc" factory in Zagreb.

Early in the morning of December 22, Pavica accompanied me to the train for Sušak. Somewhere around Ogulin there was an inspection of travel documents. I tried not to tremble or show any anxiety and everything went smoothly. While the train was approaching Plase, the last station in the NDH, I was gripped by a fear that I might encounter the Ustasha police, but there were no Ustasha uniforms to be seen. An Italian carabiniere was standing on the platform in front of the station. I got off the train and boarded the bus for Kraljevica. Moving too slowly—or so it seemed to me in my impatience—on the twisting macadam road through Heljin and Križišće, I arrived at the square in Kraljevica and fell into my mother's arms. We were together again, in the relative security of the Italian zone of occupation, liberated from the fear of a surprise nighttime arrest and cleansing.

"Now we must bring Danko here," my mother said. I knew that she was also thinking of my father, but she no longer spoke out loud about it.

18

A Story of Two Villages

I HAD BEEN in Kraljevica only a few days when the Zagreb newspapers published official reports about *Poglavnik* Ante Pavelić's tour of Ustasha units around Lasinja and about the cleansing operation that was being carried out in northern Kordun. Despite the declamatory and propagandistic vocabulary of these reports, I could sense the misfortune that had befallen this entire region.

On Saturday morning, December 20, Vjekoslav Maks Luburić arrived in Lasinja with two companies of Ustasha. They belonged to the Ustasha Defense, a special-purpose unit that performed administrative and security tasks in the Jasenovac camp system and that led death squads in "cleansings" and "reprisals" throughout the Independent State of Croatia (NDH). Immediately after, through that Saturday or Sunday morning, regular units of the Ustasha army, the gendarmes, and the Home Guard arrived on the right bank of the Kupa from Lasinja to Bučica. Among these units were two companies of the Lika Ustasha Battalion with Juco Rukavina, the commander at that time of the entire Ustasha army. Mika Mihalić had indeed rescued me at the last minute, on the last ferry that sailed freely, only a day or two before the Kupa River and all of the roads in the entire region were blocked.

Luburić set up his headquarters in Lasinja in the home of Joso Katalinić. He did not conceal his intentions from the local Ustasha and gendarmes: "We have to kill everyone, in Prkos and in all of their villages, to the last man, even children!" Responding to a comment by gendarme corporal Josip Koledić that small children were not guilty of anything, Luburić said that when children grew up they would become witnesses and avengers, so it was better to get rid of them before they could cause trouble.[1] Hearing of Luburić's threats, Anton Klasinc, the Lasinja parish priest, was horrified and warned some of his Serb acquaintances to be careful. Sergeant Petar Nikolić, the commander of the Lasinja gendarme station, could not bear to participate in Luburić's undertaking, even though he was a firm supporter of the NDH. That Saturday Nikolić sent a warning letter to Nikola Bižić, the Prkos district representative, through the popular Roma musician Franjo "Ćurak" Parapatić from Banski Kovačevac. Parapatić didn't know what the letter contained. He was stopped by two local Ustasha guards patrolling the road to Prkos. Pressed by their questions, a befuddled Parapatić admitted that he was carrying a letter and handed it over to the Ustasha guards.

The punishment was drastic: The Ustasha executed Parapatić and his wife the next morning in Banski Kovačevac. Nikolić was arrested while trying to escape with his family to Slovenia, the native country of his wife, Matilda. On the day before Christmas Eve the entire family—Nikolić, his wife, and both their sons, five-year-old Petar and three-year-old Tomislav—were executed in the forest near Kovačevac.

Luburić's first company, with about eighty soldiers, set out from Lasinja for Prkos on Sunday at five o'clock in the morning. The second company set off two or three hours later toward Dugo Selo. The winter was harsh, with nearly four feet of snow on the ground. Local Ustasha and gendarmes from Lasinja acted as guides for the columns. Dawn had broken when at the cemetery on the approach to Prkos the village guards caught sight of them. The Ustasha began to shoot at the guards, who ran to raise the alarm in the village.

The rifle and machine-gun fire from the cemetery found the residents of Prkos going about their morning chores or at the breakfast table. There were still no Partisans in Prkos and the village guards had no weapons, so resistance was out of the question. As had been agreed in the event of such a situation, the men of the village immediately took off for the forest of Bukova Glava, and the women remained in their homes with the children and the elderly. When Italian troops, the Home Guard, and gendarmes had earlier passed through the village, they had not touched the women, children, and the elderly. But no one on the morning of December 21 knew that a completely different kind of army was moving toward their village.

The Ustasha columns burst into Prkos from three sides and began the cleansing. The fourth column, which had cut off the road to the forest, was late, allowing more than one hundred men to escape. People found in their homes were brutally forced onto the road and into the snow. There were no exceptions: mothers with infants and elderly people unable to walk. Those who faltered or tried to escape were beaten or killed on the spot. Only Dragica, a Croat from Lučko, and her three children were spared. She had lived in Prkos since 1932 and was married to an enterprising blacksmith and tradesman, Milić Bastajić. But another Croatian woman, Lenka Bižić from Split, was killed with eleven members of the Bižić family.

The systematic cleansing quickly became frenzied, an uncontrollable rampage. Anything that could be stolen from the houses was stolen—and then the arson began. The wooden houses of Prkos burned to the ground and the few stone dwellings turned into burned-out shells, with no roofs, windows, or doors. Only the unfinished schoolhouse remained intact. People were loaded onto wagons and sent to Lasinja under a heavy guard. About four hundred residents of Prkos were imprisoned in the basement of the gendarme station and in some other buildings in Lasinja. Here the detainees were mistreated and beaten, and women were raped. Over the next several days and nights in groups of fifty these people were led to the nearby Brezje forest.

> According to the testimony of Nikola Orečić: The Ustasha Joža Mađer Đedera was an eyewitness to the execution of these men, women, and children in the Brezje forest. He told me that the Serbs from the surrounding villages, but mostly from Prkos, were arrested and taken to the Brezje forest; these people—men, women, and the elderly—were bound in groups of four and led to a pit, next to which stood an Ustasha who killed these unfortunate people, one by one, with a hammer. He struck each one in the back of the head and threw them into the pit... that was what Mađer told me when we were forced the next morning to fill in the pit with earth into which the Serbs of Prkos had been thrown.

At that time, Vaso Roknić was a tall and rather strong seventeen-year old boy with an enterprising character. He had very early on begun to work for the Partisans as a courier between Prkos and the Partisan bases at Sjeničak and Stipan. When the gendarmes or army would set off from Lasinja toward Prkos, Vaso would flee to the forest with the other men and would return home as soon as the danger had passed. On the morning of December 21, when the shooting started at the cemetery, Vaso was at breakfast. He grabbed the bag that he had already prepared and rushed through the snow toward Bukova Glava. His fourteen-year old brother, Milan, and his twelve-year old sister, Dragica, ran after him. Vaso barked at both of them: "Where are you going!? Go back home, stay with Mama and Grandma!" The younger brother Milan didn't listen to Vaso and continued to run after him, through Bukova Glava to Sjeničak, and thus saved his own life. Their sister listened to Vaso: she turned back home and with her mother and grandmother was taken from her home to Lasinja and into the pit in Brezje.

Sixty years later, when the mournful anniversary of the killings was observed in Prkos, Vaso confessed to me that he had never been able to recover from this loss and that he would always carry a feeling of guilt within himself for having stupidly and recklessly sent his sister to her death. Many other men from Prkos carried within themselves a similar lifelong torment, because on that morning in 1941 they had saved their own heads while abandoning their loved ones to Maks Luburić.At the memorial gravesite in Prkos there is an inscription that reads "In this common grave are the bones of 478 victims of the fascist terror." Although numbers of victims are often grossly exaggerated in Croatia, in this case I can vouch that any exaggeration is minimal, if it exists at all. More than half of the victims were infants and children under the age of eighteen, of whom twenty-two were less than one year old and seventy-four were between the ages of one and seven years.

Both in both a dry statistical sense and in the method of the killing Prkos was the most devastated village in Croatia, the forerunner of many more devastations to come.

* * *

On the morning of December 21, in Banski Kovačevac, eight-year-old Jandra Jakin was awoken by his mother, confused and frightened: "Get up, my son, Prkos is burning, it won't be good for us, either." When the cleansing and burning began in Prkos, several people or small groups from houses at the edge of the village managed to escape to Banski Kovačevac. There were no army units in Kovačevac. Gunshots echoed from Prkos from time to time and thick smoke rose into the sky.

The residents of Kovačevac were huddled in their homes behind heavily curtained windows and locked doors. In the hamlets of Mihalići and Lesari, which were closest to Prkos, people in several houses hid some of the fleeing residents of Prkos in their basements or barns. Some of the fugitives only passed through Kovačevac and continued on to Sjeničak.

At about ten o'clock in the morning, Luburić's Ustasha rushed from Prkos, burst into Kovačevac, and unleashed terror on the village. Eight boys from Prkos, who had found refuge in a barn in Lesari, sensed the danger and escaped through the forest to Sjeničak. Another group of children from Prkos, most of them girls, remained hidden in another barn in Lesari, where the Ustasha discovered them. They were sent to the pits at Brezje.

The search for the fleeing Prkos residents in Kovačevac was thorough and brutal. The Ustasha went from house to house threatening anyone hiding fugitives with execution on the spot. Under this kind of pressure the majority of fugitives were captured and no one was spared: some were killed immediately in the forest and some were killed a few days later with other residents of Prkos at Brezje. However, Jakov Mance managed to hide Đuro M. Bižić, an old carpenter from Prkos, in his cellar and he accompanied him the next night on the road to Sjeničak. Bižić's grandchildren, Draga and Rade, succeeded in hiding in Prkos itself and the next night they reached the nearest house in Mihalići, where Joža Mihalić took them in and kept them safe until the Ustasha offensive had passed. Vasilj V. Korać and his five-year-old grandson, Mirko, found refuge in a house next to the one in which Draga and Rade were hiding until one of the people in the house allegedly betrayed them to the Ustasha. They killed Korać in the Brezje forest in the first group and, it was said, his grandson in the last group.

To this day contradictory stories circulate in Prkos and Kovačevac, making it impossible to know the truth. The residents of Prkos claim that their fugitives in Kovačevac were all too easily betrayed and handed over to the Ustasha on December 21, while the residents of Kovačevac claim that there was no betrayal, with the exception of a single case, and that the Ustasha arrested the fugitives only after brutal searches of their homes. A legitimate judicial inquiry into this case was never carried out. Between 1943 and 1945 the Partisan intelligence service took away sixteen men from their homes in Mihalići and Lesari and not one of them returned. Allegedly some of the sixteen were executed because they had betrayed and handed over fugitives from Prkos to the Ustasha. No public report was ever made about this incident. In the contradictory estimates and stories the truth has remained shrouded in fog, and that fog is a most fertile ground for concocting new stories, for new hatred and renewed vengeance to grow.

The Ustasha cleansing of Prkos was underway when other army units launched a major offensive against the Orthodox villages of northern Kordun. However, the cleansing succeeded nowhere as thoroughly as in Prkos. The flames, smoke, and fugitives from Prkos raised the alarm for the entire region; people no longer waited in their homes. The columns of fleeing Kordun Serbs, with and without wagons, with cows and calves, with anything that people could lead or carry, crawled toward Petrova Gora. About fifteen thousand people abandoned their homes. The Fourth Battalion of the Kordun Partisan detachment at least managed to slow the enemy advance. It was a one-sided battle: more than two thousand Ustasha, gendarmes, and Home Guards against two hundred Partisans. Because they were natives of the area, and knew the terrain and were defending their families and villages, the Partisans were able to hold off the enemy to allow the people to make their escape.

The cleansing operation in northern Kordun lasted for about fifteen days; along the road to Vrginmost it lasted for twenty days. After Prkos, the Ustasha captured another five hundred Orthodox inhabitants from various settlements, most of them elderly people unable or unwilling to flee. If they were not killed in their villages, they were sent to Lasinja and, like the residents of Prkos, killed in the Brezje forest. The cleansing also swept up all of the Roma from the surrounding area—forty-eight of them from a settlement next to Novo Selo, thirty-four from Lasinja, and more than one hundred from the remaining Roma settlements. All were sent to Rakov Potok near Zagreb and killed, allegedly on New Year's Eve 1941. During the offensive, two Jewish women were captured in Pokupska Blatnica. They were imprisoned in the school in Banski Kovačevac and killed in the forest of Bukova Glava.

The Ustasha burned everything in sight. They torched more than two thousand houses, barns, and stables, and devastated the entire region. The burning was preceded by organized robbery: the Ustasha forced Croatian peasants from Lasinja, Banski Kovačevac, Kablar, Bučica, and the surrounding area to go to the abandoned Serbian villages with their wagons and deliver everything that could be carried away to a collection point in Lasinja. Many of the villagers, who were forced into robbery on behalf of the Ustasha, took some things for themselves. Veco Holjevac, the political commissar of the Kordun Partisan detachment of Croatia, wrote to the headquarters of the National Liberation Movement for Croatia:

> Worst of all is the fact that entire Croatian villages participated in the robberies that began after the passage of the Ustasha. Men, women, and children scavenged through the charred remains, rummaging through the potato cellars and taking away what little food remained after the fires. It is clear that by forcing these villagers into robbery the Ustasha intended to deepen

> the gulf between Croats and Serbs, and it is no accident that it has occurred in an area where our relations with Croats were friendly and where there existed a possibility that Croatian peasants might join Partisan detachments.

As a Croat with strong national sentiment, Holjevac deplored such dishonorable acts by his countrymen. However, in that area there was not much of a possibility of the Croatian peasants joining the Partisan forces. And if you ask the residents of Prkos, they will tell you that what remained after the burning was stolen by their neighbors from Kovačevac, while the people of Kovačevac will say that no one from their village voluntarily went to Prkos to rob; they were forced to do so by the Ustasha.

* * *

On the second day of Christmas, Pavelić called an urgent meeting with Ante Moškov, the commander of the *Poglavnik*'s bodyguard, and with Jura Francetić, the most capable Ustasha military officer. Pavelić ordered Moškov to immediately take command of all of the forces in action in northern Kordun. He, the *Poglavnik*, would come on New Year's Eve for an inspection with an entourage that would include senior representatives of the allied armies. Moškov's assignment was to make sure everything was in order by that time.[2]

By the next day Moškov was already in Lasinja and Bučica, where he met Luburić and Rukavina. Luburić had been informed of Pavelić's arrival for an inspection and, Moškov claimed, he had instructions to complete his part of the cleansing operation by New Year's Eve. And, indeed, on December 30, the last group of detainees from Prkos, Dugo Selo, and other places were killed in the Brezje forest. In speaking of these killings, Moškov wanted to show that there existed a second chain of command that ordered reprisals and that it ran directly to Luburić from Pavelić or through Dido Kvaternik.

On December 31, Pavelić arrived. He was accompanied by Kvaternik, Erich Lisak, and General Giovanni Battista Oxilia, the chief of the Italian military mission to the NDH. Moškov greeted them in the village of Lukinići. They then rode down to Bović, where Moškov had established his headquarters. Luburić was no longer there. Pavelić rode through abandoned villages, along endless rows of burned houses, and explained to General Oxilia in Italian that this was the result of a battle with the rebels. Allegedly, Moškov privately gave Pavelić an objective description of the situation: They had not destroyed the Partisans, it was just the opposite. The Partisans employed guerrilla tactics, putting up resistance in some places and carrying out raids in others. In the face of superior forces they would withdraw into the forests and were unreachable. The villages, Moškov claimed, were burned by members of Luburić's Ustasha Defense and Rukavina's Lika Battalion, to which Pavelić made no comment. Moškov took this silence as Pavelić's tacit approval. There was no question or discussion about the inhabitants who had been killed or who had fled.

Pavelić ordered Moškov to attack the large village of Kirin with reinforced units and to continue to advance by road in the direction of Vrginmost and Topusko. From a military standpoint these orders were a failure that is difficult to explain. Pavelić was in Bović with strong formations of Moškov's army, while only twenty kilometers away the Kordun Partisans were enjoying their greatest victory. They had just disarmed the Home Guard garrisons at the railway station in Vojnić, at Utinja, and at Vojišnica; captured 128 Home Guard members and gendarmes; seized 113 rifles, eight submachine guns, and other military equipment; and had encircled the district seat of Vojnić with its garrison of about 450 soldiers. Subjected to a two-week siege in the depth of winter, the NDH soldiers were freezing, starving, and demoralized; the garrison was on the verge of a complete breakdown.

Instead of ordering Moškov to strike the Partisan encirclement from the rear with his numerically superior forces, thus freeing the largest concentration of his army in Kordun, it was more important to Pavelić to burn a few more Serbian villages.

Between January 5 and 15, the cleansing operation in northern Kordun slowly abated, in part because of the exhaustion of the army and the impassable freshly fallen snow. Units under Moškov's command gradually withdrew from the field, but rather strong Ustasha, gendarme, and Home Guard garrisons remained in the area. In the greater part of the district of Vrginmost, however, the Partisans of the Fourth Kordun Battalion were again in full control.

Through deep snow in the dead of winter the people who had fled began to return to their burned-out homes. The men from Prkos and Dugo Selo, who had lost their wives, children, and entire families, did not go back. What was Petar Bućan, born in Prkos in 1912, to do? His biography says: "He was married in 1932 to Evica Bućan. They had two daughters, Smilja (born in 1933) and Marija (1935), and a son, Miloš (1937). The Ustasha killed his wife and children at Brezje in 1941." More than fifty residents of Prkos joined the Partisans in the waning days of 1941 and in early 1942. After capturing the Home Guard garrisons in and around Vojnić, there were suddenly plenty of weapons in Kordun: From about two hundred fighters before the cleansing operation, the Fourth Battalion grew to more than four hundred armed Partisans. On January 21, 1942, Ivan Betlehem, the director of the provincial police in Karlovac, wrote in his regular report on the situation in the province: "The Croatian army has not yet succeeded in liquidating these units. Indeed, with each passing day [they] are stronger and have more men.... Since the end of December the Ustasha have had only minor, or better to say, no successes against the Partisans."

* * *

In Banski Kovačevac there was fear of a Partisan reprisal. Jaga's neighbors in the village confided their fears to her: The massacre and burning of Prkos was a great evil that could now be visited upon Kovačevac. Certainly no one from Kovačevac had participated in the killing in Brezje or in the torching of Prkos and Sjeničak, but many people had been involved in plundering, either by force or of their own free will. And revenge doesn't distinguish between the guilty and the innocent—it strikes at will.

After the Ustasha's winter offensive, a garrison of about two hundred Home Guard engineers and a squad of gendarmes, temporarily reinforced with a small number of Ustasha, was established in Banski Kovačevac. Set in a fortified position on the hill around the school, it managed to repel several Partisan attacks in the course of 1942, but it couldn't control the entire scattered village. The Partisans were always able to raid the outlying hamlets at night and frequently during the day. One resident of Kovačevac, Rudolf Mažuran, who in the 1970s was the director of the Karlovac dairy, told me how one autumn evening in 1942 he was in his home, rather isolated on the edge of Kovačevac just below the forest, when a Partisan "courier," an old acquaintance from neighboring Sjeničak, came by. They had just prepared dinner for him when an Ustasha patrol came along. With the help of his host the Partisan hid in the attic as the three Ustasha entered the house, sat down in the warm kitchen, and waited for the family to offer them dinner. So the Ustasha ate the dinner intended for the Partisan and, sated, returned to their base at the school. After some time, the Partisan calmly came down from the attic and his hosts prepared a new dinner for him.

Kovačevac had become a battle front and the neutrality of the village residents was becoming increasingly difficult to maintain. Fearing a Partisan reprisal, several young men had volunteered to take up arms with the Home Guard and had joined the garrison at the school;

four or five enlisted in the Ustasha army. Several families sought refuge in villages closer to Karlovac, which had not yet been caught up in the war. At the same time, the first two or three residents of Kovačevac joined the Partisans, and the circle of Partisan collaborators slowly grew. Despite these divisions, people preserved solidarity within the village: Many guessed or knew of Jaga's contacts with the Partisans, but no one betrayed her to the Ustasha or the gendarmes, nor did she betray anyone to the Partisans.

The fears of the residents of Kovačevac that they would be subject to reprisals were not unfounded. During the Ustasha offensive, Nikola Vidović, the commander of the Fourth Battalion, ordered the houses of several local Ustasha in Kablar and Golinja to be burned, justifying it as necessary "to distract the Ustasha and to weaken the pressure on the other side." However, the burning of the villages, in addition to several similar incidents in Kordun, sparked an internal political controversy in the headquarters and party committees, with many discussions and immediate consequences. Srećko Manola, Vidović's superior, with the agreement of the District Committee of the Communist Party of Croatia (KPH), banned the burning of Croatian houses under the penalty of death; he warned against any further incidents and ordered that the Partisans "take particular care about their conduct, propriety, and manners" when passing through Croatian villages. I don't know how many Kordun Partisans followed these orders, willingly or unwillingly, but I do know that in the spring of 1942 discipline within the Partisan units was strict and breaking discipline was severely punished.

At that time, the Partisan leadership in central Croatia considered its main task to be "winning over Croatian villages to the antifascist struggle" and "spreading the rebellion into Croatian areas." In their directives and pronouncements, the committees of the KPH reiterated the slogan "Brotherhood and Unity." In March 1942, the District

Committee made the decision to carry out a drastic "purge" of the Partisan ranks in Kordun, which was defined as the "fight against Chetnik elements." In part, this purge had already taken on the characteristics of the communist-Bolshevik "struggle against the class enemy," but it also suppressed the willful plundering and vengeful burning of Croatian villages and other "deviations" that were a hallmark of the Chetniks. On March 19, seven Partisans were executed following a decision of the military court in Vojnić, while in a report to the Central Committee of the KPH, dated March 30, the District Committee announced that a total of twenty-three "bandits" had been executed and that thirty misguided peasants had been released. Soon after this report, two more minor purges were carried out: In the first one, nine people were executed and in the second one, four "bandits" were executed. The most notable example of discipline came in the summer of 1942, when Petar Krnjaić, the commander of the First Battalion of the Banija Partisan detachment, was executed. During an attack on Prekopa, the village in which the massacre of Glina Serbs had been carried out in May, Krnjaić had ordered the burning of the entire village and the killing of all men over the age of sixteen as an act of vengeance. With the exception of the burning of several houses, the order was not carried out; it was rescinded by Mate Jerković, Krnjaić's superior, and Šukrija Bijedić, the political commissar. The military court of the headquarters of the First Zone (Kordun, Lika, and Banija) condemned Krnjaić to death and the sentence was carried out.

* * *

Only after the capitulation of Italy, and with the sudden growth of the National Liberation Army and other changed circumstances, did the discipline of the Partisan army slacken, and in October 1943, I heard serious allegations by Croatian villagers about the robberies carried out by some Partisan units and their collaborators from nearby Orthodox villages.

From October 1943 to the end of February 1944, I was a political field worker with the District Committee of the League of Young Communists of Yugoslavia in Kordun, sent to agitate in Croatian villages. I also wrote reports on the work of the youth for the newspaper *Omladinski borac* (Youth Fighter) and traveled around Kordun, including several visits to Banski Kovačevac and Prkos.

In Banski Kovačevac I asked people if they had been robbed. Some were afraid to speak and avoided giving an answer, but Jaga's sisters Jana and Draga (Jaga was living in Karlovac from the spring of 1943 until the end of the war) and some of their neighbors spoke freely about all of this. Yes, there had been robberies, not just a few, and there still were, the sisters confirmed. Several families, whose sons or husbands were in the Ustasha army, were kicked out of Kovačevac "and almost all of their property confiscated." Some were visited by the quartermaster or storekeeper of some battalion or brigade who stole their cows. It was worse when a man from a burned-out Serbian village would show up, with or without a gun, looking for the property that had been taken from him during the cleansing. People were afraid. Several older men had been taken from their homes and were in prison, under investigation, in Lasinja or in Desni Štefanki. Because of this fear, Jana said men from the Home Guard were not returning to their homes and several had gone over to the Ustasha, where they would normally never go.

A bit of order, and even justice, was instilled by the National Liberation Committee (NOO) of the District of Vrginmost, and later the NOO of the District of Pisarovina, which made an organized effort for Croatian villages to provide assistance to their Serbian neighbors whose villages had been devastated. In Kovačevac a municipal NOO was established with some ten members and assistants that gradually succeeded in normalizing relations between the local population and the Partisan authorities. In 1943, several young people voluntarily joined the Partisan army. Far more residents of Kovačevac were still in the Home Guard, although five or six of them had left the NDH army in 1942 and 1943 after deciding that they would no longer fight for either side. In 1944, they were joined by some like-minded Kovačevac "neutrals." They were hiding in the forests and in various places around their village, a small "green cadre." The village gave them the name "deserters." The first and longest-serving deserter, actually their leader, was my friend and Jaga's brother, Mata Đerek.

In Prkos an imperfect life slowly, very slowly, returned at the beginning of the spring of 1943. There were no longer any enemy garrisons in the vicinity. Partisan commands from Lasinja and Skakavac ruled the entire region, and the surviving residents of Prkos were finally able to cultivate their fields and garden plots without fear. About eighty military-age residents of Prkos were serving in various units of the National Liberation Army, while the other seventy lived in temporary shelters on the land of their family or friends, the majority in out-of-the-way Sjeničak. The braver ones had already begun to erect huts or some kind of shelters on the charred remains of their homes. They were mostly older men unfit for military service, because barely ten Prkos women and young girls and a few small boys and girls had survived the massacre. In some Serbian villages in Kordun men were in the minority and there was an increasing number of young unmarried women and young widows. Some of the Prkos widowers, who had decided to repair their homes in Prkos and start new families, courted these women and girls. Ljuban V. Korać, who was generally well-regarded on both sides of Vezovnik Creek, had lost his wife and two sons (age five and one) in the Ustasha "cleansing" in 1941. He was the first resident of Prkos who fell in love with someone from Banski Kovačevac: as soon as he was demobilized, he proposed to Jana Đerek, the cousin of my friend Mata, and together they rebuilt Ljuban's house in Prkos. Other men from Prkos, who fought all over the country during the war and afterward remained in the army, entered mixed marriages, which after the war were no longer a rarity in Prkos. However, even this did not overcome the latent resentment between Prkos and Banski Kovačevac that continued to smolder, swept under the rug that was called "Brotherhood and unity" by politicians and the police. The "1941 syndrome" was fading away slowly, but it never vanished completely.

In contrast to their neighbors in Kovačevac, the residents of Prkos were not reluctant to complain to the Partisan government—because it was their government. For the first year of the war the Serbian villages in Kordun, Banija, and Lika alone fed the bulk of the Croatian Partisan army, while their able-bodied men served in its detachments and brigades and the women and girls made up the primary labor force. Even before the war these villages were a poorer region of Croatia: In prewar Sjeničak four hectares for a larger household was about the average, two horses or two oxen minor affluence, and more than three cows or three pigs great wealth; half of the households in 1936 didn't have shovels and one-third didn't have plows. When in 1942, and especially in 1943, the ranks of the National Liberation Army suddenly swelled, and the devastated Serbian villages that fed the army were exhausted, the Partisan authorities had no choice but to put the burden of feeding the army on the untouched Croatian villages. In these circumstances it had become increasingly difficult to suppress willful plundering by individuals and small groups. The Partisan army quickly lost its original ascetic innocence.

Feeling that the fortunes of war were favoring them, the Partisan authorities became more arrogant about the liberated territory of central Croatia in 1944. Hierarchically organized centers managed the intelligence, police, and investigative services. A Regional Intelligence Center, which for a time was headed by Rade Bastajić-Lipi from Prkos, was responsible for Banski Kovačevac, Prkos, and the surrounding villages. Bastajić-Lipi had organized the village guards in Prkos at the very beginning of the uprising. He had become the first member of the local NOO and then an intelligence officer. In the massacre of December 21, 1941, he had lost his wife and five daughters; only his son survived. The local historian Dušan Korać writes that "from that time Rade Bastajić-Lipi turned all his passion to militant struggle against the enemy, finding in this a reason to go on living."[3] From the summer of 1943 to the summer of 1944 about ten people in Banski Kovačevac were taken from their homes and tried by the military court in Desni Štefanki, or else disappeared without a trial. Some claimed that Bastajić-Lipi issued the orders for these actions, which was probably true. Some said that he did it out of a vengeful hatred of Banski Kovačevac, which I don't think is true. Bastajić-Lipi was a tough, disciplined soldier of the party who never acted out of personal motives or anti-Croatian hatred but strictly according to Bolshevik (Stalinist) principles "in the second stage of the revolution," when an even more ferocious struggle was to be waged against all enemies—real and potential, bourgeois, peasant, and profascist, and by class.

Rade was a brave man who diligently toured his area of responsibility, often exposing himself to danger. At dawn on September 26, 1944, two Ustasha from Kovačevac, Joža Lesar and Ivan Mihalić-Lindek, ambushed him at the edge of Prkos. They wanted to capture Rade alive, but he resisted. He had already overpowered Lesar when Lindek brought him down with several shots from his revolver. The two Ustasha allowed Rade's twelve-year-old son, who was accompanying his father that morning, to escape. The RIC organized a major search for Rade's killers, to no avail. On an Ustasha army retreat to Bleiburg, Joža Lesar disappeared somewhere on the *Križni put* ("Way of the Cross," see Chapter 19). Ivan Mihalić-Lindek remained hidden, even after the war, in various hideouts in his native region until the spring of 1950, when he fell into an OZNA ambush and was killed.

Much blood has been spilled in the history of Banski Kovačevac and Prkos, but the death of Rade Bastajić-Lipi and all of the circumstances surrounding it, is the only case in which residents of the two villages shot directly at one another.

* * *

In the last days of 1943, I was warming myself next to the stove in the Đereks' house when Jana suddenly asked me if I wanted to see Mata. Of course I wanted to see him, even though I knew he was a deserter, or because I knew he was a deserter. "You know he is here now, close by, and he is cold," Jana added. Soon she brought in a smiling, happy Mata. He had probably been in some well-camouflaged bunker under the hay barn or in the garden behind the house. Extending his hand, he said jestingly, "I hope you are not here to arrest me. You know, I got away from some others, I'll get away from you, too." Then he took my gun from the corner of the room and handed it to me. "Here, keep your gun by your side," he said. "I'm a deserter, I might take it from you!"

Mata told me that the Home Guard company in which he had served was transferred from Karlovac to Hrvatski Blagaj in the spring of 1942. The company commander, Stjepan Urban, was an associate professor at the university. The intelligent Mata became his confidante and favorite. In the village that was notorious for the massacre of neighboring Serbs in May 1941 and that was surrounded by the Partisans in the summer of 1942, First Lieutenant Urban quickly realized that his garrison would soon come under attack. He wrote a letter "to the Partisan commander of Kordun, Mr. Ćanica Opačić" and entrusted Mata with making sure that the letter reached the intended address at all costs. Mata carried out his assignment extremely well. Young Petra Mlađen, whom Mata had already seen several times, lived in the nearby Serbian village of Crno Vrelo on the other side of the Lisac hill. Mata passed the letter to Petra, which is how it arrived into the hands of Ćanica Opačić the very next day. Only two days later, Ćanica and Lieutenant Urban, through Mata's mediation, met at dusk at the house of Petra Mlađen. Urban condemned the Ustasha crimes, guaranteed that his company would prevent any further crimes as long as he was in command in Hrvatski Blagaj, and proposed a local non-aggression agreement. Ćanica sought the surrender of Urban's company after a feigned attack in order to avoid any bloodshed. They could not reach an agreement, but they did agree to stay in touch with each other. The exchange of correspondence went on for the entire summer, with Mata and one other Home Guard soldier from his company as the couriers. The finale was played out on September 13,1942, when the First Proletarian Battalion of Croatia, two shock battalions from Primorsko-Goranska County, and a Kordun battalion attacked Hrvatski Blagaj and Blagajski Pavlovac. Urban's company with about 120 members of the Home Guard and about thirty armed local Ustasha defended Blagaj. Despite the constant contacts, a precise agreement for the surrender had not been reached with Urban, but it was understood that resistance to a Partisan attack would not be very great. Some units in Urban's company, scattered in defensive positions around the village, attempted to defend themselves and were overpowered and fled. Urban and the main body of the company, sheltered in the school building, surrendered to the Partisans after a short siege and battle. The local Ustasha fought desperately around their homes and the church; the majority of them were killed in the battle, some committed suicide so that they would not fall into the hands of the Partisans, and seven were captured and executed by the Partisans. All captured Home Guard members were disarmed and lined up in Crno Vrelo, where Ćanica Opačić and Veco Holjevac gave speeches to them. First Lieutenant Urban and three other Home Guard soldiers remained in the Partisans; the others were stripped of their uniforms and equipment and sent home. Mata was among the first to surrender his rifle and equipment. His Home Guard uniform was exchanged for peasant clothing and he was sent home to Banski Kovačevac. He made a firm decision that he would never again join any army and he managed to honor that decision until the end of the war.

Mata didn't tell me anything about his adventures as a deserter, and I didn't ask. We were friends from opposing sides: In the beginning the Partisans tolerated deserters, but when deserters from the Home Guard began to join deserters from Partisan units in 1944, party committees included desertion in the category of "sabotage against the National Liberation Struggle." Special Partisan units, the Protiv Pete Kolone (Against the Fifth Column), hunted down the deserters or set up ambushes for them. Toward the end of the war, Mata's group fell into one such ambush. They managed to escape, except for one man who was killed while fleeing.

Today, when old people in Banski Kovačevac talk about the Second World War, the Kovačevac deserters are mentioned with great sympathy. Although there were only a few of them, some ten young men, they embodied the prevailing mood in the village: neutrality. As a Partisan, I passed several times through Hrvatski Blagaj and stayed in some other villages in Kordun and Lika that we called, with some justification, Ustasha territory. I got to know even better many Croatian villages in the regions of Gorski Kotar and Hrvatsko Primorje that already in 1942 we had reason to call Partisan, and as the war went on, they became more numerous. Banski Kovačevac was among the villages that tried to maintain neutrality the longest, though it did not last beyond the first year of the war. Their noncombative behavior in the Home Guard and their raising of the white flag in the first serious engagement with the Partisans were clear demonstrations of that neutrality. However, by 1944 the NDH army began to combine Ustasha and the Home Guard units, and newly mobilized young men and an increasing number of Home Guard troops had to dress in Ustasha uniforms. As a result, many men lost their lives after Bleiburg and on the Way of the Cross, among them ten young men from Banski Kovačevac.

When he reached the age of eighty, Mata decided to make a list of all those from Banski Kovačevac who had lost their lives during the Second World War as a way "to leave the truth as a memorial." He counted seventeen people killed in an Ustasha uniform, the majority in the last days of the war; ten killed as members of the Home Guard; sixteen who had been taken from their homes by the Partisans in 1944 and 1945 and never returned; and eight civilians killed by the Partisans after they had found refuge as displaced persons or refugees in Rečica and other villages around Karlovac. In addition, three people from Kovačevac were killed as Partisans (out of the total of twelve who had been in the National Liberation Army), four were executed by the Ustasha as Partisan sympathizers or "undesirables," and four were killed in bombing raids or as a result of other wartime circumstances. (At the same time, besides the approximately 450 victims of the Ustasha cleansing, twenty-six residents of Prkos were killed as members of the National Liberation Army, one was killed as a Chetnik, and the Partisans executed two from within their own ranks—one for dereliction of duty as a guard and one for violating discipline.)

Mata and his fellow deserters spent two or three more weeks after the end of the war in hideouts and shelters between Banska Selnica and Banski Kovačevac. After the first amnesty, Mata got in touch with the appropriate authorities in Pisarovina. As a result, when the deserters, as agreed, turned themselves in to the district NOO, the majority were immediately sent home, while the others followed several weeks later.

An excellent carpenter, Mata started to repair houses in neighboring

Prkos and that is how the Second World War between Prkos and Banski Kovačevac ended, but the trauma of 1941 remained hanging in the air above the entire region, and it was joined by the trauma of 1945. The two traumas were different, in that one was endlessly discussed and written about, frequently in a skewed way, while everyone knew to keep silent about the other.

* * *

From the time of the Military Frontier, Prkos was under the purview of the land office of the district of Banski Kovačevac, so after 1945 the two villages were joined into a single local administrative unit. In 1837, officials of the Military Frontier had founded a school in Banski Kovačevac that children from Prkos attended until 1941. In the nineteenth century both villages still had a common Catholic and Orthodox cemetery. At the beginning of the twentieth century, they jointly supported the party of the Croatian-Serbian Coalition, but after 1918 Kovačevac unanimously supported the Croatian Peasants' Party of Antun Radić and Vladko Maček. Meanwhile, Prkos was divided between supporters of the more democratic Serbian People's Independent Party of Svetozar Pribičević and radical followers of the Royalist regime. A chapter of the Yugoslav Sokol that bore Serbian national emblems was founded in Prkos in 1932; but a Croatian Sokol chapter could not be established due to a 1929 decree that disbanded and banned the Croatian Sokol Society. It was also easier for residents of Prkos than for residents of Kovačevac to find employment in services financed by the government (game wardens, inspectors, etc.).

The Serbian cultural-educational society known as *Seljačko kolo* (Peasants' Circle) was active in Prkos, while in Kovačevac it was the Croatian cultural-educational society known as *Seljačka sloga* (Peasants' Unity). A rivalry existed between the two societies that grew into a public political dispute with mutual accusations and slurs of an ethnic character during a revue of choral and dance groups in 1935. More moderate people from the leadership of both societies prevented the outbreak of a general brawl. The sharpest clash, based on political and interethnic friction, broke out on the day of the Saint Peter's Fair in Banski Kovačevac, also in 1935. Gendarmes had to intervene and disperse the crowd. However, relations between the two villages improved considerably when in 1938 they jointly supported the parties of Vladko Maček's United Opposition.

The hot-cold relationship between the two villages was influenced by the general conditions and the political parties, but it only rarely disrupted business relationships and friendships between individuals. Perhaps there was some sympathy among the boys and girls who went to school together, but until 1945 there were no mixed marriages between Prkos and Kovačevac. It was as if an invisible barrier ran along Vezovnik Creek that permanently kept the two villages at a measured distance from each other.

According to the census of 1948, Banski Kovačevac contained 570 inhabitants, about the same as before the war. That same year, Prkos had 235 inhabitants, more than half of whom were new residents (the wives and children of newly established families and people from other regions who had settled on the property of their murdered relatives).

Mata served several terms as the president of the local administration for Kovačevac-Prkos. In 1949, the people of Kovačevac were being forced into a peasant collective, but residents of Prkos managed to avoid collectivization. Just after the war, Prkos enjoyed many advantages over Kovačevac: In addition to assistance for rebuilding and other benefits to which they were entitled as veterans of the National Liberation War and victims of the fascist enemy, the survivors of Prkos retained preferences for job hirings as well as a variety of privileges for schooling their children. After the war, about fifty Prkos

Vaso Roknić (1925–2005)

survivors remained in the army as officers of the Yugoslav People's Army or in other services and almost all maintained some connection with their native village and helped in its renovation and reconstruction.

The people of Kovačevac successfully delayed the establishment of a peasant collective. In 1951, they were among the first to break out of the peasant collective, and Kovačevac's fortunes improved, albeit slowly. Focused exclusively on their work, and not on privileges, they set about cultivating their fields and working in the forests. Some even became small entrepreneurs. The skillful and capable Mata built a small mill for the entire village. For a while, he piloted a rented boat and, with his steady work as a carpenter, was able to provide a decent living for his new family, a wife and two daughters (who with Jaga's help were able to finish their schooling, including university, in Zagreb). At the beginning of the 1960s, the villagers of Banski Kovačevac began to go abroad to work, mostly to Germany. They would send home German marks, agricultural machinery, tractors, and also televisions and kitchen appliances. The wooden shanties in the village became brick homes, the one-story homes became two-story homes. Mata was among the last to live in a wooden shanty, but its carpentry and construction were outstanding, with excellent farm outbuildings in the courtyard.

The school in Prkos miraculously survived the entire conflict and was opened immediately after the war. Children from Banski Kovačevac also attended the school until 1952, when a new school was built in Kovačevac. The neighboring villages cooperated in joint projects to improve infrastructure: In 1955 the unified General Agricultural Cooperative, with an associated market and shop, began operations; an electrical power network was installed through joint efforts; access roads and asphalt sections through both villages were built and connected to the main Lasinja–Karlovac road. *Karlovački tjednik* (The Karlovac Weekly) published an article from Banski Kovačevac and Prkos entitled "Two Brotherly Villages." Weekend vacationers from Zagreb, who in the 1970s built a small vacation settlement on the Kupa River at the foot of Prkos, also improved the standards. Mata earned a good living as a carpenter from the construction of such weekend houses. Older residents of Prkos, who had reached the rank of major or colonel in the Yugoslav People's Army, were building new homes and then returning to their land as retirees. The retired colonel Vaso Roknić settled into his beautiful home and became a moving force behind road construction and other projects in the village. With the assistance of his daughter, Dragica, an architect from Pula, he opened a carpentry shop and became a successful businessman. Slowly, very slowly, life in both villages improved. On the western edge of Prkos, which jutted out toward Banski Kovačevac, the enterprising Stevo

Mata Đerek (1918–2005)

Korać opened an inn that became the liveliest meeting place for the people of both villages. "We met people from Prkos at Stevo's place, we drank, we passed the time with them, argued and fraternized, and we made business deals," one old resident of Kovačevac told me. Korać frequently organized entertainment with dancing at his inn, which was attended equally by both villages. Few from Kovačevac would travel to Lasinja and not drop in at Korać's place along the way, just as few from Prkos traveling to Skakavac or Karlovac would not drop by the inn of Mijo Paulić in Kovačevac.

Younger people, increasingly better educated, remained in the cities, and the villages' populations became older. Mata's daughters married in Zagreb and Karlovac, and when his sisters Jana and Dragica died, he and his wife, Danica, remained in the house alone. But life in Banski Kovačevac and Prkos went on. Some of the younger people still concentrated on agriculture, and the children and grandchildren now living in the cities remained tied to their birthplaces. In the cities, more and more people intermarried and spent summers in their native hills along the Kupa River. It was as if that youthful liveliness brought from the cities had dissolved the invisible barrier between the two villages.

Of course, there were disagreements and arguments between individuals, and even conflicts of interest between the two villages. In such instances, Roknić and Mata would sit at a table in a corner of the inn of Korać or Paulić, order two spritzers or two beers, and talk heart-to-heart for an hour or two. If necessary, they would seek advice from their neighbors, then meet again in a day or two until they found a mutually agreeable solution, often a rational compromise. And so there were no irreconcilable differences between Banski Kovačevac and Prkos, though such differences existed between the republics that made up Yugoslavia at the time because their leaders in the 1980s were not of the same caliber as Mata and Roknić.

The tensions that tore Yugoslavia apart in the 1980s emanated from television screens like parasites into the homes of Banski Kovačevac and Prkos. The signs of the crisis filled everyday life: shortages of detergent and gasoline, runaway inflation, restrictions on driving through the use of an "odd-even" system on alternate days of the week, and children living in the cities unable to visit their parents in the villages on weekends. And when they did, they brought explanations for the crisis based on coffeehouse humor and cleverness: No more Tito; no bank loans. The Serbs are to blame for oppressing us, the Slovenes for exploiting us, the Bosnians for sucking us dry, the Macedonians and Montenegrins for dragging us down. And on the opposite side: The Croats and Slovenes are guilty of taking everything from us and giving it to the Albanians, who in turn are pushing us out of Kosovo and tearing apart our Mother Serbia. And the Croats, especially the *Croats*, are again preparing a 1941 for us, God forbid, but this time it will not work, we will not be caught by surprise again. I don't remember if it was in the early run-up to the war that the global conspiracy against Serbia, with the strings being pulled by the Vatican, was "uncovered."

The residents of Prkos and Kovačevac talked about these topics in a "half joking, half serious" way at Korać's inn, even though the public media had to remain silent on such subjects. In socialist Yugoslavia from 1950 to 1990 necessary reforms of the socioeconomic system could be discussed in public on the condition that criticism didn't exceed certain unwritten limits known to everyone. There was no tolerance, even minimal, for critical discussions about interethnic and inter-republic relations. When in 1950 the Partisan leaders of the Serbs in Croatia, Rade Žigić, Duško Brkić, and Ćanica Opačić, complained too loudly about the postwar economic and political neglect of the devastated Serbian areas most responsible for the victory of the National Liberation War in Croatia, all three were dismissed from their ministerial positions, kicked out of the Communist Party, and imprisoned for several years on the island of Goli Otok, where Žigić died.[4] Still more frequent were discontented declarations from the Croatian side, which for forty years could result in jail sentences or banishment to prison camps up to the time of Vlado Gotovac,[5] who after four years of imprisonment at Stara Gradiška spent two more years in the prison at Lepoglava.

The pluralism of national interests and the disagreements that naturally arose from them in multiethnic socialist Yugoslavia were never freely and publicly discussed, so there could never be any mutual understanding. Everyone pushed their own interests. Open questions were repressed or "swept under the rug." The classic pressure cooker in which those disputed questions had been pushed to one side multiplied, expanded, and grew deformed until an explosion was inevitable. I think that Zoran M. Marković aptly summarized this in his picturesque claim that "a good portion of the blame for the wars that befell us in the 1990s were hidden in these blocked-up valves of dissatisfaction."[6]

That explosive, dangerous pressure cooker in which the Serbian-Croatian dispute simmered was named "Brotherhood and Unity." The slogan, which was probably devised by Tito, the master of effective sloganeering, sounded attractive but had little relation to the truth ("Power to the people," "Factories for the workers," "We don't want anybody else's, but we won't give anything away that's ours," etc.). Who would oppose those beautiful words "Brotherhood and unity," which sound so noble and well-meaning? However, the problem was in the relations between peoples and states; in the literal sense the words "brotherhood and unity" did not exist in the region and had never existed. Conceived as a way to remove the plurality of interests and pluralism in general, this exalted slogan was mendacious and unsustainable. Between two or more peoples, two or more states, understanding, harmony, cooperation, and alliance can be established, but their natural differences cannot be forcibly destroyed. The author of the slogan "Brotherhood and Unity" possessed a certain sensibility for interethnic problems in the multinational Yugoslav community.[7] However, the limitations of Tito's Bolshevik upbringing, coupled with his authoritarian character, clouded his vision and rendered him incapable of democratic dialogue—the only rational solution. I think that in the modern world multiethnic national communities can be sustained in the long term only under liberal democracy and are unsustainable under one-party systems with a totalitarian (or monistic) concept of power.

The Kingdom of Yugoslavia, at least at the very end, tried to bridge the Croat-Serb disagreements through the Cvetković-Maček Agreement of 1939. But it was already too late; too little time remained for the agreement to show any positive results or for any of its defects to be remedied. After Tito's death, socialist Yugoslavia was not capable of formulating any agreement, which would have also had to anticipate the possibility of a community of sovereign states, and moreover its peaceful dissolution.

However illusory it may have been, the slogan "Brotherhood and Unity" had a propagandist and mobilizing effect during the war. It prevented mass reprisals by Serbian Partisans against Croatian villages and, to a great extent, suppressed the spread of Chetnik ideology. Chauvinistic behavior was also suppressed and punished in the postwar period, but the fetishism connected with the slogan was counterproductive, as is every fetishism in the political sphere of a modern, pluralistic society.

My friend Ivo Škrabalo shared an insightful allegory on the theme of "brotherhood and unity," which is a bit one-sided for my taste but worth repeating here with the author's permission. "Brotherhood and Unity" is an anomaly that among humans exists only between

Siamese twins. Each of these forcibly joined unfortunates is incapable of having a normal life. They cannot help themselves—only very skillful doctors can separate them and only after long preparations and difficult operations. To find such doctors is not easy. However, Škrabalo has told me of a number of successful surgical separations of Siamese twins in recent years. The procedures were, indeed, complicated and lasted all day and night, but they were carried out in such a way that the twins felt neither pain nor torment and suffered no damage. After the operation, they could begin to live normally. Freed from their enforced "brotherhood and unity," the twins became capable of making decisions for themselves. Some twins have remained together; some have gone their separate ways in life.

In Serbia and Croatia we had no doctors capable of carrying out such a successful procedure. In key places we had medical quacks who performed the operation in the most painful way possible.

* * *

On September 24, 1986, the Belgrade daily *Večernje novosti* (The Evening News) published a portion of a "Memorandum of the Serbian Academy of Sciences and Art," a text on which sixteen academics had worked for more than a year. Although the "Memorandum" wasn't finished or edited, the publication of part of it marked a dramatic turning point in discussions about the Yugoslav crisis at that time. Instead of the earlier, rather reserved analytical texts on reforms needed for a stunted sociopolitical system, the "Memorandum" focused on interethnic relations in a one-sided and provocative manner. Slovenia and Croatia were accused of economic and political domination in implementing their nationalistic programs and economic aspirations, of "satisfying their interests at Serbia's expense," of putting Serbia in a "subordinate position," and of supporting a "physical, legal, and cultural genocide against the Serbian population of Kosovo and Metohija." Serbia was described as "the victim," the greatest victim in two world wars, and "in the new Yugoslavia as the only nation with no state"—a "worse historical defeat in peacetime cannot be conceived." The Serbs in Croatia were sent the message that they were being "subjected to the most refined and effective policy of assimilation," that they were living "under the pressure of discrimination" in areas that "remained the most undeveloped in Croatia," and that "the Serbian people, regardless of which republic or province they live in . . . must be given the opportunity to find themselves again and to become a historical entity."

When he was made undisputed "leader" at the Eighth Session of the Central Committee of the Communist Party of Serbia in 1987, Slobodan Milošević transformed the academic theses of the "Memorandum" into a destructive weapon of war in a campaign to gain power over all of Yugoslavia, or at least its major areas. Radio Television Belgrade, the daily newspaper *Politika*, and a fair number of other newspapers became effective propagators of Milošević's aggressive policies. "Special journalists who monitored the status of Serbs outside of Serbia were appointed to the editorial offices. An organized, at times hysterical, wailing about the general endangerment of Serbs began," writes Zoran Marković. The bill for 1941 was being presented to Croats and Croatia: Arbitrarily inflated numbers of those killed in the Jasenovac concentration camps were distastefully peddled, with allusions to Croats being a genocidal people, while each real or imagined incident was used as proof that the Ustasha ideology was again rising in Croatia. The Belgrade editor and publisher Ivan Čolović thinks that these were "morbid ideas" and an "obscene use" of Serbian victims with the goal of proving to Serbs that they had suffered eternally at the hands of their "ancient enemies"—and preparing them for a bloody new conflict.

The Croatian political leadership was not equal to this new situation. Incapable of making the appropriate response to Milošević's policy and propaganda, it withdrew into its well-known "Croatian silence," an unwise decision that, unfortunately, is not a rarity in the history of Croatian politics. By its cowardly silence, the Croatian political leadership essentially aided the attempts of the Belgrade media to create a sense of endangerment among Serbs in Croatia. The polemical response of some Croatian media and social organizations were not sufficiently persuasive. With the emergence of a multiparty system in Croatia in 1989, the militant rhetoric of some parties and media overstepped the bounds of political rhetoric, which could be interpreted as a blanket accusation against Serbia and the Serbs as a people. An inflammatory column in *Politika*, "Odjeci i reagovanja" (Echoes and Reactions), demagogically used the argument that the Ustasha ideology was being reawakened in Croatia and that the Ustasha crimes were being minimized and had never been sufficiently condemned.

I first had the feeling that something much worse might be born from the Serbian-Croatian skirmishes in Belgrade in October 1988 when I attended the annual book fair as the editor of the Croatian edition of the Ljubljana publishing house Cankarjeva založba. At the home of my close friends Vojo, Mina, and Planinka Kovačević I ran into the retired colonel general Pavle Jakšić, whom I had known since 1944, when he had been chief of the general staff of the National Liberation Army of Croatia. In his seemingly humorous but actually argumentative way, he immediately attacked me: "Slavko, for me you are a Croat who works for the Slovenes and that is the worst thing you can be. But you are also a Jew and were a good little Partisan, so that is why I am speaking to you as a friend: Tell your Croats and Slovenes that we Serbs liberated them twice in this century. But if we have to liberate them a third time, no one will ever have to liberate them again. Do you understand?" Of course I understood, especially when Jakšić added some comments about his birthplace, the village of Blatuša, and the fate of his fellow villagers in the Glina church in August 1941.

A day or two later, I was working as an editor with Dobrica Ćosić[8] in the building of the Serbian Academy on one of his books that was to be published by Cankarjeva založba. During a break, we walked along a spacious interior balcony with a view of the imposing atrium. I recounted my conversation with Jakšić, but Ćosić waved it off: "Well, you know Pavle, you shouldn't always take him so seriously." I insisted that I had read and heard many other less humorous and more malevolent statements from Jakšić and I said, "Dobrica, if we are to part ways in this state, I think we have to part like human beings." Ćosić stopped, leaned on the railing of the balcony, and looked into the depths of the atrium. After a long pause, he said, as if speaking to himself, "Yes, like human beings.... We will part like human beings. But it will not be easy; the borders are in question...."

When I spoke the next day with Kosta Čavoški, who had written the foreword for Ćosić's book, I brought up my fears about this topic and repeated the idea that we would have to part as human beings. Čavoški didn't brood over the question like his friend Ćosić; he responded readily, with a calm, self-confident smile: "Of course, we will part like human beings, as soon as we agree about the borders. But I'm afraid that it will not be easy."

The dissolution of Yugoslavia would indeed not be easy. However, I remained somewhat naïve. When the question of war was discussed publicly in 1989, I insisted that there would be no real war. "Some isolated incidents, fights, perhaps some armed skirmishes," I said hopefully. "However, if one or two hundred people are suddenly killed, we will recognize the insanity and we will sit down at a table and work out an agreement."

Events showed that not even one hundred thousand killed, wounded, and expelled were enough for responsible people to begin to think hard.

* * *

In the villages of Lika, Banija, and Kordun it is impossible to find a Serbian family that didn't lose at least one or more members at the hands of the Ustasha. The year 1941 had left behind painful memories and a latent fear that the same thing could happen again. Embedded in their subconscious, it was manifested in an oversensitivity to anything that would, through their deepest associations, harken to 1941. Over the years, through several generations, that latent fear gradually faded and was perhaps forgotten, but periodic "incidents" and the inability of the Croatian authorities to confront the problem in an appropriate manner kept it alive. They treated the events of 1941 and the entire phenomenon of the NDH only superficially, in propagandistic terms. In Croatia there was never anything resembling the Nüremberg trials. The postwar trials of Mile Budak and other Ustasha leaders were carried out in a superficial and accelerated way, with one day designated for joint testimony and sentencing for about ten accused men. The goal was to stage a political-propaganda event and not to establish individual guilt, while separating it from collective guilt. There was always a sense of incompleteness, leaving room for a variety of interpretations: from concern that the general tone of the indictments disguised a lack of firm evidence, to a suspicion that the courts avoided investigation of the essence of the genocide policy and precise identification of its creators and perpetrators for political reasons. The Croatian government and public didn't have a sufficient understanding of the oversensitive latent fear of Croatian Serbs in 1941; and the Croatian Serbs didn't have a sufficient understanding of the dissatisfaction the Croatian public felt for always being suspected of Ustasha tendencies.

At the annual commemorations for the victims at Prkos on December 21, there is no mention that the company commanded by Vjekoslav Maks Luburić carried out the massacre; the main perpetrator was never publicly identified (and it wasn't known until recently because a thorough investigation had never been carried out). The massacre is spoken about only in general terms as an Ustasha crime. The names of two or three known Ustasha from Lasinja are sometimes mentioned, adding to the suspicion that the neighboring Croatian villages also participated in the crime in 1941. And the people of Kovačevac were never shown documentary proof of who from their village had been an accomplice in the plundering and who may have denounced those residents of Prkos who had fled. This would have been the only way to prove convincingly that none of the people of Kovačevac had taken part in the killings, that the majority had not even taken part in the plundering, and that a considerable number had helped both those who had suffered and the Partisans.

This dichotomous and vaguely distrustful attitude toward Banski Kovačevac also appears in some of the pages of Dušan Korać's 1989 book *Prkos in Flames*. Korać conscientiously researched and described by name the fates of more than five hundred individuals from his village, but nowhere in this enormous book does he say precisely who the perpetrator of the massacre was. Although he makes many references to "brotherhood and unity," and even titles one chapter "The People of Prkos Fell for Freedom, Brotherhood, and Unity," he writes that even before December 21, 1941, Banski Kovačevac was an "Ustasha stronghold" and that during the massacre in Prkos "a unit of local Ustasha that was waiting in Banski Kovačevac was supposed to trick the refugees from Prkos and, along with the newly arrived Ustasha, to arrest everyone, which was carried out according to a preordained plan." This is not the truth. I myself was a witness to the truth because I spent time around Banski Kovačevac for a month, until December 19, and did not see a single Ustasha. Moreover, I would not be alive today if Kovačevac had been an "Ustasha stronghold" or "a unit of local Ustasha."

I believe Prkos and Sjeničak were among the last Serbian villages in central Croatia to fall under the siren's spell from Belgrade, that their lives were in danger in Croatia, that all Serbs should live in one state, and that this state should extend to the farthest reaches of any Serbian grave. Halfway between Sjeničak and Prkos lay Banski Kovačevac, which posed no threat. Many of their children were living in the cities, most in mixed marriages. The son of Vaso Roknić was a salesman in Zagreb, married to a Croatian woman with whom he had two daughters; Roknić's daughter, Dragica, an architect, lived in Pula and was married to a Croat, with whom she had a son and a daughter. As long as the children didn't feel endangered in the cities, it was difficult to convince Roknić that Prkos was in danger.

The latent fears of the Serbian population were quickly inflamed by the escalating anti-Serbian rhetoric in Croatia in 1989. The climax of this rhetoric was voiced by Franjo Tuđman at the First General Congress of the Croatian Democratic Union (HDZ) on February 24, 1990. In his words, the "NDH wasn't just a simple 'Quisling' creation or a 'fascist crime' but also the expression both of the historical aspirations of the Croatian people for an independent state and of an awareness of international factors, in this case of the government of Hitler's Germany, which on the ruins of Versailles tailored a New European Order. Thus, the NDH wasn't just a mere whim of the Axis powers but the result of precise historical factors."

For understandable reasons, in the historical memory of the Serbian people the NDH was and would be nothing more than a fascist crime, a slaughterhouse for the Serbs of Croatia and of Bosnia and Herzegovina. If the NDH was indeed the expression"of the historical aspiration of the Croatian people," then Croatian and Bosnian Serbs needed to find another state for themselves, and the slogan "All Serbs in one state" suddenly became attractive to them. None of this helps the jumbled sophistry of Tuđman's remarks, which the Serbs could only interpret as an ominous threat to their survival in Croatia.

Just eight days later, on March 4, at the monument on Petrova Gora, tens of thousands of Serbs chanted against Tuđman. The most popular slogan was "This is Serbia," but one could also hear the morbid rhyme "*Nećemo se više dati, nećete nas klati*" (We will not give in, you will not slaughter us). For the first time several people from Prkos, who until then had been vacillating, participated in public protest. It was the most difficult for people like Roknić—with his grandchildren in the cities, born into mixed marriages, his only option was Yugoslavia, but with Milošević in Belgrade and Tuđman in Zagreb, Yugoslavia could not survive.

When he became the head of the Croatian state, Tuđman still had a chance to sway many of the Serbs in Croatia. During both the war and the postwar era, he had cooperated with many Serbs and had several close Serbian friends and acquaintances. After 1989, he never spoke to any of them. Unlike his successor in the HDZ, he never greeted them with the traditional Serbian Orthodox Christmas greeting "*Hristos se rodi*" (Christ is born), and he never reassured them that Croatia was also their homeland and that 1941 would never again be repeated. Instead, he sullenly delivered small-minded, warped historical lectures and waved before them, like a toreador's red cape, Luburić's perverse idea of a "reconciliation of the Ustasha and the Croatian Partisans." With the rhetoric of combative intolerance, Tuđman encouraged anti-Serbian sentiment within the Croatian public. When the Serbian uprising began in Croatia in the summer of 1990, Tuđman sensed the danger and softened the rhetoric. He stated several times that the Serbs and other minorities in Croatia would be "guaranteed, not only de jure but also de facto, all civil and ethnic rights," but it was too late. These rare conciliatory words were in contradiction to the ever-more frequent ominous actions. As the head of state, Tuđman didn't oppose the mass firings of Serbs from the civil service, the bombing of Serbian homes, the demolition of monuments, or the killing of Serbian civilians in some Croatian cities.

With Milošević leading Serbia, I don't think a military attack against Croatia could have been avoided in 1991. However, the evil could have been considerably lessened. With a wiser policy toward Croatia's Serbs, many of them would not have felt threatened or would not have participated in the attack on Croatia, the shelling of Croatian cities, and the mass burnings of Croatian villages. The Serbs of Gorski Kotar are a good example. Former minister of internal affairs Josip Boljkovac and some local Croatian officials approached them in time with reasonable explanations and proposals, and not a single bullet was fired from Drežnica, Jasenak, Gomirje, and Moravice, and not a single home, either Serbian or Croatian, was burned.

At the beginning of 1990, Tuđman and I were in Vienna for a three-day symposium on the riverboat *Europa* with representatives of countries just making the transition from communism to multiparty democracy. During a coffee break, I brought up the topic of the Serbs in Croatia. Tuđman responded, "Please, what more is there to talk about? Someone should sit at a table with Milošević and agree on everything. The Croatian Serbs will follow him like sheep. But tell me, Slavko, is there anyone in Croatia, except me, who could sit at that table with Milošević and make such an agreement in the name of Croatia?"

Instead, the Serbs in Croatia were abandoned to Milošević, who misled them, abused them, incited them to rebel against Croatia, and finally betrayed them.

* * *

At about one thirty in the afternoon of October 4, 1991, intense machine-gun and mortar fire suddenly broke out around the forested hills above Banski Kovačevac. People immediately began to flee from their homes toward the Kupa River. Members of the Territorial Defense Forces[9] of the Serbian Autonomous Region (SAO) of Krajina and volunteer reservists from Serbia burst from the forest. The attack was part of a general offensive that began that day in a broad front toward the Kupa River and the city of Karlovac. Outmanned and outgunned by the far more powerful attackers, about ten armed residents of Kovačevac didn't put up resistance and fled toward the Kupa along with everyone else. The attackers fired over their heads to frighten them. No resident of Kovačevac was killed or wounded that day. They all crossed by ferry to Šišljavić on the other side of the Kupa. According to the spring 1991 census, of the 307 residents of Kovačevac, 16 people, mostly elderly, remained in the village. Mata and his wife, Danica, also remained. Some soldiers, said to be from the town of Loznica,[10] questioned Mata and threatened to kill him, until a Territorial Defense soldier from Trebinje named Dakić, who knew Mata, came by. He reprimanded the soldiers for behaving like wild animals. He told Mata and Danica that nothing would happen to them as long as he was there to protect them, but he could not guarantee what would happen once he left. Later that day, a Loznica man, the leader of the group, approached more peaceably and asked Danica to prepare dinner for them. "This is now Serbia, all the way to the Kupa," he then explained to Mata. "You can stay here only if you recognize Serbian authority; otherwise it would be better for you to leave. We aren't going to kill you the way you killed our people in 1941."

The possibility of an attack on Banski Kovačevac and other Croatian villages on the right bank of the Kupa River had been rumored for several weeks, but it was still a surprise when it took place. The establishment of the SAO of Krajina had been proclaimed in the small town of Knin on December 21, 1990. It incorporated the district of Vrginmost, which included Prkos, under a decision of the District Assembly of April 1, 1991. Ten young men from Prkos, members of the military wing of the Serbian Democratic Party, then received weapons and agreed to serve in the Territorial Defense Forces of the SAO of Krajina. Meanwhile, ten residents of Kovačevac, militant members of the HDZ, acquired carbines and two submachine guns. An armed peace between the two villages lasted for about six months, until October 4. There were no incidents. The residents of Kovečevac peacefully passed through armed Prkos on their way to Lasinja; residents of Prkos peacefully passed through armed Kovačevac to Sjeničak or Karlovac. However, tensions on all sides increased. They didn't arise from disagreements between the two villages, because Mata Đerek and Vaso Roknić would have been there to resolve them; outside circumstances had intruded into the relations between the two villages in the face of which both men were powerless. As there is every year, there was a celebration in 1991 for the Feast of the Assumption in front of the village Church of Saint Peter in Banski Kovačevac. And as every year, the innkeeper Stevo Korać traveled from Prkos with a supply of roasted meat to sell at the celebration. Except this time he didn't sell one ounce. He was boycotted, not because he was the innkeeper Korać but because he was a Serb. The passable barrier that had existed between the two villages had suddenly become more concrete and impassable. The people had been divided into two camps in which Janas and Anđelijas, Bastajićis and Milovcis, and the people of Prkos and Kovačevac were disappearing. They had all become Serbs or Croats.

Throughout the summer of 1991 the war in Croatia gradually spread. It still had not reached the Kupa River in northern Kordun, but emissaries for the policy that Milošević directed from Belgrade and that his yes-men carried out from Knin were arriving all the more frequently in Serbian villages. The Croatian media spread rigidly anti-Serbian statements and constantly referred to the traumatic memories of 1941, while claiming a similar danger now threatened. One resident of Prkos told me that what was most persuasive was General Dušan Pekić and General Pavle Jakšić, highly regarded Partisan military leaders from their region, aligning themselves with Belgrade and Knin.[11] Roknić was trying to avoid the worst, at least at the local level, until the last moment: At meetings with Croats in Lasinja—one meeting also took place in Banski Kovačevac—he proposed the establishment of joint guards and patrols, with one armed Croat and one armed Serb in each shift. Extremists on both sides blithely refused him. After forty-five years, Mata again withdrew into neutrality, convinced that nothing more could be done.

At that time a company of the National Guard Corps (ZNG) was encamped in Lasinja. Some of its members had behaved arrogantly and rudely toward Serbs from the neighboring villages. Feeling that a motley army of Territorial Defense Forces and paramilitary units was gathering in the Serbian villages, units of the ZNG dug trenches at the approaches to Prkos on September 29 and became engaged in the first exchange of gunfire, in the hamlet of Dobrići between Prkos and Crna Draga. No one was killed or wounded, but from that day on no one from Kovačevac approached Prkos. If someone had to go to Lasinja, they took a circuitous route, on the other side of the Kupa River. Some residents of Kovačevac were wisely cautious and shipped anything that was valuable to them to Šišljavić on the opposite side of the wide river.

Between September 29 and October 4 so many soldiers had gathered in Prkos, Sjeničak, and Dugo Selo that it was clear a major operation was in the offing. Light artillery also arrived in Prkos and was dug in on the hill facing Banski Kovačevac. However, no one from Prkos told the people in Banski Kovačevac that danger was threatening them. Obviously the people of Prkos were afraid such reports to Kovačevac might be considered treason, which in the terror that already reigned in Krajina meant putting your head on the chopping block.

* * *

As soon as the Yugoslav army occupied Banski Kovačevac on October 4, the wooden Church of Saint Peter was doused with gasoline and set afire before nightfall. It burned the entire night and into the next morning. No other fires were set because the abandoned homes had to be plundered. Danica and Mata were forbidden to leave their home or courtyard, but Mata saw an acquaintance from Sjeničak across the road with a tractor and trailer in front of the relatively prosperous home of a Kovačevac man who had been working in Germany for a time. He and an assistant calmly brought out the electric stove, the refrigerator, the television, and other items, loaded them onto the trailer, and drove off. They returned in the afternoon for the remaining spoils.

Mata was well-known and well-regarded in Sjeničak, where he had often worked as a carpenter until 1989. On the first morning of the occupation of Banski Kovačevac, a young soldier from Sjeničak visited Danica and Mata at their home, asked how they were, if they needed anything, and, as a sign of sympathy and attentiveness, brought them bread. He returned two or three more times, until one of his superiors put a stop to it. An eighteen-year-old boy from Sjeničak refused to carry out orders to round up abandoned cattle from the stalls and pastures and drive them to the quartermaster's depot of the Territorial Defense Forces. He could not, he said, participate in robbing neighbors with whom he so recently had attended school. And so, while some residents of Sjeničak did participate in the plundering of occupied Banski Kovačevac, many others avoided it and some even tried to help their Croatian neighbors.

While quite a few residents of Sjeničak roamed through Banski Kovačevac during this time, neither Mata nor Danica saw a single resident of Prkos. But Mata expected that if no one else his longtime collaborator and friend Roknić would come by. But Roknić didn't come by. Not even when the army was gathering in Prkos for the attack on Banski Kovačevac and Lasinja did he cross those six or seven hundred meters from his home to Mata's to warn his old friend to be careful. Mata never forgave him. However, I think that Mata was judging his friend too harshly. Prkos was only a microscopic part of a large invasion front dictated by authorities far higher than Roknić, using the Serbs in Croatia and leading them into arson, robbery, and war. In such circumstances, Roknić was unable to make any decision about Prkos, or even about his own family and himself. In contrast to some older residents of Prkos, he remained in Prkos, thinking he would be able to protect his ancestral property, his beautiful home, and his workshop, even if his children and grandchildren never returned from Zagreb and Pula.

Roknić didn't accept any arms when the rebel Serbs distributed abundant quantities to their supporters in the spring of 1991. He tried to the very end to achieve a truce, at least around his village and, if possible, in the entire region with his idea of mixed patrols. As a well-known conciliator and "peacemaker," he was under constant surveillance by the Krajina security services, who once carried out a thorough search of his home and workshop. (The Zagreb home of Roknić's son was also searched at about the same time.) Under the authority of the Republic of Serbian Krajina (RSK),[12] Roknić became a member of the welfare service for people who had fled war-torn areas and Croatian cities. He worked with Dmitar Obradović, the president of the Vrginmost district, and they quickly became friends. Obradović partially opposed the belligerent policies of Knin and tried to establish some degree of tolerance and compromise between the authorities of the Republic of Croatia and parts of the RSK. When he was ambushed and killed on July 4, 1992, by "unknown assailants" while leaving the town of Topusko, I don't think Roknić slept peacefully in Prkos.

Mata and Danica spent three days and two nights in occupied Banski Kovačevac. On the third day, a close boyhood friend, with whom Mata had served in the Royal Yugoslav Army in Gorski Kotar, came to visit from Sjeničak. He warned Mata to leave immediately: "They are planning to kill you because you have seen too much. You know who was plundering whose houses. They say you could testify against them."

This time Mata did not hesitate. That evening he and Danica left their home carrying nothing with them, not even a knapsack. Circling the long way around Kovačevac, they crossed the road at a suitable spot and before dawn they crossed the Kupa River near Selnica. By noon they were in Karlovac at the home of their eldest daughter and her husband, which is where they spent the next four years.

* * *

In the early spring of 1992, Mata and Danica's son-in-law drove them several times to the hamlet of Rožan Breg near Šišljavić, where the residents of Kovačevac watched the destruction of their village on the other side of the Kupa River. After the Church of Saint Peter was burned, there were no further burnings in Kovačevac for about five months. After Danica and Mata's escape and the departure of an elderly couple with the assistance of the Red Cross, only about twelve inhabitants remained in the village. They had decided to stay in their homes, come what may. Although almost the entire Croatian population of the cities and the majority of the villages of the SAO of Krajina had been forced out or had escaped from their homes (more than a hundred thousand refugees and displaced persons), the Krajina authorities didn't make any trouble for the handful of remaining inhabitants of Kovačevac until the spring of 1992. The abandoned homes were robbed, but the village passed the winter virtually intact, if eerily empty. Units of the Territorial Defense Forces of the SAO of Krajina (which from the beginning of 1992 would be known as the Army of the RSK) were quartered in several of the abandoned homes. They held positions on the right bank of the Kupa River, while the Croatian army settled on the left bank. From Karlovac to just outside the town of Sisak, the Kupa River had become the demarcation line.

In March 1992, the sounds of homes being blown up began to echo from Banski Kovačevac; barns and stalls burst into flame. These were weeks of great changes in the Krajina. Croatia was managing to defend itself militarily—it had obtained international recognition of its existing borders, and the Krajina leadership now began to fear that breaking away from Croatia would be more than difficult. They had also been betrayed by Milošević, when he summarily turned down their proposal to join the Krajina to the rump Yugoslavia, that is, Serbia, by constitutional means. Having forced the Krajina leadership to accept a truce under the peace plan negotiated by former U.S. Secretary of State Cyrus Vance, Milošević made it known that he was prepared to exchange Krajina for additional territory in Bosnia. In this critical situation many disagreements, strains, and divisions arose within the Krajina leadership. Separate chains of command also emerged—a prescription for anarchy. The original enthusiasm among the people symbolized by the slogan "All Serbs in one state" was suddenly evaporating. Optimism had dissolved into ever-increasing material privation and a sense of isolation from the rest of the world.

During this mood of frustration and resentment Banski Kovačevac was demolished in the spring of 1992. Empty houses that had until then been spared were destroyed, farm buildings disappeared in flames, and in a single night six of the twelve inhabitants of Kovačevac who had remained in their homes under the occupation were brutally murdered. The killers threw the bodies into a well. Several days later they pulled them out and took them away in a small truck. To this day, no one knows where they are. Because of the different stories that circulated about this crime, a tense situation has existed between Banski Kovačevac and Prkos for the last eleven years. In writing this story about the two villages I was permitted to review the records of the case at the police station in Karlovac. I am convinced that the investigation was conducted properly and in great detail, as I summarize below.

In the early spring of 1992, the Slatnjak Creek, which divides Banski Kovačevac in half, also served as the demarcation line for two "areas of responsibility" of the Serbian-Krajina army. The southern part of the village was the responsibility of the Eleventh Brigade, headquartered in Vojnić. The northern section was the responsibility of the Fourth Brigade, headquartered in Vrginmost (today known as Gvozd). The Third Platoon of the Fifth Company of the Third Battalion of the Vrginmost brigade was stationed in the northern part of Kovačevac. All of its soldiers and command personnel were from Slavsko Polje and the surrounding area. There wasn't a single resident of Prkos among them. One evening, a battalion security officer named Pane Bulat arrived at the company command post in Banski Kovačevac from battalion headquarters in Novo Selo Lasinjsko. He brought with him a quiet civilian dressed in black and another security officer with the same rank as Bulat. (Security officers in the Krajina army were officers or noncommissioned officers with special powers and were responsible for the intelligence services and security.) Bulat asked the platoon commander for five soldiers to help him take away several elderly Kovačevac inhabitants still living in the village. One soldier immediately volunteered, and the platoon commander ordered four others to help Bulat. According to Bulat's plan, the soldiers took six people from their homes: five women and one man. All six were elderly, between the ages of sixty-three and seventy-eight. Bulat sequestered them in the hamlet of Mihalići; in the courtyard of house number 8 he dismissed the soldiers, while he stayed behind with his two assistants to interrogate the prisoners.

The soldiers of the Third Platoon stated during the police investigation that after thirty to forty-five minutes they had heard brief but intense gunfire from an automatic rifle and a Skorpion submachine gun from the hamlet. Then after another fifteen minutes or so, Bulat's assistant—the civilian dressed in black—came for more soldiers, and the commander assigned another group to go to Mihalići. In the courtyard of the home of Zlatko Mihalić they encountered Bulat beside the six bodies. It was evident that the victims had been stripped naked and beaten before they were killed. Bulat ordered the bodies carried to a dried-up well and thrown in, then ordered the well destroyed with explosives. Parts of the bodies were still visible at the bottom of the well.

During their subsequent investigation, Karlovac police were not able to establish the exact date the crime was committed because the witness statements did not match. The record states that the murders were committed "on one of the nights between March 19 and 23, 1992." Motives for the crime likewise could not be established. Bulat's assistant, the civilian dressed in black, told the soldiers who threw the bodies into the well that it was revenge for 1941 because Bulat was from a village near Vrginmost where the Ustasha had killed his entire family. It has also been surmised that the motive might have been the announced arrival of a unit of UNPROFOR monitors who were to be stationed in Banski Kovačevac. Allegedly it had become necessary to cleanse Kovačevac of all witnesses. Indeed, in addition to the six people who were killed and thrown into the well, three other residents of Kovačevac had been killed in individual raids during that same period and three had been saved by friends from Sjeničak (they took them into their homes for three years, until after Operation Storm, the Croatian army's successful campaign to recover the Krajina in 1995). There were distinct differences in the conduct toward the Croatian population under Krajina authority: All of the above-described crimes were committed in the area monitored by the Vrginmost brigade, while there were no such crimes in the southern part of Banski Kovačevac, where Sjeničak, the Vojnić brigade, was stationed.

Some of the witnesses mentioned plundering as a motive for these crimes. Grgo Mihalić was well-to-do and was said to have saved up quite a few German marks. During the interrogations before the killings, Bulat had asked Mihalić to pay him 100,000 marks, or at least 70,000 or 80,000 to spare his life. Allegedly Mihalić handed over to Bulat all he had, barely 3,000 or 4,000 marks. Mihalić claimed that he was good friends with many Serbs from Prkos and that after the first Ustasha offensive in the spring of 1942 they had received first aid, food, and clothing from him (all of which was true), but it did nothing to dissuade Bulat.

Several days later, Milan Rabljenović, an inspector from the police station in Sjeničak, arrived in Banski Kovačevac to investigate the incident. His two brief reports were terse and objective. He saw the body parts at the bottom of the well and he drily noted the facts he obtained from soldiers of the local units. Bulat received Rabljenović in Banski Kovačevac on March 31 and angrily attacked him: "What are you doing in my region of responsibility? Get out of here and don't let me see you again!"

However, word of the crime had spread and Bulat's superiors ordered him to cover up all traces of it. In early April, Bulat drove a small truck to Banski Kovačevac and again sought the assistance of several soldiers from the local garrison. With much effort and many complications, the bodies were pulled out of the well and loaded onto the truck. With several of his trusted men he drove to an unknown destination.

Based on two reports on the murders in Banski Kovačevac by the police inspector, Milan Rabljenović, the SAO Krajina authorities launched an official investigation in May 1992. As far as is known, Pane Bulat was not questioned. When Croatia established control over the SAO Krajina after Operation Storm in the summer of 1995, the Karlovac police took over the case. Bulat and his collaborators were out of reach by then, having escaped to Serbia in the mass exodus of Croatian Serbs after Operation Storm, so the investigation concentrated on locating the site where the victims were buried. Some residents were closely questioned. After an intense interrogation, a confused Svetozar Bižić admitted that in April 1992, while hunting illegally with his neighbor Mirko Roknić in the nearby forest of Gusto Cerje, he may have seen bodies of the victims from Banski Kovačevac. Next to the forest road about one kilometer from the village they had come across a large open box used in harvesting, which poorly concealed several bodies. When Bižić and Roknić returned to the same spot, the bodies and the box were no longer there. The investigators found the address of Roknić, who had left Croatia after 1995. During a subsequent telephone conversation with the investigators, he agreed to make a statement that basically corroborated Bižić's. The graves of the six victims from the Kovačevac hamlet of Mihalići have never been found.

I obtained unofficial information from Croatian agencies responsible for these matters that during the existence of the RSK, 700 Croatian civilians were killed outside of military operations, out of a total of about 8,000—the number that remained living in the area after the persecutions and the fleeing of refugees. In *Srpska pobuna u Hrvatskoj 1990–1995* (The Serbian Rebellion in Croatia, 1990–1995), by Nikica Barić,[13] I gathered that from January 1, 1992, to September 30, 1994, the Krajina Ministry of Internal Affairs documented 440 criminal acts of murder in which 573 people—305 Serbs and 268 Croats and members of other non-Serb nationalities—were killed. For 195 of the Croats and members of other non-Serb nationalities the person or persons who committed the murders were never found. The Krajina police filed murder charges with the prosecutor against 306 people, but they kept no record of how many of these people were brought to trial and punished.

The number of Croats killed was, of course, higher than the 268 cited in the book. I believe that the number was closer to 700 because the information from Knin doesn't cover the entire period of the war, nor does it include killings that were covered up or were not officially registered. Radovan Jović, the judge of the district court of Glina, spoke about this at a meeting of prominent intellectuals of Glina on June 26, 1992. He concluded that the "Serbian people after the war must ask the forgiveness of Croats for the evil deeds they have committed against them."[14] While preparing this book, I spoke with Jović about the general conditions in the RSK at the time. According to the laws of the RSK, Serbs and Croats were equal citizens and were jointly protected by government institutions. In Jović's opinion a fair number of officials in the judicial bodies of the RSK would have been prepared to carry out such laws, but they were obstructed either because the criminal charges filed had insufficient proof for an indictment or because such procedures were halted by a variety of pressures and manipulations by higher authorities. The judiciary and the police were incapable of preventing atrocities by Serbian paramilitary units against the Serbian population, let alone the RSK's Croatian inhabitants.

Jović assisted in the investigation at Joševica near Glina, where on

December 16, 1991, one of the most serious crimes against Croatian civilians was committed. At one thirty in the afternoon a group of soldiers in camouflage uniforms attacked the village and killed nineteen women and men, including four children between the ages of ten and sixteen. The Serbs justified the crime as a reprisal for a raid by the Croatian army on the night of December 12 in Graćanica along the Kupa River that killed nineteen soldiers of the Territorial Defense Forces of the SAO of Krajina. Evidence of the crime reliably pointed to a reconnaissance-commando unit of the Territorial Defense Forces and to the Glina paramilitary unit of Siniša Martić, which for a long time had been beyond the control of both civilian and military authorities. Because of pressure "from above," further investigation of the crime at Joševica was removed from the district court in Glina and entrusted to the headquarters of the Territorial Defense Forces for the district of Glina. After a one-month investigation, Dušan Jović, the president of the Wartime Presidency of the Assembly of the District of Glina, issued a report that claimed that "a commando group of about ten men from the Ustasha forces of Croatia committed the horrible act" in Joševica. The report also stated that the "act qualified as a loathsome Ustasha-fascist deception against the Serbian people."

Further investigation into the crime at Joševica was blocked and members of the reconnaissance-commando group that was widely suspected of committing it were sent to Pančevo, outside of Belgrade, for additional military training. Under these circumstances it is no wonder that neither Bulat nor any other perpetrators were tried in the Krajina. Without the assignment of individual guilt, a collectively formed distrust and suspicion between Serbs and Croats in the Krajina spread. This distrust and suspicion deepened yet again, under similar circumstances and in the same area, after Operation Storm, but this time it would be the Croats attacking the Serbs.

* * *

A week after the end of Operation Storm, I was standing with Mata above the exposed foundations of his house in Banski Kovačevac. The barn and another large farm building had been burned down, but there was no trace of a fire where the house once stood. Someone had skillfully taken apart the well-built wooden house and carried off the timber to an unknown destination. In all likelihood, the house had experienced an unusual fate: It may have been rebuilt someplace far away in the Krajina where no one would know it as the house of Mata Đerek from Banski Kovačevac. The burning of Serbian villages in the Krajina in the wake of Operation Storm soon followed. Thus Mata's house was robbed, dismantled, and carried away by one army and likely burned by another.

Of the 119 houses in Banski Kovačevac before the war, only two remained more or less intact since they had been used by UNPROFOR peacekeepers. Everything built of wood in the village, including the church, no longer existed: It had all disappeared in flames or had been carried off, like Mata's house. All that remained of the former brick houses were pieces protruding out of the ground like jagged teeth, no roofs, windows, or doors. No one had moved back yet, but people were returning from their exile to check the situation and to clean up around their homes. The large field leading toward the Kupa River couldn't be tilled because signs had been posted warning of dangerous mines. In any case, there were no crops as for four years no one had either plowed or sown the fields. Someone told Mata that his tractor had been seen in Tesla's orchard in Lasinjski Sjeničak. With my Renault 4 we drove to Tesla's nearby hamlet and, indeed, Mata's tractor was in the orchard, totally stripped. Mata thought that Tesla, fleeing before "Operation Storm," had tried to start the tractor but didn't succeed. He removed everything useful from it and disappeared east.

Lasinjski Sjeničak was a ghost town. Below the town, around

Križ, there were freshly scorched houses. Along the road to Kovačevac, the houses were still there but not a living soul was in them. My curiosity made me take a peek into a small, beautiful brick house, its door wide open. There were randomly placed plates on the kitchen table, neatly arranged pots on the stove, scattered papers on the kitchen sideboard. It was as if someone had been living there until that morning, then hurriedly fled. Two Croatian military policemen suddenly appeared next to our car and asked what we were doing there. They checked our documents, heard us out, then told us they had orders to prevent plundering, but that they turned a blind eye to it. "In any event," they said, "this will all be ours because any Serb who doesn't return within thirty days loses his home and property." (Indeed, in the first days after Operation Storm, the Croatian government passed this law, which was quickly repealed at I don't know whose intervention.) On the return to Kovačevac we met a man on a tractor who was from the torched village of Kablar. In reply to Mata's question, he said with a roguish smile, "I'm off to look for my belongings and if I can't find mine, I'll take somebody else's!"

Mata told me about his plans: He would build a brick house on the foundations of his wooden house and his children, grandchildren, and sons-in-law would help. It would be a weekend home for them after Danica and he were gone. But first he intended to repair the big barn. This could be finished quickly and would provide a small temporary living area for Danica and him until the brick house was completed. I felt this was the moment for me to repay Mata and his family for what he, Jaga, Jana, and Draga had done for my family and me in 1941, so I suggested that our family company, Novi Liber, cover the cost of the materials. Mata transported the materials himself from the sawmill in Krašić, Novi Liber paid the bill, and then the authorities levied a 25 percent tax on the purchase price of the goods. We protested the tax, explaining that this transaction was assistance for victims of the war in the liberated areas, but the authorities maintained that such assistance is provided by the government, and that private individuals had to pay a tax—otherwise no one would be able to determine whom they were helping and why. Faced with the possibility that money might be laundered in small amounts, the government was being exceptionally cautious, even as it helped certain individuals launder money in far larger amounts.

In those days, my son, Ivo, and I traveled to Kordun and Banija almost every weekend. Along the main road we saw gasoline stations, public buildings, inns, and cooperative markets that had been systematically destroyed, while houses in the scattered villages were usually abandoned but still intact, as in Sjeničak. The plundering in the deserted Serbian villages had only just begun. Week by week the plundering and the arson increased in frequency and scope. On one such Saturday in September, Timothy Garton Ash asked if he might join us. I had published the Croatian edition of his well-known book, *We the People: The Revolution of '89 Witnessed in Warsaw, Budapest, Berlin, and Prague.*[15] Since Ivo and I admired him as a brilliant writer and historian, as someone exceptionally well-informed about the countries in transition, we gladly took him with us. In the chapter entitled "Cleansed Croatia" in his book *History of the Present*,[16] he described in five pages our Saturday excursion to Banski Kovačevac and Glina, an excerpt of which I provide below:

> With Slavko, his son Ivo, and Planinka[17] packed into a sputtering Renault 4, we drive south from Zagreb to the Krajina, under Serb rule for nearly four years but now "liberated" by the Croatian army in "Operation Storm." At Karlovac, where Slavko lived as a boy, we visit the marketplace bombed by the besieging Serb forces. Look, here's the mark of the mortar bomb on the pavement; that's where the shoppers died.

On the way out of town, we pick up Mate, an elderly Croat farmer who hid Slavko in his village during the war (the last war, that is), when the Ustasha—the Croat fascists—were rounding up the Jews of Karlovac.... The old man has a broad, nut-brown face, a ready smile beneath a cloth cap, and quiet dignity.

Leaving Karlovac, we cross what for the last four years was the Serb front line. Suddenly, all the houses are roofless, scorched, plundered, or simply reduced to rubble.... In the Croat villages, almost every house has been plundered and had the roof burned or blown out by the occupying Serbs. Here and there, we see Croats returning to their houses, starting over, with the checkerboard flag of Croatia flying from the balcony. But for the most part the villages are still deserted.... Mate and Slavko [introduce us to] a thickset farmer, grinning from ear to ear. He is a Serb, married to a Croat, and during the Serb occupation he protected the houses of his Croat neighbors. We can see their roofs along the skyline of a nearby hill, miracles of intactness. Now, we are told, he is a hero to the local Croats. But he does seem desperately eager to please. Fear lines his smile.

Mate's village, Kovačevac, has hardly a house intact. He leads us through some long grass to an area of rubble and twisted metal: all that is left of an eighteenth-century wooden church, a fine and rare example of its kind. Planinka picks up a small piece of twisted bronze and turns it over. It is beautiful. I feel that she would love to place it on her studio table. But then she puts it back. After all, she, too, is a Serb....

We drive through more eerily empty villages... to the town of Glina, scene of another Ustasha massacre during the Second World War. Here, Serbs from the local area were told they would be spared if they converted to Roman Catholicism. They marched, singing, along the road into Glina. Then they were herded into the Orthodox Church and massacred.

Today, this is a ghost town. The Croats fled in 1991; now the Serbs have fled, too, while most of the Croats have yet to return. However, the Croat administration has started the work of reconstruction by converting a memorial pavilion to the victims of the Ustasha massacre into a "Croat House." They have removed the marble tablets bearing the names of the Serb victims, raised the checkerboard flag, and held a liberation concert to inaugurate this Croat cultural institute. Western civilization has triumphed.

From Lasinja to Glina and from Glina to Petrinja we drove through the mute rows of demolished and burned-out houses on either side of the road. Ivo and I divided them into "old burnings" (from 1991) and "new burnings" (from 1995). The numbers were roughly equal: up to Glina there were more "new" charred remains, after Glina there were more "old" ones.

* * *

During Operation Storm not a single house in Prkos was burned, but the village was almost completely deserted. About 130 residents of Prkos, including Vaso Roknić, left in the stream of Krajina refugees on the road to Serbia. His younger brother, Milan, remained in the village with his bedridden wife and seventeen other people, mostly women, who didn't want to join the exodus. One Sunday, about a month after Operation Storm, we were traveling through the villages on the right bank of the Kupa River and we visited Milan at his home. He had managed the cooperative market of Prkos-Banski Kovačevac for most of his working life. When the tractor convoy for the mass flight of Krajina Serbs was hurriedly formed on August 6, Milan decided he wasn't going anywhere.

The Krajina army had abandoned its positions along the Kupa River and withdrawn through Prkos to Lasinja and Vrginmost. The approaching detonations signaled the advance of the Croatian army from Karlovac. The news on the radio and television confirmed the defeat of the RSK. Many in Prkos were gripped by panic: *The Ustasha are coming, 1941 is returning.* They quickly loaded everything they could onto trailers pulled by tractors, with the assistance and under the supervision of the army. "In 1941, I escaped in my slippers through the snow, at least now I am riding on a tractor," one elderly resident joked bitterly. But a Krajina military officer consoled him by saying that all this was only temporary, that the army would be coming from Serbia and the RSK restored.

Some residents of Prkos wavered until the last minute: If their children, sisters, or brothers had survived for five years in Zagreb under Croatian authority, why would they not survive, too? They would gladly crawl into a mousehole until the storm had passed, then greet their children, sisters, or brothers from Zagreb at home in Prkos. The soldiers were impatiently rushing them and the majority of the residents fell under the spell of the general psychosis, becoming part of an endlessly long column of about 150,000 people who were abandoning their homes.

Milan shut himself in his home with his wife, sealed the doors and windows, and listened attentively to the departure of one army and the arrival of another. When he finally dared to go into his courtyard after two days, a Croatian patrol caught sight of him and surrounded him, their rifles at the ready. Milan was the first Serbian man the Croatian army had encountered in Prkos. With crude threats and jabbing him in the back with their rifle barrels, the soldiers questioned Milan in the courtyard, until a soldier appeared from the neighboring village of Novo Selo Lasinjsko and recognized Milan and saved him. Nevertheless, the army requisitioned his tractor. It was returned to him twelve days later, still in working order. From then on, no one laid a finger on Milan; he lived in his house in peaceful retirement caring for his bedridden wife.

Milan's older brother, Vaso, joined the convoy to Serbia on August 6, 1995, while his wife, Milena, stayed behind in Prkos. Their parting was a real drama. Another retired colonel named Vaso Roknić also lived somewhere in the Krajina. He had been mentioned two or three times in the Croatian press in an unflattering light. He had in some way been involved in discrimination against the local Croatian population, which could not be said for our Vaso. Our Vaso, the Vaso Roknić from Prkos, a sober and wise man, had very early on realized that the RSK, such as it was, would not last. When he saw the military forces of the RSK fall before the onslaught of the Croatian army on August 5 without firing a shot, Vaso became concerned that as a former Yugoslav People's Army colonel he might be killed in the inevitable initial chaos. Perhaps someone would rashly confuse him with that other Colonel Vaso Roknić? Thus, Vaso decided to join the refugees, even though his wife refused to go with him. Vaso's requests, urgings, and exhortations could not dissuade her—Milena remained intransigent. Their family and close friends liked to say that though Vaso was a colonel in the army, Milena was the general of the house. She was indeed a woman with a strong will and personality. Vaso was on the tractor without her as she waited for her daughter from Pula and her son from Zagreb to hurry home in the wake of the army.

The Serbian authorities resettled the majority of Prkos refugees in Kosovo to bolster the numbers of the Serbian population there. No one from Prkos approved of this and sooner or later they all left. Vaso avoided transfer to Kosovo by taking refuge first with relatives in Vojvodina and then in a friend's isolated weekend house on Fruška Gora in eastern Serbia. At the beginning of 1998, his son, Ljubinko, from Zagreb brought him back to Prkos and Milena. About forty other residents, mostly older people, returned around the same time. Younger people adjusted to the new circumstances and settled into a new life in Serbia. The majority found jobs or started their own businesses. With the further normalization of relations between Croatia and Serbia, some former inhabitants of Prkos were happy to restore relations with their native village and from time to time visited it. Some will never return as they were involved in the plundering of Croatian villages or in some other questionable actions during the time of RSK rule in the early 1990s.

Among the last to return was the innkeeper Stevo Korać with his wife, Anđelija. He died soon after. When the tractor convoy of Serbian refugees passed through the Croatian town of Sisak after Operation Storm on August 7, the residents of Sisak lined some of the town's streets to hurl insults and abuse at the refugees. Some threw stones, one of which hit Korać in the head. The injury never healed and his health coninued to deteriorate. When his condition became critical, Anđelija brought him back to Croatia so that he might die at home.

The neighboring Serbian villages of northern Kordun suffered more than Prkos during and after Operation Storm. Not a single life was lost in Prkos after Operation Storm. In its first onslaught the Croatian army vandalized the memorial park and plundered the cooperative store, the inn, and some abandoned houses. A young man, originally from Banski Kovačevac and now living in Germany, set fire to seven farm buildings and homes about ten days after Operation Storm, but the military police stopped him and expelled him from the village. They did not arrest or charge him, but they did act decisively against reprisal burnings. A military police unit stationed in Prkos for the first six months after Operation Storm behaved correctly and villagers maintain that it deserves most of the credit for the absence of any greater evil. Young military policemen helped older women chop wood and, when necessary, provided transportation for them, and the village reciprocated with warm milk, cheese, and whatever else was available. The policemen that replaced this unit in Prkos were completely different: they were arrogant and didn't hesitate to rob or engage in petty theft.

The destruction in 1995 in Sjeničak, Dugo Selo, Čremušnica, Bović, and other Serbian villages in the surrounding area was much greater than in Prkos. According to information provided by the Croatian Helsinki Committee, more than 26,000 homes were destroyed or made uninhabitable by fire or bombing and 760 civilians of Serbian nationality were killed after the end of the military operations in the area of the failed RSK. For too long the Croatian government of the time tolerated the reign of terror that ravaged the Krajina for months and now a different government has paid the price for it—from the International Criminal Tribunal in The Hague to the heavy burdens on its annual budgets.

Thanks to its industrious people and government assistance, Banski Kovačevac raised itself from the rubble surprising quickly. Two or three years after Operation Storm, larger and better houses had sprung up on the sites of the previous homes. In place of his wooden house, Mata had built a modest brick home for Danica and himself. When I first visited them there, I was happy to see its solid construction and all of its modern appliances, but I was taken aback when Danica served the milk for my coffee from a carton. In a village that for me remained a symbol of beautiful pastures and fat cows that milled around the property, there was now not a single cow in sight. When Mata returned to the village, he was eighty years old and Danica was seventy-five, and the other people who returned were about the same age. They had neither the strength nor the will to restore the local agriculture or to raise stock. They were satisfied with cultivating their private plots. Only later did five young families with children move back from the city, restoring a sense of life to the village. Three households now raised two or three cows each and it was possible to get fresh milk in the village again. Every working day a school bus would pick up five or six children and drive them to the elementary school in Lasinja and back home. The three or four high-school students made their own arrangements to commute to school in Karlovac.

During the week, Banski Kovačevac is strangely deserted; where there were 119 households before the war, in 2006 there were close to 100 spacious, new country homes. Only on weekends did the village revive. The owners, young people from Kovačevac who lived and worked in the cities, would come by car to enjoy their homes and gardens. The fields remained uncultivated, overgrown with brambles and tall grasses, and in the former pastures and on the picturesque hills young forests were spreading and encroaching into the village. If this situation were to continue, Kovačevac would survive perhaps only as a weekend retreat with no local population. In the ten years after Operation Storm, twenty returnees died, all of them elderly people, among them Mata and Danica in the summer of 2005. In 2006, Kovačevac had ninety-two residents, only one-quarter of whom were under sixty.

It is not much different in neighboring Prkos, which has seventy inhabitants and even fewer children than Kovačevac. Only one boy was to attend the elementary school in Lasinja, but his mother was afraid that the other children would pick on her son, the only Serbian child in the class, so she chose to move to Karlovac and send him to school there. As with Kovačevac, Prkos revives on weekends in the summer months because the young people of the village return, some of them with their children. In contrast to Kovačevac, there are far fewer renovated homes and considerably more dilapidated ones. However, in the summer of 2006, people from Zagreb started to buy up the abandoned houses and land. In one hamlet alone three houses and their gardens and fields were purchased at virtually the same time. One family moved in immediately and began to farm; the other two families used the houses exclusively as weekend residences, but they have considered starting businesses. Other interested buyers are cropping up and the prices of housing and land have noticeably increased.

At the same time processed-food manufacturers and large commercial enterprises need more farms to supply ingredients. Perhaps this area will not become a complete wasteland: the scenery is quite beautiful, the unused gardens and pastures are rich, and it is only a thirty-minute drive to Karlovac and a forty-five-minute drive to Zagreb.

* * *

Immediately upon their return to Kovačevac, the families of the six people whose bodies were thrown into the well wanted to bury the remains in a common grave in the Kovačevac cemetery. An investigation was launched to try to locate the burial site, but yielded no results. Nothing could be learned from the residents of Prkos—each claimed they knew nothing about its location. The families of the victims didn't believe them, and all of Kovačevac shared this suspicion. The division hardened into one of village against village and, ultimately, into Croat against Serb.

And so we are again in the year 1941. After Operation Storm, the people of Banski Kovačevac and Prkos never tried to sit at the same table and calmly and openly, in the spirit of their former friendship, discuss the unreconciled accounts from 1991 and 1995, or even those from 1941 and 1945. Perhaps Vaso Roknić should have taken a step in this direction when he returned to Prkos in the spring of 1998. Among the few village residents, he was the only one with the unspoken authority to conduct such discussions. Perhaps he should have gone to his old friend Mata Đerek and started with him, face-to-face.

But how would he explain to Mata the burning and plundering of Banski Kovačevac and the rest of the insanity in the summer and fall of 1991? How would he explain why no one from Prkos, not even Roknić himself, tried to help the people of Kovačevac?

In the summer of 1998, Jandra Jakin accidentally ran into Roknić on the banks of the Kupa River between their two villages. They were alone, in the solitude of the riverbank. Conversation could not be avoided. The talkative Jakin wasn't one to beat around the bush and, after a slight pause, got straight to the point: "Vaso, everyone in Prkos listens to you, as do many people beyond Prkos. Why didn't you tell them not to act like lunatics? Why did they have to destroy the houses in Kovačevac? To kill old women?" Roknić replied a bit vaguely, wanting to avoid a longer conversation: "It was anger, rage, barbarity. It's easy to incite uneducated poor people when you tell them that they may plunder and go wild and that it is a justifiable revenge for '41. But I can tell you one thing, Jandra: My people did not kill anyone in Kovačevac and they did not hide the bodies from the well."

I think that "anger, rage, barbarity" is a rather accurate explanation for the wild attacks on Croatian villages in the fall of 1991, but they do not explain Roknić's silence in the first days of the autumn of that year. Perhaps the courageous old soldier had finally become frightened and withdrawn when he met the real-life invasion of "anger, rage, barbarity."

When Roknić returned to Prkos from exile, with several of his neighbors he restored the memorial park as much as was possible. During Operation Storm, the busts of the four famous Prkos residents that circled the small park had been decapitated. The mausoleum had been riddled with stray bullets. After 1998, the park was carefully maintained; the damaged inscription on the mausoleum, dedicated to the victims of Prkos in December 1941, was repaired.

On the anniversary of the massacre and on some holidays candles are lit and wreaths and flowers laid.

In 1998, Roknić restored the tradition of annual commemorations every December 21. In the first few years only about fifty to one hundred people, mostly from Prkos, would gather there. Year by year, the number of participants grew, so that now former members of the Union of Fighters (a World War II veterans' organization) and other antifascists from Zagreb and Karlovac and delegations from other places regularly attend. In 2005, an emissary of the president of the Republic of Croatia was present and laid a wreath. However, not a single person from Banski Kovačevac ever attended one of these commemorations, nor did anyone from the district headquarters of Lasinja, to which Prkos belongs.

The boycott had expanded and now even included the dead.

At the commemoration on December 21, 2001, the sixtieth anni-

A view of the Kupa River and Pokuplje from Prkos, photographed from the garden of Vaso Roknić by his son, Ljubinko

versary of the massacre, I attempted to break the ice between the two neighboring villages. I tried to arrange for Mata with four or five other residents of Kovačevac to come to the ceremony in Prkos and lay a wreath for the victims of the crime in 1941, and for Roknić to come immediately after with several of his people to lay a wreath for those killed during the Krajina occupation in 1992. Mata agreed reluctantly and only after I persisted. He would not go alone, he said, and it would not be easy to get neighbors to join him, but he would try. Roknić hesitated less and was in complete agreement but with a word of warning: "It will all work smoothly if they first come to Prkos and not insist that we first go to them in Kovačevac. Our victims were first and there were fifty times more of them."

When I stopped first at Kovačevac that day, Mata told me with much discomfort that he had been unable to get anyone to join him and that he would not go alone. People are saying, Mata explained to me, that they will go to Prkos, and to the commemoration, only when the people of Prkos reveal the location of the burial site of the Kovačevac victims from 1992.

This came as no surprise to Roknić. He shrugged, and the two of us proceeded to the commemoration. I had been announced as a speaker and I made my speech, which was intended as an announcement of the reconciliation between the two villages but instead turned into the conventional expression of piety for the victims of December 21, 1941, in Prkos. Somewhat vaguely, I added that I hoped commemorations in the years to come, at this same spot, might serve to reconcile the living.

Among our other failures, it is obvious that for too long we memorialized only the victims we consider to be ours and for too long we have been silent about the victims of the other side. Now it is all swinging, like a pendulum, in an equally offensive or more offensive manner. In the center of Lasinja, opposite the church, a richly adorned monument was erected in 2005 with the following inscription: "An eternal monument to the innocent Croatian martyrs of the Second World War and the postwar period, victims of the communist government and Partisan-Chetnik units in the period of 1941–1949." At the dedication on Saint Anthony's Day in 2006, the military bishop Monsignor Juraj dedicated a monument inscribed with the names, and dates of birth and death, of 206 victims from the area of today's district of Lasinja. The authorities in the district of Lasinja should change the inscription on the monument because it contains several crude mistakes and untruths, the most egregious being:

1. The monument lists the names of nineteen people from Lasinja who were killed during the German bombardment of the town on March 9, 1944; therefore they were not victims of the communist authorities.
2. The monument lists the names of several local Ustasha officials, war criminals who cannot be included among the "innocent victims" since on December 21, 1941, they participated in

> the Ustasha operation for the mass murder of the civilian Serbian population of the district of Lasinja and the surrounding villages.
> 3. During the Second World War, there were no Chetnik units or "Partisan-Chetnik" units in the district of Lasinja and the neighboring districts, so the text inscribed on the monument about such units is a pure fabrication.

And finally, one general comment: Today's district of Lasinja includes only two Serbian villages: Sjeničak and Prkos. During the Second World War, between 600 and 700 civilian inhabitants of these two villages and more than 100 members of the Partisan army were killed. During the same war and in the immediate postwar period, about 150 civilian residents of Lasinja and the Croatian villages in the Lasinja district were killed and several dozens more were killed in the ranks of the Home Guard and the Partisan and Ustasha armies. The war ended for these victims a long time ago. Is it not time that we stop commemorating them separately and in opposition to each other? They are not all equal victims nor are they all equal criminals, but we should stop trying to use our victims in provocations, we should establish who the criminals were and single them out from all collective entities: villages, movements, and peoples alike.

I will cite only one more example, for now still rare but encouraging nonetheless. In the town of Novska in 2005, a book was published that, unfortunately, has received scant attention: *Žrtve Drugoga svjetskoga rata i poraća na području bivše općine Novska* (Victims of the Second World War and the Postwar Period in the Area of the Former District of Novska), by Alojz Buljan and Franjo Horvat.[18] On the basis of detailed research and in more than eight hundred pages, the authors have tried to describe, factually and objectively, the general conditions and events in each village and settlement and then to list the names of all of the victims, with information about the date of birth, nationality, and date and place of death with comments about who killed them and why. There is no discrimination or priority: Croats, Serbs, and Roma are recorded, along with members of another ten nationalities, with clearly marked attempts to correct the exaggerations, deceptions, and other shortcomings of previous estimates and publications. In summary, and to my knowledge the most objective publication until now, the authors have listed 4,078 victims in the column "Victims of Fascism" and 1,581 victims in the column "Victims of Communism (the Second World War and the Postwar Period)." By nationality, 3,376 victims were Serbs, 1,811 were Croats, and 472 were other nationalities—a fair indication, to my mind, of the actual numbers of victims of the Second World War and the postwar period in one district in today's Croatia.

* * *

Mata died in July 2005. Only a month later Danica also died. In November 2005, Roknić died, followed only six days later by Milena. With their passing, my story about the two villages ends, a story for which my generation did not find the way to a happy ending. I am afraid that the burial site of the six people killed in Kovačevac will never be found and that the older inhabitants in both villages will no longer have either the will or the time to resolve their quarrel. However, neither Prkos nor Banski Kovačevac will disappear with the departed. The world of the near future will suffocate if it does not protect its lungs—the healthy rural areas like the ones on the right bank of the Kupa River. I hope the new residents of Prkos and Banski Kovačevac will not repeat this story, as we repeated 1941 and 1945 in 1991 and in 1995.

19

Kraljevica and the Partisans

WHEN I REACHED my mother in Kraljevica a few days before Christmas in 1941, she was already comfortably settled in this beautiful small coastal town. She had rented two rooms on the first floor of a small family home in an area known as Vrtić. The owner, Mrs. Pravdica, lived alone on the ground floor—the war had broken out while her husband, a sailor, was overseas and he never returned. They didn't have children.

The next day my mother took me to the local Italian carabinieri station. In her strange mixture of Italian, Croatian, and German she explained to the sergeant major on duty, whom she obviously knew, that according to this-and-that regulation she was allowed to bring her underage son to Kraljevica on her residence permit. The sergeant major looked at my travel papers and some of my mother's papers, and without further ado I was granted a residence permit for thirty days.

There were about two hundred Jews in Kraljevica, refugees from the territory of the Independent State of Croatia (NDH) controlled by the Ustasha authorities; in Crikvenica there were three or four times that number. Although this part of the Croatian coast nominally belonged to the NDH, all authority had been in the hands of the Italian occupation forces (Zone B) since the beginning of September. The Ustasha NDH was not permitted to keep either its army or its police on this territory. Indeed, there was a district administration that acted as an organ of the NDH, but its authority was confined to a land office, a registrar's office, and other administrative services. Only the Italian occupation authorities were responsible for any security issues, including the supervision of refugees. At the beginning, the Italians grudgingly issued residence permits to refugees and returned some of them to areas under Ustasha control. By August, they had changed the policy: In their territories they curbed the Ustasha persecutions of Serbs and were a little more tolerant toward Jewish and other refugees who had escaped Ustasha persecution. The Jews were under constant surveillance in Kraljevica: They had to report once a week to the carabinieri station; they had to renew their residence permits every month; and at first they were not permitted to travel without special permission.

It is difficult to describe the Italians occupiers as unambiguously "good," "bad," "gentle," or "brutal." Massed into an army, they were frequently merciless; in raids against the Partisans they ruthlessly set fire to entire villages; they sent whole families to jail or to camps; they also executed people for the most innocent collaboration with the Partisans and sometimes executed hostages. At the same time, as individuals—with the exception of the Blackshirts—many of the officers and soldiers could be cordial and willing to help. Some units adopted and cared for Serbian children who had been orphaned by the Ustasha massacres. From documents released after the war, we have learned that from the fall of 1941 until the summer of 1943, the Ustasha authorities, and then the Nazi representatives, persistently demanded that Jews being sheltered in the northern Croatian coastal regions and Dalmatia be handed over to them, which the Italian military command skillfully avoided, thereby saving many lives.

During the two months my mother spent in Kraljevica before my arrival, she became close with several local people: Dorica Švrljuga, the matron of a reputable old family, was a friend; my mother was frequently invited to the Villa Carevo, the home of Ivan Kosić and his family; but most important was her old acquaintance, from the Karlovac days, with Branka Šantić. Before the war Branka had been a maid in the home of a Karlovac industrialist. She had become friends with our Jaga through the United Workers' Union and sometimes dropped by to see us at home. She married Marko Šantić, a housepainter, and when Branka became pregnant, they moved to Kraljevica. They lived with Branka's mother in the family home, which had a well-maintained garden. By the time my mother arrived in Kraljevica at the end of October, Branka had given birth to a daughter, Ljiljana, but her husband was no longer at home. An ardent United Workers' Union activist—he had probably become a member of the Communist Party while still in Karlovac—Šantić had organized a group of sympathizers among the workers of the Kraljevica shipyard at the beginning of 1941. I don't know how the Italian occupation authorities discovered their group. The military tribunal in Rijeka sentenced five of them to prison terms of ten to twenty years. After a year, Branka received news that her husband had died in prison, somewhere far away in Italy.

Through Branka my mother got in touch with some of Šantić's friends, Partisan sympathizers and perhaps already collaborators. By the time I arrived in Kraljevica, my mother was closely connected with these people, making her the first of the Jewish refugees in Kraljevica to join the organized activities to assist the Partisans.

At the end of 1941 and the beginning of 1942, I think the majority of Kraljevica residents were silent Partisan sympathizers. Several young locals had been mobilized into the Home Guard, but not a single person was in the Ustasha army. The Italians enjoyed no sympathy as occupiers. The people along the coast could not forgive them the annexation of Sušak, Bakar, the islands of the Gulf of Kvarner, and the occupation of the entire Croatian coast. In Bribir, Hreljin, Križišće, and the region around Vinodol collaboration with the Partisans was virtually public; Partisan emissaries were visiting these places in broad daylight. But in the coastal towns, where there were strong Italian garrisons, active support for the Partisans developed clandestinely.

The local population of Kraljevica treated Jewish refugees correctly—some were a bit restrained and some friendly, with openly expressed compassion for the unjustly persecuted. During my four-month residence in Kraljevica, I never experienced animosity for the Jews from the locals and I don't remember a single anti-Semitic incident.

In the total absence of tourism, which for half a century had been an important source of income for Kraljevica, the Jewish refugees were unexpected guests. They filled the small hotels and pensions on the Oštro peninsula, and they rented rooms in family homes. Mima, a large restaurant on the coast, was always filled with Jewish guests who used it as their social center—here they met, drank tea and coffee, played chess, and some even regularly lunched. Many Jewish refugees ate their meals with their host families. Close friendships were develped that lasted well beyond the war. Such was our friendship with Tonica Jakovčić and her daughter, Branka, and granddaughter, Ljiljana. My wife, Vera, and son, Ivo, spent the entire summer in both 1959 and 1960 with Grandma Tonica in Kraljevica after Branka had remarried and moved to Kostrena and Ljiljana was working in Rijeka. We continued visiting her until the late 1960s, when death took her and the house at Vrtić No. 9 became sadly empty.

In their spare time, Jewish refugees in Kraljevica met, confided, conspired, and gossiped, always talking about the same topics: what was happening on the faraway battlefields and what would happen to them. I remember how Mr. Bijelić, formerly Weiss, the father of my friend Beni, once told me in confidence that the Chetnik commander Draža Mihailović and the Partisan commander Rus Lebedev[1] had met at the top of Mount Romanija and concluded an alliance against the Ustasha and the Germans, but they would no longer wage war against the Italians—which, of course, as the joke went, was good for us Jews.

My mother kept company with several Jewish refugee families and became close friends with Šarlota-Lolika Robiček, a graduate chemistry student and the daughter of the former director of the Zagreb brewery. The Robičeks lived with Marija and Kosta Pribilović, where we also ate our meals. Before or after lunch, Lolika and my mother always chatted for a few minutes alone and so Lolika became the first of the Jewish refugees in Kraljevica to join my mother in working with the Partisans.

My mother was also always happy to see Ančica Čerić and her husband, the painter Vili Čerić, and she would walk with them along the road to Fara, the open sea on one side and Mount Učka on the other. She often visited Mrs. Gottlieb and her husband, Hinko, a lawyer, the respected editor of Jewish magazines, and the most successful Croatian translator of Heinrich Heine's poetry. The Gottliebs' eldest son, Vlado, lived with them in Kraljevica. He called me Mustafa, probably after the main character in the classic Russian film *The Road to Life*. A brilliant graduate student in chemistry and a well-known chessmaster, he taught me nearly the entire course of high-school mathematics in four months. Their younger son, Danko, was among the 180 young Jewish boys from Zagreb taken to Jadovno. My mother and the Gottliebs shared one subject that they spoke little about but which was always on their minds: the fate of our people at Jadovno. In conversations with Mr. Gottlieb, and still more in his silences, one could feel a barely stifled pain, mixed with rare surges of false hope. Mrs. Gottlieb and my mother were more realistic: They understood that all hope was lost, but they still dared not say so.

After the war I learned the fate of the Gottliebs. They were interned in Italian camps for Jews, first in Kraljevica and then on the island of Rab. In both camps Hinko Gottlieb had been an influential member of various camp committees and a leading representative of the inmates in negotiations with the camp authorities. In September 1943, they somehow managed to reach the liberated territory of Italy and all three started to work at the Yugoslav Partisan base in Bari. Vlado had an accident while driving a motorcycle on an assignment and was killed instantly. Without their sons the Gottliebs no longer wished to return to Zagreb after the war and took the first opportunity to emigrate to Israel. They settled in the then-small, nondescript town of Holon, surrounded by the sandy desert that only much later was transformed into green gardens and a luxurious settlement. Alone and overcome with grief, they both died in 1948, barely sixty-two years old.

* * *

A week after my arrival in Kraljevica, Josip Đerđa, the secretary of the District Committee of the Communist Party of Croatia (KPH) for the Croatian Primorje, unexpectedly appeared at our doorstep. Of course, at the time I didn't know who he was, but it was clear that he had come to us through a party connection. My mother could no longer hide anything from me and slowly drew me into her work for the Partisans. She introduced me to an acquaintance of hers, a shoemaker in the town of Hreljin. Two or three weeks later I delivered some medical supplies for the Partisans to him and brought back Partisan newspapers and leaflets. I cannot remember the man's name, but I think that even today I would be able to find his shop, if it still exists.

Đerđa stayed with us about a week. I clearly remember that he celebrated New Year's Day 1942 with us. My mother moved me into her room and gave Đerđa mine. He didn't go out much, but when he did, he would be out the entire day, returning in the evening just before curfew. Some people came to see him, singly or in pairs, some of whom my mother knew and others whom she didn't.

For New Year's Day 1942, my mother invited Lolika Robiček, the pharmacist Kornel Bauer, Vili Čerić, and perhaps some others. She introduced them to Đerđa, using a false name, and described him as our friend from Karlovac. They talked for two or three hours—of course, only about politics. I was pleased and flattered that I was permitted to listen to the discussion. I absorbed every word. Đerđa dealt superbly with those questions that were not easy to answer: Why had the Germans penetrated so easily and deeply into Russia? How was it possible that the powerful Red Army had found it difficult to subdue little Finland? Why do you speak so poorly of the Chetniks? Isn't it better that we all unite against Hitler and Pavelić? The most unpleasant question was about Stalin's pact with Hitler in 1939: Wasn't it a great mistake on Stalin's part to allow Hitler to subjugate Europe? Đerđa dodged the questions with communist propaganda: It was, in fact, a cunning political move by Stalin; Great Britain and France opened the door to the east for Hitler in Munich in 1938 and encouraged him to go after Russia, while Stalin outsmarted them and turned Hitler back to the west, thereby gaining two years to expand his territory and strengthen his defenses.

Đerđa's forceful explanations about the necessity of the antifascist struggle and the advantages of the Partisan method of waging war had a persuasive effect on his listeners, or so it seemed to me. I was surprised that he spoke in detail in front of an unknown audience about the many Partisan operations and successes, as it became obvious that he was not only a sympathizer of the Partisan movement but a man of influence. I had the same impression when I saw him in the Partisans as the chief of agitprop for the Central Committee of the KPH and after the war as the deputy minister of foreign affairs of the Socialist Federal Republic of Yugoslavia. His originality and passionate eloquence impressed me, while the cynicism of his logic and the cold, harsh way in which he communicated with people repelled me. He was a man of fervent activism and radical action. His resignation in 1972 as the vice president of the National Assembly of Yugoslavia over his disagreement with the actions of the Central Committee of the Communist Party of Yugoslavia (KPJ) against the leaders of the Croatian Spring and the Serbian liberals didn't surprise me as much as the fact that in the remaining eighteen years of his life he managed to live the quiet, secluded life of a pensioner.

After Đerđa's departure, my mother's collaboration with the antifascist movement and the Partisans intensified. Đerđa had provided her with contacts through whom she received messages, assignments, and propaganda leaflets. She also began to entrust me with some assignments, which I gladly accepted. I remember the day when creeping through the forest with Lolika above the Hreljin ruins I made my first contact with a Partisan patrol. My mother also sent me to the nearby town of Crikvenica with letters and messages to Dr. Gradišnik at the local health clinic. The carabinieri did not usually issue Jewish refugees permits to move outside of their assigned area, but my mother had obtained a statement from Dr. Kosić that I required examination by a specialist and I obtained the permit without difficulty. I introduced myself to Dr. Gradišnik with an identifying sentence in code, and he received me very kindly. I don't think it was unusual for clandestine Partisan collaborators to use adolescents as their couriers—the carabinieri would not suspect them. After he quickly looked at the papers I had brought him, Dr. Gradišnik handed me a letter for my mother. He then sent me to another address in Crikvenica, where I had to contact a bricklayer named Car, who would pass me Partisan newspapers to be delivered to Kraljevica.

Car was a garrulous young man of eighteen or nineteen. He told me immediately that he was a member of the League of Young Communists of Yugoslavia (SKOJ), that he was fed up with the "work behind the scenes," and that he was getting ready to join the Partisans. He asked about our situation in Kraljevica, if we were active and if so how active, and if we were in close contact with the District Committee and the Partisans. Abiding by the rules of conspiratorial work, he didn't ask for names and details. I answered in a general way and perhaps a little too optimistically, to which Car suddenly said, "But I've heard that it's bad and dangerous for you in Kraljevica!"

Confused, I asked him what he meant.

"They say that one woman runs the show there, that everything goes through her. That may not be so bad, but she has a young son whom she sends all over the place, and he knows too much. When the carabinieri catch him and slap him three times, he'll tell them everything!"

I must have turned red, which Car probably didn't notice in the darkness of the back room. I don't know how I managed to collect myself and calmly continue the conversation. I told Car that I knew the woman, that I thought her "boy" knew very little, and that the danger wasn't excessive. Nevertheless, I had to promise I would relay to "that woman" the fears circulating among people in the organization.

Car was probably a member of the District Committee of SKOJ, and in that capacity he was concerned with the organization's security throughout the area. I don't think he had any idea that I might be the "young son" who threatened such mortal danger. Perhaps I seemed too precocious and serious in appearance and behavior. He talked some more, but I could barely follow him and was happy when it was time for me to catch the boat back to Kraljevica. I rolled up the Partisan newspapers into my school bag and took my leave from the hardworking Car.

I cautiously told my mother what I had heard about us in Crikvenica. This certainly wasn't pleasant for her to hear, but I don't think she was concerned because she continued to entrust assignments to me.

* * *

Among all of my mother's worries, her greatest by far was how to bring Danko from Tuzla as soon as possible. She and my grandmother corresponded regularly, and I think she could sense from the terse postcards that it was no longer as safe there as it had been. It was probably Lolika's idea that we engage Joško Pribilović. Lolika had been living with the Pribilović family for two months and had gotten to know Joško well. He was a polite, well-dressed, likable nineteen-year-old. Just before the war he had graduated from the maritime high school in Split and then languished, unemployed, at his parents' home in Kraljevica. I don't know how he avoided mandatory service in the Home Guard. Like many young Croatian boys, in the first days of the NDH he was ecstatic that Croatia had become an independent state and signed up for the Ustasha Youth Movement, but he quickly cooled to it. By the end of the summer of 1941, the small group of Ustasha Youth in Kraljevica no longer met and had practically ceased to exist. However, Joško still carried a valid membership card, which Lolika considered a fortunate circumstance.

Early in the new year Lolika acted as the intermediary between my mother and the Pribilović family, and Joško agreed to travel to Tuzla to bring Danko to Kraljevica. Joško's father, Kosta, was known in town as an intelligent, brave man who was prepared to help Jews and other refugees cross the border to Kostrena or Praputnjak in the Italian zone. Perhaps Joško was encouraged by his father's example to become involved in a courageous enterprise, or maybe his father encouraged him. It was known that Kosta was helping people across the border for a small compensation, so my mother offered it to Joško, but he refused. Not long ago he explained to me that his primary motive for taking on this risky mission was to show that he and his friends from Kraljevica didn't support the Ustasha and, in fact, opposed the Ustasha's actions.

My mother provided Joško with a letter for my grandparents and other proof of his trustworthiness. She also covered his travel and incidental costs. Joško obtained Croatian and Italian travel documents without difficulty. Two weeks after New Year's Day he bravely set out on the long journey, with a forced smile that concealed his nervousness. Those of us who had to wait the five days until Joško's return were even more anxious than he was. We were relying on his resourcefulness and his Ustasha Youth membership card.

Joško traveled without complications for two days and a night to reach Tuzla. His arrival would not have been a surprise: To prevent drawing the attention of the censors, which would have endangered Joško's mission, my mother couldn't directly inform my grandparents by mail of his trip, but we had a well-developed method of corresponding in code. As Joško discovered, Aron and Adolfa Goldstein were no longer in their beautiful, spacious home opposite the train station. In December 1941, their house had been confiscated, along with its outlying buildings and large garden. Though they had been given a relatively nice apartment in town, my grandfather's confidence that nothing bad would happen to them in Tuzla had been shaken. Not even the intercession of the Ursuline nuns, their former neighbors, helped. They only managed to obtain assurances from "the authorities" that the Goldsteins would not be arrested or sent to a camp, which had been the fate of many Tuzla Jews. Perhaps my grandfather still believed in these promises, but his eldest son, Oto, did not. When they received the order to leave their home, Oto managed to obtain permits to leave with his wife, Greta, and eight-year-old son, Darko, for Makarska, a small town on the Adriactic coast, which was occupied by the Italians. My grandfather remained in Tuzla to care for his bedridden wife, his sickly daughter, Berta, and his grandson Danko. Fortunately the Ursuline sisters accepted Danko as a third-grade student in their school. And so Danko was around children his own age under the careful attention the Ursuline nuns gave to all of the Goldsteins.

Danko's recollection is that his grandfather hesitated to turn him over to Joško for the trip to Kraljevica; Joško remembers that my mother's detailed letter immediately convinced my grandfather that Kraljevica was better and safer for Danko than Tuzla. But my grandfather dismissed my mother's suggestion that he also come to Kraljevica with my grandmother and Berta: He wasn't going anywhere with a paralyzed woman in a wheelchair. Besides, no one in Tuzla would arrest him or his family.

Joško stayed the night with my grandparents and the next afternoon set off for the train station with Danko and two suitcases. Today, Danko says that he wasn't frightened about leaving with Joško—he immediately trusted him. He was also looking forward to joining his mother and brother, though sorry to leave two elderly people and a sickly aunt, with whom he had felt safe and comfortable for five months. For them the parting with Danko was certainly more difficult—they were left without that bit of cheerfulness their carefree grandson and nephew added to those gloomy days.

Upon their departure, Joško explained to Danko that he would present him as his younger brother, and Danko understood that he would need to play the role convincingly. These unnatural times had taught even children how to behave unnaturally. At the beginning of the journey problems arose: The train stood on an open track and they waited a long time for repairs to be made. That first night they slept squeezed together like sardines into the coach with other passengers. After they changed trains in Slavonski Brod, they were crowded into a coach with a small group of Ustasha, dressed in all black. Danko was frightened and the quick-witted Joško moved them to another car. During the document check, Joško explained that Danko was his younger brother. Children below a certain age in the company of parents or an older person required no travel permits, and Joško's Ustasha Youth membership card helped.

They were forced to stay overnight in Zagreb because they had arrived too late to catch the evening train for Sušak. Fearing strict controls in the Zagreb hotels, they decided to go with a woman standing in front of the station offering overnight accommodations. The two of them slept in one bed in a room where a fat man snored in another bed.

In Karlovac they were stopped for a long time at the station. Danko recognized a well-known detective named Košir, who entered their coach to check travel documents. Joško repeated the story about the younger brother he was taking to Kraljevica; Košir carried out his routine document check, paying no attention to Danko. He probably would not recognize Danko, who to this day remembers this encounter as the moment of his greatest fear. They again had to wait at the station in Liče because the tracks had to be repaired after a Partisan attack the night before. By the time they arrived in Kraljevica, it was dark. Danko at last reached his mother's embrace, Joško his parents, and we all breathed a sigh of relief.

I don't know if Joško was aware at the time of all of the dangers during that trip from Tuzla to Kraljevica or how fortunate his decision was not to spend the night in a Zagreb hotel with a smuggled Jewish child. Between January 8 and 15, 1942 the largest roundup of Jews in Zagreb was carried out. About 1,500 people were arrested; the men were sent to Jasenovac, the women and children to Loborgrad.

The roundup targeted homes, hospitals, hotels, and even people on the street.

In the spring of 1943, Joško joined the Partisans and by the end of the war had the rank of lieutenant. After the war, he got a degree in economics from the University of Zagreb and in the 1970s became the secretary of the Secretariat for Finance of the Municipal Assembly of Zagreb. He retired in 1982. In 1999, Danko described in detail for Yad Vashem how Joško had rescued him from the Ustasha. Yad Vashem investigated Danko's statement and the circumstances in which those events had occurred, and in 2001 Joško was awarded the honor of Righteous Among the Nations.

No one in our family in Tuzla survived the war. Immediately after the war, we sent letters from Karlovac and asked about our relatives in Tuzla, Sarajevo, Vinkovci, Dorna Vatra, Bucharest, Černovic, and Palestine. We learned that our grandfather, grandmother, and Berta had been taken away in the summer of 1942. As we never heard from them, we think that they ended up in the camp at Jasenovac, as did the majority of Jews from Croatia and Bosnia. I also wrote a chapter about this for *Obitelj* (Family), co-published in 1996 by the Miroslav Shalom Freiberger Cultural Society and our firm Novi Liber. In the list of 59,188 victims of the Jasenovac concentration camp published in 1997, I found the names of my aunt Alma Rosenberg (mistakenly written as Ulma), her husband, Aco, and their eleven-year-old son, Feliks, from Vinkovci, but I could never find the names of my grandfather, grandmother, and Berta. In the spring of 2001, while helping my son with his book *Holokaust u Zagrebu* (The Holocaust in Zagreb), I learned that between August 13 and 24, 1942, 4,792 Jews had been sent in four large transports from Zagreb, Osijek, and Bosnia to death camps in occupied Poland. There are lists of the victims in all of these camps, but they are incomplete, as is the list for Jasenovac. So even today we don't know if my grandmother, grandfather, and Berta were killed in Jasenovac, Treblinka, Sobibor, or Auschwitz.

In the summer of 1943, my uncle Oto, along with his wife and son and about 3,200 other Jews, was sent to the large Italian camp of Kampor on the island of Rab. When the camp was liberated after the capitulation of Italy, the family crossed over to Partisan territory. An excellent glazier, Oto was employed in the workshops of the Economic Section of the National Anti-Fascist Council of the People's Liberation of Croatia (ZAVNOH) in Otočac. There he met my brother, Danko, who in the summer and autumn of 1943 was also in Otočac as an auxiliary laborer and courier at the printing press of the Central Committee of Agitprop. When the Germans launched an offensive in October, Danko obtained permission from Josip Đerđa, the chief of agitprop, to find a place on the press's truck for Uncle Oto and his wife and son. However, Uncle Oto and Aunt Greta hesitated. They had a number of possessions that they could not take with them on the truck, so they tried to hire a wagon in a nearby village to evacuate them and everything they owned. In vain Danko urged them to come with him. On the road from Otočac German tanks caught up with the wagon and for more than half a century we did not hear anything more about Uncle Oto and his family. We assumed that the Germans had handed them over to the Ustasha, who probably sent them to Jasenovac. I also wrote about this in my contribution to *Obitelj*. A year or two later, a stranger, speaking with a Belgrade accent, contacted me by telephone. Without introducing himself he said that he was calling from Sweden and that for family reasons he was carrying out research on Yugoslav Jews killed in Auschwitz. He had read my contribution in *Obitelj* and wished to inform me that in the Auschwitz *Sterbebücher* (Death Books) he had found that Oto, Greta, and Darko Goldstein had been sent from Rižana in April 1944 and that they had been killed at Auschwitz. Now I must correct the inaccurate information in my text in *Obitelj*: Uncle Oto and his wife and son were not killed at Jasenovac. The German tank unit that captured them sent them to Rižana, a major concentration camp near Trieste commanded by the infamous SS general Odilo Globocnik. They spent about six months in the camp. In the spring of 1944 they were sent to Auschwitz, and then to the gas chambers.

* * *

The icy winter winds that descended on Kraljevica from Tuhobić and Plase slowly died down and the spring sun lured idle Jewish strollers to Fara and Oštro. Contacts with the Partisans also revived and my mother was receiving their newspapers more frequently. I would take these to the local pharmacist Bauer and to several others whom I don't remember. Bauer, a Jewish refugee from Osijek, obtained medicine and medical supplies for the Partisans. I would sometimes accompany my mother or Lolika to visit our Partisan contacts in Križišće or Hreljin. Danko became aware of our strange comings and goings and was curious. I don't know how much my mother explained to him, I just know that sometimes she would take him to see her contact in Križišće. This partly served as camouflage, since a mother walking with a child aroused less suspicion than a lone traveler, and Danko knew very well what he should say if someone asked where he was going and why. "He has learned the rules of conspiracy," my mother joked.

We frequently passed time in the courtyard and garden of Grandma Tonica Jakovčić's, our neighbor in Vrtić. The painter Ivo Rein, a Jewish refugee from Osijek, would also come to visit. He tirelessly drew pastel and ink portraits of little Ljiljana, a lively one-year old child with an alluring smile, luxuriant curly hair, and big eyes that cheerfully took in the world around her. With nervously impulsive movements, as if in a trance, Rein sketched portraits, landscapes, and motifs of seaside life. Danko and I liked to watch him draw and to listen to his captivating stories about Paris. Everything that he drew he took with him through the camps in Kraljevica and on Rab and then to the Partisans. He was detailed to work in the Propaganda Section of ZAVNOH. During the German offensive in October 1943, Rein put his sketches and drawings—said to number several hundred—into a box and hid them somewhere in Lika. He was killed in December 1943 while on assignment somewhere near Sisak. His drawings from Kraljevica—of camp life, of the Partisans—have never been found. Apparently Rein entrusted no one with the location of his treasure chest.[2]

With every new family that found refuge in Kraljevica, increasingly bad news arrived. In January or February, we heard about the major roundup in Zagreb and the mass deportations to Jasenovac and Loborgrad. The gruesome stories about Jasenovac were circulating. Many of the detainees sent to Jasenovac in the early autumn were never heard from again. Then news from Osijek arrived about a typhus epidemic and mass deaths in the Đakovo camp. At the end of winter my mother talked for the first time about Jadovno in a way that made it clear her last sliver of hope was disappearing. Was it possible that for six months not one of them had been able to get in touch? We decided that we had to tell Danko, who often asked when his father would come back. Danko vividly remembers how one day we sat down with him in my mother's room and she told him of our fear that our father was no longer alive. I had come to this realization slowly over the course of four or five months, but for Danko this was a blow from which we could no longer spare him.

For two hundred Jewish refugees, Kraljevica was a seemingly peaceful oasis in which everyone was in a state of constant anxiety. The brief winter counteroffensive in Russia ground to a halt in February 1942; Rommel was again advancing in Libya toward Egypt and the Suez Canal; German submarines in the Atlantic continued to sink Allied convoys; the Japanese conquered island after island in the Pacific, and before the end of March they subjugated the entire Malay Peninsula (including Singapore), captured Rangoon, and reached the gates of India. News of the Partisan successes was of little comfort because the final outcome would be decided on faraway battlefields and not in Kordun.

In the early spring of 1942, Hans Helm, the newly appointed German police attaché in Zagreb, began to be directly involved in the "final solution to the Jewish question" in the NDH. With the agreement of his superiors in Berlin, he was preparing the deportation of all of the remaining Jews from Croatia and Bosnia to Nazi death camps. He was also planning to include in this deportation about five thousand Jews who had fled the NDH to Zone B and to Italy. The German Ministry of Foreign Affairs, through its ambassador in Rome, ordered that these five thousand people be handed over to German and Ustasha police forces. Italian diplomats skillfully dragged out making a response to the Germans. General Mario Roatta, the commander of the Italian Second Army, refused to carry out the extradition, with the justification that neither the Germans nor the Ustasha had any authority over territory that was under the administration of his army. If the Jews had to go to camps, Roatta concluded, then they should be sent to camps under Italian command on Italian territory and not handed over to the Germans.

This tug-of-war between the Nazi authorities, Italian diplomats, and the military command lasted from early spring until late autumn of 1942. At one point the fate of the Jewish refugees hung by a thread: Concerning one request from Berlin that sought the extradition of the Jews, Mussolini wrote by hand "*nulla osta*" (no objection), but his commanders convinced him that Italian concentration camps should be established for the Jewish refugees and that they should not be handed over to the Nazi SS.

We in Kraljevica knew nothing about how our fates were being negotiated, although we felt there was something "in the air." Various rumors were passed on "in confidence," but we weren't sure how credible they were. Aleksandar Goldštajn, in the name of a group of Zagreb Jews who had sought refuge in Hreljin, wrote an elegantly composed and detailed request in Italian to General Roatta personally. He painstakingly described what was happening to the Jews in the NDH and concluded: "Any decision to extradite us will also be a death sentence, for it is widely known what can be expected when we are handed over to the Ustasha authorities in Karlovac."

At that time, the early spring of 1942, a powerfully built man with thick eyeglasses made an unannounced visit to us in Kraljevica. He was about thirty years old and introduced himself to my mother with a password, saying he was our new contact with the Partisan District Committee. As proof, he had brought a letter from Josip Cuculić, who had been our primary contact and with whom my mother had met in Križišće. Our new contact had been an engineer employed by the Banovina Electrical Company at the construction site of the Vinodol plant in Tribalj. He arrived on a powerful motorcycle, as he would for every visit, and enthusiastically greeted Lolika, who responded in kind. They said they were pretending to be in love, but I don't think it was just a pretense. Through this man my mother received a message from either Cuculić or Đerđa that if she felt unsafe in Kraljevica she could join the Partisans and bring her children.

In early May that moment arrived. During a routine weekly appearance at the carabinieri station, my mother chatted with the sergeant major, as was her custom. She asked him about the barracks the army was building in Carevo on the edge of Kraljevica. The friendly Italian answered without equivocation: "That will be a camp for Slovenes. And perhaps for you Jews if necessary. But don't worry, Mrs. Goldstein, nothing bad is going to happen to you. We are not the Ustasha or the Germans."

My mother didn't hesitate. Since Danko's arrival in Kraljevica, she had decided she would never again wait for someone else to determine the fate of her and her children. That same day she proposed that we join the Partisans, and I agreed. Through our contact my mother requested a meeting with Cuculić. She also brought Danko to that meeting in Križišće, not as camouflage but to introduce him to Cuculić and ask one more time if she could join the Partisans with such a young child. My mother again received an assurance that she could come with both boys. Cuculić showed Danko photographs from either the Grižanski or the Bribir camp with children of Danko's age. Danko thus knew where we were going and followed strict orders not to say anything to anyone.

Our flight to the Partisans worked out smoothly, "like a Swiss watch." My mother and Lolika packed rucksacks for us, as if we were going on a long excursion. We gave all of the more valuable posessions we could not carry to Tonica. Then two young men arrived and took our rucksacks. In the afternoon of the same day the three of us and Lolika set off on a walk to Križišće. At the edge of the settlement we entered the first house on the left where our two helpers were waiting with the rucksacks. As soon as darkness fell, they led us through the settlement, steeply downhill then steeply uphill, across the Križišće–Hreljin road, and twenty or thirty meters into the forest where two Partisans with rifles and tricorn caps were waiting for us. They took some of the rucksacks while we carried the rest, and after about an hour we were in the Drivenik Partisan camp. About twenty Partisans were fast asleep under a shelter and in one large tent, with only two others awake and on watch. They showed us the cots that had been prepared in a separate small tent, in which the four of us peacefully spent our first night with the Partisans.

A day or two later, via the same route, Kornel Bauer, Leo Ripp, and Pavle Mahler arrived. Lolika and my mother had invited more of the Jewish refugees to join us, but only these three appeared. The rest of the refugees were later sent to the Carevo camp in Kraljevica. About two hundred from Kraljevica, along with about three thousand Jewish refugees from Croatian Primorje and Dalmatia, were transferred in 1943 to the large camp of Kampor on the island of Rab. After the capitulation of Italy, they crossed into liberated Partisan territory in Lika. About eight hundred of them volunteered for Partisan combat and auxiliary units; approximately two thousand survived the war on liberated territory in Lika, Kordun, and Banija; another two hundred managed to get to Italy; and two hundred more remained on Rab, convinced they would survive there. But with the German autumn offensive, they were forced into the camp at Rižana, just like Uncle Oto.

Of the seven of us from Kraljevica, five survived the war in the Partisans. The handsome Mahler, a courageous and much-loved soldier of the First Primorsko-Goranski Shock Battalion, was killed in August 1942 during the attack on Modruš. Bauer, a highly regarded pharmacist in the medical corps of the Seventh Banija Division, was killed in June or July 1943 in Sutjeska. Ripp returned to Osijek, Lolika to Zagreb, and the three of us to Karlovac.

* * *

Perhaps what I remember of our first days with the Partisans is idyllic. In the dazzling spring sunshine we walked through the green freshness of mountain meadows with a view of Vinodol below us and the peak of Mount Viševica above us. On the road from the Drivenik camp to the Grižanski camp, Tomo Strižić, a Partisan veteran from Bribir, patiently answered our questions and instructed us on the unwritten rules of the Partisan way of life. No one asked who we were, where we were from, why we had come, and no one was interested in whether we were Croats, Serbs, or Jews. At the Grižanski camp there were several refugee families with children, so Danko had friends to play with, while my mother had proof that she was not the only one to burden the Partisans with caring for underage children. At the headquarters of the Matija Gubec battalion in Bitoraj, I received my first rifle as a Partisan, a small Italian one. With a boyish feeling of pride, I stood my first watch at the lookout post facing Mrkopalj and at the guard post in front of the camp. One night I accompanied a group of local Partisans to Ličko Polje, where sacks full of potatoes were waiting for us. Of course they gave me the smallest bag, which I carried with great effort up to Bitoraj. When I arrived back in camp, exhausted and sweaty, my mother heroically controlled herself from showing too much pity for the trials of her poor son. But let it be said that in the next three years she saw Danko and me in much more difficult circumstances, and she bore that with equal heroism. She must have possessed great willpower and courage to make the decision to join the Partisans with two young children and to withstand all she had to withstand without self-pity. However, I don't think she ever regretted it.

Along the road from Bitoraj to Drežnica we met Ivo Vejvoda, the political commissar of the Fifth Operational Zone of the National Liberation Army of Croatia. My mother and Vejvoda, old acquaintances from Karlovac, agreed on our assignments. My mother was given the task of organizing an ambulatory clinic for the wounded and the ill in Drežnica and, enterprising and communicative as she was and able to handle impossible situations, she performed her job superbly. A new challenge arrived with the major Italian offensive against Drežnica in September 1942: Along with Jela Jančić and Vera Schwabenitz, my mother courageously cared for the wounded in the main hospital of the Fifth Operational Zone, spending seventeen days in the limestone hollows and makeshift hideouts in the trackless forest of Javornica. She was then given the very demanding job of hygienist for the surgical team of the general staff of the National Liberation Army of Croatia. Under the leadership of Dr. Franz Kleinhappel, the famous Partisan surgeon, the team visited almost every Partisan hospital in central Croatia in the course of two and a half years, but it stayed the longest at Petrova Gora. My mother assumed responsibility for hygienic conditions in the hospitals, which given the conditions of that time was not an easy task. During some major battles, the surgical team was positioned directly behind the front line so that it could operate more quickly on the seriously wounded. My mother faced all of this with strength and never showed that anything was too difficult for her, with the exception of her separation from us. During my Partisan wanderings, I would drop by the hospital to visit my mother and Danko whenever I had the chance. Several times I received permission from my superiors to stay for two or three days, and Veco Holjevac, the political commissar in my corps, granted me a seven-day leave in Petrova Gora to be with them. When I left to return to my unit, my mother accompanied me to the edge of a meadow that descended toward the road. As I walked farther away, I turned around several times and waved, while she just stood there. She was alone; perhaps she allowed herself a quiet moment, overcome as she must have been by a single thought: Will we ever see each other again?

Although he was only ten years old when we joined the Partisans, Danko performed a variety of auxiliary tasks in the Partisan forces during the remaining three years of the war. While he was with my mother in hospitals in Drežnica, Slunj, Bijeli Potoci, Turki, and Petrova Gora, he served as a courier, guard, and telephone operator. In the last year of the war he was the telephone operator for the central hospital in Petrova Gora, working at the switchboard that connected several regional hospitals with the corps headquarters and with the general staff of Croatia. For almost all of 1943 he was separated from our mother. During the Fourth Anti-Partisan Offensive,[3] he crossed all of Lika with the wounded and was then temporarily placed with the Gerovac family in the liberated town of Jezerane. They treated him as a member of the family. He took the cows to pasture, he brought his own rations from the command post in Stajnica, and Mile Gerovac, the head of the household, would sometimes take him hunting. Not long ago Danko told me how one day in the pasture, in a deserted meadow at the foot of the wooded Mala Kapela, he was overwhelmed by the sadness of total isolation. Somewhere in another part of Lika, in Bijeli Potoci, our mother was suffering from typhus and had not been in touch for some time. Danko was afraid she would die. His brother was imprisoned in Ogulin and also had not been in touch for a while, and there was a question as to whether they would ever see each other again. So eleven-year-old Danko felt that he no longer had any family and that he was alone in the world. He breathed a sigh of relief when a courier from the general staff, a man named Maljković, arrived with a report that our mother had passed through the crisis period of typhus and that she was slowly recovering. Maljković took Danko to Otočac, where for another five months he worked in the Central Committee of Agitprop of the KPH, whose chief at that time was Josip Đerđa. Danko was a paper loader in the printing office and also worked as a courier—every morning he distributed a news bulletin to the general staff, to ZAVNOH, to the area command, and to other Partisan institutions located at that time in Otočac.

As soon as we arrived in Drežnica in June 1942, Miron Cesarec, the adopted son of August Cesarec,[4] accepted me into SKOJ and had me work in the organization's District Committee for Ogulin, where

At a Partisan youth meeting in Ribnik on October 16, 1944, a group of Karlovac high-school students from the Karlovac Partisan detachment with girls who were Partisan collaborators and who had come to the meeting from Karlovac and Novigrad. Left to right: Slavko Goldstein, Mirko Humski, Ljiljana Gener, Dušan Benini, Beba Vešović, Ivo Pavliško, Josip Hagendorfer, Ljubica Erdeljac (later Blažević), Josip "Papiga" Butković, Marijan Trepo, and Danka Grgurić (later Draganjac)

Miron was the temporary secretary. I had my baptism of fire during the attack on Jezerane on August 12, 1942. I had been ordered to maintain contact with the auxiliary youth service from Drežnica (responsible for supplying food to the army, the transport of the wounded, etc.) and the headquarters of the First Brigade of the National Liberation Army of Croatia. In the fog around the Jezerane church, from whose barricaded bell tower gendarmes were shooting, I ducked instinctively as each bullet whistled past. Stevan Opsenica, the brigade commander, was laughing at me stooped over so low, while he, from his height of more than two meters, protected by the fog, calmly stood upright. "Don't duck, comrade!" he said. "The one that you hear will never hit you; the one that hits you is the one you never hear!" After that day I tried never to show fear, even when, as with every soldier in war, fear overwhelmed me. During the major Italian-Chetnik offensive against Drežnica in September 1942, I served as a soldier defending the hospital and rescuing the wounded. As a reward for my courage I was made a member of the District Committee of the SKOJ. For about six months I was engaged in organizational work and agitation among the youth in the Serbian villages around Drežnica and in the Croatian villages between Modruš and Ogulin. I frequently joined the Ogulin unit, led by Boro Sušanj and Luka Čemeljić, and participated in minor skirmishes against the Italians, Ustasha, and Chetniks. I was a delegate to the founding congress of the United Alliance of Anti-Fascist Youth of Yugoslavia in the last days of 1942 in Bihać and at the conference of the SKOJ Croatia in the first days of 1943 in Slunj. For part of the spring and almost all of the summer of 1943, I was imprisoned by the Italians in Ogulin. From October 1943 until the end of February 1944, I crisscrossed Kordun and a part of Pokuplje, organizing in Serbian and Croatian villages at the direction of the SKOJ District Committee for Karlovac. At the end of February 1944, I was reassigned to the Karlovac Partisan detachment at my own request. For the last fourteen months of the war, I served mostly as a soldier and the battalion secretary for the SKOJ. I quickly became the political commissar of the unit and, in the absence of a commanding officer, I led the unit for six months. I was decorated with the Order of Bravery and demobilized in Karlovac on May 15, 1945, with the rank of commissar lieutenant of the Karlovac Shock Brigade.

I started the war with the Croatian Partisans of Gorski Kotar and the Croatian Primorje, and ended it with units of the Croatian Partisans, living in and moving through the Croatian villages of the Karlovac and Ozalj regions and the regions of Žumberak and Pokuplje. In the meantime, I lived for a long time in Serbian villages with the Serbian Partisans of Kordun and Lika. I fought against the Ustasha,

Chetniks, Italians, and at the end of the war also against the Germans. Through the bars of a jail cell in Ogulin, I listened to and partly saw the peculiar Ustasha-Chetnik "singing" war that could not be transformed into an actual war because both sides were under the control of the Italians. On the sidewalk in front of the jail the Ustasha would sing to the imprisoned Serbs "*Zeleni se Trebević / Pije vino Pavelić / Vino pije, peče janjca, kolje Srbijance*" (Trebević is getting green / Pavelić is drinking wine / He is drinking wine, roasting lamb, and slaughtering Serbs), while the Chetniks would respond to the Ustasha from their cells with "*Oj, Hrvati, al' ćemo vas klati / kad se Pero iz Londona vrati*" (Hey, Croats, we are going to slaughter you / When Pero [King Peter] comes back from London). I know from personal experience that the Partisans and the National Liberation Army were the only army in which Croats and Serbs were on the same side of the battle front. At the same time I clearly felt in Serbian and Croatian villages the pathetic hollowness of the slogan "Brotherhood and Unity." I joined the Partisan army in its infancy, when plundering by its soldiers was punished, when it delivered speeches to its captured enemies and generously allowed them to return to their homes. In the winter of 1943–1944, I encountered units of that army for which the plundering of non-Partisan villages had become a custom that was tolerated and the killing of captured enemies a form of revenge that was sometimes encouraged. I was fortunate to spend the last fourteen months of the war in an army unit and in an area where there was no unlawful vengeance, and other incidents were the exception.

I emerged from the war convinced that my mother had led the three of us to the right side in the spring of 1942; that we were not sacrificial lambs left to their fate but had defied fate, even if only by our modest participation in the struggle against evil. Without doubting the basic values of the national liberation struggle, I also took from the war vague and unformed uncertainties about some groups and some of the methods used. In the decades after the war I frequently discussed these misgivings with many colleagues who had participated in the conflict. But I spoke gladly with those who during the war had participated in making key decisions or who had been close to those who originated them and then after the war, sooner or later, had become dissidents and thought in critical terms about all that had happened (people such as Milovan Đilas, Koča Popović, Gojko Nikoliš, Veljko Mićunović, Mijalko Todorović, Mina and Veljko Kovačević, Ivan Šibl, Veco Holjevac, Olga Hebrang, Zora and Stjepan Steiner). My editorial and publishing experience also helped because I read countless manuscripts and books on such topics. I have addressed some of my concerns at various points in this book, and now I would like to summarize my views regarding the Partisans.

1. The uprising in 1941 on the territory of prewar Yugoslavia was a heroic act that had no equal in wartime Europe under the domination of the Third Reich. In Croatia and Bosnia and Herzegovina the uprising had specific qualities in relation to other regions of the dismembered country, in particular the successful symbiosis of self-sacrificing communist revolutionary fervor and the threat to their lives felt by the Serbian population, especially the peasants. These two components, along with the patriotic sentiment in the Croatian regions ceded to Italy, were united by the force of circumstances into an antifascist concept that had been completely incorporated into the political principles of the wartime alliance of Great Britain, the USSR, and the United States. Thus Croatia, as well as all of Yugoslavia, became a part of the winning side in the Second World War, with all of the favorable consequences that this inclusion brought (the return to Croatia of Istria, the Kvarner islands, Zadar, and Lastova).

2. The uprising partially suppressed genocidal actions by the Ustasha regime in rural areas of the NDH populated by Serbs. The union

of Croatian communists and the Serbian peasantry, and the gradual inclusion of Croatian antifascists in the National Liberation War, considerably reduced the division between Croats and Serbs, which on one hand was created by the Ustasha regime and on the other hand by the Chetnik movement. Therefore, the Chetnik movement in the NDH was much less influential than in Serbia and Montenegro in 1942 and 1943. In addition, the national liberation movement in Croatia didn't condone massive retribution against the Croatian people for the Ustasha crimes such as those the Chetniks advocated and partially carried out. The Croatian people and the country were saved from identification with the Ustasha NDH and spared the catastrophic consequences that such identification might have brought.

3. Having assumed leadership of the uprising from the start, the communists expanded and consolidated that position during the course of the war. The Partisan war, or the national liberation struggle, had a double character for the communists: It was a radical antifascist movement because the communists were committed antifascists; it was also a war for the establishment of a new order, a revolutionary war, and a socialist revolution patterned in many ways after the October Revolution in Russia. With its successful conduct of the antifascist war, the Communist Party gained authority and expanded its circle of followers.

4. The Communist Party's slogan "There is no return to the old way!" promised the Croats and other people dissatisfied with their unequal position within the Kingdom of Yugoslavia that they would have a federal state—that is, equality within the framework of a common postwar state. The same slogan also had the power to attract poor peasants who were hoping for a more just distribution of land and who in most regions were the main source of manpower for the national liberation struggle. To the urban population "There is no return to the old way!" could sound like a promise of the democracy

that was absent in the Kingdom of Yugoslavia and which would be achieved by the new "people's power." However, the primary factor for the uninterrupted strengthening of the national liberation struggle was the continued Ustasha terror, and especially its genocidal character. Pavelić's occasional conciliatory proclamations and decrees had no real effect because the reign of terror didn't stop. While in the other parts of dismembered Yugoslavia the national liberation struggle developed more slowly or experienced serious reversals, and at one time came to a complete standstill, as in Serbia and Montenegro, it was constantly growing in Croatia and Bosnia and Herzegovina. During the three key years of the war, Bosnia and Croatia were the linchpins and the focus of the Partisan war for all of Yugoslavia.

5. At the beginning of 1943, after Stalingrad and the Allied invasion of North Africa, it was becoming increasingly clear who was winning and who was losing the Second World War, and the communist leadership of the Yugoslav and Croatian national liberation struggle reoriented all of its political and military tactics to capturing postwar power. Some separatist schemes for the postwar separation of Croatia or Slovenia from Yugoslavia were completely illusory. In all of their declarations the victorious Allies had clearly stated that they would not recognize any changes that had been made to the political map of Europe under the domination of the Third Reich. In the struggle for power in Yugoslavia the only real rival of the communists were the Chetniks. At the beginning of 1942, they still enjoyed support from London and Washington, and even the USSR still recognized their king and their government in exile.

6. The main shortcoming of the Chetniks was that after the autumn of 1941 they no longer contributed to the Allied war effort. With their slogans "Protecting Serbian blood" and "Waiting for the right moment," the Chetniks didn't fight against the occupying

forces. In Croatia, Herzegovina, and Montenegro they openly collaborated with the occupiers and fought against the Partisans. In contrast, the National Liberation Army waged an aggressive war at the cost of major losses in its own ranks: revolutions do not spare casualties—theirs or others. The National Liberation Army attacked and captured strong garrisons, considerably expanded liberated territory, and from the spring of 1943 quickly obtained international recognition.

7. The year 1943 was the real turning point. The war was drawing closer to the Balkans from the southwest and the northeast, and territory liberated by the Partisans was becoming desirable as a base for the future military operations of the Allies. The traditional monarchical sympathies of Churchill receded in the face of unassailable military logic, and in the spring and summer of 1943, Great Britain began to send military advisers and assistance to the Partisans and halted its assistance to the Chetniks. At the Tehran Conference in late November and early December 1943, Churchill, Stalin, and Roosevelt confirmed the battle-tested National Liberation Army as a military ally. The Chetniks had lost the battle for postwar power in Yugoslavia.

8. In May 1945 the majority of the population of the failed NDH was liberated from the Ustasha terror and wartime suffering ended. For a portion of the population, however, it brought new hardships and suffering, and they still refer to May 1945 as the "fall" or the "overthrow," and not the "liberation." The antifascist army and policy under communist leadership would win the war, but the new regime didn't possess the skill to be a wise victor in peacetime. It began its postwar rule with a crime that in time became known as "Bleiburg and the Way of the Cross." This traumatic site of the more recent Croatian past is a direct consequence of 1941, so I will devote several of the next, slightly more detailed points to it, convinced that

one cannot analyze 1941 without mentioning 1945, in the same way that 1945 cannot be explained without examining its roots in 1941.[5]

9. The first stage of Bleiburg, which was characterized by spontaneous vengeance, unfolded between May 9 and 14, 1945. Germany had surrendered, the war was over, and only the army of the NDH was still fighting. It was making its way through northern Slovenia toward the Austrian border with elements of Army Group E of the Wehrmacht, Slovenian White Guards,[6] Montenegrin Chetniks and smaller groups of supporters of Milan Nedić and Dimitrije Ljotić,[7] and members of the Muslim Legion. Veteran Ustasha units commanded by Maks Luburić and Rafael Boban were leading the NDH army, plundering and burning Slovenian hamlets northwest of Celje, refusing to surrender their weapons to the Yugoslav army "out of fear that the Partisans would behave toward them the way they behaved four years earlier toward the Partisans and the pro-Partisan civilian population" (according to Jozo Tomasevich). A multitude of relatives and other civilians (a mass of more than several tens of thousands, and perhaps close to one hundred thousand) accompanied the army. Six divisions of the Third Yugoslav Army, the Fourteenth Slovenian Division, several Slovenian Partisan detachments, and a powerful mechanized unit of the Fourth Army were ordered to block the disparate throng of army and civilians. Heavy fighting broke out northwest of Celje, in the area of Mislinja-Slovenj Gradec-Dravograd-Prevalje. According to a report of the Third Army headquarters, 142 of its soldiers and officers were killed, 374 were wounded, and 55 were missing. These figures didn't include the slightly lower losses among the Slovenian division and the local detachments, so the total Partisan losses might have reached as many as 1,000 killed and wounded. At the same time, in a column headed "Enemy Losses," the report cites 25,000 killed and 4,000 wounded. The disproportionate numbers speak for themselves: captives were

killed on a massive scale. It was an orgy of vengeful wrath. War crimes against prisoners of war have no moral, political, or legal justification, but in view of the circumstances it is not completely incomprehensible. Soldiers of the Third Army and the Slovenian Partisans were being killed by enemy soldiers who had mercilessly ravaged the entire country for four years and who had not stopped fighting, even once peace had been declared.

10. In a handwritten dispatch dated May 14, Supreme Commander Josip Broz Tito ordered an immediate halt to the killing of prisoners. He demanded compliance with the Geneva Conventions, as the general staff of the Yugoslav army had previously ordered regarding the treatment of prisoners on May 3. Tito's order sought neither an investigation into nor punishment for the killings that had been committed up to that time, but the order to halt the liquidations was generally respected over the next several days. Scattered units of the Yugoslav army in Carinthia were in almost daily contact with elements of the Fifth Corps of the British Eighth Army, which at least partially influenced Tito's command and the more disciplined behavior of the Yugoslav army.

11. A major battle near the Austrian border near Dravograd and Prevalje culminated on May 14. Veterans of the Ustasha Black Legion, the Ustasha Defense, and the *Poglavnik*'s personal bodyguards, for whom a breakthrough to British units in Carinthia was the sole remaining hope for salvation, led the NDH forces in the battle. On the other side were Vojvodina, Slovenian, Slavonian, and eastern Bosnian Yugoslav army units that were more numerous but depleted by combat and could barely wait for the shooting to stop so they could return to their homes. At the rear of the Ustasha-lead group came a slow-moving, immense mass of worn-out Home Guards in tattered uniforms and Home Guards forced to wear Ustasha uniforms; recently mobilized young boys and men unfit for military service;

starving and frightened civilians—a sixty-kilometer-long column in which desperation was rampant under the merciless artillery fire of the Yugoslav army's Seventeenth Eastern Bosnian Division. By a skillful circling movement on the night of May 14, the lead Ustasha units broke through the positions of the Fifty-first Vojvodina Division around Dravograd and through the valley of the Meža River, through Prevalje and Poljana, opening the road to the Austrian border. By the morning of May 15, about 30,000 NDH soldiers—mostly Ustasha with a relatively small number of civilians—had arrived as far as a spacious field on the approaches to Bleiburg, finally encountering strong forces of the British army. A considerably smaller part of the Ustasha advance units, perhaps about 2,500 soldiers and officers, had crossed the Austrian border farther east, around Lavamünde, and surrendered to British units on the road to Wolfsberg. The Fourteenth Slovenian Division on the road between the villages of Poljana and Bleiburg cut off further retreat for the largest portion of the NDH forces and its accompanying civilians, and the main column remained surrounded and dispersed on the Slovenian side of the border in an area from Celje to the banks of the Drava and Meža Rivers.

12. During negotiations at the Bleiburg Castle on May 15, Brigadier T. C. Scott, serving as the representative of the British headquarters of the Fifth Corps, refused to accept the surrender of General Ivo Herenčić and Colonel Danijel Crljen in the name of the forces of the NDH. Contrary to their expectations, the Ustasha delegates were treated rudely by Scott, as representatives of forces that had fought against the Allies for four years and which, contrary to the rules of war, had continued to fight after the surrender that the German high command had signed on May 8 in the name of its army and "of the armies of all countries that are under German domination." Based on interallied agreements, Scott ordered the Ustasha delegation to

surrender their weapons to the Allied forces against which they had been directly engaged, that is, the Yugoslav army, and declared an ultimatum: that the deadline for doing so was one hour and twenty minutes. In that short period of time several thousand Ustasha who felt the most threatened scattered in all directions into the nearby Carinthia forests, many of them to make a new life as émigrés. A smaller group headed by Luburić made it back to Slovenia and for several months continued to roam the forests as far as Mount Papuk in Slavonia. On the Bleiburg field and its immediate vicinity there were minor skirmishes with the fugitives in which twenty-seven Ustasha were reported killed. The great majority of the NDH forces surrendered their weapons within the allotted time without further resistance. The Twelfth Slavonia Division of the Yugoslav army, on orders from the headquarters of the Third Army, took the disarmed soldiers and civilians to Maribor in Slovenia. They were housed in improvised camps in and around the city. The same thing happened to the main body of the NDH forces and civilians who had not managed to reach Bleiburg and remained encircled on the approaches to the Drava River and between the Mislinja and Meža Rivers. Demoralized and dispersed into many smaller groups, only some put up sporadic resistance and tried to save themselves by fleeing to the nearby forests. In the next two to three days most of the soldiers surrendered their weapons and were sent to camps set up in Celje or to Maribor. There were no mass liquidations before their departure to the camps, but there was abuse and some individual killings, allegedly because of attempted escapes and other incidents.

13. During these events in May there were tensions and diplomatic rows between the erstwhile wartime allies Great Britain and Yugoslavia about taking over power in Carinthia. In some instances the disputes directly influenced the positions and actions of both parties, and they indirectly influenced the fate of the NDH forces. At the end

of February 1945, Field Marshal Harold Alexander, the British commander of the Allied Mediterranean theater of operations, visited Belgrade for five days and negotiated with Tito, agreeing on all of the important points for cooperation in the final operations of the war. In the spirit of the decisions reached by Churchill, Stalin, and Roosevelt at Tehran and Yalta, Alexander and Tito agreed that the Yugoslav army would conduct operations in and occupy the area up to Yugoslavia's prewar borders and Istria, while Allied forces under the command of Alexander would occupy Trieste and Carinthia, where a British zone of occupation would be established. Yugoslav demands for a change of the postwar border would be resolved at the peace conference. Following the decisions of the three major allies at the Moscow Conference in October 1943, it was also confirmed in Belgrade that captured members of collaborationist armed forces would be handed over to the authorities of the Allied countries from where they had originated. However, in the first days of May 1945, it had become apparent that Tito was not keeping to these agreements. At his urgent orders, the Fourth Yugoslav Army quickly occupied Trieste, and Slovenian and Vojvodina units of the Yugoslav army occupied Carinthia. On May 9, in Klagenfurt, Austria, a civilian Slovenian government was established with Vida Tomšič, a member of the Central Committee of the Communist Party of Slovenia and Yugoslavia, as president. British military commanders in Carinthia immediately protested and requested that Yugoslavia honor the agreements they had signed. The British government waged a diplomatic war against the actions of the new Yugoslav government. Churchill, once well-disposed toward Tito, was prepared to order Alexander to kick the Yugoslav army out of Carinthia by military force. He also appealed to Stalin to persuade Tito to withdraw. Tito relented and ordered units of the Third Army and the Slovenian National Liberation Army to return to their side of the border on May 18. Within five days all

Yugoslav military forces had withdrawn from Carinthia, carrying with them a great deal of the spoils. But Yugoslav's acquiescence also meant that the British had to fulfill their part of the agreements: They refused to accept the surrender of the Ustasha army at Bleiburg, and after May 23 they also handed over to Yugoslav authorities the approximately 25,000 remaining White Guards, Chetniks, Ljotić supporters, Ustasha, and Home Guards who were being held in camps not far from Klagenfurt.

14. Beginning on May 17, Department for the Protection of the People (OZNA) secret police officers carried out expedited interrogations and made the first selection of prisoners, a process that marked the start of the second stage of the Bleiburg–Way of the Cross syndrome—the programmed selective killing of larger groups of prisoners who were identified as "bandits," "criminals," "enemies of the people," or simply "enemies." In the Maribor camps officers from the OZNA section of the Third Army headquarters carried out the selection. Several times they warned their superiors that there were too few of them for such a huge job, so the decisions were frequently made on a group basis rather than individually. Almost all of the civilians from the area of the NDH received one-way permits to return to their native towns, with an order to report to the local authorities within twenty-four hours of their return. Under an order of the general staff of May 21, the more than sixty thousand German prisoners were formed into labor battalions and sent to work in Slovenian mines, to repair the railway lines and bridges, and to work in the forests or on farms. The youngest Ustasha soldiers were under twenty, soldiers with minimal experience in the Ustasha army and in the Home Guard. Junior Home Guard officers and civilian officials of various institutions of the Ustasha movement and the NDH as a rule were sent to camps that had been prepared in the interior of the country, where further interrogation and selection were being planned.

Senior Ustasha and Home Guard officers were immediately sent to an improvised military tribunal that in the majority of cases sentenced them to death; in the Maribor and Celje camps, lower-ranking Ustasha officers and Ustasha soldiers and noncommissioned officers with longer service in the Ustasha army (from 1941 and 1942) were immediately separated out for group liquidation, without a trial and frequently without interrogation. A similar fate befell almost all of the Chetniks, Ljotić supporters, and Slovenian White Guards who had been captured or handed over by the British.

15. Prisoners separated out from the Maribor camps were killed in large groups over several nights in the last week of May. The killing site was part of a three-kilometer-long antitank trench that passed through a forest and next to the cemetery in the suburb of Tezno. Two battalions from two brigades of the Seventeenth Eastern Bosnia Division of the Yugoslav army carried out the executions. A report dated May 20 from one of these brigades to divisional headquarters stated that one of its battalions "has the assignment to liquidate five hundred Ustasha with the First Battalion, Sixth Brigade," and another report later the same day said it was "to liquidate Chetniks and Ustasha of whom there are 2,500." The next day's report laconically stated that "today we continued with the executions," while on May 23, 24, and 25 a battalion from another brigade continued the operation "of liquidating traitors to the people." When a new highway was being constructed in this area in 1999, 72 meters of this trench were excavated and closely examined. A total of 1,179 bones of murdered Ustasha soldiers and Chetniks were discovered and counted. In August 2007, two days of investigations along 950 meters of the antitank trench in Tezno were carried out, and it was surmised that the trench contained considerably more victims. Many organized executions were also carried out in the wider area around Celje, where victims from the Teharje camp were taken in groups to various kill-

ing sites, while others were killed in the camp itself. The largest burial site is probably at Kočevski Rog, where at the end of May and in early June the organized execution of a great majority of the fleeing Slovenian White Guards and smaller groups of collaborationists turned over by the British to the Yugoslav authorities in the second half of May took place. On the basis of now available documentation, there is no doubt that massive liquidations of prisoners in May 1945 on Slovenian territory were carried out by units of the Yugoslav army and the People's Defense Corps at the order of OZNA. Senior organs of the military and government were informed of everything through official channels and nothing important occurred without their agreement. This was confirmed by Milovan Đilas in the final pages of his memoir, *Wartime*.[8]

16. On May 18, the Twelfth Krajiška Brigade of the Yugoslav army reported that it "had to take about 40,000 prisoners" from Celje in the direction of Samobor and Zagreb. After a fifty-two-hour march, without food for the majority of the prisoners, according to the report, "there were no losses in dead or wounded either on our side or on the enemy side." In Zagreb and the surrounding camps the prisoners were closely interrogated—some were sent to the military tribunal, smaller groups were sentenced to liquidation without a trial, a small number was freed, some were ordered to OZNA prisons for further investigation, many members of the Home Guard and civilians were conscripted for military service in the Yugoslav army, while the great majority were dispatched on further marches to distant forced labor camps. When the camps in Maribor were disbanded, long columns of prisoners marched through Podravina and Posavina to Osijek, Srijem, and Vojvodina. The escorts for the columns were regular units of the Yugoslav army. They had written orders from senior commands regarding strict supervision of the prisoners, and probably verbal instructions for the execution of anyone who broke

off from the column or lagged too far behind. "Way of the Cross" is an apt metaphor for the tortuous, several-hundred-mile-long march of starving and thirsty prisoners, many of whom could not withstand the torment and were killed. The degree of torture mostly depended on the commander of the Yugoslav army unit that made up the escort. Frequently there were willful acts of vengeance and even robbery. Such excesses were usually criticized afterward at brigade or divisional party conferences, which is how one brigade of my division was admonished because some of its members had killed villagers who had given food and drink to Home Guard members or to Ustasha in the column. However, such reprimands were few, disciplinary punishment was the exception, and serious punishment, as far as I know, was nonexistent.

17. It has been most difficult for me to write about estimates of the number of victims of war and genocidal crimes. So much bad blood has been stirred up by the political manipulations of these numbers: Arbitrarily inflating them has led to irresponsible accusations against entire nations, while hypocritically downplaying them has served to cover up crimes and has deeply insulted the descendants of the victims. Excessive exaggerations of the number of victims of Bleiburg and the Way of the Cross have frequently been politically manipulated in order to cloud the truth about the victims of 1941 and all that happened in the four years that preceded Bleiburg. The number of victims in Slovenia was also sharply polemicized, until a more precise listing of names for the entire country was made, which provided more reliable numbers: between 14,000 and 15,000 members of the Slovenian collaborationist army were killed in the spring and summer of 1945. Croatian authorities should follow this example. Until then, I suggest that we temporarily accept those estimates that I think are closest to the truth because they come from two conscientious researchers: Jozo Tomasevich and Vladimir Žerjavić. Indepen-

dent of each other and using different research methods, they have arrived at the same conclusions. They estimate the total number of victims of Bleiburg and the Way of the Cross to be about 70,000, more than 20,000 of whom were Slovenes, Serbs, and members of the Bosnian Legion, while close to 50,000 were soldiers, noncommissioned officers, and officers of the NDH army and civilians.

18. According to some credible witnesses (Milovan Đilas, Stjepan Steiner, and others), in private conversations and within the narrowest leadership circles in May and June 1945, Tito complained that in his opinion the executions had gone too far. At his initiative an internal order had been issued on May 28 to no longer treat members of the Croatian Home Guard as prisoners, and thus they should be selectively released, mobilized into the Yugoslav army as conscripts, or appear before military tribunals to serve short sentences at forced labor camps. But they were no longer to be killed. In the meantime, many Home Guard members had been murdered because they had been forced to dress in the Ustasha uniform following a decision by Pavelić on December 11, 1944, to unify all of the NDH military units into a combined Croatian Armed Forces. Tito rubber-stamped the liquidations that had been carried out until then at a meeting in Ljubljana: "But regarding these traitors . . . that is a thing of the past. The hand of justice, the hand of revenge of our people has reached the great majority." The exterminations on the marches and in the camps continued for about another month, although on an ever-smaller scale. During this time, central government agencies were receiving an increasing number of warnings from local governments and communities that people were complaining "we are the same as the Ustasha" or "as Chetniks" because suspected citizens were killed without a trial and in secret, and prisoners on the Way of the Cross were killed arbitrarily in public view. Even the politburo of the Central Committee of the Communist Party of Slovenia complained to the

Central Committee of the KPJ about the behavior of OZNA, and the academic Petar Strčić has claimed that in the archive of the presidency of the Socialist Federal Republic of Yugoslavia, in the 1980s, he saw a letter dated June 1945 that had been sent personally to Tito and Edvard Kardelj in which Vladimir Bakarić draws attention to "a great deal of constant and frequent news about the very bad treatment of tens of thousands of people arriving in prisoner columns from Austria and Slovenia," adding that "we are now also creating hundreds of thousands of new enemies." At the first meeting of OZNA Croatia in July 1945, Ivan Krajačić-Stevo, the chief of the organization, concluded his remarks with the following: "Comrades, it is time you finally stop the liquidations!" Also in July, departments for general supervision were established within the state prosecutors' offices to control the activities of OZNA. This was followed by the Law on Granting Amnesty and Reprieves of August 5, after which group executions stopped, but the law also strictly banned the investigation and public discussion of what had occurred previously. Under this enforced silence, the trauma of Bleiburg and the Way of the Cross deepened with time. Among émigrés it was nurtured as a memory for political and propaganda purposes. Within the families of those who had been killed it was the source of homegrown mythologies, until at the first opportunity, after more than forty-five years, the trauma flared up as misdirected vengeance against Serbs in Croatia.

19. Thanks to the participation of a large portion of the Croatian people in the National Liberation War, Croatia avoided the danger of being included after the war in a mini buffer zone between a Greater Serbia and a small Slovenia, and so the Croatian people weren't exposed to Chetnik vengeance. At the same time, the defeat of the Chetniks and the Ustasha meant the establishment of a communist Croatia in a communist Yugoslavia, with all of the consequences that we have experienced in the last sixty years. Stalinism in Yugoslavia

was born of the wartime victory of antifascism. Tito laid the groundwork when he uncompromisingly bolshevized the KPJ in the years before the war. He explained this process in a famous article in 1940, "For the Purging and Bolshevization of the Party": "Today, when it is necessary to exert all our strength to create a single powerful and monolithic Party able to stand at the forefront of events, anyone who does not submit to that work and these tasks in a disciplined fashion belongs on the other side of the barricade, i.e., on the side of the enemies of the working class...Our Party grows stronger every day. It is capable of crushing everything that stands in its way and obstructs its development. Today, it is already capable of moving with closed ranks to meet all difficulties, of traveling the same road as the heroic Bolshevik party of the Soviet Union." Many of the young people who joined the party before the war, believing it stood for freedom and social justice, had to submit to a Bolshevization that was contrary to their ideals. They did so with the classic self-consoling justification in the name of "higher goals," for a "great, noble goal also justifies the use of some unpleasant means," but the means swamped the goals and led to deformations, both of individuals and of the party.

20. A party so constituted was fit for waging war and revolution and unfit for building a healthy society and a modern state. At the end of the war Stalin's USSR quickly established dominance over eastern and southeastern Europe, and in all of those countries (except Greece) it brought communist parties to power. The exception was the KPJ. It had not been installed in power by the Red Army but had taken control of the state through its own resources and with far greater support from its people than the miniature parties in other countries that relied on the Soviet Union. The KPJ entered the war with approximately 9,000 members (two-thirds of whom were killed) and it celebrated victory as a mighty power with 141,066 members, tested in battle and proven in war. Instead of using these comparative

advantages to seek their own initiatives in the postwar world, the KPJ and the KPH used their power to bolshevize the country more quickly and more thoroughly than all of the other new communist governments in the Soviet bloc. Yugoslavia was the most vocal antagonist of the Western allies and in the Western media it deservedly acquired the epithet "Satellite No. 1." This is all the more difficult to understand since Tito and some of his comrades were in Moscow during Stalin's infamous purges, and they were personally acquainted with the most brutal forms of Stalinist Bolshevism. Despite this, between 1944 and 1948 they blindly followed Stalin.

21. The KPJ and the KPH had already been exercising absolutist, single-party rule during the war. Roughly half of the members of ZAVNOH were members of the Croatian Peasants' Party (HSS) or the Serbian Democratic Party of Croatia; the rest were not members of any political party. Even Vladimir Nazor, the president of ZAVNOH, didn't belong to any party. But the ruling mechanism was designed so that all decisions were made by Andrija Hebrang (the vice president) and other prominent communists. The situation in the Anti-Fascist Council of the National Liberation of Yugoslavia was similar. Behind the façade that was called "people's power" all the local communities were ruled by the party committees, which treated the national liberation committees—that is, the local governing authorities—as their auxiliary bodies. The intelligence centers were already carrying out purges on liberated territory of actual and perceived "collaborators of the occupiers" and other "enemies of the people." They also prepared lists for such purges before they ever entered a town.

22. Among the people and within the Communist Party there were many who expected the new government to soften its revolutionary activities with victory and in peacetime. But the opposite happened: The single-party political dictatorship became more radi-

cally rigid and ruthless than during the war, with the obvious intention of extending totalitarian power over all segments of society. In his book *Conversations with Stalin*,[9] Milovan Đilas vividly describes the paranoid source of such a policy: the Kremlin. The morbid suspicion of everything and everyone, a suspicion that wartime victory against an external enemy had turned into a war against an internal "class" enemy, turned "into a dreadful unceasing battle" that knows no lulls and has no end. "A revolution in progress," a revolution that had ceased to be the means to achieve a great ideal, had been transformed into the ideal itself, the ideal unto itself, an unattainable holy grail: All that is done in the name of the revolution is valuable, progressive, and positive because the value and progress of the revolution is unquestionable. It is an inviolable fetish and cult. During the war, the most important virtue for a member of the Communist Party was bravery; after the war it became "revolutionary spirit." And this meant the uncompromising (and ruthless) execution of party decisions, regardless of whether they matched the convictions of the person carrying them out, whether in his opinion they were useful or harmful, wise or stupid, whether they carried within themselves good or evil. Such a revolution, and perhaps every revolution, by its victory carries within itself its own death.

23. For four years after the war the KPJ and the KPH introduced in their respective areas an almost complete Stalinist system, excluding some of its paranoias, such as the continual purges at the upper levels of power and Stalin's monstrous anti-Semitism. With great fervor the communists were in the forefront of the reconstruction of the devastated country, but with equal fervor they cemented their one-party government, and conformism became an unwritten law. Already before the end of 1945, weak attempts by remnants of the HSS to resurrect at least a rudimentary form of political pluralism were crushed. Victorious vengeance in the early weeks after the war

quickly grew into systematic political repression against the "collaborators of the occupiers," "war profiteers," "exploiters of the working class," "kulaks," "smugglers," "bureaucrats," "saboteurs," and suspicious people of all types. The Catholic Church was repressed. The courts were transformed into an expedited service for the government's policy. The efficiency of industry and commerce was destroyed by massive expropriations and ill-advised nationalization. The forced introduction of peasant labor cooperatives modeled after the Soviet *kolkhoz* seriously damaged agriculture. The postwar enthusiasm of a good portion of the population was destroyed by the terror of political conformism; the initial joyous zeal gave way to listless obedience. From a respected military leader, Tito had turned into an untouchable icon. The extent of the damage inflicted on the people and the country in the course of four years would still be felt forty years later. These four years were the greatest historical error of the Croatian and Yugoslav communists' Partisan generation.

24. I know that many members of the Communist Party at the time were not satisfied with the postwar actions of a government they considered their own. This dissatisfaction was reflected in the conversations of former wartime comrades or in the confidences shared among close friends. To speak publicly about it could be fatal, especially for party members. Unquestioned fidelity and self-denying dedication to the party's goals and policies set by a "wise leadership" were all they were entitled to. If a party member dared to express some doubts or to make mildly heretical comments at a party meeting, the least he could expect would be an accusation of "a weak revolutionary spirit" or "un-communist behavior." While self-reliance and self-initiative on the part of the local party organizations and individuals was a necessity in wartime, and criticism and relatively free speech were tolerated to some degree within the party, in the early postwar years it was as if the spirit of Tito's prewar threat

that "anyone who doesn't submit to these tasks in a disciplined fashion belongs on the other side of the barricade, that is, on the side of the enemies of the working class," had come back to haunt us. The party and OZNA had become the chief instruments of a state dictatorship, and conformism within the party meant conformism throughout society. Without the freedom to criticize within the party and without a political opposition in public, the regime became more entrenched in its own self-absorption.

25. The disillusionment began in 1948 with Stalin's personal attack on Tito, on his closest associates, and on the independence of Yugoslavia. It wasn't enough for the Kremlin masters that the KPJ and the KPH recognized their leading role and followed their foreign and domestic policies. They demanded absolute obedience, the servile relationship with the communist governments of other satellite states of the Soviet bloc. But to demand humiliating servility from self-assured victors in the war was a major error on the part of the Kremlin. Stalin recklessly intruded upon the better part of the traditions of the KPJ and the KPH, carried over from the Partisan war of 1941–1945. The primary bearers of these traditions were the party elite, those roughly three thousand surviving prewar communists and *prvoborci* from 1941 who, carefully assigned to key positions in the party and government apparatus, carried out the decisions of the central party leadership and de facto managed the country. The great majority remained faithful to their leadership, thereby contributing to the success of Tito, the KPJ, and Yugoslavia itself in resisting the powerful community of communist governments and parties around the world. It was yet another victory, and also the last victory, achieved by the generation of leaders from the uprising of 1941.

26. The people considered the anti-Stalin resistance of the threatened Tito and his followers to be resistance to foreign domination. There were no democratic elections or polls of public opinion, so we

can rely only on elementary personal conjectures. I believe that the victors in 1945 would have also been convincing winners in free multiparty elections in Croatia and Yugoslavia in the first months after the war, but that they would have quickly lost the wide support of the people. For several years after the war the ruling minority had forcibly implemented measures against the will of the majority of the people. The Stalinist Soviet attack on Tito personally, and on the KPJ and Yugoslavia, had again, to a certain degree, brought the interests of the communist leadership and the people closer together.

27. With an active and tacit majority in the party, the leadership of the KPJ used Stalinist methods to crush Stalinism and other deviations of the minority in its own ranks (about fifteen thousand male prisoners on Goli Otok and women prisoners on Sveti Grgur), but further opposition to Stalin without distancing themselves from Stalinism itself was unsustainable. The total economic blockade from the East, accompanied by military threats, dictated radical changes in foreign policy, specifically reliance on the Western powers, on the former wartime allies the United States, Great Britain, and France. Under the pressure of the serious economic situation and tensions in society, reforms had become necessary. For resistance to Stalin to be convincing, one had to be different from Stalin. In the summer of 1949, senior party forums had begun internal discussions about "decentralization and liberalization" and "new paths to socialism." A few of these deliberations were made public for the first time, but in a restrained way, at the Third Plenum of the KPJ on the island of Brioni in December 1949.[10] Then in 1950, the first laws on workers' councils and self-management were passed, revealing that within the revolutionary party, even when it had been transformed into a hard-line government, aspirations for freedom with democratic political potential still smoldered. Nevertheless, for the next

forty years that same party would be a limiting factor that prevented self-management and other pluralistic ideas born within it to flourish and to achieve their original intent.

28. In 1951 and 1952, people could feel that the government and the Communist Party had begun to loosen the reins on cultural and public life: within a period of only several months in Zagreb—at the exhibitions of the group EXAT, at the joint exhibition of Stančić-Vaništa, and with Murtić's *Doživljaj Amerike* (The American Experience)—there was a definitive break in Croatian painting with the mandatory socialist realism; art, culture, and science require freedom of expression and were seeping into the cracks of monolithic power. A generation of young Croatian writers started the freethinking journal *Krugovi* (Circles), and a group of intellectuals at the University of Zagreb started the journal *Pogledi* (Views); Ive Mihovilović and Frane Barbieri injected new life into Croatian journalism with the newly launched weekly *Vjesnik u srijedu* (Vjesnik on Wednesday) and the reorganized *Vjesnik*. At the kiosk on the main square people could suddenly buy *Le Monde*, *The Guardian*, and *Corriere della Sera*; for the first time student groups traveled to Western countries and it was possible to obtain passports for unhindered personal travel. Miroslav Krleža's paper at the Congress of Writers in Ljubljana opened new vistas. The organ of the KPH, the weekly *Naprijed* (Forward), demonstrated the freethinking aspirations of some party intellectuals in critically intoned articles, but it was quickly shown that they didn't have the support of the party leadership. The Communist Party had permitted a liberalization of everyday life to specified limits and could stop such liberalization if those limits were exceeded.

29. From the 141,066 members that it could count on the day the war ended, the Communist Party swelled to 468,175 members by the Fifth Congress in July 1948 and to about 600,000 members by the

fall of 1952. It was no longer a party of self-sacrificing, battle-tested visionaries and disciplined soldiers of the revolution. Its ranks had been swelled by opportunists, careerists, the power-hungry, sycophants, and small-time schemers, along with younger people of the postwar period who still believed in the optimism of the slogan "We will build a new world." Although diluted and heterogeneous, the party, with its massiveness, had permeated all aspects of society and strictly controlled it. Organized with harsh hierarchical subordination, it routinely issued directives "from above" and blocked initiatives "from below." As long as such a party monopolistically dominated government and society, liberalization and democratization in the full sense were unachievable, and the healthy concept of a federally run state remained only rudimentary.

30. The wave of limited liberalization, in spite of various obstacles, slowly spread over four years. By July 1953, Yugoslavians had begun to hope that they were on the threshold of what today is called Euroatlantic integration: Yugoslavia had signed agreements and published declarations on a Balkan alliance with Greece and Turkey, with members of NATO, and with close partners in the emerging western European Economic Community. It seemed as if Yugoslavia was moving toward the West in a roundabout way. In the party daily *Borba* in the fall of that same year, one of Tito's three closest associates, the leading party ideologue Milovan Đilas, known as the defender of rigid revolutionary methods in the war and firm ideological dogmatism just before and after it, suddenly supported pluralism, the democratization of political life, and essentially a multiparty system. By the end of the year, eighteen of Đilas's articles had been published in *Borba* and with each of those articles enthusiasm grew among those intellectuals, inside and outside the party, who until then had stifled their sympathies for free critical thinking. Valika Stein-Singer—a longtime friend of my mother who was then a deputy re-

public minister of social policy and before the war the hostess in the salon of Beno Stein, which brought together Zagreb's left-wing intelligentsia—approached me on the street. She hugged and kissed me, tears of happiness in her eyes, and whispered in my ear that because of Đilas's articles "life is worth living again." A poll on Đilas's articles, which I conducted as the editor of *Vjesnik u srijedu*, was flooded with expressions of enthusiasm, or at least of approval. But the first ominous sign also appeared: Zvonko Brkić, the organizational secretary of the Central Committee of the League of Communists of Croatia, and prior to that Tito's chief of staff for many years, refused to make any statement about Đilas's articles. He coldly explained to Zlatko Glik, his wartime colleague and the deputy editor of our newspaper, that he would not make a statement because he didn't agree with Đilas's ideas. Several days later we read a terse report in the newspapers that an extraordinary plenum of the Central Committee of the League of Communists of Yugoslavia would be held on January 16, 1954, to discuss the "case of Comrade Milovan Đilas." The great wave of liberalization had come to an end.

31. For three or four months, approximately the length of Đilas's heyday, the latent aspirations for freedom among the prewar communists experienced its last great eruption. Although these ideas of freedom within the Communist Party were killed off by the fetish of revolution, dogma, and party discipline, they had survived among many as distant, hazy ideals, forbidden fruits that had suddenly become attainable. The extraordinary plenum of the Central Committee of the League of Communists of Yugoslavia in January 1954 served as the crude burial of the awakened illusions. State radio broadcast all of the sessions of the two-day meeting live. It was sad to listen to Đilas vacillating, agonizing, giving in, and repenting under pressure from the dogmatists and to hear the dogmatism still alive within him. It was even sadder to listen to the leading party

intellectuals, Edvard Kardelj, Moša Pijada, Vladimir Bakarić, Veljko Vlahović, Krste Crvenkovski, and others, who until only a few days before had publicly supported Đilas's ideas. At the plenum they accused and defamed him and tore him to pieces both intellectually and personally in the crudest manner possible in order to prove their loyalty to the dogma, the party, and Tito. To those of us listening on the radio it vividly demonstrated how far we could tread with heresy, and that if we dared tread further, we would hear the thunder.

32. Before, during, and after the plenum, the ultimate arbitrator was Tito. In *War and Peace*, Tolstoy tried to determine to what extent the victory over Napoleon should be attributed to Kutuzov and to what extent it should be attributed to all of the other participants and the general circumstances. Of course, he couldn't give a clear answer, just as many other writers, historians, and philosophers who have examined the "role of the individual in history" cannot. But I believe Tito's influence on our lives for forty years was immense. From 1950 to 1953, he tolerated controlled liberalization because at the time of crisis he needed to win the support of the people and the democratic world. He felt that he had to be different from Stalin. Later he decisively halted the wave of liberalization when he understood that it might threaten the ruling monopoly of the League of Communists of Yugoslavia (as the communist party became known after 1952) and his undisputed personal power. However, he didn't abolish some of the freedoms that the first liberalization had given us. He continued to rule in a hot-and-cold manner—a small dose of freedom followed by a tightened grip, sometimes with kid gloves, sometimes with a firm hand, and sometimes with the gloves off. He was a hedonist who bathed in luxury, but at the same time he felt a responsibility for the economic and social standards of the populace and tried to improve it. He liked to build roads, to improve schools, to expand social but not civil and political rights. He had a great

ambition to be an influential world leader, which he partly achieved. With the slightly expanded freedoms at home he succeeded in deceiving us that under his rule we could perhaps expect more, but the periodic crackdowns reminded us that the limits of that freedom were still firm and definitively drawn at the extraordinary plenum of the Central Committee of the League of Communists of Yugoslavia in January 1954. Some people have said that "Titoism is communism with a human face." I would rather define it as a "milder communism." In some circumstances the face of that communism, sometimes called "Titoism," wasn't exactly human; it embittered the lives of many people. However, the circle of freedom had expanded: From Satellite No. 1, we had become the most liberal communist country, but still communist. The standard of living increased, faster than in the countries of the Soviet bloc, although much slower than in the world of economic freedom and liberal democracy. When we dissatisfied Yugoslav citizens wanted a little consolation, we only had to glance across the border to Bulgaria, Romania, and Hungary, where until the end of the 1980s "Yugoslavia" was an unachievable dream, practically the land of milk and honey. On the other hand, if we needed a reality check, we only had to glance across the border at Austria or Italy. For more than thirty years we enjoyed the privilege of freedom of movement to the East and to the West. In the world of communist tyranny—to which in some degree we belonged—we were still an exception, the only communist country outside the iron curtain, outside the collective prison of a billion and a half people, a country in the slippery area of prescribed freedoms in which so much was permitted, but in which it was dangerous to seek freedom without a prescription.

33. To return to the initial question: What did the Partisans and the communists leave as legacy? How much good, how much evil? In major historical events and epochs it is difficult to define a clear border

between good and evil. There are few things that are unambiguously evil, just as there are even fewer that are unambigousously good. The French Revolution committed a variety of evils, but it left behind many good things. Mindful of T. S. Eliot's verse, "only with time does time win," we can say that in the war years of 1941–1945 the Partisans and the communists created more good than evil, in the early postwar years more evil than good, and in the period 1950–1953 they tried to make amends, at least partially, for the evil that was committed, so perhaps there was more good than evil. Regarding the entire forty-year period of milder communism, from 1950 to 1989, it is difficult to judge reliably because the consequences still endure, and the final outcome cannot be evaluated. Our experiences, like our perceptions, are varied, and I dare to state mine.

34. I think it is clear that the milder communism under Tito's government and for ten years after Tito wasn't the same as the communism of the Soviet Union and the states under its domination. There were some common characteristics (one-party government and limited political and civil rights), but there were also some distinct differences that made our lives different from those of the countries of the Soviet bloc. I think that the harsh condemnation of communism as a social order that the Council of Europe announced in 2005 can only in some ways relate to the former Yugoslavia. We lived in the shadow of the iron curtain, under its constant threat, but for forty years we were beyond its reach.

35. A generation of fanatically brave prewar communists led the uprising of 1941 and helped to bring about a unique military victory in Europe at that time. The awareness of that victory allowed them several years later to stand up to Stalin and the entire communist world, to keep their hold on power, and to establish an independent state. For the next few decades it wasn't always easy for them to

maintain that independence with a regime of mild communism, on that slippery terrain between the two opposing blocs. Tito skillfully steered a middle course and even succeeded in promoting himself as the leader of nonaligned states, but all of this was possible only with the loyalty of the older generation of prewar communists with whom he had won the war. But these efforts exhausted the powers of that generation and of Tito. To a great extent they remained prisoners of the prewar hard-line Bolshevization, of rigid conformist dogmas, of Comintern courses and schooling. With such obstacles it was impossible to build a society of lasting civil and political rights—the only healthy exit from the contradictions of mild communism. At the end of the 1960s, the younger generation of communists-Partisans realized this. They weren't burdened by the prewar Comintern schools, and mild communism had provided them with more systematic schooling and a broader view of the world. The Croatian Spring reformers, the Serbian liberals, the Slovenian street protesters, and supporters of reform and liberalization in other Yugoslav republics appeared. They openly called for constitutional reforms, the advancement of civil rights, and the further democratization of public life. They were stopped by Tito and the yes-men of his regime. The last chance had passed for reform to be carried out under the aegis of the communist government that would have forestalled the sufferings of the 1991–1995 war and might have led to an agreement for peaceful dissolution or joint entry into a democratic Europe. Unreformed Yugoslav communism, incapable of surviving the impending crisis, fell into the hopeless agony of the 1980s. Through its failures in multiethnic Croatia and Yugoslavia, it opened the way for nationalism and all of the consequences that followed. The years 1991–1995 returned us to the years 1941–1945. The dangers of further historical repetition have not passed, as long as in many hearts and minds prejudices still smolder that human beings can be persecuted and even killed only because they were born into another nationality or faith or because they dared to think differently.

20

Liberation

"GERMANY HAS SURRENDERED! The war is over!" coursed through the battalions of the Karlovac Shock Brigade at noon on May 8, 1945. We were quartered in homes and courtyards along the Karlovac–Zagreb road between Draganić and Jastrebarsko, preparing to move out. We were supposed to be "chasing bandits" over Žumberak toward Slovenia, where the fighting was still going on. We received the news of the war's end without much enthusiasm—what kind of ending could it be when just yesterday we were being shot at on the approaches to Draganić and tomorrow we would be shot at in Slovenia? The explosion of joy came only two or three days later when the order came from divisional headquarters: "Karlovac Brigade to Karlovac!" In unrestrained celebration the men fired volleys and salvos into the air until a strict order stopped them, "Cease-fire! Are you all crazy? A man has been wounded, cease-fire!" A stray bullet had hit the deputy commander of a squad, a young man from Duga Resa, in the buttocks and the medics hurried over to him. The wounded man laughed: "It's nothing. I'll walk to Karlovac if I have to, and even to Duga Resa! We're going home, that's what counts!"

Karlovac was about twenty kilometers away by road, but the brigade happily marched and sang without pause. Twelve hundred young men were returning from the war to their homes, to their city, which had been liberated for two days. Three nights earlier, on the banks of the Kupa River below Ozalj, we listened to the echoes of the artillery fire in the battle for Karlovac. Under the nighttime shelling, I crawled into an abandoned bunker just before the railway bridge at Zorkovac Field, thinking it could be my last combat assignment. I was suddenly gripped by a cold fear that perhaps the bunker was rigged with explosives or that I might step on a mine when I was on the verge of reaching home and at the very end of the war. In the ranks of the brigade as it approached the city I felt relief in knowing that it was finally over; no longer would there be heavy bursts of fire whistling overhead or mined bunkers on the banks of the Kupa.

About six weeks before the end of the war, my mother was assigned to lead a large convoy of wounded soldiers from the Partisan hospital in Petrova Gora to "real" hospitals in liberated Dalmatia. As a reward for successfully completing this assignment, she was permitted to enter liberated Karlovac with the first rear-echelon troops. Of course, she took Danko with her. They arrived in the city on the morning of May 7, barely twelve hours after the German and Ustasha troops had retreated and about thirty-six hours before the Karlovac Shock Brigade arrived. They immediately found Pavica Vine and Jaga, and with the latter they went to our apartment. No one was there. Franjo Družak and his wife had probably left the city in a hurry because some of their clothes and other items remained in the apartment. My mother and Jaga discovered that very few of our possessions were missing: Most of the furniture was there, as were all of the pictures and most of the carpets, kitchen items, and vases, and even a good portion of the books. "He didn't have to put his name in them," my mother complained when she noticed Družak's signature on some of the nicer editions of the books, including my father's bound set of Goethe's works with the picturesque Gothic lettering.

In the first days after liberation throngs of people inundated the newly established headquarters for the city, seeking information about their children, husbands, sisters, brothers, and friends still scattered around the country in Partisan units. Here my mother was among the first to learn that the Karlovac Shock Brigade was returning to the city. She stood the entire evening at the wrecked bridge in Banija and waited for the brigade to arrive. It was close to midnight when Boris Balaš, the popular Karlovac sportsman and the commander of our brigade, appeared on horseback at the head of the column. My mother breathed a sigh of relief when she heard from him that her son was alive and well, somewhere in the rear of the column with the staff of the Fourth Battalion. Nor could he refuse my mother's request to take me home that very evening.

As we approached Karlovac I had the feeling my mother would be waiting for me. When she pulled me from the ranks "at the order of the brigade commander," I was a bit confused in her embrace. I couldn't even dream that I would sleep in my own room, in my own bed that night. Jaga had brought home many of our things that had been stored with Pavica. With Danko's help she had cleaned the apartment and arranged it more or less the way we had left it four years earlier. Danko and I again had our room; Jaga had her room, and my mother had the bedroom. Alone in a room in which she had never been alone, in the evening hours my mother may have given herself over to a sadness that during the day was suppressed by tireless activity. Too many things in the apartment reminded her of her Ivo. All of us—Danko, Jaga, and me—felt a great unspoken emptiness, a wound that we would have to live with.

For the next week I had to report for duty every morning to the political department of the brigade, but like the other members of the Karlovac Shock Brigade, I slept at home. I worked on editing the brigade newspaper and the battalion's news flyers. Some of my superiors had considered nominating me for training at higher military schools in Belgrade and the Soviet Union, but I didn't like the idea. In Slunj three months before the end of the war Veco Holjevac, the political commissar of our corps, brought up the subject.

"Slavko, we're getting ready to enter the cities. A Municipal Committee for the SKOJ is being set up in Karlovac and they are asking that I release you from the Karlovac detachment. What do you say?"

I said that I would rather stay in the detachment, but only until the end of the war. I would feel like a deserter if I were to abandon friends in whose company I had been through so much, especially since all that remained was for us to march together into Karlovac. I explained that I had no desire to work in the committee after the war, but that I wanted to make up for the four school years I had lost, to finish gymnasium and enroll at the university. Holjevac liked my answer. He stuck out his hand as if confirming an agreement.

Later my mother found a nice way to remind Holjevac of his wartime promise, and so on May 15, 1945, one week after my return to Karlovac, I became the first soldier of the Karlovac Shock Brigade to be demobilized. For a brief time, I still paraded around town in my uniform with its officer's insignia as I didn't have any civilian clothes, until one day the man who was our tailor before the war called out to me: "Hey, Slavko, I can't call you little Goldstein anymore now that you're an officer. Your father left some cloth with me and I saved it. Come by and I'll make you a suit."

* * *

The country came out of the war devastated, impoverished, and hungry. The people had had to feed the armies of two foreign occupiers and four different homegrown armies for four years, while the best manpower was in jail, in concentration camps, on the battlefield, or in the ground. About 200,000 working-age people from Croatia and Bosnia had to labor in Germany for Hitler's war machine, while at home there was no one left to cut the grass. The railway network was paralyzed, with half of the bridges destroyed and more than half of the equipment disabled. "The citizens of the city of Zagreb have begun to receive rationed bread," *Vjesnik* announced on May 16, 1945, but only 150 to 250 grams per day, while almost no other foodstuffs were available in the markets. A month later the newspapers announced that "the first deliveries of food for the city of Zagreb have begun to arrive," which included fifty railway wagons of flour, fifteen wagons of potatoes, and seven wagons of beans. This translated to about half a kilogram of potatoes and one-quarter of a kilogram of beans per resident. On June 6, the correspondent of *Vjesnik* wrote that "the people of Karlovac will provide abundant assistance to the people of Kordun," but that assistance was modest because the needs of the battered people of Kordun were huge, while the capabilities of the people of Karlovac were proportionally small.

The most depressing items in the newspapers were the personal ads: "All former prisoners in Lepoglava until the end of the war, if you know anything about Josip Grdenić, please contact his wife, Jurjevska Street 31, Zagreb" or "Anyone who knows anything about our son Marijan Borčić, please contact his parents." In the first months after the war such cries for help flooded the newspapers. My mother was the director of foster homes in Karlovac and Ozalj, and several times she wrote such personal ads searching for the lost parents of her charges, knowing that happy replies would be few.

We learned from Sarajevo that my aunt Danica Grof (née Goldstein) had survived the war in the Partisans, and my cousins Mirko and Ita Haler in Italian internment camps. Their mother, Valika, my father's eldest sister, had died in a camp, while their sister, Ivana, who was my age, had died as a Partisan nurse from wounds she had suffered at a battle on the Pelješac peninsula in 1944. All of the remaining members of my father's family had disappeared in Ustasha and Nazi concentration camps, but we had heard about their fates some time earlier: In regard to my uncle Oto, his wife, Greta, and their son, Darko, we again received confirmation that they had been sent to Jasenovac in 1943, and it was only much later that I found out that they had ended up in Auschwitz in 1944; we learned that my grandmother, grandfather, and aunt Berta from Tuzla had been taken somewhere in the summer of 1942 and to this day we don't know where; Aunt Alma, her husband, Aco, and their son, Feliks, were on the list of Jasenovac victims from 1942. The survivors from my mother's family were scattered around the world. After many difficulties, most of them reached Israel, where my mother's sister Rut and brother Oto-Jehošua Bril, both Palestinian veterans, had brought them with much personal sacrifice. Their mother, my grandmother Sabina, died in 1942 in the Ukrainian village of Đurin, near Mogilev, after she had been exiled there by the Romanian fascist government, along with my mother's eldest sister, Elza, her husband, Moše Greif, and their daughter, Gerda. Greif also died in exile, while Elza and Gerda, after suffering their "calvary" through Bessarabia, somehow reached Bucharest. With a reckless scheme and the assistance of Aunt Rut, they reached Israel via Paris in 1949. My mother's youngest sister, Šošana, survived the war in Bucharest with her husband and son, thanks to some exceptional circumstances. With the assistance of Uncle Oto, they moved to Israel in 1951. The greatest tragedy struck my mother's youngest brother, Berthold-Holcju Bril, and his wife and two-year old daughter. In 1941, the Germans sent them to a concentration camp in Ukraine after cleansing Chernowitz of Jews. Their daughter died there of starvation and disease. The Gestapo then killed Berthold's wife before his eyes and in anger and desperation he intentionally instigated his own death. Wresting himself from the hands of the Gestapo, he rushed toward the barbed-wire fence and was shot. Although I have never read the book, my cousin Gerda Greif has told me that Berthold's dramatic suicide was described by an eyewitness, the Romanian writer Arnold Daghani, in his book *Grob u višnjiku* (The Grave is in the Cherry Orchard).[1] My mother's eldest brother, Herman, his wife, and their daughter found refuge in a village not far from Chernowitz, where he somehow survived the war as a merchant. With the return of the Red Army to Chernowitz in 1944, Herman continued his commercial activities, which the communist government considered "illegal speculation," sending Uncle Herman to a camp for "criminal-correctional forced labor." When he was released from the camp a year and a half later and reached home, he suffered a heart attack the day he arrived and died. His daughter, Rut, whom I met in New York in 1978, thinks her father died of a heart ailment he developed in the camp, combined with the excitement of finally being home.

My mother's brother Šaju, a watchmaker by profession, passed through the longest "calvary." When the Russians occupied Chernowitz in 1940, they proclaimed him a "bourgeois element" and deported him to the Siberian taiga with his wife and one-year-old son, Dani. They spent sixteen years in an isolated village about three hundred kilometers north of Tomsk. Uncle Šaju's "golden hands" saved them as he made repairs in the neighboring villages and received food in return. Occasional packages from Israel that Aunt Rut and Uncle Oto managed to send despite many obstacles also helped. With the assistance of Golda Meir, the first woman Israeli ambassador to the Soviet Union, and after a huge number of expected and unexpected complications, Rut and Oto finally managed to get Šaju out of Siberia and to settle him in Riga. After ten more years of further complications, Oto and Rut obtained a visa for Šaju to emigrate from the USSR to Israel with his family. Uncle Šaju and Aunt Erna could finally enjoy a peaceful old age and live to see Dani establish a happy and successful family in Raanana, one of the greenest of Israel's new cities.

Of the approximately 330 members of the Karlovac Jewish Community before the war, I know of only 53 who returned after the war. Perhaps ten to fifteen survived the war overseas and no longer wanted to return, or if they did return, they didn't get back in touch. Of the 2,750 Serbian Orthodox people in Karlovac before the war, 1,196 didn't live to see the end of the war. Most were killed in the Ustasha camps at Jasenovac, Jadovno, and Pag, many on the battlefield as Partisans, and more than two hundred in exile, as refugees, or as prisoners. Karlovac's Croatian families weren't spared either: almost every one of them mourned the loss of a family member or a good friend who had been killed as a Partisan, or as a member of the Home Guard or the Ustasha. And the news had spread in whispers that the jails were again full and that people were disappearing overnight.

* * *

Returning to my thoughts of what happened more than sixty years ago, the paradoxes of that early postwar period still confound me. The joy of victory clashed with the first disappointments; the drunkenness of great expectations was shattered by a brutal reality. It seemed that the sadness and misery the war had bequeathed to us was starting to fade away in the enthusiasm of a new era, but that new era brought new sadnesses and miseries, rooted in the horrors of the past. I think of Charles Dickens, writing in *A Tale of Two Cities* sixty years after the great revolution: "It was the best of times, it was the worst of times, it was the age of wisdom, it was the age of foolishness, it was the epoch of belief, it was the epoch of incredulity, it was the season of Light, it was the season of Darkness, it was the spring of hope, it was the winter of despair, we had everything before us, we had nothing before us...."

Much of what had been destroyed in the devastated country was rebuilt remarkably quickly. The demolished bridges in Karlovac and the surrounding area were able to handle traffic after several weeks. High-school students volunteered to cut wood, working the saws at full speed, and wooden huts for temporary accommodations rose on the charred remains of Kordun's homes. After four years, the harvest was completed in peace, undisturbed. For a portion of the population, food provided by the United Nations Relief and Rehabilitation Administration was a lifesaver.

Much of the population was caught up in the enthusiasm of reconstruction, and the slogan "*Nema odmora dok traje obnova*" (No rest while the reconstruction is in progress) was for many people more than just an empty phrase. Factories that had enough raw materials were working overtime at full capacity. Massive actions of so-called volunteer laborers and a variety of competitions to break the records weren't only compulsory events for propaganda purposes but also a reflection of a normal human need to participate in the rebuilding and renovation. This mix of the compulsory and voluntary, the organized and spontaneous, also permeated the massive entertainments that were staged in quick succession. The Croatia House in Karlovac, always filled to overflowing, staged choral performances and recitations, appearances by amateur companies, and at least one boring political speech every evening that degenerated into wild parties until the early-morning hours.

On May 27, 1945, *Vjesnik* reported that "at a magnificent gathering in Karlovac the Croatian and Serbian people of Kordun, Karlovac, and the surrounding area celebrated the birthday of Marshal Tito." The reporter probably exaggerated the total number of celebrants at thirty-five thousand, but columns bearing flags and banners were immensely long and flooded the city on all sides. They were loudly singing patriotic tributes to Tito for fighting for justice and people's rights. In the groups of young members of the League of Young Communists of Yugoslavia (SKOJ) I recognized girls from Prilišće and Hrašće, whom I had known and liked during the war, and I wondered whether they were shouting those slogans so diligently at the orders of SKOJ or because they were elated at having taken part in conquering the city. I think it was both because such were the times, the times of interwoven contrasts. At the meetings that were endlessly multiplying throughout the country unimaginative speakers using tired phrases were promising a brighter future. Nevertheless, the people clamored with approval because many believed in a brighter future; many others were indifferent but were carried along by the enthusiastic masses, and there were certainly those who didn't believe in a brighter future but clamored on because it was inexpedient to be out of step with the crowd. Seventy-year-old Vladimir Nazor was one of the rare speakers who, with his captivating rhetoric, succeeded in enthralling the residents of Zagreb. On May 16, 1945, residents flooded Ban Jelačić Square to hear him speak:

> We are bringing to you, the city of Zagreb, a new spirit, a new national life... that is, freedom and equality among all people. We are bringing to you a youth that is always prepared to resist and fight against evil. We are bringing to you faith in our ability and in our ideals. We bring love for every Croat, all men regardless of their language, faith, job, social strata, or the color of their skin. It is our desire that the unemployed, the neglected elderly and children, the lame, and the ill disappear from our city streets and village yards. Each of them, and any other unfortunate person in our country, will have the right to be cared for by the collective. Handouts humble a man, but to achieve all of this, comrades, we need your cooperation; we need your

> hard work and your patience because after so much destruction and devastation, we cannot achieve this overnight.... With suffering and blood we have preserved Croatia's national honor.... But there is something else that we are bringing to you. We are bringing to you the renunciation of every vengeful hatred. We will try only the obvious oppressor, traitor, and exploiter of someone else's efforts. All those who are able and prepared to work for the good of the federal state of Croatia, and who have not been tainted by criminal, political, or social misdeeds, will have before them an open path in collaborating with, in working for the homeland, in the free profession of their faith, and in the continued enjoyment of the property they have acquired through their own honest work.[2]

After such great promises and expectations, disappointments inevitably arose.

* * *

With my return to civilian life, I also returned to my old crowd—friends, colleagues, and the bookshop. I went to school and took walks on the promenade and along the Korana. I again played football and Ping-Pong. Already, in these early days after the war, I heard many questioning the new government: Why was it so ruthlessly evicting people from their apartments? Why was it appointing incompetent people "from the sticks" to positions of responsibility? Why have they arrested so-and-so who was never an Ustasha or an Ustasha sympathizer? I heard many complaints from our Jaga, who grumbled about the new government just as she had grumbled about all of the previous governments, and even more so, because she felt that this new government belonged, at least in part, to her. I voiced some of these complaints at the first postwar conference of Karlovac communists, which took place at the Croatia House in early June. I spoke in particular about the injustice in the market, where peasants from Rečica and Draganić had to maintain the maximum prices under threat of severe punishment, while the authorities turned a blind eye toward peasants from the Partisan areas of Kordun. Mane Trbojević, a member of the District Committee and a schoolteacher by profession, responded: "I am sorry that Comrade Slavko has so quickly fallen under the influence of the Karlovac bourgeoisie and is representing their positions at this conference."

In August 1944, I had just turned sixteen when Rudolf Pruner, the deputy commissar of the Karlovac Partisan movement, informed me that I was being promoted to a member of the Communist Party of Croatia (KPH). I felt quite honored because the main criteria for party membership at that time were courage in battle and good behavior as a comrade in the company and in the battalion. Acceptance into the Communist Party was considered a great recognition. With naïve ambition, I thought that, among my other duties as a communist, was the obligation to speak openly at party meetings and conferences, even about our own weaknesses. Indeed, this duty was written in the handbooks for party members where the section for "criticism and self-criticism" occupied an important place. This relatively free intraparty criticism was tolerated to a certain extent during the war, only to be curtailed in the first weeks after it.

At that time, I was volunteering in the agitprop division of the Municipal Committee of the KPH. I organized courses for new members and candidates, and I wrote the text for municipal proclamations. I worked at my job diligently and conscientiously but without the enthusiasm that had sustained me in the war years. I was more interested in returning to a normal life: working in the bookshop and studying for the examinations that would compensate for school years lost to the war. But everything in that springtime of freedom seemed easier and nicer to me with my first happy love.

Late on a warm summer evening I was walking Ljiljana home through the deserted Zrinski Square. An unusual group was approaching from the direction of the Kupa, where the headquarters of the Department for the Protection of the People (OZNA) was located, five or six men dejectedly walking, surrounded by three or four armed soldiers. This ominous scene was underscored by the naked bayonets the soldiers had fitted to their rifles and which were pointing threateningly to the sky. One of the group desperately waved at us. It was Professor Gorodecki, the father of one of Ljiljana's friends and a frequent visitor to our bookstore before the war. He had recognized us, or at least Ljiljana, and tried to call out to us, but one of the soldiers silenced him and pushed him back into the group. It was a painful scene. In the stillness of night we watched the group heading toward the Rijeka or Senj road through the empty Zrinski Square, as Gorodecki continued to look over his shoulder and tried to convey something to us through hand signs.

The next day I sought out a man from Karlovac I had met during the war, who I knew worked in the district office of OZNA. I asked him what was going on with Professor Gorodecki, but he only shrugged his shoulders. I said that Gorodecki was a favorite teacher of French and philosophy, a widely educated and fine man, popular in the cultural life of the city, a staunch antifascist, that his daughter worked in the municipal organization of SKOJ. The reticent officer muttered, "What can you do, that's the way it is, a Russian emigrant. You can't do anything, that's the directive." Although the man had not told me in so many words, it was clear that Gorodecki was no longer alive. I left, feeling deeply despondent. I had liked Gorodecki when he was my French teacher before the war, I was sorry for his daughter, and I was struck by the realization that people were being killed without establishing their guilt, with no judicial procedure, based on a crudely issued directive that suffered no objections.

The Veličkovićes' trial was an even harder blow, although it was not a matter of life or death. They were the friends who had helped my family and me in the most difficult of times, and now they were subjected to the injustice of my party and government, and I could do little to help. They were realistic people and knew that under the communist regime they would not be able to keep their 66 percent ownership in the Podvinec leatherworks, the largest factory in our city. They were preparing to donate the factory with all of its inventory to the state, which was not unusual in those days, and request that they remain in their positions as technical director and financial adviser until retirement. By making this donation, they would avoid the unpleasantness of expropriation or nationalization laws that were already in force, and at the same time continue to work in the factory as they had for their whole working lives. A married couple with no children, they were closely identified with the factory and its reputation.

My mother and I were at the Veličkovićes' reading the text they had prepared for the donation when Stevo Tomić arrived with bad news. Until joining the Partisans, Tomić had been an outstanding leatherworker in their factory. In 1943, he was the secretary of the clandestine Municipal Committee of the KHP. Somehow the police had discovered this and two detectives went to the factory to arrest him. They called Mr. Veličković from the gate and demanded that he take them to Tomić, but the resourceful Veličković told them that Tomić "had not come to work that day." Tomić came out of his hiding place that same evening and went directly to Kordun, to the Partisans. He returned to liberated Karlovac as the secretary of the temporary National Liberation Council for Karlovac. In that capacity he was also invited to a meeting of the Municipal Committee of the KPH. There he witnessed the discussion on how the confiscation of Karlovac factories from their current private owners should be accelerated by means of the Court for the Protection of National

Honor. Among the first factories mentioned was Podvinec and its majority owners, Mia and Aleksandar Veličković.

According to the legal decree for the protection of national honor issued by ZAVNOH in April 1945, "economic assistance to the occupier and his auxiliaries, especially placing economic enterprises at the service of the occupier" was among the things that would be considered "a crime or offense against national honor."[3] The decree called for the loss of civil rights, forced labor, and the confiscation of some or all property. With such general formulations, a court could confiscate the property of any businessman whose production, commercial, or banking enterprise had been operating on the territory of the Independent State of Croatia (NDH) during the war.

The Podvinec leather factory the Veličkovićes managed operated under the NDH at reduced capacity, with at most two hundred workers. Of course, it had also been ordered to make deliveries to NDH government institutions, perhaps even to the army. At the same time, the Veličkovićes had found a way to secretly deliver leather to the Partisans. I had personally acted as an intermediary during one such delivery. Of even greater value was the material assistance the Veličkovićes had provided to persecuted people, some of whose lives they had saved. It was an insulting idea that people such as the Veličkovićes could be sentenced for insulting national honor, lose their civil rights, and face the prospect of forced labor. Who, then, in Karlovac or in all of Croatia would remain unpunished? Only we who were Partisans? Or perhaps only those who had property that wasn't worth confiscating?

Under the circumstances, could the authorities be persuaded to accept the donation and give up the idea of confiscating the factory through the court? Tomić said that he would try to persuade the authorities in the Municipal Committee and the local OZNA to accept such an agreement. However, the Court for the Protection of National

Honor was a district institution and the district government would have the final say. He suggested that I go to the leading people in the District Committee and other district agencies where they knew me and with whom I still enjoyed a good reputation.

At the District National Liberation Committee I spoke with Mane Trbojević, the secretary, and then with Dušan Rkman, the president; at the District Committee of the Unified National Liberation Front I spoke with Marko Polović, the president. At the District Committee of the KPH I had a long and detailed discussion with Božo Rkman, the secretary. I pointed out that the Veličkovićes' donation was ready to proceed and everywhere made more or less the same arguments: Wasn't it better to accept a factory honorably from such people as a gift rather than to accuse them falsely of collaborating with the occupier? Wouldn't it be better to keep them as valuable experts instead of kicking them out as enemies and thereby compromising the court?

Not one of the officials with whom I met refuted my arguments. If the public prosecutor had not yet gone too far in issuing the indictment, the question of accepting the donation could be discussed.

Milutin Košarić, the public prosecutor for the district, was very direct with me. "The Court for the Protection of National Honor *is* a revolutionary court," he repeated several times. "Why would we accept gifts from the bourgeoisie when we have the court?" And then Comrade Košarić explained a little more calmly that he couldn't drop the indictment against the Veličkovićes because the prosecutor's office would be criticized for bringing the fewest indictments in all of Croatia before the Court for the Protection of National Honor.[4] But he would take into account the mitigating circumstances for the Veličkovićes: A donation or a court trial would amount to the same thing. One way or another the Veličkovićes would only lose the factory and no more.

Neither Tomić nor my mother accomplished much more than I

had in their efforts with municipal institutions in Karlovac or the republic ones in Zagreb. If someone intervened with Košarić, he showed no signs of wavering. But he kept his word: In the public trial against the Veličkovićes, he read out an indictment that was brief and that mentioned the extenuating circumstances. There were not many people in the courtroom. Tomić and I sat in the first row and informed the judge (whose name I have forgotten) that we were ready to testify. After the reading of the indictment, the judge allowed Aleksandar Veličković to speak. He was surprisingly bewildered. He held some papers in his trembling hands and was barely able to read. The public prosecutor interrupted him: "Tell me, Veličković, did your factory manufacture and deliver leather goods during the occupation? Yes or no?" The befuddled Veličković mumbled, "Well, yes, but—" before the public prosecution jumped in, "Well, that's the only thing I want to know; nothing else interests me."

The judge stated that the accused had admitted his guilt on the essential point of the indictment and that further evidence and possible testimonies were unnecessary. He then read the decision that had obviously been prepared in advance: Aleksandar Veličković, born in Pančevo in 1896, a resident of Karlovac, was sentenced to the loss of his civil rights for a period of two years and the confiscation of part of his property, that is, the ownership share of Podvinec. The entire trial lasted barely ten minutes. So it turned out that Košarić had kept to his interpretation: A donation or a conviction, it was all the same to him. The Veličkovićes had lost their factory but they kept their private property.

After the sentence was read, an uneasy stillness descended on the courtroom. The crestfallen Aleksandar sat next to Mia, who consolingly held his hand. The judge read Mia's sentence, which was the same as her husband's, except that she was sentenced to the loss of her civil rights for only one year.

There is an interesting epilogue to this story. The Veličkovićes had many acquaintances and were highly regarded in Slovenia—Mia in leftist-oriented circles of Slovenian intellectuals and artists, and Aleksandar among industrialists and leather merchants. Mia went to Ljubljana and spoke with Josip Vidmar, the president of the National Assembly of Slovenia. Vidmar called Luka Leskovšek, the minister of industry and also a secretary of the Central Committee of the Communist Party of Slovenia, who in turn invited Aleksandar to Ljubljana. After an hour's conversation with Aleksandar and another hour's consultation with his closest assistants, Leskovšek appointed Aleksandar as a special adviser for the leather industry and leather clothing in the Slovenian Ministry of Industry. Aleksandar enjoyed the trust of Leskovšek, who gave him great authority. When in 1948–49 there were shortages of raw materials because of the break in trade relations with the Soviet bloc countries, Aleksandar managed to use his old connections to arrange the purchase of raw leather on credit from Argentina and immediately to conclude the sale of the finished products in Switzerland and other countries. The Slovenian leather industry had survived its most serious crisis of the year through the immense professional and business expertise of Aleksandar Veličković, and it has continued to thrive ever since.

However, the former Podvinec leather factory no longer exists. It was taken over as a state enterprise and quickly experienced problems. It was incorporated into a business consortium, only to see its crisis deepen. It finally declared bankruptcy and was liquidated. All that is now left of the former Podvinec factory, where as many as four hundred people once worked, are its empty, gaping workshops.

In Ljubljana, Aleksander quickly recovered from the torments suffered in Karlovac, and true to his entrepreneurial spirit he diligently went around to all of the leather factories in Slovenia. Mia no longer wanted to work and almost never left the house. My mother frequently went to see her in Ljubljana, and I too was happy to visit them. Mia died of a heart attack in the spring of 1960, sitting at a table, playing her thirty daily hands of patience and smoking thirty cigarettes. Aleksandar outlived her by sixteen years.

* * *

I first heard about the events of May 1945 that became known as "Bleiburg" from Zvonko Pasek and Borivoj Kasumović, both members of SKOJ. The Ustasha had mobilized them on the last day of April, along with about twenty other high-school students, when they were withdrawing from Karlovac in early May, and ordered them to put on new light-blue Ustasha uniforms. Thus, about twenty Karlovac high-school students, among them seven or eight SKOJ members, found themselves in Podsused, a Zagreb suburb, in an immense column of soldiers and civilians fleeing toward Austria. In that mass of humanity were many members of the Home Guard and young boys, like ours from Karlovac, who had been mobilized and forced to join the march, but the majority were Ustasha with their families and other refugees who had reason to flee before the advancing Partisans. Two of the Karlovac students tried to escape, but the Ustasha escort caught and killed them. Stanko Lasić and Velimir Zgaga escaped in the village of Pojatno, and Lasić later described their wanderings in his *Autobiographical Notes*. Pasek and Kasumović, with several other Karlovac SKOJ members in Ustasha uniforms, escaped in Slovenia when the rapidly fleeing column began to fall apart. Only four of our boys from Karlovac reached Bleiburg, passed through the Way of the Cross and the camps, and after a month or two returned to Karlovac.

In June 1945, my mother gathered some information about Bleiburg from Mrs. Družak, who unexpectedly appeared at our door holding her young daughter by the hand. Mrs. Družak had come to ask if she could retrieve some things she had left in our apartment when they had fled Karlovac. At the outset, my mother was restrained and cold, but she led them into the kitchen and handed over some clothing and other items that we had come across in the apartment. Both women then relaxed a bit and Mrs. Družak told her story. She had gone all the way to Austria with her husband, but then they had become separated. She and her daughter had a torturous journey on foot to Maribor and several days in a camp, where she received a permit to return home. Mrs. Družak may already have had some news from her husband, but she didn't say so given the circumstances of his survival; he later settled in Argentina.

Then one hot summer day my friend Joško Hagendorfer arrived from Topusko. An otherwise cheerful, humorous character, Joško was in no mood for joking that day. In Topusko he was serving as a clerk in a company of the People's Defense Corps of Yugoslavia (KNOJ). It was insufferable, he complained, and asked if I could help him get out of Topusko and the KNOJ, and out of the army altogether.

Joško was one of the group of slightly older Karlovac high-school students who had drawn me into their circle in the summer of 1941, to ease a bit of the misery I was going through. They helped me take books from my family's lending library that was about to be confiscated by the Ustasha government. I divided some of these books among them, and we hid the rest, which I recovered after the war. Most of the boys from this group joined the Partisans. Joško had been in my company from the time it was formed in August 1944 until it was disbanded in April 1945. Among the friendships made during my three years in the Partisans, the one with Joško was and remained the closest. Together we had gone through some difficult times, and at one particularly dangerous moment we had literally saved each other's lives. Joško was popular in the unit for being funny at rest and calm under fire. We were all sorry when the unit disbanded right before the end of the war, Joško leaving with a small group to join the KNOJ.

Assigned to the KNOJ unit in Kordun, he experienced quite an ordeal. He was quartered with a group of soldiers who made up the guard unit in the local jail and carried out "special" assignments. At nightfall, the duty officer would come to the guardhouse and ask for volunteers to carry out executions. Two or three people usually volunteered; the rest were coerced by the duty officer. Some Bosnians from the Cazin region cited religious reasons that forbade them to carry out such orders. Surpisingly the duty officer usually accepted these reasons. As the unit's clerk, Joško enjoyed the privilege of being spared from guard duty and from the "special" night assignments. However, in the morning he had to write the unit's report that often stated, "Five bandits liquidated, two bullets used."

During the war, on numerous occasions I witnessed two or more Ustasha prisoners led away for execution. Several times I heard the volleys from such executions. I always felt very uneasy, but I managed to calm myself by rationalizing them as inevitabilities of wars. However, listening to stories about the slaughters—most frequently by Ustasha, then Chetniks, and sometimes even by our own soldiers—was deeply painful. I would picture that terrible, inhuman act, and a hundred times I would return to Ivan Goran Kovačić's *Jama* (The Pit). I published a special illustrated edition of this book of poems, but I could never read it all the way through because I couldn't bear the images it brought to mind. I once heard that the commissar of a company in our brigade, with whom I had been friendly, had "slit the throat" of a seriously wounded Ustasha during the assault on Mondekar Castle near Netretić. After hearing the story, I avoided this man. It was difficult for me to accept that an officer in our brigade would do something that I wanted to attribute only to the Ustasha and the Chetniks.

Of course, each new realization became more sobering than the last in these first months after the war. For at least a year I consoled myself by saying that this was only a childhood disease, a painful disease but a temporary one. Then for some time I tried to convince myself and my close friends that it was a mistake arising from the inability of many of our leaders to implement a brilliant idea and was not part of the idea of socialism. First loves are not extinguished quickly or suddenly. We often need a great deal of time to recover our balance and sanity.

I initially acquired a rather vague notion about Bleiburg and the Way of the Cross syndrome in 1945, but I sensed that it was a trauma of great proportions. Nor did I have a complete picture of that trauma twenty or more years later, when I first read about it in London and Paris in various émigré writings. These were one-sided depictions with many credible and shocking details of the killings but without an objective picture of the events surrounding it. I found it especially disturbing that these texts consistently remained silent about the direct roots of Bleiburg and the Way of the Cross, about the year 1941. Moreover, I felt that a politicized myth had been created about the Bleiburg crime to put the more serious crime of 1941 into the background. As a journalist, publisher, and participant in public life, I knew that such a trauma couldn't be overcome without bringing to light the entire documented truth and that 1945 couldn't be judged independently from 1941, just as no definitive judgment could be passed on 1941 in isolation from 1945. In 1969, in my capacity as the editor in chief of NIP *Stvarnost* and in 1979 as the director of Liber University Publishing, I tried to initiate objective research and publishing on Bleiburg and the Way of the Cross through discreet interviews with people from the senior political leadership. But in both instances I was adamantly refused. The taboo was untouchable, probably on orders from the most senior of all of the senior leaderships.

The enforced silence was not eased until 1989 or 1990, by which time it was too late for calm investigation and level-headed discussion. The traumas of 1941 and 1945 had returned in altered incarnations.

Paradoxically, in the huge amount of literature about Bleiburg and the Way of the Cross there has not been a single study that comprehensively and objectively presents the tragedy based on research of all relevant sources, taking into account the various aspects and components of the events. Nevertheless, some publications have recently appeared that provide a more thorough, if still incomplete, view of the events. The magisterial work of Jozo Tomasevich, *War and Revolution in Yugoslavia, 1941–1945*, might set the standard, but it is also worth mentioning that antifascist veterans, after sixty years of voluntary or enforced silence, have finally decided to confront this trauma of Croatian and Yugoslav antifascism publicly. In 2006, the Council of the Alliance of Anti-Fascist Fighters of Croatia organized a roundtable on the theme of Bleiburg and the Way of the Cross. In addition to several self-serving papers and statements in the discussion, which did little to help the purpose of the roundtable, there were some well-argued papers, primarily from younger authors and supporters of antifascism, that respected the truth.

* * *

My gradual break with the Communist Party took two to three years, but my discontent became public in the spring of 1946, when Vlado Sokač, the secretary of the Municipal Committee of the KPH, assigned me to requisition produce in the outlying village of Hrnetić. He handed me a list of the village's households with the exact amounts that I had to "requisition" from each. I have put the word "requisition" in quotation marks because this was, in fact, forced confiscation of the stocks from otherwise impoverished peasants in return for unrealistically low monetary compensation. I felt I wasn't suited for such a task and I immediately said so to Sokač, but he persuaded me that this was important, we all had to participate. Without requisitioning we would not be able to feed the urban population until the harvest, and the peasants had to be told openly that if they didn't voluntarily turn over the assigned quantities, they would be confiscated with an additional punishment of forced labor.

We had already heard the unpleasant news of the "requisitioning operation" from various people, but Jaga learned the details from her family in the village. She claimed that the requisition lists had been drawn up "either off the cuff or through connections," most often to extract revenge on someone or to pluck some alleged kulak or political undesirable naked. "It's simple robbery! Get away from this, Slavko, get out of it however you can, it's not a job for honest people," Jaga implored me.

When I biked to Hrnetić the next morning, I felt uneasy and had butterflies in my stomach as never before, whether on a military or a peacetime assignment. I knew that Mića Katarinčić lived in Hrnetić and I went directly to see him to get his advice. He wasn't on my requisition list, so to some extent I believed that he would be an objective judge. He was horrified when I gave him the list to review: "What is this, are you crazy? You'll create bad blood among the villagers and turn them into a collective enemy of your party and government!" The anonymous author of the list, he believed, was either completely uninformed or ill-intentioned. Some people were more or less spared, while others were being asked for more than they had and would have to sell everything they owned to meet the prescribed quota. Many of them would be impoverished and their willingness to engage in agricultural production would be destroyed. Everyone would be embittered.

Before the war Mića Katarinčić had been the secretary of the Karlovac URS, a bricklayer, and a self-educated man, well read in literature, politics, and Marxism, and a respected leftist intellectual in

Karlovac. He married into a worker-peasant family in Hrnetić. In the middle or late 1930s, he was a member of the Communist Party but was then pushed out in 1940 because of his support of Krleža and his followers. He frequently came to our bookshop and was an assiduous reader of books from our lending library. Katarinčić also harbored obvious feelings for our Jaga, who remained rather reserved, holding firmly to her opinion that it was stupid to become involved with a married man. Banned from the party, Mića joined the Partisans rather late, but his prewar comrades in the unions still offered him a modest job in the postwar unions. With his average salary and part-time income from agricultural work, Mića was able to live relatively comfortably, if rather isolated, in Hrnetić.

Having finished his polemic about my requisition list, Mića dwelled on the quota prescribed for one man, whose name I have forgotten. They were neighbors and Mića knew the man and his circumstances at home. He confidently told me that this household had nowhere near the amount of grain that it would have to turn over based on the requisition list. "You will ruin a man who was most valuable to you during the war," Mića said. He told me that the man had helped the Partisans throughout the war and his home was the secret hiding place of the saboteurs led by Ilija Gromovnik.[5] "You Partisans speak humanely to a peasant when you need him to feed you and carry you to victory, and now that you are the government, you have mercilessly pounced on the village, as if you don't need it anymore. This will come back to haunt you," Mića warned, even though I needed no further convincing. I went back to the city, straight to the Municipal Committee, turned in the bicycle, and handed the requisition list to Sokač. I told him I couldn't carry out this assignment and the party could punish me as it saw fit.

Perhaps Sokač held me in some regard because we had served together in the Partisans; perhaps he harbored some veiled sympathy because of my open manner or his understanding of my arguments in favor of the peasants, so he continued to speak to me in a friendly way, as if it didn't involve a serious breach of party discipline. He said I was obviously not cut out for assignments that required a revolutionary's behavior so he would have to find someone else for the task. He was pleased that I had been able to get through four years of high school in less than a year, all with very good marks, and he agreed to relieve me of my duties in the agitprop division so I could sit for more exams. That is how, with the benevolent agreement of the head of the party for Karlovac, I stopped being a party activist.

I didn't join the Karlovac Youth to help build the Brčko–Banovići railway line or to labor elsewhere. The leaders in the committee left me in peace to continue my accelerated high-school testing. When in the summer of 1946 we finally turned over the bookshop to the Kultura enterprise, I looked for a new job so I could help my mother keep our apartment. I was appointed director of the Karlovac movie theaters Edison and Banija. I did my job diligently and enthusiastically. Friends from my prewar class helped me get through the final year of high school and I graduated with them. That group of young men—Josip Vaništa,[6] Božidar Fancev, and others—again pulled me into their group, just as in 1941. Of course, my priority for the entire time was Ljiljana and taking walks with her in the Karlovac parks and along the Korana. I don't know how I managed to read the piles of books, trying to compensate for the lack of reading in those years when it is most beneficial. Ljiljana introduced me to Cesarić and Ujević, and in no time I became a follower of Krleža and have remained one until today. Even now, during our long evening discussions, Vaništa and I always return to two unavoidable themes—Karlovac and Krleža.

All of this quickly distanced me from the rigid party ideology and from the politics of the day. This was the five-year period of Yugoslav and Croatian Stalinism, of intolerable conformism, of firm control, and of the repression of cultural and political and public life, a time when an offensive propaganda had obtrusively taken the place of ideology. The government was quickly losing the support of the people and the fervor of the former communist visionaries had cooled, but such things were spoken of only in the narrow circle of family and close friends because any heresy might be deadly. Renegades immediately became suspect, candidates for various types of discrimination at work and in public life. It was a time of humiliating obedience to a hypocrisy that disgusted me, a time of lying to ourselves and to everyone. I managed to avoid party functions and assignments, but I was still attending meetings of my party cell, in part out of fear of the discriminatory measures and in part out of a shabby self-justification that it was better "to be inside," with the possibility here and there at the local level of repairing, or at least of softening, the party's harshness.

When we moved to Zagreb in the fall of 1947, I decided that in this new environment in the Faculty of Philosophy and at Jadran Films I would keep my party affiliation under wraps and that my membership would simply expire. Opportunistically, I continued to sit in on party meetings, holding my tongue. I felt intensely that I no longer belonged. I confided this only to my closest new friends in Zagreb, especially in the film community. And then the break came: In the fall of 1948, the Communist Party of Yugoslavia (KPJ) and the KPH imposed upon their memberships and the entire country the most drastic Stalinist methods to defend against the Cominform, the USSR, and Stalin himself. Anyone could be sent to jail or to Goli Otok for the smallest careless allusion or joke. Friends were forced to denounce friends, wives to give up their husbands, children to spy on parents. Of course, I didn't have one whit of sympathy for the Cominform and Stalin, to the contrary, but such measures were unacceptable to me.

At a party meeting I didn't attend, a screenwriter accused the artistic director of Jadran Films, my friend Drago Zdunić, of spreading bad jokes at the expense of Tito. Zdunić was expelled from the KPH and was automatically sentenced to two years on Goli Otok and then a job in "purgatory" as a night watchman in a factory before he was allowed to return to public life with his brilliant business and publishing ideas. Several people who defended Zdunić from the political accusations, claiming that he was only a harmless jokester, were also expelled from the KPH and spent several months at forced labor in the former Miler brickworks on the outskirts of Zagreb.

For the next several days I heard from my friends the details of that party meeting and was horrified. It reinforced my earlier decision: I had no desire to live under such communism, be it Tito's or Stalin's. Distraught by such brutal persecutions, I came to the incorrect conclusion that Yugoslav socialism was sinking into the worst kind of Stalinism and that it would never be free of it. With my mother's wholehearted support, I decided to go to Israel, an option made posssible for all Jews in Yugoslavia in the fall of 1948. I also had one other, more intimate reason: After three and a half years of happy love, Ljiljana had left me. In the summer of 1949, my mother, Danko, and I set sail on the large transport ship *Radnik* (Worker) from Rijeka to a new life and a new world. My mother was happy because she had two sisters and a brother in Israel, and they were expecting another sister and a brother to arrive, whom she was more deeply attached to than to anyone in Croatia. Danko didn't share my mother's joy because he was leaving his first love in Zagreb, but he hoped that he would create a new and better life in Israel and that his beloved might be able to join him (and indeed in a circuitous way under other circumstances this happened). In my pocket I carried my party identity card for the District Committee of the KPH for the area of Zagreb known as Maksimir. I was to present this to the Communist

Party of Israel to be included in its political activities. As we were passing through the Strait of Otranto, and after a brief hesitation, I tossed the card into the sea and severed forever my membership in any Communist Party.

I lived in Israel for almost two years. I started out working in housing and highway construction, followed by a brief stint editing short news items for a film journal, and then I won a scholarship to study for two semesters at the University of Jerusalem. I became close with my mother's family, especially with Uncle Oto-Jehošua, a commissioner for culture and education for the district of Petah Tikva. I quickly realized several things that influenced me in later years: First, I was introduced to political democracy and immediately sensed its great advantages over one-party socialism, and so I voted for one of the two Israeli social democratic parties; second, I came to admire the constructive enthusiasm of Israel's early pioneers and the well-being of its many new immigrants, who after all the persecutions and wartime sufferings had finally found a home; third, I learned much about the war that led to this newly created state and witnessed the nation's "growing pains," the influx of new immigrants populating the villages and urban quarters from which 600,000 Arabs had fled in 1948, already clear signs of future trouble; fourth, I had brought a large box of Croatian books to Israel that I eagerly read, especially Krleža, and I was constantly reminded that I was more deeply immersed in Croatian culture than I would ever be in Jewish or Israeli culture (my closest friend in Israel, Harry Frank, jokingly called me a Croatian nationalist with a Jewish identity, and I called him, a native of Belgrade, a Serbian nationalist who was in love with Israel); and fifth, I recognized that my social life and work life would be better in Croatia and Yugoslavia as my abilities could reach a fuller potential there than in Israel, but I was determined to not return to the Yugoslavia I had left.

In Israel many books were available that opened my eyes to the actual state of affairs in the USSR and the essence of Stalinist communism, and to a certain extent to socialist-communist ideology in general. I was especially impressed by the work of Arthur Koestler, and devoured his books. Letters from Zagreb in the early spring of 1951 revealed that circumstances had begun to change for the better, and I decided to spend my summer holiday on a trip to Rome and Zagreb. With the good salary I earned as a night watchman in the demilitarized zone of Jerusalem I could afford the trip. In July 1951, armed with an Israeli passport, I spent a week tirelessly roaming Rome's attractions and then I got on a train for Trieste and Zagreb.

In the compartment from Trieste to Ljubljana there was only me and a Slovenian. He spoke fluent Croatian, and a rather lively conversation slowly developed. The man was well-informed, perhaps a businessman or a diplomat returning from Italy. With undisguised satisfaction he spoke about a "controlled liberalization" in Yugoslavia and how quickly it was advancing. He cited some persuasive examples and optimistically predicted that Yugoslavia could soon become the first proof that freedom and socialism were not incompatible.

During my two-year absence, Zagreb had been transformed into a completely different city. Perhaps I experienced this in an exaggerated way, but some of the changes were obvious. The streets had come alive; people were lingering on the main square to converse and the mood seemed optimistic. The coffeehouses were full. Even the shop windows looked more appealing as the country had begun to pull out of the economic crisis caused by the blockade of the USSR and its satellites. Ration cards had been abolished and freer commercial activity was evident everywhere. The daily newspapers offered more information and less stereotypical propaganda. Acquaintances

I met on the street spoke more casually and openly, some optimistically, others with skepticism, because "Yes, really, things are heading in the right direction, but you never know how far it will go, and who might suddenly say 'Halt!'"

I stayed in an apartment with a beautiful balcony on Novak Street, the residence of the family of General Franz Kleinhappel, our Partisan friends, who welcomed me warmly. I met my old, close friends and talked incessantly with them, trying to get a real sense of the extent of the promising developments. I began to flirt with an idea that perhaps my place was in this country—I knew that I was more at home in Zagreb than in Tel Aviv. If this wave of liberalization continued for several more years, perhaps I could experience here the freedom that gave me such joy in Israel and perhaps I could do more here than anywhere else for myself, my family, and for what I believed in. I hesitated—in my own way I had fallen in love with Israel, and also I wanted to be certain that the unbearable repression I had escaped would never again return to Yugoslavia.

Perhaps the key discussions for me were with Veco Holjevac and his wife, Nada, and with Maca Gržetić and her husband, Joso. I knew all four of them well from our Partisan days. In 1951, Veco was a minister in the Croatian government, Maca was a member of the Central Committee of the KPH, and Joso was the assistant minister of internal affairs. Sensing my dilemma, all of them, using almost identical arguments, urged me to stay in Zagreb. They promised to help me find work and anything else that would be necessary, even assistance for my mother and brother if they also decided to return. The place for old Partisans was here, in this country, and not somewhere else in the world. They adamantly claimed that the liberalization was a "long-term strategic course" of the leadership because a return to Stalinism would endanger the leadership itself. The effect was rather persuasive, especially when Joso spoke because I knew that the Stalinist purges in Moscow in 1937 had swallowed up his brother, the representative of the Central Committee of the KPJ to the Comintern.

I recall reaching my decision while speaking with Krešo Golik during lunch in the shady garden of the Gradski Podrum restaurant. Among my friends at that time Krešo was the closest. He was by then a total film addict and removed from politics, so we talked little about the latter. When Krešo asked me about Israel, and I gave him detailed explanations, it suddenly dawned on me: I love Israel, but it is not my home. One is always better off in his own home, able to do more, and my home is here.

The next day I went to the Ministry of Internal Affairs with Joso. Within twenty-four hours I had received the decision on the reversion of my Yugoslav citizenship and other necessary documents. Without delay I threw myself into the wave of general liberalization that was then in full swing. Gifts for friends I had brought with me from Israel included Arthur Koestler's *Darkness at Noon*, Alexander Weissberg-Cybulski's *The Conspiracy of Silence*, and Margarete Buber-Neumann's *Under Two Dictators*. Frane Barbieri, then editor-in-chief of *Vjesnik*, accepted my proposal to review these books and to translate some excerpts from them. The translation of the key chapter from *Darkness at Noon* appeared in *Naprijed*, the journal of the KPH. Over coffee at the Theater coffee shop, Ive Mihovilović warned me—apparently in jest but also with the wisdom of a man of experience—not to get carried away with such a drastic unmasking of Stalinist socialism because someone might get the "wrong impression," that what I was writing might also apply to us in Yugoslavia. It felt satisfying to be actively participating in the development of freedom in a society that had happily accepted me. My good fortune continued when Mihovilović and Barbieri included me in the founding editorship of *Vjesnik u srijedu* in the spring of 1952. We injected liveliness into Croatian journalism and to some extent expanded the barriers for freedom in public life.

Danko was happy to return to Zagreb, and even my mother wasn't displeased when she saw how good her sons felt about returning. For a time she commuted between Israel and Yugoslavia, but when her grandsons were born, she moved in permanently with us in Zagreb. She died in 1974 from heart disease.

We enjoyed the wave of Yugoslav liberalization for two and a half years. It peaked in the late fall of 1953 with Milovan Đilas's visionary articles in *Borba*. I even believed that we were on the verge of complete democratization. Then we received a shock—a true bolt from the blue, one might say. The Third Plenum of the Central Committee of the Communist Party of Yugoslavia, held January 16 and 17, 1954, sent a clear message: "Halt!" That period, when the Milovan Đilas affair reached its resolution, was the only time I regretted not having stayed in Israel.

From the maelstrom of political journalism I withdrew into the relative calm of Radio Zagreb, and then to the cultural and entertainment sections of *Vjesnik u srijedu* and to writing film scripts. These weren't exactly my true callings, but I had to live and, I have to admit, the work was not unbearable. I demonstrated my political position passively—by refusing to join the Communist Party again. This had been suggested to me several times, most directly by Joža Vrhovec, when he was my editor at *Vjesnik u srijedu*, and Predrag Vranicki, when he was the president of the council of Liber University Publishing in the 1960s. Vrhovec warned me that because I was outside the party I could not become *Vjesnik*'s correspondent in Bonn or London, positions that I was seeking at the time. Vranicki also thought that as a party member I would eventually be appointed the director of Liber University Publishing, thereby ensuring the future of this successful business. I was pleased that neither Vrhovec nor Vranicki sought more detailed explanations for my refusal to join the party. Lacking the privilege of a party membership card, I could still draw on other occasional privileges as one of the youngest Partisan veterans. This could open doors in the event of trouble with some of the powers that be, former comrades from the "grand old days." My dual Jewish-Croatian background helped too: When I wrote articles in the journal *Kritika* and elsewhere, expressing sympathy for the Croatian Spring, it was difficult to accuse me, a Jew, of being a Croatian nationalist.

During the second wave of liberalization of Yugoslav communism that followed the fall of Minister of Interior Aleksandar Ranković in the late 1960s, and with my establishment first of Liber University Publishing and then of Novi Liber, I entered a profession that immediately felt made for me or I for it. For close to forty years I have published books I like and have avoided pubishing books I don't like. In a varied working career there are usually moments of glory—mine were the twelve years as head of Novi Liber and of Liber University Publishing, where more than two hundred people had a pleasant, secure existence, and where we published books that broadened the horizons of free thought, among them books no one else dared to publish at the time in Yugoslavia. Moreover, we were able to assist some people who were returning from prison and others suffering political discrimination, providing them with part-time employment that allowed them to survive. I believe that I was at the time the only person outside the party to head one of the more important publishing houses in Yugoslavia.

But I must also temper this self-praise: There were times when I had to make compromises and when I was not a fearless hero. I did have to turn down some authors with valuable ideas or completed works because they had veered too far over the limit of the controlled freedom. At times I had to forsake my own ideas because they were too daring and might have endangered the company. Once, because of a threat from the Municipal Committee of the KPH, I halted publication of an important book that had already gone to press, which made things hard for me with the author. Feeling responsible for the existence of the company and its employees, I suppressed my inclination to state my heretical ideas in public. I maintained a balance between boldness and caution, between faithfulness to my ideas and compromises within the limits of controlled freedom. Only after 1982, when I was no longer the director, did I begin to make long-considered proposals for the radical reform of the sociopolitical system—in the spirit of a free market, political democracy, and a European orientation. These ideas led me to a brief, and not particularly successful, excursion into active politics in 1989–1990, before I returned again to ten years of defending independent thought and interethnic tolerance as an editor and publisher. I don't think I was especially successful, but at least I had the satisfaction of taking the opportunity, under new circumstances in contrast to those earlier ones under mild communism, to state my opinions freely, even when those opinions didn't please either the current government or a great portion of the Croatian public.

* * *

In Israel I met Hilel Livni, the founder of the Yugoslav kibbutz Šaar Haamakim, and Zvi Rotem, the editor of the daily newspaper *Davar*. Both knew my father from his pre-Palestine days in the Zionist movement and they had a lot to say about the breakup and disappointments of his group in Palestine in 1925–1928. Rotem had in his library a complete set of the Zagreb Jewish journal *Gideon* from the 1920s. He showed me several articles by my father, including one of his speeches to Zionist supporters in Slavonski Brod in 1920:

> Jewish youth are preparing for necessary action. But the work is difficult and even more difficult tasks await. They must

> physically and spiritually renew their people. They must build a homeland for their people in Palestine, they must raise that homeland to such heights that it will be the equal of and an example to other nations in order to fulfill the words of the prophecy: because learning will emerge from Zion and the Word of God from Jerusalem.

The ardent enthusiasm of my father and his ten-member group cooled rather quickly when faced with the hardships, shortages, and general crisis in Palestine at that time. The young people were obviously ill-prepared and the organization for receiving new immigrants was still weak. Under the pressure of such difficulties internal squabbling broke out in the group, accelerating its breakup. My father also had some other, deeper reasons for returning from Palestine, which I came across in some of his letters to my mother, letters that were more emotionally and reflectively written than those from later times. While building roads and laboring in the fields, he frequently worked with Arabs and befriended them. He learned their songs and enough Arabic for basic communication. At that time, the first Arab-Jewish conflicts had temporarily subsided, but there were signs of new ones. In his talks with Arabs my father felt an understanding for some of their arguments. He probably had a few doubts about the basic Zionist concept that a Jewish national state should be built in Palestine, which was populated by Arabs. Shouldn't we first come to an agreement with the Arabs about this, perhaps convince them to build a joint state, a joint binational democratic state, the most economically and politically advanced state in the entire Middle East, an example and a model to others in the area, which is choking on backwardness and poverty?

In one of my father's books of Silvije Strahimir Kranjčević's poems and in one of his diary entries I have found thickly underlined verses from the poem "Moses": "*Mrijeti ti ćeš kada počneš sam u ideale svoje sumnjati*" (You will die when you begin to doubt your ideals). Returning from Palestine with these doubts, my father didn't completely distance himself from the Zionist movement, but he was no longer a fervent activist. Only after 1933, faced with the flood of Jewish refugees from Nazi Germany whom he tried to help, did my father again draw near to the Zionist principle that Jews must have a state of their own. In his writings from 1932, I found a line: "Perhaps the light is coming from the East," (that is, from Russia). People who have lived through a disappointing experience holding on to their early political ideas reach for new ones reluctantly, which is probably what happened to my father. His sympathies for communism were remote and I think completely extinct after the Moscow show trials of 1936–1938, and especially after the Hitler-Stalin pact in the summer of 1939. I know that he brought back from Palestine a distrust of Great Britain and a certain intolerance of its imperial policies, but I once heard him say in the summer or fall of 1940 how sad it was that our only hope was the English (who at that time were the only people fighting Hitler).

Today, as I am sketching my hot-and-cold road through political ideas and ideals, it seems to me that in many ways I have mimicked my father's wavering between enthusiasm and coolness, through hesitation and doubt. In 1947, I also avidly read Kranjčević's poems and knew large parts of "Moses" by heart, always with the emphasis on the stanza "You will die when you begin to doubt your ideals."

But today I have already lived almost twice as long as my father. Like him, I have had time to doubt my ideals, but also time to doubt Kranjčević's verses. The twentieth century produced the greatest hopes for mankind, but it buried most of them. It became the graveyard of great ideals. It taught us that ideals are most often a seductive chimera and that doubt is not a fatal weakness but a necessary defense against fatal beliefs.

This book was written with such thoughts in mind.

LIST OF ACRONYMS

HDZ	Croatian Democratic Union
HSS	Croatian Peasants' Party
KNOJ	People's Defense Corps
KPH	Communist Party of Croatia
KPJ	Communist Party of Yugoslavia
NDH	Independent State of Croatia
RAVSIGUR	Directorate for Public Order and Security
OZNA	Department for the Protection of the People
SKOJ	League of Young Communists of Yugoslavia
UDBA	State Security Administration
ZAVNOH	National Anti-Fascist Council of the People's Liberation of Croatia

NOTES

CHAPTER ONE: THE TWO RANKS (1941–1945)

1. Sokols were originally youth sports organizations that sought to instill physical, moral, and intellectual values similar to the Boy Scouts. Sokols also existed in interwar Yugoslavia, but each of the country's major ethnic groups—Croats and Serbs—also sought to establish their own sokols, which could be used to highlight the cultural values and sometimes the political aspirations of their nationality.

2. Stanko Lasić, *Autobiografski zapisi* (Autobiographical Notes) (Zagreb: Globus, 2000).

3. Frankists were followers of Josip Frank, the founder of an extreme right-wing Croatian separatist movement at the beginning of the twentieth century.

CHAPTER TWO: IN THE JAIL OF THE DISTRICT COURT

1. Dido Kvaternik (1910–1962), the Ustasha equivalent of Heinrich Himmler, was the chief of the Ustasha security services and police until the autumn of 1942 and the chief organizer of the mass genocidal crimes in the Independent State of Croatia (NDH). He was the son of Slavko Kvaternik (1878–1947), who was Ante Pavelić's first deputy and the commander of the Croatian armed forces of the NDH in 1941–1942.

Sjećanja i zapažanja 1925–1945 (Memories and Observations 1925–1945), ed. Jare Jereb (Zagreb: Starčević, 1995).

2. Because of the events that will be described in several chapters of this book, I think that it is worth noting here that Pavelić spent his first two nights in the homeland after a twelve-year absence with a friend from his student days, Dr. Ante Nikšič, the president of the district court in Karlovac, who was at this time appointed the Ustasha commissioner for the city and county of Karlovac.

3. Miroslav Krleža (1893–1981) is the central Croatian literary figure of the twentieth century. He wrote more than fifty major works as a poet, playwright, novelist, essayist, and journalist. He joined the Communist Party of Yugoslavia in 1919 but left it in the late 1930s because of his liberal views on art and unwillingness to support the Stalinist purges. He spent the war in Zagreb, where he refused to cooperate with either the Ustasha government or the Partisans. After the war, he renewed his old friendship with Tito, cooperated with the communist authorities, and wrote his most important novel, the five-volume *Zastave* (Flags). In 1950, he founded the Yugoslav Institute for Lexicography, now called Lexicographical Institute Miroslav Krleža, which he headed until his death.

4. Kajkavian is a Croatian dialect found primarily in the northwestern part of the country, especially around Zagreb.

5. Milan Radeka, *Memories of the Year 1941*, in Yearbook for 2000 (Zagreb: Prosvjeta, 2000).

6. Danica is Croatian for the alternative name of the planet Venus—the morning star.

CHAPTER THREE: CELL NO. 15

1. The term *purger* is a colloquial expression derived from the German word *burgher* and frequently used by residents of Zagreb. It was used originally for fans of the Zagreb soccer club Građanski but has more recently been applied to any resident of the city. It is pronounced with a hard *g*.

2. Radeka, *Memories*, 24–25.

3. Mihajlo Mihajlov (1934–2010) was a prominent dissident in the former Yugoslavia. In 1966, he was imprisoned for three and a half years for publishing an article about camps for dissidents in the Soviet Union, which was punishable under Yugoslav law as "damaging the reputation of a foreign state." He was again put on trial in 1975 for "disseminating hostile propaganda" and sentenced to seven years in prison but was released in 1978. He then taught at Harvard, Yale, Ohio State University, and the University of Virginia until his return to Serbia in 2000.

4. Radeka, *Memories*, 31.

5. Radeka, *Memories*, 34.

6. See William L. Shirer's classic work, *The Rise and Fall of the Third Reich* (New York: Simon & Schuster, 1960).

CHAPTER FOUR: THE CAMP WITH THE BEAUTIFUL NAME

1. Radeka, *Memories*, 37–38.

2. Šibl (1917–1989) was one of the leaders of the resistance movement in Zagreb and a leader of Partisan units in the surrounding area. After the war, he became a member of the Central Committee of the Communist Party of Croatia and the general manager of Zagreb Radio and Television.

3. Radeka, *Memories*, 38

4. The National Liberation Struggle, sometimes called the National Liberation War, is the name given to the fight against the Axis powers by broad segments of Yugoslav society. The KPJ, led by Josip Broz Tito, was the main organizer of the NOB and assumed a leading role in waging it.

5. Radeka, *Memories*, p. 47–49

6. For this and the majority of the other information about the Danica camp, I have relied on the work of Dr. Zdravko Dizdar, "Human Losses at the 'Danica' Camp Near Koprivnica, 1941–1942," *Journal of Modern*

History 2 (2002).While I was writing this book, Dizdar was preparing a book about the Danica camp, the result of several years of research. I am grateful to him that during our collegial conversations he filled in some of the gaps in my knowledge about the camp.

7. Levi wrote *If This Is a Man* in 1946. Fifty years later, Jorge Semprun, in a book about his camp experience, *Literature or Life*, still claims that "Primo Levi expressed our common anxiety with unattainable conciseness." When Theodor Adorno once wrote that after Auschwitz poetry could no longer be written, Levi responded that "as the ultimate consequence, after Auschwitz poetry can no longer be written—except about Auschwitz." Although hyperbolic, and at first glance contradictory, I think that the claims are really complementary: In a paradoxical interpretation they are the distant echo of a cathartic shock that the concentration camps of the twentieth century have impressed on the historical memory of civilized humanity.

8. My father, in fact, was not "a rich Jew," although I think that he had quite a bit of money with him. I remember that during that time my mother sold everything in the house and took money and whatever was of value out of the bookshop. Our rich friends, the Veličkovićes, also offered money, as much and whenever needed.

9. Đuro Zatezalo, *Radio sam svoj seljački i kovački posao—Svjedočanstva genocida* (I Was Working At My Farmer's and Blacksmith's Job: Testimonies Of Genocide) (Zagreb: Prosvjeta, 2005), 206.

CHAPTER FIVE: THE LETTER

1. English translation based on *Faust*, trans. Alice Raphael (Norwalk, CT: Easton Press, 1980).

2. There is no accurate equivalent in English for the Croatian word that Nikolić used, *sinčić*, which is a diminutive form of the Croatian word *sin* (son). The suffix attached to the word denotes a degree of emotion, perhaps even sympathy, deeper than or beyond the ability of the English "small son" or "younger son" to define.

3. Maks Luburić (1914–1969) was born in Humac in present-day Bosnia-Herzegovina. Before the Second World War, he was a petty criminal who went abroad and joined the Ustasha movement. After the establishment of the NDH, he became the commandant of the Jasenovac concentration camp and the architect of the mass killings at this and other camps in the NDH. He escaped to Spain at the conclusion of the war. He remained active in extreme Croatian nationalist organizations and also founded his own organization, known as the Croatian National Resistance. He was murdered by an agent of the Yugoslav security service on April 20, 1969, in Carcaixent, Spain.

CHAPTER SIX: THE "VUJIČIĆ AFFAIR" AND THE ROOTS OF EVIL

1. The Croatian Home Guard was the name used for the regular armed forces in the Independent State of Croatia.

2. On January 6, 1929, King Alexander I of Yugoslavia abolished the country's constitution, outlawed all political parties, disbanded its parliament, and established a royal dictatorship in an attempt to quell the political turmoil that had gripped the country after the assassination of Stjepan Radić, the leader of the Croatian Peasants' Party in the Yugoslav parliament in 1928.

3. The Krajina Serbs of Croatia (*Krajishniks*) were ethnic Serbs who first migrated from Serbia proper in the sixteenth century and settled in a geographic area south and west of present-day Zagreb known as Krajina. They retained their ethnic and linguistic identity and Orthodox faith and continued to push for greater autonomy within Croatia after the creation of Yugoslavia in 1918.

4. The Cvetković-Maček Agreement created new administrative divisions within the Kingdom of Yugoslavia. It was concluded on August 23, 1939, by Yugoslav Prime Minister Dragiša Cvetković and Vladko Maček. The agreement established a new *Banovina* of Croatia. This administrative unit was specifically intended to include as many ethnic Croats as possible and granted Croatia substantial autonomy, for which Croatian politicians had lobbied since 1918. The agreement became obsolete

when Germany invaded the Kingdom of Yugoslavia in April 1941 and established the Independent State of Croatia on the territory of Croatia, Bosnia, and Herzegovina.

5. Ivan Šubašić (1892–1955) a Yugoslav politician who became the last governor of Croatia under the Cvetković-Maček Agreement of 1939.

6. Bogoljub Jevtić (1886–1960) served briefly as prime minister of Yugoslavia from December 22, 1934, to June 24, 1935.

7. The file on Dr. Vladimir Židovec is located in the Croatian National Archive, File MUP SRP 013.0.56, and contains about 330 pages with an autobiographical section, *My Participation in Political Life*, and notes from his interrogation in the investigative detention. Židovec's writings related to the Vujičić affair, which I cite several times in this text, can be found on pages 24–36 of the autobiographical section. Its content corresponds to the notes from his statements during the investigation.

8. The NDH had essentially two distinct civilian police organizations—the municipal police (*redarstvo*) and the gendarmerie, which was a holdover from the prewar Yugoslav state. The gendarmes were trained professionals, but they were assigned to towns, villages, or hamlets in the countryside and not to the larger urban areas. The gendarmerie was supportive of the NDH, but it was not necessarily pro-Ustasha and was at times considered unreliable by the Ustasha military and police, often because of the reluctance of some of its members to participate directly in the Ustasha's mass killings.

9. King Alexander I of Yugoslavia was assassinated in Marseilles, France, during a state visit on October 9, 1934. He was shot by Vlado Chernozemski, a member of the Internal Macedonian Revolutionary Organization. The assassination was organized by Pavelić and the Ustasha leadership when they were in exile in Italy.

10. Dušan Lukač, *Ustanak u Bosanskoj krajini* (The Uprising in Bosnian Krajina) (Belgrade: Vojnoizdavački Zavod, 1967), 60–62.

11. In Serbian *hajduk* is a brigand or outlaw, often romanticized, especially in the Serbian oral tradition, as a heroic, Robin-Hood-like figure, as in

the legends of Kraljević Marko. Saint George's Day is celebrated in both Orthodox Serbia and Catholic Croatia. It informally marks the beginning of spring, or the time of year when outlaw activities might begin anew.

12. Croatian State Archives, "Dizdar" file, MUP SRH, 013.0.3, 64.

13. Peter Broucek, *Ein General im Zwielicht: Die Erinnerungen Edmund Glaises von Horstenau* (Vienna, Cologne, Graz: Böhlau Verlag, 1988), 431. Glaise von Horstenau was an exceptionally well-informed observer of the general situation and events in the NDH. He belonged to a group of senior German officers who had called for curbing the Ustasha's terrorist methods, which they argued were creating instability in the entire region, forcing the German army to keep several divisions permanently in the area that were needed on other fronts. Glaise von Horstenau's exhaustive diaries and memoirs about the NDH are collected in Broucek's book, while his official reports and documents are included and cited in Vasa Kazimirović, *NDH u svetlu nemačkih dokumenta i dnevnika Gleza fon Horstenau 1941–1945* (Belgrade: Nova knjiga, 1987).

14. According to the daily newspaper *Jutarnji list* of July 30, 2003, this was noted in the dossier of Dido Kvaternik in the national archive of Argentina, which became accessible to researchers and the general public in July 2003.

15. Dr. Branko Pešelj, the personal secretary of Dr. Vladko Maček, wrote about Dido Kvaternik's "missionary assignment" in 1961 in exile. Because they were friends from their student days, Kvaternik freed Pešelj from jail on July 21, 1941, and had an unusually open conversation with him. Kvaternik spoke about the required "cleansing of the field of the Serbs," and as Pešelj states: "I could not restrain myself and not notice how 'cleansing the field of Serbs' would never lead to anything good, and that we could all one day pay for that policy because, I blurted out, the war is still not over and no one knows who will win.... Strangely, Kvaternik remained calm and told me: 'I know you think and expect that the English will win. I agree with you; and I maintain that

the English will win the war in the end, but there will be no more Serbs in Croatia. Accordingly, whoever wins the war will have to accept the situation as it is.'"

16. The diary of the late Starčević is still in the possession of his family, who made parts of this fascinating manuscript available to me.

17. Jozo Tomasevich recounts Kasche's report on Lorković's intervention in his magisterial work *War and Revolution in Yugoslavia, 1941–1945* (Palo Alto, CA: Stanford University Press, 2001), 398. He cites documents from the Ministry of Foreign Affairs of the Third Reich, a microfilmed copy of which is in the National Archives of the United States, No. T-120, Roll 5787, Fr. E301, 722.

18. This is the official name of the village, but for the sake of convenience and clarity I refer to it in the text more simply as Blagaj.

19. Kordun is a region in central Croatia extending along the Korana and Slunjčica Rivers. Its southern boundary touches Bosnia and Herzegovina and the Lika region.

20. Even today no one knows who the killers of the Mravunac family were. According to the first version, it was a murder-robbery by unknown assailants; according to a second version, it was a politically motivated crime and perhaps even a signal for an uprising by some unidentified members of a prewar Chetnik organization in the Veljun and Poloj area; while according to a third version, the Mravunac murders were a provocation designed by some Ustasha from Karlovac and the local Ustasha to incite retaliation against Serbs in the Kordun region. Arguments about the incident are still being waged today by people from the region, and even among some memoir writers and historians, without any firm proof. Based on discussions I had with people from Veljun and Blagaj in 1969; with Josina Mravunac's surviving daughter, Milka; with Nikola Lasić, the investigating judge, and Milan Stilinović, his deputy; and after reviewing the documents, I am most inclined to believe that there were two or three assailants whose motive was robbery. Knowing the Ustasha and even some Chetnik atrocities in the region, I cannot completely exclude a "conspiracy theory," whether it is Ustasha

or Chetnik, but there are arguments that make such a theory very improbable.

21. In 1991, the Kordun area became part of the Republic of Serbian Krajina, which was declared by ethnic Serbs in the regions of northern Dalmatia, Kordun, Lika, Banija, and some parts of Slavonia who refused to accept Croatia's declaration of independence from Yugoslavia. The region's ethnic Croatian population fled or was forced from the new, unrecognized republic. In 1995, the roles were essentially reversed. In July 1995, the new Croatian Army launched a major offensive known as Operation Storm, which recaptured much of the lost territory and led to a mass exodus of ethnic Serbs from central Croatia to northern Bosnia and Serbia.

22. I first wrote about the crime at Hrvatski Blagaj as a contribution to the book *Okrug Karlovac 1941* (The District of Karlovac in 1941) (Zagreb: Institute for the History of the Workers' Movement, 1965), 42–45. I had only some incomplete, simple documents and relied too heavily on a single statement that I subsequently learned was made under duress and was unreliable. The reactions to this book encouraged me to go to Veljun and Blagaj to talk to people and to search for more complete documentation. The result was apparent in the ten-part serialization about Veljun and Blagaj that was published in *Politika*. While preparing this book, I had available considerably greater and more recently processed documentation from the Croatian National Archive, so that I was able to verify, confirm, amplify, and correct my data. Based on the conscientious research of my late friend Tomo Žalac, who was a teacher in Veljun before the war, I began to doubt the number of victims buried in the memorial cemetery (520). In this chapter I cite a number that seems to me to be more realistic, but still with due reservation, because of the unreliability of the sources and the all too frequent arbitrary inflation and reduction of that number.

23. Stojan Pribičević (1875–1936) was an ethnic Serbian politician from Croatia. Before World War I, he was active in promoting Croat-Serb cooperation to achieve a "Yugoslav" agenda. In the 1920s, he served in the Yugoslav parliament and filled ministerial posts, including minister

of the interior, as a member of the Serbian Democratic Party. In 1924, he formed the Independent Democrat Party and went into opposition with the Croatia Peasants Party of Stjepan Radić, continuing to promote the idea of Croat-Serb cooperation and a federal, republican Yugoslav state. He was imprisoned in 1929 and released and sent into exile in 1931. He died in Prague in 1936.

24. The Yugoslav Radical Community was a coalition of Serbian political parties whose leader, Milan Stojadinović, became prime minister after elections in 1935. He was replaced as prime minister on February 5, 1939, by Dragiša Cvetković.

25. Juraj Rebok, *Sjećanja* (Memoirs) (Split: Journal Harulić, Nos. 2 and 3), 118-119.

26. Much has been written about the murder of the Glina Serbs, but the most telling facts have been collected in Đuro Roksandić, *Ustaški zločini u glinskom kotaru od 1941 do 1945, Zbornik GLINA* (Anthology GLINA 1941–1945) (Glina: District Assembly of Glina, 1988), 283–304, and in the article "Glina 13 May 1941—U povodu 60. godišnjice ustaškog zločina," *Ljetopis* 6 (2001). I also took into account the memoirs of Dr. Juraj Rebok, published in the Split journal *Marulić* 2 and 3 (2000), as the only direct testimony from an Ustasha source about the crime. Rebok's descriptions are very rudimentary, but they confirm the basic facts about the crime. He tries to minimize his personal responsibility and to downplay the number of victims, but I think some of the details are credible and make an interesting supplement to the overall picture.

27. *Marulić* 6 (1991). This disease that clouds the comprehension and blocks the consciousness, which I have already called in this book the "fetishism of the state," did not abandon the author in her later days. Despite her unequivocal criticisms of the Ustasha leadership for its political conformity, genocidal terror, and traitorous ceding of Croatian territory, Zelić-Bučan, in articles published in *Marulić* in 1991 and 2000, was still very proud that she had so zealously assisted in the establishment of the Ustasha NDH. In 2005, I read in the newspapers that she had led a group of residents from Zadar to the jail in Glina,

where they visited General Mirko Norac, who had been sentenced to twelve years imprisonment for the genocidal murder of Serbs in the town of Gospić during the 1991–1995 war in Croatia, and expressed her sympathy for him—a sad example of the enduring practice of making peace with a crime when the perpetrator is from your own ranks.

28. Hebrang (1899–1949) was a prominent Croatian communist. He joined the KPJ in 1920 and was sentenced to twelve years imprisonment in 1928 for party activities. He was the general secretary of the Communist Party of Croatia—the political chief of the very strong antifascist movement in Croatia—between 1942 and 1944. Because of increasing criticism of his support for Croatian political autonomy within Yugoslavia, the Politburo of the KPJ withdrew him from Croatia in the fall of 1944. He was assigned the responsibility of managing the country's postwar economic policy but was dismissed from most of his duties in 1946 because of personal disagreements with Tito. In 1948, at the height of the Stalin-Tito confrontation, Hebrang was accused of maintaining secret contacts with the Soviet Union. He was arrested in May 1948, expelled from the KPJ, and then charged with wartime collaboration with the Ustasha and the Gestapo and with sabotaging the economic policies of the Federal People's Republic of Yugoslavia. He died in prison in 1949 under mysterious circumstances. In 1992, the Croatian national assembly proclaimed him a "victim of the communist system."

29. Singer, an intelligence chief in the spring and summer of 1941, was nevertheless naïve in believing that despite his Jewish background he would be able to remain in a senior position in the Ustasha movement. In September 1941, Pavelić suddenly ordered Singer's surprise arrest, allegedly because he had interceded on behalf of a communist saboteur, a former friend, but really because Pavelić was trying to curry favor with Himmler's SS representatives in the NDH, who didn't want to work with a man of Jewish background. Singer spent more than a year as a detainee with special treatment at the Jasenovac camp, sending Pavelić confidential reports on Vladko Maček, who was also being held there. Finally, at the end of 1942, Pavelić ordered that Singer be killed. Maks Luburić obediently carried out the order, allegedly with a knife.

30. Hermann Neubacher, *Sonderauftrag Südost 1940–1945* (Special Mission Southeast 1940–1945) (Göttingen: Musterschmidt, 1956), 18 and 31.

31. Pavelić never replied to this letter, and Archbishop Stepinac (1898–1960) didn't insist on a response, but he did complain several times in writing to Pavelić and Artuković, the minister of internal affairs, about the Ustasha crimes against the Jews and Serbs. In his sermons in 1942 and 1943, Stepinac for the first time spoke critically in public about the Ustasha racial policy and about the Jasenovac concentration camp, which he described as "a shameful stain for the NDH." Stepinac was considerably more energetic in his declarations against the communist authorities in the early postwar years, protesting its discriminatory acts against the Catholic Church. Because of this, he was sentenced to sixteen years in prison, five of which he spent in jail and nine of which, until his death, he spent confined to his birthplace in the village of Krašić. Pope Pius XII made him a cardinal and Pope John Paul II beatified him in 1998, but among historians and the public there is still dispute about Stepinac's attitude toward the Ustasha government, some critics feeling he was too accommodating.

32. Under the Rome agreements of 1941, Italy would have the right to nominate a member of the Italian royal family as king of the NDH. On May 18, 1941, King Victor Emmanuel III named his cousin Prince Aimone of Savoy-Aosta to fill the post. While Aimone formally accepted the nomination, he refused to be coronated and, in fact, never set foot in the country that he nominally ruled. He gave up the throne on July 31, 1943, and formally renounced all rights to it in October 1943.

33. Radeka, *Memories*, 43.

34. National Archive of Split, in the collection Main Districts of the NDH in Dalmatia, Box 4.

35. The writer Ervin Šinko was living in Drvar as a Jewish émigré at the time. In his diary entries for July 3, 8, and 13, he described the arrival of the refugee column in Drvar and the impression that it made on the local population. See *Drvarski dnevnik* (Drvar Diary), Volume 19 (Zagreb: Yugoslav Academy of Sciences and Arts, 1987), 470–71.

36. Jakov Blažević, *Prva godina narodnooslobodilačkog rata* (The First Year of the National Liberation War) (Karlovac: Historical Archive of Karlovac, 1971), 663.

37. Ivan Nikšić, *Spomenici o župi Slunjksoj* (Testimonies About the County of Slunj) (Zagreb: Prosvjeta, Yearbook 2007), 575–577. Nikšić and his *Testimonies About the County of Slunj* are discussed in greater detail in Chapter 16.

38. With the promulgation of the June 10 decision, the NDH now had three levels of administrative divisions: province, district, and municipality. There were 22 provinces, 142 districts, and 1,006 municipalities. The highest level of administration was the province, each of which was headed by a provincial governor.

39. Vladimir Židovec, *My Participation in Political Life*, 24–36.

CHAPTER SEVEN: THE YELLOW SYMBOL THAT I DID NOT WEAR

1. The *bersaglieri* are an elite corps of the Italian army originally established in 1836. Chosen for their physical stature and stamina, they are capable of serving as mobile light infantry and as mountain troops. *Bersaglieri* are known for their distinctive wide-brimmed hats and helmets decorated with the black feathers of the wood grouse. Another distinctive feature is the fast jogging pace that they keep in parades instead of more traditional marching.

2. Lopašić (1835–1893), a Croatian historian and topographer, was born in Karlovac.

3. All citations from the German reports are taken from Peter Broucek, *Ein General im Zwielicht: Die Erinnerungen Edmund Glaises von Horstenau* (Vienna, Cologne, Graz: Böhlau Verlag, 1988), and Vasa Kazimirović, *NDH u svetlu nemačkih dokumenta i dnevnika Gleza fon Horstenau 1941–1945* (The NDH in Light of German Documents and the Diary of General Glaise von Horstenau, 1941–1944) (Belgrade: Nova knjiga, 1987).

4. "*Na bijelome hljebu*" literally translates as "on white bread." It is a Serbian expression that was common among prison inmates condemned to death. A prisoner awaiting execution enjoyed the right to be served more expensive white bread with his last meal before his execution instead of the more common dark bread or corn bread. The nearest English equivalent for the expression would be that "they never had it so good," but the Serbian expression implies an added, and more ominous, realization among the refugees in Draganić that death, if not imminent, was lurking nearby.

CHAPTER EIGHT: THE STRANGE SUICIDE OF FILIP REINER

1. The Illyrian Movement was a nineteenth-century intellectual movement in Croatia that mirrored the rise of national consciousness among the peoples of Central and Eastern Europe in post-Napoleonic Europe. Its main objectives were to revive Croatian as a literary language and to promote unity among the southern Slavs.

2. Banjica was a German concentration camp from June 1941 to September 1944. Located on the outskirts of Belgrade, it initially served as a center for holding hostages but later housed Jews, Serbian communists, Roma, and captured Partisans.

CHAPTER NINE: THE SEALED AND UNSEALED BOOKSHOP

1. Marija Vrbetić, *Karlovac Anthology, 1579–1979* (Karlovac: Historical Archive of Karlovac, 1979), 297–298.

2. This was the official name of the country from its creation in 1918 until 1929, when it became the Kingdom of Yugoslavia.

3. Among my documents, I have a photocopy of a letter from the headquarters of the Women's Ustasha Youth to the city hall of Karlovac from August 26, 1942, that announces, verbatim, with all its grammatical errors and abbreviations: "In connection with the removal of Jews of Karlovac the above named is requested to share with this headquarters all goods and clothing for the impoverished Ust. Yth. The goods are much needed since we do not have the resources to procure

the same, and the impoverished Ust. Yth. has a great need and it is in the interest and for the advancement of the homeland to assist it. Since Ust. Yth. has received the goods of removed Jews in all other places, we hope that the above named will do the same—*Za dom spremni*! [Ready for the Homeland!]—Hqs. Dept. Admin. for Soc. Econ. Welfare: Dragica Brstilo."

4. My mother and father always spoke German between themselves, so for all of us my mother was "Muti" and my father was "Fati."

5. This is an abbreviation of *Smrt fašizmu, sloboda narodu* (Death to Fascism, Freedom for the People), a popular Partisan slogan that during the war and the early postwar years was the obligatory closing on all official documents of the Partisan Army and the postwar government.

6. Edvard Kardelj (1910–1979) was a Yugoslav political leader, economist, and writer. He worked for the Comintern in Moscow in the 1930s, surviving Stalin's purge of the Yugoslav Communist Party leadership of that time. During World War II, he organized Partisan resistance in his native Slovenia. In the 1950s, he became prominent as one of the authors of the new economic policy of Yugoslavia known as workers' self-management. Upon Milovan Đilas's removal in 1954, Kardelj was considered the chief party ideologist. His power and influence diminished in the 1960s and early 1970s, but he returned to prominence in the mid-1970s as one of the main authors of the 1974 constitution that decentralized decision-making in the country.

7. The Law on the Nationalization of Private Enterprises was passed on November 6, 1946. Thus, by donating the bookshop to the government, we preempted its takeover, but we had also denied ourselves one more school year that would have allowed us to raise our standard of living even more.

CHAPTER TEN: CHERCHEZ LES JUIFS

1. The equivalent in English would be, "Peter Piper picked a peck of pickled peppers."

2. The earliest trials of Jews accused of the ritual killing of Christian children were recorded in England (Norwich in 1144, Gloucester in 1168), France (Blois in 1171), and Spain (Zaragoza in 1182). They led to the mass expulsion of Jews from individual cities and counties and were accompanied by mistreatment, the theft of property, and even killing. The Jews demonstrated in vain that their religion was in fact the first religion to strictly forbid any rituals that included the murder of children, from the time of their forefathers Abraham and Isaac. Around 1235, Frederick II Hohenstaufen, the King of Germany, King of Sicily, and Holy Roman Emperor, the most powerful and well-educated European ruler of his time, ordered investigations in all of his dominions that established that there were no ritual murders and that such accusations had been fabricated or corroborated by witnesses who made their statements under the cruelest torture. In 1247, Pope Innocent IV also publicly warned that these accusations were false, but that did not stop the wave of accusations and trials, which led to the great exodus of Jews from Germany to Poland and Russia. Although nothing was ever proven, in the perceptions of medieval suspiciousness, superstition, mythomania, and mysticism a prejudice took root that "there must be something to it" or "where there is smoke there is fire," so that Jews occupied a prominent place in medieval demonology beside satanical heretics, trouble-making witches, and perfidious evil spirits. Through the Enlightenment and the growth of urban society, the medieval horror stories of ritual killings abated, only to be reincarnated in the race theories of modern anti-Semitism.

The trial in Tiszaeszlar in 1883 was the last accusation of Jews for ritual killing in Austria-Hungary. Two such trials were recorded on the territory of today's Croatia, both of them in Dubrovnik. In 1502, after the torture and a forced and false confession of a Jew in Dubrovnik, seven Jews in Dubrovnik were condemned to death for the alleged ritual murder of a woman. As a consequence of this trial, and after several years of discussion and delays, all the Jews were expelled from Dubrovnik in 1515. However, the decision was not rigidly enforced because of commercial interests and the Jews quickly began to return. In 1538, their permanent residence in the city was legalized. When another accusation of ritual killing was made against a Jew in Dubrovnik in 1622, people again demanded the expulsion of Jews from the city. However, when the accused, Isaac Ješurum, was found innocent, their demand was forgotten. Jews in the Dubrovnik Republic then acquired a status more satisfactory than in the great majority of European states of the time.

3. At the beginning of the investigation in Tiszaeszlar investigators used crude pressure tactics to force Moric Scharf, a psychologically unstable fourteen-year-old boy, to testify how he had seen his father and several other Jews from the village and the surrounding area butcher the Catholic girl Eszter Solymosi in the synagogue and collect her blood in a large pitcher. Moric suffered a nervous breakdown during the trial and admitted that his testimony against his father was false. After the trial, the boy lived with his parents in Budapest, recovered psychologically, moved to Amsterdam, and became a diamond cutter. He started a family and lived according to the strictest tenets of Orthodox Judaism. In 1927, he published his recollections of the trial in Tiszaeszlar in which he confessed to and movingly described his false testimony against his father, a trauma that stayed with him for the rest of his life.

CHAPTER ELEVEN: "WE ARE ALL HOSTAGES NOW"

1. I heard the story about the murder of Ljudevit Tiljak in the fall of 1942 during the Italian-Chetnik offensive in Drežnica from Mojmir Martin, a participant in the events. Tiljak had at one time been a communist, but several years before the war "he had changed sides," "become a traitor," and worked for the Yugoslav royal police in Belgrade. With the establishment of the NDH, the Ustasha government took him into their police service. He knew many activists and members of the Communist Party. He posed the greatest danger to them after June 22, 1941, when the police raids against communists began. According to Martin's account, it was enough for Tiljak to recognize some communist on the street and give the signal to his team, and an arrest was immediately made. When the party organization lost several members in this way, it ordered Tiljak's liquidation. Martin mentioned that "Comrade Šiljo" was the person

who organized this action. I later learned that this was the pseudonym of Pavel Pap, a member of the Central Committee of the KPJ, who was at that time operating illegally in Zagreb. "Comrade Šiljo" ordered an attractive woman party member to lure Tiljak to an apartment in the Zagreb neighborhood of Trešnjevka, where a group of activists, which included Martin, was waiting. Tiljak was disarmed, interrogated under torture until midnight, beaten, and killed. The next night his body was dumped in the Petruševac Pond.

2. For the great majority of Kuhn's colleagues—Jewish lawyers from Zagreb—their release from Kerestinec was only an illusory and brief freedom in which they curiously and naïvely believed. A new wave of arrests awaited them at their homes in Zagreb and they ended up in the camps on the island of Pag, Velebit, and Jasenovac. Only a few of them were able to reach the Italian zone of occupation and then Italy, or the Partisans, or some other refuge where they had a good chance for survival.

3. Zvonimir Richtmann, *Sigmund Freud* (Zagreb: Orbis, 1937).

4. In his book *Power/Knowledge*, the French philosopher and historian of ideas Michel Foucault describes these frequent polemics among European philosophical and literary leftists that lasted until the 1960s as conflicts of "universal intellectuals" and "specific intellectuals." The former acted as "masters of truth and justice" and gave precedence to an ideology-infected philosophy over to the exact results of modern science. The latter started from one of the basic natural sciences and created their philosophical view of the world. He cites the physicists Robert Oppenheimer, Werner Heisenberg, and Albert Einstein as examples of "specific intellectuals," but if he had been aware of our conflict on the left, he would have called Richtmann a "specific" and Prica a "universal" intellectual.

CHAPTER TWELVE: ON THE ROAD TO JADOVNO

1. Somewhat later there was an indirect explanation of why my mother, Jaga, and several other women from Karlovac were arrested on July 14,

Bastille Day. A detailed *Obavijest broj 1* (Notice No. 1) "on Communist-Chetnik Disturbances" of August 6 begins with these words: "Around July 10 of this year several English radio stations began to spread the rumor that an uprising would break out on July 14 in all countries engaged in the war against the Axis Powers." Although such a general European uprising was not being prepared, it happened that on the night of July 13 the communist prisoners at Kerestinec disarmed the guards and escaped from the camp. This was probably the reason for the accelerated arrests of people on the list of "suspects," which included my mother and Jaga. For Jaga, there was probably an additional legal reason for her arrest. The Legal Decree on the Preservation of the Aryan Blood and Honor of the Croatian People of April 30, 1941, forbade women "of Aryan origin" under the age forty-five to be employed in Jewish homes, which Jaga ignored.

2. In Chapter 5, I provide greater detail on Družak.

3. Ivo Goldstein, *Holokaust u Zagrebu* (The Holocaust in Zagreb) (Zagreb: Novi Liber, 2001).

CHAPTER THIRTEEN: THE VELEBIT DEATH CAMP

1. "Greco-easterners" is an Ustasha euphemism for Serbs and/or those of the Serbian Orthodox faith.

2. Ilija Jakovljević, *Konclogor na Savi* (Concentration Camp on the River Sava) (Zagreb: Konzov, 1999).

3. HDA, USIKS 337, 41.

4. After the publication of my book in Croatian in February 2007, Đuro Zatezalo published his complete research in the book *Jadovno—Kompleks Ustaških logora* (Jadovno—The Complex of Ustasha Camps) (Belgrade: Museum of the Victims of Genocide, 2007). Here I have quoted the preliminary results of his investigations that were published in different journals and periodicals before 2007.

5. HDA Karlovac, Jadovno Box.

6. Franjo Zdunić Lav in the anthology *Kotar Gospić i Kotar Perušić u Narodno oslobodilačkom ratu 1941–1945* (The District of Gospić and the District of Perušić in the National Liberation War, 1941–1945) (Karlovac and Gospić: Historical Archive of Karlovac and District Assembly of Gospić, 1989), 195–96.

7. Ibid., 168–200.

8. In his book *Ustaški logori* (Ustasha Camps) (Zagreb: Globus, 1990), Mirko Peršen maintains that the "number of victims throughout the Gospić camps could be between fifteen and twenty thousand," while Đuro Zatezalo speaks of a number greater than forty thousand. According to Rubinić's statements, recorded by Ilija Jakovljević in the camp at Stara Gradiška, the county police in Gospić carried out detailed identification of the arriving prisoners, 28,700 of which were received from June 18 to August 23, 1941. Since about 3,500 prisoners from Gospić were sent to other camps (Jastrebarsko, Jasenovac, Loborgrad) at the end of August, and several hundred (500 at most) were released, it follows that more than 24,000 prisoners were killed in the Gospić-Velebit-Pag camp system, at least half of whom were killed at the Velebit caves and in the Jadovno camp.

9. Reports of two Italian sanitary groups are published in their entirety in the Italian original and in a Croatian translation in Ante Zemljar, *Haron i sudbine* (Charon and the Fates) (Belgrade: July Fourth, 1988), 222–48.

10. Pavle M. Babac, *Velebitsko podgorje* (The Velebit Foothills) (Belgrade: Balby International, CD edition, www.balby.com, 2003).

CHAPTER FOURTEEN: CELL NO. 20

1. Veco Holjevac, *Zapisi iz rodnog grada* (Notes from My Birthplace) (Zagreb: Nakladni zavod Matice Hrvatske, 1972).

2. During the time of socialist Yugoslavia, republic- and national-level ministries were known as "secretariats."

3. Jakša Kušan, *Bitka za Novu Hrvatsku* (The Battle for New Croatia) (Rijeka: Otokar Keršovani, 2000).

CHAPTER FIFTEEN: FANATICS, YES-MEN, KILLERS, AND SAVIORS

1. *Prvoborci*, or literally "first fighters," was the term used in postwar Yugoslavia for people who had fought with the Partisans from the beginning of the war. Designation as a *prvoborac* (singular) brought honor and many privileges to its bearer.

2. Joachim Fest, *Das Gesicht des Dritten Reiches—Profile einer totalitären Herrschaft* (The Face of the Third Reich: Portraits of the Nazi Leadership) (Munich: Piper Verlag, 2004).

CHAPTER SIXTEEN: THE UPRISING IN BANIJA AND KORDUN

1. Stanko Bjelajac, *The Glina Anthology* (Glina: District Assembly of Glina, 1988), 225. According to one document in *The Glina Anthology*, there were 717 members and candidates for membership in the Communist Party of Croatia in Kordun and Banija in April 1941. There was approximately the same number of people who were members of SKOJ and active communist sympathizers. Compared to the total population in this area in 1941 (more than 250,000), the number of potential communist activists was relatively small, less than 0.5%. But these were people who were well-organized, prepared to fight, and prepared to carry out the assignments of their committees. However, at the meeting in the Abez Forest, Končar and Kraš overestimated the capabilities of their membership.

2. See Milan Bekić, Ivo Butković, and Slavko Goldstein, *The District of Karlovac in 1941*, 79–80.

3. Bjelajac, *The Glina Anthology*, 230.

4. Židovec, *My Participation in Political Life*, 86.

5. Of the documents that I reviewed, this one is the only document that mentions the presence of Kvaternik in Kordun during this time. But which Kvaternik? Eugen Dido, Slavko, or Ljubomir? Eugen Dido Kvaternik, the architect of the genocide campaign, would spend a day or two "in the field" during some of the earlier "cleansing" or "reprisal" operations—as at Grubišno Polje, Gudovac, or Banski Grabovac.

Perhaps he was in Kordun on July 31, but I cannot confirm it with certainty.

6. Đuro Zatezalo, *Radio sam svoj seljački i kovački posao—Svjedočanstva genocida* (I Was Working At My Farmer's and Blacksmith's Job: Testimonies Of Genocide) (Zagreb: Prosvjeta, 2005), 66–68.

7. Đuro Zatezalo, Milan Romčević, and Mirjana Peremin, eds., *Kotar Vojnić u narodnooslobodilačkom ratu i socijalističkoj revoluciji* (The District of Vojnić in the National Liberation War and the Socialist Revolution) (Karlovac: Historical Archive of Karlovac, 1989).

8. The District Committee of the KPH (Kraš and Marinković) criticized Čuić's behavior as "opportunism" because he had missed the critical moment for a mass uprising. Because of this failure and other actions, the District Committee banished Čuić from the party and sent him as an ordinary soldier to the Slunj region. Čuić very quickly demonstrated personal courage and became the commissar of his unit and had a good reputation among the soldiers and supporters throughout the region. He was killed on November 12, 1941, during an attack on an Italian garrison in Plavča Draga, not far from Plaško, while trying to rescue his wounded comrade Stjepan Milašinčić. The District Committee (Marinković) posthumously recognized Čuić's extraordinary courage in battle and rescinded his exclusion from the party.

9. Ventura Baljak was a participant in the 1932 Velebit uprising and was the thirteenth arrival in the Ustasha émigré camp in Italy.

10. Ivan Nikšić, *Spomenici o župi Slunjskoj.*

11. Đuro Zatezalo, *Kotar Slunj i kotar Veljun u NOR-u i socijalističkoj izgradnji* (The Counties of Slunj and Veljun in the National Liberation War and the Socialist Revolution) (Karlovac: Historical Archive of Karlovac, 1988).

12. *Zbornik dokumenata i podataka o NOB* (Collected Documents and Information on the National Liberation War), vol. 5, book 1 (Belgrade: Vojno-istoriski Institut JNA, 1979), 340–43.

13. Father Štimac was executed in Slunj on January 31, 1943, for collaborating with the Partisans. According to Partisan sources, the Ustasha executed him, while Ustasha sources claim that the Germans executed him.

14. See Čedomir Višnjić, *Kordunaški proces* (The Kordun Trial) (Zagreb: Prosvjeta, 1997).

15. Bleiburg and the Way of the Cross refer to a massacre and forced repatriation of Croatian Ustasha, soldiers, and civilian sympathizers centered on the Austrian town of Bleiburg and in nearby areas in Slovenia in mid-May 1945, and to the forced repatriation of survivors to the new communist state of Yugoslavia. See Chapter 19.

16. Milovan Đilas, *Wartime*, trans. by Michael B. Petrovich (New York: Harcourt Brace and Jovanich, 1977).

17. Vladimir Maček, *Memoari* (Memoirs) (Zagreb: Croatian Peasant Party, 1992), 170–72.

CHAPTER SEVENTEEN: THE REFUGE AT BANSKI KOVAČEVAC

1. *Jasenovac: žrtve rata prema podacima Statističkog zavoda Jugoslavije* (Jasenovac: Victims of the War Based on Information of the Statistical Bureau of Yugoslavia) (Zurich, Sarajevo: Bošnjački institut, 1992).

2. Gavazzi (1895–1992) was one of the foremost Croatian ethnologists of the twentieth century.

3. Sava Mrkalj (1783–1833) was born in Sjeničak and educated in Zagreb and Budapest. He is best known for his attempt to reform the Serbian language before Vuk Karadžić. His proposed reform to reduce the number of letters in the Serbian alphabet from forty-two to twenty-six met stiff resistance from the Serbian Orthodox Church, which based its opposition on the fact that the alphabet had been created by Saint Cyril and Saint Methodius in the ninth century.

4. Dušan Korać, *Prkos u plamenu* (Prkos in Flames) (Zagreb: Radničke Novine, 1989), 245.

5. I have established all of the dates cited in this chapter, by which I follow

the course of events, by comparing Partisan and gendarme reports from that time and information from Korać, *Prkos u plamenu*.

6. During the war, Germany formed six divisions or legions manned by Croats, but which often had German commissioned and noncommissioned officers. These units included the Croatian Air Force Legion; the Croatian Naval Legion; the 369th Croatian Reinforced Regiment, which fought on the eastern front, including Stalingrad, where it was virtually wiped out; the 369th Croat Infantry Division, the successor to the Reinforced Regiment, but which fought primarily in central and southern Bosnia; the 373rd Croat Infantry Division, which carried out the bulk of its operations in the area between Bihać and Banja Luka; and the 392nd Croat Infantry Division, whose area of operations embraced southern Slovenia and the Croatian Adriatic coast to the city of Knin.

7. Milan Bekić, Ivo Butković, and Slavko Goldstein, *Okrug Karlovac 1941* (The District of Karlovac in 1941) (Zagreb: Institute for the History of the Workers' Movement, 1965).

CHAPTER EIGHTEEN: A STORY OF TWO VILLAGES

1. All of this has been recorded by Nikola Orečić, who was mobilized by Luburić's Ustasha troops with about twenty other Croats from Lasinja and the surrounding area to assist in some auxiliary tasks, among which was filling in the pits containing murdered Serbs. While working for about a week under the supervision of local gendarmes and among Luburić's Ustasha, Orečić heard and saw much of what was happening and later wrote about it. His testimony, which in my opinion is credible, was published in *Svjedočenja učesnika NOB 1941–1942*, (Testimonies of Participants in the National Liberation Struggle, 1941–1942), volume 6 (Belgrade: Vojnoizdavački zavod, 1975). In 1942, Orečić was the main Partisan contact on the Kupa River in his native village of Desni Stefanki, where he awaited Vladimir Nazor and Ivan Goran Kovačić when they were taken across the river, which Nazor later celebrated in verse in "Čamac na Kupi" ("Boat on the Kupa").

2. Information about Pavelić's inspection in Kordun is based on the statement of Moškov during his interrogation by the State Security Administration in May 1947 and on reports in the Ustasha press and Partisan documents.

3. Dušan Korać, *Prkos u plamenu.*

4. This was probably the earliest anticipation of the 1980s Serbian author Dobrica Ćosić's well-known slogan that the Serbs were always "victors in war and losers in peace."

5. Vlado Gotovac (1930–2000) was a politician and poet. He came to prominence in 1971 during the Croatian Spring and as editor of *The Croatian Weekly*, a newspaper whose influence reached beyond the borders of Croatia. Gotovac was arrested and imprisoned in 1972 on charges of being a separatist and nationalist, both of which were anathema to the communist regime then ruling the country. In 1989, he joined the newly established Croatian Socialist Liberal Party. A passionate public speaker, Gotovac served in the Croatian parliament, but a lack of political prowess led to his defeat in the 1997 presidential elections, when he finished third. He died in Rome in 2000 of complications from hepatitis.

6. Zoran M. Marković, in the anthology, *Srpska strana rata* (The Serbian Side of the War), ed. Nebojša Popov (Belgrade: Journal Republika and Municipal Library of Zrenjanin, 1996), 639.

7. See Tito's December 1942 text in *Nacionalno pitanje u svetlosti narodnooslobodilačke borbe* (The National Question in Light of the National Liberation Struggle), Proleter No. 16, December 1942, published by the Central Committee of the Communist Party of Yugoslavia.

8. Dobrica Ćosić (b. 1921) is a Serbian writer, politician, and theorist. He joined the Communist Party during World War II and remained active in the party during the postwar era. He became close to Tito in the 1960s. But in the 1970s he became disenchanted with Tito's policy for decentralizing the Yugoslav government and the diminishing influence that Serbia would have within the Yugoslav federation. By the 1980s,

Ćosić had become the intellectual champion of a revived Serbian national consciousness, particularly as it was applied to the status of Serbs in Kosovo, which became increasingly intense and aggressive. He was an early supporter of Slobodan Milošević and assumed the largely ceremonial position of President of the Federal Republic of Yugoslavia (consisting of the former Yugoslav republics of Serbia and Montenegro) in 1992. He broke with Milošević in 1999–2000 but continued to support the actions of the Bosnian Serb military and political leaders during the 1992–1995 war in Bosnia.

9. The Territorial Defense Forces were a separate part of the armed forces of the former Yugoslavia. They were envisioned as a military reserve force that would conduct irregular or guerrilla operations in the event of war. Each of Yugoslavia's constituent republics had its own Territorial Defense military units, whose members received regular training. Their doctrine drew extensively on the Partisan experience of World War II with small, lightly armed infantry units fighting defensive actions on familiar local terrain.

10. Loznica is located in Serbia on the banks of the Drina River, which forms part of the boundary between Serbia and Bosnia.

11. I feel obligated to mention here two colonel generals who were oriented completely differently than Pekić and Jakšić. My friend Dr. Gojko Nikoliš, the son of the previously mentioned Sjeničak Orthodox priest Mihajlo Nikoliš, the wartime chief of the Partisan medical corps, was among the first academics who opposed the membership and leadership of the Serbian Academy of Sciences and Art when it began to support the aggressive policy of Milošević. When open war against Croatia then broke out, Gojko left Belgrade and lived the rest of his life in France. In 1994, he wrote to me from there: "To my people in Belgrade, I am an Ustasha. To your people in Zagreb, I am a Chetnik. What is left to me is that I die here in France." He died two years later at Le Ferté Bernard, a small town about two hundred kilometers from Paris. My first senior Partisan military commander, whom I briefly served as courier and escort, the Montenegrin Veljko Kovačević, the wartime commander of the Fifth Operational Zone of Croatia (made up of Gorski

Kotar and Hrvatsko Primorje), and the postwar author of *Kapelski kresovi* and several other books, could not bear that his Yugoslav People's Army was attacking his Gorski Kotar and his Slavonia, so in 1993 in Belgrade—already seriously ill—he committed suicide. I heard that in his farewell letter to his daughters he pointed to exactly these reasons: an unbearable illness and the unbearable policy that had led to a war between "his people" and "his people."

12. The RSK, the successor to the SAO of Krajina, was the name of the self-proclaimed Serbian entity within Croatia. It took its name from the medieval Military Frontier under the Hapsburgs and lasted from 1991 until 1995. The territory of this separatist state was comprised of a broad arc of land that ran along the Croatian border with Bosnia and Herzegovina, roughly from Okučani in the east to below Knin in the south, which was also the capital of the self-styled republic. The RSK also incorporated a wide strip of land along Croatia's eastern border with Serbia that ran roughly from Beli Manastir in the north to the point where the borders of Croatia, Serbia, and Bosnia and Herzegovina intersect in the south. The RSK was overrun by Croatian forces in the summer of 1995.

13. Nikica Barić, *Srpska pobuna u Hrvatskoj 1990–1995* (The Serbian Rebellion in Croatia, 1990–1995) (Zagreb: Tehnička knjiga, 2005).

14. After making this statement, Jović was invited to several international symposia, roundtables, and other gatherings, where he regularly put forward ideas and proposals about the need to improve relations between Croats and Serbs in Croatia. Because of these activities, he was interrogated several times by the Krajina police and plastic explosives were once put under his house. In 1994, he was dismissed, stripped of his judicial immunity, and spent a month in jail in Glina. After Operation Storm in August 1995, the Croatian police arrested him and charged him with spying for the RSK. "Not only was I not convicted but the court did not even produce a single piece of evidence from the indictment...which only degrades its credibility," he wrote in his biography. From 1997 until the end of 2003, Jović worked as a legal adviser to the OSCE mission in Sisak, Petrinja, and Zagreb. He was

then selected as an international judge with the UN mission in Kosovo. With outstanding evaluations and recommendations, he submitted his name four times as a candidate for the vacant judgeship in Gvozd beginning in 2004, but each time Croatian candidates, primarily people with considerably fewer qualifications, were selected. He submitted his name several more times for other positions on the bench, but always with the same results. I believe the National Judiciary Council violated the constitution's Law on the Rights of National Minorities (Article 22), which calls for the proportional representation of all national communities in the judiciary and government administration. I agree with the opinion of the OSCE mission in Croatia that concluded its recommendation: "The reintegration of Mr. Jović as a judge in the Croatian legal system would be beneficial in terms of the application of European standards and it would be an excellent example of Croatia's progress in the direction of reconciliation." Finally, in the spring of 2008, Jović was hired as a legal expert in the Sisak branch office of INA (the national oil company in Croatia).

15. Timothy Garton Ash, *We the People: The Revolution of '89 Witnessed in Warsaw, Budapest, Berlin, and Prague* (Zagreb: Biblioteka Erasmus, 1993).

16. Timothy Garton Ash, *History of the Present* (London: Penguin Books, 2002).

17. Planinka Kovačević, a painter from Belgrade and a collaborator in Novi Liber, now lives in Israel.

18. Alojz Buljan and Franjo Horvat, *Žrtve Drugoga svjetskoga rata i poraća na području bivše općine Novska* (Victims of the Second World War and the Postwar Period in the Area of the Former District of Novska) (Novska: Novska Branch of Matice Hrvatske, 2006).

CHAPTER NINETEEN: KRALJEVICA AND THE PARTISANS

1. At that time, no one knew for sure who the Partisan commander was. Rumors circulated that he was a Russian, perhaps a former diplomat in the Kingdom of Yugoslavia named Lebedev.

2. Much was written about Rein in Yugoslavia after the war and his works became well known. Several exhibitions of his paintings were held in Zagreb and Osijek, including the pictures he produced during his stay in Paris.

3. The Fourth Anti-Partisan Offensive, known as the Fourth Enemy Offensive among the Partisans and sometimes as the Battle of the Neretva, was a combined attack by the Axis powers launched in early 1943 against the Partisans throughout Yugoslavia.

4. August Cesarec (1893–1941) was a Croatian writer and political figure. Although a staunch Croatian nationalist as a youth—he participated in a botched attempt to assassinate the Hungarian viceroy Slavko Cuvaj, for which he was imprisoned for two years—he became an enthusiastic communist after serving with the Austro-Hungarian army during World War I. In the 1920s and 1930s he became one of Croatia's leading literary figures, publishing poems, plays, and novels, all demonstrating his abhorrence of capitalism and its social class structure. He was arrested in March 1941 along with many other prominent left-wing intellectuals and imprisoned at Kerestinec. He was executed by the Ustasha in July 1941 after being caught in a prison break organized by the Croatian Communist Party.

5. I have drawn information on Bleiburg and the Way of the Cross from the following sources: the concluding chapter from Jozo Tomasevich, *War and Revolution in Yugoslavia, 1941–1945* (Stanford University Press, 2001); Franci Strle, *Veliki finale na Koroškem* (The Grand Finale in Carinthia) (Ljubljana: 1977); Milan Basta, *Rat je završen 7 dana kasnije* (The War Ended 7 Days Later) (Zagreb: Globus, 1977); Roman Leljak, *Teharske žive rane* (The Open Wound of Teharje) (Ljubljana: Cankarjeva založba, 1990); collected documents entitled *Partizanska i komunistička represija i zločini u Hrvatskoj 1944–1946* (Partisan and Communist Repression in Croatia, 1944–1946), eds. Zdravko Dizdar, Vladimir Geiger, Milan Pojić, and Mate Rupić (Slavonski Brod: Croatian Institute of History, 2006); *Otvoreni dossier Bleiburg* (The Open File on Bleiburg), ed. Marko Grčić (Zagreb: Start, 1990, second expanded edition); *Bleiburška tragedija hrvatskog naroda* (The Bleiburg

Tragedy of the Croatian People), ed. Vinko Nikolić (Zagreb: Library of the Croatian Review, 1993); Jera Vodušek, *Kako su komunisti osvojili vlast 1944–1946* (How the Communists Came to Power) (Zagreb: Naklada Pavičić, 2006); Josip Jurčević, *Bleiburg* (Zagreb: 2005); Simo Dubajić, *Kočevski rog* (Zagreb: Ljetopis SKD Prosvjeta, 2007); papers from the symposium "Bleiburg i Križni put 1945," organized by the Council of the Alliance of Anti-Fascist Fighters of Croatia in June 2006, which was published as a book at the beginning of 2007; documents from the Military Museum in Belgrade, which the late Jure Bilić collected and permitted me to review; numerous memoirs published in various newspapers and magazines; and discussions with several participants in the events.

6. The White Guards was the name given by the Partisans to anticommunist paramilitary groups that were formed in Slovenia after the German invasion of Yugoslavia.

7. Milan Nedić (1877–1946) and Dimitrije Ljotić (1891–1945) were Serbian political leaders in the rump Serbian state that remained after the German invasion of Yugoslavia. Nedić served as the head of the puppet government, but Ljotić did not fill any political office, instead preferring to work behind the scenes.

8. Milovan Đilas, *Wartime*, trans. by Michael B. Petrovich (New York: Harcourt Brace Jovanovich, 1977).

9. Milovan Đilas, *Conversations with Stalin*, trans. by Michael B. Petrovich (New York: Harcourt Brace & Company, 1962).

10. My brother, Danko, who as a memorial to our father changed his surname to Ivin, wrote a historical analysis of this plenum in 1965 as preparation for his doctoral dissertation, on which he was working at the Institute for the History of the Workers' Movement of Croatia. Because of criticism that his thesis was too bold, in other words heretical, he was not able to publish the text in Zagreb. In 1968, it was translated into German and published by the Ost-Institut in Bern, Switzerland, as an eighty-five-page pamphlet.

CHAPTER TWENTY: LIBERATION

1. Arnold Daghani, *Grob u višnjiku* (The Grave is in the Cherry Orchard) (Middlesex: Eden Press, 1961).

2. From the daily newspaper, *Vjesnik*, May 17, 1945.

3. See "Komunistièka represija i zloèini u Hrvatskoj," 1944–1946 (Communist Repression and Crimes in Croatia, 1944–1946) Documents, 94–96.

4. I have convinced myself that Milutin Košarić was telling the truth. After reviewing a report of the Ministry of Justice from September 18, 1945, in the book *Partizanska i komunistička represija i zločini u Hrvatskoj, 1944–1946* (Partisan and Communist Repression and Crimes in Croatia, 1944–1946), it is apparent that the thirty sentences handed down by the Karlovac court were among the fewest issued by such courts.

5. "Ilija Gromovnik" was the wartime pseudonym of Ivan Hariš-Gromovnik (1903–1989). A veteran of the Spanish Civil War, he carried out several of the most significant acts of sabotage in the early days of the war. After the war, he rose to senior positions in the general staff of the Yugoslav People's Army.

6. Josip Vaništa is one of the rare friends from my childhood whom I still often see. Now eighty-eight years old, he is among the most prominent artists in Croatia.

Acknowledgments

FOR THIS ENGLISH edition of my book I am most grateful to Robert Silvers who discovered the original publication on a trip to Zagreb in 2009; to Rea Hederman and Edwin Frank who accepted it for publication; to Chares Simic who provided the introduction; and to Drenka Willen and Jeffrey Yang who edited the book.

I am also grateful to Michael Gable who ably translated the text into straightforward English; to Nikola Djuretić who was the first person to read the entire English translation and helped to shape the final text; and to Lara Hölbling Matković, Pavle Goldstein, and Thao Nguyen-Goldstein who read the manuscript and offered many useful suggestions.

INDEX

Page numbers in *italics* refer to illustrations.